SOLIDWORKS 2017:
A Power Guide for Beginners and Intermediate Users

CADArtifex

The premium provider of learning products and solutions
www.cadartifex.com

SOLIDWORKS 2017: A Power Guide for Beginners and Intermediate Users

Published by
CADArtifex
www.cadartifex.com

Copyright © 2017 CADArtifex

This textbook is copyrighted and the publisher reserves all rights. No part of this publication may be reproduced, stored in a retrieval system, transmitted, transcribed, stored in a retrieval system or translated into any language, in any form or by any means, electronic, mechanical, photocopying, recording, scanning or otherwise without the prior written permission of the Publisher.

ISBN-13: 978-1543059793
ISBN-10: 1543059791

NOTICE TO THE READER
The publisher and the author make no representations or warranties with respect to the accuracy or completeness of the contents of this work/text and specifically disclaim all warranties, including without limitation warranties of fitness for a particular purpose. Publisher does not guarantee any of the products described in the text or perform any independent analysis in connection with any of the product information contained in the text. No warranty may be created or extended by sales or promotional materials. This work is sold with the understanding that the publisher is not engaged in rendering legal, accounting, or other professional services. Neither the publisher nor the author shall be liable for damages arising herefrom. Further, readers should be aware that Internet Websites listed in this work may have changed or disappeared between when this work was written and when it is read.

Examination Copies
Textbooks received as examination copies in any form such as paperback and eBook are for review only and may not be made available for the use of the student. These files may not be transferred to any other party. Resale of examination copies is prohibited.

Electronic Files
The electronic file/eBook in any form of this textbook is licensed to the original user only and may not be transferred to any other party.

Disclaimer
The author has made sincere efforts to ensure the accuracy of the material described herein, however the author makes no warranty, expressed or implied, with respect to the quality, correctness, accuracy, or freedom from error of this document or the products it describes.

www.cadartifex.com

Dedication

First and foremost, I would like to thank my parents for being a great support throughout my career and while writing this book.

Heartfelt thanks go to my wife and my sisters for their patience and support in taking this challenge, and letting me spare time for it.

I would also like to acknowledge the efforts of the employees at CADArtifex for their dedication in editing the content of this textbook.

Content at a Glance

Part 1. Introducing to SOLIDWORKS and Drawing Sketches
Chapter 1. Introduction to SOLIDWORKS .... 19 - 38
Chapter 2. Drawing Sketches with SOLIDWORKS .... 39 - 104
Chapter 3. Editing and Modifying Sketches .... 105 - 152
Chapter 4. Applying Geometric Relations and Dimensions .... 153 - 208

Part 2. Creating 3D Models/Components
Chapter 5. Creating First/Base Feature of Solid Models .... 209 - 242
Chapter 6. Creating Reference Geometries .... 243 - 276
Chapter 7. Advanced Modeling - I .... 277 - 338
Chapter 8. Advanced Modeling - II .... 339 - 430
Chapter 9. Patterning and Mirroring .... 431 - 484
Chapter 10. Advanced Modeling - III .... 485 - 558
Chapter 11. Working with Configurations .... 559 - 576

Part 3. Working with Assemblies
Chapter 12. Working with Assemblies - I .... 577 - 652
Chapter 13. Working with Assemblies - II .... 653 - 702

Part 4. Creating Drawings
Chapter 14. Working with Drawings .... 703 - 758

Index .... 759 - 768

Table of Contents

Dedication 3
Preface 15

Part 1. Introducing to SOLIDWORKS and Drawing Sketches

Chapter 1. Introduction to SOLIDWORKS .... 19 - 38

Installing SOLIDWORKS 20
Getting Started with SOLIDWORKS 20
    Task Pane 21
    Standard Toolbar 21
    SOLIDWORKS Menus 21
    SOLIDWORKS Search 22
Invoking the New SOLIDWORKS Document 22
    Part Environment 23
    Assembly Environment 23
    Drawing Environment 24
Identifying SOLIDWORKS Documents 24
Invoking the Part Modeling Environment 24
    CommandManager 25
    FeatureManager Design Tree 29
    View (Heads-Up) Toolbar 30
    Status Bar 30
    Task Pane 30
Invoking the Assembly Environment 31
    Assembly CommandManager 32
Invoking the Drawing Environment 32
    View Layout CommandManager 33
    Annotation CommandManager 34
Invoking a Shortcut Menu 34
Customizing the Context Toolbar of the Shortcut Menu 35
Customizing the CommandManager 36
Working with Mouse Gestures 37
Saving Documents 38
Opening Existing Documents 38
Summary 38
Questions 38

Chapter 2. Drawing Sketches with SOLIDWORKS .... 39 - 104

Invoking the Part Modeling Environment 41
Invoking the Sketching Environment 43
Working with Selection of Planes 45
Specifying Units 45

6 Table of Contents

- Specifying Grids and Snaps Settings 47
- Drawing a Line Entity 49
  - Procedure for Drawing a Line 50
- Example 1 51
- Hands-on Test Drive 1 55
- Drawing an Arc by using the Line tool 55
  - Procedure for Drawing an Arc by using the Line tool 55
- Example 2 56
- Hands-on Test Drive 2 61
- Drawing a Centerline 61
- Drawing a Midpoint Line 62
  - Procedure for Drawing a Midpoint Line 62
- Drawing a Rectangle 62
  - Corner Rectangle 63
  - Center Rectangle 65
  - 3 Point Corner Rectangle 65
  - 3 Point Center Rectangle 66
  - Parallelogram 67
- Drawing a Circle 68
  - Circle 68
  - Perimeter Circle 69
- Drawing an Arc 70
  - Centerpoint Arc 70
  - 3 Point Arc 71
  - Tangent Arc 71
- Drawing a Polygon 73
  - Procedure for Drawing a Polygon 75
- Drawing a Slot 75
  - Straight Slot 75
  - Centerpoint Straight Slot 77
  - 3 Point Arc Slot 77
  - Centerpoint Arc Slot 78
- Drawing an Ellipse 79
  - Procedure for Drawing an Ellipse 79
- Drawing an Elliptical Arc 80
  - Procedure for Drawing an Elliptical Arc 80
- Drawing a Parabola 81
  - Procedure for Drawing a Parabola 81
- Drawing Conic Curves 82
  - Procedure for Drawing Conic Curves 82
- Drawing a Spline 83
  - Spline 83
  - Equation Driven Curve 84
  - Style Spline 86
  - Fit Spline 87

Editing a Spline 90
Tutorial 1 91
Tutorial 2 97
Hands-on Test Drive 3 103
Hands-on Test Drive 4 103
Summary 104
Questions 104

Chapter 3. Editing and Modifying Sketches .... 105 - 152

Trimming Sketch Entities 106
    Procedure for Trimming Entities by using the Trim Entities Tool 109
Extending Sketch Entities 109
    Procedure for Extending Entities by using the Extend Entities Tool 110
Offsetting Sketch Entities 110
    Procedure for Offsetting Entities 113
Mirroring Sketch Entities 113
    Mirroring Entities by using the Mirror Entities Tool 113
    Mirroring Entities by using the Dynamic Mirror Tool 115
Patterning Sketch Entities 116
    Linear Sketch Pattern 116
    Circular Sketch Pattern 120
Creating a Sketch Fillet 123
Creating a Sketch Chamfer 125
Moving a Sketch Entity 126
    Procedure for Moving Sketch Entities 127
Creating a Copy of Sketch Entities 128
    Procedure for Creating a Copy of Sketch Entities 128
Rotating an Entity 128
    Procedure for Rotating Sketch Entities 130
Scaling Sketch Entities 130
    Procedure for Scaling Sketch Entities 131
Stretching an Entity 131
    Procedure for Stretching Sketch Entities 132
Tutorial 1 133
Tutorial 2 140
Tutorial 3 148
Hands-on Test Drive 1 152
Summary 152
Questions 152

Chapter 4. Applying Geometric Relations and Dimensions .... 153 - 208

Working with Geometric Relations 153
Applying Geometric Relations 156
    Applying Geometric Relation by using the Add Relation Tool 156
    Applying Geometric Relation by using the Pop-up Toolbar 157
Controlling the Display of Geometric Relations 158

8 Table of Contents

    Applying Dimensions 158
        Working with Smart Dimension tool 159
        Working with Horizontal Dimension and Vertical Dimension tools 165
        Working with Ordinate Dimension tool 166
    Modifying/Editing Dimensions 167
    Modifying Dimension Properties 168
    Working with Different States of a Sketch 179
        Under defined Sketch 179
        Fully defined Sketch 180
        Over defined Sketch 180
    Tutorial 1 181
    Tutorial 2 191
    Tutorial 3 200
    Hands-on Test Drive 1 207
    Hands-on Test Drive 2 207
    Summary 208
    Questions 208

Part 2. Creating 3D Models/Components

Chapter 5. Creating First/Base Feature of Solid Models .... 209 - 242

    Creating an Extruded Feature 210
    Creating a Revolved Feature 218
    Navigating a 3D Model in Graphics Area 223
        Zoom In/Out 223
        Zoom To Fit 224
        Zoom to Area 224
        Zoom to Selection 225
        Pan 225
        Rotate 225
    Manipulating View Orientation of a Model 225
        Manipulating View Orientation by using the View Orientation flyout 226
        Manipulating View Orientation by using the Orientation dialog box 227
        Manipulating View Orientation by using the View Selector Cube 228
        Manipulating View Orientation by using the Reference Triad 229
    Changing the Display Style of a Model 229
        Shaded With Edges 229
        Shaded 230
        Hidden Lines Removed 230
        Hidden Lines Visible 230
        Wireframe 230
    Changing the View of a Model 231
        Shadows In Shaded Mode 231
        Perspective 231
        Ambient Occlusion 232
        Cartoon 232

Tutorial 1 232
Tutorial 2 234
Tutorial 3 237
Hands-on Test Drive 1 241
Hands-on Test Drive 2 241
Summary 242
Questions 242

Chapter 6. Creating Reference Geometries .... 243 - 276

Creating Reference Planes 244
    Creating a Plane at an Offset Distance 247
    Creating a Parallel Plane 248
    Creating a Plane at an Angle 248
    Creating a Plane passing through Three Points/Vertices 248
    Creating a Plane Normal to a Curve 249
    Creating a Plane at the middle of two Faces/Planes 249
    Creating a Plane Tangent to a Cylindrical Face 250
    Creating a Plane Parallel to the Screen 250
    Creating a Projected Plane onto a Non-Planar Face 251
Creating a Reference Axis 252
Creating a Reference Coordinate System 254
    Procedure for Creating a Reference Coordinate System 255
Creating a Reference Point 256
Tutorial 1 259
Tutorial 2 266
Tutorial 3 273
Hands-on Test Drive 1 276
Summary 276
Questions 276

Chapter 7. Advanced Modeling - I .... 277 - 338

Using Advanced Options of the Extruded Boss/Base Tool 277
Using Advanced Options of the Revolved Boss/Base Tool 281
Creating Cut Features 282
    Creating Extruded Cut Features 282
    Creating Revolved Cut Features 283
Working with Different Types of Sketches 285
    Close Sketches 285
    Open Sketches 285
    Nested Sketches 285
    Intersecting Sketch 287
Working with Contours of a Sketch 287
    Procedure for Extruding Contours by using the Selected Contours Rollout 288
    Procedure for Extruding Contours by using the Contour Select Tool 289
Displaying Shaded Sketch Contours 292
Projecting Edges onto the Sketching Plane 292
    Procedure for Projecting Edges onto the Sketching Plane 294

Editing a Feature 294
  Procedure for Editing a Feature 294
  Procedure for Editing the Sketch of a Feature 295
Measuring the Distance between Entities/Faces 296
  Procedure for Measuring Distance between Entities/Faces 300
Assigning Appearance/Texture 300
  Assigning Predefined Appearance/Texture 300
  Assigning Customized Appearance 302
Applying Material 305
  Procedure for Applying Standard Material 305
  Procedure for Applying Customized Material Properties 307
Calculating Mass Properties 308
  Procedure for Calculating Mass Properties 312
Tutorial 1 313
Tutorial 2 320
Tutorial 3 330
Hands-on Test Drive 1 336
Hands-on Test Drive 2 337
Summary 338
Questions 338

Chapter 8. Advanced Modeling - II .... 339 - 430

Creating a Sweep Feature 339
  Procedure for Creating a Sweep Feature with Sketch Profile 354
  Procedure for Creating a Sweep Feature with Circular Profile 354
  Procedure for Creating a Sweep Feature with One Guide Curve 354
  Procedure for Creating a Sweep Feature with Two Guide Curves 354
  Procedure for Creating a Twisted Sweep Feature 355
Creating a Sweep Cut Feature 355
  Procedure for Creating a Sweep Cut Feature with Sketch Profile 357
  Procedure for Creating a Sweep Cut Feature with Circular Profile 357
  Procedure for Creating a Sweep Cut Feature with Solid Profile 358
Creating a Lofted feature 358
  Procedure for Creating a Lofted Feature 367
  Procedure for Creating a Lofted Feature by using Guide Curves 368
  Procedure for Creating a Lofted Feature by using Centerline 368
Creating a Lofted Cut Feature 368
Creating a Boundary Feature 369
  Procedure for Creating a Boundary Feature 373
Creating a Boundary Cut Feature 374
Creating Curves 374
  Creating Projected Curves 374
  Creating Helical and Spiral Curves 377
  Creating Curves by Specifying XYZ Points 382
  Creating Curves by Selecting Reference Points 384
  Creating a Composite Curve 385

Splitting Faces of a Model 386
    Procedure for Splitting Faces by using the Projection Method 390
    Procedure for Splitting Faces by using the Intersection Method 390
    Procedure for Splitting Faces by using the Silhouette Method 390
Creating 3D Sketches 390
    Using the Line Tool in the 3D Sketching Environment 391
    Using the Spline Tool in the 3D Sketching Environment 393
Tutorial 1 395
Tutorial 2 402
Tutorial 3 414
Tutorial 4 419
Hands-on Test Drive 1 428
Hands-on Test Drive 2 429
Summary 429
Questions 430

Chapter 9. Patterning and Mirroring .... 431 - 484

Patterning Features/Faces/Bodies 431
    Creating a Linear Pattern 432
    Creating a Circular Pattern 444
    Creating a Curve Driven Pattern 447
    Creating a Sketch Driven Pattern 452
    Creating a Table Driven Pattern 454
    Creating a Fill Pattern 456
    Creating a Variable Pattern 460
Mirroring a Feature 464
    Procedure for Creating a Mirror Feature 466
Tutorial 1 466
Tutorial 2 474
Hands-on Test Drive 1 481
Hands-on Test Drive 2 482
Summary 482
Questions 483

Chapter 10. Advanced Modeling - III .... 485 - 558

Working with Hole Wizard 485
    Procedure for Creating a Hole by using Hole Wizard 491
Creating Advanced Holes 492
Adding Cosmetic threads 496
    Procedure for Adding a Cosmetic Thread 499
Creating Threads 499
    Procedure for Creating a Thread 504
Creating Fillets 504
    Creating a Constant Radius Fillet 505
    Creating a Variable Radius Fillet 511
    Creating a Face Fillets 514
    Creating a Full Round Fillet 516

Creating Chamfers 518
    Procedure for Creating a Chamfer 522
Creating Rib Features 523
    Procedure for Creating a Rib Feature 525
Creating Shell Features 525
    Procedure for Creating a Shell Feature with Uniform Thickness 527
    Procedure for Creating a Shell Feature with Multi-Thickness 527
Creating Wrap Features 528
Tutorial 1 531
Tutorial 2 545
Hands-on Test Drive 1 556
Hands-on Test Drive 2 557
Summary 557
Questions 557

Chapter 11. Working with Configurations .... 559 - 576

Creating Configurations by using the Manual Method 559
    Procedure for Creating Configurations by using the Manual Method 564
Creating Configurations by using the Design Table 564
    Procedure for Creating Configurations by using the Design Table 569
Suppressing and Unsuppressing Features 569
Tutorial 1 570
Hands-on Test Drive 1 575
Summary 576
Questions 576

Part 3. Working with Assemblies

Chapter 12. Working with Assemblies - I .... 577 - 652

Bottom-up Assembly Approach 578
Top-down Assembly Approach 578
Creating Assembly by using Bottom-up Approach 578
    Inserting Components in the Assembly Environment 580
    Inserting Components by using the Insert Components Tool 582
Working with Degrees of Freedom 584
Applying Relations or Mates 584
    Working with Standard Mates 586
    Working with Advanced Mates 590
    Working with Mechanical Mates 598
Moving and Rotating Individual Components 605
    Moving a Component by using the Move Component Tool 606
    Rotating a Component by using the Rotate Component Tool 609
Working with SmartMates 610
Tutorial 1 611
Tutorial 2 626

Hands-on Test Drive 1 648
Summary 651
Questions 652

Chapter 13. Working with Assemblies - II .... 653 - 702

Creating Assembly by using the Top-down Approach 654
    Procedure for Creating Assembly by using the Top-down Approach 654
Editing Assembly Components 661
    Editing Assembly Components within the Assembly Environment 661
    Editing Assembly Components in the Part Modeling Environment 662
Editing Mates 663
Patterning Assembly Components 664
    Creating a Pattern Driven Component Pattern 664
    Creating a Chain Component Pattern 667
Mirroring Components of an Assembly 672
    Procedure for Mirroring Components of an Assembly 674
Creating Assembly Features 674
Suppressing or Unsuppressing Components 675
Inserting the Parts having Multiple Configurations 676
Creating and Dissolving Sub-Assemblies 677
Creating an Exploded View 678
    Procedure for Creating the Regular Exploded View 683
    Procedure for Creating the Radial Exploded View 683
Collapsing an Exploded View 683
Animating an Exploded View 684
Editing an Exploded View 684
Adding Explode Lines in an Exploded View 685
    Procedure for Creating Exploded Lines 685
Creating Bill of Material (BOM) of an Assembly 686
Tutorial 1 687
Hands-on Test Drive 1 698
Summary 700
Questions 701

Part 4. Creating Drawings

Chapter 14. Working with Drawings .... 703 - 758

Invoking Drawing Environment by using the New Tool 704
    Creating the Base/Model View of a Model 707
Invoking Drawing Environment from the Part or the Assembly Environment 711
Creating a Model View 712
    Procedure for Creating a Model/Base View 713
Creating a Projected View 713
    Procedure for Creating Projected Views 714
Creating 3 Standard Views 715
Working with Angle of Projection 715

Table of Contents

Defining the Angle of Projection 717
Editing the Sheet Format 718
Creating other Drawing Views 718
    Creating a Section View 719
    Creating an Auxiliary View 724
    Creating a Detail View 725
    Creating a Broken-out Section View 727
    Creating a Break View 728
    Creating a Crop View 729
    Creating the Alternate Position View 730
Applying Dimensions 731
    Applying Reference Dimensions 731
    Applying Driving Dimensions 732
Modifying the Driving Dimension 734
Controlling the Dimension and the Arrow Style 734
Adding Notes 735
Adding the Surface Finish Symbol 736
Adding the Weld Symbol 737
Adding the Hole Callout 738
Adding the Center Mark 738
Adding Centerlines 740
Creating the Bill of Material (BOM) 740
    Procedure for Creating Bill of Material (BOM) 744
Adding Balloons 744
    Adding Balloons Automatically 744
    Adding Balloons Manually 747
Tutorial 1 747
Hands-on Test Drive 1 757
Summary 757
Questions 758

Index .... **759 - 768**

Preface

SOLIDWORKS, developed by Dassault Systèmes SOLIDWORKS Corp., one of the biggest technology providers to engineering, offers complete 3D software tools that let you create, simulate, publish, and manage data. The products of SOLIDWORKS are easy to learn and use, and are integrated with each other to help you design products accurately, fast, and cost-effectively.

SOLIDWORKS delivers a rich set of integrated tools that are powerful and intuitive to use. It is a feature-based, parametric solid-modeling mechanical design, and automation software that allows you to create real-world 3D components and assemblies by using simple but highly effective tools. The 3D components and assemblies created in SOLIDWORKS can be converted into 2D drawings within few mouse clicks. In addition, you can validate your designs by simulating their real-world conditions and assess the environmental impact of your products.

SOLIDWORKS 2017: A Power Guide for Beginners and Intermediate Users textbook is designed for instructor-led courses as well as for self-paced learning. It is intended to help engineers and designers interested in learning SOLIDWORKS for creating 3D mechanical design. Taken together, this textbook can be a great starting point for new SOLIDWORKS users and a great teaching aid in classroom training. This textbook consists of 14 chapters, total 768 pages covering major environments of SOLIDWORKS: Sketching environment, Part modeling environment, Assembly environment, and Drawing environment, which teach you how to use the SOLIDWORKS mechanical design software to build parametric models and assemblies, and how to make drawings of those parts and assemblies. Moreover, this textbook includes the topic of Configurations.

This textbook not only focuses on the usages of the tools/commands of SOLIDWORKS but also on the concept of design. Every chapter of this textbook contains tutorials which instruct users how things can be done in SOLIDWORKS step by step. Moreover, every chapter ends with hands-on test drives which allow users to experience themselves the ease-of-use and powerful capabilities of SOLIDWORKS.

Who Should Read This Book

This book is written with a wide range of SOLIDWORKS users in mind, varying from beginners to advanced users and SOLIDWORKS instructors. The easy-to-follow chapters of this book allow you to easily understand different design techniques, SOLIDWORKS tools, and design principles.

What Is Covered in This Textbook

SOLIDWORKS 2017: A Power Guide for Beginners and Intermediate Users textbook is designed to help you learn everything, you need to know to start using SOLIDWORKS 2017 with easy to understand, step-by-step tutorials. This textbook covers the following:

Chapter 1, "Introduction to SOLIDWORKS," introduces SOLIDWORKS interface, different SOLIDWORKS environments, various components SOLIDWORKS, invoking and customizing the shortcut menu, saving documents, and opening documents in SOLIDWORKS.

Chapter 2, "**Drawing Sketches with SOLIDWORKS**," discusses how to invoke Sketching environment, specify unit system and, grids and snaps settings. Also, it introduces you with various sketching tools such as Line, Arc, Circle, Rectangle, and Spline for creating sketches.

Chapter 3, "**Editing and Modifying Sketches**," introduces various editing and modifying operations such as trimming unwanted sketched entities, extending sketch entities, mirroring, patterning, moving, and rotating sketch entities by using various editing/modifying tools of the Sketching environment.

Chapter 4, "**Applying Geometric Relations and Dimensions**," introduces the concept of fully defined sketches, creating fully defined sketches by applying geometric relations and dimensions. Also, it introduces different methods of applying geometric relations and dimensions. You can modify the already applied dimensions and dimension properties such as dimension style, tolerance, and precision. This chapter also introduces you with different sketch states.

Chapter 5, "**Creating First/Base Feature of Solid Models**," discusses how to create extruded and revolved base features by using the Extruded Boss/Base and Revolved Boss/Base tools. This chapter also introduces you with various navigating tools such as Zoom In/Out and Zoom To Fit. Moreover, it introduces how to manipulate the orientation of a model. Additionally, this chapter introduces you with changing the display style and view of the model.

Chapter 6, "**Creating Reference Geometries**," introduces that the three default planes: Front, Top, and Right may not be enough for creating models having multiple features: therefore, you need to create additional reference planes. In addition, this chapter discusses how to create a reference axis, reference coordinates system and reference point.

Chapter 7, "**Advanced Modeling - I**," introduces advanced options for creating extruded and revolved features. In addition, this chapter discusses how to create cut features and, how to work with different type of sketches. This chapter also introduces you with creating multiple features by using a single sketch having multiple contours, projecting edges of the features, editing individual features of a model. Moreover, in this chapter you learn how to measure distance and angle between lines, points, faces, planes, and so on by using the Measure tool, as well as how to assign appearance and material properties to a model. Additionally, how to calculate the mass properties of a model.

Chapter 8, "**Advanced Modeling - II**," discusses how to create sweep features, sweep cut features, lofted features, lofted cut features, boundary features, boundary cut features, curves, split faces, and 3D Sketches.

Chapter 9, "**Patterning and Mirroring**," introduces various patterning and mirroring tools. After the successfully completing this chapter, you can create different type of patterns such as linear pattern, circular pattern, and curve driven pattern. Also, you can mirror features, faces, or bodies.

Chapter 10, "**Advanced Modeling - III**," discusses how to create standard and customized holes such as counterbore and countersink. You will learn about creating cosmetic thread. In addition, you will learn about creating real threads on holes, fasteners, and cylindrical features. Besides this, you learn how to add constant and variable radius fillets. Moreover, in this chapter you learn how to create chamfer, rib features, and shell features.

Chapter 11, "*Working with Configurations*," discusses how to create multiple variations of a model within a single file by using the configurations. You will learn about creating configurations by using the Manual method and the Design Table method. Moreover, this chapter introduces you how to suppress and unsuppress features of a model.

Chapter 12, "*Working with Assemblies - I*," discusses how to create assemblies by using the bottom-up assembly approach and how to work with standard, advanced, and mechanical mates. This chapter also introduces you how to move and rotate the individual component within the Assembly environment, detect collisions between the components of an assembly, and working with SmartMates.

Chapter 13, "*Working with Assemblies - II*," discusses how to create assemblies by using the top-down assembly approach. You can also edit the individual components of an assembly within the Assembly environment or in the Part environment. This chapter also introduces you to edit the existing mates applied between the components and create different type of patterns such as linear component pattern and pattern driven component pattern. Also, it introduces you to mirror components in the Assembly environment, creating assembly features, suppressing or unsuppressing the components of an assembly, and inserting components in the Assembly environment having multiple configurations. You can also create and dissolve sub-assemblies. In addition, this chapter introduces you with creating, editing, or collapsing the exploded view of an assembly. You can also animate the exploded/collapse view and add exploded lines in an exploded view and create BOM.

Chapter 14, "*Working with Drawings*," discusses how to create 2D drawings from parts and assemblies. This chapter also introduces the concept of angle of projections, defining the angle of projection, and editing sheet format. In addition, this chapter introduces you with applying reference and driving dimensions, adding notes, surface finish symbol, weld symbols, hole callouts, and so on in drawing views. In this chapter, adding Bill of Material (BOM) and balloons have also been introduced.

Icons/Terms used in this Textbook

The following icons and terms are used in this textbook:

Note

Note: Notes highlight information requiring special attention.

Tip

Tip: Tips provide additional advice, which increases the efficiency of the users.

New

New New icons highlight new features of this release.

Update

Updated Updated icons highlight updated features of this release.

Flyout
A Flyout is a list in which a set of tools are grouped together, see Figure 1.

Drop-down List
A drop-down list is a list in which a set of options is grouped together, see Figure 2.

Rollout
A rollout is an area in which drop-down list, fields, buttons, check boxes is available to specify various parameters, see Figure 2. A rollout can be either in the expanded or in the collapsed form. You can expand/collapse a rollout by clicking on the arrow available on the right of its title bar.

Field
A Field allows you to enter new value, or modify existing/default value, as per your requirement, see Figure 2. Also, a field allows you to select entities from the graphics area.

Check box
A Check box allows you to turn on or off the uses of a particular option, see Figure 2.

Button
A Button appears as a 3D icon and is used to turn on or off the uses of a particular option.

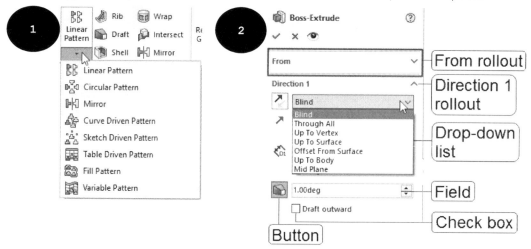

How to Contact the Author
We welcome your valuable feedback and suggestions. Please email us at *info@cadartifex.com* or *cadartifex@gmail.com*. You can also login to our website *www.cadartifex.com* and write your feedback about the textbook as well as download the free learning resources.

Thank you very much for purchasing SOLIDWORKS 2017: A Power Guide for Beginners and Intermediate Users textbook, we hope that the information and concepts introduced in this textbook help you to accomplish your professional goals.

CHAPTER 1

Introduction to SOLIDWORKS

In this chapter, you will learn the following:

- Installing SOLIDWORKS
- Getting Started with SOLIDWORKS
- Invoking the New SOLIDWORKS Document
- Identifying SOLIDWORKS Documents
- Invoking the Part Modeling Environment
- Invoking the Assembly Environment
- Invoking the Drawing Environment
- Invoking a Shortcut Menu
- Customizing the Context toolbar of the Shortcut Menu
- Customizing the CommandManager
- Working with Mouse Gestures
- Saving Documents
- Opening Existing Documents

Welcome to the world of Computer Added Design (CAD) with SOLIDWORKS. SOLIDWORKS, the product of Dassault Systemes SOLIDWORKS Corp., one of the biggest technology provider to engineering, which offers complete 3D software tools that let you create, simulate, publish, and manage your data. By providing advanced solid modeling techniques, SOLIDWORKS help engineers to optimize performance while designing with capabilities, that cut down on costly prototypes, eliminate rework and delays, and save engineers time and development costs.

SOLIDWORKS delivers a rich set of integrated tools that are powerful and intuitive to use. It is a feature-based, parametric solid-modeling mechanical design and automation software which allows you to convert 2D sketches into solid models by using simple but highly effective modeling tools. SOLIDWORKS provides a wide range of tools that allow you to create real-world components and assemblies. These real-world components and assemblies can then be converted into engineering 2D drawings for production, used to validate designs by simulating their real world conditions and assess the environmental impact of your products.

SOLIDWORKS utilizes a parametric feature-based approach for creating models. With SOLIDWORKS you can share your designs with your partners, subcontractors and colleagues in smart new ways, which improve knowledge transfer and shorten the design cycle.

Installing SOLIDWORKS

If you do not have SOLIDWORKS installed in our system, you first need to get it installed. However, before you start installing SOLIDWORKS, you need to evaluate the system requirements and make sure that you have a system capable of running SOLIDWORKS adequately. Below are the system requirement for installing SOLIDWORKS 2017.

1. Operating Systems: Windows 10, 8.1, or 7 SP1 - 64-bit
2. RAM: 8 GB or more
3. Disk Space: 10 GB or more
4. Processor: Intel or AMD with SSE2 support, 64-bit operating system
5. Graphics Card: SOLIDWORKS certified graphics card drivers

For more information about the system requirement for SOLIDWORKS, visit SOLIDWORKS website at *https://www.solidworks.com/sw/support/SystemRequirements.html*.

Once the system is ready, install SOLIDWORKS by using the SOLIDWORKS DVD or by using the downloaded SOLIDWORKS data.

Getting Started with SOLIDWORKS

Once the SOLIDWORKS 2017 is installed on your system, start SOLIDWORKS 2017 by double-clicking on the **SOLIDWORKS 2017** icon on the desktop of your system. As soon as you double-click on the SOLIDWORKS 2017 icon, the system prepares for starting SOLIDWORKS by loading all required files. Once all the required files have been loaded, the initial screen of SOLIDWORKS 2017 appears, see Figure 1.1. If you are starting SOLIDWORKS first time after installing the software, the **SOLIDWORKS License Agreement** window appears, see Figure 1.2. Click on the **Accept** button in the **SOLIDWORKS License Agreement** window to accept the license agreement and start SOLIDWORKS 2017.

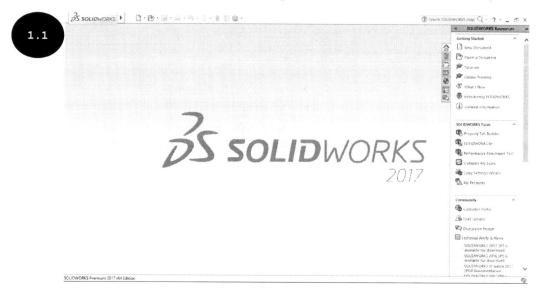

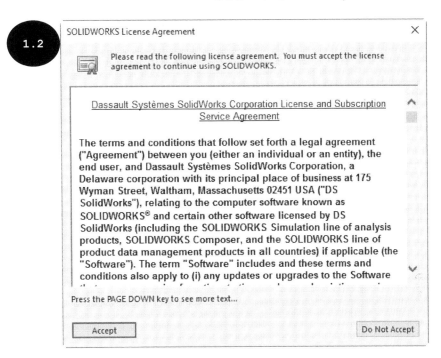

It is evident from the initial screen of SOLIDWORKS 2017 that SOLIDWORKS is very user-friendly and easy to use. The components of the initial screen of SOLIDWORKS 2017 are as follows:

Task Pane
Task Pane appears on the left side of the screen with various tabs for accessing various resources of SOLIDWORKS. You can access SOLIDWORKS resources, start a new file, open an existing file, access tutorial help file, several applications, communities, library, and so on by using the Task Pane. Different tabs of the Task Pane are discussed later in this chapter.

Standard Toolbar
The **Standard** toolbar contains a set of the most frequently used tools such as **New**, **Open**, and **Save**, see Figure 1.3.

SOLIDWORKS Menus
The SOLIDWORKS menus contain different menus such as **File**, **View**, and **Tools** for accessing different tools, see Figure 1.4.

Note that the SOLIDWORKS menus appears when you move the cursor on the SOLIDWORKS logo, which is available at the top left corner of the screen. You can keep the SOLIDWORKS menus visible all time by clicking on the push-pin button that is available at the end of the SOLIDWORKS menus. The tools in different menus of the SOLIDWORKS menus are dependent upon the type of environment invoked.

SOLIDWORKS Search
The SOLIDWORKS Search is a search tool for searching command (tool), knowledge base (help topic), community forum, files, models, and so on, see Figure 1.5.

Invoking the New SOLIDWORKS Document
The new SOLIDWORKS document such as Part, Assembly, and Drawing can be invoked by using the **New SOLIDWORKS Document** dialog box. This dialog box can be invoked by clicking on the **New** tool in the **Standard** toolbar or by clicking on the **New Document** tool in the **SOLIDWORKS Resources** task pane. You can also invoke this dialog box by choosing **File > New** in the SOLIDWORKS menus.

Click on the **New** tool in the **Standard** toolbar. The **New SOLIDWORKS Document** dialog box appears, see Figure 1.6. If you are invoking the **New SOLIDWORKS Document** dialog box for the first time after installing the software then the **Units and Dimension Standard** dialog box appears as soon as you click on the **New** tool, see Figure 1.7. In this dialog box, specify the unit system as the default unit system for SOLIDWORKS and then click on the **OK** button to invoke the **New SOLIDWORKS Document** dialog box. By using the buttons available in this dialog box, you can invoke the Part environment, Assembly environment, and Drawing environment of SOLIDWORKS. The method of invoking different environments of SOLIDWORKS are as follows:

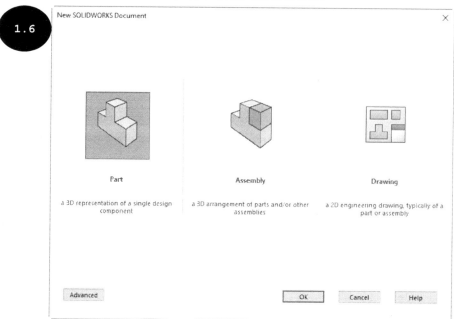

SOLIDWORKS 2017 A Power Guide > 23

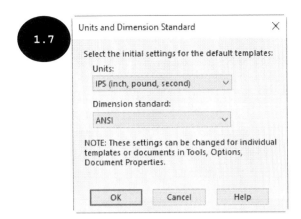

Note: In this textbook, the metric unit system and ANSI standard have been used. You can change the unit system at any point of time in your design as per the requirement. You will learn more about setting unit system in later chapters.

Part Environment

The Part environment is used to create 3D solid models, surface models, and sheet metal models. You can invoke the Part environment by using the **Part** button of the **New SOLIDWORKS Document** dialog box. By default, the **Part** button is activated in the dialog box. As a result, clicking on the OK button in the dialog box, the Part environment gets invoked, see Figure 1.8. You will learn more about invoking the Part modeling environment and various components of its initial screen later in this chapter.

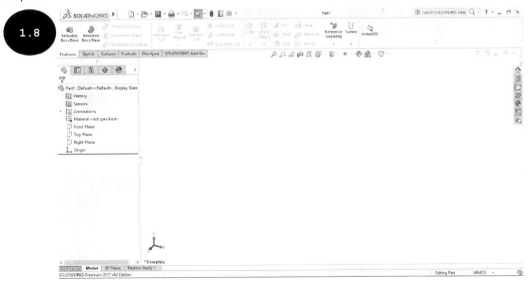

Assembly Environment

The Assembly environment of SOLIDWORKS is used to assemble different components of an assembly with respect to each other by applying required mates, see Figure 1.9. To invoke the Assembly environment, click on the **Assembly** button and then on the **OK** button in the **New SOLIDWORKS Document** dialog box. The Assembly environment gets invoked. You will learn more about invoking the Assembly environment and various components of its initial screen later in this chapter.

Drawing Environment

The Drawing environment of SOLIDWORKS is used to create 2D drawings of a component or an assembly, see Figure 1.10. To invoke the Drawing environment, click on the **Drawing** button and then on the **OK** button in the **New SOLIDWORKS Document** dialog box. The Drawing environment gets invoked. You will learn more about invoking the Drawing environment and various components of its initial screen later in this chapter.

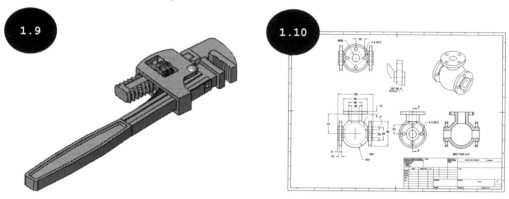

Identifying SOLIDWORKS Documents

The documents created in different environments (Part, Assembly, and Drawing) of SOLIDWORKS have a different file extension, see the table given below.

Environments	File Extension
Part Modeling Environment	*.sldprt
Assembly Modeling Environment	*.sldasm
Drawing Modeling Environment	*.slddrw

Invoking the Part Modeling Environment

To invoke a Part modeling environment, click on the **New** tool in the **Standard** toolbar. The **New SOLIDWORKS Document** dialog box appears. In this dialog box, make sure that the **Part** button is activated. Next, click on the **OK** button. The Part modeling environment gets invoked. The initial screen of the Part modeling environment appears, see Figure 1.11.

Some of the components of the initial screen of SOLIDWORKS such as SOLIDWORKS menus, the Standard toolbar, and SOLIDWORKS Search have been discussed earlier. The remaining components of the initial screen of the Part modeling environment are as follows:

SOLIDWORKS 2017 A Power Guide > 25

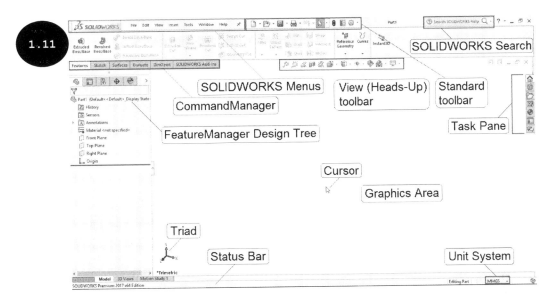

CommandManager

CommandManager is available at the top of the graphics area. It provides access to different SOLIDWORKS tools. There are various CommandManagers such as **Features CommandManager**, **Sketch CommandManager**, **Evaluate CommandManager**, and so on are available in the Part modeling environment. When the **Features** tab is activated in the CommandManager, the **Features CommandManager** appears, which provides access to different tools for creating solid 3D models. On clicking on the **Sketch** tab, the **Sketch CommandManager** appears, which provides access to different tools for creating sketches.

Note: The different environments (Part, Assembly, and Drawing) of SOLIDWORKS are provided with different sets of CommandManagers.

Some of the CommandManagers of the Part modeling environment are as follows:

Features CommandManager

The **Features CommandManager** is provided with different sets of tools that are used for creating 3D models. To invoke the tools of the **Features CommandManager**, click on the **Features** tab in the CommandManager. Note that initially, most of the tools of the **Features CommandManager** are not activated. These tools are activated as soon as you create a base or a first feature of a model. Figure 1.12 shows the **Features CommandManager** and Figure 1.13 shows a 3D model for your reference only.

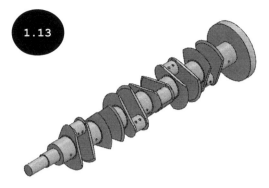

Sketch CommandManager

The **Sketch CommandManager** is provided with different sets of tools that are used for creating 2D and 3D sketches. To invoke the tools of the **Sketch CommandManager**, click on the **Sketch** tab in the CommandManager. Figure 1.14 shows the **Sketch CommandManager** and Figure 1.15 shows a 2D sketch for your reference only.

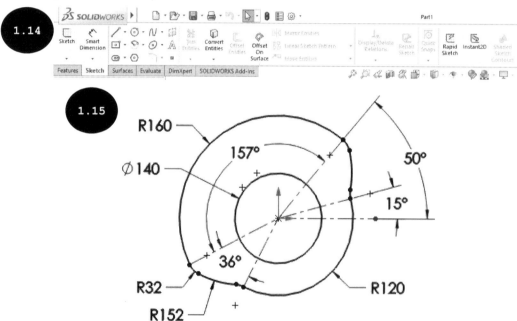

Evaluate CommandManager

The tools of the **Evaluate CommandManager** are used to evaluate the model by measuring entities, calculating mass properties, checking the tangent or curvature continuity, draft analysis, calculating section properties, geometry analysis, and so on. To invoke the tools of the **Evaluate CommandManager**, click on the **Evaluate** tab in the CommandManager, see Figure 1.16.

Note: The Surface modeling environment as well as the Sheet Metal environment of SOLIDWORKS can also be invoked within the Part modeling environment by using the respective CommandManagers.

Surfaces CommandManager

The **Surfaces CommandManager** is provided with different sets of tools that are used for creating surface models. To invoke the tools of the **Surfaces CommandManager**, click on the **Surfaces** tab in the CommandManager. If the **Surfaces** tab is not available in the CommandManager then right-click on any CommandManager tab. A shortcut menu appears. In this shortcut menu, click on the **Surfaces** option. The **Surfaces** tab becomes available in the CommandManager. Figure 1.17 shows the **Surfaces CommandManager** and Figure 1.18 shows a surface model for your reference only. Note that initially, most of the tools of the **Surfaces CommandManager** are not activated. These tools are activated as soon as you create a base or first surface feature of a surface model.

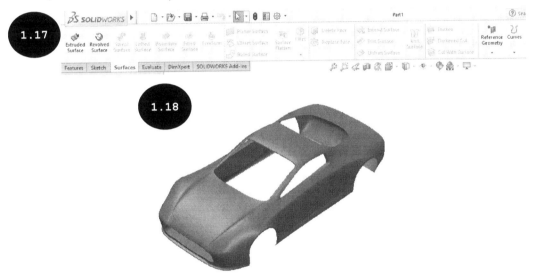

Note: In addition to the default CommandManagers such as **Features CommandManager** and **Sketch CommandManager**, you can also add additional CommandManagers that are not available by default. To add a CommandManager, right-click on any of the available CommandManager tab. A shortcut menu appears, see Figure 1.19. This shortcut menu displays a list of available CommandManagers. Also, a tick mark on the front of the CommandManager indicates that the respective CommandManager is already added. Click on the required CommandManager in the shortcut menu. The respective CommandManager tab is added in CommandManager.

28 Chapter 1 > Introduction to SOLIDWORKS

Sheet Metal CommandManager

The **Sheet Metal CommandManager** is provided with different sets of tools for creating sheet metal components. If the **Sheet Metal** tab is not available in the CommandManager then right-click on a CommandManager tab to display a shortcut menu. Next, click on the **Sheet Metal** option in the shortcut menu. Figure 1.20 shows the **Sheet Metal CommandManager** and Figure 1.21 shows a sheet metal component for your reference only.

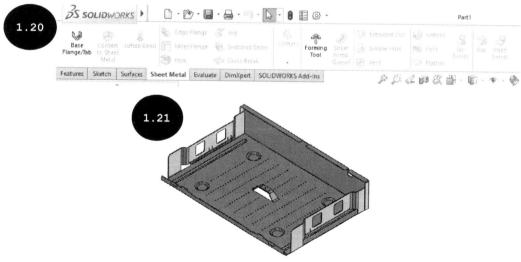

Weldments CommandManager

The **Weldments CommandManager** is provided with different sets of tools for creating weldments structures. Figure 1.22 shows the **Weldments CommandManager** and Figure 1.23 shows a weldments component for your reference only.

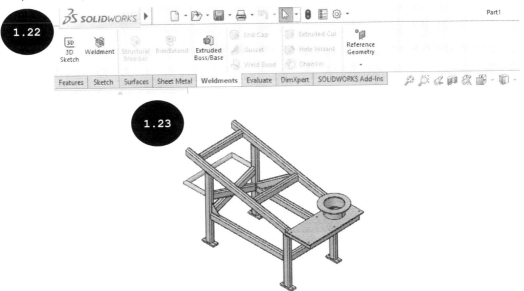

FeatureManager Design Tree

FeatureManager Design Tree appears on the left of the graphics area and keeps a record of all operations or features used for creating a model, see Figure 1.24. Note that the first created feature appears at the top and the next created features appear one after another in an order in the FeatureManager Design Tree. Also, in the FeatureManager Design Tree, three default planes, and an origin appear, by default, see Figure 1.24.

Tip: The features are the logical operations that are performed to create a component. In other words, a component can be designed by creating number of features such as extrude, sweep, hole, fillet, draft, and so on.

View (Heads-Up) Toolbar
The **View (Heads-Up)** toolbar is available at the top center of the graphics area, see Figure 1.25. It is provided with different sets of tools that are used to manipulate the view and display of a model available in the graphics area.

Status Bar
The Status Bar is available at the bottom of the graphics area and provides the information about the action to be taken based on the currently active tool. It also displays the current state of the sketch being created, coordinate system, and so on.

Task Pane
As discussed earlier, the Task Pane is used to access SOLIDWORKS resources and documents, start a new file, and so on. It appears on the left of the graphics area with various tabs such as **SOLIDWORKS Resources**, **Design Library**, **File Explorer**, **View Palette**, **Appearances, Scenes, and Decals**, and **Custom Properties** for accessing various resources of SOLIDWORKS, see Figure 1.26. Some of the tabs of the Task Pane are as follows:

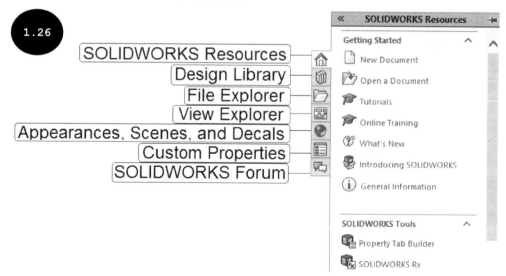

SOLIDWORKS Resources
The **SOLIDWORKS Resources Task Pane** is provided with tools to get started with SOLIDWORKS, and links to access SOLIDWORKS Community and Online Resources. To display the **SOLIDWORKS Resources Task Pane**, click on the **SOLIDWORKS Resources** tab in the Task Pane, refer to Figure 1.26.

The **SOLIDWORKS Resources Task Pane** is provided with various rollouts such as **Getting Started**, **SOLIDWORKS Tools**, **Community**, and **Online Resources**. Some of these rollouts are as follows:

Getting Started
The **Getting Started** rollout of the **SOLIDWORKS Resources Task Pane** is provided with tools that are used to start a new file, open an existing file, what's new, tutorials, and so on.

SOLIDWORKS Tools
The **SOLIDWORKS Tools** rollout is used to access several applications such as **Property Tab Builder**, **SOLIDWORKS Rx**, **Performance Benchmark Test**, and so on.

Community
The **Community** rollout is used to access SOLIDWORKS customer portals, various SOLIDWORKS user groups, discussion forum, and updates about technical alerts and news.

Design Library
The **Design Library Task Pane** is used to access SOLIDWORKS design library, toolbox components, 3D Content Central, and SOLIDWORKS Content.

Appearances, Scenes, and Decals
The **Appearances, Scenes, and Decals Task Pane** is used to change or modify the appearance of the model and the graphics display area.

Invoking the Assembly Environment

To invoke the Assembly environment, click on the **New** tool in the **Standard** toolbar. The **New SOLIDWORKS Document** dialog box appears. In this dialog box, click on the **Assembly** button and then click on the **OK** button. The Assembly environment is invoked with the display of the **Open** dialog box along with the **Begin Assembly PropertyManager**, see Figure 1.27.

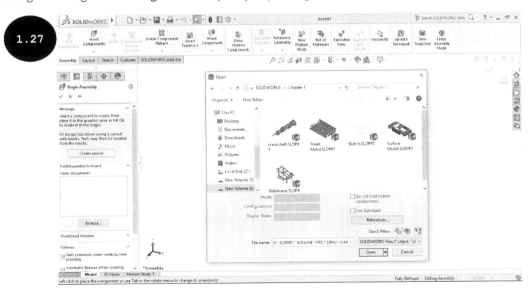

The **Open** dialog box is used to insert a component in the Assembly environment and appears automatically on invoking the Assembly environment, if no components are opened in the current session of SOLIDWORKS. You will learn about inserting components in the Assembly environment and different methods of creating assemblies in the later chapters.

Most of the components of the initial screen of the Assembly environment are the same as those of the Part modeling environment. The **Assembly CommandManager** is as follows:

Assembly CommandManager

The **Assembly CommandManager** is provided with different sets of tools that are used to insert components in the assembly environment, apply mates between the inserted components, create exploded views, pattern, and so on. Figure 1.28 shows the **Assembly CommandManager** and Figure 1.29 shows an assembly for your reference only.

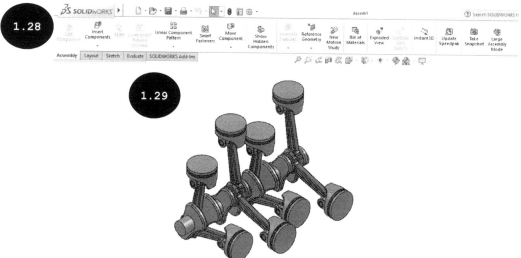

Invoking the Drawing Environment

To invoke the Drawing environment, click on the **New** tool in the **Standard** toolbar. The **New SOLIDWORKS Document** dialog box appears. In this dialog box, click on the **Drawing** button and then click on the **OK** button. The **Sheet Format/Size** dialog box appears, see Figure 1.30. In this dialog box, select the sheet size and format for creating drawings. Once you have defined sheet size and format in the dialog box, click on the **OK** button. The initial screen of the Drawing environment appears with the display of the **Model View PropertyManager** on the left of the drawing sheet, see Figure 1.31. The **Model View PropertyManager** is used to insert a component or an assembly in the Drawing environment for creating its drawing views. You will learn about creating drawing views of a component and an assembly in the later chapters.

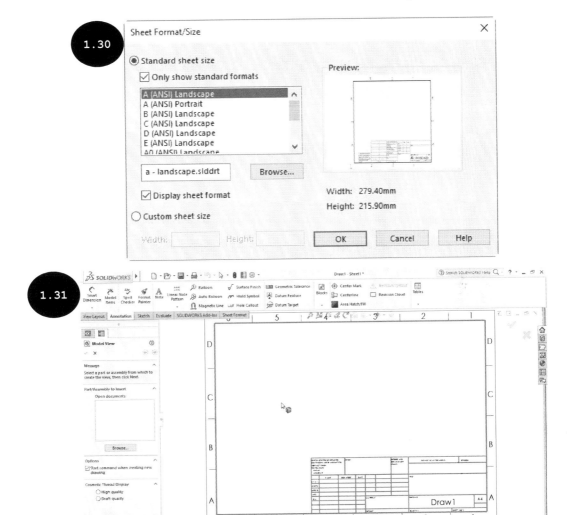

Most of the components of the initial screen of the Drawing environment are the same as of the Part modeling environment. The **View Layout CommandManager** and **Annotation CommandManager** of the Drawing environment are as follows:

View Layout CommandManager

The **View Layout CommandManager** is provided with different sets of tools that are used to create different drawing views such as orthogonal views, section views, and detail view of a component or an assembly. Figure 1.32 shows the **View Layout CommandManager** and Figure 1.33 shows different drawing views of a component for your reference only.

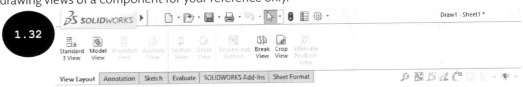

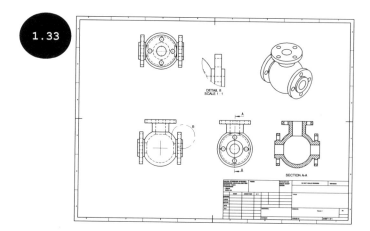

Annotation CommandManager

The **Annotation CommandManager** is provided with different sets of tools that are used to apply dimensions, note, surface/welding symbols, create BOM, and so on. Figure 1.34 shows the **Annotation CommandManager**.

Invoking a Shortcut Menu

A shortcut menu invokes when you right-click in the graphics area. It provides quick access to the most frequently used tools such as **Zoom to Fit**, **Zoom In/Out**, and **Pan**, see Figure 1.35. A shortcut menu also contains the **Context** toolbar, see Figure 1.35. Note that the availability of the tools in the **Context** toolbar and the shortcut menu depends on the entity selected to invoke the shortcut menu. Figure 1.36 shows a shortcut menu, which appeared after selecting a face of a feature in the Part modeling environment.

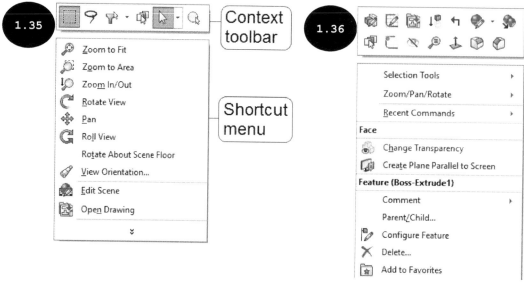

You can also customize to add frequently used tools in the **Context** toolbar of a shortcut menu, as required. The method to customize the **Context** toolbar is discussed next.

Customizing the Context Toolbar of the Shortcut Menu

In addition to the display of default tools in the **Context** toolbar, you can also customize it to add frequently used tools. To customize the **Context** toolbar, move the cursor over the **Context** toolbar in the shortcut menu and then right-click. The **Customize** option appears, see Figure 1.37. Next, click on the **Customize** option. The **Customize** dialog box appears along with the **Graphics Area** toolbar, see Figure 1.38.

36 Chapter 1 > Introduction to SOLIDWORKS

In the **Categories** area of the **Customize** dialog box, select the required category of tools. The tools of the selected category appear on the right side of the dialog box in the **Buttons** area. You can drag and drop tools from the **Buttons** area of the dialog box to the **Graphics Area** toolbar. Note that the tools added to the **Graphics Area** toolbar appear in the **Context** toolbar of the shortcut menu. Once you have added the required tools in the **Graphics Area** toolbar, click on the OK button in the dialog box.

Customizing the CommandManager

In addition to the default set of tools in a CommandManager, you can customize to add more tools in a CommandManager, as required. To customize a CommandManager, right-click on a tool of a CommandManager to be customized. A shortcut menu appears, see Figure 1.39. Next, click on the **Customize** tool in the shortcut menu. The **Customize** dialog box appears, see Figure 1.40. Next, click on the **Commands** tab in the **Customize** dialog box, see Figure 1.40.

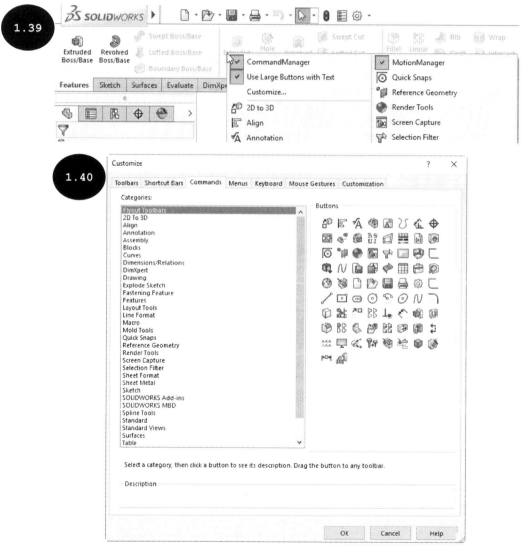

Next, select the required category of tools in the **Categories** area of the dialog box. The tools in the selected category appear on the right side of the dialog box in the **Buttons** area. Now, you can drag and drop the tools from the **Buttons** area of the dialog box to the CommandManager. You can also drag and drop the tools back to the **Buttons** area of the dialog box from the CommandManager. Once you have added the required tools in the CommandManager, click on the **OK** button in the dialog box.

Working with Mouse Gestures

Mouse Gestures act as a shortcut to quickly access the frequently used tools. To display the Mouse Gestures, press and hold the right mouse button in the graphics area and then drag the cursor a small distance, see Figure 1.41. Note that different default tools in the Mouse Gestures appear in different environments of SOLIDWORKS. Also, by default, the four tools are displayed in the Mouse Gestures. You can display either four tools or eight tools in the Mouse Gestures. To display eight tools in the Mouse Gestures, click on the **Tools > Customize** in the SOLIDWORKS menus. The **Customize** dialog box appears. In this dialog box, click on the **Mouse Gestures** tab and then select the **8 gestures** radio button, see Figure 1.42. You can also customize the tools of the Mouse Gestures for different environments of SOLIDWORKS by using the table displayed in the **Mouse Gestures** tab of the **Customize** dialog box. For example, to customize the tools of the Mouse Gestures for the Part environment, click on the field corresponding to a respective tool row and the **Part** column in the table of the **Mouse Gestures** tab in the dialog box. An arrow appears in the field. Click on this arrow to display the drop-down list. In this drop-down list, you can select the required option to add the tool at the respective location of the Mouse Gestures.

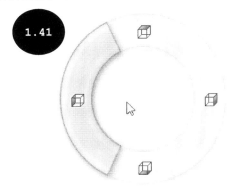

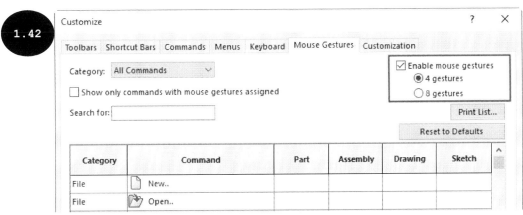

Saving Documents

To save a document created in any of the environment of SOLIDWORKS, click on the **Save** button in the **Standard** toolbar or click on **File > Save** in the SOLIDWORKS menus. The **Save As** dialog box appears. Enter the name of the document in the **File name** field of the dialog box and then browse to the location where you want to save the document. Next, click on the **Save** button.

Opening Existing Documents

To open an existing SOLIDWORKS Document, click on the **Open** button in the **Standard** toolbar or click on **File > Open** in the SOLIDWORKS menus. The **Open** dialog box appears. In this dialog box, select the **SOLIDWORKS Files (*.sldprt; *.sldasm; *.slddrw)** file extension from the **File Type** drop-down list. Note that you can select the file extension from the **File Type** drop-down list depending upon the document to be opened. After selecting the required file extension, browse to the location where the SOLIDWORKS document is saved and then click on the document to be opened. Next, click on the **Open** button in the dialog box. The selected document gets opened.

Similar to opening existing SOLIDWORKS documents, you can also open/import documents created in other CAD applications. SOLIDWORKS allows you to open documents created in CATIA V5, ProE/Creo, Unigraphics/NX, Inventor, Solid Edge, CADKEY, Rhino, DWG, and so on by selecting the respective file type from the **File Type** drop-down list of the **Open** dialog box. In addition to this, you can also open documents saved in universal CAD formats such as IGES, STEP, SLT, and Parasolid.

Summary

In this chapter, you have learned about system requirements for installing SOLIDWORKS. You have also learned how to invoke different SOLIDWORKS environments, identifying SOLIDWORKS documents, various components of the initial screen of SOLIDWORKS, invoking and customizing the shortcut menu, saving documents, and opening documents in SOLIDWORKS.

Questions

- The surface modeling environment and the Sheet Metal environment of SOLIDWORKS can be invoked within the _____ modeling environment.

- The file extension of the documents created in the Part modeling environment is _____, the Assembly environment is _____, and the Drawing environment is _____.

- In SOLIDWORKS, a component can be designed by creating all its _____ one by one.

- The FeatureManager Design Tree is used to a keep record of all operations/features in an order.

CHAPTER 2

Drawing Sketches with SOLIDWORKS

In this chapter, you will learn the following:

- Invoking the Part Modeling Environment
- Invoking the Sketching Environment
- Working with Selection of Planes
- Specifying Units
- Specifying Grids and Snaps Settings
- Drawing a Line Entity
- Drawing an Arc by using the Line tool
- Drawing a Centerline
- Drawing a Midpoint Line
- Drawing a Rectangle
- Drawing a Circle
- Drawing an Arc
- Drawing a Polygon
- Drawing a Slot
- Drawing an Ellipse
- Drawing an Elliptical Arc
- Drawing a Parabola
- Drawing Conic Curves
- Drawing a Spline
- Editing a Spline

SOLIDWORKS is a feature-based, parametric, solid modeling mechanical design and automation software. Before you start creating solid 3D components in SOLIDWORKS, you need to understand it. To design a component in this software, you need to create all its features one by one, see Figures 2.1 and 2.2. Note that features are divided in two main categories: sketch based features and placed features. A feature created by using a sketch is known as sketch based feature, whereas a feature created by specifying placement on an existing feature and a sketch is not required is known as placed feature. Of these, two categories, the sketch based feature is the first feature of any real world component to be designed. Therefore, drawing sketch is important to be learned first.

40 Chapter 2 > Drawing Sketches with SOLIDWORKS

Figure 2.1 shows a component consists of extruded feature, cut feature, chamfer, and fillet. Of all these features, extruded and cut features are created by using a sketch. Therefore, these features are known as sketch based features. On the other hand, the fillet and the chamfer are known as placed features because no sketch is used for creating these features.

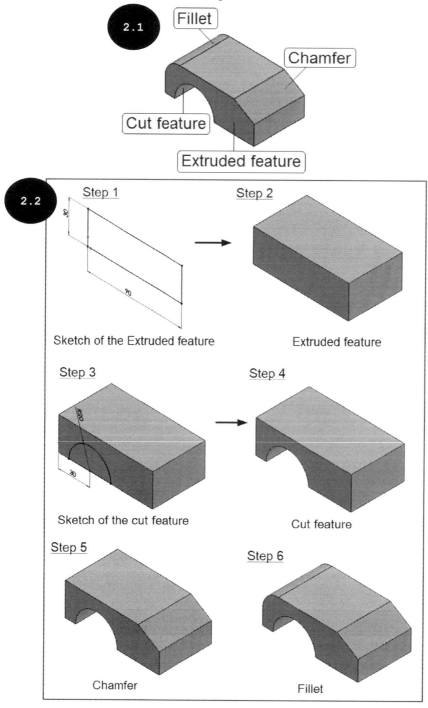

As the first feature of any component is a sketch based feature, you need to first learn how to create sketches in the Sketching environment. In SOLIDWORKS, the Sketching environment can be invoked within the Part modeling environment.

Invoking the Part Modeling Environment

Start SOLIDWORKS by double-clicking on the SOLIDWORKS 2017 icon on your desktop. After loading all required files, the initial screen of SOLIDWORKS appears as shown in Figure 2.3. Once the initial screen of SOLIDWORKS has been invoked, click on the **New** tool in the **Standard** toolbar or click on the **New Document** tool in the **SOLIDWORKS Resources Task Pane**, see Figure 2.3. The **New SOLIDWORKS Document** dialog box appears, see Figure 2.4.

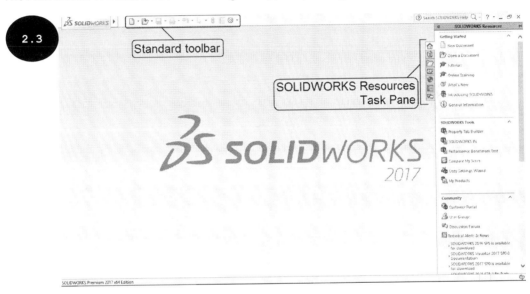

Note: If you are invoking the **New SOLIDWORKS Document** dialog box for the first time after installing the software, the **Units and Dimension Standard** dialog box appears. You can specify the unit system as the default unit system for SOLIDWORKS by using this dialog box.

In this textbook, the metric unit system and ANSI standard have been used. Therefore, select the **MMGS (millimeter, gram, second)** option from the **Units** drop-down list and **ANSI** option from the **Dimension standard** drop-down list of the **Units and Dimension Standard** dialog box.

42 Chapter 2 > Drawing Sketches with SOLIDWORKS

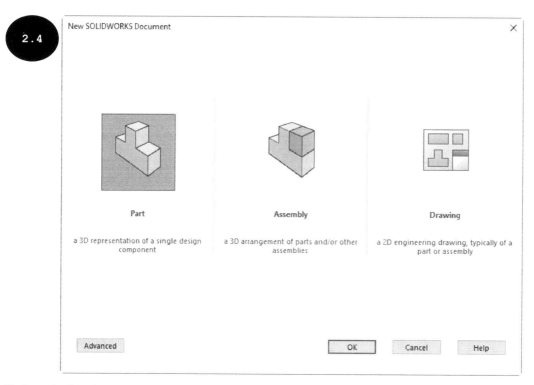

Click on the **Part** button in the **New SOLIDWORKS Document** dialog box and then click on the **OK** button. The initial screen of the Part modeling environment of SOLIDWORKS appears, see Figure 2.5. Various components of the Part modeling environment have been discussed in Chapter 1. Once the Part modeling environment is invoked, you can invoke the Sketching environment for creating the sketch of the first feature of a model.

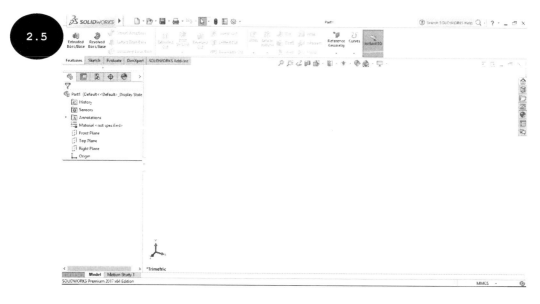

Invoking the Sketching Environment

After the Part modeling environment is invoked, you need to invoke the Sketching environment for creating the sketch of the first feature of a model. To invoke the Sketching environment, click on the **Sketch** tab in the CommandManager. The tools of the **Sketch CommandManager** appear, see Figure 2.6.

Click on the **Sketch** tool in the **Sketch CommandManager** to invoke the Sketching environment, see Figure 2.6. The three default planes: Front, Top, and Right, which are mutually perpendicular to each other appear in the graphics area, see Figure 2.7. Also, the **Edit Sketch PropertyManager** appears on the left of the graphics area. Now, you can select any of the three default planes as the sketching plane for creating the sketch. To select a plane, move the cursor over the plane to be selected. Next, click the left mouse button when the boundary of the plane highlights in the graphics area. As soon as you select a plane, the Sketching environment gets invoked with a Confirmation corner at the top right corner in the graphics area, see Figure 2.8. Also, the selected plane becomes the sketching plane for drawing the sketch and it is oriented normal to the viewing direction, so that you can create the sketch easily. Note that the Confirmation corner consists of two icons: **Exit Sketch** and **Cancel Sketch**. The **Exit Sketch** icon is used to confirm the creation of the sketch successfully and to exit the Sketching environment. Whereas, the **Cancel Sketch** icon is used to discard the sketch created.

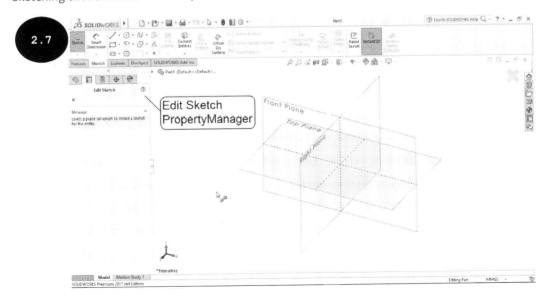

44 Chapter 2 > Drawing Sketches with SOLIDWORKS

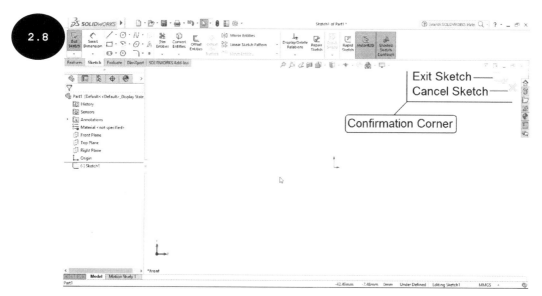

The Sketching environment also displays a red color point with two perpendicular arrows in the center of the graphics area. The red color point represents the origin (0,0) of the Sketching environment and the perpendicular arrows represent the X axis and Y axis of the sketching plane. If the red color point does not appear by default in the graphics area, turn on its appearance by clicking on **Hide/Show Items > View Origins** in the **View (Heads-Up)** toolbar, see Figure 2.9. The **View Origins** tool of the **View (Heads-Up)** toolbar is a toggle button.

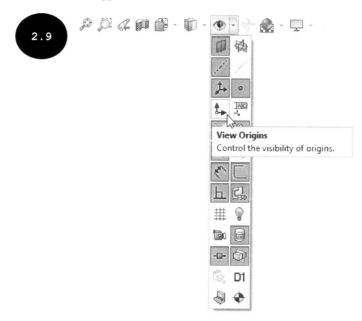

Working with Selection of Planes

As discussed earlier, the Sketching environment can be invoked by selecting a plane as the sketching plane. Selection of correct plane is very important to define the right orientation of the model. Figure 2.10 shows the isometric view of a model having length 200 mm, width 100 mm, and height 40 mm. To create this model with the same orientation, select the Top plane as the sketching plane and then draw a rectangular sketch of 200X100. However, if you select the Front plane as the sketching plane for creating this model, you need to draw a rectangular sketch of 200X40. Likewise, if you select the Right plane as the sketching plane, you need to draw a rectangular sketch of 100X40.

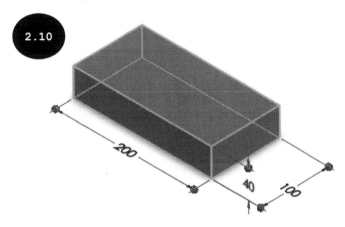

Once the Sketching environment has been invoked, you can start drawing the sketch by using different sketching tools in the **Sketch CommandManager**. However, before you start drawing the sketch, it is important to understand the procedure for setting the units of measurement and grids.

Specifying Units

When you invoke the SOLIDWORKS software first time after the installation, the **Units and Dimension Standard** dialog box appears. This dialog box allows you to specify units and measuring standard as the default settings. Note that the units and measuring settings specified in the **Units and Dimension Standard** dialog box become the default units for all new documents to be opened. However, SOLIDWORKS allows you to modify the default unit settings at any point of your design for any particular document.

To modify the default unit settings, click on the **Options** tool in the **Standard** toolbar. The **System Options** dialog box appears, see Figure 2.11.

The **System Options** dialog box contains two tabs: **System Options** and **Document Properties**. By default, the **System Options** tab is activated in the dialog box. Click on the **Document Properties** tab of the dialog box. The name of the dialog box changes to **Document Properties**. Also, all options for setting document properties appear in the dialog box. Click on the **Units** options on the left panel in the dialog box. The options for setting the units appear on the right panel of the dialog box, see Figure 2.12.

46 Chapter 2 > Drawing Sketches with SOLIDWORKS

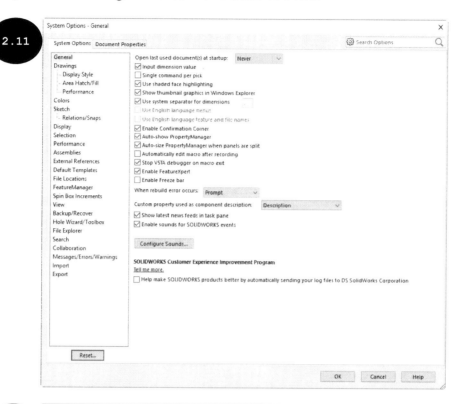

Note that the **Unit system** area of the dialog box displays a list of predefine standard unit systems. In this area, you can select the required predefined unit system for the document that has currently been opened. For example, to set the metric unit system for the currently opened document, click on the **MMGS (millimeter, gram, second)** radio button. Note that in the metric unit system, the length is measured in millimeters, mass is calculated in grams, and time is represented in seconds.

You can also specify the unit system for the currently opened document other than the default predefined standard unit systems by clicking on the **Custom** radio button. On clicking the **Custom** radio button, the fields in the table available at the bottom of the dialog box get activated. Now, you can change the unit of length measurement, angle measurement, mass calculation, and time as per your requirement other than the standard combination. For example, to change the unit of length measurement, click on the field corresponding to the **Unit** column and the **Length** row in the table. A down arrow appears. Next, click on the down arrow. A drop-down list appears with a list of different units for length measurement. Now, you can select the required unit from this drop-down list. Similarly, you can change units for other measurements in this table. You can also specify decimal places for the measurement as per the requirement by using this table. Once you have set all the required units of measurements for the currently opened document, click on the **OK** button to accept the changes made in the dialog box.

Specifying Grids and Snaps Settings

Grids help you specify points in the drawing area for creating sketch entities and act as reference lines. By default, the display of grids is turned off in the drawing area. You can turn on the display of grids in the drawing area and specify snap settings such that the movement of the cursor is restricted at specified intervals.

To turn on the display of grids and specifying snap settings, click on the **Options** tool in the **Standard** toolbar, which is available next to the SOLIDWORKS logo in the upper left corner. The **System Options - General** dialog box appears. Click on the **Document Properties** tab in the dialog box. The options related to document properties appear and the name of the dialog box changes to **Document Properties - Drafting Standard**. Next, click on the **Grid/Snap** option in the left panel of the dialog box. The options related to grids and snaps settings appear on the right panel of the dialog box. Also, the name of the dialog box changes to **Document Properties - Grid/Snap**, see Figure 2.13.

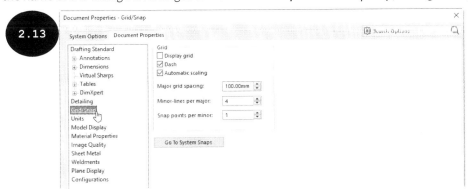

In the **Major grid spacing** field of the **Grid** area in the dialog box, specify the distance between two major grid lines. In the **Minor-lines per major** field of the dialog box, specify the number of minor lines

48 Chapter 2 > Drawing Sketches with SOLIDWORKS

between two major grid lines. Note that the value entered in the **Minor-lines per major** field defines the number of division between two major grid lines. For example, if you enter 5 in the **Minor-lines per major** field, then two major grid lines will be divided into 5 smaller areas horizontally or vertically. In the **Snap points per minor** field, you can specify the number of snap points for the cursor between two minor grid lines.

You can turn on the display of grids in the drawing area by selecting the **Display grid** check box in the **Grid** area of the dialog box. Similarly, you can turn the snap mode on for snapping the cursor to the specified snap settings. To do so, click on the **Go To System Snaps** button in the dialog box. The name of the dialog box changes to **System Options - Relations/Snaps**. In this dialog box, you can select the **Grid** check box for turning the snap mode on. If you select the **Snap only when grid appears** check box of this dialog box, the cursor snaps only when the display of grids is turned on. Note that snapping of the cursor at specific intervals is very useful for defining exact points in the drawing area for creating sketch entities. Once you have specified the grid and snap settings in the dialog box, click on the **OK** button to accept the changes made in the dialog box. Figure 2.14 shows the drawing area with the display of grids turned on.

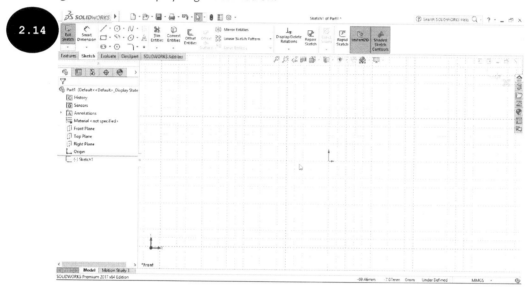

2.14

Note: In this textbook, the background color of the graphics area has been changed to white for clarity. To change the background color, click on the **Option** tool in the **Standard** toolbar to invoke the **System Options - General** dialog box. Next, click on the **Colors** option in the left panel of the dialog box. The options to specify color scheme settings appear on the right panel of the dialog box. Select the **Plain (Viewport Background color above)** radio button in the **Background appearance** area of the dialog box. Make sure that the **Viewport Background** option is selected in the **Color scheme settings** area of the dialog box. Next, click on the **Edit** button available in the right of the **Color scheme settings** area. The **Color** swatch window appears. In this window, select the white color and then click on the **OK** button. Next, click on the **OK** button in the **System Options - General** dialog box. The background color of the drawing area is changed to white.

Drawing a Line Entity

A line is defined as the shortest distance between two points. To draw a line, click on the **Line** tool in the **Sketch CommandManager**. The **Insert Line PropertyManager** appears on the left of the drawing area, see Figure 2.15. Also, the appearance of the cursor changes to line cursor. The line cursor appears with the symbol of a pencil and a line. You can click in the drawing area to specify a start point and then an endpoint for drawing a line. Note that you can draw a chain of continuous lines by clicking the left mouse button one by one in the drawing area. To end the creation of a continuous chain of lines, press the ESC key. Alternatively, right-click in the drawing area and then click on the **Select** option in the shortcut menu appeared. The options in the **Insert Line PropertyManager** are used to control the settings for drawing lines. The options are as follows:

Message

The **Message** rollout of the **Insert Line PropertyManager** displays appropriate information about the required action to be performed for creating a line entity.

Orientation

The **Orientation** rollout is used to control the orientation of a line. The options in the **Orientation** rollout are as follows:

As sketched

By default, the **As sketched** radio button is activated in the **Orientation** rollout. As a result, you can draw a line of required orientation by clicking the left mouse button in the drawing area. In this case, the orientation of the line depends upon the points you specify by clicking the left mouse button in the drawing area.

Horizontal

On selecting the **Horizontal** radio button in the **Orientation** rollout, you can draw a horizontal line only by clicking the left mouse button in the drawing area. Notice that when you select this radio button, the **Parameters** rollout appears below the **Options** rollout in the PropertyManager, see Figure 2.16. In the **Parameters** rollout, the **Length** field is activated, by default. You can specify the required length value of the horizontal line in this field. By default, value 0 is entered in this field. As a result, you can draw a horizontal line of required length by specifying two points in the drawing area.

Vertical
Similar to drawing a horizontal line by selecting the **Horizontal** radio button, you can draw vertical lines by selecting the **Vertical** radio button in the **Orientation** rollout of the PropertyManager.

Angle
The **Angle** radio button is used to draw a line at an angle. As soon as you select this radio button, the **Parameters** rollout appears in the PropertyManager with the **Length** and **Angle** fields. You can specify the required length and angle values of the line in the respective fields of this rollout. By default, value 0 is entered in both the fields. As a result, you can draw a line of required length and angle by specifying the points in the drawing area.

> **Note:** The angle values of the line entered in the **Angle** field of the **Parameters** rollout, is measured from the X axis of the plane.

Options
The options in the **Options** rollout of the **PropertyManager** are as follows:

For construction
The **For construction** check box of the **Options** rollout is used to draw a construction or reference line.

Infinite length
The **Infinite length** check box is used to draw a line of infinite length. On selecting the **Infinite length** check box, you can draw a line of infinite length by specifying two points in the drawing area.

Midpoint line
The **Midpoint line** check box is used to draw a symmetric line about a point. On selecting the **Midpoint line** check box, you need to first specify the midpoint of a line and then an endpoint by clicking the left mouse button in the drawing area. A line symmetric about the midpoint is drawn.

Procedure for Drawing a Line
1. Click on the **Line** tool in the **Sketch CommandManager**. The **Line** tool gets activated.
2. Click to specify the start point of the line in the drawing area.
3. Move the line cursor away from the start point. A rubber band line appears with one of its ends fixed at the start point and the other end attached to the cursor. Notice that as you move the cursor, the length of the rubber band line changes and appears near the cursor, see Figure 2.17.

Note: If you move the cursor horizontally or vertically after specifying the start point of the line, the symbol of horizontal — or vertical ∣ relation appears near the cursor. The symbol of relation indicates that if you click the left mouse button to specify the second point of the line, the corresponding relation will be applied. You will learn more about the relations in later chapters.

4. Click the left mouse button to specify the second point of the line when the length of the line appears near the cursor, closer to the required one. A line between the specified points is drawn. Also, notice that the rubber band line is still displayed with one of its ends fixed to the last specified point and the other end attached to the cursor. It indicates that a chain of continuous lines can be drawn by clicking the left mouse button in the drawing area.

Tip: As SOLIDWORKS is a parametric, 3D solid modeling software, you can first draw a sketch in which measurements of the entities may not be exact. Once the sketch has been drawn without dimensions, you need to apply dimensions. You will learn about dimensioning sketch entities in later chapters.

5. Once all the line entities have been drawn, right-click in the drawing area. A shortcut menu appears. In this shortcut menu, click on the **Select** option to exit the **Line** tool.

Example 1

Draw the sketch of the model shown in Figure 2.18. The dimensions and the model shown in the figure are for your reference only.

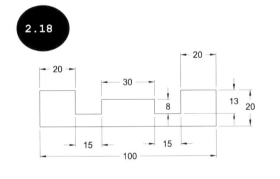
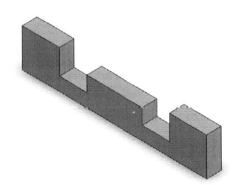

2.18

Section 1: Starting SOLIDWORKS
1. Start SOLIDWORKS by double-clicking on the SOLIDWORKS icon on your desktop.

Section 2: Invoking the Part Modeling Environment
1. Click on the **New** tool in the **Standard** toolbar, which is available next to the SOLIDWORKS logo in the upper left corner. The **New SOLIDWORKS Document** dialog box appears.

52   Chapter 2 > Drawing Sketches with SOLIDWORKS

2. Click on the **Part** button and then click on the **OK** button in the dialog box. The Part modeling environment is invoked, see Figure 2.19.

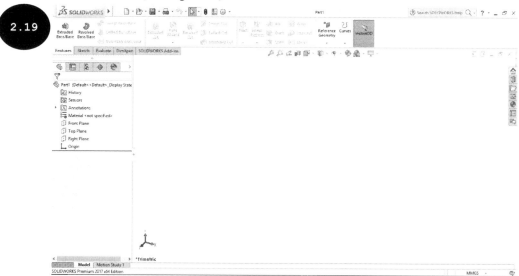

Section 3: Invoking the Sketching Environment

1. Click on the **Sketch** tab in the CommandManager. The tools of the **Sketch CommandManager** are displayed.

2. Click on the **Sketch** button in the **Sketch CommandManager**. The three default planes mutually perpendicular to each other appear in the graphics area.

3. Move the cursor over the Front plane and then click the left mouse button when the boundary of the plane gets highlighted. The Sketching environment is invoked. Also, the Front plane is orientated normal to the viewing direction and the Confirmation corner appears at the upper right corner of the drawing area, see Figure 2.20.

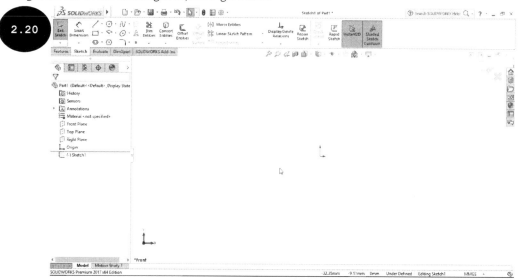

Note: In this example, the display of grids and snaps settings have been turned off.

Section 4: Drawing the Sketch

1. Click on the **Line** tool in the **Sketch CommandManager**. The **Line** tool gets activated and the **Insert Line PropertyManager** appears on the left of the drawing area. Also, the appearance of the cursor changes to line cursor.

2. Move the cursor to the origin and then click to specify the start point of the line when the cursor snaps to the origin.

3. Move the cursor horizontally toward right and click to specify the endpoint of the line when the length of the line appears close to 100 mm near the cursor, see Figure 2.21.

4. Move the cursor vertically upward and then click the left mouse button when the length of the line appears close to 20 mm near the cursor, see Figure 2.22.

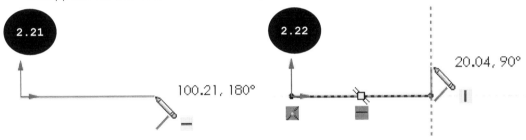

5. Move the cursor horizontally toward left and click when the length of the line appears close to 20 mm.

6. Move the cursor vertically downward and click when the length of the line appears close to 13 mm near the cursor, see Figure 2.23.

7. Move the cursor horizontally toward left and click when the length of the line appears close to 15 mm.

8. Move the cursor vertically upward and click when the length of the line appears close to 8 mm, see Figure 2.24.

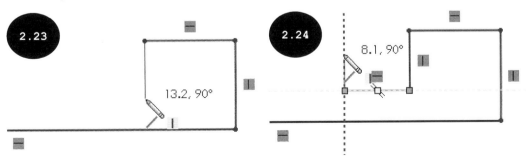

9. Move the cursor horizontally toward left and click when the length of the line appears close to 30 mm, see Figure 2.25.

10. Move the cursor vertically downward and click when the length of the line appears close to 8 mm, see Figure 2.26.

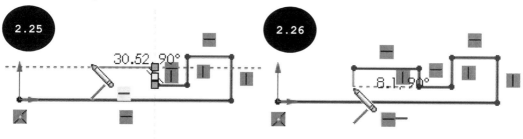

11. Similarly, draw the remaining sketch entities. Figure 2.27 shows the sketch after all the sketch entities have been drawn.

12. Right-click in the drawing area. A shortcut menu appears. In this shortcut menu, click on the **Select** option to exit the **Line** tool.

Tip: In the Figure 2.27, the display of automatic applied relations such as horizontal and vertical is turned off. To turn off or on the display of relations in the drawing area, click on **Hide/Show Items > View Sketch Relations** in the **View (Heads-Up)** toolbar, see Figure 2.28. The **View Sketch Relations** button is a toggle button.

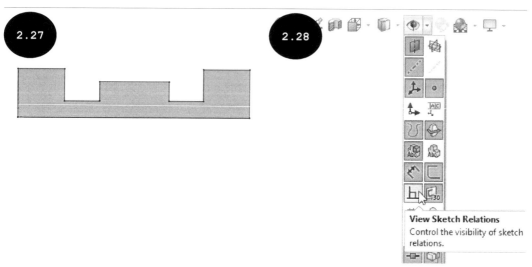

13. Click on the **Save** tool in the **Standard** toolbar. The **Save As** dialog box appears. Next, browse to the location where you want to save the sketch.

14. Enter **Example 1** in the **File name** field of the dialog box and then click on the **Save** button. The sketch is saved in the specified location.

Hands-on Test Drive 1

Draw a sketch of the model shown in Figure 2.29. The dimensions and the model shown in the figure are for your reference only.

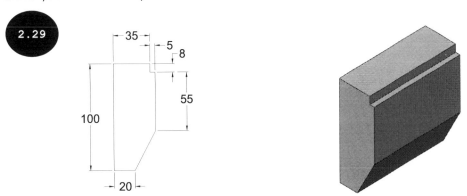

Drawing an Arc by using the Line tool

SOLIDWORKS is provided with different set of tools for drawing arcs: **Centerpoint Arc**, **3 Point Arc**, and **Tangent Arc**. The tools for drawing arcs are discussed later in this chapter. In addition to drawing arcs by using these tools, you can also draw a tangent arc by using the **Line** tool. Note that in order to draw a tangent arc by using the **Line** tool, at least one line or arc entity has to be drawn in the drawing area. The procedure to draw a tangent arc by using the **Line** tool is as follows:

Procedure for Drawing an Arc by using the Line tool

1. Invoke the Sketching environment.
2. Invoke the **Line** tool and then draw a line by specifying two points in the drawing area. Once the line is drawn, do not exit the **Line** tool.
3. Move the cursor away from the last specified point and then move it back to the last specified point. An orange color dot appears in the drawing area, see Figure 2.30.
4. Move the cursor away from the point. The arc mode is activated and the preview of a tangent arc appears in the drawing area, see Figure 2.31.

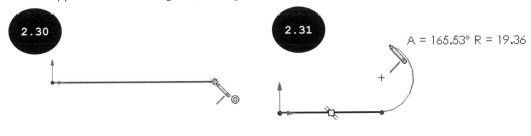

Note: The creation of arc depends on how you move the cursor from the last specified point in the drawing area. Figure 2.32 shows movements of the cursor and the creation of arcs.

56 Chapter 2 > Drawing Sketches with SOLIDWORKS

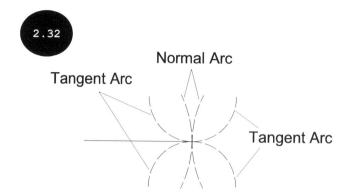

5. Click the left mouse button to specify the endpoint of the arc when the angle and radius values appear close to the required one. An arc is drawn and the line mode is activated again. You can continue with the creation of line entities or move the cursor back to the last specified point to invoke the arc mode for drawing an arc.
6. Once you have created all entities, right-click in the drawing area and then click on the **Select** option in the shortcut menu to exit the **Line** tool.

Example 2

Draw a sketch of the model shown in Figure 2.33 by using the **Line** tool. The dimensions and the model shown in this figure are for your reference only.

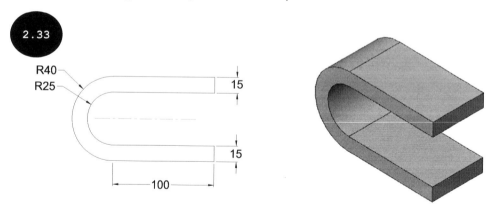

Section 1: Starting SOLIDWORKS
1. Start SOLIDWORKS by double-clicking on the SOLIDWORKS icon on your desktop, if not started already.

Section 2: Invoking the Part Modeling Environment
1. Click on the **New** tool in the **Standard** toolbar. The **New SOLIDWORKS Document** dialog box appears.

2. Click on the **Part** button and then click on the **OK** button. The Part modeling environment is invoked.

Section 3: Invoking the Sketching Environment

1. Click on the **Sketch** tab in the CommandManager. The tools of the **Sketch CommandManager** are displayed.

2. Click on the **Sketch** button in the **Sketch CommandManager**. The three default planes mutually perpendicular to each other appear in the graphics area.

3. Move the cursor over the Front plane and click when the boundary of the plane is highlighted. The Sketching environment is invoked and the Front plane is orientated normal to the viewing direction, see Figure 2.34.

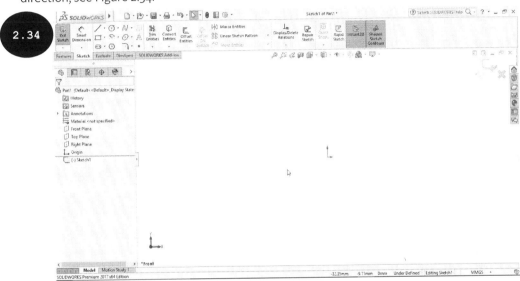

It is evident from Figure 2.33 that all the sketch entities are multiples of 5 mm. Therefore, you can set the snap settings such that the cursor snaps to the increment of 5 mm only.

Section 4: Specifying Grid and Snap Settings

1. Click on the **Options** tool in the **Standard** toolbar, which is available next to the SOLIDWORKS logo in the upper left corner. The **System Options - General** dialog box appears.

2. Click on the **Document Properties** tab in the dialog box. The name of the dialog box changes to **Document Properties - Drafting Standard**.

3. Click on the **Units** option in the left panel of the dialog box. The options to specify the unit system appear on the right panel of the dialog box.

4. Click on the **MMGS (millimeter, gram, second)** radio button in the **Unit system** area of the dialog box, if not selected by default.

58 Chapter 2 > Drawing Sketches with SOLIDWORKS

Now, you need to specify the grid and snap settings such that the cursor snaps to the increment of 5 mm.

5. Click on the **Grid/Snap** option in the left panel of the dialog box. The options for grid and snap settings appear on the right panel of the dialog box. Also, the name of the dialog box changes to **Document Properties - Grid/Snap**.

6. Enter **20** in the **Major grid spacing** field; **4** in the **Minor -lines per major** field; and **1** in the **Snap points per minor** field of the **Grid** area in the dialog box.

7. Select the **Display grid** check box in the **Grid** area of the dialog box to turn on the display of grids in the drawing area based on the grid settings specified in the above step.

8. Click on the **Go To System Snaps** button in the **Document Properties - Grid/Snap** dialog box. The name of the dialog box changes to **System Options - Relations/Snaps**.

9. Click on the **Grid** check box in the **Sketch snaps** area of the dialog box to turn on the snap mode.

10. Click on the **OK** button in the dialog box. The grid and snap settings have been specified and the dialog box is closed. Also, the drawing area appears similar to the one shown in Figure 2.35.

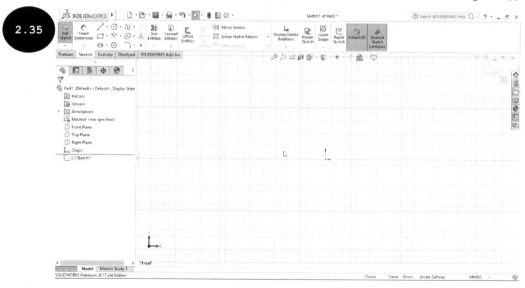

Once the units, grid, and snap settings have been specified, you can start creating the sketch by using the **Line** tool.

Section 5: Drawing the Sketch

1. Click on the **Line** tool in the **Sketch CommandManager**. The **Line** tool gets activated and the **Insert Line PropertyManager** appears on the left of the drawing area. Also, the appearance of the cursor changes to the line cursor .

2. Move the cursor to the origin and click to specify the start point of the line when the cursor snaps to the origin.

3. Move the cursor horizontally toward left and then click to specify the second point of the line when the length of the line appears 100 mm near the cursor, see Figure 2.36. Notice that the cursor is snapping incrementally to the distance of 5 mm.

4. Move the cursor away from the last specified point and then move it back to the last specified point. An orange color dot appears in the drawing area, see Figure 2.37.

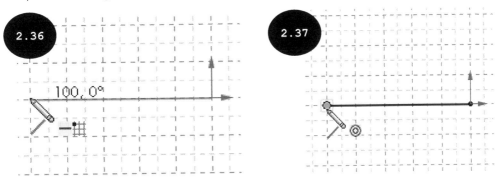

5. Move the cursor horizontally toward left for a little distance and then move it vertically upward. The arc mode is activated and the preview of the tangent arc appears in the drawing area, see Figure 2.38.

6. Click to specify the endpoint of the tangent arc when the angle and radius values of the arc appear 180 degrees and 40 mm, respectively, near the cursor, see Figure 2.39. The tangent arc is created and the preview of a line is attached to the cursor.

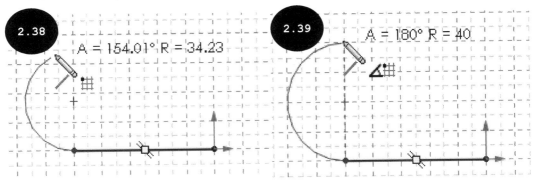

7. Move the cursor horizontally toward right and click when the length of the line appears 100 mm near the cursor.

8. Move the cursor vertically downward and click when the length of the line appears 15 mm.

9. Move the cursor horizontally toward left and click when the length of the line appears 100 mm.

10. Move the cursor for a little distance and then move it back to the last specified point. An orange color dot appears in the drawing area, see Figure 2.40.

11. Move the cursor horizontally toward left for a little distance and then move it vertically downward. The arc mode is activated and the preview of the tangent arc appears in the drawing area, see Figure 2.41.

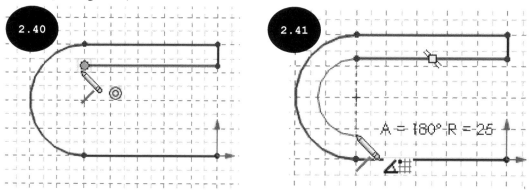

12. Click to specify the endpoint of the tangent arc when the angle and radius values of the arc appear 180 degrees and 25 mm, respectively, see Figure 2.41. The tangent arc is created and the line mode is activated.

13. Move the cursor horizontally toward right and click when the length of the line appears 100 mm near the cursor.

14. Move the cursor vertically downward and click when the cursor snaps to the start point of the first sketch entity.

15. Right-click in the drawing area. A shortcut menu appears. In this shortcut menu, click on the **Select** option to exit the **Line** tool. The final sketch is drawn, see Figure 2.42.

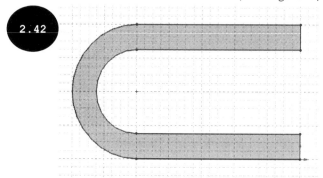

16. Click on the **Save** tool in the **Standard** toolbar. The **Save As** dialog box appears. Next, browse to the location where you want to save the sketch.

17. Enter **Example 2** in the **File name** field of the dialog box and then click on the **Save** button. The sketch is saved in the specified location.

Hands-on Test Drive 2

Draw a sketch of the model shown in Figure 2.43. The dimensions and the model shown in the figure are for your reference only. Draw all entities of the sketch by using the **Line** tool. As all the dimensions of the sketch are multiples of 5 mm, you can set the snap setting such that the cursor snaps to the increment of 5 mm.

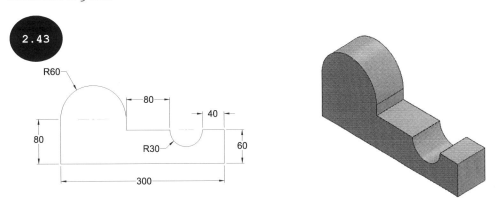

Drawing a Centerline

Centerlines are defined as reference or construction lines, which are drawn for the aid of sketches. In SOLIDWORKS, you can draw a centerline by using the **Centerline** tool. To draw a centerline, click on the down arrow next to the **Line** tool in the **Sketch CommandManager**. The **Line** flyout appears, see Figure 2.44. In this flyout, click on the **Centerline** tool. The **Centerline** tool gets activated and the **Insert Line PropertyManager** appears, in which the **For construction** check box is selected, by default, see Figure 2.45. The options in this PropertyManager are same as those discussed earlier while drawing line entities. Also, the procedure of drawing centerlines is the same as that of drawing lines. Figure 2.46 shows a horizontal centerline drawn by specifying two points in the drawing area.

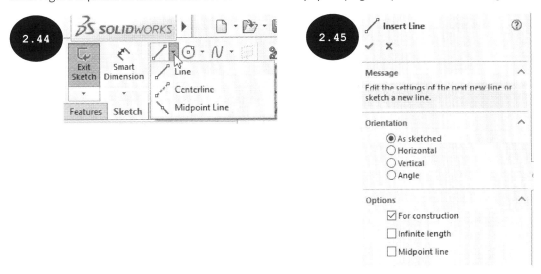

Drawing a Midpoint Line

A midpoint line is created symmetrically about its midpoint. In SOLIDWORKS, you can draw midpoint lines by using the **Midpoint Line** tool in the **Line** flyout. To invoke the **Midpoint Line** tool, click on the down arrow next to the **Line** tool in the **Sketch CommandManager**. The **Line** flyout appears, refer to Figure 2.44. In this flyout, click on the **Midpoint Line** tool. The **Midpoint Line** tool gets activated and the **Insert Line PropertyManager** appears, in which the **Midpoint line** check box is selected, by default, see Figure 2.47. The options in this PropertyManager are the same as those discussed earlier while drawing line entities. The procedure to draw a midpoint line is as follows:

Procedure for Drawing a Midpoint Line
1. Invoke the **Line** flyout and then click on the **Midpoint Line** tool.
2. Click to specify the midpoint of a line in the drawing area, see Figure 2.48.
3. Move the cursor to the required location for defining the endpoint of the line. Note that as you move the cursor, the preview of a line symmetry about the midpoint appears, see Figure 2.48.
4. Click to specify the endpoint of the line. A line symmetry about the midpoint is created.

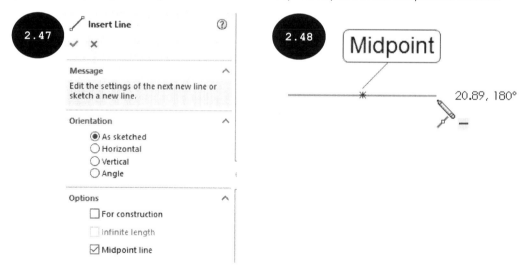

Drawing a Rectangle

In SOLIDWORKS, you can draw a rectangle by different methods using the tools in the **Rectangle** flyout of the **Sketch CommandManager**, see Figure 2.49. To invoke the **Rectangle** flyout, click on the down arrow next to the active rectangle tool in the **Sketch CommandManager**, see Figure 2.49. The tools for drawing a rectangle are as follows:

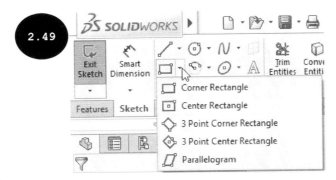

Corner Rectangle

The **Corner Rectangle** tool is used to draw a rectangle by specifying two diagonally opposite corners. The first specified corner defines the position of the rectangle and the second corner defines the length and width of the rectangle, see Figure 2.50.

To create a rectangle by using the **Corner Rectangle** tool, invoke the **Rectangle** flyout, see Figure 2.49, and then click on the **Corner Rectangle** tool. The **Corner Rectangle** tool gets activated and the **Rectangle PropertyManager** appears on the left of the drawing area, see Figure 2.51. The options in the **Rectangle PropertyManager** are as follows:

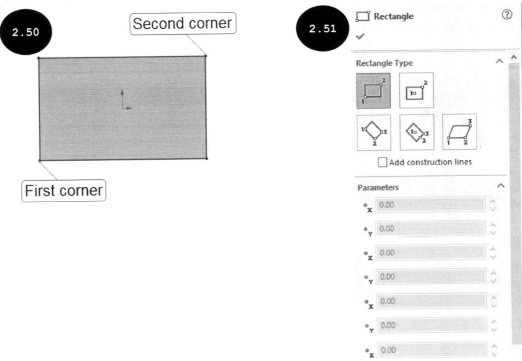

Rectangle Type

The **Rectangle Type** rollout of the PropertyManager is used to switch between different methods of drawing rectangle. By default, depending upon the rectangle tool invoked, the respective button is activated in this rollout.

The **Add construction lines** check box of the **Rectangle Type** rollout is used to add construction lines in a rectangle. On selecting this check box, the **From Corners** and **From Midpoints** radio buttons become available, see Figure 2.52. When the **From Corners** radio button is selected, the construction lines connecting corner to corner are added in the rectangle, see Figure 2.53. By selecting the **From Midpoints** radio button, the construction lines connecting the midpoint of the line segments are added in the rectangle, see Figure 2.54.

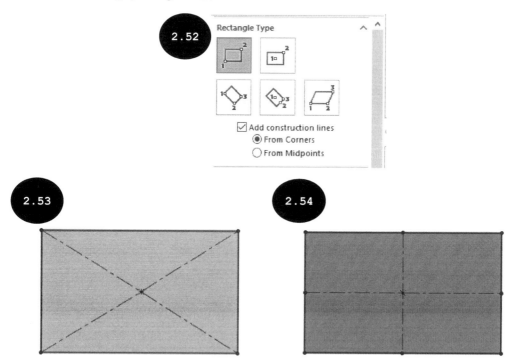

Parameters
The options in the **Parameters** rollout of the **Rectangle PropertyManager** are used to display or control parameters of the rectangle. Note that all the options of the rollout get activated once a rectangle has been drawn and is selected in the drawing area.

Procedure for Drawing a Rectangle by using the Corner Rectangle Tool
1. Invoke the **Rectangle** flyout and then click on the **Corner Rectangle** tool. The **Rectangle PropertyManager** appears.
2. Click to specify the first corner of the rectangle in the drawing area.
3. Move the cursor away from the first specified corner to specify the diagonally opposite corner of the rectangle, see Figure 2.55.
4. Click to specify the second corner of rectangle when the required length and width values of the rectangle appear near the cursor. A rectangle is drawn.

Note: The length of the rectangle is measured in the X axis of the plane and the width is measured in Y axis.

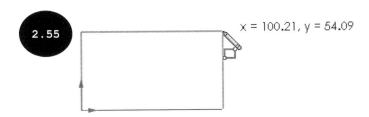

Center Rectangle

The **Center Rectangle** tool is used to draw a rectangle by specifying a center point and a corner point, see Figure 2.56.

Procedure for Drawing a Rectangle by using the Center Rectangle Tool
1. Invoke the **Rectangle** flyout and then click on the **Center Rectangle** tool.
2. Click to specify the center point of the rectangle in the drawing area.
3. Move the cursor for a little distance. The preview of the rectangle appears, see Figure 2.57.
4. Click to specify the corner of rectangle in the drawing area. A rectangle is drawn.

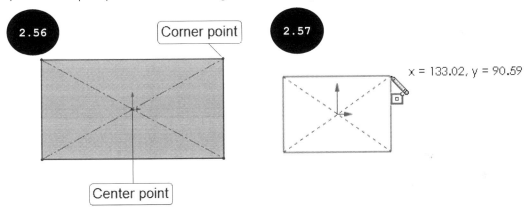

3 Point Corner Rectangle

The **3 Point Corner Rectangle** tool is used to draw a rectangle by specifying 3 corners. The first two corners, define the width and orientation of the rectangle and the third corner defines the length of the rectangle, see Figure 2.58.

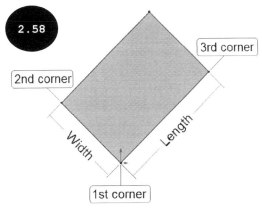

Procedure for Drawing a Rectangle by using the 3 Point Corner Rectangle Tool
1. Invoke the **Rectangle** flyout and then click on the **3 Point Corner Rectangle** tool.
2. Click to specify the first corner of rectangle in the drawing area.
3. Move the cursor for a little distance in the drawing area. An interfacing line attached to the cursor appears, see Figure 2.59.
4. Click to specify the second corner of rectangle in the drawing area.
5. Move the cursor for a little distance in the drawing area. The preview of the rectangle appears, see Figure 2.60.
6. Click to specify the third corner of rectangle. A rectangle is drawn.

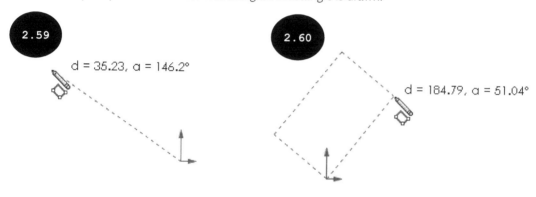

3 Point Center Rectangle
The **3 Point Center Rectangle** tool is used to draw a rectangle at an angle by specifying three points. The first point defines the center of the rectangle; the second point defines the width and orientation of the rectangle; and the third point defines the length of the rectangle, see Figure 2.61.

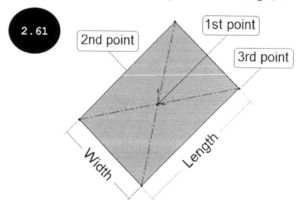

Procedure for Drawing a Rectangle by using the 3 Point Center Rectangle Tool
1. Invoke the **Rectangle** flyout and then click on the **3 Point Center Rectangle** tool.
2. Click to specify a point (first point) as the center point of rectangle.
3. Move the cursor for a little distance in the drawing area. An interfacing line attached to the cursor appears, see Figure 2.62.
4. Click to specify the second point of rectangle.

5. Move the cursor for a little distance in the drawing area. The preview of rectangle appears in the drawing area, see Figure 2.63.
6. Click to specify the third point of rectangle in the drawing area. A rectangle is drawn.

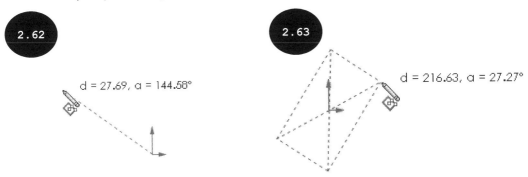

Parallelogram

The **Parallelogram** tool is used to draw a parallelogram, whose sides are not perpendicular to each other. You can draw a parallelogram by specifying three corners. The first two corners, define the width and orientation of the parallelogram and the third corner defines the length and the angle between the parallelogram sides, see Figure 2.64.

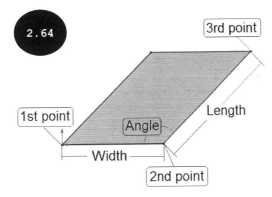

Procedure for Drawing a Parallelogram
1. Invoke the **Rectangle** flyout and then click on the **Parallelogram** tool.
2. Click to specify the first corner of parallelogram, refer Figure 2.64.
3. Move the cursor away from the first specified corner in the drawing area. An interfacing line attached to the cursor appears.
4. Click to specify the second corner of parallelogram in the drawing area, refer to Figure 2.64.
5. Move the cursor away from the second specified corner in the drawing area. The preview of the parallelogram appears in the drawing area.
6. Click to specify the third corner of parallelogram when the required distance and angle values appear near the cursor. A parallelogram is drawn.

Drawing a Circle

In SOLIDWORKS, you can draw a circle by using the **Circle** and **Perimeter** tools available in the **Circle** flyout of the **Sketch CommandManager**, see Figure 2.65. To invoke the **Circle** flyout, click on the down arrow next to an active circle tool in the **Sketch CommandManager**, see Figure 2.65. The tools for drawing a circle are as follows:

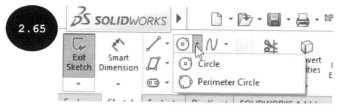

Circle

The **Circle** tool is used to draw a circle by specifying the center point and a point on the circumference of a circle, see Figure 2.66.

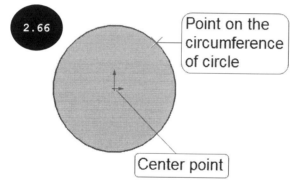

Procedure for Drawing a Circle by using the Circle Tool

1. Click on the **Circle** tool in the Sketch CommandManager. The **Circle PropertyManager** appears, see Figure 2.67.
2. Click to specify the centerpoint of the circle in the drawing area.
3. Move the cursor for a little distance in the drawing area. The preview of a circle attached to the cursor appears, see Figure 2.68.
4. Click to specify a point on the circumference of the circle in the drawing area. A circle is drawn.

Perimeter Circle

The **Perimeter Circle** tool is used to draw a circle by specifying three points on the circumference of circle, see Figure 2.69.

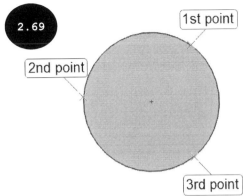

Procedure for Drawing a Circle by using the Perimeter Circle Tool

1. Invoke the **Circle** flyout and then click on the **Perimeter Circle** tool. The **Circle PropertyManager** appears.
2. Click to specify the first point on the circumference of circle, see Figure 2.70.
3. Move the cursor away from the first specified point. The preview of the circle appears in the drawing area.
4. Click to specify the second point on the circumference of circle, see Figure 2.70.
5. Click to specify the third point on the circumference of circle. The circle is drawn by defining three points on its circumference.

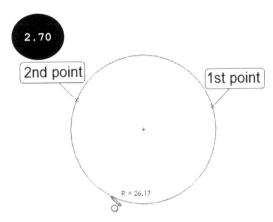

Tip: You can also convert a circle into a construction circle. To do so, click on the circle drawn in the drawing area. The **Circle PropertyManager** and a Pop-up toolbar appear. Click on the **For construction** check box in the **Options** rollout of the **Circle PropertyManager**. The circle converts to a construction circle. Alternatively, click on the **Construction Geometry** tool in the Pop-up toolbar to convert the circle into a construction circle.

Drawing an Arc

In SOLIDWORKS, you can draw an arc by different methods using the tools in the **Arc** flyout of the **Sketch CommandManager**, see Figure 2.71. To invoke the **Arc** flyout, click on the down arrow next to the active arc tool in the **Sketch CommandManager**, see Figure 2.71. The tools for drawing arc are as follows:

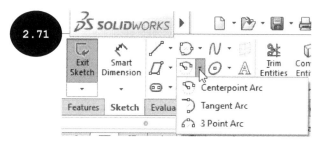

Centerpoint Arc

The **Centerpoint Arc** tool is used to draw an arc by defining the center point, start point, and endpoint, see Figure 2.72.

Procedure for Drawing an Arc by using the Centerpoint Arc Tool

1. Click on the **Centerpoint Arc** tool. The **Arc PropertyManager** appears, see Figure 2.73.
2. Click to specify the center point of arc in the drawing area.
3. Move the cursor for a little distance. A construction circle attached to the cursor appears.
4. Click in the drawing area to define the start point of the arc.
5. Move the cursor clockwise or anti-clockwise. The preview of arc appears in the drawing area.
6. Click to specify the endpoint of arc in the drawing area. An arc is drawn.

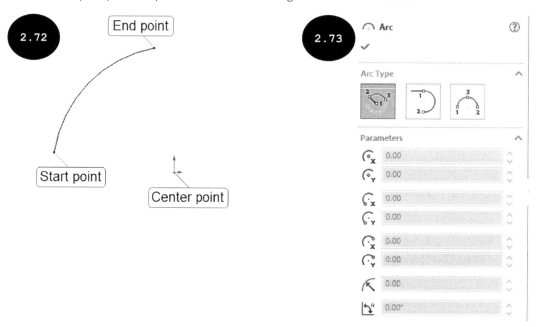

3 Point Arc
The 3 Point Arc tool is used to draw an arc by defining three points on the arc length, see Figure 2.74.

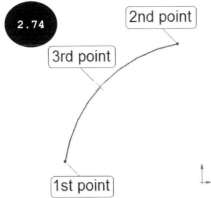

Procedure for Drawing an Arc by using the 3 Points Arc Tool
1. Invoke the **Arc** flyout and then click on the **3 Point Arc** tool.
2. Click to specify the first point of arc in the drawing area, see Figure 2.75.
3. Move the cursor away from the first specified point and then click to specify the second point of the arc in the drawing area, see Figure 2.75.
4. Move the cursor for a little distance. The preview of the arc appears in the drawing area, see Figure 2.75. Next, click to specify a point on the arc length. An arc is drawn.

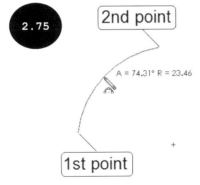

Tangent Arc
The **Tangent Arc** tool is used to draw an arc tangent to an existing entity, see Figure 2.76. To draw a tangent arc by using the **Tangent Arc** tool, at least a line, an arc, or a spline entity must be available in the drawing area.

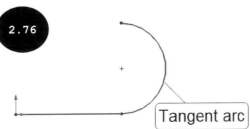

Procedure for Drawing a Tangent Arc

1. Click on the **Tangent Arc** tool in the **Arc** flyout.
2. Move the cursor to the endpoint of an existing entity in the drawing area and then click to specify the start point of the tangent arc when the cursor snaps to the endpoint of the existing entity.
3. Move the cursor for a little distance. The preview of the tangent arc appears in the drawing area and its endpoint is attached to the cursor.

Note: The tangency of arc depends upon how you move the cursor from the specified point in the drawing area. Figure 2.77 shows possible movements of the cursor and the creation of arcs in the respective movement.

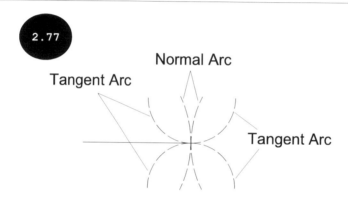

4. Click to specify the endpoint of the tangent arc in the drawing area, see Figure 2.78. A tangent arc is drawn and the **Tangent Arc** tool remains active. Also, the preview of another tangent arc appears in the drawing area. It indicates that you can continue drawing tangent arcs, one after another by clicking the left mouse button.
5. Once you have drawn tangent arcs, right-click in the drawing area. A shortcut menu appears. In this shortcut menu, click on the **Select** option to exit the **Tangent Arc** tool.

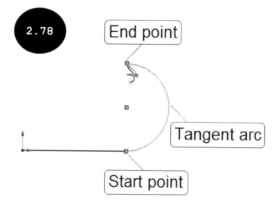

Drawing a Polygon

In SOLIDWORKS, you can draw a polygon of sides ranging from 3 to 40. A polygon is a multi-sided geometry having all sides of equal length and equal angle, see Figure 2.79.

To draw a polygon, click on the **Polygon** tool in the **Sketch CommandManager**. The **Polygon PropertyManager** appears, see Figure 2.80. The options in the **Polygon PropertyManager** are as follows:

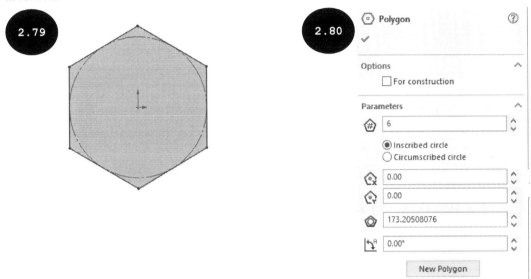

Options

By default, the **For construction** check box is unchecked in the **Options** rollout of the PropertyManager, see Figure 2.80. As a result, the drawn resultant polygon has solid sketch entities, see Figure 2.81. If you select the **For construction** check box, the drawn resultant polygon has construction entities, see Figure 2.82.

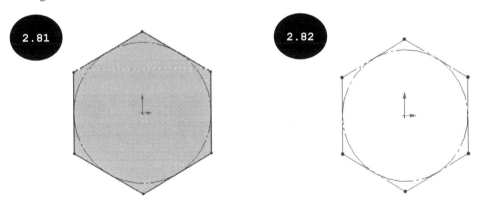

Parameters

The options in the **Parameters** rollout are used to specify parameters of a polygon. The options are as follows:

Number of Sides
The **Number of Sides** field is used to specify the number of sides of a polygon. You can specify the number of sides of a polygon ranging from 3 to 40.

Inscribed circle
The **Inscribed circle** radio button is used to draw a polygon by drawing an imaginary construction circle inside the polygon. In this case, the midpoint of all sides of the polygon touches the imaginary construction circle, see Figure 2.83.

Circumscribed circle
The **Circumscribed circle** radio button is used to draw a polygon by drawing an imaginary construction circle outside the polygon. In this case, all vertices of the polygon touch the imaginary construction circle, see Figure 2.84.

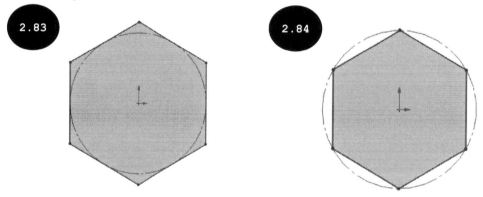

Center X Coordinate
The **Center X Coordinate** field of the **Parameters** rollout is used to display or control the X coordinate value of the center of a polygon.

Center Y Coordinate
The **Center Y Coordinate** field is used to display or control the Y coordinate value of the center of a polygon.

Center Diameter
The **Center Diameter** field is used to display or control the diameter of the inscribed or circumscribed imaginary construction circle of a polygon.

Angle
The **Angle** field is used to display or control the angle value between polygon sides with respect to the X axis of the plane.

New Polygon
The **New Polygon** button is used to draw a new polygon.

Procedure for Drawing a Polygon
1. Click on the **Polygon** tool. The **Polygon PropertyManager** appears.
2. Enter the number of sides of the polygon in the **Number of Sides** field of the PropertyManager.
3. Click on the **Inscribed circle** or **Circumscribed circle** radio button, as required.
4. Click to specify the center point of the polygon in the drawing area.
5. Move the cursor for a little distance in the drawing area. The preview of the polygon with an imaginary construction circle appears in the drawing area.
6. Click to specify a point in the drawing area to define the diameter of the imaginary circle. The polygon is drawn. You can also enter the diameter of the imaginary circle in the **Center Diameter** field of the PropertyManager.
7. Click on the green tick mark ✓ button in the PropertyManager.

Drawing a Slot
In SOLIDWORKS, you can draw straight and arc slots by using the tools in the **Slot** flyout, see Figure 2.85. To invoke the **Slot** flyout, click on the down arrow next to the active slot tool in the **Sketch CommandManager**, see Figure 2.85. The tools for drawing slots are as follows:

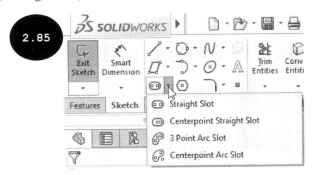

Straight Slot
The **Straight Slot** tool is used to draw a straight slot by defining the start point, endpoint, and a point to define the width of the slot, see Figure 2.86. To draw a straight slot, click on the **Straight Slot** tool in the **Slot** flyout. The **Slot PropertyManager** appears, see Figure 2.87. The options in the **Slot PropertyManager** are as follows:

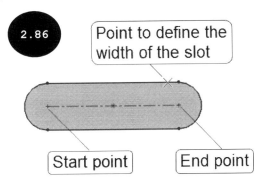

Slot Types

The **Slot Types** rollout is used to switch between different methods of drawing a slot. By default, depending upon the slot tool invoked, the respective button becomes active in this rollout.

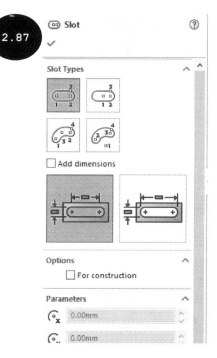

The **Add dimensions** check box in the **Slot Types** rollout is unchecked, by default. As a result, the dimension values are not applied to the slot drawn, refer to Figure 2.86. On selecting this check box, the dimension values are automatically applied to the slot drawn in the drawing area, see Figure 2.88.

The **Center to Center** button of the **Slot Type** rollout is activated by default. As a result, the straight slot measures the length from center to center of the slot. On choosing the **Overall Length** button, the straight slot measures the overall (end to end) length of the slot.

Parameters

The options in the **Parameters** rollout of the PropertyManager are used to display or control the parameters of the slot. Note that the options of this rollout get activated once the slot is drawn and selected in the drawing area. You can modify the X and Y coordinate values of the center point of the slot, the width of the slot, and length of the slot by using their respective fields of this rollout.

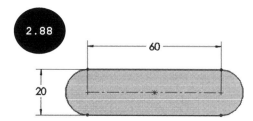

Procedure for Drawing a Slot by using the Straight Slot Tool

1. Click on the **Straight Slot** tool. The **Slot PropertyManager** appears.
2. Click to specify the start point of the slot, refer Figure 2.86.
3. Move the cursor for a little distance in the drawing area. A straight rubber band construction line with its one end attached to the cursor appears.
4. Click the left mouse button in the drawing area to define the endpoint of the slot.
5. Move the cursor for a little distance in the drawing area. The preview of the slot appears.
6. Click to specify a point in the drawing area to define the width of the slot. The straight slot is drawn.

Centerpoint Straight Slot

The **Centerpoint Straight Slot** tool is used to draw a straight slot by defining center point, endpoint, and a point to define the width of the slot, see Figure 2.89.

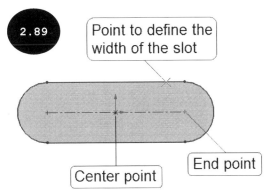

Procedure for Drawing a Slot by using the Centerpoint Straight Slot Tool
1. Click on the **Center Point Straight Slot** tool in the **Slot** flyout.
2. Click to specify the center point of slot, see Figure 2.90.
3. Move the cursor for a little distance in the drawing area. A straight rubber band construction line with its one end attached to the cursor appears.
4. Click the left mouse button in the drawing area to define the endpoint of the slot.
5. Move the cursor for a little distance. The preview of the slot appears, see Figure 2.90.
6. Click to specify a point in the drawing area to define the width of the slot. The straight slot is drawn.

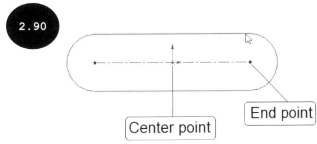

3 Point Arc Slot

The **3 Point Arc Slot** tool is used to draw an arc slot by defining three points on the arc length, see Figure 2.91.

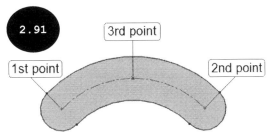

Procedure for Drawing an Arc Slot by using the 3 Point Arc Slot Tool
1. Click on the **3 Point Arc Slot** tool in the **Slot** flyout.
2. Click to specify the first (start) point of the arc slot, see Figure 2.92.
3. Move the cursor for a little distance. A construction arc appears in the drawing area.
4. Click to specify the second (end) point of the arc slot, see Figure 2.92.
5. Move the cursor for a little distance and click to specify the third point of the slot, see Figure 2.92.
6. Move the cursor for a little distance. The preview of the arc slot appears, see Figure 2.92.
7. Click to specify a point in the drawing area to define the width of the slot. The arc slot is drawn.

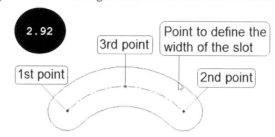

Centerpoint Arc Slot
The **Centerpoint Arc Slot** tool is used to draw an arc slot by defining center point, start point, and endpoint of the arc slot, see Figure 2.93.

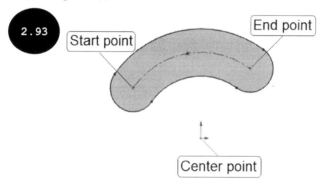

Procedure for Drawing an Arc Slot by using the Centerpoint Arc Slot Tool
1. Click on the **Centerpoint Arc Slot** tool in the **Slot** flyout.
2. Click to specify the center point of the arc slot, see Figure 2.94.
3. Move the cursor for a little distance in the drawing area. A rubber band construction circle appears.
4. Click to specify the start point of the arc slot, see Figure 2.94.
5. Move the cursor clockwise or counterclockwise in the drawing area. A construction arc appears.
6. Click to specify the endpoint of the arc slot, see Figure 2.94.
7. Move the cursor for a little distance in the drawing area. The preview of the arc slot appears, see Figure 2.94.
8. Click to specify a point in the drawing area to define the width of the arc slot. The arc slot is drawn.

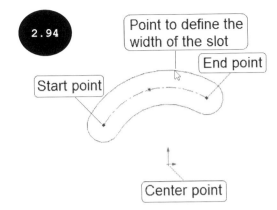

Drawing an Ellipse

An ellipse is drawn by defining its major axis and minor axis, see Figure 2.95. You can draw an ellipse by using the **Ellipse** tool in the **Sketch CommandManager**.

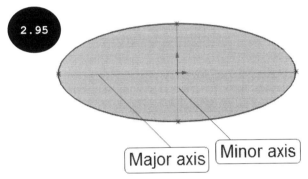

Procedure for Drawing an Ellipse

1. Click on the **Ellipse** tool in the **Sketch CommandManager**. The **Ellipse** tool gets activated.
2. Click to specify the center point of the ellipse, see Figure 2.96.
3. Move the cursor for a little distance in the drawing area. A construction circle appears.
4. Click to define the major axis of the ellipse, see Figure 2.96.
5. Move the cursor for a little distance. The preview of the ellipse appears, see Figure 2.96.
6. Click to specify the minor axis of the ellipse. The ellipse is drawn.
7. Right-click in the drawing area and then click on the **Select** option in the shortcut menu to exit the **Ellipse** tool.

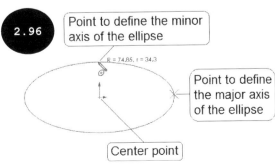

Drawing an Elliptical Arc

You can draw an elliptical arc by using the **Partial Ellipse** tool in the **Ellipse** flyout, see Figure 2.97. To invoke the **Ellipse** flyout, click on the down arrow in the right of the **Ellipse** tool in the **Sketch CommandManager**, see Figure 2.97. Figure 2.98 shows an elliptical arc.

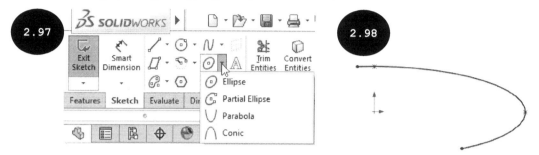

2.97

2.98

Procedure for Drawing an Elliptical Arc

1. Invoke the **Ellipse** flyout and then click on the **Partial Ellipse** tool, refer to Figure 2.97.
2. Click to specify the center point of the elliptical arc in the drawing area.
3. Move the cursor for a little distance in the drawing area. A reference circle appears.
4. Click to define the major axis of the elliptical arc in the drawing area and then move the cursor a distance in the drawing area. The preview of an imaginary ellipse appears, see Figure 2.99.
5. Click to specify the start point of the elliptical arc in the drawing area, see Figure 2.100.
6. Move the cursor for a little distance in the drawing area. The preview of the elliptical arc appears, see Figure 2.100.
7. Click to specify the endpoint of the elliptical arc. The elliptical arc is created, see Figure 2.101.
8. Right-click in the drawing area and then click on the **Select** option in the shortcut menu to exit the **Partial Ellipse** tool.

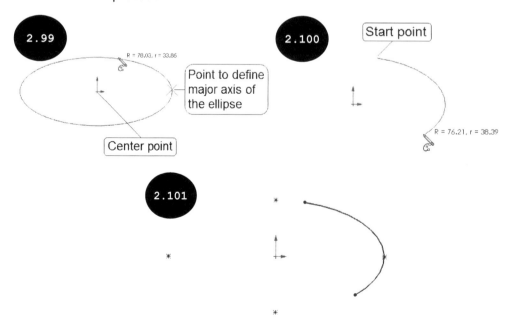

Drawing a Parabola

A Parabola is a symmetrical plane curve formed by the intersection of a cone and a plane parallel to its side. You can draw a parabola by defining its focus point, apex point, and two points (start point and end point) on the parabolic curve, see Figure 2.102. You can draw a parabola by using the **Parabola** tool in the **Ellipse** flyout.

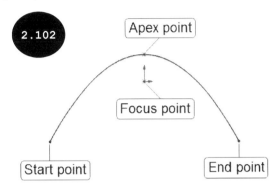

Procedure for Drawing a Parabola

1. Invoke the **Ellipse** flyout and then click on the **Parabola** tool. The **Parabola** tool gets activated.
2. Click to specify the focus point of the parabola in the drawing area, see Figure 2.103.
3. Move the cursor for a little distance. A construction parabola appears and the cursor is attached at its apex, see Figure 2.103.
4. Click to specify the apex of the parabola. The preview of the imaginary parabola appears.
5. Move the cursor over the imaginary parabola and then click to specify the start point of the parabola, see Figure 2.104.
6. Move the cursor clockwise or counterclockwise. The preview of the parabolic arc appears in the drawing area, depending upon the movement of the cursor.
7. Click to specify the endpoint of the parabola. The parabola is drawn, see Figure 2.104.
8. Right-click in the drawing area and then click on the **Select** option in the shortcut menu to exit the tool.

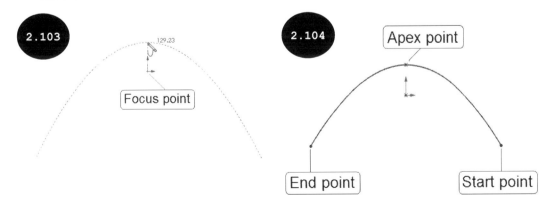

Drawing Conic Curves

SOLIDWORKS allows you to draw conic curves by specifying the start point, end point, top vertex, and Rho value, see Figure 2.105. You can draw conic curves by using the **Conic** tool in the **Ellipse** flyout.

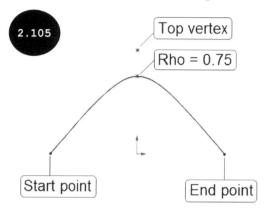

Procedure for Drawing Conic Curves

1. Click on the **Conic** tool in the **Ellipse** flyout. The **Conic** tool gets activated.
2. Click to specify the start point of the curve in the drawing area, see Figure 2.106.
3. Move the cursor for a little distance in the drawing area. A construction line appears.
4. Click to specify the endpoint of the curve, see Figure 2.106.
5. Move the cursor a distance in the drawing area. The preview of the conic curve appears, see Figure 2.106.
6. Click to specify the top vertex of conic curve, see Figure 2.107.
7. Move the cursor up or down for a little distance. The preview of the conic curve appears in the drawing area. Also, the current Rho value of the curve appears near the cursor, see Figure 2.107.

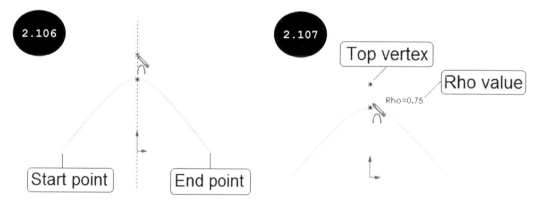

8. Move the cursor at the location where the Rho value appears closer to the required value, and then click to specify the apex of the conic curve, see Figure 2.108.

Note: The Rho value of the conic curve defines the type of curve. If the Rho value is less than 0.5 then the conic curve will be an ellipse; if the Rho value is equal to 0.5 then the conic curve will be a parabola; if the Rho value is greater than 0.5 then the conic curve will be a hyperbola.

9. Right-click in the drawing area and then click on the **Select** option in the shortcut menu to exit the **Conic** tool.

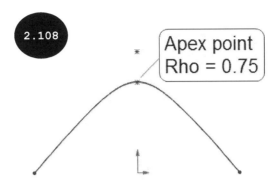

Drawing a Spline

A Spline is defined as a curve having a high degree of smoothness and is used to create free form features. You can draw a spline by specifying two or more than two control points in the drawing area. In SOLIDWORKS, you can also draw a spline by defining mathematical equations. The different tools for drawing splines are as follows:

Spline

The **Spline** tool is used to create a spline by defining two or more than two control points in the drawing area, see Figure 2.109. Note that the spline is created such that it passes through the specified control points.

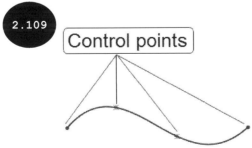

Procedure for Drawing a Spline by using the Spline Tool

1. Click on the **Spline** tool in the **Sketch CommandManager**. The **Spline** tool gets activated and the cursor changes to spline cursor .

84   Chapter 2 > Drawing Sketches with SOLIDWORKS

2. Click to specify the first control point of the spline in the drawing area.
3. Move the cursor for a little distance. A reference curve appears in the drawing area whose one end is fixed at the specified point and the other end is attached to the cursor.
4. Click to specify the second control point of the spline and then move the cursor for a little distance. The preview of the spline curve appears in the drawing area such that it passes through the specified control points, see Figure 2.110.
5. Click to specify the third control point of the spline. The preview of the curve, passing through the three control points, appears in the drawing area. Similarly, you can keep on specifying the control points for drawing the spline.
6. Once all control points have been specified for drawing the spline, right-click and then click on the **Select** option in the shortcut menu to exit the tool. Figure 2.111 shows a spline drawn by specifying five control points in the drawing area.

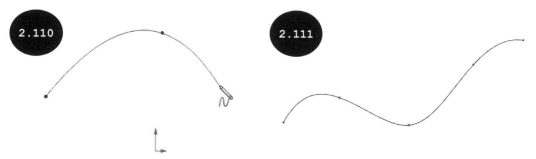

Equation Driven Curve

The **Equation Driven Curve** tool is used to create an equation driven spline. To draw an equation driven spline, click on the down arrow next to the **Spline** tool in the **Sketch CommandManager**. The **Spline** flyout appears, see Figure 2.112. Next, click on the **Equation Driven Curve** tool in the **Spline** flyout. The **Equation Driven Curve PropertyManager** appears on the left of the drawing area, see Figure 2.113. The options in this PropertyManager are as follows:

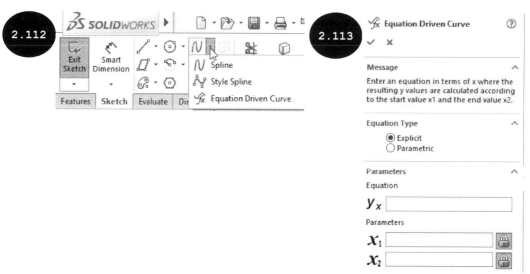

Message
The **Message** rollout of the PropertyManager is used to display appropriate information about the action to be taken for drawing the equation driven spline.

Equation Type
The **Equation Type** rollout is used to select the type of equation for drawing a spline. The options in this rollout are as follows:

Explicit
The **Explicit** radio button is selected by default. As a result, you can define an equation for calculating 'Y' values of spline control points as the function of 'X' in the **Parameters** rollout of the PropertyManager.

Parametric
The **Parametric** radio button is used to define two equations. First one is used for calculating 'X' values and the other one is used for calculating 'Y' values of control points as the function of 't' in the **Parameters** rollout of the PropertyManager.

Parameters
The **Parameters** rollout is used to define driving equations, and the start and end function values. The options displayed in this rollout depend on the type of equation (**Explicit** or **Parametric**) selected in the **Parametric** rollout of the PropertyManager, see Figures 2.114 and 2.115.

When the **Explicit** radio button is selected, you can define an equation for 'Y' as the function of 'X' in the **Yx** field of the **Equation** area in the rollout. Also, you can define the start and end values for the function 'X' in the **X1** and **X2** fields of the rollout.

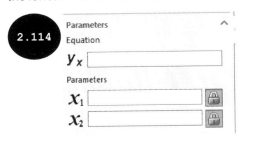 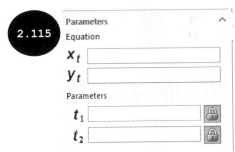

When the **Parametric** radio button is selected, you can define equations for 'X' and 'Y' as the function of 't' in the **Xt** and **Yt** fields of the **Parameters** rollout. Also, you can define the start and end values for the function 't' in the **t1** and **t2** fields. The procedures to draw equation driven spline by using the explicit and parameter equation types are as follows:

Procedure for Drawing an Explicit Equation Spline
1. Click on the **Equation Driven Curve** tool in the **Spline** flyout. The **Equation Driven Curve** PropertyManager appears.
2. Make sure that the **Explicit** radio button is selected in the **Equation Type** rollout.
3. Enter the equation for 'Y' as the function of 'X' in the **Yx** field of the **Parameters** rollout. For example, enter the equation '2* sin(x)^12' in the **Yx** field.

4. Enter start and end values of the function 'X' in the x1 and x2 fields. For example, enter '0' in the X1 field and '38' in the X2 field as the start and end function values, respectively.
5. Press ENTER. The preview of the equation driven spline appears in the drawing area.
6. Click on the green tick mark ✓ button in the PropertyManager. An equation driven spline is drawn, see Figure 2.116.

Procedure for Drawing a Parametric Equation Spline

1. Click on the **Equation Driven Curve** tool in the **Spline** flyout. The **Equation Driven Curve** PropertyManager appears.
2. Click on the **Parametric** radio button in the **Equation Type** rollout.
3. Enter equations for 'X' and 'Y' as the function of 't' in the **Xt** and **Yt** fields of the **Parameters** rollout, respectively. For example, enter '(t + sin(t)^2)' in the **Xt** field and '2* sin(t)' in the **Yt** field of the PropertyManager.
4. Enter start and end values of the function 't' in the **t1** and **t2** fields of the **Parameters** area. For example, enter '0' in the **t1** field and '38' in the **t2** field as the start and end values, respectively.
5. Press ENTER. The preview of the equation driven spline appears in the drawing area.
6. Click on the green tick mark ✓ button in the PropertyManager to accept the creation of spline and to exit the PropertyManager. Figure 2.117 shows a spline drawn by using the parametric equation type.

Style Spline

The **Style Spline** tool is used to create bezier splines of 3 degrees, 5 degrees, and 7 degrees by defining control points in the drawing area, see Figure 2.118. A bezier spline is created such that it passes near the control points specified in the drawing area and is used to create smooth and complex shaped features. Note that minimum number of control points required to create bezier splines of 3 degrees, 5 degrees, and 7 degrees are 4, 6, and 8, respectively.

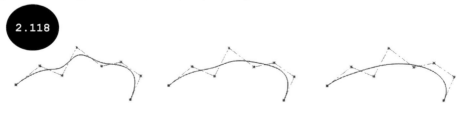

3 degrees bezier spline   5 degrees bezier spline   7 degrees bezier spline

Procedure for Drawing a Style/Bezier Spline

1. Click on the **Style Spline** tool in the **Spline** flyout. The **Insert Style Spline PropertyManager** appears, see Figure 2.119.
2. Click on the **Bezier, B-Spline: Degree 3, B-Spline: Degree 5,** or **B-Spline: Degree 7** radio button in the PropertyManager, see Figure 2.119.
3. Click to specify the first control point of the spline in the drawing area.
4. Move the cursor for a little distance and then click to specify the second control point of the spline.
5. Move the cursor for a little distance and then click to specify the third control point of the spline. The preview of the spline appears in the drawing area such that it passes near the specified control points, see Figure 2.120. Similarly, you can keep on specifying control points for drawing the spline in the drawing area.

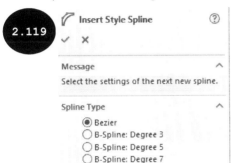

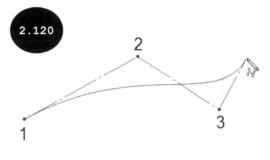

6. Once all control points have been specified for drawing the spline, right-click and then click on the **Select** option in the shortcut menu to exit the tool.

Fit Spline

The **Fit Spline** tool is used to convert multiple sketch entities into a single spline curve. To convert sketch entities into a spline, click on the **Tools > Spline Tools > Fit Spline** in the SOLIDWORKS menus. The **Fit Spline PropertyManager** appears, see Figure 2.121. The options in the **Fit Spline PropertyManager** are as follows:

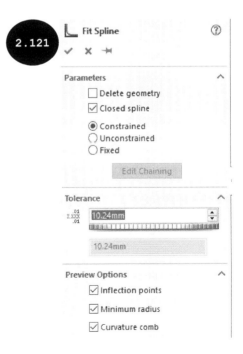

Parameters

The options in the **Parameters** rollout of the PropertyManager are used to specify different parameters for converting sketch entities into a single spline curve. The options are as follows:

Delete geometry
On selecting the **Delete geometry** check box, the original selected entities get deleted from the drawing area and the resultant spline is created.

Constrained

By default, the **Constrained** radio button is selected. As a result, the parametric links are applied between the original sketch entities and the resultant spline curve. Therefore, a change made in the original entities will also be reflected in the spline and vice-versa.

Unconstrained

On selecting the **Unconstrained** radio button, the parametric links between the original sketch entities and the resultant spline curve get broken. As a result, a change made in the original entities will not be reflected in the spline and vice-versa.

Fixed

On selecting the **Fixed** radio button, the fixed relation is applied to the resultant spline. As a result, the changes such as position, dimensions, and so on cannot be made to the resultant spline. However, the original entities will be free to change, which is unconstrained with the spline curve created.

Closed spline

By default, the **Closed spline** check box is selected. As a result, a closed spline is created by closing the open ends of the selected entities. Figures 2.122 and 2.123 show the preview of a resultant spline with the **Closed spline** check box unchecked and checked, respectively.

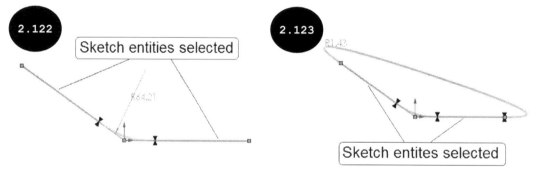

Edit Chaining

The **Edit Chaining** button is used to alter the creation of a chain of contiguous splines. Note that this button is activated only on selecting non-contiguous entities. Figure 2.124 shows non-contiguous entities (entities that are not in contact with each other). Figure 2.125 shows the preview of the default resultant contiguous spline and Figure 2.126 shows the preview of the resulting contiguous spline appeared on clicking the **Edit Chaining** button.

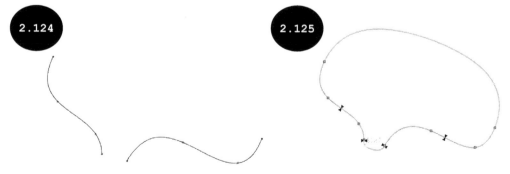

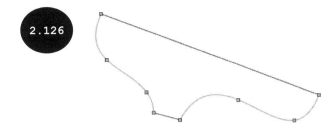

2.126

Tolerance
The **Tolerance** rollout is used to specify the maximum deviation allowed for the original sketch entities. You can enter tolerance value in the **Tolerance** field of this rollout. You can also drag the thumbwheel on the bottom of the **Tolerance** field to set the tolerance value.

Preview Options
The options in this rollout are used to control the preview of the resultant spline and are as follows:

Inflection points
By default, the **Inflection points** check box is selected. As a result, the preview of the spline appears with inflection points where the concavity of the spline changes. You can click on an inflection point to check for alternative solution.

Minimum radius
By default, the **Minimum radius** check box is selected. As a result, the preview of the spline appears with minimum radius measurement on the spline.

Curvature comb
By default, the **Curvature comb** check box is selected. As a result, the visual enhancement of the slope as well as the curvature appears in the drawing area.

Procedure for Drawing a Fit Spline
1. Click on the **Tools > Spline Tools > Fit Spline** in the SOLIDWORKS menus. The **Fit Spline PropertyManager** appears.
2. Select sketch entities to be converted into a spline, see Figure 2.127. The preview of the fit spline appears in the drawing area.
3. Specify parameters for creating fit spline, as required, by using the options in the **Fit Spline PropertyManager**.
4. Click on the green tick mark ✓ button in the PropertyManager. The fit spline is created. Figure 2.128 shows an open fit spline created with its original sketched entities deleted.

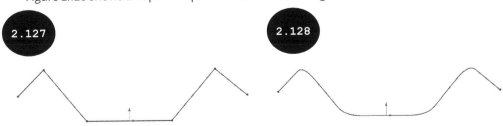

2.127   2.128

Editing a Spline

Editing a spline is important in order to achieve the complex shape and maintain a high degree of smoothness and curvature. You can edit a spline by using its control points and spline handle. Control points are the points which are specified in the drawing area for drawing the spline. To modify or edit a spline by using control points, click on the control point of the spline to be modified. The selected control point gets highlighted and appears with spline handles in the drawing area, see Figure 2.129. Also, the **Point PropertyManager** appears on the left of the drawing area. You can drag the selected control point by pressing and holding the left mouse button to change its location in the drawing area. Alternatively, enter the new X and Y coordinate values of the selected control point in the respective fields of the **Parameters** rollout of the **Point PropertyManager**.

You can use the spline handle to edit the curvature of a spline. Figure 2.130 shows the spline handle components. The different components of a spline handle are as follows:

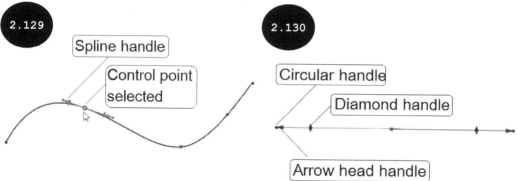

Circular handle

The circular handles of a spline handle is used to control the tangency, curvature, and angle of inclination of the spline, asymmetrically about the control point by dragging the spline handle. If you drag a circular handle by pressing the ALT key, the tangency, curvature, and angle of inclination of the spline are controlled, symmetrically about the control point.

Arrow head handle

The arrow head handles of a spline handle is used to control the tangency of the spline, asymmetrically about the control point by dragging it. If you drag the arrow head handle by pressing the ALT key, the tangency is controlled, symmetrically about the control point.

Diamond handle

The diamond handles of a spline handle is used to control the tangent vector or the tangency angle of the spline by dragging it.

Tutorial 1

Draw the sketch shown in Figure 2.131. The dimensions and the model shown in the figure are for your reference only. All dimensions are in mm. You will learn about applying dimensions and creating a model in later chapters.

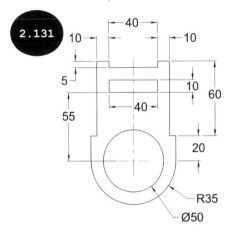
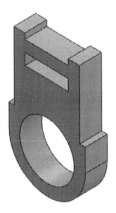

Section 1: Starting SOLIDWORKS
1. Start SOLIDWORKS by double-clicking on the SOLIDWORKS icon on your desktop.

Section 2: Invoking the Sketching Environment
1. Click on the **New** tool in the **Standard** toolbar. The **New SOLIDWORKS Document** dialog box appears.

2. Make sure that the **Part** button is activated in the dialog box and then click on the **OK** button. The Part modeling environment is invoked.

3. Click on the **Sketch** tab in the CommandManager, see Figure 2.132. The tools of the **Sketch CommandManager** are displayed.

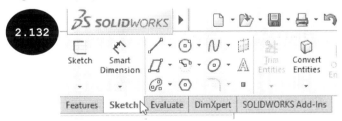

4. Click on the **Sketch** tool in the **Sketch CommandManager**. The three default planes mutually perpendicular to each other appear in the graphics area.

92 Chapter 2 > Drawing Sketches with SOLIDWORKS

5. Move the cursor over the Front plane and then click the left mouse button when the boundary of the plane gets highlighted. The Sketching environment is invoked. Also, the Front plane orientated normal to the viewing direction and the Confirmation corner appears at the upper right corner of the drawing area.

As all the sketch entities are multiples of 5 mm, you need to set the snap settings such that the cursor snaps to the increment of 5 mm only. Also, specify the metric unit system for measurement.

Section 3: Specifying Grid/Snap and Unit Settings

1. Click on the **Options** tool in the **Standard** toolbar. The **System Options - General** dialog box appears.

2. In the **System Options - General** dialog box, click on the **Document Properties** tab. The name of the dialog box changes to **Document Properties - Drafting Standard**.

3. Click on the **Units** option in the left panel of the dialog box. The options for specifying the unit system appear on the right panel of the dialog box.

4. Make sure that the **MMGS (millimeter, gram, second)** radio button is selected in the **Unit system** area of the dialog box.

    Now, you need to specify the grid and snap settings such that the cursor snaps to the increment of 5 mm.

5. Click on the **Grid/Snap** option in the left panel of the dialog box. The options for specifying the grid and snap settings appear on the right panel of the dialog box. Also, the name of the dialog box changes to **Document Properties - Grid/Snap**.

6. Enter **20** in the **Major grid spacing** field, **4** in the **Minor -lines per major** field, and **1** in the **Snap points per minor** field of the **Grid** area in the dialog box.

7. Select the **Display grid** check box of the **Grid** area in the dialog box to turn on the display of grids in the drawing area.

8. Click on the **Go To System Snaps** button in the **Document Properties - Grid/Snap** dialog box. The name of the dialog box changes to **System Options - Relations/Snaps**.

9. Select the **Grid** check box in the **Sketch snaps** area of the **System Options - Relations/Snaps** dialog box, if not selected by default to turn on the snap mode.

10. Click on the **OK** button in the dialog box. The grid and snap settings are specified and the dialog box is closed. Also, grids appear in the drawing area, see Figure 2.133.

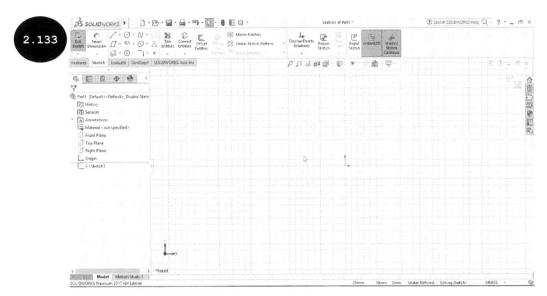

Section 4: Drawing the Sketch

Once the units, grids, and snap settings have been specified, you need to start drawing the sketch.

1. Click on the **Circle** tool in the **Sketch CommandManager**. The **Circle** tool gets activated and the **Circle PropertyManager** appears on the left of the drawing area. Also, the appearance of the cursor changes to circle cursor.

2. Move the cursor to the origin and then click to specify the center point of the circle when the cursor snaps to the origin.

3. Move the cursor horizontally toward right and then click to specify a point when the radius of the circle appears 25 mm near the cursor, see Figure 2.134. A circle of radius 25 mm is drawn. Next, press the **ESC** key to exit the **Circle** tool.

4. Invoke the **Arc** flyout by clicking on the down arrow next to the active arc tool in the **Sketch CommandManager**, see Figure 2.135.

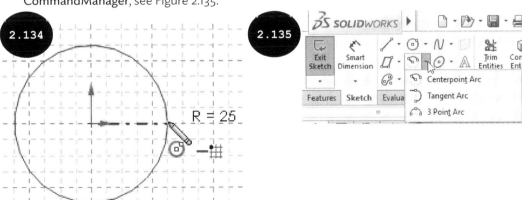

5. Click on the **Centerpoint Arc** tool in the **Arc** flyout. The **Centerpoint Arc** tool gets activated and the **Arc PropertyManager** appears on the left of the drawing area. Also, the appearance of the cursor changes to arc cursor.

6. Move the cursor to the origin and then click to specify the center point of the arc when cursor snaps to the origin.

7. Move the cursor horizontally toward right. The preview of an imaginary circle appears in the drawing area, see Figure 2.136. Next, click to specify the start point of the arc when the radius of the imaginary circle appears 35 mm near the cursor, see Figure 2.136.

8. Move the cursor in the clockwise direction. The preview of an arc appears in the drawing area. Next, click to specify the endpoint of the arc when the angle value appears 180 degrees near the cursor, see Figure 2.137. An arc is drawn. Press the **ESC** key to exit the tool.

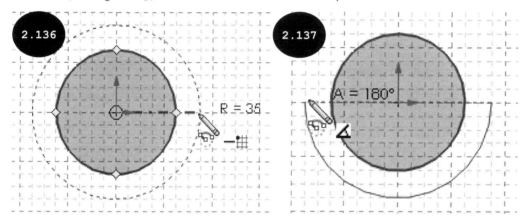

9. Click on the **Line** tool in the **Sketch CommandManager**. The **Line** tool gets activated and the **Insert Line PropertyManager** appears on the left of the drawing area. Also, the appearance of the cursor changes to line cursor.

10. Move the cursor to the start point of the previously drawn arc and then click the left mouse button when the cursor snaps to the start point of the previously drawn arc, see Figure 2.138.

11. Move the cursor vertically upward and click when the length of the line appears 20 mm near the cursor. A line of length 20 mm is drawn.

12. Move the cursor horizontally toward left and click when the length of the line appears 5 mm.

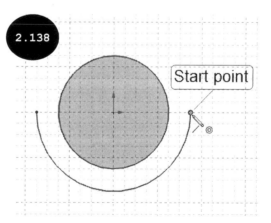

13. Move the cursor vertically upward and click when the length of the line appears 60 mm, see Figure 2.139.

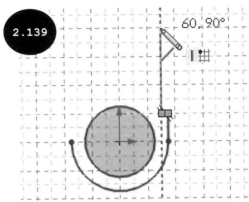

14. Move the cursor horizontally toward left and click when the length of the line appears 10 mm.

15. Move the cursor vertically downward and click when the length of the line appears 5 mm.

16. Move the cursor horizontally toward left and click when the length of the line appears 40 mm.

17. Move the cursor vertically upward and click when the length of the line appears 5 mm.

18. Move the cursor horizontally toward left and click when the length of the line appears 10 mm.

19. Move the cursor vertically downward and click when the length of the line appears 60 mm.

20. Move the cursor horizontally toward left and click when the length of the line appears 5 mm.

21. Move the cursor vertically downward and click when the cursor snaps to the endpoint of the arc drawn earlier. The sketch appears similar to one shown in Figure 2.140. Next, press the **ESC** key to exit the **Line** tool.

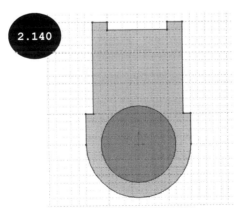

22. Invoke the **Rectangle** flyout, see Figure 2.141 and then click on the **Corner Rectangle** tool. The **Corner Rectangle** tool gets activated and the **Rectangle PropertyManager** appears.

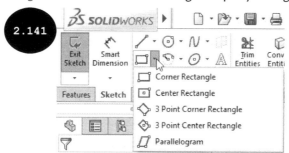

23. Move the cursor in the drawing area and then click the left mouse button when the coordinates (X, Y, Z) appear "20, 65, 0" respectively, in the Status Bar, see Figure 2.142.

24. Move the cursor toward left and click to specify the second corner point of the rectangle when "X = 40" and "Y = 10" appear near the cursor, see Figure 2.143. Next, press the ESC key to exit the tool. Figure 2.144 shows the final sketch of Tutorial 1.

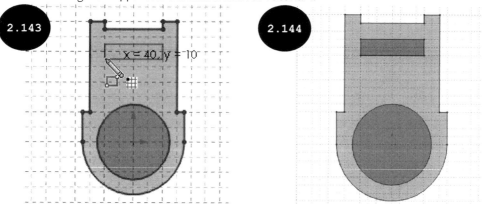

Section 5: Saving the Sketch

After creating the sketch, you need to save it.

1. Click on the **Save** tool in the **Standard** toolbar. The **Save As** dialog box appears.

2. Browse to the local drive of your system and create a folder with the name **SOLIDWORKS**.

3. Create another folder with the name **Chapter 2** in the *SOLIDWORKS* folder. Next, enter **Tutorial 1** in the **File name** field of the dialog box.

4. Click on the **Save** button in the dialog box. The sketch is saved with the name Tutorial 1.

Tutorial 2

Draw the sketch shown in Figure 2.145. The dimensions and the model shown in the figure are for your reference only. All dimensions are in mm. You will learn about applying dimensions and creating a model in later chapters.

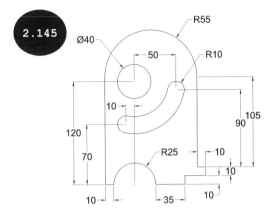

Section 1: Starting SOLIDWORKS
1. Start SOLIDWORKS by double-clicking on the SOLIDWORKS icon on your desktop.

Section 2: Invoking the Sketching Environment
In SOLIDWORKS, the Sketching environment is invoked within the Part modeling environment. Therefore, you first need to invoke the Part modeling environment.

1. Click on the **New** tool in the **Standard** toolbar. The **New SOLIDWORKS Document** dialog box appears.

2. Make sure that the **Part** button is activated in the dialog box and then click on the **OK** button. The Part modeling environment is invoked.

3. Click on the **Sketch** tab in the CommandManager, see Figure 2.146. The tools of the **Sketch CommandManager** are displayed.

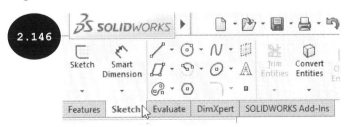

4. Click on the **Sketch** tool in the **Sketch CommandManager**. The three default planes mutually perpendicular to each other appear in the graphics area.

98   Chapter 2 > Drawing Sketches with SOLIDWORKS

5. Move the cursor over the Front plane and then click the left mouse button when the boundary of the plane gets highlighted. The Sketching environment is invoked. Also, the Front plane is orientated normal to the viewing direction and the Confirmation corner appears at the upper right corner of the drawing area.

    As all the sketch entities are multiples of 5 mm, you need to set the snaps setting such that the cursor snaps to the increment of 5 mm only. Also, specify the metric unit system for the measurement.

Section 3: Specifying Grid/Snap and Unit Settings

1. Click on the **Options** tool in the **Standard** toolbar. The **System Options - General** dialog box appears.

2. In the **System Options - General** dialog box, click on the **Document Properties** tab. The name of the dialog box changes to **Document Properties - Drafting Standard**.

3. Click on the **Units** option in the left panel of the dialog box. The options for specifying the unit system appear on the right panel of the dialog box.

4. Make sure that the **MMGS (millimeter, gram, second)** radio button is selected in the **Unit system** area of the dialog box.

    Now, you need to specify the grid and snap settings.

5. Click on the **Grid/Snap** option in the left panel of the dialog box. The options for specifying the grid and snap settings appear on the right panel of the dialog box. Also, the name of the dialog box changes to **Document Properties - Grid/Snap**.

6. Enter **20** in the **Major grid spacing** field, **4** in the **Minor -lines per major** field, and **1** in the **Snap points per minor** field of the **Grid** area in the dialog box.

7. Select the **Display grid** check box in the **Grid** area of the dialog box to turn on the display of grids in the drawing area.

8. Click on the **Go To System Snaps** button in the **Document Properties - Grid/Snap** dialog box. The name of the dialog box changes to **System Options - Relations/Snaps**.

9. Make sure the **Grid** check box is selected in the **Sketch snaps** area of the dialog box.

10. Click on the **OK** button in the dialog box. The grid and snap settings are specified and the dialog box is closed. Also, grids appear in the drawing area, see Figure 2.147.

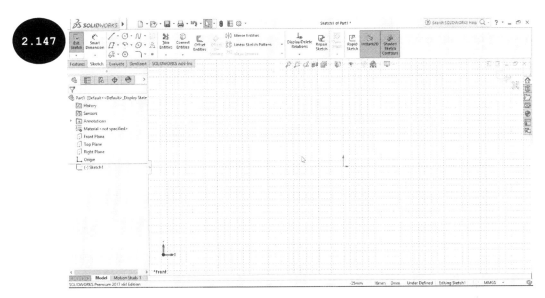

2.147

Once the units, grid, and snap settings have been specified, you can start drawing the sketch. First, you need to draw the outer loop of the sketch and then the inner slot and the circle of the sketch.

Section 4: Drawing the Outer Loop of the Sketch

1. Invoke the **Arc** flyout in the **Sketch CommandManager**, see Figure 2.148.

2. Click on the **Centerpoint Arc** tool in the **Arc** flyout. The **Centerpoint Arc** tool gets activated and the **Arc PropertyManager** appears.

3. Move the cursor to the origin and then click when the cursor snaps to the origin.

4. Move the cursor horizontally toward the right. The preview of an imaginary circle appears in the drawing area. Next, click the left mouse button when the radius of the imaginary circle appears 25 mm near the cursor.

5. Move the cursor in the anti-clockwise direction. The preview of an arc appears in the drawing area. Next, click the left mouse button when the angle value appears 180 degrees near the cursor, see Figure 2.149. Next, press the ESC key to exit the **Centerpoint Arc** tool.

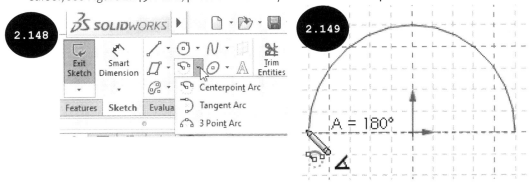

2.148

2.149

6. Click on the **Line** tool in the **Sketch CommandManager**. The **Line** tool gets activated.

7. Move the cursor to the start point of the previously drawn arc and then click the left mouse button when the cursor snaps to it, see Figure 2.150.

8. Move the cursor horizontally toward right and click when the length of the line appears 35 mm near the cursor, see Figure 2.151.

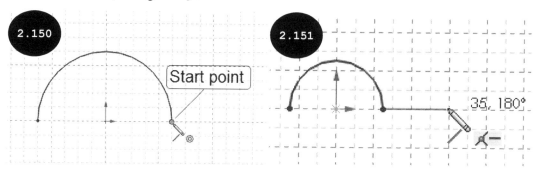

9. Move the cursor vertically upward and click when the length of the line appears 10 mm.

10. Move the cursor horizontally toward right and click when the length of the line appears 25 mm.

11. Move the cursor vertically upward and click when the length of the line appears 10 mm.

12. Move the cursor horizontally toward left and click when the length of the line appears 10 mm.

13. Move the cursor vertically upward and click when the length of the line appears 105 mm.

14. Move the line cursor away from the last specified point and then move it back to the last specified point. An orange color dot appears in the drawing area, see Figure 2.152.

15. Move the cursor vertically upward for a little distance and then move the cursor horizontally toward left. The arc mode is activated and the preview of the tangent arc appears, see Figure 2.153.

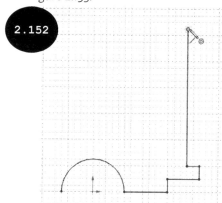
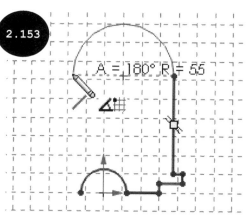

16. Click to specify the endpoint of the arc when the angle and radius values of the arc appear 180 degrees and 55 mm, respectively near the cursor, see Figure 2.153.

17. Move the cursor vertically downward and click when the length of the line appears 125 mm.

18. Move the cursor horizontally toward right and click when the cursor snaps to the endpoint of the arc. The outer loop of the sketch is drawn, see Figure 2.154. Next, press the **ESC** key to exit the **Line** tool.

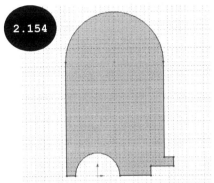

Section 5: Drawing the Inner Slot and the Circle of the Sketch

1. Click on the **Circle** tool in the **Sketch CommandManager**. The **Circle** tool gets activated and the **Circle PropertyManager** appears on the left of the drawing area.

2. Move the cursor in the drawing area and then click the left mouse button when the coordinates (X, Y, Y) appear "0, 120, 0" respectively, in the Status Bar, see Figure 2.155.

3. Move the cursor horizontally toward right and click when the radius of the circle appears 20 mm, see Figure 2.156. A circle of radius 20 mm is drawn. Next, exit the **Circle** tool.

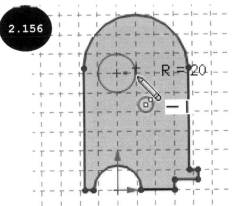

102 Chapter 2 > Drawing Sketches with SOLIDWORKS

After creating the circle, you need to create the slot of the sketch.

4. Invoke the **Slot** flyout in the **Sketch CommandManager** and then click on the **Centerpoint Arc Slot** tool, see Figure 2.157. The **Centerpoint Arc slot** tool gets activated.

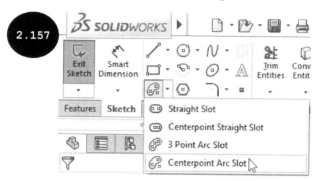

5. Move the cursor to the center point of the previously drawn circle and then click the left mouse button when the cursor snaps to it.

6. Move the cursor to the location where coordinates "-10, 70, and 0" appear in the Status Bar and then click the left mouse button.

7. Move the cursor for a little distance in the anti-clockwise direction. The preview of an arc appears. Next, click the left mouse button when coordinates "50, 110, 0" appear in the Status Bar.

8. Move the cursor for a little distance in the drawing area. The preview of the slot arc appears in the drawing area. Next, click the left mouse button when the width of the slot appears close to 20 mm in the **Slot Width** field of the **Slot PropertyManager**.

9. Enter **20** in the **Slot Width** field of the **Slot PropertyManager**, see Figure 2.158. The slot of width 20 mm is drawn, see Figure 2.159.

10. Click on the green tick mark ✓ button in the PropertyManager. The final sketch of Tutorial 2 is shown in Figure 2.159.

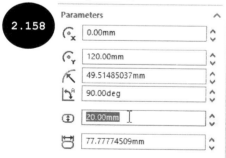

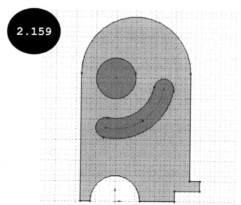

Section 6: Saving the Sketch

After creating the sketch, you need to save it.

1. Click on the **Save** tool in the **Standard** toolbar. The **Save As** dialog box appears.

2. Browse to the *Chapter 2* folder, which is created in the *SOLIDWORKS* folder. If these folders have not been created in Tutorial 1 of this chapter then you need to first create these folders in the local drive of your system.

3. Enter **Tutorial 2** in the **File name** field of the dialog box and then click on the **Save** button. The sketch is saved with the name Tutorial 2.

Hands-on Test Drive 3

Draw the sketch of the model shown in Figure 2.160. The dimensions and the model shown in the figure are for your reference only. All dimensions are in mm.

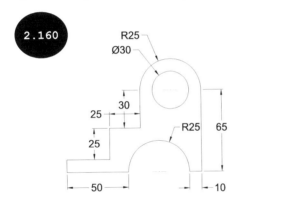

Hands-on Test Drive 4

Draw the sketch of the model shown in Figure 2.161. The dimensions and model shown in the figure are for your reference only. All dimensions are in mm.

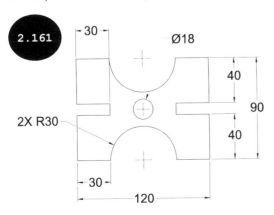
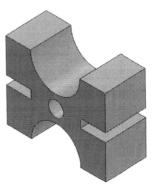

Summary

In this chapter, you have learned that the Sketching environment can be invoked within the Part modeling environment. To invoke the Sketching environment, you need to select a plane as the sketching plane. Once the Sketching environment has been invoked, you can specify the unit system as per your requirement by using the **Document Properties - Units** dialog box as well as specify the grids and snaps settings. You have also learned about drawing sketches by using different sketching tools such as **Line**, **Arc**, **Circle**, **Rectangle**, and **Spline**.

Questions

- Features are divided into two main categories: _____ and _____ .

- The _____ feature of any real world component is a sketch based feature.

- A polygon has number of sides ranging from _____ to _____.

- To draw an ellipse, you need to define its _____ axis and _____ axis.

- If the Rho value of a conic curve is less than 0.5 then the conic is an _____.

- A parabola is a symmetrical plane curve which is formed by the intersection of a cone with a plane parallel to its side (True/False).

- You cannot draw a tangent arc by using the **Line** tool (True/False).

- A fillet feature is known as placed feature (True/False).

CHAPTER 3

Editing and Modifying Sketches

In this chapter, you will learn the following:

- Trimming Sketch Entities
- Extending Sketch Entities
- Offsetting Sketch Entities
- Mirroring Sketch Entities
- Patterning Sketch Entities
- Creating a Sketch Fillet
- Creating a Sketch Chamfer
- Moving a Sketch Entity
- Creating a Copy of Sketch Entities
- Rotating an Entity
- Scaling Sketch Entities
- Stretching an Entity

Editing and modifying a sketch is very important to give the sketch a desired shape. In SOLIDWORKS, various editing operations such as trimming unwanted sketched entities, extending sketch entities, mirroring, patterning, moving, and rotating sketch entities can be performed by using the editing/modifying tools in the Sketching environment. These tools are discussed next.

Trimming Sketch Entities

You can trim the unwanted sketch entities by using the **Trim Entities** tool in the **Sketch CommandManager**. Besides using this tool for trimming unwanted sketch entities, you can also use this tool to extend sketch entities up to the next intersection. However, in SOLIDWORKS, a separate tool named as **Extend Entities** is available for extending sketch entities. The **Extend Entities** tool is discussed later in the chapter.

To trim sketch entities by using the **Trim Entities** tool, click on the **Trim Entities** tool in the **Sketch CommandManager**. The **Trim PropertyManager** appears, see Figure 3.1. The options in the **Trim PropertyManager** are as follows:

Message

The **Message** rollout of the PropertyManager is used to display the information about the action to be taken. The display of information in the **Message** rollout depends on the options selected in the **Options** rollout of the PropertyManager.

Options

The **Options** rollout is provided with various options for trimming sketch entities. The options are as follows:

Power trim

The **Power trim** button of the **Options** rollout is used to trim sketch entities by holding and dragging the cursor across the entities to be trimmed. Notice that when you hold the left mouse button and drag the cursor after activating this button, a light color tracing line following the cursor is displayed and the sketch entities coming across the tracing line get trimmed from their nearest intersection. Figure 3.2 shows a sketch before trimming the sketch entities and Figure 3.3 shows the same sketch after trimming the entities coming across the tracing line.

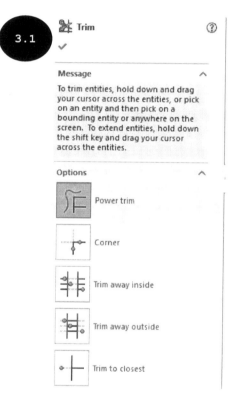

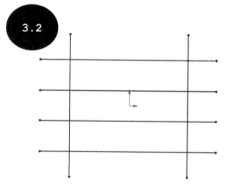

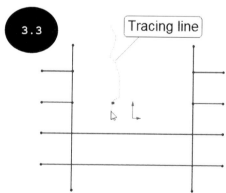

In addition to trimming sketch entities by using the **Power trim** button, you can also extend sketch entities up to their nearest intersection. To extend sketch entities using this tool, activate the **Power trim** button. Next, press and hold the SHIFT key plus the left mouse button and then drag the cursor. A light color tracing line following the cursor appears and the entities coming across this tracing line get extended up to their nearest intersection. Figure 3.4 shows a sketch before extending a sketch entity and Figure 3.5 shows the same sketch after extending the entity coming across the tracing line.

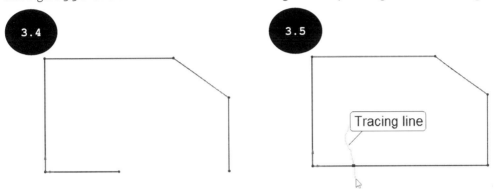

Tip: You can also extend a sketch entity up to a particular distance by using the **Power trim** button. To extend an entity up to a distance, click on the entity to be extended in the drawing area and then move the cursor in the required direction. The preview of the extended sketch entity appears. Next, click the left mouse button to specify the endpoint. The selected entity is extended to the specified point.

Corner

The **Corner** button is used to create a corner between two selected entities by trimming or extending them. To create a corner between entities, click on the **Corner** button in the **Trim PropertyManager** and then select the two sketch entities one by one. As soon as you select the two entities, a corner is created between the selected entities either by trimming or extending them, see Figures 3.6 and 3.7.

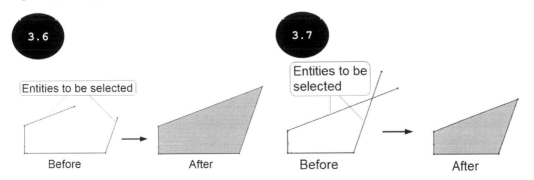

Trim away inside

The **Trim away inside** button is used to trim entities that lie inside a defined boundary. To trim inside a defined boundary, click on the **Trim away inside** button and then select two entities as the boundary entities one by one. Next, select the entities to be trimmed. The portion of the entities lying inside the boundary gets trimmed. Figure 3.8 shows the boundary entities and the entities to be trimmed and Figure 3.9 shows the resultant sketch after trimming the portion of the entity that lie inside the boundary.

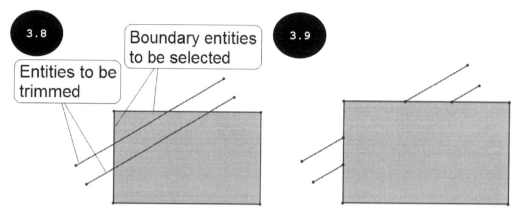

Trim away outside

The **Trim away outside** button of the **Options** rollout is used to trim the entities that lie outside a defined boundary. To trim outside a defined boundary, click on the **Trim away outside** button and then select two entities as the boundary entities one by one. Next, select the entities to be trimmed. The portion of the entities that lie outside the boundary gets trimmed. Figure 3.10 shows the boundary selected and the entities to be trimmed and Figure 3.11 shows the resultant sketch after trimming the portion of the entities that lie outside the boundary.

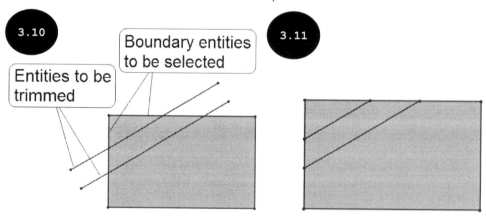

Trim to closest

The **Trim to closest** button is used to trim sketch entities from their nearest intersection by clicking the left mouse button. To trim a sketch entity by using this option, click on the **Trim to closest** button and then click on the entity to be trimmed. The selected entity is trimmed from its nearest intersection, see Figures 3.12 and 3.13.

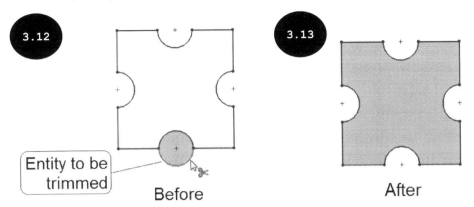

Procedure for Trimming Entities by using the Trim Entities Tool

1. Click on the **Trim Entities** tool. The **Trim PropertyManager** appears.
2. Select the required method of trimming entities by clicking on the respective button in the **Options** rollout of the PropertyManager.
3. Depending upon the button selected in the **Options** rollout, you can trim the sketch entities.

Extending Sketch Entities

You can extend sketch entities up to their nearest intersection by using the **Extend Entities** tool. The entities that can be extended by using this tool are line, centerline, ellipse, spline, arc, and so on. The Extend Entities tool is available in the **Trim** flyout of the **Sketch CommandManager**, see Figure 3.14. To invoke the Trim flyout, click on the down arrow available below the **Trim Entities** tool in the **Sketch CommandManager**. Figure 3.15 shows

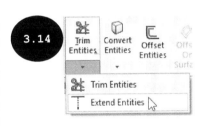

a sketch entity to be extended and Figure 3.16 shows the resultant sketch after extending the entity. The procedure to extend entities by using the **Extend Entities** tool is as follows:

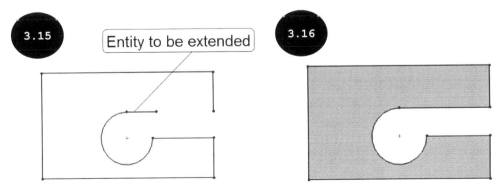

Procedure for Extending Entities by using the Extend Entities Tool

1. Click on the down arrow below the **Trim Entities** tool in the **Sketch CommandManager**. The **Trim** flyout appears, refer to Figure 3.14. Next, click on the **Extend Entities** tool. The appearance of the cursor changes to extend cursor.
2. Move the cursor over the entity to be extended. The preview of the extended line, up to the next intersection appears in the drawing area, see Figure 3.17.

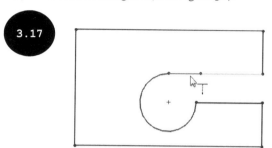

3.17

3. Click the left mouse button when the preview of the extended line appears. The selected entity is extended up to the next intersection.
4. Similarly, you can extend other sketch entities. Once you have extended all the sketch entities, press the ESC key to exit the **Extend Entities** tool.

> **Note:** The direction of the extension depends upon the position of the cursor over the entity to be extended. The endpoint of the entity, which is closer to the position of the cursor will be extended. To change the direction of extension, move the cursor to the other side of the sketch entity.

Offsetting Sketch Entities

You can offset sketch entities or edges of an existing feature at a specified offset distance by using the **Offset Entities** tool. To offset sketch entities or edges, click on the **Offset Entities** tool in the **Sketch CommandManager**. The Offset Entities PropertyManager appears, see Figure 3.18.

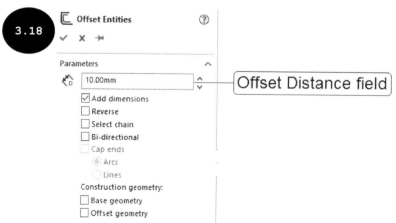

3.18

Once the **Offset Entities PropertyManager** has been invoked, select the entity to be offset from the drawing area. The preview of the offset entity appears with default parameters. You can modify the default parameters as required by using the options in the PropertyManager. The options of the PropertyManager are as follows:

Parameters

The options in the **Parameters** rollout of the PropertyManager are used to specify parameters for offsetting the selected sketch entities. The options of this rollout are as follows:

Offset Distance

The **Offset Distance** field of the **Parameters** rollout is used to specify the offset distance.

Tip: Besides controlling the offset distance by using the **Offset Distance** field, you can also dynamically control the offset distance. To do so, press and hold the left mouse button in the drawing area and then drag the cursor. Note that as you drag the cursor, the offset distance gets modified dynamically in the drawing area. Once the required distance has been achieved, release the left mouse button. The offset entity is created at the specified offset distance.

Add dimensions

The **Add dimensions** check box is selected to apply the specified offset distance value (dimension) in the resultant offset sketch. If this check box is unchecked, the offset distance value (dimension) is not applied in the resultant offset sketch, see Figure 3.19.

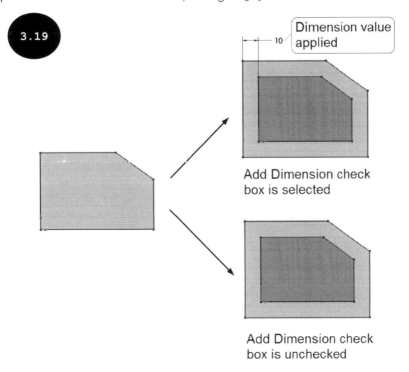

Reverse
The **Reverse** check box is used to reverse the direction of offset.

Select chain
If the **Select chain** check box is selected, on selecting a sketch entity in the drawing area, all the contiguous entities of the selected entity will be selected, automatically.

Bi-directional
The **Bi-directional** check box is used to offset selected entity/entities bi-directionally (both sides of the parent entity/entities), see Figure 3.20.

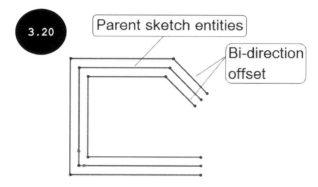

Cap ends
The **Cap ends** check box is used to cap the open ends of offset entities with lines or arcs, see Figures 3.21 and 3.22.

On selecting the **Cap ends** check box, the **Arcs** and **Lines** radio buttons get enabled in the PropertyManager. On selecting the **Arcs** radio button, the offset entities get capped with arcs, see Figure 3.21. If you select the **Lines** radio button, the offset entities will be capped with lines, see Figure 3.22.

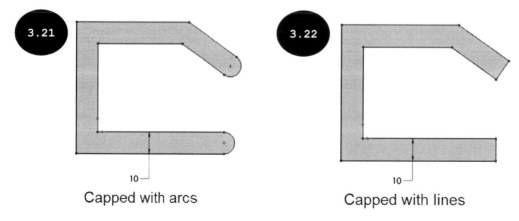

Capped with arcs   Capped with lines

Construction geometry

On selecting the **Base geometry** check box in the **Construction geometry** area, the original/base sketch entities are converted into construction entities, see Figure 3.23 (a). If you select the **Offset geometry** check box, then the offset entities are converted to construction entities, see Figure 3.23 (b).

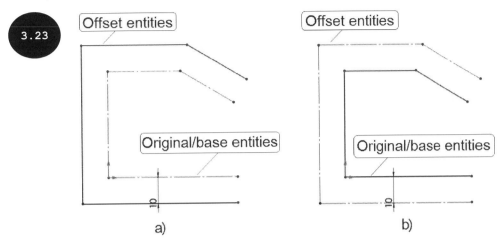

Figure 3.23

Procedure for Offsetting Entities

1. Invoke the **Offset PropertyManager** by clicking on the **Offset Entities** tool.
2. Select the sketch entities to be offset from the drawing area. The preview of the offset entities appears in the drawing area.
3. Enter the required offset distance value in the **Offset distance** field.
4. Select the **Reverse** check box to reverse the direction of offset, if required.
5. Specify the other parameters for offsetting the sketch entities in the PropertyManager.
6. After specifying all parameters, click on the green tick mark button in the PropertyManager. The offset entities are created.

Mirroring Sketch Entities

In SOLIDWORKS, you can mirror sketch entities about a mirroring line and create their mirror images by using the **Mirror Entities** and **Dynamic Mirror** tools. Both the tools are as follows:

Mirroring Entities by using the Mirror Entities Tool

The **Mirror Entities** tool is used to create a mirror image of the selected entities about a mirroring line. You can select a line, a centerline, or a linear edge of an existing feature as a mirroring line. To mirror sketch entities, click on the **Mirror Entities** tool in the **Sketch CommandManager**. The **Mirror PropertyManager** appears, see Figure 3.24. The options in this PropertyManager are as follows:

Tip: The **Message** rollout of the PropertyManager is used to display information about the action to be taken.

Entities to mirror

The **Entities to mirror** field of the **Options** rollout in the PropertyManager is used to select entities to be mirrored. By default, this field is activated. As a result, you can select entities by clicking the left mouse button or by using the window selection method. Note that as soon as you select entities, the names of the selected entities appear in this field. You can select entities to be mirrored before or after invoking the PropertyManager.

3.24

Copy

By default, the **Copy** check box is selected. As a result, the original sketch entities are retained and the mirror image of the selected entities is created in the resultant sketch. However, on unchecking this check box, the original sketch entities get removed and the mirror image of the selected entities is created in the resultant sketch.

Mirror about

The **Mirror about** field is used to select a mirroring line about which the selected entities get mirrored. Click on the **Mirror about** field in the PropertyManager and then select a line, a centerline, or a linear edge of existing features as the mirroring line. The preview of the mirror image appears in the drawing area. Next, click on the green tick mark ✓ button in the PropertyManager. The mirror image of the selected entities is created. Figure 3.25 shows entities to be mirrored and a mirroring line. Figure 3.26 shows the resultant sketch after mirroring the entities about the mirroring line.

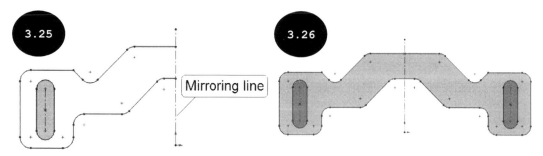

3.25 3.26 Mirroring line

Note: When you mirror entities, the symmetric relation is applied between the original entities and the mirror image with respect to the mirroring line. As a result, on modifying the original entities, the mirror image gets automatically modified and vice-versa. You will learn more about the relations in later chapters.

Procedure for Mirroring Entities by using the Mirror Entities Tool

1. Click on the **Mirror Entities** tool. The **Mirror PropertyManager** appears.
2. Select the entities to be mirrored from the drawing area.
3. Make sure that the **Copy** check box is selected in the PropertyManager.
4. Click on the **Mirror about** field and then click on a line, a centerline, or a linear edge as the mirroring line in the drawing area. The preview of the mirror image appears.
5. Click on the green tick mark button in the PropertyManager. The mirror image of the selected entities is created.

Mirroring Entities by using the Dynamic Mirror Tool

The **Dynamic Mirror** tool is used to mirror entities about a mirroring line similar to mirroring entities using the **Mirror Entities** tool with the only difference that this tool dynamically mirrors entities while drawing them.

Procedure for Mirroring Entities by using the Dynamic Mirror Tool

1. Click on **Tools > Sketch Tools > Dynamic Mirror** in the SOLIDWORKS menus. The **Dynamic Mirror** tool gets activated and the **Mirror PropertyManager** appears.
2. Select a mirroring line. The symbol of dynamic mirror appears on both ends of the selected mirroring line, see Figure 3.27. This symbol indicates that if you draw a sketch entity on either side of the mirroring line, the respective mirror image will automatically be created on the other side of the mirroring line.
3. Draw entities on one side of the mirroring line by using the sketching tools such as **Line** and **Circle**. The respective mirror images are created dynamically on the other side of the mirroring line, see Figure 3.28.
4. Once you have created the sketch, click on **Tools > Sketch Tools > Dynamic Mirror** in the SOLIDWORKS menus again to exit the **Dynamic Mirror** tool.

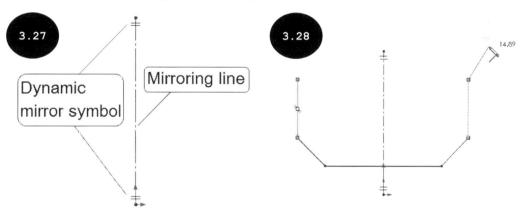

116 Chapter 3 > Editing and Modifying Sketches

Patterning Sketch Entities

In SOLIDWORKS, you can create linear and circular patterns of sketch entities by using the **Linear Sketch Pattern** and **Circular Sketch Pattern** tools, respectively. Both the tools are as follows:

Linear Sketch Pattern

Creating multiple instances of a sketch entity in a linear manner, along the X and Y axes, using the **Linear Sketch Pattern** tool is known as a linear sketch pattern. To create a linear sketch pattern, click on the **Linear Sketch Pattern** tool in the **Sketch CommandManager**. The **Linear Pattern PropertyManager** appears, refer to Figure 3.29.

Once the **Linear Pattern PropertyManager** has been invoked, select the sketch entity or entities to be patterned from the drawing area. The preview of the linear pattern with default parameters appears in the drawing area. Also, the names of the selected sketch entities appear in the **Entities to Pattern** field of the **Entities to Pattern** rollout in the PropertyManager. You can select the sketch entity to be patterned before or after invoking the PropertyManager. The options in the **Linear Pattern PropertyManager** are used to define the parameters for creating a linear sketch pattern and are as follows:

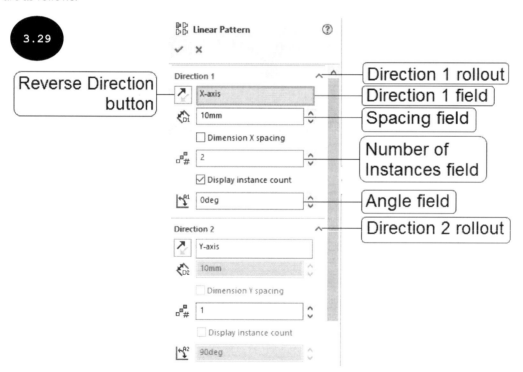

Direction 1

The options in the **Direction 1** rollout of the PropertyManager are used to specify the parameters for patterning sketch entities in direction 1 that is the X axis. The options are as follows:

Direction 1
By default, the X axis is selected in the **Direction 1** field of the **Direction 1** rollout. As a result, the patterning direction is along the X axis. You can also select a linear edge of a model or a linear entity of an existing sketch as the direction of the pattern.

Reverse Direction
The **Reverse Direction** button is used to reverse the direction of the pattern.

Spacing
The **Spacing** field is used to specify the distance/spacing between two pattern instances.

Number of Instances
The **Number of Instances** field is used to specify the number of pattern instances to be created in direction 1 (along the X axis).

> **Note:** The number of pattern instances specified in the **Number of Instances** field is counted along with the parent or original instance. For example, if 6 is specified in the **Number of Instances** field, then the 6 pattern instances will be created including the parent instance.

Angle
The **Angle** field is used to specify an angle for direction 1 with respect to the horizontal X axis. By default, 0 degree angle is specified in this field. As a result, the linear pattern is created along the X axis at 0 degree angle, see Figure 3.30. Figure 3.31 shows the preview of the linear pattern along the X axis at 12 degrees angle.

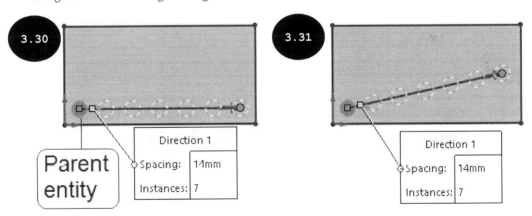

> **Note:** In the preview of the linear pattern, an arrow appears with a dot at its tip, refer to Figures 3.30 and 3.31. You can also change the orientation or the angle of the pattern direction by dragging this dot in the drawing area. For dragging the dot, press and hold the left mouse button over the dot and then drag the cursor.

Dimension X spacing
On selecting the **Dimension X spacing** check box, the distance/spacing specified between two pattern instances is applied in the resulting pattern sketch, see Figure 3.32.

Display Instance count
On selecting the **Display instance count** check box, the number of pattern instances specified in the direction 1 displayed in the resultant pattern sketch, see Figure 3.32.

Direction 2
The options in the **Direction 2** rollout of the PropertyManager are same as the options of the **Direction 1** rollout with the only difference that the options of the **Direction 2** rollout are used to specify the parameters for the linear pattern in the second direction that is the Y axis, by default, see Figure 3.33.

Note: By default, all the options in the **Direction 2** rollout are not enabled except the **Number of Instances** field. This is because 1 is specified in the **Number of Instances** field as the number of pattern instances. On specifying the number of pattern instances, two or more than two in this field, the other options of the **Direction 2** rollout get enabled.

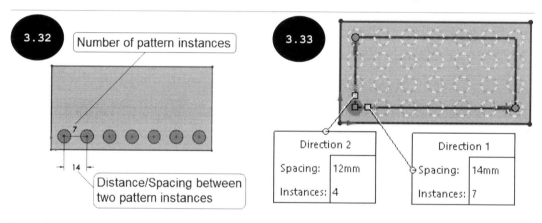

Entities to Pattern
The **Entities to Pattern** field in the **Entities to Pattern** rollout displays the list of entities selected for patterning. You can select the entities to be patterned before or after invoking the PropertyManager.

Instances to Skip
The **Instances to Skip** rollout of the PropertyManager is used to skip or remove the unwanted instances of a pattern. To skip instances of a pattern, click on the down arrow available in the title bar of the **Instances to Skip** rollout to expand the rollout. Next, click on the field in the expanded **Instances to Skip** rollout. The pink dots appear in all the instances of the pattern in the drawing area, see Figure 3.34. Next, move the cursor over the pink dot, of the instance to be skipped and then click the left mouse button. The preview of the selected instance is disabled and is no longer a part of the resultant pattern, see Figure 3.35. Also, the pink dot changes to orange dot and the skipped instance appears in the field of the **Instances to Skip** rollout. Similarly, you can skip multiple instances of pattern by clicking the left mouse button on the pink dots of instances to be skipped.

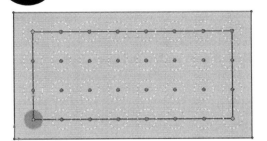
3.34

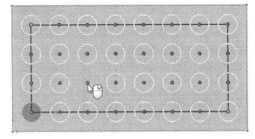
3.35

Note: To recall the skipped instances of the pattern, click on the orange dots of the skipped instances that appear in the preview of the pattern. Alternatively, you can select the instance to be recalled from the field in the **Instances to Skip** rollout and then right-click to display a shortcut menu. Next, click on the **Delete** option in the shortcut menu to remove the respective instance from the list of skipped instances.

After defining the required parameters for patterning the sketch entities in the **Linear Pattern PropertyManager**, click on the green tick mark ✓ button in the PropertyManager. The linear pattern is created.

Procedure for Creating a Linear Pattern

1. Click on the **Linear Sketch Pattern** tool. The **Linear Pattern PropertyManager** appears.
2. Select the entities to be patterned from the drawing area. The preview of the linear pattern along the X axis appears with the default settings.
3. Reverse the direction of the pattern, if required, by clicking on the **Reverse Direction** button.
4. Specify the distance between pattern instances in the **Spacing** field of the **Direction 1** rollout.
5. Specify the number of pattern instances to be created along the X axis in the **Number of Instances** field of the **Direction 1** rollout.
6. Specify the number of pattern instances to be created along the Y axis in the **Number of Instances** field of the **Direction 2** rollout.
7. Specify other parameters such as distance between instances and the number of instances for direction 2 in the respective fields of the **Direction 2** rollout.
8. After specifying all the parameters for the direction 1 and direction 2 pattern instances, click on the green tick mark ✓ button in the PropertyManager. The linear pattern is created.

Circular Sketch Pattern

Creating multiple instances of a sketch entity in a circular manner about a center point by using the **Circular Sketch Pattern** tool is known as a circular sketch pattern. To create a circular sketch pattern, invoke the **Pattern** flyout by clicking on the down arrow next to the **Linear Sketch Pattern** tool in the **Sketch CommandManager**, see Figure 3.36 and then click on the **Circular Sketch Pattern** tool. The **Circular Pattern PropertyManager** appears, refer to Figure 3.37.

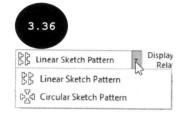

3.36

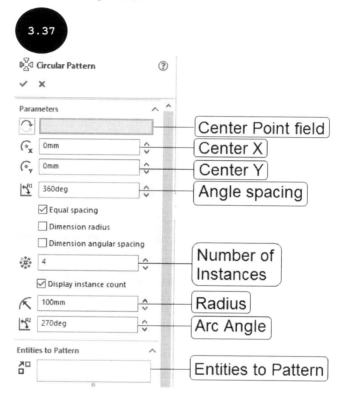

3.37

Once the **Circular Pattern PropertyManager** has been invoked, select the sketch entity/entities to be patterned in the drawing area. The preview of the circular pattern with default parameters appears, see Figure 3.38. Also, the names of the selected entities appear in the **Entities to Pattern** field of the PropertyManager. You can select entities to be patterned before or after invoking the PropertyManager. The options in the **Circular Pattern PropertyManager** are used to define parameters for creating the circular sketch pattern. The options of the PropertyManager are as follows:

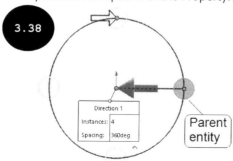

3.38

Parameters

The options in the **Parameters** rollout are used to specify parameters for patterning sketch entities in a circular manner. The options of this rollout are as follows:

Center Point

The **Center Point** field is used to specify the center point for the pattern instances. Note that as soon as you select entities to be patterned, the origin point (0,0) is selected as the center point for pattern instances, by default, see Figure 3.38. You can specify any other point as the center point of the circular pattern by using the **Center X** and **Center Y** fields of the PropertyManager.

Center X

The **Center X** field is used to specify the X coordinate of the center point.

Center Y

The **Center Y** field is used to specify the Y coordinate of the center point.

Note: Besides specifying the X and Y coordinates for defining the center point of the pattern, you can define the center point of the pattern by dragging the dot appeared at the tip of the arrow in the preview of the circular pattern, refer to Figure 3.38. As you change the location of the dot by dragging it, the coordinates of the center point change accordingly in the **Center X** and **Center Y** fields, dynamically. In addition, you can also select a sketch point as the center point of the pattern.

Angle spacing

The **Angle spacing** field is used to specify the total angle value of the pattern. By default, the value entered in this field is 360 degrees. As a result, the circular pattern is created such that it covers 360 degrees in the pattern and the number of pattern instances are adjusted within the total 360 degrees, equally. This is because the **Equal spacing** check box is selected, by default, in this rollout.

Equal spacing

By default, the **Equal spacing** check box is selected. As a result, the total angle value specified in the **Angle spacing** field is arranged equally among all the pattern instances. However, on unchecking this check box, the angle value entered in the **Angle spacing** field is used as the angle between two instances of the pattern.

Dimension radius

On selecting the **Dimension radius** check box, the pattern radius with respect to the center point is displayed in the resultant pattern, see Figure 3.39.

Dimension angular spacing

On selecting the **Dimension angular spacing** check box, the angular distance between the two instances is applied in the resultant pattern, see Figure 3.39.

Number of Instances

The **Number of Instances** field is used to specify the total number of instances in the pattern.

Note that the number of instances specified in this field is counted along with the parent instance.

Display instance count
On selecting the **Display instance count** check box, the pattern instances count appears in the resultant pattern, see Figure 3.39.

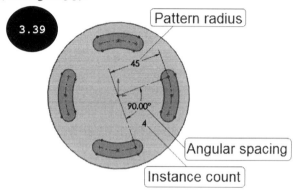

Radius
The **Radius** field is used to specify the pattern radius. As the origin is defined as the center point of the circular pattern, by default, the **Radius** field displays the pattern radius by keeping the origin as the center point for measurement. You can change the default radius value by entering the new radius value in this field.

Arc Angle
The **Arc Angle** field is used to specify the angle measured value from the center of the selected entities to the center point of the pattern.

Instances to Skip
The **Instances to Skip** rollout of the PropertyManager is used to skip pattern instances of a circular pattern. To skip instances of the pattern, click on the down arrow available in the title bar of the **Instances to Skip** rollout to expand it. Next, click on the field in the expanded **Instances to Skip** rollout. The pink dots appear in all the instances of the pattern in the drawing area, see Figure 3.40. Next, move the cursor over the pink dot, of the instance to be skipped and then click the left mouse button. The preview of the selected instance is disabled and it is no longer a part of the resultant pattern, see Figure 3.41. Also, the pink dot changes to orange dot and the respective instance number is displayed in the field of the **Instances to Skip** rollout.

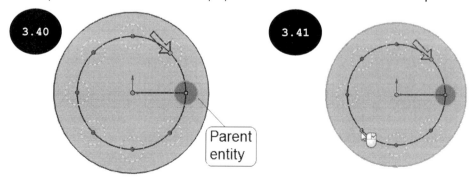

After defining the required parameters for patterning the sketch entities in the **Circular Pattern PropertyManager**, click on the green tick mark button. The circular pattern is created.

Procedure for Creating the Circular Pattern

1. Click on the **Circular Sketch Pattern** tool in the **Pattern** flyout. The **Circular Pattern PropertyManager** appears.
2. Select the entities to be patterned. The preview of the circular pattern appears such that the origin is selected as the center point of the pattern.
3. Click on the **Reverse Direction** button to reverse the direction of the pattern, if needed.
4. Change the center point of the pattern by dragging the dot available at the arrow tip in the preview or by specifying coordinates of the center point in the **Center X** and **Center Y** fields of the PropertyManager, if needed.
5. Specify the total pattern angle value or the angle between two instances in the **Angle spacing** field.

> **Tip:** If the **Equal spacing** check box is selected, the angle specified in the **Angle spacing** field measures the total angle between which all the pattern instances are arranged, equally. However, if the **Equal spacing** check box is unchecked, the angle specified in the **Angle spacing** field measures the angle between two pattern instances.

6. Specify the number of pattern instances to be created in the **Number of Instances** field.
7. After specifying all the parameters, click on the green tick mark button. The circular pattern is created.

Creating a Sketch Fillet

A sketch fillet is used to remove the corner at the intersection of two sketch entities by creating a tangent arc of constant radii, see Figure 3.42. In the Sketching environment, you can create fillets by using the **Sketch Fillet** tool.

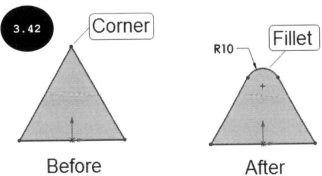

To create sketch fillets, click on the **Sketch Fillet** tool in the **Sketch CommandManager**, see Figure 3.43. The **Sketch Fillet PropertyManager** appears, see Figure 3.44. Next, enter the fillet radius in the **Fillet Radius** field of the **Fillet Parameters** rollout in the PropertyManager. By default, the **Keep constrained corners** check box is selected in the **Fillet Parameters** rollout. As a result, if the corner/vertex to be filleted has dimensions, then a virtual intersection point is created at the corner to maintain dimensions, whereas if the corner/vertex has relations, then the SOLIDWORKS message window appears which informs you that if the fillet is created, the applied relation will be deleted. The **Dimension each fillet** check box of the PropertyManager is used to apply radius dimension to all the fillets created in the drawing area.

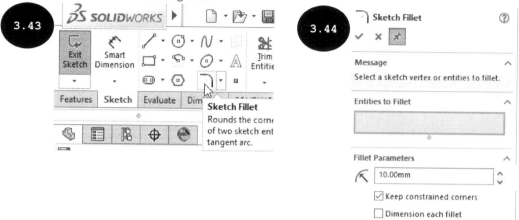

After specifying the fillet radius, move the cursor over the corner/vertex of the sketch to be filleted, see Figure 3.45. The preview of fillet appears in the drawing area, see Figure 3.45. Next, click the left mouse button to accept the fillet preview. Similarly, click on the other corners of the sketch to create fillets of specified radius, see Figure 3.46. Next, click on the green tick mark button ✓ in the PropertyManager. The fillets of specified radius are created at the selected corners of the sketch, see Figure 3.47. Note that the fillet radius is applied to one of the fillets and the equal relation is applied to all the fillets. If the **Dimension each fillet** check box is selected in the **Fillet Parameters** rollout of the PropertyManager then the fillet radius will be applied to all the fillets created in the drawing area.

Tip: Instead of selecting a corner/vertex, you can also select two intersecting sketch entities to create a fillet of specified radius at their intersection.

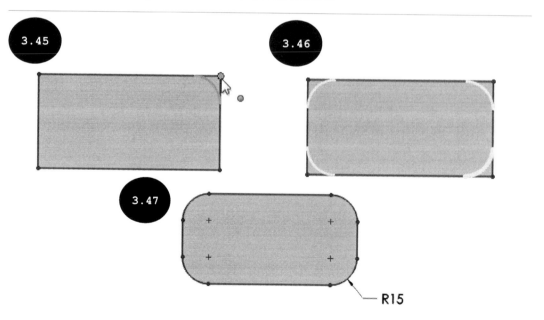

Creating a Sketch Chamfer

A chamfer is a bevel edge that is non perpendicular to its adjacent sketch entities. You can create a chamfer to the adjacent entities of a sketch by using the **Sketch Chamfer** tool, see Figure 3.48.

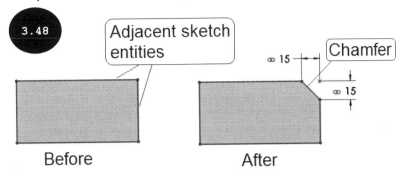

To create a sketch chamfer, click on the down arrow next to the **Sketch Fillet** tool in the **Sketch CommandManager**. A flyout appears, see Figure 3.49. In this flyout, click on the **Sketch Chamfer** tool. The **Sketch Chamfer PropertyManager** appears, see Figure 3.50.

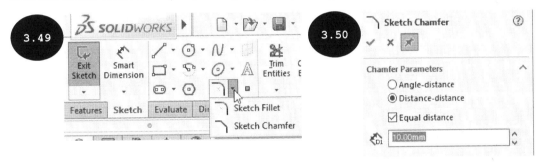

The **Distance-distance** radio button of the PropertyManager is used to create a chamfer by specifying distance values from both the adjacent sketch entities in the **Distance 1** and **Distance 2** fields of the PropertyManager, see Figure 3.51. Note that if the **Equal distance** check box is selected in the PropertyManager then the **Distance 2** field is not available in the PropertyManager and the distance value specified in the **Distance 1** field is applied to both sides of the sketch entities, see Figure 3.52.

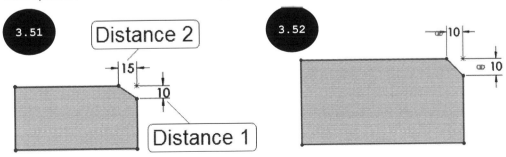

126 Chapter 3 > Editing and Modifying Sketches

The **Angle-distance** radio button of the PropertyManager is used to create a chamfer by specifying the angle and distance values in the **Distance 1** and **Direction 1 Angle** fields of the PropertyManager, respectively, see Figure 3.53. After selecting the required radio button (**Distance-distance** or **Angle-distance**) and specifying the required parameters (distance-distance or angle-distance) in the PropertyManager, select the adjacent entities of the sketch one by one. The chamfer is created between the selected entities. Note that instead of selecting adjacent entities of a sketch, you can also select a vertex at the intersection of two adjacent sketch entities for creating a chamfer. After creating the chamfer, press the ESC key to exit the **Sketch Chamfer** tool.

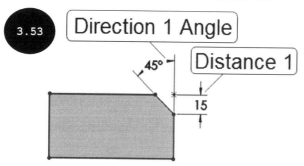

Moving a Sketch Entity

You can move a sketch entity from one position to another in the drawing area by using the **Move Entities** tool. To move a sketch entity or entities, click on the **Move Entities** tool. The **Move PropertyManager** appears, see Figure 3.54. The options in the PropertyManager are as follows:

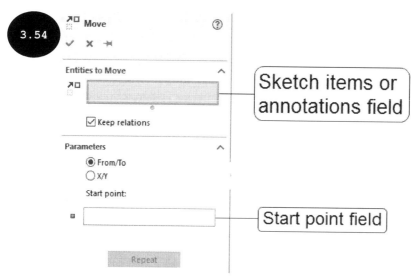

Entities to Move

The options in the **Entities to Move** rollout are used to select entities to be moved and are as follows:

Sketch items or annotations
The **Sketch items or annotations** field of the **Entities to Move** rollout is used to select entities to be moved. By default, this field is activated. As a result, you can select entities to be moved from the drawing area. You can select entities to be moved before or after invoking the PropertyManager. The names of the selected entities are displayed in this field.

Keep relations
The **Keep relations** check box is used to maintain relations between the entities. If the **Keep relations** check box is selected, the existing relations between the sketch entities to be moved and the other entities of the sketch will be maintained. However, on unchecking this check box, the relations between the sketch entities to be moved and the other entities of the sketch will be broken.

Parameters
The options in the **Parameters** rollout are used to specify parameters for moving the entities and are as follows:

From/To
By default, the **From/To** radio button is selected in the **Parameters** rollout. As a result, you can move the selected entities from one location to the other with respect to a base point. To move entities, when this radio button is selected, click on the **Start point** field and then specify a point in the drawing area as the base point for moving the selected entities. As soon as you specify a base point, the selected entities get attached to the cursor and as you move the cursor, the entities move dynamically into the drawing area with respect to the specified base point. Now, specify a new position for the selected entities in the drawing area by clicking the left mouse button.

X/Y
The **X/Y** radio button is used to move sketch entities by specifying a translation distance along the X and Y axes with respect to the original location of the sketch entities. When you select the **X/Y** radio button, the △X and △Y fields get enabled in the rollout. In these fields, you can specify a translation distance along the X and Y axes. Note that the distance specified in the △X and △Y fields is measured from the center point of the original location of the sketch entities.

Repeat
The **Repeat** button is used to move sketch entities with the incremental distance specified in the △X and △Y fields. Note that every time you click on the **Repeat** button, the selected entities move to the incremental distance specified in the △X and △Y fields.

Procedure for Moving Sketch Entities
1. Click on the **Move Entities** tool. The **Move PropertyManager** appears.
2. Select the entities to be moved.
3. Select the **From/To** or **X/Y** radio button for moving the entities. By default, the **From/To** radio button is selected. As a result, you can move the sketch entities with respect to a base point.
4. Depending upon the radio button selected in Step 3, specify a new position for the sketch entities in the drawing area.

Creating a Copy of Sketch Entities

You can create a copy of a set of sketch entities by using the **Copy Entities** tool. To copy sketch entities, click on the down arrow next to the **Move Entities** tool. A flyout appears, see Figure 3.55. Next, in this flyout, click on the **Copy Entities** tool. The **Copy PropertyManager** appears, see Figure 3.56. The options in this PropertyManager are same as of the **Move PropertyManager** with the only difference that the options in this PropertyManager are used to create a copy of the original sketch entities in the specified location.

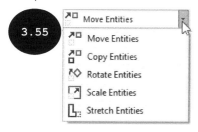

Procedure for Creating a Copy of Sketch Entities

1. Click on the down arrow next to the **Move Entities** tool and then click on the **Copy Entities** tool in the flyout appeared. The **Copy PropertyManager** appears.
2. Select the sketch entities to be copied.
3. Select the **From/To** or **X/Y** radio button from the **Parameters** rollout, as required.
4. Depending upon the radio button selected in the Step 3, specify a new location for the entities in the drawing area. The copy of selected entities is created at the specified location.

Rotating an Entity

You can rotate a sketch entity or entities at an angle by using the **Rotate Entities** tool. To rotate sketch entities, click on the down arrow next to the **Move Entities** tool. A flyout appears, refer to Figure 3.55. In the flyout, click on the **Rotate Entities** tool. The **Rotate PropertyManager** appears, see Figure 3.57. The options in this PropertyManager are as follows:

Entities to Rotate

The options of the **Entities to Rotate** rollout are used to select entities to be rotated. The options are as follows:

Sketch items or annotations

The **Sketch items or annotations** field of this rollout is used to select entities. Select entities to be rotated from the drawing area. The names of the selected entities appear or get listed in this field. You can select entities before or after invoking the PropertyManager.

Keep relations

The **Keep relations** check box is used to maintain relations between sketch entities. If this check box is selected, the existing relations between sketch entities to be rotated and the other entities of the sketch will be maintained. However, on unchecking this check box, the relations between the sketch entities to be rotated and the other entities of the sketch will be broken.

Parameters

The **Parameters** rollout of the PropertyManager is used to specify parameters for rotating sketch entities. The options in this rollout are as follows:

Center of rotation

The **Center of rotation** field is used to specify a base point or a center point of rotation. To specify a base point for rotating sketch entities, click on the **Center of rotation** field and then specify a point in the drawing area by clicking the left mouse button. A triad appears in the drawing area, see Figure 3.58. Also, the **Angle** field gets enabled below this field in the PropertyManager. Now, you can specify the angle of rotation in the **Angle** field and then press ENTER. The preview of rotated sketch entities appears in the drawing area. You can also use the spinner arrows ≎ in the **Angle** field to specify the angle of rotation. Next, click on the green tick mark button ✓ in the PropertyManager. The selected entities get rotated at the specified angle. Figure 3.58 shows a sketch before or after rotating a slot at an angle of 30 degrees with respect to its center point.

Tip: When you specify a positive angle value, the direction of rotation will be in the anti-clockwise direction. Whereas, on specifying a negative angle value, the direction of rotation will be in the clockwise direction.

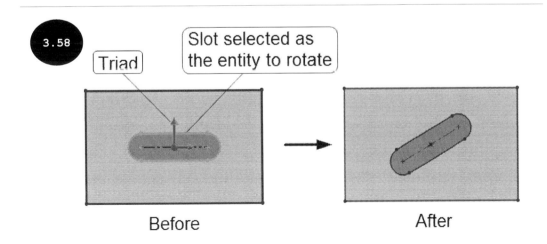

Procedure for Rotating Sketch Entities

1. Click on the down arrow next to the **Move Entities** tool and then click on the **Rotate Entities** tool in the flyout appeared. The **Rotate PropertyManager** appears.
2. Select the sketch entities to be rotated.
3. Click on the **Center of rotation** field in the PropertyManager to activate it and then specify a center point of rotation.
4. Specify the angle of rotation in the **Angle** field of the PropertyManager.
5. Click on the green tick mark ✓ button in the PropertyManager. The selected entities are rotated at the specified angle.

Scaling Sketch Entities

You can increase or decrease the scale of sketch entities by using the **Scale Entities** tool. To scale sketch entities, click on the down arrow next to the **Move Entities** tool. A flyout appears. In this flyout, click on the **Scale Entities** tool. The **Scale PropertyManager** appears, see Figure 3.59. The options in this PropertyManager are as follows:

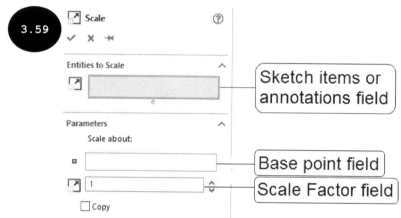

Entities to Scale

The **Sketch items or annotations** field of the **Entities to Scale** rollout is used to select entities to be scaled. Select the entities to be scaled from the drawing area. The names of the entities appear in the **Sketch items or annotations** field.

Parameters

The options in the **Parameters** rollout are used to specify parameters for scaling the selected sketch entities. The options are as follows:

Base point and Scale Factor

The **Base point** field of the **Parameters** rollout is used to specify a base point or center point for scaling the selected entities. To specify a base point, click on the **Base point** field and then click the left mouse button in the drawing area for scaling the entities. A dot filled with yellow color appears in the drawing area, which is representing the base point, see Figure 3.60. Next, specify the scale factor in the **Scale Factor** field. You can use the spinner arrows ↕ of the **Scale Factor** field to specify the scale factor. The preview of the scaled sketch of the specified scale factor appears in the drawing area, see Figure 3.60. Next, click on the green tick mark ✓ button in the PropertyManager. The selected entities are scaled.

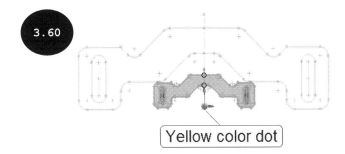
Figure 3.60

Copy

By default, the **Copy** check box is unchecked. As a result, the selected entities are scaled to the new scaled factor without retaining a copy of the original entities. However, if you select the **Copy** check box, the original entities are retained and a copy of scaled entities is created in the drawing area. Note that on selecting the **Copy** check box, the **Number of Copies** field gets enabled in the rollout. In this field, you can specify the number of copies of the scaled entities to be created.

Note: A set of original sketch entities is excluded or not counted in the number of copies specified in the **Number of Copies** field. For example, if you specify 2 in this field, then two sets of copies of the scaled entities are created in addition to the original sketch entities. Also, note that every scaled copy will be created with the incremental scale factor.

Procedure for Scaling Sketch Entities

1. Click on the down arrow next to the **Move Entities** tool and then click on the **Scale Entities** tool in the flyout appeared. The **Scale PropertyManager** appears.
2. Select the entities to be scaled.
3. Click on the **Base point** field to activate it.
4. Select a base point for scaling the sketch entities.
5. Enter the scale factor for scaling the entities in the **Scale Factor** field.
6. Click on the green tick mark ✓ button in the PropertyManager. The selected entities are scaled.

Stretching an Entity

You can stretch entities of a sketch by using the **Stretch Entities** tool. To stretch entities, click on the down arrow next to the **Move Entities** tool. A flyout appears. In this flyout, click on the **Stretch Entities** tool. The **Stretch PropertyManager** appears, see Figure 3.61. The options in this PropertyManager are as follows:

Figure 3.61

Entities to Stretch
The **Sketch items or annotations** field of the **Entities to Stretch** rollout is used to select entities to be stretched. By default, this field is activated. As a result, you can select entities to be stretched from the drawing area. The names of the selected entities appear in the **Sketch items or annotations** field.

Parameters
The options in the **Parameters** rollout are used to specify parameters for stretching the entities. The options are as follows:

From/To
The **From/To** radio button is used to stretch entities with respect to a base point. On selecting this radio button, the **Base point** field gets enabled in the **Parameters** rollout. Click on this field to activate it and then select a base point for stretching the entities. After specifying a base point, move the cursor. The preview of the stretched entities appears in the drawing area. Next, specify a new position for the stretched entities by clicking the left mouse button in the drawing area.

X/Y
The **X/Y** radio button is used to stretch entities by specifying a translation distance along the X and Y axes with respect to the original location of the entities. When you select the **X/Y** radio button, the $\triangle$X and $\triangle$Y fields get enabled in the **Parameters** rollout. In these fields, you can specify a translation distance along the X and Y axes.

Repeat
The **Repeat** button is used to stretch entities into the incremental distance specified in the $\triangle$X and $\triangle$Y fields.

Procedure for Stretching Sketch Entities
1. Click on the down arrow next to the **Move Entities** tool and then click on the **Stretch Entities** tool in the flyout appeared. The **Stretch PropertyManager** appears.
2. Select the entities to be stretched.
3. Select the **From/To** or **X/Y** radio button from the **Parameters** rollout.
4. Depending upon the radio button selected in the Step 3, specify a new position for the stretched entities in the drawing area.

Tutorial 1

Draw the sketch shown in Figure 3.62. The dimensions and the model shown in this figure are for your reference only. You will learn about applying dimensions and creating a model in later chapters.

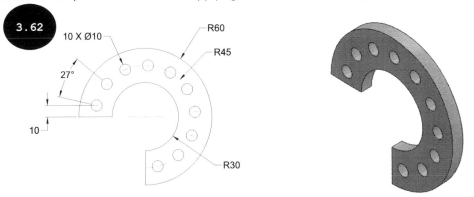

Section 1: Starting SOLIDWORKS

First, you need to start the SOLIDWORKS software.

1. Double-click on the SOLIDWORKS icon on your desktop to start SOLIDWORKS, if not started already.

Section 2: Invoking the Sketching Environment

Now, invoke the Sketching environment by selecting the Front plane as the sketching plane.

1. Click on the **New** tool in the **Standard** tool. The **New SOLIDWORKS Document** dialog box appears.

    In this dialog box, the **Part** button is activated by default. As as result, you can directly click on the OK button to invoke the Part modeling environment.

2. Click on the **OK** button to invoke the Part modeling environment.

    Once the Part modeling environment has been invoked, you can invoke the Sketching environment and create the sketch of this tutorial.

3. Click on the **Sketch** tab in the CommandManager. The tools of the **Sketch CommandManager** are displayed.

4. Click on the **Sketch** button in the **Sketch CommandManager**. The three default planes mutually perpendicular to each other appear in the graphics area.

5. Move the cursor over the Front plane and click when the boundary of the plane is highlighted. The Sketching environment is invoked. Also, the Front plane is orientated normal to the viewing direction and the confirmation corner appears at the upper right corner of the drawing area.

Section 3: Specifying the Snap and Unit Settings

Once the Sketching environment has been invoked, you need to set the snap settings such that the cursor snaps to the increment of 5 mm. Also, specify the metric unit system for measurement.

1. Click on the **Options** tool in the **Standard** toolbar. The **System Options - General** dialog box appears.

2. In this dialog box, click on the **Document Properties** tab. The name of the dialog box changes to **Document Properties - Drafting Standard**.

3. Click on the **Units** option in the left panel of the dialog box. The options for specifying the unit system are displayed on the right of the dialog box.

4. Click on the **MMGS (millimeter, gram, second)** radio button in the **Unit system** area of the dialog box, if not selected by default. Once the unit system has been specified, do not exit the dialog box.

   Now, you need to specify snap settings such that the cursor snaps to the increment of 5 mm.

5. Click on the **Grid/Snap** option in the left panel of the dialog box. The options for specifying the grid and snap settings are displayed on the right panel of the dialog box. Also, the name of the dialog box changes to **Document Properties - Grid/Snap**.

6. Enter **20** in the **Major grid spacing** field; **4** in the **Minor -lines per major** field; and **1** in the **Snap points per minor** field of the **Grid** area in the dialog box.

7. Uncheck the **Display grid** check box of the **Grid** area in the dialog box to turn off the display of grids in the drawing area.

8. Click on the **Go To System Snaps** button in the dialog box. The name of the dialog box changes to **System Options - Relations/Snaps**.

9. Select the **Grid** check box in the **Sketch snaps** area of the dialog box to turn on the snap mode, if not selected by default.

10. Make sure that the **Snap only when grid appears** check box, available below the **Grid** check box is unchecked.

11. Click on the **OK** button in the dialog box. The snap settings are specified and the dialog box is closed.

Section 4: Drawing Sketch Entities

Once the units and snap settings have been specified, you need to start drawing the sketch.

1. Click on the **Circle** tool in the **Sketch CommandManager**. The **Circle** tool gets activated and the **Circle PropertyManager** appears on the left of the drawing area.

2. Move the cursor to the origin and then click to specify the center point of the circle when the cursor snaps to the origin.

3. Move the cursor horizontally toward right for a little distance. The preview of the circle attached to the cursor appears. Also, the radius of the circle is displayed near the cursor tip. Notice that as you move the cursor, the preview of the circle and its radius is modified dynamically.

4. Move the cursor to the location where the radius of the circle appears 60 mm, see Figure 3.63, and then click on that location. A circle of radius 60 mm is created. Note that after creating a circle, the **Circle** tool remains active.

5. Move the cursor to the origin and click to specify the center point of the second circle when cursor snaps to the origin.

6. Move the cursor horizontally to the right and click when the radius of the circle appears 30 mm, see Figure 3.64.

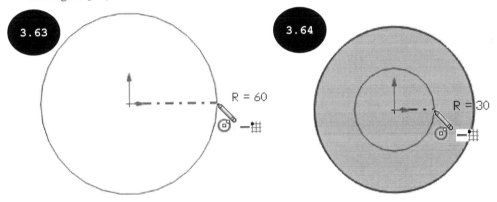

After creating the circles of radius 60 mm and 30 mm, you need to create a construction circle of radius 45 mm that will define the PCD of holes.

7. Create a circle of radius 45 mm whose center point is at the origin, see Figure 3.65. After creating the circle of radius 45 mm, right-click in the drawing area and click on the **Select** option in the shortcut menu displayed, to terminate the creation of the circle and to exit the **Circle** tool.

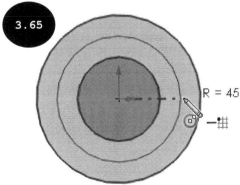

136 Chapter 3 > Editing and Modifying Sketches

Once you have created the circle of radius 45 mm, you need to convert it into a reference/construction circle.

8. Click on the circle of radius 45 mm in the drawing area to select it. The **Circle PropertyManager** appears on the left of the drawing area. Also, a Pop-up toolbar appears near the cursor, see Figure 3.66.

9. Click on the **Construction Geometry** tool in the Pop-up toolbar, see Figure 3.66. The selected circle of radius 45 mm is converted into a construction circle, see Figure 3.67. Alternatively, select the **For construction** check box in the **Options** rollout of the PropertyManager to convert the circle into a construction circle.

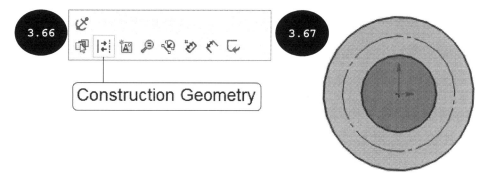

10. Click on the **Line** tool in the **Sketch CommandManager**. The **Insert Line PropertyManager** appears.

11. Specify the start point of the line at the origin and then move the cursor horizontally toward left.

12. Click to specify the endpoint of the line when the length of the line appears 60 mm and the cursor snaps to the outer circle, see Figure 3.68.

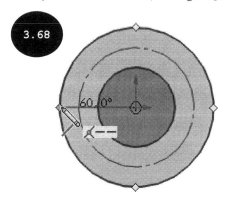

13. Right-click in the drawing area. A shortcut menu appears. Next, click on the **End chain (double-click)** option in the shortcut menu to terminate the creation of a continuous chain of lines. However, the **Line** tool is still active for creating other line entities.

> **Tip:** To exit the **Line** tool, click on the **Select** option in the shortcut menu, which appears on right-clicking on the drawing area. On clicking the **End chain (double-click)** option in the shortcut menu, only the creation of a continuous chain of lines gets terminated and the **Line** tool remains active.

14. Move the cursor to the origin and click to specify the start point of the line when cursor snaps to the origin.

15. Move the cursor vertically downward and click to specify the endpoint of the line when the length of the line appears 60 mm and the cursor snaps to the outer circle, see Figure 3.69.

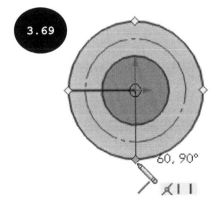

16. Right-click in the drawing area. A shortcut menu appears. Next, click on the **Select** option in the shortcut menu to exit the **Line** tool.

   Now, you need to create a circle of diameter 10 mm. It is evident from Figure 3.62 that the circles of diameter 10 mm are 10 in the count. As the diameter of all the circles is same and are on the same PCD (Pitch Circle Diameter), you can create one circle and then create a circular pattern to create remaining circles.

17. Click on the **Circle** tool. The **Circle PropertyManager** appears.

18. Move the cursor in the drawing area, where the coordinates (X, Y, Z) appear "-45, 10, 0" respectively, in the Status Bar, see Figure 3.70. The construction circle gets highlighted, see Figure 3.71.

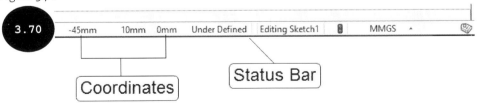

19. Click the left mouse button to specify the center point of the circle when the coordinates appear "-45, 10, 0" in the Status Bar and the construction circle gets highlighted, see Figure 3.71.

138   Chapter 3 > Editing and Modifying Sketches

20. Move the cursor horizontally toward right and click when the radius of the circle appears close to 5 mm near the cursor, see Figure 3.72. A circle of radius close to 5 mm is created and is selected in the drawing area. Also, the options in the **Circle PropertyManager** are enabled to control the parameters of the selected circle.

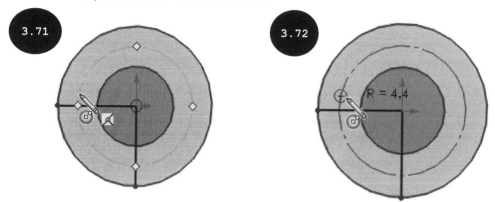

21. Enter **5** as the radius of the selected circle in the **Radius** field of the **Parameters** rollout of the PropertyManager. Next, press ENTER. The radius of the circle is modified to 5 mm.

22. Right-click in the drawing area and then click on the **Select** option in the shortcut menu to exit the **Circle** tool.

Section 5: Trimming Sketch Entities

Now, you need to trim the unwanted sketch entities of the sketch.

1. Click on the **Trim Entities** tool in the **Sketch CommandManager**. The **Trim PropertyManager** appears on the left of the drawing area.

2. Click on the **Trim to closest** button in the **Options** rollout of the PropertyManager. The appearance of cursor changes to trim cursor.

3. Move the cursor over the portion of the entity to be trimmed, see Figure 3.73 and then click the left mouse button when it is highlighted in the drawing area. The selected portion of the entity is trimmed, see Figure 3.74.

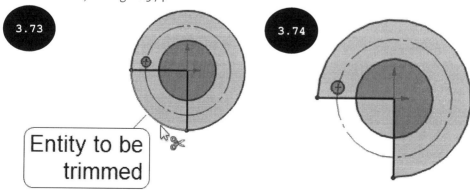

4. Similarly, trim the other unwanted portions of the entities of the sketch. Figure 3.75 shows entities to be trimmed and Figure 3.76 shows the sketch after trimming all the unwanted entities.

5. Click on the green tick mark in the PropertyManager to exit the **Trim Entities** tool.

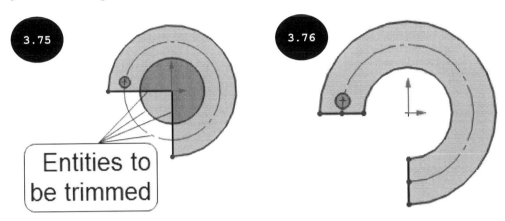

Section 6: Creating the Circular Pattern

Now, you need to create a circular pattern of the circle having radius 5 mm for creating remaining circles of the sketch.

1. Select the previously created circle of radius 5 mm from the drawing area.

2. Click on the down arrow next to the **Linear Sketch Pattern** tool. The **Pattern** flyout appears, see Figure 3.77.

3. Click on the **Circular Sketch Pattern** tool in the **Pattern** flyout. The preview of the circular pattern with default parameters appears in the drawing area. Also, the **Circular Pattern** PropertyManager appears on the left of the drawing area.

4. Uncheck the **Equal spacing** check box in the **Parameters** rollout of the PropertyManager.

5. Enter **27** in the **Angle** field of the **Parameter** rollout as the angle between two instances.

6. Enter **10** in the **Number of Instances** field as the number of pattern instances to be created.

7. Click on the green tick mark in the PropertyManager. A circular pattern is created, see Figure 3.78.

Note: The circular pattern shown in Figure 3.78 has been created with the **Dimension angular spacing** and **Display instance count** check boxes are selected in the PropertyManager.

140   Chapter 3 > Editing and Modifying Sketches

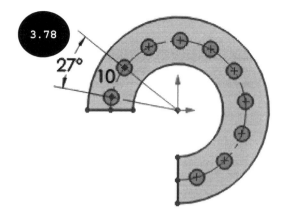

Section 7: Saving the Sketch

1. Click on the **Save** tool in the **Standard** toolbar. The **Save As** dialog box appears.

2. Browse to the *SOLIDWORKS* folder and then create a folder with the name **Chapter 3** in the *SOLIDWORKS* folder.

3. Enter **Tutorial 1** in the **File name** field of the dialog box. Next, click on the **Save** button. The sketch is saved with the name Tutorial 1.

Tutorial 2

Draw the sketch shown in Figure 3.79. The dimensions and the model shown in the figure are for your reference only.

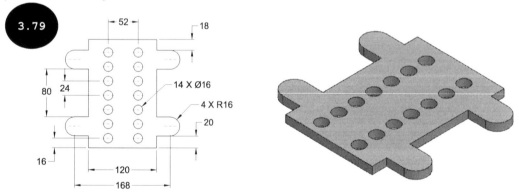

Section 1: Starting SOLIDWORKS

First, you need to start the SOLIDWORKS software.

1. Double-click on the **SOLIDWORKS** icon on your desktop to start SOLIDWORKS.

Section 2: Invoking the Sketching Environment

Now, you need invoke the Part modeling environment and then the Sketching environment by selecting the Top plane as the sketching plane.

1. Click on the **New** tool in the **Standard** toolbar. The **New SOLIDWORKS Document** dialog box appears.

   In this dialog box, the **Part** button is activated by default. As as result, you can directly click on the **OK** button to invoke the Part modeling environment.

2. Click on the **OK** button to invoke the Part modeling environment.

   Once the Part modeling environment has been invoked, you can invoke the Sketching environment and create the sketch of this tutorial.

3. Click on the **Sketch** tab in the CommandManager. The tools of the **Sketch CommandManager** are displayed.

4. Click on the **Sketch** tool in the **Sketch CommandManager**. The three default planes mutually perpendicular to each other appear in the graphics area.

5. Move the cursor over the Top plane and then click the left mouse button when the boundary of the plane gets highlighted. The Sketching environment is invoked. Also, the Top plane is orientated normal to the viewing direction.

Section 3: Specifying the Snap and Unit Settings

Once the Sketching environment has been invoked, you need to set the snap settings such that the cursor snaps to the increment of 2 mm. This is because all dimensions of the sketch are multiples of 2 mm. Also, specify the metric unit system for measurement.

1. Click on the **Options** tool in the **Standard** toolbar. The **System Options - General** dialog box appears.

2. Click on the **Document Properties** tab in this dialog box. The name of the dialog box changes to **Document Properties - Drafting Standard**.

3. Click on the **Units** option in the left panel of the dialog box. The options for specifying the unit system are displayed on the right of the dialog box.

4. Click on the **MMGS (millimeter, gram, second)** radio button in the **Unit system** area, if not selected by default.

   Now, you need to specify the snap settings such that the cursor snaps to the increment of 2 mm.

5. Click on the **Grid/Snap** option in the left panel of the dialog box. The options related to the grid and snap settings are displayed on the right panel of the dialog box.

142 Chapter 3 > Editing and Modifying Sketches

6. Enter 10 in the Major grid spacing field, 5 in the Minor-lines per major field, and 1 in the Snap points per minor field of the Grid area in the dialog box.

7. Uncheck the Display grid check box in the Grid area of the dialog box to turn off the display of grids in the drawing area, if not unchecked by default.

8. Click on the Go To System Snaps button in the dialog box. The name of the dialog box changes to System Options - Relations/Snaps.

9. Click on the Grid check box in the Sketch snaps area of the dialog box in order to turn on the snap mode. Also, make sure that the Snap only when grid appears check box below the Grid check box is unchecked.

10. Click on the OK button. The snap settings have been specified and the dialog box is closed.

Section 4: Drawing the Sketch

It is evident from the Figure 3.79 that the sketch is symmetric about its center line, therefore, you can draw the right half of the outer loop of the sketch and then mirror it about a centerline to create the left half of the outer loop by using the Mirror Entities tool.

1. Click on the Line tool in the Sketch CommandManager. The Line tool is invoked and the Insert Line PropertyManager appears on the left of the drawing area. Also, the appearance of the cursor changes to line cursor .

2. Move the cursor to the origin and click to specify the start point of the line when the cursor snaps to the origin.

3. Move the cursor horizontally toward right and click to specify the endpoint of the first line when the length of the line appears 60 mm near the cursor, see Figure 3.80.

4. Move the cursor vertically upward and click to specify the endpoint of the second line entity when the length of the line appears 20 mm, see Figure 3.81.

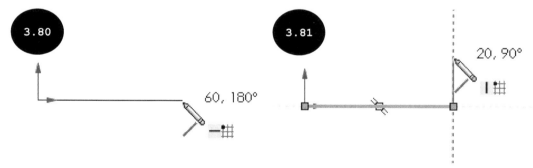

5. Move the cursor horizontally toward right and click to specify the endpoint of the line when the length of the line appears 24 mm, see Figure 3.82.

Now, you need to create an arc of radius 16 mm. To create an arc, you can use the arc tools. However in this tutorial, you will create arcs by using the **Line** tool.

6. Move the cursor away from the last specified endpoint and then move the cursor back to the endpoint. An orange color dot appears, see Figure 3.83.

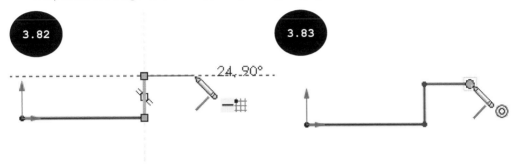

7. Move the cursor horizontally toward right for a little distance and then vertically upward. The arc mode is invoked and the preview of the arc appears in the drawing area, see Figure 3.84.

8. Click to specify the endpoint of the arc when the radius and angle values of the arc appear 16 mm and 180 degrees, respectively, near the cursor, see Figure 3.84. The arc is created and the line mode invoked again.

9. Move the cursor horizontally toward left and click when the length of line appears 24 mm, see Figure 3.85.

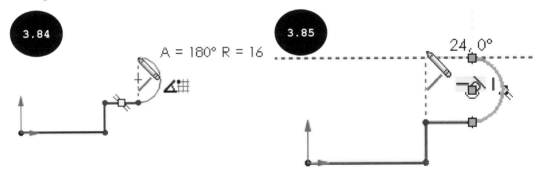

10. Move the cursor vertically upward and click when the length of the line appears 80 mm.

11. Move the cursor horizontally toward right and then click when the length of the line appears 24 mm.

    Now, you need to create an arc of radius 16 mm.

12. Move the cursor away from the last specified endpoint and then move the cursor back to the endpoint again. An orange color dot appears, see Figure 3.86.

144   Chapter 3 > Editing and Modifying Sketches

13. Move the cursor horizontally toward right for a little distance and then vertically upward. The arc mode is invoked and the preview of the arc appears in the drawing area, see Figure 3.87.

14. Click to specify the endpoint of the arc when the radius and angle values of the arc appear 16 mm and 180 degrees, respectively, near the cursor, see Figure 3.87. The arc is created and the line mode is invoked again.

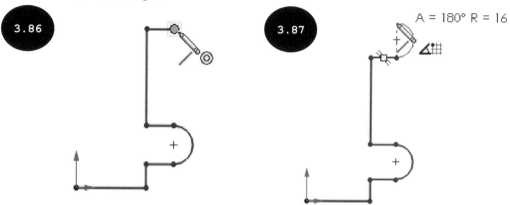

15. Move the cursor horizontally toward left and click when the length of the line appears 24 mm.

16. Move the cursor vertically upward and click when the length of the line appears 18 mm.

17. Move the cursor horizontally toward left and click when the length of the line appears 60 mm. The right half of the sketch is created, see Figure 3.88. Next, right-click in the drawing area and then click on the **Select** option in the shortcut menu displayed, to exit the **Line** tool.

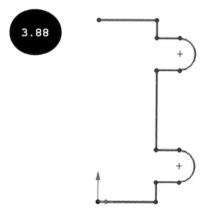

Section 5: Drawing the Centerline

After creating the right half of the sketch, you can mirror it about a centerline to create the left half of the sketch.

1. Click on the down arrow next to the **Line** tool. The **Line** flyout appears, see Figure 3.89.

2. Click on the **Centerline** tool in the **Line** flyout. The **Insert Line PropertyManager** appears with the **For construction** check box selected in it.

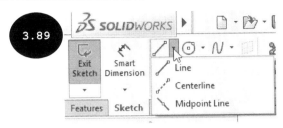

3.89

3. Move the cursor to the origin and then click to specify the start point of the centerline when the cursor snaps to the origin.

4. Move the cursor vertically upward and then click to specify the endpoint of the vertical centerline of any length, see Figure 3.90. Next, right-click, and then click on the **Select** option in the shortcut menu to exit the **Centerline** tool.

Section 6: Mirroring Sketch Entities

After creating the centerline, you need to mirror the sketch about the centerline.

1. Click on the **Mirror Entities** tool in the **Sketch CommandManager**. The  **Mirror PropertyManager** appears.

2. Select all the sketch entities except the centerline. The names of the selected entities appear in the **Entities to mirror** field of the PropertyManager.

3. Click on the **Mirror about** field in the PropertyManager to activate it.

4. Click on the centerline as the mirroring line in the drawing area. The preview of the mirror image appears.

5. Make sure that the **Copy** check box is selected in the PropertyManager.

6. Click on the green tick mark ✓ in the PropertyManager. The mirror image of the selected sketch entities is created, see Figure 3.91.

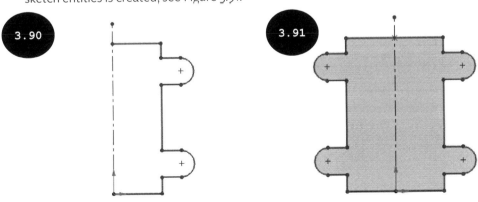

3.90

3.91

Section 7: Creating the Circle

Now, you need to create a circle of diameter 16 mm and then create a linear pattern along the X and Y axes to create the remaining circles.

1. Click on the **Circle** tool. The **Circle PropertyManager** appears.

2. Move the cursor in the drawing area, where the coordinates (X, Y, Z) appear "-26, 16, 0" respectively, in the Status Bar, see Figure 3.92.

3. Click to specify the center point of the circle when the coordinates "-26, 16, 0" appear in the Status Bar.

4. Move the cursor horizontally toward right and click when the radius of the circle appears 8 mm, see Figure 3.93. The circle of radius 8 mm is created.

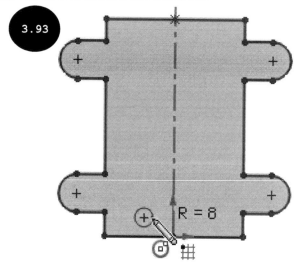

5. Right-click in the drawing area. A shortcut menu appears. Next, click on the **Select** option in the shortcut menu to exit the **Circle** tool.

Section 8: Creating the Linear Pattern

Now, you need to create the linear pattern of the circle to create remaining circles of the sketch.

1. Make sure that the previously created circle of radius 8 mm is selected in the drawing area.

2. Click on the **Linear Sketch Pattern** tool. The **Linear Pattern PropertyManager** appears. Also, the preview of the linear pattern in the X axis appears with the default parameters.

3. Enter **2** in the **Number of Instances** field of the **Direction 1** rollout in the PropertyManager.

4. Enter **52** in the **Spacing** field of the **Direction 1** rollout as the distance between two instances.

5. Enter **7** in the **Number of Instances** field of the **Direction 2** rollout as the number of instances to be created in the Y axis. Next, click anywhere in the drawing area. The preview of the linear pattern in the Y axis appears.

6. Enter **24** in the **Spacing** field of the **Direction 2** rollout as the distance between two instances in the Y axis.

7. Click on the green tick mark in the PropertyManager. The linear pattern is created, see Figure 3.94.

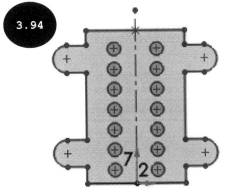

3.94

Note: Figure 3.94 shows the display of instance counts (7 and 2) in direction 1 and direction 2 of the linear pattern, respectively. This is because the **Display instance count** check box was selected in the **Direction 1** and **Direction 2** rollouts of the **Linear Pattern PropertyManager** while creating the linear pattern.

Section 9: Saving the Sketch

1. Click on the **Save** tool in the **Standard** toolbar. The **Save As** dialog box appears.

2. Browse to the *Chapter 3* folder in the *SOLIDWORKS* folder.

3. Enter **Tutorial 2** in the **File name** field of the dialog box. Next, click on the **Save** button. The sketch is saved with the name Tutorial 2.

148 Chapter 3 > Editing and Modifying Sketches

Tutorial 3

Draw the sketch shown in Figure 3.95. The dimensions and the model shown in the figure are for your reference only. You will learn about applying dimensions and creating a model in later chapters.

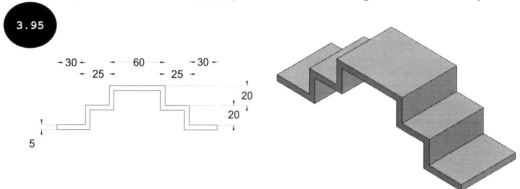

Section 1: Starting SOLIDWORKS
1. Double click on the SOLIDWORKS icon on your desktop to start SOLIDWORKS.

Section 2: Invoking the Sketching Environment
Invoke the Sketching environment by selecting the Front plane as the sketching plane.

1. Click on the New tool in the Standard toolbar. The New SOLIDWORKS Document dialog box appears.

2. Double-click on the Part button in the dialog box. The Part modeling environment is invoked.

   Now, you need to invoke the Sketching environment for creating the sketch of this tutorial.

3. Click on the Sketch tab in the CommandManager. The tools of the Sketch CommandManager are displayed.

4. Click on the Sketch tool in the Sketch CommandManager. The three default planes mutually perpendicular to each other appear in the graphics area.

5. Select the Front plane as the sketching plane. The Sketching environment is invoked and the Front plane gets orientated normal to the viewing direction.

Section 3: Specifying the Unit and Snap Settings
Once the Sketching environment has been invoked, you need to set the snap settings such that the cursor snaps to the increment of 5 mm. This is because the dimensions of all the sketch entities are multiples of 5 mm. Also, specify the metric unit system for measurement.

1. Click on the Options tool in the Standard toolbar. The System Options - General dialog box appears.

2. Click on the **Units** option in the left panel of the dialog box.

3. Make sure that the **MMGS (millimeter, gram, second)** radio button is selected in the **Unit system** area of the dialog box.

4. Click on the **Grid/Snap** option in the left panel of the dialog box.

5. Enter **50** in the **Major grid spacing** field, **10** in the **Minor-lines per major** field, and **1** in the **Snap points per minor** field in the **Grid** area of the dialog box.

6. Uncheck the **Display grid** check box in the **Grid** area of the dialog box to turn off the display of grids in the drawing area, if not unchecked by default.

7. Click on the **Go To System Snaps** button in the dialog box.

8. Select the **Grid** check box in the **Sketch snaps** area of the dialog box to turn on the snap mode. Also, make sure that the **Snap only when grid appears** check box below the **Grid** check box is unchecked.

9. Click on the **OK** button in the dialog box. The snap settings are specified and the dialog box is closed.

Section 4: Drawing the Upper Loop of the Sketch

In this tutorial, you will create the left half of the upper sketch loop and mirror it dynamically about the center line to create the right half of the upper loop.

1. Click on the down arrow next to the **Line** tool. The **Line** flyout appears, see Figure 3.96.

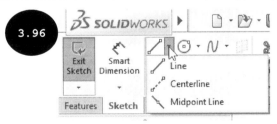

2. Click on the **Centerline** tool in the flyout. The **Insert Line PropertyManager** appears with the **For construction** check box selected.

3. Move the cursor to the origin and then click to specify the start point of the centerline when the cursor snaps to the origin.

4. Move the cursor vertically upward and then click to specify the endpoint of the vertical centerline of any length in the drawing area, see Figure 3.97. Next, press ESC key.

After creating a vertical centerline, you need to invoke the **Dynamic Mirror** tool so that on creating entities on one side of the centerline, the respective mirror images are created dynamically on the other side.

5. Click on **Tools > Sketch Tools > Dynamic Mirror** in the SOLIDWORKS menus. The **Mirror PropertyManager** appears.

6. Move the cursor over the centerline in the drawing area and then click on it. The symbol of dynamic mirror represented by two small horizontal lines appears on both sides of the centerline, see Figure 3.97.

7. Click on the **Line** tool. The **Insert Line PropertyManager** appears.

8. Move the cursor in the drawing area, where the coordinates appear "-85, 0, 0" respectively, in the Status Bar and then click the left mouse button at that location to specify the start point of the line.

9. Move the cursor horizontally toward right and click to specify the endpoint of the first line when the length of the line appears 30 mm near the cursor. A horizontal line of length 30 mm is created. Also, its mirror image is created on the other side of the centerline, automatically, see Figure 3.98.

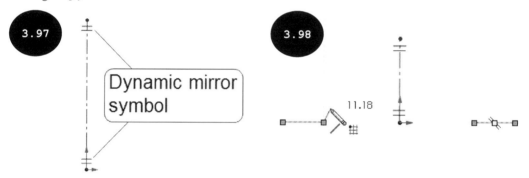

10. Move the cursor vertically upward and then click to create a line of length 20 mm. The line of length 20 mm is created on the other side of the centerline as well, see Figure 3.99. Note that as you are creating entities on the left of the centerline, the respective mirror images are being created on the right of the centerline. This is because the **Dynamic Mirror** tool is invoked.

11. Move the cursor horizontally toward right and then click to create a line of length 25 mm.

12. Move the cursor vertically upward and then click to create a line of length 20 mm.

13. Move the cursor horizontally toward right and click when the cursor snaps to the centerline. The upper loop of the sketch is created, see Figure 3.100.

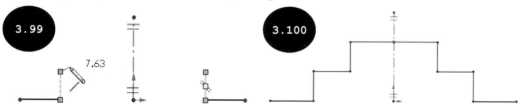

14. Right-click in the drawing area and then click on the **Select** option in the shortcut menu to exit the **Line** tool.

    Now, you need to exit the **Dynamic Mirror** tool.

15. Click on **Tools > Sketch Tools > Dynamic Mirror** in the SOLIDWORKS menus to exit the **Dynamic Mirror** tool.

Section 5: Offsetting the Sketch Entities

After creating the upper loop of the sketch, you need to create the lower loop by offsetting entities of the upper loop to a distance of 5 mm by using the **Offset Entities** tool.

1. Click on the **Offset Entities** tool. The **Offset Entities PropertyManager** appears.

2. Make sure that the **Select chain** check box is selected in the PropertyManager.

3. Select an entity of the upper loop. All contiguous entities of the selected entity get selected and the preview of offset entities appear in the drawing area, see Figure 3.101.

4. Make sure that the direction of offset entities is on the lower side of the sketch, see Figure 3.101. If not so, select the **Reverse** check box to reverse the direction of offset entities.

5. Enter **5** in the **Offset Distance** field of the PropertyManager.

6. Select the **Cap ends** check box. The **Arcs** and **Lines** radio buttons get enabled.

7. Click on the **Lines** radio button in order to cap the open ends of offset entities with lines.

8. Make sure that the **Base geometry** and **Offset geometry** check boxes are unchecked.

9. Click on the green tick mark button. The sketch is created, see Figure 3.102.

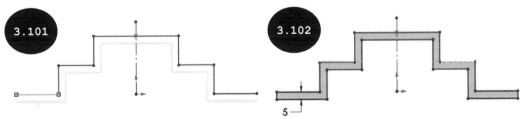

Section 6: Saving the Sketch

1. Click on the **Save** tool in the **Standard** toolbar. The **Save As** dialog box appears.

2. Browse to the *Chapter 3* folder in the *SOLIDWORKS* folder.

3. Enter **Tutorial 3** in the **File name** field of the dialog box. Next, click on the **Save** button. The model is saved with the name Tutorial 3.

Hands-on Test Drive 1

Draw the sketch shown in Figure 3.103. The dimensions and the model are for your reference only.

3.103

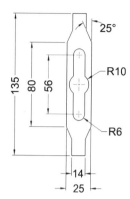

Summary

So far in this chapter, you have learned about editing and modifying sketch entities by using various editing tools such as **Trim Entities, Extend Entities, Offset Entities, Mirror Entities,** and **Linear Sketch Pattern**. The pattern tools discussed in this chapter allow you to create the linear and circular patterns. Also, the mirror tools allow you to create the mirror image of the selected entities about a mirroring line. You can also dynamically mirror sketch entities while drawing them using the **Dynamic Mirror** tool. Moreover, you have learned how to move sketch entities from one position to the other, copy sketch entities, rotate sketch entities, scale, and stretch sketch entities by using the respective tools.

Questions

- The _____ tool is used to offset sketch entities at a specified offset distance.

- You can rotate sketch entities at an angle by using the _____ tool.

- You can stretch the sketch entities of a sketch by using the _____ tool.

- To rotate sketch entities anti-clockwise, you need to define the _____ angle value.

- While offsetting sketch entities, if you select the _____ check box, all the contiguous entities of the selected entity get selected.

- The number of pattern instances specified in the **Number of Instances** field include the parent or original instance selected to pattern (True/False).

- You cannot recall the skipped pattern instances (True/False).

- In addition to trimming sketch entities, you can extend sketch entities by using the **Trim Entities** tool (True/False).

CHAPTER 4

Applying Geometric Relations and Dimensions

In this chapter, you will learn the following:

- Working with Geometric Relations
- Applying Geometric Relations
- Controlling the Display of Geometric Relations
- Applying Dimensions
- Modifying/Editing Dimensions
- Modifying Dimension Properties
- Working with Different States of a Sketch

Once you are done with creating a sketch by using sketching tools, you need to make your sketch fully defined by applying proper geometric relations and dimensions. A fully defined sketch is a sketch, whose all degrees of freedoms are fixed and its shape and positions cannot be changed by simply dragging its entities. You will learn more about fully defined sketches later in this chapter. Before that you need to understand geometric relations and dimensions.

Working with Geometric Relations

Geometric relations are used to restrict some degrees of freedom of a sketch. You can apply geometric relations on a sketch entity, between sketch entities, and between sketch entities and planes, axes, edges, or vertices. Some geometric relations such as horizontal, vertical, and coincident are applied automatically while drawing sketch entities. For example, after specify the start point a line entity, if you move the cursor horizontally toward left or right, a symbol of horizontal relation appears near the cursor, see Figure 4.1. It indicates that if you specify the endpoint of the line, the horizontal relation will be applied to the line entity. Likewise, on moving the cursor vertically upward or downward after specifying the start point of a line, a symbol of vertical relation appears, see Figure 4.1 and gets applied immediately after specifying the end point of the line. Various geometric relations are as follows:

154 Chapter 4 > Applying Geometric Relations and Dimensions

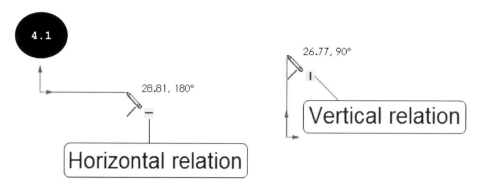

Horizontal Relation
Horizontal relation is used to change the orientation of an entity to horizontal and then to force the entity to remain horizontal. This relation can be applied to a line, centerline, or between two points or vertices.

Vertical Relation
Vertical relation is used to change the orientation of an entity to vertical and then to force the entity to remain vertical. This relation can be applied to a line, centerline, or between two points or vertices.

Coincident Relation
Coincident relation is used to coincide a sketch point with a line/arc/elliptical entity and then to force them to remain coincident with each other. You can apply this relation between a point and a line/arc/ellipse. You can also apply the coincident relation between a sketch point and the origin/a vertex.

Collinear Relation
Collinear relation is used to make two or more than two lines collinear with each other and then to force them to remain collinear. You can also make line entities collinear to a linear edge or a reference plane.

Perpendicular Relation
Perpendicular relation is used to make two line entities perpendicular to each other and then to force them to remain perpendicular. You can also make a line perpendicular to a linear edge or a plane.

Parallel Relation
Parallel relation is used to make two or more than two line entities parallel to each other and then to force them to remain parallel. You can also make line entities parallel to a linear edge or a plane.

Tangent Relation
Tangent relation is used to make two sketch entities such as a circle and a line tangent to each other. You can also make two circles, two arcs, two ellipses, two splines, and a combination of these entities tangent to each other. In addition, you can make sketch entities tangent to a linear or a circular edge of a model.

Concentric Relation

Concentric relation is used to make two or more than two arcs or circles; a point and an arc; and a point and a circle concentric to each other. In concentric relation, the selected entities share the same center point. You can also make sketch entities such as arcs/circles concentric to a vertex or cylindrical edge of a model.

Coradial Relation

Coradial relation is used to make two or more than two arcs or circles coradial to each other. In coradial relation, the selected entities share the same center point as well as radius. You can also make sketch entities such as arcs/circles coradial to a cylindrical edge of a model.

Equal Relation

Equal relation is used to make two or more than two arcs/circles/lines equal to each other. In equal relation, the length of line entities and radii of arc entities become equal.

Equal Curve Length Relation

Equal Curve Length relation is used to make curved segments equal to each other. This relation can be applied between a circle and an arc; two circles; two arcs; a line and a circle; a circle and a spline; and a spline and a line.

Midpoint Relation

Midpoint relation is used to make a point coincident at the middle of a line entity. You can apply the midpoint relation between a sketch point and a line; a vertex and a line; and a sketch point and a linear edge.

Symmetric Relation

Symmetric relation is used to make two points, two lines, two arcs, two circles, and two ellipses symmetric/equidistant about a centerline.

Merge Relation

Merge relation is used to merge two points together to share a single point. You can merge endpoints of two lines.

Pierce Relation

Pierce relation is used to coincide a sketch point to the axis/edge/curve of the other sketch which has been created on a different sketching plane.

Fix Relation

Fix relation is used to fix the current position and the size of a sketch entity. However, in case of fixed line, arc, circle, or ellipse entity, their endpoints are free to move without disturbing the position.

Applying Geometric Relations

In SOLIDWORKS, you can apply geometric relations either by using the **Add Relation** tool or by using the Pop-up toolbar. Both the methods of applying geometric relations are as follows:

Applying Geometric Relation by using the Add Relation Tool

To apply the geometric relation by using the **Add Relation** tool, click on the arrow in the lower side of the **Display/Delete Relations** tool in the **Sketch CommandManager**. A flyout appears, see Figure 4.2. In this flyout, click on the **Add Relation** tool. The **Add Relations PropertyManager** appears, see Figure 4.3. Notice that in the **Add Relations PropertyManager**, only the **Selected Entities** rollout is available. This rollout is used to display the list of entities selected for applying relation.

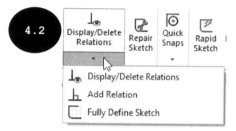

As soon as you select entities from the drawing area for applying relation, the **Add Relations PropertyManager** gets modified and the names of selected entities appear in the **Selected Entities** rollout. Figure 4.4 shows the modified PropertyManager after selecting two circles. Different rollouts in the modified PropertyManager are as follows:

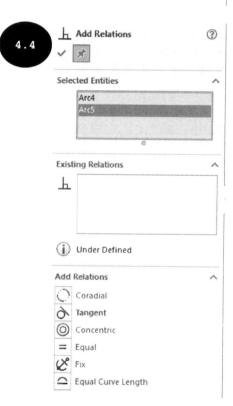

Selected Entities

The **Selected Entities** rollout displays the list of entities selected for applying relations. You can select entities from the drawing area. You can also remove an entity from the list of entities appeared in the **Selected Entities** field of the rollout. To remove an entity, select it from the field and then right-click. A shortcut menu appears. In this shortcut menu, click on the **Delete** option. The selected entity is removed from the list. If you click on the **Clear Selections** option in the shortcut menu, all the entities listed in the field get removed from the selection.

Existing Relations

The **Existing Relations** rollout is used to display the list of already applied relations between the selected entities.

> **Tip:** You can delete the relations that are already applied between the selected entities. To delete existing relations, select them from the **Existing Relations** field of the rollout and then right-click. A shortcut menu appears. In this shortcut menu, click on the **Delete** option. The selected relations get deleted and removed from the list. If you click on the **Delete All** option in the shortcut menu, all the existing applied relations between the selected entities get deleted.

Add Relations

The **Add Relations** rollout displays the list of all possible relations that can be applied between the selected entities. Also, the most suitable relation is highlighted by default, see Figure 4.4.

Procedure for Applying Relations by using the Add Relation Tool

1. Click on the arrow in the lower side of the **Display/Delete Relations** tool in the **Sketch CommandManager**. A flyout appears, refer to Figure 4.2.
2. Click on the **Add Relation** tool in the flyout. The **Add Relations PropertyManager** appears.
3. Select sketch entities by clicking the left mouse button in the drawing area to apply relation.
4. Click on the relation to be applied between the selected entities in the **Add Relations** rollout. The selected relation is applied.
5. Click on the green tick mark ✓ button in the PropertyManager.

Applying Geometric Relation by using the Pop-up Toolbar

In addition to applying geometric relations by using the **Add Relations PropertyManager**, you can apply relations by using the Pop-up toolbar. It is a time saving method. To apply geometric relations by using the Pop-up toolbar, select entities directly from the drawing area by pressing the CTRL key without invoking any tool. Next, release the CTRL key and do not move the cursor. A Pop-up toolbar appears near the tip of the cursor, see Figure 4.5. Click on the relation to be applied in the Pop-up toolbar. The selected relation is applied between the entities.

> **Note:** The availability of relations in the Pop-up toolbar depends upon the type of entities selected for applying relation. Figure 4.5 shows a Pop-up toolbar appeared on selecting two circle entities.

Procedure for Applying Relations by using the Pop-up Toolbar

1. Select sketch entities from the drawing area by pressing the CTRL key.
2. Release the CTRL key and do not move the cursor. A Pop-up toolbar appears.
3. Click on the required relation in the Pop-up toolbar. The selected relation is applied.

158 Chapter 4 > Applying Geometric Relations and Dimensions

Controlling the Display of Geometric Relations

You can control the display or visibility of the applied geometric relations by using the **View Sketch Relations** tool in the **View (Heads-Up)** toolbar. To turn on or off the display of the applied geometric relations, click on the **Hide/Show Items** arrow in the **View (Heads-Up)** toolbar, see Figure 4.6. A flyout appears, see Figure 4.6. In this flyout, click on the **View Sketch Relations** tool, see Figure 4.6. The display of all the applied geometric relations is turned on or off. Note that this is a toggle tool. You can also delete the already applied relation by selecting the relation to be deleted from the drawing area and then pressing the DELETE key.

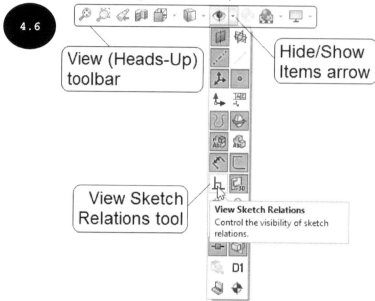

Applying Dimensions

Once a sketch has been drawn and required geometric relations have been applied, you need to apply dimensions by using dimension tools. As SOLIDWORKS is a parametric software, the parameters of sketch entities such as length and angle are controlled or driven by dimension values. On modifying a dimension value, the respective sketch entity also gets modified accordingly. The tools used to apply dimensions are grouped together in the **Dimensions** flyout. To invoke this flyout, click on the down arrow in the bottom of the **Smart Dimensions** tool in the **Sketch CommandManager**, see Figure 4.7. The dimension tools are as follows:

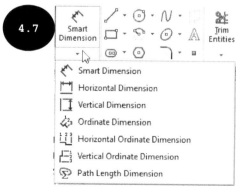

Working with Smart Dimension tool

The **Smart Dimension** tool is used to apply dimension, depending upon the type of entity selected. For example, if you select a circle, the diameter dimension is applied and if you select a line entity, the linear dimension is applied. To apply dimensions by using the **Smart Dimension** tool, click on the **Smart Dimension** tool in the **Sketch CommandManager**. The cursor changes to dimension cursor and you are prompted to select the entity to be dimensioned. Select an entity in the drawing area. A dimension with the current dimension value is attached to the cursor depending upon the type of entity selected, see Figure 4.8. In Figure 4.8, diameter dimension is attached to the cursor on selecting a circle, radius dimension is attached to the cursor on selecting an arc, and linear dimension is attached to the cursor on selecting a line, respectively. Notice that after selecting an entity if you move the cursor, the attached dimension also moves accordingly in the drawing area. Move the cursor to a location where you want to place the dimension and then click the left mouse button at that location. The **Modify** dialog box appears, see Figure 4.9. By default, the **Modify** dialog box displays the current dimension value of the sketch entity. Enter the required dimension value and then click on its green tick mark button. The dimension is applied to the selected entity. You can select an entity to be dimensioned before or after invoking the **Smart Dimension** tool. Figure 4.9 shows various components of the **Modify** dialog box. These components are as follows:

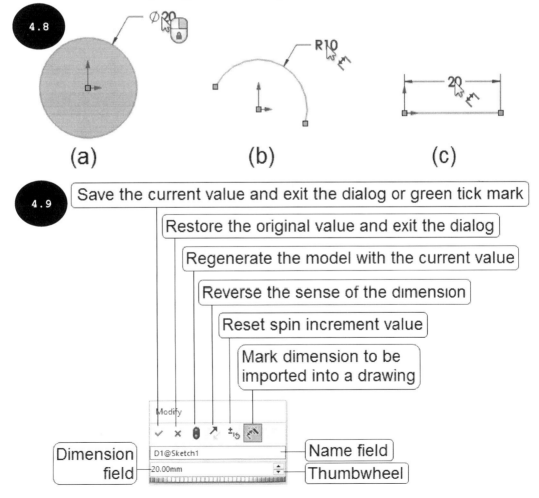

Name Field

The **Name** field of the **Modify** dialog box displays the name of the dimension. By default, the names for dimensions are assigned as D1, D2, D3 ..., and Dn. You can specify a required name other than the default one. To specify a name, click on the **Name** field and then enter the required name in this field.

Dimension field

The **Dimension** field is used to specify the dimension value for the sketch entity. By default, this field displays the current dimension value of the sketch entity. You can enter a new dimension value in this field.

Spinner

You can also set or control the dimension value by using the Spinner, refer to Figure 4.9. On clicking the up arrow of the Spinner, the dimension value increases by adding the predefined spin increment value. Similarly, on clicking the down arrow of the Spinner, the dimension value decreases or subtracts. Note the increment or decrement of the dimension value is based on the default, the predefined spin increment value set. You can control the predefined spin increment value by using the **Reset spin increment value** button of the dialog box, which is discussed next.

Reset spin increment value

The **Reset spin increment value** button is used to reset the spin increment value for dimension. To set it, click on the **Reset spin increment value** button, refer to Figure 4.9. The **Increment** window appears with the default spin increment value. Enter the required spin increment value in the field of this window and then press the **ENTER** key. The newly entered value is set as the current spin increment value for the dimension and the window is closed.

Note: On selecting the **Make Default** check box in the **Increment** window, the specified spin increment value is set to default for other dimensions as well.

You can also set the spin increment value by using the **System Options - Spin Box Increments** dialog box. To invoke the **System Options - Spin Box Increments** dialog box, click on the **Options** tool of the **Standard** toolbar. The **System Options - General** dialog box appears. Select the **Spin Box Increments** option from the left panel of the dialog box. The name of the dialog box changes to **System Options - Spin Box Increments** and the options for setting the spin increment value appear on the right panel of the dialog box. Next, set the required spin increment value for linear dimensions by using the **English units** field and the **Metric units** field of the **Length increments** area of the dialog box.

You can specify the spin increment value for angle and time measurements by using the **Angle increments** field and the **Time increments** field of the dialog box, respectively.

Thumbwheel

You can also set or control the dimension value by sliding the thumbwheel.

Regenerate the model with the current value
The **Regenerate the model with the current value** button is used to regenerate or refresh drawing with the current dimension value entered in the **Dimension** field. You can regenerate or refresh your drawing if the change in the dimension value is not reflected in the drawing area.

Reverse the sense of the dimension
The **Reverse the sense of the dimension** button is used to flip or reverse dimension value from the positive dimension value to negative dimension value and vice versa. Note that this button is enabled only when the selected dimension is a linear dimension.

Save the current value and exit the dialog
The **Save the current value and exit the dialog** button or green tick mark button of the dialog box is used to accept change in the dimension value entered in the **Dimension** field and exit the dialog box.

Restore the original value and exit the dialog
The **Restore the original value and exit the dialog** button or red cross mark button is used to discard the change made in the dimension value. On clicking this button, the original dimension value is restored and the **Modify** dialog box is closed.

As discussed earlier, the **Smart Dimension** tool is used to apply dimensions depending upon the type of sketch entity or entities selected. You can apply horizontal, vertical, aligned, angular, diameter, radius, and linear diameter dimensions by using this tool. The methods of applying dimensions using the **Smart Dimension** tool are as follows:

Applying Horizontal Dimension by using the Smart Dimension tool
To apply horizontal dimension by using the **Smart Dimension** tool, click on the **Smart Dimension** tool and then select the required sketch entity or entities. You can select a horizontal sketch entity, an aligned sketch entity, two points, or two vertical sketch entities for applying the horizontal dimension, see Figure 4.10. As soon as you select a horizontal sketch entity, an aligned sketch entity, two points, or two vertical sketch entities, the current dimension value of the selected entity or entities is attached to the cursor. Next, move the cursor vertically up or down and then click the left mouse button in the drawing area to specify the placement point for the horizontal dimension. The **Modify** dialog box appears. Next, enter the required dimension value in the **Dimension** field of the **Modify** dialog box and then click on the green tick mark button. The horizontal dimension is applied, see Figure 4.10.

> **Tip:** After selecting an aligned entity or two sketch points, if you move the cursor in a direction other than vertically up or down, then notice that the vertical or aligned dimension is attached to the cursor.

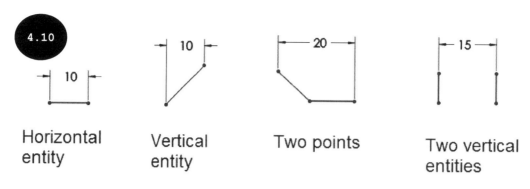

Note: You can select entities to be dimensioned before or after invoking the **Smart Dimension** tool.

Applying Vertical Dimension by using the Smart Dimension tool

Similar to applying horizontal dimension by using the **Smart Dimension** tool, you can apply vertical dimension to a vertical sketch entity, aligned sketch entity, between two points, and between two horizontal sketch entities, see Figure 4.11. Note that to apply a vertical dimension by using the **Smart Dimension** tool, you need to move the cursor horizontally toward right or left after selecting a vertical sketch entity, an aligned sketch entity, two points, or two horizontal entities.

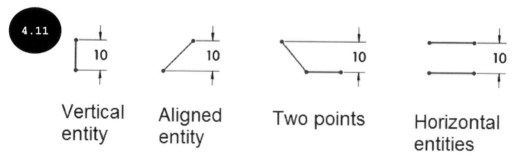

Applying Aligned Dimension by using the Smart Dimension tool

Similar to applying horizontal and vertical dimensions by using the **Smart Dimension** tool, you can apply aligned dimension to an aligned sketch entity or between two points, see Figure 4.12. The aligned dimension is generally used to measure the aligned length of an inclined line. Note that after selecting an entity or entities for applying aligned dimension, you need to move the cursor perpendicular to the selected entity for specifying the placement point.

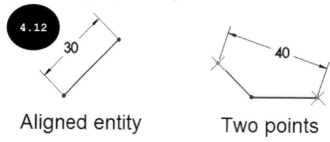

Applying Angular Dimension by using the Smart Dimension tool

You can apply angular dimension between two non-parallel line entities or three points by using the Smart Dimension tool. To apply angular dimension between two non-parallel line entities, invoke the Smart Dimension tool and then select two non-parallel line entities in the drawing area. The angular dimension between the selected entities is attached to the cursor, see Figure 4.13. Next, move the cursor to a location where you want to place the dimension and then click to specify the placement point. The **Modify** dialog box appears. Enter the required angular value in this dialog box and then press ENTER or click on the green tick mark button. The angular dimension is applied between the two selected line entities. Note that the angular dimension applied between the selected entities depends upon the location of the placement point specified, see Figure 4.13.

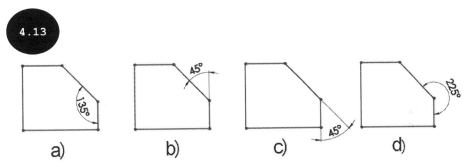

To apply angular dimension between three points, invoke the Smart Dimension tool and then select three points in the drawing area, see Figure 4.13. The angular dimension between the selected points is attached to the cursor. Next, move the cursor to a location where you want to place the attached angular dimension and then click to specify the placement point. The **Modify** dialog box appears. Enter the required angular value in this dialog box and then press ENTER. The angular dimension is applied between the three selected points, see Figure 4.14.

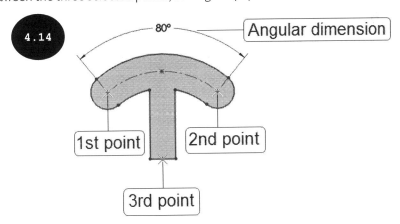

Applying Diameter Dimension by using the Smart Dimension tool

The diameter dimension can be applied to a circle by using the **Smart Dimension** tool. To apply the diameter dimension, click on the **Smart Dimension** tool and then select a circle. The diameter dimension is attached to the cursor. Next, move the cursor to a required location and click to specify the placement point. The **Modify** dialog box appears. Enter the diameter value in this dialog box and then press ENTER. The diameter dimension is applied, see Figure 4.15.

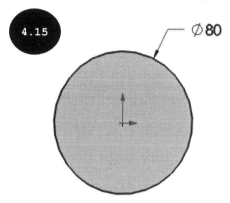

Note: You can also apply radius dimension to a circle. To do so, first apply the diameter dimension to a circle, as discussed. Next, right-click on the applied diameter dimension. A shortcut menu appears. In this shortcut menu, click on **Display Options > Display As Radius**. The selected diameter dimension is converted into the radius dimension. Note that if the **Smart Dimension** tool is active and you right-click on a diameter dimension, then you can directly select the **Display As Radius** option from the shortcut menu displayed.

Applying Radius Dimension by using the Smart Dimension tool

The radius dimension can be applied to an arc by using the **Smart Dimension** tool. To apply radius dimension, click on the **Smart Dimension** tool and then select an arc. The radius dimension is attached to the cursor. Move the cursor to the required location and click to specify the placement point. The **Modify** dialog box appears. Enter the radius value in this dialog box and then press ENTER. The radius dimension is applied, see Figure 4.16.

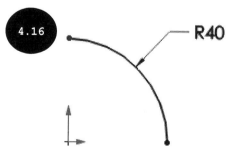

Note: You can also apply diameter dimension to an arc. To do so, first apply the radius dimension to an arc, as discussed. Next, right-click on the applied radius dimension. A shortcut menu appears. In this shortcut menu, click on **Display Options > Display As Diameter**. The selected radius dimension is converted into the diameter dimension. Note that if the **Smart Dimension** tool is active and you right-click on a radius dimension, then you can directly select the **Display As Diameter** option from the shortcut menu displayed.

Applying Linear Diameter Dimension by using the Smart Dimension tool

The Linear diameter dimension can be applied to a sketch of a revolved feature, see Figure 4.17. To apply the linear diameter dimension, click on the **Smart Dimension** tool and then select a linear sketch entity of the sketch. The linear dimension is attached to the cursor. Next, select the centerline or revolving axis of the sketch. The linear dimension between the sketch line and the centerline is attached to the cursor. Move the cursor to the other side of the centerline or the revolving axis. The linear diameter dimension is attached to the cursor. Next, click to specify the placement point. The **Modify** dialog box appears. Enter the linear diameter value in the dialog box and then press ENTER. The linear diameter dimension is applied.

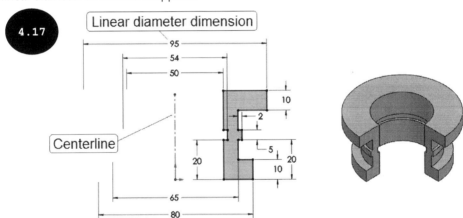

Working with Horizontal Dimension and Vertical Dimension tools

In additional to applying horizontal and vertical dimensions by using the **Smart Dimension** tool, you can also apply these dimensions by using the **Horizontal Dimension** and **Vertical Dimension** tools In the **Dimension** flyout, see Figure 4.18.

To apply horizontal dimension by using the **Horizontal Dimension** tool, click on the down arrow below the **Smart Dimension** tool. The **Dimension** flyout appears, see Figure 4.18. Next, click on the **Horizontal Dimension** tool in the flyout. Next, move the cursor over the sketch entity to be dimensioned and when the entity is highlighted, click on it. The horizontal dimension is attached to the cursor. Move the cursor to a location where you want to place the dimension and then click to specify the placement point. The

166 Chapter 4 > Applying Geometric Relations and Dimensions

Modify dialog box appears. Enter the required dimension value in the Modify dialog box and then press ENTER. The horizontal dimension is applied.

The way you applied horizontal dimension by using the Horizontal Dimension tool, you can apply vertical dimension by using the Vertical Dimension tool of the Dimension flyout.

Working with Ordinate Dimension tool

The Ordinate Dimension tool is used to apply ordinate dimensions to a sketch. Ordinate dimensions are measured from a base entity. The base entity is defined as the starting point from where all other sketch entities are measured, see Figure 4.19. Generally, the ordinate dimensions are used for the components created by using CNC machines. Figure 4.20 shows a component and Figure 4.21 shows a sketch used for creating this model. Notice that in Figure 4.21, the horizontal dimensions applied to the sketch have symmetric tolerance value of 0.1. It means the maximum accepted length of entities measuring 100 mm, 30 mm, and 40 mm are 100.1 mm, 30.1 mm, and 40.1 mm, respectively. If you sum the maximum accepted dimension of the entities (2, 4, and 6) measuring 30 mm, 40 mm, and 30 mm, you will get the maximum accepted horizontal length of the component is 100.3 mm (30.1+40.1+30.1). However, the actual maximum accepted horizontal length of the component is 100.1 mm, see Figure 4.21. It is a difference of 0.2 mm, therefore you need to apply ordinate dimensions to overcome the difference in the dimension values. Figure 4.19 shows a sketch with ordinate dimensions applied and shows 100.1 mm as the maximum accepted horizontal length of the component.

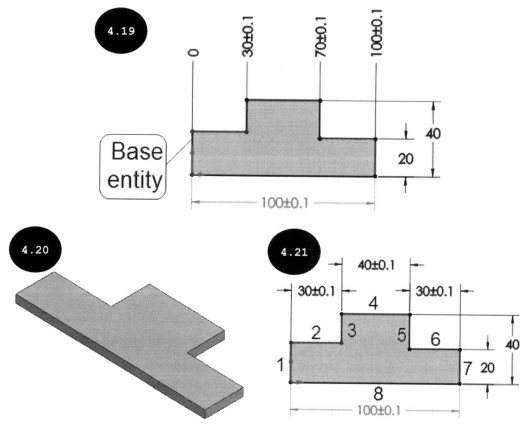

You can apply horizontal and vertical ordinate dimensions by using the **Ordinate Dimension** tool. The methods of applying horizontal and vertical ordinate dimensions are as follows:

Applying Horizontal Ordinate Dimensions

To apply horizontal ordinate dimension, click on the down arrow below the **Smart Dimension** tool. The **Dimension** flyout appears, refer to Figure 4.18. In the **Dimension** flyout, click on the **Ordinate Dimension** tool. The cursor changes to the ordinate dimension cursor and you are prompted to select an entity as the base entity to measure all dimensions. Click on a vertical entity (1) as the base entity, see Figure 4.22. The 0 (zero) dimension value is attached to the cursor. Move the cursor to a required location and then click to specify the placement point. Next, select the second vertical entity (2), see Figure 4.22. The horizontal distance measured from the 0 (zero) dimension value is applied and appears in the drawing area, see Figure 4.22. Similarly, select other vertical entities of the sketch to be measured from the 0 (zero) dimension value, see figure 4.22.

Applying Vertical Ordinate Dimensions

Similar to applying horizontal ordinate dimension, you can apply vertical ordinate dimension by using the **Ordinate Dimension** tool. To apply vertical ordinate dimension, invoke the **Ordinate Dimension** tool and then select a horizontal entity as the base entity. The 0 (zero) dimension value is attached to the cursor. Move the cursor to a required location and then click to specify the placement point for the attached 0 (zero) dimension value, see Figure 4.23. Next, select the second horizontal entity. The vertical distance measured from the 0 (zero) dimension value to the newly selected entity is applied and appears in the drawing area. Similarly, select other entities of the sketch to be measured from the 0 (zero) dimension value, see Figure 4.23.

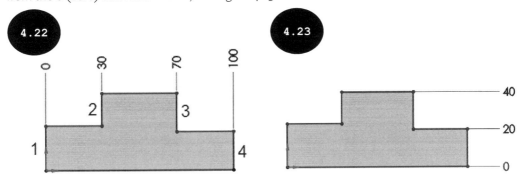

Tip: Similar to applying horizontal and vertical ordinate dimensions by using the **Ordinate Dimension** tool, you can apply horizontal and vertical ordinate dimensions by using the **Horizontal Ordinate Dimension** and **Vertical Ordinate Dimension** tools, respectively.

Modifying/Editing Dimensions

After applying dimensions, you may need to modify them due to changes in the design, revisions in the design, and so on. To modify the already applied dimension, click on the dimension to be modified. The **Dimension Input Value** box appears with the display of current dimension value in the drawing area, see Figure 4.24. Enter the new dimension value in this box and then press ENTER. The selected dimension value has been modified. Note that if you double click on a dimension, then the **Modify** dialog box appears. In this dialog box, you can specify the new dimension value and then press ENTER or click on the green tick mark button in the **Modify** dialog box to apply the modified dimension value.

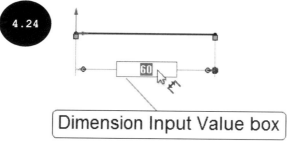

Note: When you click on a dimension, the **Dimension Input Value** box appears only if the **Instant2D** tool is activated in the **Sketch CommandManager**.

Modifying Dimension Properties

In SOLIDWORKS, when you apply a dimension, it is applied with default properties. You can modify default dimension properties such as dimension style, tolerance, and precision by using the **Dimension PropertyManager**. To invoke the **Dimension PropertyManager**, select a dimension whose properties is to be modified. The **Dimension PropertyManager** appears on the left of the drawing area, see Figure 4.25. Note that if the **Dimension Input Value** box appears on selecting a dimension, then you need to click on the **Instant2D** tool in the **Sketch CommandManager** to deactivate it. The options in the **Dimension PropertyManager** are as follows:

Value Tab

By default, the **Value** tab is activated in the **Dimension PropertyManager**. The options in the tab are used to modify the properties related to the dimension value. The options are as follows:

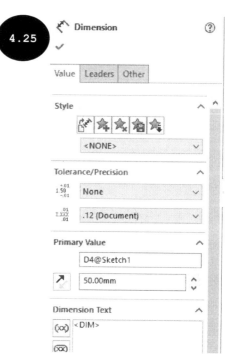

Style

The **Style** rollout of the **Value** tab is used to restore default attributes such as dimension height, fonts, and arrow type. You can also add a new style, update existing style, delete added style, save style, and load existing style in the current document by using the options of this rollout. The options of this rollout are as follows:

Apply the default attributes to selected dimensions
The **Apply the default attributes to selected dimensions** button of the **Style** rollout is used to apply the default dimension attributes such as dimension height, fonts, arrow type to the selected

dimension. If you have modified dimension attributes, then on clicking this button, the dimension attributes will be restored to the default.

Add or Update a Style

The **Add or Update a Style** button is used to add new dimension style or update the existing dimension style. To add new dimension style, click on the **Add or Update a Style** button. The **Add or Update a Style** dialog box appears, see Figure 4.26. Enter the name of the style to be added in the **Enter a new name or choose an existing name** field of this dialog box and then click the **OK** button. The new style is added and set as the current style for the document. Also, its name appears in the **Set a current Style** drop-down list of the **Style** rollout. Now, you can specify different attributes for this newly added style such as dimension height, fonts, arrow type. You will learn more about specifying dimension attributes later in this chapter.

To update the existing dimension style attributes, click on the **Add or Update a Style** button of the **Style** rollout to display the **Add or Update a Style** dialog box. In this dialog box, click on the down arrow on the right of the **Enter a new name or choose an existing name** field. A drop-down list appears. Select the dimension style to be updated. The **Update all annotations linked to this style** and **Break all links to this style** radio buttons are enabled in this dialog box. By default, the **Update all annotations linked to this style** radio button is selected. As a result, the modifications made in the attributes of the selected style of a selected dimension are also reflected in other dimensions of the same style as soon as you click on the **OK** button.

Note: If the modifications are not reflected in other dimensions of the same style after choosing the **OK** button, then click on the dimensions in the drawing area to update them.

On selecting the **Break all links to this style** radio button, the link between the selected dimension and the other dimensions assigned to the style will be broken. In other words, the other dimensions associated with the selected dimension style will no longer be associated with the same dimension style and modifications are only made in the selected dimension.

Delete a Style

The **Delete a Style** button of the **Style** rollout is used to delete an existing style, which is no longer required. To delete an existing style, select the style from the **Set a current Style** drop-down list of the **Style** rollout and then click on the **Delete a Style** button. The selected style is deleted from the current document.

Save a Style

The **Save a Style** button is used to save a style as an external file so that the same style can be loaded in other documents as well. To save a style, select the style from the **Set a current Style** drop-down list and then click on the **Save a Style** button. The **Save As** window appears. Browse the location where the style is to be saved and then click on the **Save** button. The selected style is saved in the specified location in the *.sldstl* file extension.

Load Style

The **Load Style** button is used to load the existing saved style in the current document. To load a style, click on the **Load Style** button. The **Open** window appears. Browse the location where the style has been saved and then select the style. Next, click on the **Open** button of the dialog box. The selected style is loaded in the current document and set as the current style.

Set a current Style

The **Set a current Style** drop-down list displays the list of all the added styles in the current document. By default, the **None** option is selected in this drop-down list. As a result, the default dimension style is used. You can select any dimension style from this drop-down list as the current dimension style for the document.

Tolerance/Precision

The options in the **Tolerance/Precision** rollout are used to specify the tolerance and precision values for the selected dimension style and dimensions. The options in this rollout are as follows:

Tolerance Type

The **Tolerance Type** drop-down list is used to select the type of tolerance for the selected dimension style and dimensions. By default, the **None** option is selected in this drop-down list. As a result, no tolerance has been applied. Depending upon the type of tolerance selected in this drop-down list, the corresponding fields are enabled below this drop-down list in the **Tolerance/Precision** rollout in order to specify tolerance values.

Unit Precision

The **Unit Precision** drop-down list is used to select the unit of precision or number of digits after the decimal point in a dimension value.

Primary Value

The **Primary Value** rollout is used to control the information of the primary dimension value. The primary dimension value is the original dimension value of entities. It drives entities when a modification is made in the primary dimension value. The options in this rollout are as follows:

Name

The **Name** field of the **Primary Value** rollout is used to display the name of the dimension selected. By default, the default names are assigned to the dimensions. You can enter a new name for the selected dimension in this field. Note that the name entered in this field is automatically followed by *@Sketch1*. It can be Sketch1, Sketch2, Sketch3, ... or Sketch 'n' depending upon the number of sketch you are working on in the current document.

Dimension value

The **Dimension Value** field of the **Primary Value** rollout is used to control the current dimension value of the selected dimension. You can enter a new dimension value in this field for the selected dimension. The value entered in this field drives the sketch entity of the dimension.

Dimension Text

The **Dimension Text** rollout is used to add text and geometric symbols for the selected dimension style and dimensions. The options in this rollout are as follows:

Add Parentheses

The **Add Parentheses** button of the **Dimension Text** rollout is used to display dimension value or text as a driven or reference dimension with parentheses, see Figure 4.27 (a).

Inspection Dimension

The **Inspection Dimension** button is used to display dimension value or text with inspection, see Figure 4.27 (b).

Center Dimension

The **Center Dimension** button is used to display dimension value or text at the center of the extension lines of the dimension. Note that when you drag dimension text, the text snaps to the center of the extension line, see Figure 4.27 (c).

Offset Text

The **Offset Text** button is used to display dimension value or text at an offset distance from the dimension line by using a leader, see Figure 4.27 (d).

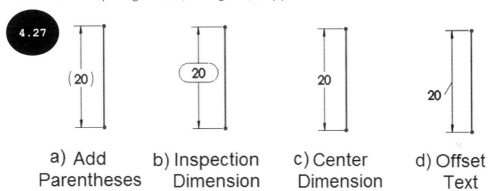

a) Add Parentheses   b) Inspection Dimension   c) Center Dimension   d) Offset Text

Text Field

The **Text** field displays <DIM>, where **DIM** represents dimension value. You can add text, prefixes, and suffixes before or after <DIM> in the field. Figure 4.28 shows a dimension value after adding 'L -' in front of <DIM> in the **Text** field.

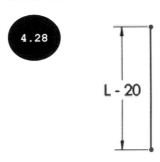

172 Chapter 4 > Applying Geometric Relations and Dimensions

Note: If you delete <DIM> from the Text field, the dimension value will also be deleted or removed from the drawing area. Also, the Add Value button gets enabled in the Dimension Text rollout. On choosing the Add Value button, the dimension value gets restored in the drawing area. Also <DIM> is displayed again in the Text field.

Left Justify/Center Justify/Right Justify
The Left Justify, Center Justify, and Right Justify buttons are used for the justifications of dimension value to left, center, right, respectively.

Symbols
The Symbols area of the rollout is used to add different types of symbols to the selected dimensions, see Figure 4.29. To add a symbol, click to place the cursor where you want to insert or add symbol in the Text field and then click on the respective symbol button. The selected symbol is added in the field as well as displayed in the drawing area. On clicking on the More Symbols button of this area, a flyout appears with the display of additional symbols. You can click on the required symbol to be added in the dimension. If you click on the More Symbols option in this flyout. The Symbol Library dialog box appears, see Figure 4.30.

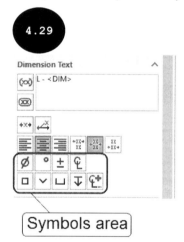

Dual Dimension

The **Dual Dimension** rollout is used to display dual or alternative dimension measurement for sketch entities. By default, this rollout is collapsed. As a result, the dimension values for sketch entities are displayed only in the document's unit system. To display dimensions in dual dimension unit, expand the **Dual Dimension** rollout by clicking on the arrow in the **Dual Dimension** rollout. After expanding the **Dual Dimension** rollout, select the check box in the title bar of the **Dual Dimension** rollout. The options of the **Dual Dimension** rollout gets enabled. Also, the default dual dimension unit along with the current document unit are displayed in the selected dimension in the drawing area, see Figure 4.31. You can specify a precision value and tolerance as required for the dual dimension by using the **Unit Precision** and **Tolerance Precision** drop-down lists of the expanded **Dual Dimension** rollout.

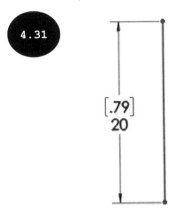

Note: You can also specify a unit system for dual dimensions by using the **Document Properties - Units** dialog box. To invoke this dialog box, click on the **Options** tool in the **Standard** toolbar. The **System Options - General** dialog box appears. In this dialog box, click on the **Document Properties** tab and then select the **Units** option. The **Document Properties - Units** dialog box appears. Next, specify the dual dimension unit in the field respective to the **Unit** column and the **Dual Dimension Length** field of the dialog box.

Leaders Tab

The options in the **Leaders** tab of the **Dimension PropertyManager** are used to control the properties of dimension leader. Figure 4.32 shows the PropertyManager with the **Leader** tab activated. The options in this tab are as follows:

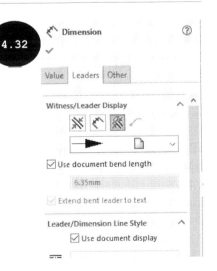

Withness/Leader Display

The **Withness/Leader Display** rollout is used to specify parameters for dimension arrows. The options in this rollout are as follows:

174 Chapter 4 > Applying Geometric Relations and Dimensions

Outside
The **Outside** button in this rollout is used to place dimension arrows outside the dimension extension lines, see Figure 4.33 (a).

Inside
The **Inside** button in this rollout is used to place dimension arrows inside the dimension extension lines, see Figure 4.33 (b).

Smart
By default, the **Smart** button is activated in this rollout. As a result, the placement of the arrows is either inside or outside the extension lines depending on the availability of space between the extension lines of dimensions. For example, if the space available between the extension lines of a dimension is not adequate to place arrows inside, then the arrows are placed automatically outside the extension lines.

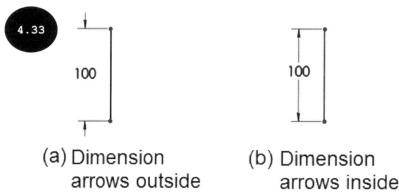

(a) Dimension arrows outside (b) Dimension arrows inside

Directed Leader
The **Directed Leader** button is used to change the orientation a leader at an angle with respect to the surface on which it is applied, see Figure 4.34. The leaders that can be oriented by using this button are applied using the tools available in the **DimXpert CommandManager**. Also, note that this button gets enabled in the **Withness/Leader Display** rollout only when the selected leader is applied on a cylindrical surface.

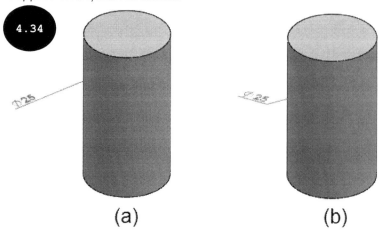

(a) (b)

Style Drop-down List

The **Style** drop-down list of the rollout is used to select the type of arrow style to be used for the selected dimension.

Radius

The **Radius** button is used to apply radius dimension even if the selected dimension is a diameter dimension of a circle. Note that this button gets enabled only if the selected dimension is either a diameter dimension or a radius dimension. On selecting the **Radius** button, the selected diameter dimension changes to radius dimension. Also, three buttons: **Foreshorten**, **Solid Leader**, and **Open Leader** get enabled bellow this button in the rollout, see Figure 4.35. By using these buttons, you can specify the type of leader for the radius dimension, see Figure 4.36.

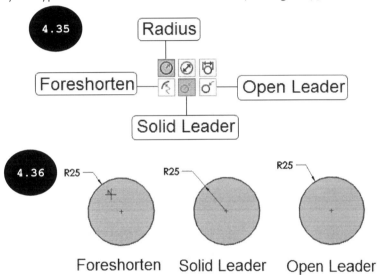

Diameter

The **Diameter** button is used to apply diameter dimension even if the selected dimension is a radius dimension. Note that this button gets enabled only if the selected dimension is either a diameter dimension or a radius dimension. On selecting the **Diameter** button, the selected dimension changes to diameter dimension. Also, four buttons: **Two Arrows / Solid Leader**, **Two Arrows / Open Leader**, **One Arrow / Solid Leader**, and **One Arrow / Open Leader** appear below the **Diameter** button, see Figure 4.37. These buttons are used to specify the type of leader, see Figure 4.38. Note that the **Two Arrows / Solid Leader** and **Two Arrows / Open Leader** buttons are enabled only when the **Use document second arrow** check box is unchecked in the rollout.

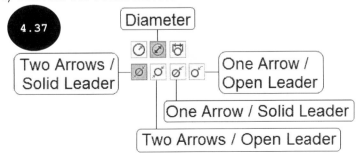

 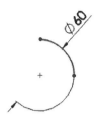

Figure 4.38 Two Arrows / Solid Leader   Two Arrows / Open Leader   One Arrow / Solid Leader   One Arrow / Open Leader

Note: The availability of the buttons in the rollout also depends upon the type of drafting standard selected in the **Document Properties - Drafting Standard** dialog box. To set the drafting standard, click on the **Options** tool in the **Standard** toolbar and then click on the **Document Properties** tab in the **System Options - General** dialog box appeared. Next, select the required drafting standard in the **Overall drafting standard** drop-down list of the dialog box.

Linear

The **Linear** button is used to display the diameter dimension as a linear diameter dimension. On selecting the **Linear** button, the selected diameter dimension changes to linear diameter dimension in the drawing area. Also, two buttons: **Perpendicular To Axis** and **Parallel To Axis** get enabled. By using these buttons you can define whether the linear diameter dimension is perpendicular or parallel to the axis of the object.

Use document second arrow

The **Use document second arrow** check box is used to specify the second arrow style for diameter dimension. By default, this check box is selected. As a result, the second arrow of the diameter dimension is specified as per the default document settings.

Note: To specify default document settings for the second arrow of the diameter dimension, invoke the **Document Properties - Diameter** dialog box. To invoke this dialog box, click on the **Options** tool in the **Standard** toolbar. The **System Options - General** dialog box appears. Next, click on the **Document Properties** tab and then expands the **Dimensions** node by clicking on the plus (+) sign available in front. Next, select the **Diameter** option from the expanded **Dimensions** node. The name of the dialog box is changed to **Document Properties - Diameter**. Now, you can specify the document settings for the second arrow of diameter dimensions by using the **Display second outside arrow** and **Display with solid leader** check boxes of the dialog box. On selecting the **Display second outside arrow** check box, the second arrow of the diameter dimension appears outside. If you select the **Display with solid leader** check box, then the second arrow for diameter dimension appears with solid leader.

Use document bend length
The **Use document bend length** check box is used to specify the leader length after the bend. If this check box is selected, then the default bend length, which is specified in the **Document Properties - Dimensions** dialog box is used. However, if you uncheck this check box, you can specify the bend length for the selected leader in the field available below this check box.

Note: To specify the default bend settings for leaders, you need to invoke the **Document Properties - Dimensions** dialog box. To invoke this dialog box, click on the **Options** tool in the **Standard** toolbar. The **System Options - General** dialog box appears. In this dialog box, click on the **Document Properties** tab and then select the **Dimensions** node. The options related to dimension styles appear on the right of the dialog box. Also, the name of the dialog box changes to the **Document Properties - Dimensions**. In this dialog box, specify the default bend length for dimension leaders in the **Leader length** field of the **Bent leaders** area.

Leader/Dimension Line Style
The options in the **Leader/Dimension Line Style** rollout are used to specify leader style and thickness properties for leader. By default, the **Use document display** check box is selected in this rollout. As as result, the default properties of the leader style specified in the **Document Properties** dialog box are used. On unchecking this check box, the **Leader Style** and **Leader Thickness** drop-down lists get enabled in this rollout. By using these drop-down lists, you can specify the leader style and the leader thickness for the selected dimension leader.

You can also specify default leader style and thickness for angle dimensions, arc length, chamfer, hole, linear, ordinate, and radius dimensions. To specify the default leader style and thickness for angle dimension, you need to invoke the **Document Properties - Angle** dialog box. To invoke this dialog box, click on the **Options** tool in the **Standard** toolbar. The **System Options - General** dialog box appears. In this dialog box, click on the **Document Properties** tab and then expands the **Dimensions** node by clicking on the plus (+) sign available in front. Next, select the **Angle** option from the expanded **Dimensions** node. The name of the dialog box changes to **Document Properties - Angle**. In this dialog box, you can specify default leader style and thickness for angular dimensions by using the **Leader Style** and **Leader Thickness** drop-down lists of the **Leader Style** area. Similarly, you can specify the default leader style and thickness for arc length, chamfer, hole, linear, ordinate, and radius dimensions by invoking the respective dialog boxes.

Custom Text Position
The options of the **Custom Text Position** rollout are used to customize the position of dimension text with respect to dimension leader. By default, this rollout is collapsed. As a result, the dimension text and leader are placed as per the default settings. Expand the **Custom Text Position** rollout by selecting the check box available in front of the title bar of this rollout. If you click on the **Solid Leader, Aligned Text** button in the expanded rollout, the selected dimension will have the solid dimension leader with aligned dimension text. On clicking the **Broken Leader, Horizontal Text** button, the selected dimension will have the broken dimension leader with horizontal dimension text. On the other hand, if you click on the **Broken Leader, Aligned Text** button, the selected dimension will have the broken dimension leader with aligned dimension text, see Figure 4.39.

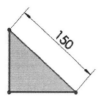 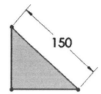 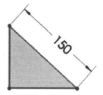

Solid Leader, Aligned Text   Broken Leader, Horizontal Text   Broken Leader, Aligned Text

Other Tab
The options in the **Other** tab of the **Dimension PropertyManager** are as follows:

Override Units
The **Override Units** rollout is used to override the default unit specified in the **Document Properties - Units** dialog box. To override the default unit, expand the **Override Units** rollout by selecting the check box in front of the title bar, see Figure 4.40. Once the **Override Units** rollout has been expanded, select the unit type as the override unit for the selected dimension from the **Length Units** drop-down list of the rollout.

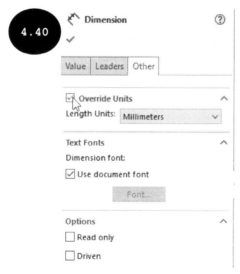

Note: The availability of other options in the **Override Units** rollout depends upon the type of unit selected in the **Length Units** drop-down list. For example, if the **Inches** is selected in the **Length Units** drop-down list, then the **Decimal** and **Fractions** radio buttons become available in the **Override Units** rollout of the PropertyManager. You can select the required radio button from the rollout to display the override unit either in decimal or fractions.

Text Fonts

The **Text Fonts** rollout is used to specify the font for the selected dimension. By default, the **Use document font** check box is selected in the rollout. As a result, the default dimension font in the **Document Properties - Dimensions** dialog box is used for all dimensions. However, if you uncheck the **Use document font** check box, then the **Font** button gets enabled below this check box. Click on the **Font** button. The **Choose Font** dialog box appears, see Figure 4.41. By using this dialog box, you can specify the required font, font style, and dimension text height for the selected dimension.

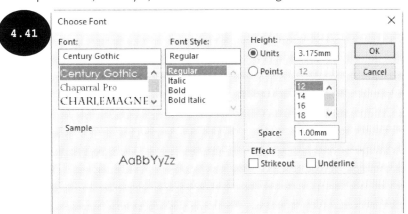

To specify the default dimension font for dimensions, you need to invoke the **Document Properties - Dimension** dialog box. To invoke this dialog box, click on the **Options** tool in the **Standard** toolbar. The **System Options - General** dialog box appears. In this dialog box, click on the **Document Properties** tab and then select the **Dimensions** option. The options related to dimension styles appear on the right of the dialog box. Also, the name of the dialog box changes to **Document Properties - Dimensions**. In this dialog box, click on the **Font** button in the **Text** area of the dialog box. The **Choose Font** dialog box appears. Now, you can specify default font, font style, text height for dimensions by using this **dialog** box. Once the default dimension font for dimensions has been set, click on the **OK** button in the dialog box.

Options

The **Options** rollout is provided with the **Read only** and **Driven** check boxes. On selecting the **Read only** check box, the selected dimension becomes read only and cannot be modified. Similarly, on selecting the **Driven** check box, the selected dimension becomes driven or reference dimension which cannot drive the sketch entity.

Working with Different States of a Sketch

In SOLIDWORKS, a sketch can be either **Under defined**, **Fully defined**, or **Over defined**. All these states of the sketch are as follows:

Under defined Sketch

An under defined sketch is a sketch, whose all degrees of freedoms are not fixed. It means entities of the sketch can change their shape, size, and position by dragging them. Figure 4.42 shows a rectangular sketch in which the length of the rectangle is defined as 40 mm. However, the width and position with respect to the origin of the rectangle are not defined. It means that the width and position of the rectangle can be changed by dragging the respective entities of the rectangle. Note that the current status of the sketch appears on the right of the Status Bar, which is available on the lower side of the drawing area. By default, the entities of an under defined sketch appear in blue color in the drawing area.

Fully defined Sketch

A fully defined sketch is a sketch, whose all degrees of freedoms are fixed. It means the entities of the sketch cannot change their shape, size, and position by dragging them. Figure 4.43 shows a rectangular sketch in which the length, width, and position with respect to the origin of the sketch is defined. Note that the entities of a fully defined sketch appear in black color.

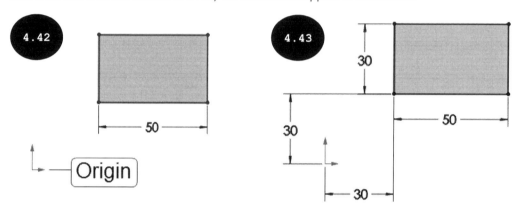

Tip: The sketch shown in Figure 4.43 is a fully defined as all its entities are dimensioned and the required geometrical relations have been applied. The required geometrical relations applied in this sketch are horizontal to the horizontal entities and vertical to the vertical entities. The relations such as horizontal and vertical apply automatically to the entities while drawing them.

Over defined Sketch

An over defined sketch is a sketch that is over defined by dimensions or geometric relations. Figure 4.44 shows an over defined rectangular because the length of both sides of the rectangle is same; therefore, applying dimension to both sides of the rectangle makes it over defined. Note that entities of an over defined sketch appear in yellow color. Also, when you apply an over defined dimension to an entity, the **Make Dimension Driven?** dialog box appears, see Figure 4.45. In this dialog box, if you select the **Make this dimension driven** radio button and click on the **OK** button, then the newly applied dimension becomes a driven dimension and acts as a reference dimension only. As a result, the sketch cannot become an over defined sketch. However, if you select the **Leave this dimension driving** radio button and click on the **OK** button, then the newly applied dimension becomes a driving dimension. As a result, the sketch becomes over defined.

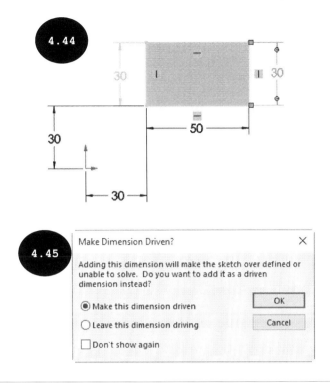

Tutorial 1

Draw the sketch shown in Figure 4.46 and make it fully defined by applying all dimensions and relations. The model shown in this figure is for your reference only. You will learn how to create 3D models in the later chapters. All dimensions are in mm.

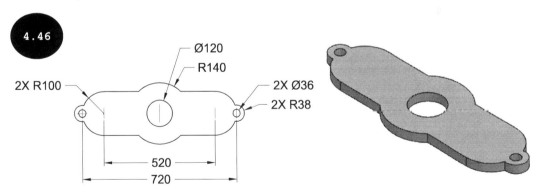

Section 1: Starting SOLIDWORKS

First, you need to start the SOLIDWORKS software.

1. Double-click on the SOLIDWORKS icon on your desktop to start SOLIDWORKS.

182   Chapter 4 > Applying Geometric Relations and Dimensions

Section 2: Invoking the Sketching Environment

Now, first invoke the Part modeling environment and then the Sketching environment by selecting the Top plane as the sketching plane.

1. Click on the **New** tool in the **Standard** toolbar. The **New SOLIDWORKS Document** dialog box appears.

2. Make sure that the **Part** button is activated in the dialog box. Next, click on the **OK** button. The Part modeling environment is invoked.

   Once the Part modeling environment has been invoked, you can invoke the Sketching environment and create the sketch of this tutorial.

3. Click on the **Sketch** tab in the CommandManager. The tools of the **Sketch CommandManager** are displayed, see Figure 4.47.

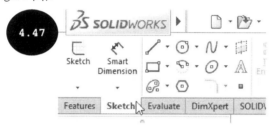

4. Click on the **Sketch** tool in the **Sketch CommandManager**. The three default planes mutually perpendicular to each other appear in the graphics area.

5. Move the cursor over the Top plane and then click on it as the sketching plane when the boundary of the plane gets highlighted. The Sketching environment is invoked. Also, the Top plane is orientated normal to the viewing direction and the Confirmation corner appears at the upper right corner of the drawing area.

Section 3: Specifying Unit Settings

Once the Sketching environment has been invoked, you need to specify the metric unit system for measurement.

1. Click on the **Options** tool in the **Standard** toolbar. The **System Options - General** dialog box appears.

2. Click on the **Document Properties** tab in the dialog box. The name of the dialog box changes to **Document Properties - Drafting Standard**.

3. Click on the **Units** option in the left panel of the dialog box. The options related to specifying the unit system appear on the right of the dialog box.

4. Make sure that the **MMGS (millimeter, gram, second)** radio button is selected in the **Unit system** area of the dialog box.

Now, you need to make sure that the snap mode is turned off. As SOLIDWORKS is a parametric software, you can turn off the snap mode and create sketches by specifying points arbitrary in the drawing area and then apply required dimensions.

5. Click on the **Grid/Snap** option in the left panel of the dialog box. The options related to grid and snap settings appear.

6. Make sure the **Display grid** check box is unchecked in the **Grid** area.

7. Click on the **Go To System Snaps** button. The name of the dialog box changes to **System Options - Relations/Snaps**.

8. Make sure the **Grid** check box in the **Sketch snaps** area of the dialog box is unchecked.

9. Click on the **OK** button to accept the changes made and close the dialog box.

Section 4: Creating the Sketch

Now, you need to create the sketch by using the sketching tools.

1. Click on the **Circle** tool in the **Sketch CommandManager**. The **Circle** tool is invoked and the **Circle PropertyManager** appears.

2. Move the cursor to the origin and then click the left mouse button to specify the center point of the circle when the cursor snaps to the origin.

3. Move the cursor horizontally toward right and click when the radius of the circle appears close to 60 mm near the cursor, see Figure 4.48. A circle of radius 60 mm is created and the **Circle** tool is still active.

4. Move the cursor to the origin and click to specify the center point of another circle when the cursor snaps to the origin.

5. Move the cursor horizontally toward right and click when the radius of the circle appears close to 140 mm near the cursor, see Figure 4.49. A circle of radius 140 mm is created and the **Circle** tool is still active.

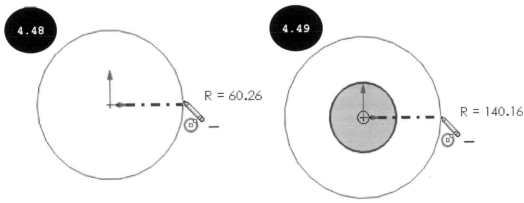

184 Chapter 4 > Applying Geometric Relations and Dimensions

> **Tip:** While drawing sketch entities, you may need to zoom in/out the drawing display area. To zoom in/out the drawing display area, scroll the middle mouse button. Alternatively, click on the **View > Modify > Zoom In/Out** in the SOLIDWORKS menus. To exit the **Zoom In/Out tool**, press the ESC key.

6. Right-click in the drawing area. A shortcut menu appears. Next, click on the **Select** option in the shortcut menu to exit the **Circle** tool.

7. Invoke the **Slot** flyout, see Figure 4.50. Next, click on the **Centerpoint Straight Slot** tool in the **Slot** flyout.

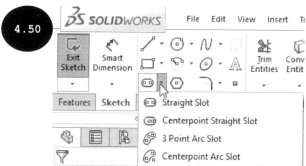
4.50

8. Move the cursor to the origin and then click the left mouse button to specify the center point of the slot when the cursor snaps to the origin.

9. Move the cursor horizontally toward right and click when the half length of the slot appears close to 260 mm (520/2 = 260) near the cursor, see Figure 4.51. Next, move the cursor for a little distance in the drawing area. The preview of the slot appears.

10. Click the left mouse button when the width of the slot appears close to 200 mm in the **Parameters** rollout of the **Slot PropertyManager**, see Figure 4.52. A slot is created, see Figure 4.53. Next, press the ESC key to exit the **Centerpoint Straight Slot** tool.

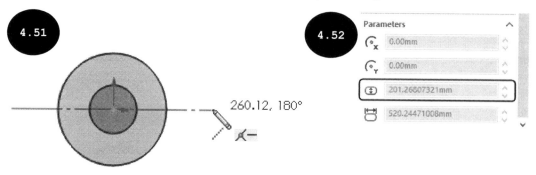
4.51   4.52

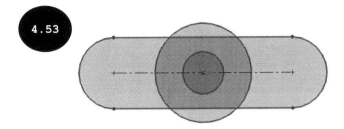

4.53

11. Click on the **Zoom to Fit** tool in the **View (Heads-Up)** toolbar to fit the sketch completely inside the screen.

12. Click on the **Circle** tool and then move the cursor toward the midpoint of the right slot arc, see Figure 4.54.

13. Click to specify the center point of the circle when the circle snaps to the midpoint of slot arc, see Figure 4.54.

14. Move the cursor horizontally toward right and click when the radius of the circle appears close to 18 mm near the cursor, see Figure 4.55. A circle of radius 18 mm is created and the **Circle** tool is still active.

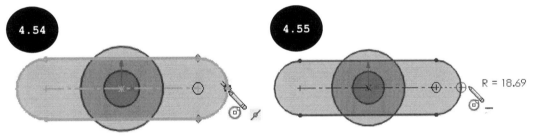

4.54   4.55

15. Move the cursor to the center point of the previously created circle of radius close to 18 mm and then click to specify the center point of another circle when the cursor snaps to it.

16. Move the cursor horizontally toward right and click when the radius of the circle appears close to 38 mm near the cursor, see Figure 4.56. A circle is created.

17. Similarly, create two circles on the left side of the slot, see Figure 4.57. Next, press the ESC key to exit the **Circle** tool.

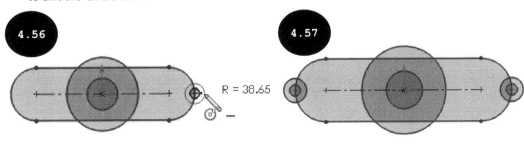

4.56   4.57

18. Click on the down arrow available next to the **Line** tool. The **Line** flyout appears, see Figure 4.58.

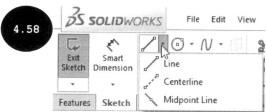

19. Click on the **Centerline** tool in the **Line** flyout and then create a vertical centerline of any length starting from the origin, see Figure 4.59. Next, press the ESC key to exit the **Centerline** tool.

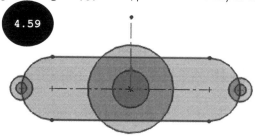

Section 5: Trimming Sketch Entities

Now, you need to trim the unwanted entities of the sketch.

1. Click on the **Trim Entities** tool in the **Sketch CommandManager**. The **Trim PropertyManager** appears on the left of the drawing area.

2. Click on the **Trim to closest** button in the **Options** rollout of the PropertyManager. The appearance of the cursor changes to trim cursor.

3. Move the cursor over the portion of the lower horizontal slot entity which lies inside the circle, see Figure 4.60. Next, click the left mouse button when it is highlighted. The **SOLIDWORKS** window appears informing you that the trim operation will destroy the slot entity.

4. Click on the **OK** button in the **SOLIDWORKS** window. The selected portion of the entity is trimmed, see Figure 4.61. Also, the **Trim Entities** tool is still active.

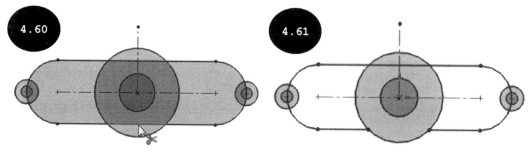

5. Similarly, click on the other unwanted entities of the sketch one by one to trim them. Figure 4.62 shows the sketch after trimming all the unwanted entities. Note that while trimming the sketch entities, if the **SOLIDWORKS** message window appears, then click on the **Yes** button of the **SOLIDWORKS** message window to continue the process of trimming sketch entities.

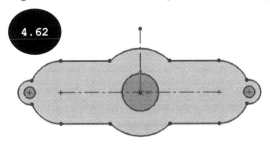

Tip: While trimming sketch entities, you may need to zoom in or zoom out the drawing display area. To zoom in/out the drawing display area, scroll the middle mouse button. Alternatively, click on the **View > Modify > Zoom In/Out** in the SOLIDWORKS menus.

6. Once you have completed the trimming operation, press the ESC key to exit the tool.

Section 6: Applying Relations

After creating the sketch, you need to make it fully defined by applying proper relations and dimensions to the sketch entities.

1. Select two smaller circles of diameter 36 mm (radius 18 mm) by pressing the CTRL key to apply equal relation between them, see Figure 4.63. Next, release the CTRL key and do not move the cursor. The Pop-up toolbar appears, see Figure 4.64. Also, the **Properties PropertyManager** appears on the left of the drawing area.

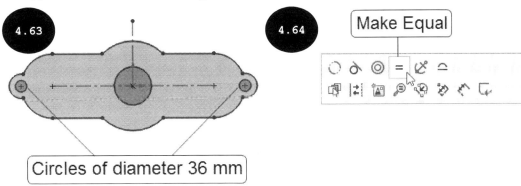

2. Click on the **Make Equal** tool = in the Pop-up toolbar, see Figure 4.64. The equal relation is applied between the selected circles.

3. Similarly, select arcs of radius 38 mm by pressing the CTRL key and then apply the equal relation between them, see Figure 4.65.

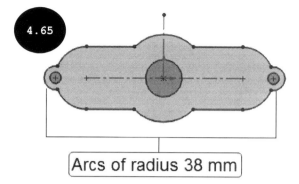

Arcs of radius 38 mm

4. Select the center points of slot arcs and the vertical centerline by pressing the CTRL key, see Figure 4.66. Next, release the CTRL key to display the Pop-up toolbar.

5. Click on the **Make Symmetric** tool in the Pop-up toolbar. The symmetric relation is applied between center points of slot arcs and the vertical centerline.

6. Similarly, select the center points of two circles of diameter 36 mm and the vertical centerline by pressing the CTRL key, see Figure 4.67 and then apply symmetric relation between them.

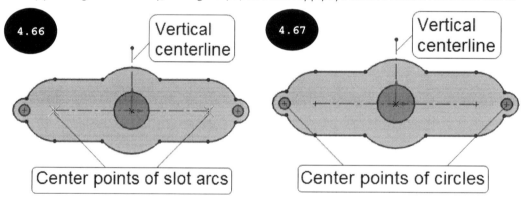

7. Similarly, apply tangent relations between four set of connecting horizontal lines and arcs one by one, see Figure 4.68.

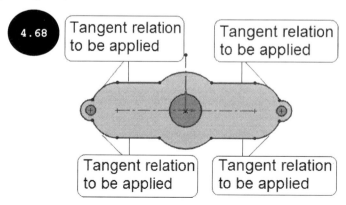

8. Select the horizontal centerline and the origin by pressing the CTRL key, see Figure 4.69 and then release the CTRL key. A Pop-up toolbar appears.

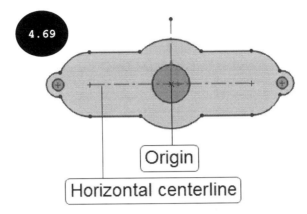

9. Click on the **Make Coincident** tool in the Pop-up toolbar. The coincident relation is applied between the horizontal centerline and the origin.

10. Similarly, apply the horizontal relation to all horizontal lines (four) of the sketch.

11. Also, apply the horizontal relation between the center points of two circles of diameter 36 mm and the origin, see Figure 4.70. To apply the horizontal relation between the center points of two circles of diameter 36 mm and the origin, select the center points of circles and origin by pressing the CTRL key and then click on the **Make Horizontal** tool in the Pop-up toolbar.

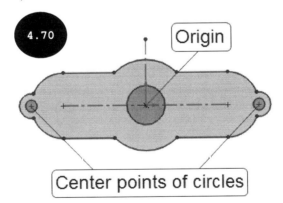

Note: You can turn on or off the display of the applied relations in the drawing area by clicking on the **View Sketch Relations** tool in the **Hide/Show Items** flyout of the **View (Heads-Up)** toolbar, see Figure 4.71.

190 Chapter 4 > Applying Geometric Relations and Dimensions

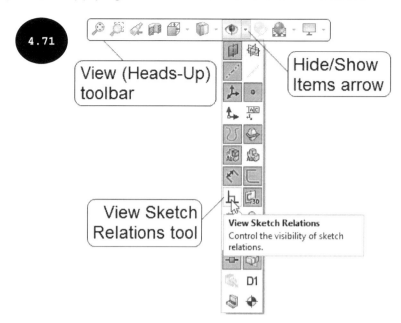

4.71

Section 7: Applying Dimensions

After applying the required relations, you need to apply dimensions to make the sketch fully defined.

1. Click on the **Smart Dimension** tool in the **Sketch CommandManager**.

2. Select the circle whose center point is at the origin, see Figure 4.72. The diameter dimension of the selected circle is attached to the cursor, see Figure 4.72.

3. Move the cursor to the location where you want to place the dimension in the drawing area and then click to specify the placement point. The **Modify** dialog box appears, see Figure 4.73.

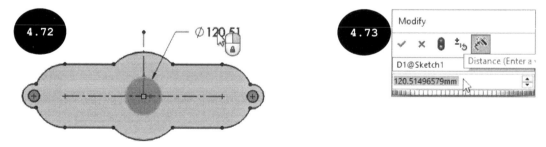

4. Enter **120** in the **Modify** dialog box and then click on the green tick mark button. The diameter of the circle is modified to 120 mm and the diameter dimension is applied, see Figure 4.74.

5. Similarly, apply the remaining dimensions of the sketch. Figure 4.75 shows the fully defined sketch after applying all dimensions.

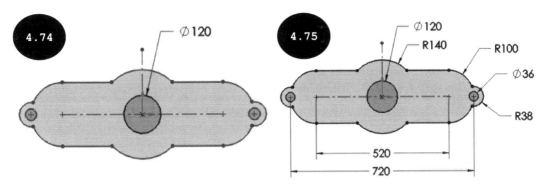

Section 8: Saving the Sketch

After creating the sketch, you need to save it.

1. Click on the **Save** tool in the **Standard** toolbar. The **Save As** dialog box appears.

2. Browse to the SOLIDWORKS folder and then create a folder with the name **Chapter 4** in the SOLIDWORKS folder. Next, save the sketch with the name Tutorial 1 in the *Chapter 4* folder.

Tutorial 2

Draw the sketch shown in Figure 4.76 and make it fully defined by applying all the dimensions and relations. You will learn how to create a 3D model in the later chapters. All dimensions are in mm.

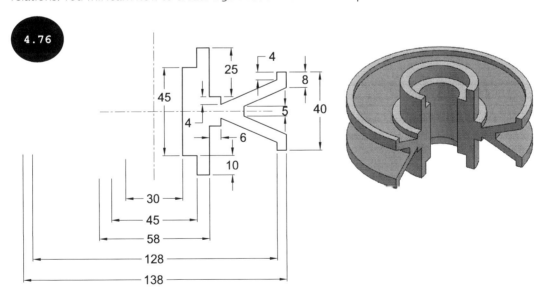

Section 1: Starting SOLIDWORKS

First, you need to start the SOLIDWORKS software.

1. Double-click on the SOLIDWORKS icon on your desktop to start SOLIDWORKS, if not started already.

Section 2: Invoking the Sketching Environment

Now, first invoke the Part modeling environment and then the Sketching environment by selecting the Front plane as the sketching plane.

1. Click on the **New** tool in the **Standard** toolbar. The **New SOLIDWORKS Document** dialog box appears.

2. Double-click on the **Part** button in the dialog box. The Part modeling environment is invoked.

   Once the Part modeling environment has been invoked, you can invoke the Sketching environment and create the sketch of this tutorial.

3. Click on the **Sketch** tab in the CommandManager. The tools of the **Sketch CommandManager** are displayed, see Figure 4.77.

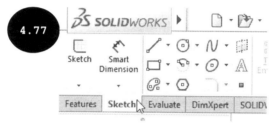

4. Click on the **Sketch** tool in the **Sketch CommandManager**. The three default planes mutually perpendicular to each other appear in the graphics area.

5. Move the cursor over the Front plane and then click on it as the sketching plane when the boundary of the plane is highlighted. The Sketching environment is invoked and the Front plane is orientated normal to the viewing direction.

Section 3: Specifying Unit Settings

Once the Sketching environment has been invoked, you need to specify the metric unit system for measurement.

1. Click on the **Options** tool in the **Standard** toolbar. The **System Options - General** dialog box appears.

2. Click on the **Document Properties** tab in the dialog box. The name of the dialog box changes to **Document Properties - Drafting Standard**.

3. Click on the **Units** option in the left panel of the dialog box. The options for specifying the unit system appear on the right of the dialog box.

4. Make sure that the **MMGS (millimeter, gram, second)** radio button is selected in the **Unit system** area of the dialog box.

Now, you need to make sure that the snap mode is turned off. As SOLIDWORKS is a parametric software, you can turn off the snap mode and create sketches by specifying points arbitrary in the drawing area and then apply the required dimensions.

5. Click on the **Grid/Snap** option in the left panel of the dialog box and then make sure that the **Display grid** check box in the **Grid** area is unchecked.

6. Click on the **Go To System Snaps** button and then make sure that the **Grid** check box in the **Sketch snaps** area of the dialog box is unchecked.

7. Click on the **OK** button to accept the changes made and close the dialog box.

Section 4: Drawing the Upper Half of the Sketch

In this section, you need to draw the upper half of the sketch.

1. Click on the down arrow next to the **Line** tool. The **Line** flyout appears, see Figure 4.78.

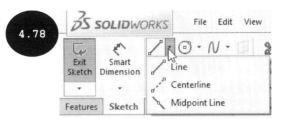

2. Click on the **Centerline** tool in the flyout. The **Centerline** tool is invoked.

3. Create a vertical and a horizontal centerlines of any length starting from the origin one by one, see Figure 4.79. Next, exit the **Centerline** tool.

4. Press and hold the right mouse button and then drag the cursor for a little distance toward left. The **Mouse Gestures** appears in the drawing area, see Figure 4.80.

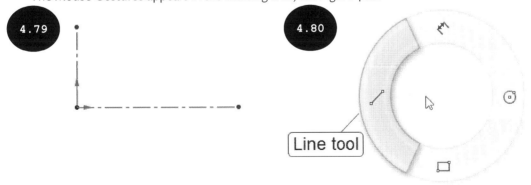

5. Drag the cursor over the **Line** tool in the **Mouse Gestures** by pressing and holding the right mouse button. The **Line** tool gets activated and the **Mouse Gestures** gets disabled. Also, the **Insert Line PropertyManager** appears on the left of the drawing area. Next, release the right mouse button.

6. Move the cursor over the horizontal centerline in the drawing area, see Figure 4.81, at a location whose X, Y, Z coordinates appear close to "15, 0, 0" respectively, in the Status Bar, see Figure 4.82. For X, Y, Z coordinates of a point, you can refer to the Status Bar.

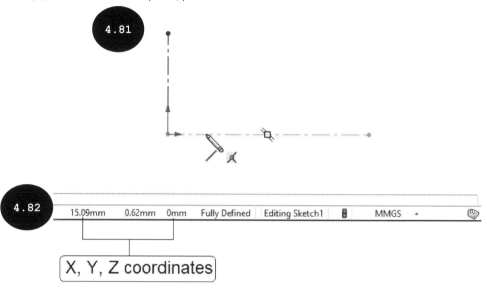

7. Click to specify the start point of the line when coordinates appear close to "15, 0, 0" in the Status Bar, see Figure 4.82.

8. Move the cursor vertically upward and click to specify the endpoint of the line when the length of the line appears close to 22.5 mm near the cursor, see Figure 4.83. A vertical line of the length close to 22.5 mm is created.

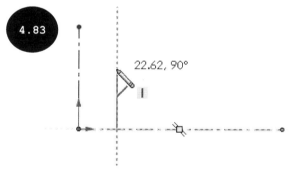

9. Move the cursor horizontally toward right and click to specify the endpoint of the second line when the length of the line appears close to 7.5 mm. A horizontal line of length close to 7.5 mm is created.

10. Move the cursor vertically upward and click to specify the endpoint of the line when the length of the line appears close to 10 mm. A vertical line of the length close to 10 mm is created.

11. Move the cursor horizontally toward right and click when the length of the line appears close to 6.5 mm. A horizontal line of the length close to 6.5 mm is created.

12. Move the cursor vertically downward and click when the length of the line appears close to 25 mm.

13. Move the cursor horizontally toward right and click when the length of the line appears close to 6 mm.

14. Move the cursor vertically downward and click when the length of the line appears close to 4 mm.

15. Move the cursor toward right at an angle, see Figure 4.84 and then click to specify the endpoint of the inclined line when the line appears similar to the one shown in Figure 4.84.

16. Move the cursor vertically upward and click when the length of the line appears close to 4 mm, see Figure 4.85.

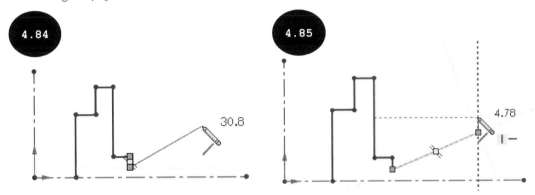

17. Move the cursor horizontally toward right and click when the length of the line appears close to 5 mm.

18. Move the cursor vertically downward and click when the length of the line appears close to 8 mm.

19. Move the cursor parallel to the inclined line toward left, see Figure 4.86 and then click the left mouse button just above the horizontal centerline, see Figure 4.86.

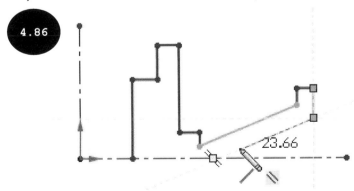

20. Move the cursor vertically downward and then click the left mouse button when the cursor snaps to the horizontal centerline. Next, press the ESC key to exit the **Line** tool. Figure 4.87 shows the sketch after creating the upper half.

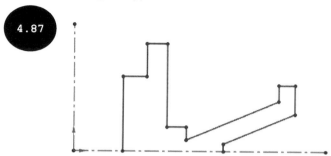

4.87

Section 5: Mirroring Sketch Entities

After creating the upper half of the sketch, you need to mirror it to create the lower half of the sketch.

1. Click on the **Mirror Entities** tool in the **Sketch CommandManager**. The  **Mirror PropertyManager** appears on the left of the drawing area.

2. Select all the sketch entities except the vertical and horizontal centerlines as the entities to be mirrored.

3. Click on the **Mirror about** field in the PropertyManager and then click on the horizontal centerline as the mirroring line in the drawing area. The preview of the lower half of the sketch appears.

4. Make sure that the **Copy** check box is selected in the PropertyManager. Next, click on the green tick mark ✓ button in the PropertyManager. The lower half of the sketch is created, see Figure 4.88.

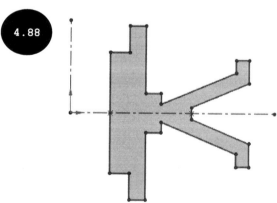

4.88

Section 6: Applying Dimensions

Now, you need to apply dimensions to make the sketch fully defined.

1. Press and hold the right mouse button and then drag the cursor vertically upward for a little distance. The **Mouse Gestures** appears in the drawing area, see Figure 4.89.

2. Drag the cursor over the **Smart Dimension** tool in the **Mouse Gestures** by pressing and holding the right mouse button, see Figure 4.89. The **Smart Dimension** tool gets activated and you are prompted to select the entities to be dimensioned. Now, release the right mouse button.

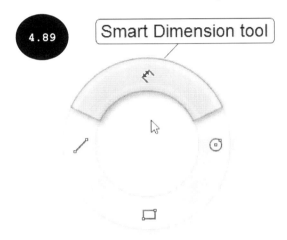

3. Click the left mouse button on the left most vertical line of the sketch, see Figure 4.90. The linear dimension of the selected line is attached to the cursor.

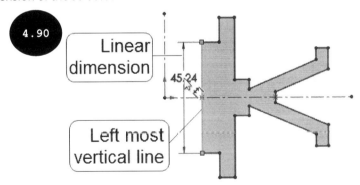

4. Move the cursor toward left for a little distance and then click to specify the placement point. The **Modify** dialog box appears, see Figure 4.91.

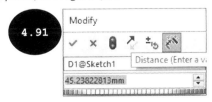

5. Enter 45 in the Modify dialog box and then click on the green tick mark ✓. The length of the line is modified to 45 mm and the linear dimension is applied, see Figure 4.92.

6. Similarly, apply the remaining linear dimensions, see Figure 4.93.

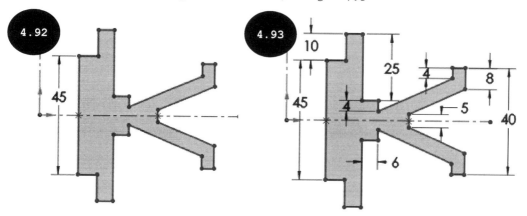

After applying the linear dimensions, you need to apply linear diameter dimensions to the sketch.

7. Make sure that the Smart Dimension tool is activated, and then select the left most vertical line of length 45 mm. The linear dimension is attached to the cursor. Next, select the vertical centerline and then move the cursor to the left of the vertical centerline. The linear diameter dimension is attached to the cursor, see Figure 4.94.

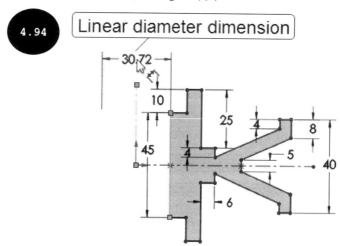

8. Click the left mouse button to specify the placement point for the linear diameter dimension. The Modify dialog box appears.

9. Enter 30 in the Modify dialog box and then click on the green tick mark ✓. The linear diameter dimension is applied, see Figure 4.95.

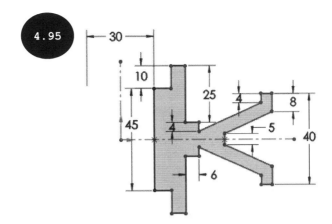

4.95

10. Select the vertical line of length 10 mm, see Figure 4.96 and then move the cursor above the previously applied dimension. The linear diameter dimension is attached to the cursor, see Figure 4.96.

11. Click to specify the placement point for the linear diameter dimension. The **Modify** dialog box appears.

12. Enter **45** in the **Modify** dialog box and then click on the green tick mark ✓. The linear diameter dimension is applied, see Figure 4.97.

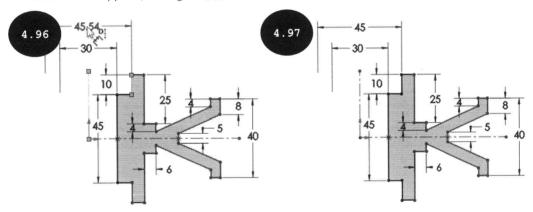

4.96   4.97

13. Similarly, apply the remaining linear diameter dimensions to the sketch, see Figure 4.98.

14. Press the ESC key to exit the **Smart Dimensions** tool. Figure 4.98 shows the fully defined sketch.

200   Chapter 4 > Applying Geometric Relations and Dimensions

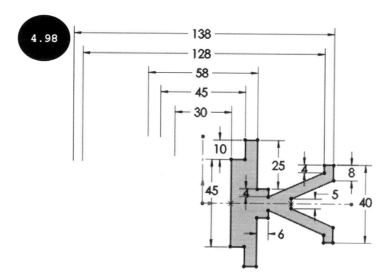

4.98

Section 7: Saving the Sketch
After creating the sketch, you need to save it.

1. Click on the **Save** tool of the **Standard** toolbar, the **Save As** window appears.

2. Browse to the *Chapter 4* folder and then save the sketch with the name Tutorial 2. If the folder is not created, create a folder with name **Chapter 4** in the *SOLIDWORKS* folder.

Tutorial 3

Draw the sketch shown in Figure 4.99 and make it fully defined by applying all dimensions and relations. The model shown in this figure is for your reference only. You will learn about creating a model in later chapters. All dimensions are in mm.

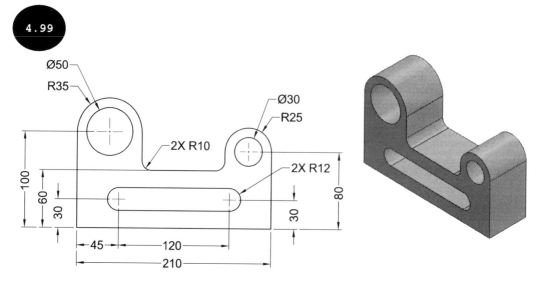

4.99

Section 1: Starting SOLIDWORKS

1. Start SOLIDWORKS, if not started already.

Section 2: Invoking Sketching Environment

Now, you need to invoke the Sketching environment by selecting the Front plane as the sketching plane.

1. Click on the **New** tool in the **Standard** toolbar. The **New SOLIDWORKS Document** dialog box appears.

2. Double-click on the **Part** button in the dialog box. The Part modeling environment is invoked.

3. Click on the **Sketch** tab in the CommandManager. The tools of the **Sketch CommandManager** are displayed, see Figure 4.100.

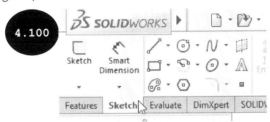

4. Click on the **Sketch** tool in the **Sketch CommandManager**. The three default planes mutually perpendicular to each other appear in the graphics area.

5. Move the cursor over the Front plane and then click the left mouse button when the boundary of Front plane highlights. The Sketching environment is invoked and the Front plane is orientated normal to the viewing direction.

Section 3: Specifying Unit Settings

Once the Sketching environment has been invoked, specify the metric unit system for measurement.

1. Click on the **Options** tool in the **Standard** toolbar. The **System Options - General** dialog box appears.

2. Click on the **Document Properties** tab in this dialog box.

3. Click on the **Units** option in the left panel of the dialog box.

4. Make sure that the **MMGS (millimeter, gram, second)** radio button is selected in the **Unit system** area of the dialog box.

5. Click on the **OK** button to accept the change and close the dialog box.

202   Chapter 4 > Applying Geometric Relations and Dimensions

Section 4: Drawing Sketch Entities
Now, you need to create the sketch by using the sketching tools.

1. Press and hold the right mouse button and then drag the cursor for a little distance toward left. The **Mouse Gestures** appears in the drawing area, see Figure 4.101.

2. Drag the cursor over the **Line** tool in the **Mouse Gestures** by pressing and holding the right mouse button. The **Line** tool gets activated and the **Mouse Gestures** gets disabled. Next, release the right mouse button.

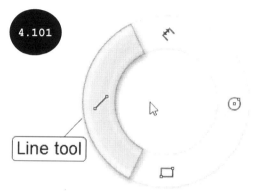

3. Move the cursor to the origin and then click to specify the start point of the line when the cursor snaps to the origin and the coincident symbol appears, see Figure 4.102.

Note: While drawing an entity, if you click the left mouse button when a relation symbol such as coincident, horizontal, or vertical appears, the respective relation will be applied.

4. Move the cursor horizontally toward right and click to specify the endpoint of the line when the length close to 210 mm and the symbol of horizontal relation appears near the cursor, see Figure 4.103. A horizontal line of length close to 210 mm is created. Also, the horizontal relation is applied to the line.

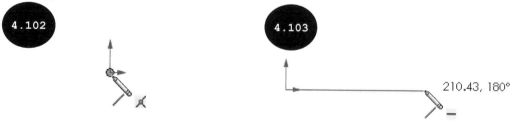

Tip: While drawing sketch entities, you may need to increase or decrease the drawing display area. You can Zoom in or Zoom out the drawing display area by scrolling the middle mouse button. Alternatively, click on the **View > Modify > Zoom In/Out** in the SOLIDWORKS menus. Next, press and hold the left mouse button and drag it upward or downward.

5. Move the cursor vertically upward and create a vertical line of length close to 80 mm.

   Now, you need to create a tangent arc.

6. Move the cursor away from the last specified point and then move it back to the last specified point. An orange color dot appears, see Figure 4.104.

7. Move the cursor vertically upward for a little distance and then move it horizontally toward left. The arc mode is activated and the preview of a tangent arc appears, see Figure 4.105.

8. Click to specify the endpoint of the tangent arc at the location where the angle and radius of the arc appear close to 180 degrees and 25 mm, respectively, see Figure 4.105. The tangent arc of radius close to 25 mm is created and the line mode is activated again.

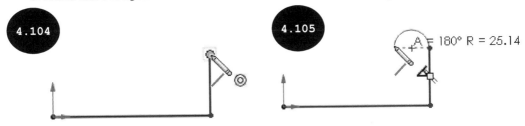

9. Move the cursor vertically downward and create a vertical line of length close to 20 mm.

10. Move the cursor horizontally toward left and create a horizontal line of length close to 90 mm.

11. Move the cursor vertically upward and create a vertical line of length close to 40 mm.

12. Create a tangent arc of radius close to 35 mm, 180 degrees, and aligned to the start point of the first line entity, see Figure 4.106.

13. Move the cursor vertically downward and click to specify the endpoint of the line when the cursor snaps to the start point of the first line entity, see Figure 4.107.

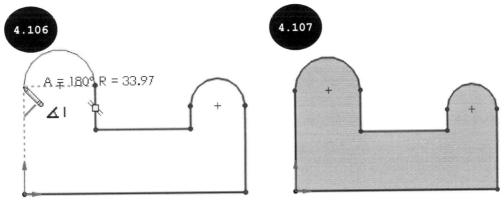

204 Chapter 4 > Applying Geometric Relations and Dimensions

14. Right-click in the drawing area. A shortcut menu appears. Next, click on the **Select** tool in the shortcut menu to exit the **Line** tool.

    Now, you need to create circles of the sketch.

15. Press and hold the right mouse button and then drag the cursor for a little distance toward right. The **Mouse Gestures** appears in the drawing area, see Figure 4.108.

16. Drag the cursor over the **Circle** tool in the **Mouse Gestures** by pressing and holding the right mouse button. The **Circle** tool gets activated and the **Mouse Gestures** gets disabled. Next, release the right mouse button.

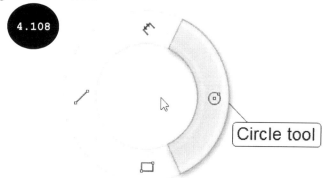

17. Create two circles of radius close to 50 mm and 30 mm, see Figure 4.109. Next, exit the **Circle** tool.

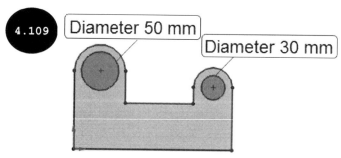

18. Invoke the **Slot** flyout, see Figure 4.110, and then click on the **Straight Slot** tool in the flyout.

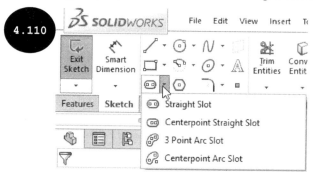

19. Create a straight slot similar to the one shown in Figure 4.111 and then exit the tool. You can create the slot of any parameters. This is because later in this tutorial, you need to apply dimensions in order to make the sketch fully defined.

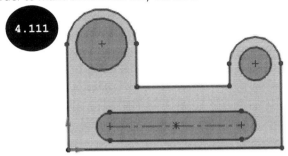

Now, you need to create fillets in the sketch.

20. Click on the **Sketch Fillet** tool. The **Sketch Fillet PropertyManager** appears.

21. Enter **10** in the **Fillet Radius** field of the **Fillet Parameters** rollout in the PropertyManager.

22. Move the cursor over the upper right vertex of the sketch, see Figure 4.112. The preview of the fillet appears, see Figure 4.112. Next, click the left mouse button to accept the fillet preview.

23. Move the cursor over the upper left vertex of the sketch, see Figure 4.113. The preview of the fillet appears, see Figure 4.113. Next, click the left mouse button to accept the fillet preview.

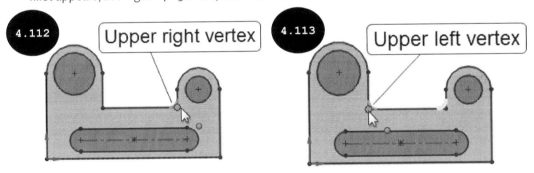

24. After selecting the vertices to create fillets, click on the green tick mark button ✓ twice in the PropertyManager. The fillets of radius 10 mm are created, see Figure 4.114. Also, a radius dimension to the fillet and the equal relation between both the fillets are applied.

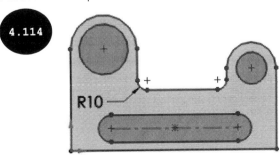

Section 5: Applying Dimensions

After creating the sketch, you need to apply the required relations and dimensions to make the sketch fully defined. In this sketch, all the required relations have been applied automatically while creating the entities. Therefore, you need to apply dimensions only.

1. Click on the **Smart Dimension** tool in the **Sketch CommandManager**.

2. Click on the lower horizontal line of the sketch and then move the cursor downward. The linear dimension is attached to the cursor, see Figure 4.115.

3. Click to specify the placement point for the attached linear dimension in the drawing area. The **Modify** dialog box appears, see Figure 4.116.

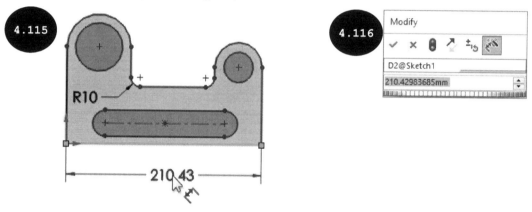

4. Enter **210** in the **Modify** dialog box and then click on the green tick mark button ✓. The length of the line is modified to 210 mm and the linear dimension is applied.

5. Similarly, apply remaining dimensions to the sketch by using the **Smart Dimension** tool, see Figure 4.117. Next, press the ESC key to exit the tool. Figure 4.117 shows the final sketch.

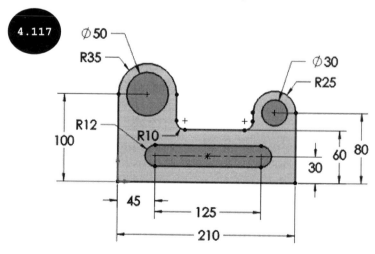

Tip: After placing a dimension in the required location, you may need to further change its location in order to place other dimensions. To change the location of an existing dimension, press and hold the left mouse button over the dimension whose location has to be changed and then drag the cursor to the new location. Next, release the left mouse button.

Section 6: Saving the Sketch

1. Click on the **Save** tool in the **Standard** toolbar. The **Save As** dialog box appears.

2. Browse to the *Chapter 4* folder and then save the sketch with the name Tutorial 3.

Hands-on Test Drive 1

Draw the sketch shown in Figure 4.118 and apply dimensions to make it fully defined. The model shown in the figure is for your reference only. You will learn about creating a model in later chapters.

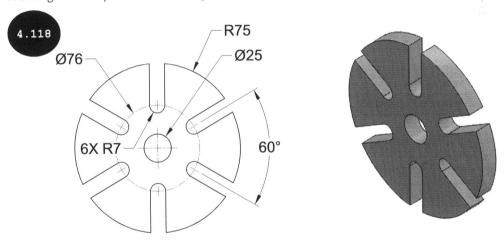

Hands-on Test Drive 2

Draw the sketch shown in Figure 4.119 and apply dimensions to make it fully defined. The model shown in the figure is for your reference only. You will learn about creating a model in later chapters.

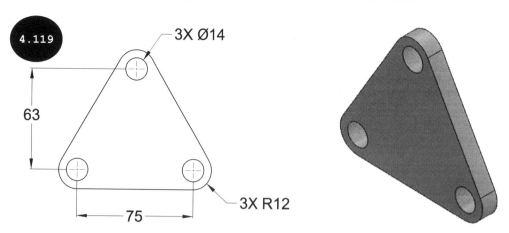

4.119

Summary

In this chapter, you have learned about creating fully defined sketches by applying geometric relations and dimensions. Also, you have learned about applying geometric relations by using the **Add Relation** tool and the Pop-up toolbar. Once the sketch has been drawn and the required geometric relations have been applied, dimensions need to be applied by using various dimension tools. The already applied dimensions and dimension properties such as dimension style, tolerance, and precision can also be modified. In this chapter, you have also learned about different sketch states such as under defined, fully defined, and over defined.

Questions

- The _____ relation is used to coincide a sketch point on to a line, an arc, or an elliptical entity.

- You can control the display or visibility of the applied geometric relations by using the _____ tool.

- The _____ dimension is applied to a sketch representing revolve features.

- The _____ dimensions are measured from a base entity.

- All degrees of freedoms of a _____ sketch are fixed.

- The availability of the suggested relations in the Pop-up toolbar depends upon the type of entities selected. (True/False).

- You cannot modify the dimensions once they have been applied. (True/False).

- You cannot delete the relations that have already been applied between the selected entities. (True/False).

- Geometric relations are used to restrict some degree of freedom of a sketch (True/False).

CHAPTER 5

Creating First/Base Feature of Solid Models

In this chapter, you will learn the following:

- Creating an Extruded Feature
- Creating a Revolved Feature
- Navigating a 3D Model in Graphics Area
- Manipulating View Orientation of a Model
- Changing the Display Style of a Model
- Changing the View of a Model

Once a sketch has been created and fully defined by using different sketching tools, you can convert the sketch into a solid feature by using the feature modeling tools. All the feature modeling tools are available in the **Features CommandManager** in the Part modeling environment, see Figure 5.1.

Note that most of the tools in the **Features CommandManager** are not activated, initially. These tools get activated after creating the base feature of a model. The base feature of a model is also known as the first feature, or parent feature of a model. In SOLIDWORKS, you can create the base feature of a model by using the **Extruded Boss/Base**, **Revolved Boss/Base**, **Swept Boss/Base**, **Lofted Boss/Base**, or **Boundary Boss/Base** tool. The names of these tools end with Boss/Base, which suggests that these tools are the base and boss tools for creating features. Note that the **Swept Boss/Base**, **Lofted Boss/Base**, and **Boundary Boss/Base** tools are not activated in the **Features CommandManager**, initially. These tools get activated only after creating the profiles or sketches required for creating

210 Chapter 5 > Creating First/Base Feature of Solid Models

features by using these tools. You will learn more about these tools in the later chapters. In this chapter, you will learn about creating a base feature by using the **Extruded Boss/Base** and **Revolved Boss/Base** tools.

Creating an Extruded Feature

An extruded feature is created by adding material normal or at an angle to the sketching plane. In SOLIDWORKS, you can create an extruded feature by using the **Extruded Boss/Base** tool. Note that the sketch of the extruded feature defines its geometry. Figure 5.2 shows different extruded features created from the respective sketches.

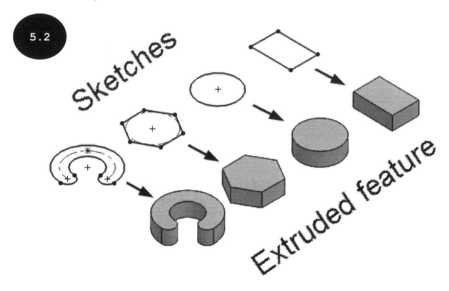

After drawing the sketch by using the sketching tools in the Sketching environment, click on the **Features** tab in the CommandManager. The tools of the **Features CommandManager** are displayed, refer to Figure 5.1. In the **Features CommandManager**, click on the **Extruded Boss/Base** tool. The preview of the extruded feature by adding material normal to the sketching plane, appears in the graphics area with default extrusion parameters and the orientation of the model is changed to Trimetric. Also, the **Boss - Extrude PropertyManager** appears on the left of the graphics area, see Figure 5.3. Figure 5.4 shows a rectangular sketch created on the Top Plane in the Sketching environment and Figure 5.5 shows the preview of the resultant extruded feature in Trimetric orientation.

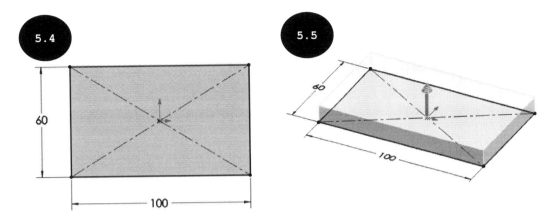

Note: If you exit the Sketching environment after creating the sketch and the sketch has not been selected in the graphics area, then on invoking the **Extruded Boss/Base** tool, the **Extrude PropertyManager** appears, see Figure 5.6. Also, you are prompted to select either a sketch to be extruded or a sketching plane to create a sketch. Select the sketch to be extruded in the graphics area. The preview of the extruded feature appears in the graphics area with default parameters and the **Boss - Extrude PropertyManager** appears on the left of the graphics area. Note that if the sketch to be extruded is not created then you can select the sketching plane for creating the sketch and once the sketch has been created exit the Sketching environment.

You can exit the Sketching environment by clicking on the **Exit Sketch** tool in the **Sketch CommandManager**. You can also click on the **Exit Sketch** icon in the Confirmation corner, which is available at the top right of the graphics area to exit the Sketching environment.

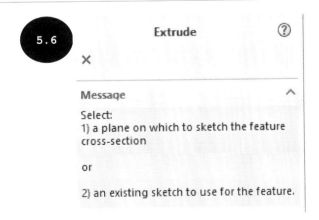

The options in the **Boss-Extrude PropertyManager** are used to specify parameters for the extruded feature. Some of the options of this PropertyManager are as follows:

From

The options in the **Start Condition** drop-down list of the **From** rollout are used to specify the start condition for the extruded feature, see Figure 5.7. The options of this drop-down list that are used while creating the second and further features of a model are discussed in later chapters. The options which are used for creating the base feature are as follows:

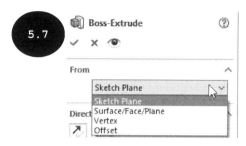

Sketch Plane

By default, the **Sketch Plane** option is selected in the **Start Condition** drop-down list of the **From** rollout. As a result, extrusion starts exactly from the sketching plane of the sketch. Figure 5.8 shows the preview of the extruded feature from its front view when the **Sketch Plane** option is selected.

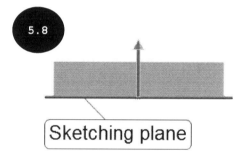

Offset

The **Offset** option is used to create an extruded feature at an offset distance from the sketching plane. On selecting this option, the **Enter Offset Value** field and the **Reverse Direction** button appear in the **From** rollout, see Figure 5.9. By default, the value entered in the **Enter Offset Value** field is 0 (zero). You can enter the required offset value in this field. You can also use the up and down arrows of the Spinner available on the right of this field to set the offset value. Figure 5.10 shows the preview of the extruded feature from its front view after specifying an offset distance. To reverse the offset direction, click on the **Reverse Direction** button in the **From** rollout.

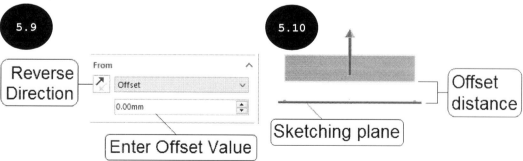

Note: The **Surface/Face/Plane** and **Vertex** options of the **Start Condition** drop-down list are discussed in later chapters.

Direction 1

The options in the **Direction 1** rollout of the PropertyManager are used to specify the end condition for the extruded feature in direction 1. The options are as follows:

End Condition

The options in the **End Condition** drop-down list are used to define the end condition for the extruded feature, see Figure 5.11. The options of this drop-down list that are used while creating the second and further extruded features are discussed in later chapters. The options which are used for creating the base feature are as follows:

Blind

The **Blind** option of the **End Condition** drop-down list is used to specify the end condition of the extrusion by specifying the depth value in the **Depth** field of the **Direction 1** rollout, see Figure 5.12.

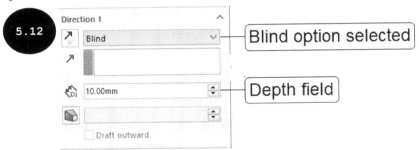

Mid Plane

The **Mid Plane** option of the **End Condition** drop-down list allows you to extrude the feature symmetrically about the sketching plane, see Figure 5.13. After selecting this option, you can enter the value for the depth of extrusion in the **Depth** field of the rollout. The depth value specified in this field is divided equally and creates symmetrical extrusion in both sides of the sketching plane. For example, if the depth value specified in the **Depth** field is 100 mm then the resultant feature is created by adding material 50 mm in each side of the sketching plane.

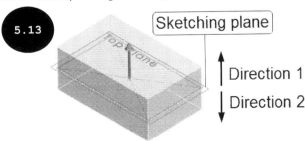

Note: The other options such as **Up To Vertex**, **Up To Surface**, and **Offset From Surface** of the **End Condition** drop-down list are discussed in later chapters.

Reverse Direction

The **Reverse Direction** button of the **Direction 1** rollout is used to reverse/flip the direction of extrusion from one side of the sketching plane to the other side.

Depth

The **Depth** field of the **Direction 1** rollout is used to specify the depth of extrusion. You can enter the value for the depth of extrusion in this field or use the Spinner up and down arrows available on the right of this field to set the depth value. Note that when you click on the down arrow of the Spinner, the depth value decreases and when you click on the up arrow of the Spinner, the depth value increases. Also note that the **Depth** field appears only when the **Blind** or **Mid Plane** option is selected in the **End Condition** drop-down list.

Direction of Extrusion

The **Direction of Extrusion** field is used to define the direction of extrusion for the extruded feature other than the direction normal to the sketching plane. Note that, by default, the direction of extrusion is normal to the sketching plane. To specify the direction of extrusion other than the normal direction to the sketching plane, click on the **Direction of Extrusion** field to activate it. Next, select a linear sketch entity, a linear edge, or an axis as the direction of extrusion. Figure 5.14 shows a sketch to be extruded and a sketch line as the direction of extrusion. Figure 5.15 shows the preview of the resultant extruded feature.

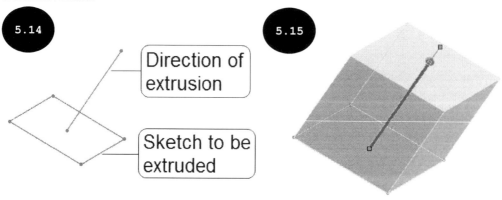

Tip: In Figure 5.14, the sketch to be extruded has been created on the Top plane and the sketch to be used as the direction of extrusion is created on the Front plane at an angle 60 degrees from the X axis.

Draft On/Off

The **Draft On/Off** button is used to add tapering in the extruded feature. By default, the **Draft On/Off** button is not activated. As a result, the resultant extruded feature is created without having any tapering in it. To add tapering in an extruded feature, click on the **Draft On/Off** button. The preview of the feature with default draft angle appears in the graphics area. Also, the **Draft Angle** field and the **Draft outward** check box are enabled in the rollout of the PropertyManager.

You can enter a draft angle in the **Draft Angle** field. By default, the **Draft outward** check box is unchecked in the rollout. As a result, the draft is added in the inward direction of the sketch, see Figure 5.16. If you select this check box, the draft will be added, outward direction of the sketch, see Figure 5.17.

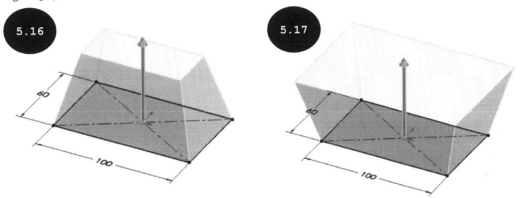

Direction 2

The options in the **Direction 2** rollout are same as those in the **Direction 1** rollout of the PropertyManager with the only difference that the options of the **Direction 2** rollout are used to specify the end condition in the second direction of the sketching plane. Note that by default, this rollout is collapsed. As a result, extrusion takes place only in one direction of the sketching plane. To add material in the second direction of the sketching plane, expand this rollout by selecting the check box in its title bar, see Figure 5.18. Figure 5.19 shows the preview of a feature, extruded on both sides of the sketching plane with different extrusion depths. Note that the **Direction 2** rollout will not be available if the **Mid Plane** option is selected in the **End Condition** drop-down list of the **Direction 1** rollout.

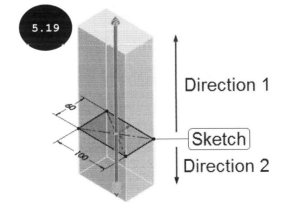

Thin Feature

The options in the **Thin Feature** rollout of the PropertyManager are used to create a thin solid feature of specified wall thickness, see Figure 5.20. By default, this rollout is collapsed. To expand the **Thin Feature** rollout, select the check box in the title bar of this rollout, see Figure 5.21. As soon as this rollout is expanded, the preview of the thin feature with the default wall thickness appears in the graphics area. The options in this rollout are as follows:

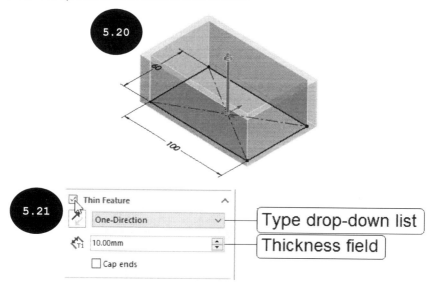

Type

The options in the **Type** drop-down list of the **Thin Feature** rollout are used to select a method to add material thickness and are as follows:

One-Direction

By default, the **One-Direction** option is selected in the **Type** drop-down list, see Figure 5.21. As a result, the thickness is added in one direction of the sketch. You can enter thickness value for the thin feature in the **Thickness** field of this rollout. To reverse the direction of thickness in either side of the sketch, click on the **Reverse Direction** button of this rollout. Figures 5.22 and 5.23 show the previews of a thin feature with material added in outward and inward directions of the sketch, respectively.

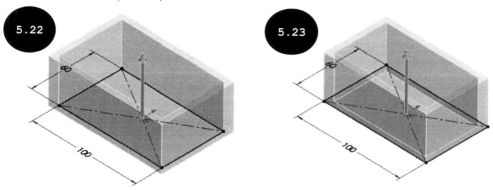

Mid-Plane
The **Mid-Plane** option of the **Type** drop-down list is used to add thickness symmetrically on both sides of the sketch. You can enter thickness value in the **Thickness** field of the rollout. Note that the thickness value entered in the **Thickness** field is divided equally on both the sides of the sketch and creates a thin feature.

Two-Direction
The **Two-Direction** option is used to add different thickness in both the directions of a sketch. As soon as you select this option, the **Direction 1 Thickness** and **Direction 2 Thickness** fields are available in the rollout. You can enter different thickness values in direction 1 and direction 2 of a sketch in the respective fields.

> **Note:** You can create a thin feature from a closed or an open sketch. Figures 5.22 and 5.23 show the preview of thin features by using closed sketches. Figure 5.24 shows the preview of a thin feature by using an open sketch. Note that if the sketch is an open sketch, then the **Thin Feature** rollout of the PropertyManager is expanded automatically for creating the thin extruded feature.

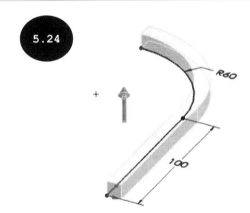

5.24

Cap ends
The **Cap ends** check box is used to close the thin feature by adding caps on its both open ends. On selecting this check box, the open ends of the thin feature are capped and a hollow thin feature is created. You can also specify required thickness for cap ends of the hollow thin feature in the **Cap Thickness** field. Note that the **Cap ends** check box is available only when you create a thin feature by using a closed sketch.

Selected Contours
The **Selected Contours** rollout of the PropertyManager is used to select the contour or closed region of a sketch for extrusion. Figure 5.25 shows a sketch with multiple contours/closed regions (3 contours/regions). Note that by default, when you extrude a sketch having multiple contours/regions, the most suitable contour/region of the sketch gets extruded, see Figure 5.26. In this figure, the contour 1 of the sketch shown in Figure 5.25 has been extruded, by default, and the remaining contours are left unextruded.

218 Chapter 5 > Creating First/Base Feature of Solid Models

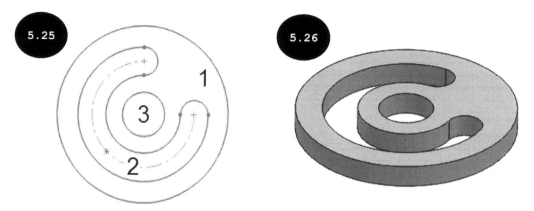

In addition to the default extrusion of the most suitable closed region of a multi-contour sketch, SOLIDWORKS allows you to select a required contour/region of a sketch to be extruded by using the **Selected Contours** rollout. To extrude a required contour of a multi-contour sketch, expand the **Selected Contours** rollout of the PropertyManager and then move the cursor over the closed region/contour of the sketch to be extruded in the graphics area and then click the left mouse button when it highlights, see Figure 5.27. As soon as you select a region, the preview of the extruded feature appears such that the material has been added to the selected closed region. You can select multiple contours/regions of a sketch to be extruded at the same time.

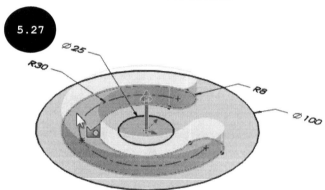

After specifying the required parameters for extruding the sketch, click on the green tick mark ✓ button in the **Boss-Extrude PropertyManager** to accept the defined parameters and create the extruded feature.

Creating a Revolved Feature

A revolved feature is a feature created such that the material is added by revolving a sketch around an axis of revolution. Note that the sketch to be revolved should be on either side of the axis of revolution. You can create a revolved feature by using the **Revolved Boss/Base** tool. Figure 5.28 shows sketches and the resultant revolved features created by revolving the sketch around the respective axes of revolution.

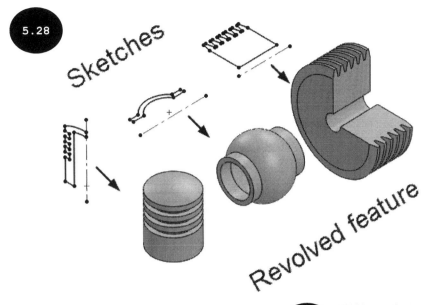

5.28

After drawing the sketch of a revolved feature and a centerline as the axis of revolution by using the sketching tools in the Sketching environment, do not exit the Sketching environment. Next, click on the **Features** tab in the CommandManager and then click on the **Revolved Boss/Base** tool. The preview of the revolved feature appears in the graphics area with default parameters. Also, the **Revolve PropertyManager** appears on the left of the graphics area, see Figure 5.29. If the preview does not appear, select a centerline as the axis of revolution. Figure 5.30 shows a sketch with a centerline created on the Front plane and Figure 5.31 shows the preview of the resultant revolved feature.

5.29

Note: If the sketch to be revolved has only one centerline, then the centerline drawn will automatically be selected as the axis of revolution and the preview of the resultant revolved feature appears in the graphics area. However, if the sketch does not have any centerline, or have two or more than two centerlines then on invoking the **Revolved Boss/Base** tool, the preview of the revolved feature does not appear and you are prompted to select a centerline as the axis of revolution. As soon as you select a centerline, the preview of the revolved feature appears in the graphics area. You can select a linear sketch entity, a centerline, an axis, or an edge as the axis of revolution.

220 Chapter 5 > Creating First/Base Feature of Solid Models

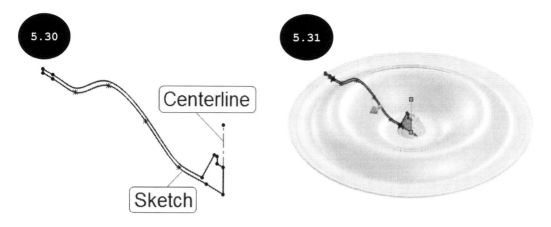

Note: If you exit the Sketching environment after creating the sketch of the revolved feature and the sketch is not selected in the graphics area, then on clicking the **Revolved Boss/Base** tool, the **Revolve PropertyManager** appears, see Figure 5.32. Also, you are prompted to select either the sketch to be revolved in the graphics area or a sketching plane for creating the sketch. As soon as you select the sketch to be revolved, the preview of the revolved feature appears in the graphics area. Also, the **Revolve PropertyManager** gets modified and appears as shown in Figure 5.29. Note that if the sketch to be revolved is not created then you can select the sketching plane for creating the sketch of the revolved feature and once the sketch has been created exit the Sketching environment.

The options in the **Revolve PropertyManager** are used to specify the parameters for the revolved feature. Some of the options of the **Revolve PropertyManager** are as follows:

Axis of Revolution
The **Axis of Revolution** field of the **Axis of Revolution** rollout in the PropertyManager is used to select the axis of revolution of the revolved feature. You can select a linear sketch entity, a centerline, an axis, or a linear edge as the axis of revolution. Note that if the sketch to be revolved is having only one centerline, then the centerline of the sketch is automatically selected as the axis of revolution on invoking the **Revolve PropertyManager**. However, if the sketch is having two or more than two centerlines then you are prompted to select the axis of revolution.

Direction 1

The options in the **Direction 1** rollout of the PropertyManager are used to define the end condition of the revolved feature in one direction. The options are as follows:

Revolve Type

The **Revolve Type** drop-down list of the **Direction 1** rollout is used to select a method for revolving the sketch, see Figure 5.33. The options of this drop-down list that are used while creating the second and further revolved features are discussed in later chapters. The options which are used for creating the base feature are as follows:

Figure 5.33

Blind

The **Blind** option of the **Revolve Type** drop-down list is used to define the end condition or termination of the revolved feature by specifying the angle of revolution. By default, this option is selected in this drop-down list. As a result, the **Direction 1 Angle** field is available in the **Direction 1** rollout. You can enter the required angle value in this field.

Mid Plane

The **Mid Plane** option is used to revolve a sketch about a centerline, symmetrically in both sides of the sketching plane, see Figure 5.34. After selecting this option, you can enter the angle of revolution in the **Direction 1 Angle** field of the rollout. Depending upon the angle value entered in this field, material is added symmetrically on both sides of the sketching plane by revolving the sketch about the axis of revolution.

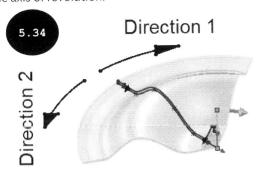

Figure 5.34

> **Note:** The **Up To Vertex**, **Up To Surface**, and **Offset From Surface** options of the **Revolve Type** drop-down list are discussed in the later chapters.

Reverse Direction

The **Reverse Direction** button of the rollout is used to reverse the direction of revolution from one side of the sketching plane to the other side. This option is not available if the **Mid Plane** option is selected in the **Revolve Type** drop-down list of the PropertyManager.

Direction 2

The options in the **Direction 2** rollout are same as those in the **Direction 1** rollout of the PropertyManager with the only difference that the options of the **Direction 2** rollout are used to specify the end condition of the revolved feature in the second direction of the sketching plane. Note that by default, this rollout is collapsed. As a result, the material is added only in one direction of the sketching plane by revolving the sketch. To add material in the second direction of the sketching plane, expand this rollout by selecting the check box in its title bar, see Figure 5.35. Figure 5.36 shows a preview of a revolved feature with different revolving angles in direction 1 and direction 2 of the sketching plane. Note that the **Direction 2** rollout will not be available if the **Mid Plane** option is selected in the **Revolve Type** drop-down list of the **Direction 1** rollout.

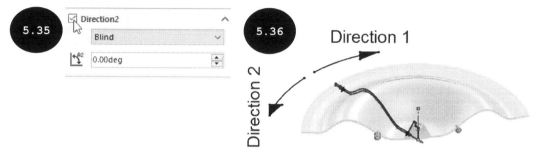

Thin Feature

The options in the **Thin Feature** rollout are used to create a thin revolved feature with a uniform wall thickness, see Figure 5.37. By default, this rollout is collapsed and the options in this rollout are not activated. To expand the **Thin Feature** rollout, click on the check box in its title bar. As soon as the **Thin Feature** rollout expands, the preview of the thin feature with default parameters appears in the graphics area. The options in this rollout are the same as discussed earlier, while creating the thin extruded feature.

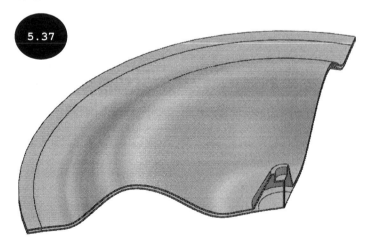

Selected Contours

The **Selected Contours** rollout is used to select contours or closed regions of a multi-contour sketch. To revolve a contour of a multi-contour sketch, expand the **Selected Contours** rollout of the PropertyManager and then move the cursor over a closed contour of the sketch to be revolved. Next, click on the closed contour when it highlights in the graphics area. The preview of the revolved feature appears such that material has been added by revolving the selected contour about the centerline.

Navigating a 3D Model in Graphics Area

In SOLIDWORKS, you can navigate a model by using the mouse buttons and the navigating tools. You can access the navigating tools in the **View (Heads-Up)** toolbar, see Figure 5.38. You can also access the navigating tools in the SOLIDWORKS menus or in the shortcut menu which appears on right-clicking in the graphics area. Different navigating tools are as follows:

Zoom In/Out

You can zoom in or out the graphics area, dynamically, by using the **Zoom In/Out** tool. In other words, you can enlarge or reduce the view of the model, dynamically, by using the **Zoom In/Out** tool. To zoom in or out a model in the graphics area, invoke the **Zoom In/Out** tool either from the SOLIDWORKS menus or the shortcut menu. You can also use the middle mouse button to zoom in or out in the graphics area.

To invoke the **Zoom In/Out** tool from the SOLIDWORKS menus, click on the **View** menu in the SOLIDWORKS menu and then move the cursor over the **Modify** option. A cascading menu appears, see Figure 5.39. Next, click on the **Zoom In/Out** tool in the cascading menu. The cursor changes to the **Zoom In/Out** cursor. Once the **Zoom In/Out** tool has been invoked, move the cursor in the graphics area and then press and hold the left mouse button. Next, drag the cursor upward or downward in the graphics area. On dragging the cursor upward, the view gets enlarged; and on dragging the cursor downward, the view gets reduced. Note that in the process of zoom in or zoom out the view, the scale of the model remains the same. However, the viewing distance gets modified in order to enlarge or reduce the view of the model.

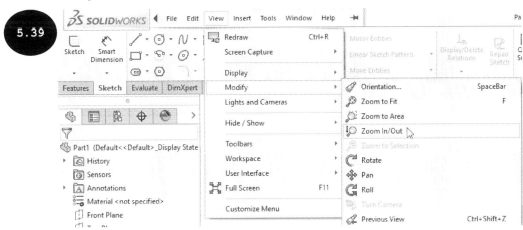

Alternatively, you can invoke the **Zoom In/Out** tool from the shortcut menu. To invoke the **Zoom In/Out** tool from the shortcut menu, right-click in the graphics area. A shortcut menu appears, see Figure 5.40. In the shortcut menu, click on the **Zoom In/Out** tool. Once the tool has been invoked, the procedure to zoom in or out a model in the graphics area is the same as discussed earlier.

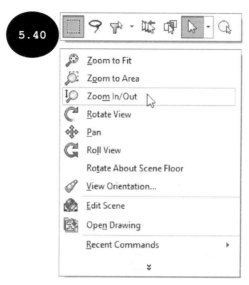

You can also zoom in or zoom out the graphics area by scrolling the middle mouse button. In addition, you can press and hold the SHIFT key plus the middle mouse button and then drag the cursor in the graphics area up and down to zoom in or zoom out the graphics area, respectively.

Zoom To Fit

The **Zoom To Fit** tool is used to fit a model completely inside the graphics area. To fit the model in the graphics area, invoke the **Zoom To Fit** tool from the SOLIDWORKS menus, shortcut menu, or **View (Heads-Up)** toolbar. You can also press the **F** key to fit the model completely inside the graphics area.

To fit the model completely inside the graphics area, click on the **Zoom To Fit** tool in the **View (Heads-Up)** toolbar. Alternatively, click on **View > Modify > Zoom to Fit** in the SOLIDWORKS menu. You can also invoke this tool from the shortcut menu which is displayed on right-clicking in the graphics area.

Zoom to Area

The **Zoom to Area** tool is used to zoom a particular portion or area of a model by defining a boundary box. To zoom a particular area of a model, invoke the **Zoom to Area** tool from the **View (Heads-Up)** toolbar, the SOLIDWORKS menus, or shortcut menu.

Once the **Zoom To Area** tool has been invoked, define a boundary box by dragging the cursor around the portion or area of a model to be zoomed, the area inside the boundary box gets enlarged.

Zoom to Selection

The **Zoom to Selection** tool is used to fit a selected object or geometry completely in the graphics area. To fit a selected object or geometry in the graphics area, invoke the **Zoom to Selection** tool by clicking on **View > Modify > Zoom to Selection** in the SOLIDWORKS menu. Note that this tool gets enabled only if the object to be fitted is selected in the graphics area.

Pan

The **Pan** tool is used to pan/move a model in the graphics area. You can invoke this tool from the SOLIDWORKS menus as well as from the shortcut menu. Once the **Pan** tool has been invoked, you can pan the model in the graphics area by dragging the cursor after pressing and holding the left mouse button. Alternatively, you can also pan the model by pressing the **CTRL** key and the middle mouse button.

Rotate

The **Rotate** tool is used to rotate a model freely in the graphics area. To rotate a model, invoke the **Rotate** tool by clicking on **View > Modify > Rotate** in the SOLIDWORKS menus. You can also invoke this tool from the shortcut menu that appears on right-clicking in the graphics area. After invoking the **Rotate** tool, press and hold the left mouse button and then drag the cursor to rotate the model freely in the graphics area.

Manipulating View Orientation of a Model

The manipulation of view orientation of a 3D model is very important in order to review a model from different views and angle. In SOLIDWORKS, you can manipulate the orientation of a 3D model to predefined standard views such as front, top, right, side, bottom, and isometric by using the **View Orientation** flyout, **Orientation** dialog box, **Reference Triad**, or **View Selector Cube**, see Figure 5.41. In addition to the predefined standard views, you can also create custom views. Various methods to manipulate the orientation of a model are as follows:

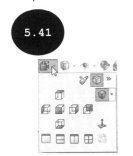
View Orientation flyout

Orientation dialog box

Reference Triad

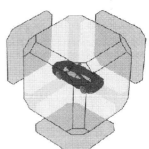
View Selector Cube

Manipulating View Orientation by using the View Orientation flyout

To manipulate the orientation of a model by using the **View Orientation** flyout, click on the down arrow next to the **View Orientation** tool in the **View (Heads-Up)** toolbar. The **View Orientation** flyout appears, see Figure 5.42. By using the tools of the **View Orientation** flyout, you can manipulate the orientation of a model. The tools are as follows:

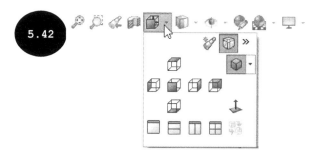

Top/Front/Right/Left/Bottom/Back/Isometric

The **Top**, **Front**, **Right**, **Left**, **Bottom**, **Back**, and **Isometric** tools of the **View Orientation** flyout are used to display predefined standard views such as front, top, right, and isometric of a model in the graphics area.

Normal To

The **Normal To** tool of the **View Orientation** flyout is used to display the selected face of a 3D model normal to the viewing direction. If you are in the Sketching environment, then you can use this tool to make the current sketching plane normal to the viewing direction.

View Drop-Down list

The tools in the **View** drop-down list of the **View Orientation** flyout are used to display the isometric, dimetric, or the trimetric view of a model. Figure 5.43 shows the **View** drop-down list of the **View Orientation** flyout. By default, the **Trimetric** tool is activated in this drop-down list. As a result, on invoking the **View Orientation** flyout, the trimetric view of the model is displayed in the graphics area. You can activate the required tool to display the respective view of the model.

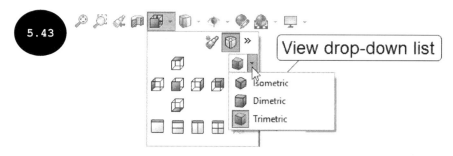

View Selector tool

The **View Selector** tool of the **View Orientation** flyout is used to display the **View Selector Cube** around the 3D model available in the graphics area, refer to Figure 5.44. By default, this tool is activated. As a result, on invoking the **View Orientation** flyout, the **View Selector Cube** appears in the graphics area around the model. Note that the orientation of the model inside the **View Selector Cube** depends upon the tool activated in the **View** drop-down list of the flyout.

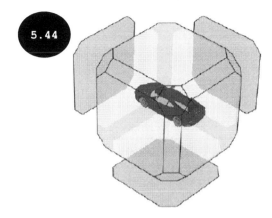

5.44

You can use the faces of the **View Selector Cube** to manipulate the orientation of the model. You will learn more about manipulating the orientation of the model by using the **View Selector Cube** later in this chapter.

New View

The **New View** tool is used to create a custom or user defined view of a model. To create a custom view, first set the orientation of the model, as required, by using different navigating tools. Once it is done, click on the **New View** tool. The **Named View** dialog box appears. In the **View name** field of this dialog box, enter the name of the custom view and then click on the **OK** button. The view is created and the name of the view created is added in the **View Orientation** flyout. You can display the model as per the custom view created at any time by clicking on its name in the **View Orientation** flyout. Similarly, you can create multiple custom views of a model.

Manipulating View Orientation by using the Orientation dialog box

To manipulate the view orientation of a model by using the **Orientation** dialog box, press the SPACEBAR key. As soon as you do so, the **Orientation** dialog box appears in the graphics area with the **View Selector** tool activated by default. As a result, the **View Selector Cube** appears around the 3D model available in the graphics area, refer to Figure 5.44. Most of the tools available in the **Orientation** dialog box are the same as discussed earlier and the remaining tools are as follows:

Pin/Unpin the dialog

The **Pin/Unpin the dialog** tool is used to pin the dialog box in the graphics area. By default, this tool is not activated. As a result, when you invoke a view such as front, top, or right of a model by clicking on the respective tool in the **Orientation** dialog box. The view of the model is invoked and the dialog box is disappeared or closed. If you do not want to exit the dialog box, click to active the **Pin/Unpin the dialog** tool in the dialog box.

Previous View
The **Previous View** tool is used to orient a model to its previous orientation. Note that you can undo the last ten views of the model by using this tool.

Update Standard Views
The **Update Standard Views** tool is used to update or change the default view of predefined standard views such as top, front, and right of a model. To update or change a standard view, first orient the 3D model in the graphics area according to your requirement and then click on the **Update Standard Views** tool. Next, click on the required standard tool such as **Top** and **Front** in the **Orientation** dialog box. The SOLIDWORKS message window appears. The message window informs that changing the standard view will change the orientation of the standard orthogonal view of this model. Click on the **Yes** button to make this change. The selected standard view gets updated to the current display of the model in the graphics area.

Reset Standard Views
The **Reset Standard Views** tool is used to reset all the standard views back to the default settings. If you have updated any of the standard views as per your requirement and you want to back to the default standard view orientation, click on the **Reset Standard Views** tool. The SOLIDWORKS message window appears. The message window asks you whether you want to reset all the standard views to the default settings. In this message window, click on the **Yes** button to reset all the views to the default settings.

Manipulating View Orientation by using the View Selector Cube
You can manipulate the view orientation of a model by using the **View Selector Cube**. Manipulating the view orientation of a model by using the **View Selector Cube** is one of the easiest ways to achieve different views such as right, left, front, back, top, and isometric of a 3D model. By default, on invoking the **View Orientation** flyout and the **Orientation** dialog box, the **View Selector Cube** appears around the 3D model available in the graphics area because the **View Selection** tool is activated in the **View Orientation** flyout as well as in the **Orientation** dialog box by default.

To manipulate the orientation of a 3D model by using the **View Selector Cube**, move the cursor to a face of the **View Selector Cube**. The face gets highlighted and the **Preview** window appears at the upper right corner of the graphics area. Next, click on the face, see Figure 5.45. The model is oriented depending upon the face of the **View Selector Cube** selected.

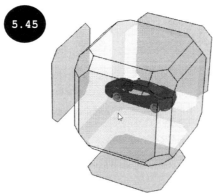
5.45

Note: The default orientation of a model inside the **View Selector Cube** depends upon the tool activated in the **View** drop-down list of the **View Orientation** flyout as well as in the **Orientation** dialog box.

Manipulating View Orientation by using the Reference Triad

The reference triad appears at the lower left corner of the graphics area and guides you while orienting a model in different views. You can also use the reference triad to manipulate the view orientation of a model normal to the screen, 180 degrees, or 90 degrees about an axis.

To orient the model normal to the screen, click on an axis of the triad. The model gets oriented normal to the screen with respect to the selected axis of the triad. Note that the direction of axis selected becomes normal to the screen. To orient the model by 180 degrees, click on the axis that is normal to the screen. To orient the model by 90 degrees about an axis, press the SHIFT key and then click on an axis as the axis of rotation.

You can also rotate the model at a predefined angle specified in the **System Options - View** dialog box. For rotating the model at a predefined angle, press the ALT key and then click on an axis of the triad. To specify the predefined angle, click on the **Options** tool in the **Standard** toolbar. The **System Options - General** dialog box appears. In this dialog box, click on the **View** option in the left panel of the dialog box. The name of the dialog box changes to **System Options - View**. By using the **Arrow keys** field of this dialog box, you can specify the predefined angle for rotation by using the triad.

Changing the Display Style of a Model

You can change the display style of a 3D model to wireframe, hidden lines visible, hidden lines removed, shaded, and shaded with edges display styles. The tools used to change the display style of the model are available in the **Display Style** flyout of the **View (Heads-Up)** toolbar, see Figure 5.46. The tools are as follows:

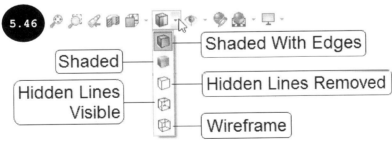

Shaded With Edges

The **Shaded With Edges** tool is used to display a model in 'shaded with edges' display style. In this style, the model is displayed in shaded mode with the display of outer edges turned on, see Figure 5.47. This tool is activated by default. As a result, the model is displayed in 'shaded with edges' display style in the graphics area, by default.

Shaded

The **Shaded** tool is used to display a model in 'shaded' display style. In this style, the model is displayed in shaded mode with the display of edges turned off, see Figure 5.48.

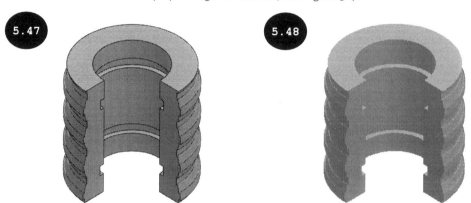

Hidden Lines Removed

The **Hidden Lines Removed** tool is used to display a model in 'hidden lines removed' display style. In this style, the hidden lines of the model are not visible in the display of the model, see Figure 5.49.

Hidden Lines Visible

The **Hidden Lines Visible** tool is used to display a model in 'hidden lines visible' display style. In this style, the visibility of the hidden lines of the model is turned on and appears in dotted lines, see Figure 5.50.

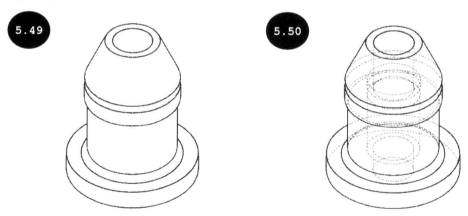

Wireframe

The **Wireframe** tool is used to display a model in 'wireframe' display style. In this style, the hidden lines of the model are displayed in solid lines, see Figure 5.51.

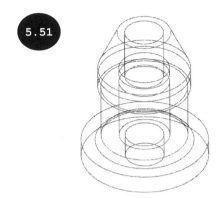

Changing the View of a Model

In SOLIDWORKS, you can change the view of a model to perspective, shadows, ambient occlusion, and cartoon effect by using the tools in the **View Settings** flyout of the **View (Heads-Up)** toolbar, see Figure 5.52. The tools are as follows:

Shadows In Shaded Mode

The **Shadows In Shaded Mode** tool is used to display a model with its shadow, see Figure 5.53. In this view of the model, the shadow appears at the bottom of the model as the light appears from the top. Note that the shadow of the model rotates in accordance with the rotation of the model.

Perspective

The **Perspective** tool is used to display the perspective view of a model, see Figure 5.54. A perspective view appears as it is viewed normally from the eyes. Note that the perspective view depends upon the size of the model and the distance between the model and the viewer.

Ambient Occlusion

The **Ambient Occlusion** tool is used to display the ambient view of a model. The ambient view is displayed due to the attenuation of the ambient light.

Cartoon

The **Cartoon** tool is used to display the cartoon rendering view of a model. The cartoon rendering view is displayed by adding a non-photorealistic cartoon effect to a model.

Tutorial 1

Open the sketch created in Tutorial 1 of Chapter 4, see Figure 5.55, and then create the model by extruding it to the depth of 40 mm, see Figure 5.56.

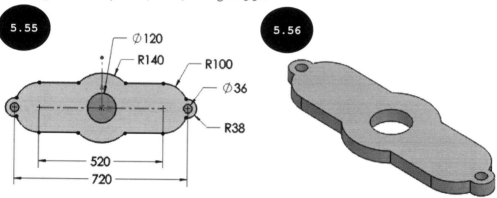

Section 1: Starting SOLIDWORKS

Start SOLIDWORKS software.

1. Double-click on the SOLIDWORKS icon on your desktop to start SOLIDWORKS, if not started already.

Section 2: Opening the Sketch of Tutorial 1, Chapter 4

Now, you need to open the sketch of Tutorial 1 created in Chapter 4.

1. Click on the **Open** tool in the **Standard** toolbar. The **Open** dialog box appears.

2. Browse to the *Tutorial* folder of *Chapter 4* and then select the **Tutorial 1** file.

3. Click on the **Open** button in the dialog box. The sketch of Tutorial 1 created in Chapter 4 is opened in the current session of SOLIDWORKS, see Figure 5.57.

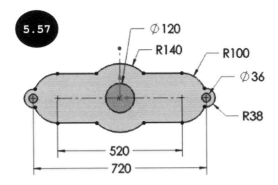

Figure 5.57

Section 3: Saving the Sketch

Now, you need to save the sketch with the name "Tutorial 1" in *Chapter 5* folder.

1. Click on **File > Save As** in the SOLIDWORKS menus. The **Save As** dialog box appears.

2. Browse to the *SOLIDWORKS* folder and then create a folder with the name **Chapter 5** in it. Next, create another folder with the name **Tutorial** in the *Chapter 5* folder.

3. Click on the **Save** button to save the sketch in the *Tutorial* folder of *Chapter 5*.

Note: It is important to save the sketch in different locations or different names before making any modification, so that the original file does not get modified.

Section 4: Extruding the Sketch

Now, you can extrude the sketch and convert it into a feature.

1. Click on the **Features** tab in the CommandManager. The tools of the **Features** CommandManager are displayed, see Figure 5.58.

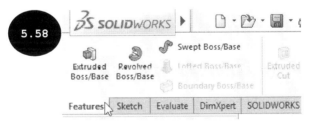

Figure 5.58

2. Click on the **Extruded Boss/Base** tool in the **Features Command Manager**. The **Boss-Extrude** PropertyManager and the preview of the extruded feature appear, see Figure 5.59. Also, the orientation of the model changes to Trimetric.

Note: If the **Extruded Boss/Base** tool is invoked without exiting the Sketching environment, then the preview of the feature appears in the graphics area, automatically. However, if you invoke the **Extruded Boss/Base** tool after exiting the Sketching environment, then you need to select the sketch to be extruded before or after invoking the tool.

234 Chapter 5 > Creating First/Base Feature of Solid Models

3. Enter 40 in the Depth field of the Direction 1 rollout in the PropertyManager and then press ENTER. The default depth of the extruded feature changes to 40 mm.

4. Click on the green tick mark ✓ in the PropertyManager. The extruded feature is created, see Figure 5.60.

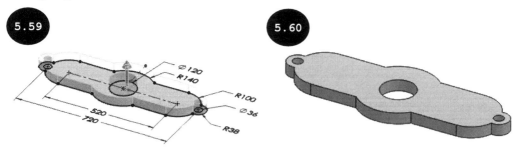

Section 5: Saving the Model
Now, you need to save the model.

1. Click on the **Save** tool in the **Standard** toolbar. The model is saved with the name **Tutorial 1** in the *Tutorial* folder of *Chapter 5*.

Tutorial 2

Open the sketch created in Tutorial 2 of Chapter 4, see Figure 5.61, and then revolve it around the vertical centerline to an angle of 270 degrees, see Figure 5.62. Also, change the display style of the model to the 'hidden lines removed' display style.

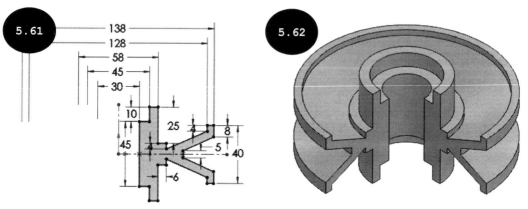

Section 1: Starting SOLIDWORKS
Start SOLIDWORKS software.

1. Double-click on the SOLIDWORKS icon on your desktop to start SOLIDWORKS, if not started already.

Section 2: Opening the Sketch of Tutorial 2, Chapter 4

Now, you need to open the sketch of Tutorial 2 created in Chapter 4.

1. Click on the **Open** tool in the **Standard** toolbar. The **Open** dialog box appears.

2. Browse to the *Tutorial* folder of *Chapter 4* and then select the **Tutorial 2** file.

3. Click on the **Open** button in the dialog box. The sketch of Tutorial 2 created in Chapter 4 is opened in the current session of SOLIDWORKS, see Figure 5.63.

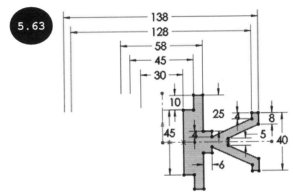

Section 3: Saving the Sketch

Now, you need to save the sketch.

1. Click on **File > Save As** in the SOLIDWORKS menus. The **Save As** dialog box appears.

2. Browse to the *Tutorial* folder of *Chapter 5* and then save the sketch in it. If these folders are not created then you need to first create these folders in the *SOLIDWORKS* folder.

Section 4: Revolving the Sketch

1. Click on the **Features** tab in the CommandManager. The tools of the **Features** CommandManager are displayed, see Figure 5.64.

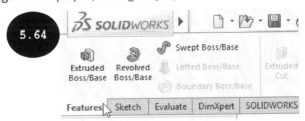

2. Click on the **Revolved Boss/Base** tool in the **Features Command Manager**. The **Revolve PropertyManager** appears and the orientation of the sketch changes to Trimetric orientation.

236 Chapter 5 > Creating First/Base Feature of Solid Models

Note: If the sketch to be revolved has only one centerline, then the centerline drawn will automatically be selected as the axis of revolution and the preview of the resultant revolved feature appears in the graphics area. However, if the sketch has two or more than two centerlines then on invoking the **Revolved Boss/Base** tool, you are prompted to select a centerline as the axis of revolution.

3. Select the vertical centerline as the axis of revolution. The preview of the revolved feature appears in the graphics area, see Figure 5.65.

4. Enter **270** degrees in the **Direction 1 Angle** field of the **Direction 1** rollout in the PropertyManager and then press the ENTER key.

5. Click on the green tick mark ✓ in the PropertyManager. The revolved feature is created, see Figure 5.66. You can change the orientation of the model by using the tools available in the **View Orientation** flyout of the **View (Heads-Up)** toolbar, see Figure 5.67.

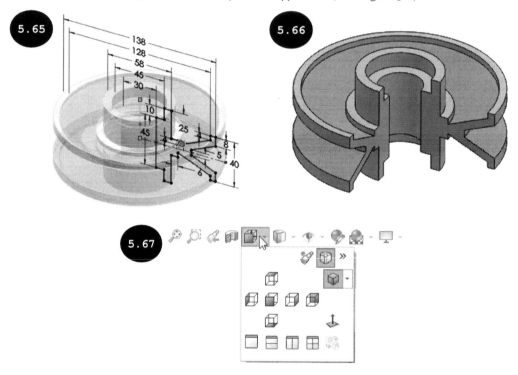

Section 5: Changing the Display Style

As mentioned in the tutorial description, you need to change the display style of the model to the 'hidden lines removed' display style.

1. Invoke the **Display Style** flyout of the **View (Heads-Up)** toolbar, see Figure 5.68.

2. Click on the **Hidden Lines Removed** tool in the **Display Style** flyout. The display style of the model is changed to 'hidden lines removed' display style, see Figure 5.69.

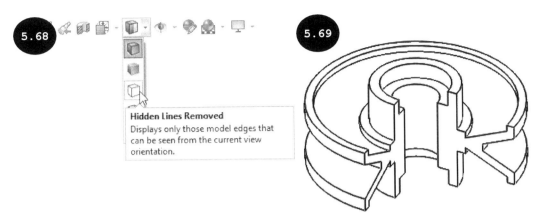

Section 6: Saving the Model

Now, you need to save the model.

1. Click on the **Save** tool in the **Standard** toolbar. The model is saved with the name **Tutorial 2** in the *Tutorial* folder of *Chapter 5*.

Tutorial 3

Open the sketch created in Tutorial 3 of Chapter 4, see Figure 5.70, and then extrude it to the depth of 60 mm symmetrically about the sketching plane, see Figure 5.71. Also, change the view orientation of the model to isometric and navigate the model in the graphics area.

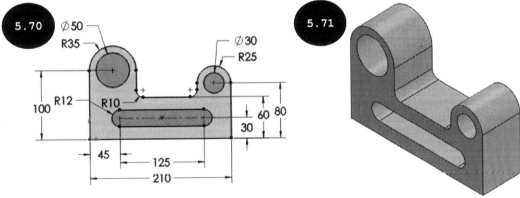

Section 1: Starting SOLIDWORKS

Start SOLIDWORKS software.

1. Start SOLIDWORKS, if not started already.

Section 2: Opening the Sketch of Tutorial 3, Chapter 4

Now, you need to open the sketch of Tutorial 3 created in Chapter 4.

1. Click on the **Open** tool in the **Standard** toolbar. The **Open** dialog box appears.

238 Chapter 5 > Creating First/Base Feature of Solid Models

2. Browse to the *Tutorial* folder of *Chapter 4* and then open the **Tutorial 3** file, see Figure 5.72.

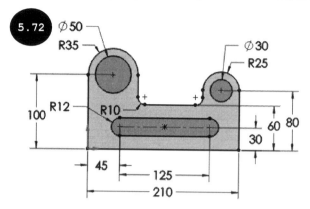

Section 3: Saving the Sketch
Now, you need to save the sketch as the Tutorial 3 of Chapter 5.

1. Click on **File > Save As** in the SOLIDWORKS menus. The **Save As** dialog box appears.

2. Browse to the *Tutorial* folder of *Chapter 5* and then save the sketch in it with the name **Tutorial 3**.

Section 4: Extruding the Sketch
Now, you can extrude the sketch and convert it into an extruded feature.

1. Click on the **Features** tab in the CommandManager to display the tools of the **Features** CommandManager.

2. Click on the **Extruded Boss/Base** tool in the Features Command Manager. The **Boss-Extrude** PropertyManager and the preview of the extruded feature appear, see Figure 5.73.

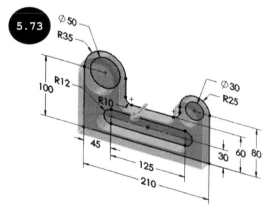

3. Enter **60** in the **Depth** field of the **Direction 1** rollout and then press the ENTER key. The depth of the extruded feature is modified to 60 mm.

4. Invoke the **End Condition** drop-down list of the **Direction 1** rollout, see Figure 5.74.

5. Click on the **Mid Plane** option in the **End Condition** drop-down list. The depth of the extrusion is modified such that it is added symmetrically on both sides of the sketching plane, see Figure 5.75.

6. Click on the green tick mark ✓ in the PropertyManager. The extruded feature is created symmetrically about the Sketching plane, see Figure 5.76.

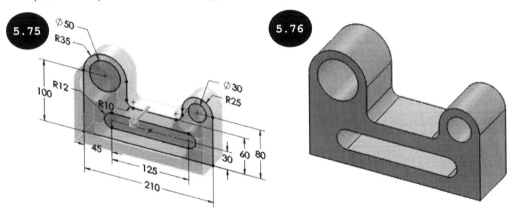

Section 5: Changing the Orientation to Isometric

1. Invoke the **View Orientation** flyout in the **View (Heads-Up)** toolbar, see Figure 5.77. The **View Selector Cube** appears around the model in the graphics area, see Figure 5.78.

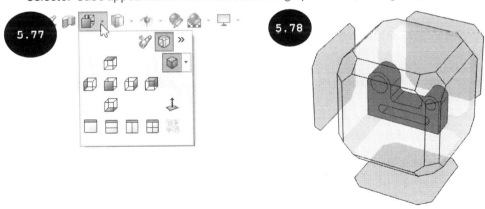

240   Chapter 5 > Creating First/Base Feature of Solid Models

Tip: You can change the view orientation of the model by using the tools of the **View Orientation** flyout or by using the **View Selector Cube**.

2. Invoke the **View** drop-down list in the **View Orientation** flyout, see Figure 5.79. Next, click on the **Isometric** option. The view orientation of the model changes to isometric.

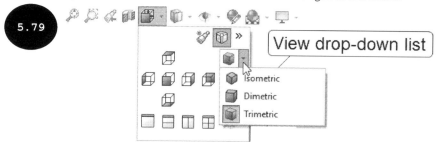

Section 6: Navigating the Model
Now, you need to navigate the model.

1. Right-click in the graphics area. A shortcut menu appears, see Figure 5.80.

2. Click on the **Zoom In/Out** tool in the shortcut menu. The **Zoom In/Out** tool is invoked and the cursor changes to zoom cursor.

3. Press and hold the left mouse button and then drag the cursor upward or downward in the graphics area. On dragging the cursor upward, the view of the model enlarges and on dragging the cursor downward, the view of the model reduces.

4. Once you are done with zoom in and out, right-click and then click on the **Select** tool from the shortcut menu displayed to exit the tool.

5. Similarly, you can invoke the remaining navigating tools such as **Rotate View** and **Pan** to navigate the model.

Section 7: Saving the Model
Now, you need to save the model.

1. Click on the **Save** button in the **Standard** toolbar. The model is saved with the name **Tutorial 3** in the *Tutorial* folder of *Chapter 5*.

Hands-on Test Drive 1

Create the revolved model as shown in Figure 5.81.

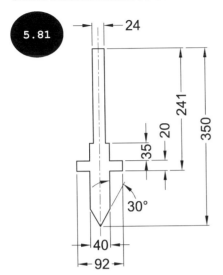

Hands-on Test Drive 2

Create the extruded model as shown in Figure 5.82.

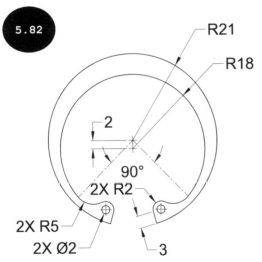
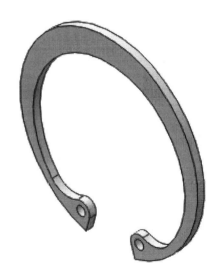

Summary

In this chapter, you have learned about creating the solid and thin extruded as well as revolved base features by using the **Extruded Boss/Base** and **Revolved Boss/Base** tools. An extruded feature is created by adding material normal or at an angle to the sketching plane. A revolved feature is created by revolving a sketch around an axis of revolution. You have also learned how to navigate a model by using the mouse buttons and the navigating tools such as **Zoom In/Out** and **Zoom To Fit**. You can also manipulate the view orientation of the model to the predefined standard views such as front, top, right, side, and custom views. Moreover, in this chapter, you have learned about changing the display style and view of the model.

Questions

- The _____ tool is used to create feature by adding material normal to the sketching plane.

- The _____ tool is used to create feature by revolving the sketch around a centerline as the axis of revolution.

- The _____ tool is used to fit a model completely inside the graphics area.

- The _____ tool of the **View Orientation** flyout is used to display the **View Selector Cube** around the 3D model available in the graphics area.

- The _____ button of the **Boss-Extrude PropertyManager** is used to taper the extrude feature.

- The _____ option is used to extrude/revolve a feature symmetrically about the sketching plane.

- You can only create a thin feature from an open sketch. (True/False).

- In SOLIDWORKS, manipulating the view orientation of a model by using the **View Selector Cube** is one of the easiest ways to achieve different views such as right, left, and isometric. (True/False).

- In SOLIDWORKS, you cannot navigate a model by using the mouse buttons. (True/False).

- While creating a revolved feature, if the sketch to be revolved has only one centerline, then the drawn centerline is automatically selected as the axis of revolution (True/False).

CHAPTER 6

Creating Reference Geometries

In this chapter, you will learn the following:

- Creating Reference Planes
- Creating a Reference Axis
- Creating a Reference Coordinate System
- Creating a Reference Point

In SOLIDWORKS, three default reference planes such as Front, Top, and Right are available, by default. You can use these reference planes to create the base feature of a model by extruding or revolving the sketch, as discussed in earlier chapters. However, to create a real world model having multiple features, you may need additional reference planes. In other words, the three default reference planes may not be enough for creating all features of a real world model and you may need to create additional reference planes. SOLIDWORKS allows you to create additional reference planes for creating real world models, as required. You can create additional reference planes by using the **Plane** tool, which is available in the **Reference Geometry** flyout of the **Features CommandManager**, see Figure 6.1.

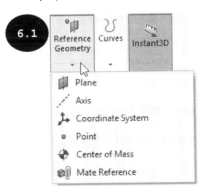

244 Chapter 6 > Creating Reference Geometries

Figure 6.2 shows a multiple-feature model, which is created by creating all its features one by one. This model has six features. Its first feature is an extruded feature created on the Top plane; the second feature is an extruded feature created on the top planar face of the first feature; the third feature is a cut feature created on the top planar face of the second feature; the fourth feature is a user-defined reference plane created by using the **Plane** tool; the fifth feature is an extruded feature created on the user-defined reference plane; and the sixth feature is a circular pattern of the fifth feature.

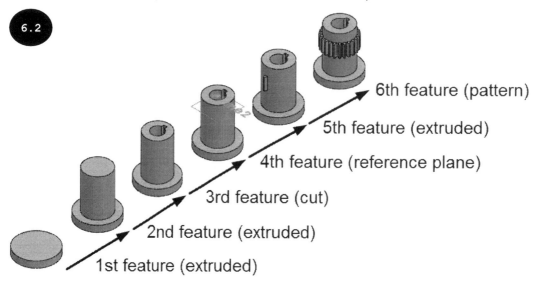

Note: It is clear from the above figure that additional reference planes may be required for creating features of a model.

Creating Reference Planes

In SOLIDWORKS, you can create reference planes at an offset distance from an existing plane or planar face; parallel to an existing plane or planar face; at an angle to an existing plane or planar face; normal to a curve by using the **Plane** tool.

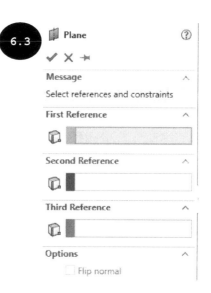

To create a reference plane, click on the down arrow in the **Reference Geometry** tool of the **Features** CommandManager. The **Reference Geometry** flyout appears, refer to Figure 6.1. In this flyout, click on the **Plane** tool. The **Plane PropertyManager** appears, see Figure 6.3. The options in this PropertyManager are used to create different types of reference planes and are as follows:

Message

The **Message** rollout of the PropertyManager displays appropriate information about the action to be taken in creating a reference plane as well as displays the current status of the reference plane. If the current status of the plane is displayed as fully defined, then it means all the required references for creating the plane have been defined. Note that the background color of the rollout changes to green as soon as the status of the plane becomes fully defined. Also, note that for creating a fully defined reference plane, maximum three references are required.

First Reference

The **First Reference** rollout is used to define the first reference for a plane. You can select a face, a plane, a vertex, a point, an edge, or a curve as the first reference for creating a plane. Note that the selection of a reference depends upon the type of plane to be created. For example, to create a plane at an offset distance from a planar face of a model, you need to select the planar face of the model as the first reference. As soon as you select the first reference, the **First Reference** rollout expands with the display of all possible relations and options that can be applied between the selected reference and the plane, see Figure 6.4. Also, the most suitable relation is selected by default in the expanded rollout. Figure 6.4 shows the expanded **First Reference** rollout when a planar face is selected as the first reference. If you select a planar face or a plane as the first reference, then the **Offset distance** button gets selected, by default in the rollout, which allows you to specify the offset distance between the selected planar face and the plane. The different relations and options of the expanded **First Reference** rollout are as follows:

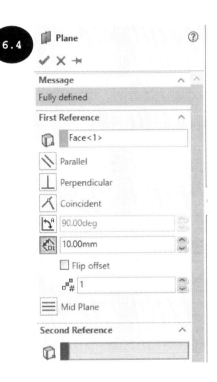

6.4

Coincident

The **Coincident** button is used to create a reference plane that passes through a selected reference (a planar face, a plane, a vertex, or a point). Note that on selecting the **Coincident** button, the coincident relation is applied between the selected reference and the plane.

Parallel

The **Parallel** button is used to create a reference plane parallel to a selected reference (a planar face or a plane). On selecting the **Parallel** button, the parallel relation is applied between the selected reference and the plane. Note that for creating a plane parallel to a planar face or a plane, you also need to select a second reference. You will learn more about creating parallel planes later in this chapter.

Perpendicular

The **Perpendicular** button is used to create a reference plane perpendicular to a selected reference (a planar face or a plane). On selecting the **Perpendicular** button, the perpendicular relation is applied between the selected reference and the plane. Note that for creating a plane perpendicular to a planar face or a plane, you also need to select a second reference. You will learn more about creating perpendicular planes later in this chapter.

Tangent

The **Tangent** button is used to create a reference plane tangent to a selected reference (a cylindrical, a conical, a non-cylindrical, or a non-planar face). On selecting the **Tangent** button, the tangent relation is applied between the selected reference and the plane. Note that for creating a plane tangent to a cylindrical, a conical, a non-cylindrical, or a non-planar face, you also need to select a second reference (an edge, an axis, or a sketch line). You will learn more about creating tangent planes later in this chapter.

At angle

The **At angle** button is used to create a reference plane at an angle to a selected reference (a planar face, a cylindrical face, or a plane). Note that for creating a plane at an angle to a cylindrical face, a planar face, or a plane, you also need to select a second reference (an edge, an axis, or a sketch line). You will learn more about creating planes at an angle later in this chapter.

Mid Plane

The **Mid Plane** button is used to create a reference plane in the middle of two planar faces. Note that for creating a mid plane, you need to select two planar faces as the first and second references.

Project

The **Project** button is used to create a reference plane by projecting a point, a vertex, an origin, or a coordinate system into a non-planar face.

Offset distance

The **Offset distance** button is used to create a reference plane at an offset distance from the selected reference.

Parallel to screen

The **Parallel to screen** button is used to create a plane normal to the viewing direction and passing through a vertex. Note that this button is enabled in the PropertyManager when you select a vertex as the first reference.

Number of planes to create

You can specify the number of planes to be created in the **Number of planes to create** field of the PropertyManager. By default, the value entered in this field is 1. As a result, only one reference plane is created with the specified parameters. Note that this field is enabled only when the **At angle** or **Offset distance** button is selected in the PropertyManager.

Second Reference

The **Second Reference** rollout is used to define the second reference for creating a reference plane. The options in this rollout are same as those discussed in the **First Reference** rollout. You need to define the second reference while creating planes such as plane at an angle, plane tangent to a cylindrical face, plane perpendicular to a planar face, and so on. You will learn more about creating different types of planes by specifying second reference later in this chapter.

Third Reference

The **Third Reference** rollout is used to define the third reference for creating a reference plane. The options in this rollout are same as those discussed in the **First Reference** rollout. You need to define the third reference while creating a reference plane, which passes through three points or vertices.

In SOLIDWORKS, you need to focus more on creating reference planes rather than selecting options in the **Plane PropertyManager**. This is because when you select a reference geometry for creating a plane, the most suitable option gets automatically selected in the PropertyManager. Also, the preview of the respective reference plane appears in the graphics area. The procedure to create different types of reference planes are as follows:

Creating a Plane at an Offset Distance

1. Click on the down arrow in the **Reference Geometry** tool of the **Features CommandManager**. The **Reference Geometry** flyout appears.
2. Click on the **Plane** tool in the **Reference Geometry** flyout. The **Plane PropertyManager** appears.
3. Click on a planar face or a plane in the graphics area as the first reference. The preview of the offset plane appears, see Figure 6.5.
4. Enter the required offset distance value in the **Distance** field, which is available in front of the **Offset distance** button.
5. To flip the direction of the creation of plane, click on the **Flip offset** check box, see Figure 6.6.
6. Click on the green tick mark ✓ in the PropertyManager. The reference plane at the specified offset distance is created.

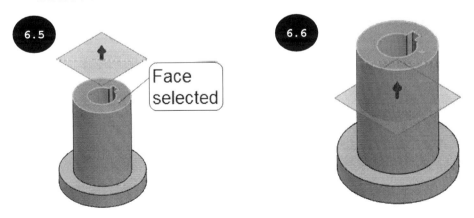

Creating a Parallel Plane

1. Invoke the **Reference Geometry** flyout and then click on the **Plane** tool.
2. Select a planar face or a plane in the graphics area as the first reference.

> **Note:** As soon as you select a planar face or a plane, the preview of an offset plane appears in the graphics area with the default offset value. Also, the **Offset distance** button gets selected automatically in the **First Reference** rollout of the PropertyManager.

3. Select a point, a vertex, or an edge in the graphics area as the second reference. The preview of the reference plane parallel to the selected face and passing through the vertex/point selected, appears in the graphics area.
4. Click on the green tick mark ✓ in the PropertyManager. The parallel plane is created, see Figure 6.7.

> **Note:** On selecting an edge as the second reference, you need to click on the **Parallel** button in the **First Reference** rollout of the PropertyManager.

Creating a Plane at an Angle

1. Invoke the **Plane PropertyManager**.
2. Select a planar face or a plane in the graphics area as the first reference. Next, click on the **At angle** button in the **First Reference** rollout of the PropertyManager.
3. Enter the required angle value in the **Angle** field available in front of the **At angle** button.
4. Select an edge, an axis, or a sketch line as the second reference. The preview of the reference plane appears, see Figure 6.8.
5. To flip the direction of the angle, click on the **Flip offset** check box.
6. Click on the green tick mark ✓ in the PropertyManager. The reference plane at the specified angle is created.

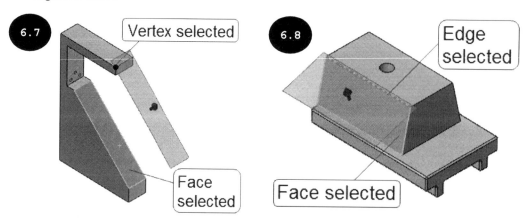

Creating a Plane passing through Three Points/Vertices

1. Invoke the **Plane PropertyManager**.
2. Select a point or a vertex from the graphics area as the first reference.
3. Select the second point or vertex as the second reference.

4. Select the third point or vertex as the third reference. The preview of the reference plane passing through three points/vertices appears in the graphics area, see Figure 6.9.
5. Click on the green tick mark ✓ in the PropertyManager. The reference plane passing through three specified points/vertices is created.

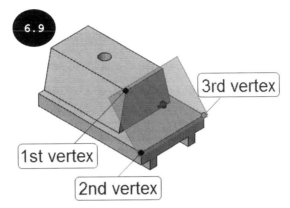

Creating a Plane Normal to a Curve
1. Invoke the **Plane PropertyManager**.
2. Select a curve in the graphics area as the first reference, see Figure 6.10.
3. Select a point of the curve as the second reference, see Figure 6.10. The preview of the reference plane normal to the curve and passing through the selected point appears, see Figure 6.11.
4. Click on the green tick mark ✓ in the PropertyManager. The reference plane normal to the curve and passing through the point is created.

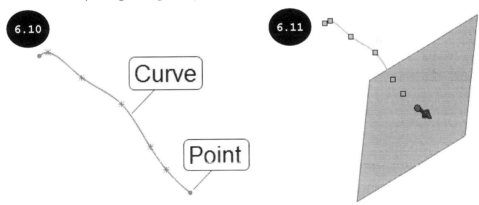

Creating a Plane at the middle of two Faces/Planes
1. Invoke the **Plane PropertyManager**.
2. Select a planar face of the model as the first reference, see Figure 6.12.
3. Select the second planar face of the model as the second reference, see Figure 6.12. The preview of the plane passing through the middle of the two selected faces appears in the graphics area, see Figure 6.12.
4. Click on the green tick mark ✓ in the PropertyManager. The reference plane in the middle of the two selected faces is created.

250 Chapter 6 > Creating Reference Geometries

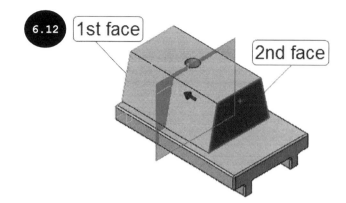

Creating a Plane Tangent to a Cylindrical Face

1. Invoke the **Plane PropertyManager**.
2. Select a cylindrical face of the model as the first reference, see Figure 6.13. The preview of the plane tangent to the selected cylindrical face appears in the graphics area.
3. Select a planar face or a plane as the second reference, see Figure 6.13. The preview of the plane tangent to the cylindrical face and perpendicular to the planar face appears, see Figure 6.14.

Note: As soon as you specify the second reference (a planar face), the **Perpendicular** button activates automatically in the **Second Reference** rollout. As a result, the preview of the reference plane appears tangent to the cylindrical face and perpendicular to the selected planar face. If you click on the **Parallel** button of the **Second Reference** rollout, the preview of the tangent plane gets modified and appears as tangent to the cylindrical face and parallel to the selected planar face. You can also flip the direction of the creation of plane by selecting the **Flip offset** check box in the **First Reference** rollout.

4. Click on the green tick mark ✓ in the PropertyManager. The reference plane tangent to the selected cylindrical face and perpendicular/parallel to the planar face is created.

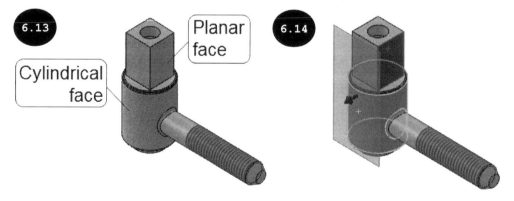

Creating a Plane Parallel to the Screen

1. Invoke the **Plane PropertyManager**.
2. Select a vertex as the first reference, see Figure 6.15.

3. Click on the **Parallel to screen** button in the **First Reference** rollout. The preview of the plane normal to the viewing direction and passing through the vertex appears, see Figure 6.16.
4. Enter the offset distance in the **Offset distance** field of the PropertyManager, if needed.

Note: If the value entered in the **Offset distance** field is 0 (zero) then the plane will be created normal to the viewing direction and passes through the vertex selected. To create a plane at an offset distance from the vertex and normal to the viewing direction, you need to enter the offset distance value in the **Offset distance** field of the PropertyManager.

5. Click on the green tick mark in the PropertyManager. The reference plane normal to the viewing direction (parallel to the screen) and passing through the vertex is created.

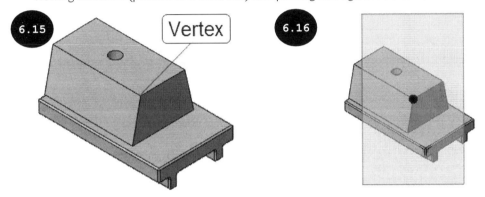

Note: Alternatively, you can create a reference plane parallel to the screen without invoking the **Plane PropertyManager**. To do so, right-click on a face, an edge, or a vertex of a model in the graphics area and then click on the **Create Plane Parallel to Screen** option in the shortcut menu appeared. A 3D point is created where you right-clicked on the model and a reference plane parallel to the screen is created at that point.

Creating a Projected Plane onto a Non-Planar Face

1. Invoke the **Plane PropertyManager**.
2. Select a point to be projected onto a non planar face as the first reference, see Figure 6.17.
3. Select the non planar face of the model to create a projected plane, see Figure 6.17. The preview of the projected plane appears in the graphics area, see Figure 6.18.

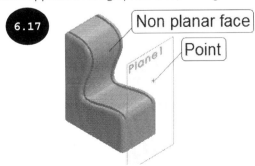

252 Chapter 6 > Creating Reference Geometries

Note: By default, the preview of a projected plane appears by projecting the selected point to the nearest location on the non planar face, see Figure 6.18. This is because the **Nearest location on surface** radio button is selected by default in the **First Reference** rollout. On selecting the **Along sketch normal** radio button, the preview of the plane appears by projecting the selected point normal to the non planar face, see Figure 6.19. You can also flip the project direction of the plane by selecting the **Flip offset** button. Note that the **Flip offset** button will be enabled only when the **Along sketch normal** radio button is selected.

4. Select the required radio button from the **First Reference** rollout (**Nearest location on surface** or **Along sketch normal**). The preview of the projected plane appears.
5. Click on the green tick mark ✓ in the PropertyManager. A projected plane is created.

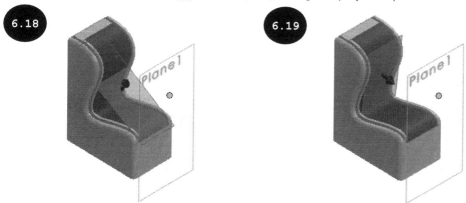

Creating a Reference Axis

Similar to creating a reference plane, you can create a reference axis. Reference axis is used as the axis of revolution for creating features such as revolved and circular pattern. To create a reference axis, click on the **Axis** tool in the **Reference Geometry** flyout, see Figure 6.20. The **Axis** PropertyManager appears, see Figure 6.21. The options in the **Axis** PropertyManager are used to create different types of axes and are as follows:

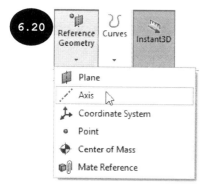

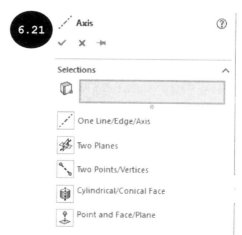

One Line/Edge/Axis

The **One Line/Edge/Axis** button of the PropertyManager is used to create an axis along an existing line, edge, or axis. To create such a reference axis, click on the **One Line/Edge/Axis** button in the PropertyManager. Next, select an existing line, edge, or an axis in the graphics area. The preview of the axis on the selected entity appears in the graphics area. Next, click on the green tick mark ✓ in the PropertyManager. The reference axis is created. Figure 6.22 shows a reference axis created along an existing edge of the model.

Two Planes

The **Two Planes** button is used to create an axis at the intersection of two planar faces or planes. To create such a reference axis, click on the **Two Planes** button of the PropertyManager and then select two planar faces or planes. The preview of the axis at the intersection of the selection appears in the graphics area. Next, click on the green tick mark ✓ in the PropertyManager. The reference axis is created. Note that the planes or faces selected need to be non-parallel to each other. Figure 6.23 shows a reference axis created at the intersection of two selected faces.

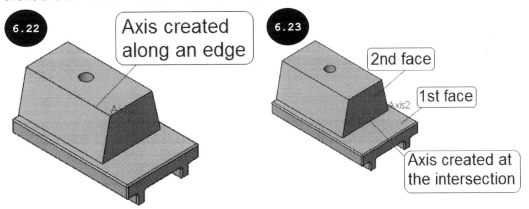

Two Points/Vertices

The **Two Points/Vertices** button is used to create an axis that passes through two points or vertices. To create such a reference axis, click on the **Two Points/Vertices** button and then select two points or vertices. The preview of the resultant axis appears in the graphics area, see Figure 6.24. Next, click on the green tick mark ✓ in the PropertyManager. The reference axis is created such that it passes through the selected vertices.

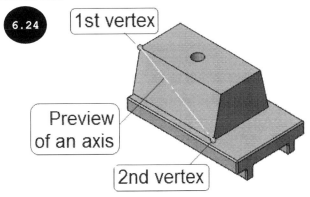

Cylindrical/Conical Face

The **Cylindrical/Conical Face** button is used to create an axis along the axis of a cylindrical/conical face. To create such a reference axis, click on the **Cylindrical/Conical Face** button and then select a cylindrical or a conical face. The preview of the resultant axis appears in the graphics area, see Figure 6.25 and Figure 6.26. Next, click on the green tick mark ✔ in the PropertyManager. The reference axis is created.

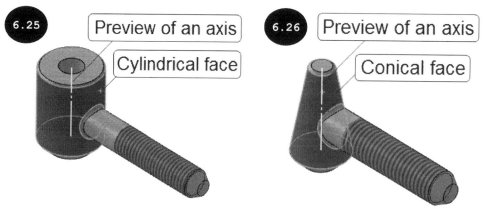

Point and Face/Plane

The **Point and Face/Plane** button is used to create an axis normal to a face or a plane and passing through a point or a vertex. To create such a reference axis, click on the **Point and Face/Plane** button and then select a planar face or a plane and a point or a vertex, see Figure 6.27. The preview of an axis normal to the selected face and passing through the selected point appears in the graphics area, see Figure 6.28. Next, click on the green tick mark ✔ in the PropertyManager. The reference axis is created.

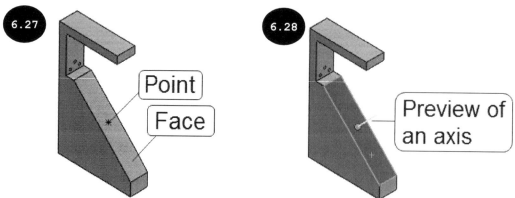

Creating a Reference Coordinate System

In addition to creating reference plane and axis, you can also create reference coordinate systems by using the **Coordinate System** tool in the **Reference Geometry** flyout, see figure 6.29. The coordinate system is mainly used for machining or analyzing a model by positioning the origin of the model relative to its features. You can also use a reference coordinate system for applying relations, calculating mass properties, measurement, and so on.

Procedure for Creating a Reference Coordinate System

1. Invoke the **Reference Geometry** flyout and then click on the **Coordinate System** tool, see Figure 6.29. The **Coordinate System PropertyManager** appears, see Figure 6.30. Also, the preview of the coordinate system appears at the origin of the graphics area.

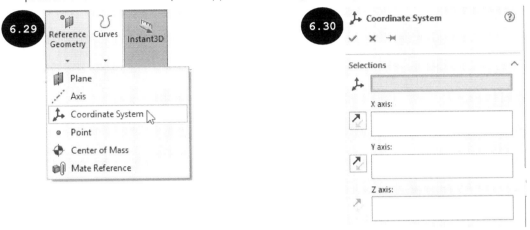

2. Select a point or a vertex as the origin of the coordinate system. Next, you need to define the direction of its axis.
3. Click on the **X Axis Direction Reference** field in the PropertyManager. Next, select a linear edge of the model. The X axis of the coordinate system is aligned along with the selected linear edge. You can also reverse the direction of axis by clicking on the **Reverse X Axis Direction** button on the left of the **X Axis Direction Reference** field.
4. Similarly, specify the direction of the Y axis and the Z axis of the coordinate system by using the **Y Axis Direction Reference** and the **Z Axis Direction Reference** fields of the PropertyManager, respectively.
5. Click on the green tick mark ✓ in the PropertyManager. The resultant coordinate system is created, see Figure 6.31.

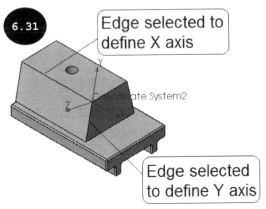

Creating a Reference Point

A reference point can be created anywhere in a 3D model or space and is used as a reference for measuring distance, creating planes, and so on. To create a reference point, invoke the **Reference Geometry** flyout and then click on the **Point** tool. The **Point PropertyManager** appears, see Figure 6.32. The options in this PropertyManager are as follows:

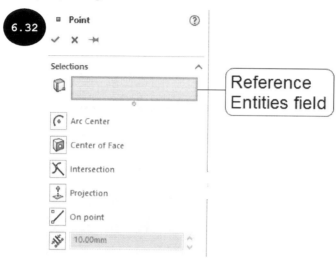

Reference Entities

The **Reference Entities** field is used to select entities as reference entities for creating points.

Arc Center

The **Arc Center** button is used to create a point at the center of a circular or semi-circular edge, see Figure 6.33. As soon as you select a circular edge or a semi-circular edge, the preview of the reference point at its center appears and the **Arc Center** button gets activated in the PropertyManager.

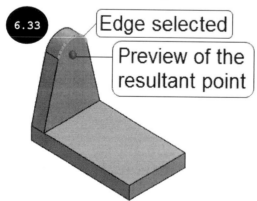

Center of Face

The **Center of Face** button is used to create a point at the center of a selected planar or a non-planar face, see Figure 6.34. As soon as you select a planar or a non-planar face, the preview of the reference point at the center of selected face appears and the **Center of Face** button gets activated in the PropertyManager.

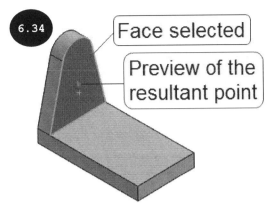

Intersection

The **Intersection** button is used to create a point at the intersection of two entities. You can select edges, curves, sketch segments, or a combination of these and a face as the entities to create a point. As soon as you select entities, the preview of a reference point at the intersection of the selected entities appears in the graphics area. Also, the **Intersection** button gets activated in the PropertyManager. Figure 6.35 shows the preview of a reference point at the intersection of two edges.

Projection

The **Projection** button is used to create a point by projecting one entity onto another entity of a model. You can select sketch points, end points of curves, or vertices as the entities to be projected and a planar or a non planar face as the entity onto which you want to project the selected point/vertex. Figure 6.36 shows the preview of a reference point after projecting a vertex onto a planar face.

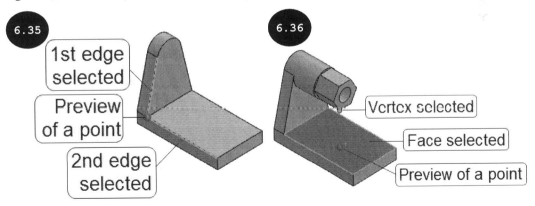

On point

The **On point** button is used to create a reference point onto a sketch point or on a point of a sketch. On selecting a sketch point or a point of the sketch, see Figure 6.37, the **On point** button gets activated in the PropertyManager and the preview of the resultant reference point appears in the graphics area, see Figure 6.38.

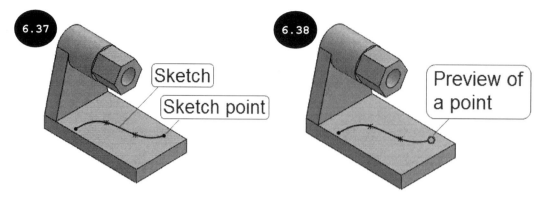

Along curve distance or multiple reference point

The **Along curve distance or multiple reference point** button is used to create a reference point on an edge, a curve, or a sketch entity. As soon as you select an edge, a curve, or a sketch entity, this button gets activated and the preview of reference point appears in the graphics area with default settings, see Figure 6.39. Also, three radio buttons: **Distance**, **Percentage**, and **Evenly Distribute** appear in the PropertyManager, see Figure 6.40. These radio buttons are as follows:

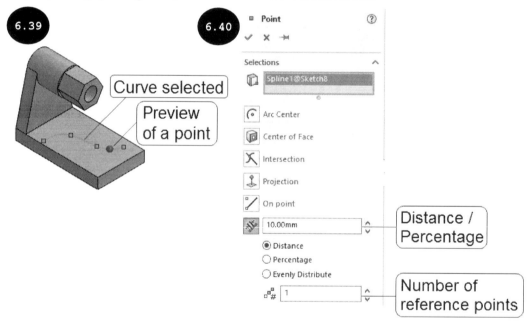

Distance Radio button
The **Distance** radio button is used to specify the position of a reference point by specifying a distance value in the **Distance/Percentage** field of the PropertyManager.

Percentage
The **Percentage** radio button is used to specify the position of a reference point by specifying a percentage value in the **Distance/Percentage** field. Note that percentage value is calculated in terms of the total length of the selected entity.

Evenly Distribute

The **Evenly Distribute** radio button is used to evenly distribute the number of reference points on the entity.

Number of reference points

The **Number of reference points** field is used to specify the number of reference points to be created on a selected entity. By default, 1 is displayed in this field. As a result, only one reference point is created on the selected entity. You can create multiple reference points on the selected entity by specifying the required number in this field.

Once the preview of the reference points has been displayed in the graphics area, click on the green tick mark ✓ in the PropertyManager. The respective reference point is created.

Tutorial 1

Create the multi-feature model shown in Figure 6.41. You need to create the model by creating all its features one by one. All dimensions are in mm.

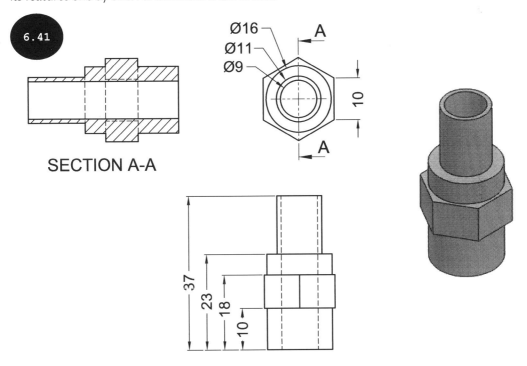

260   Chapter 6 > Creating Reference Geometries

Section 1: Starting SOLIDWORKS
1. Double-click on the SOLIDWORKS icon on your desktop to start SOLIDWORKS.

Section 2: Invoking the Part Modeling Environment
1. Click on the **New** tool in the **Standard** toolbar. The **New SOLIDWORKS Document** dialog box appears.

2. Double-click on the Part button in the dialog box. The Part modeling environment is invoked.

   Once the Part modeling environment has been invoked, you can set the unit system and create the base/first feature of the model.

Section 3: Specifying Unit Settings
1. Move the cursor toward the lower right corner of the screen over the Status Bar and then click on the **Unit System** area, see Figure 6.42. The **Unit System** flyout appears, see Figure 6.42.

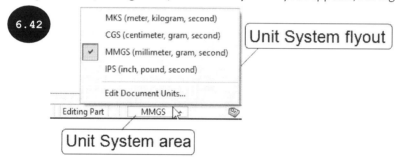

2. Make sure that the **MMGS (millimeter, gram, second)** option is tick-marked in the flyout, see Figure 6.42. If not tick-marked, click on it.

Tip: A tick-mark in front of any unit system in the **Unit System** flyout indicates that it has been selected as the unit system for the current document of SOLIDWORKS. You can also open the **Document Properties - Units** dialog box to specify the unit system for the current document by selecting the **Edit Document Units** option in the flyout.

Section 4: Creating the Base/First Feature
1. Invoke the Sketching environment by selecting the Top plane as the sketching plane and then create two circles as the sketch of the base feature and apply dimensions, see Figure 6.43. Make sure that the center points of the circles are at the origin.

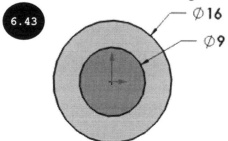

2. Click on the **Features** tab in the CommandManager, see Figure 6.44. The tools of the **Features CommandManager** are displayed, see Figure 6.44.

6.44

3. Click on the **Extruded Boss/Base** tool in the **Features Command Manager**. The **Boss-Extrude PropertyManager** and the preview of the extruded feature appear, see Figure 6.45.

4. Enter **10** in the **Depth** field of the **Direction 1** rollout and then press ENTER. The depth of the extruded feature is changed to 10 mm.

5. Click on the green tick mark ✓ in the PropertyManager. The base/first extruded feature of depth 10 mm is created, see Figure 6.46.

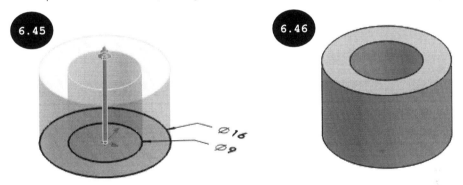
6.45
6.46

Section 5: Creating Second Feature

1. Click on the **Sketch** tab to invoke the **Sketch CommandManager**, see Figure 6.47. Next, click on the **Sketch** tool. The **Edit Sketch PropertyManager** appears and you are prompted to select a sketching plane for creating the sketch of the second feature.

2. Click on the top planar face of the base/first feature as the sketching plane, see Figure 6.48. The Sketching environment is invoked.

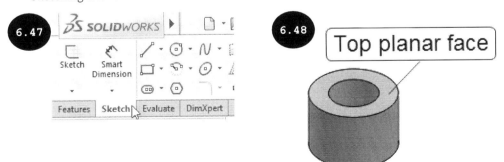
6.47
6.48

3. Invoke the **View Orientation** flyout by clicking on the **View Orientation** tool in the **View (Heads-Up)** toolbar, see Figure 6.49. Next, click on the **Normal To** tool in the flyout to change the orientation of the model as normal to the viewing direction.

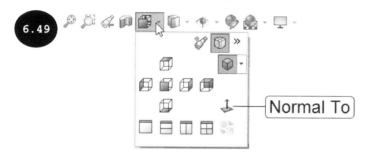

4. Create a polygon of 6 sides and a circle of diameter 9 mm by using the **Polygon** and **Circle** tools as the sketch of the second feature, see Figure 6.50. Also, apply required dimensions and relations to make the sketch fully defined.

Tip: To make the sketch fully defined, you need to apply the vertical relation to a vertical line of the polygon.

5. Click on the **Features** tab in the CommandManager to display the tools of the **Features** CommandManager.

6. Click on the **Extruded Boss/Base** tool in the **Features Command Manager**. The **Boss-Extrude PropertyManager** and the preview of the extruded feature appear. Next, change the orientation of the model to isometric, see Figure 6.51. You can change it by clicking on the **Isometric** tool in the **View Orientation** flyout of the **View (Heads-Up)** toolbar.

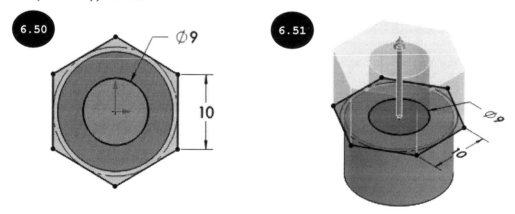

7. Enter **8** in the **Depth** field of the **Direction 1** rollout and then press ENTER.

8. Click on the green tick mark ✓ in the PropertyManager. The extruded feature is created, see Figure 6.52.

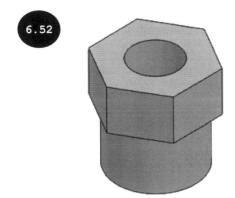

6.52

Section 6: Creating the Third Feature

1. Invoke the Sketching environment by selecting the top planar face of the second feature as the sketching plane. The Sketching environment is invoked.

2. Change the orientation of the model as normal to the viewing direction. To change the orientation of the model, click on the **View Orientation** tool in the **View (Heads-Up)** toolbar and then click on the **Normal To** tool in the **View Orientation** flyout appeared, see Figure 6.53.

3. Create the sketch of the third feature by creating two circles of diameter 9 mm and 16 mm by using the **Circle** tool and then apply required dimensions to the sketch, see Figure 6.54.

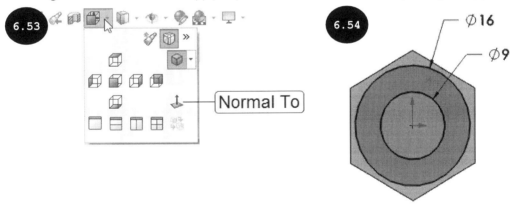

6.53   6.54

4. Click on the **Features** tab in the CommandManager to display the tools of the **Features** CommandManager.

5. Click on the **Extruded Boss/Base** tool in the **Features Command Manager**. The preview of the extruded feature appears. Next, change the orientation of the model to isometric, see Figure 6.55.

6. Enter 5 in the **Depth** field in the **Direction 1** rollout and then press ENTER.

7. Click on the green tick mark ✓ in the PropertyManager. The extruded feature is created, see Figure 6.56.

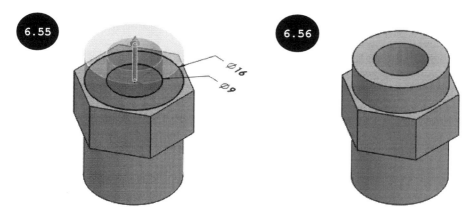

Section 7: Creating the Fourth Feature

1. Invoke the Sketching environment by selecting the top planar face of the third feature as the sketching plane, see Figure 6.57.

2. Invoke the **View Orientation** flyout by clicking on the **View Orientation** tool in the **View (Heads-Up)** toolbar, see Figure 6.58. Next, click on the **Normal To** tool in the flyout. The orientation of the model changed as normal to the viewing direction.

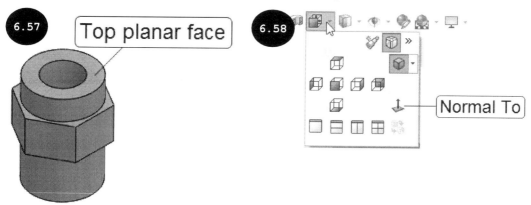

3. Create the sketch of the fourth feature by creating two circles of diameter 9 mm and 11 mm by using the **Circle** tool, see Figure 6.59. Also, apply required dimensions to the sketch.

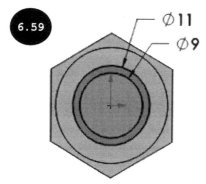

4. Click on the **Features** tab in the CommandManager to display the tools of the **Features** CommandManager.

5. Click on the **Extruded Boss/Base** tool in the **Features Command Manager**. The **Boss-Extrude PropertyManager** and the preview of the extruded feature appear. Next, change the orientation of the model to isometric, see Figure 6.60.

6. Enter **14** in the **Depth** field of the **Direction 1** rollout and then press ENTER.

7. Click on the green tick mark ✓ in the PropertyManager. The extruded feature is created. Figure 6.61 shows the model after creating all features of the model.

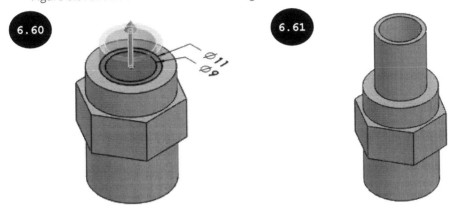

Section 8: Saving the Sketch

After creating the sketch, you need to save it.

1. Click on the **Save** tool in the **Standard** toolbar. The **Save As** dialog box appears.

2. Browse to the *SOLIDWORKS* folder and then create a folder with the name **Chapter 6**. Next, create another folder with the name **Tutorial** in the *Chapter 6* folder.

3. Enter **Tutorial 1** in the **File name** field of the **Save As** dialog box as the name of the file to be saved and then click on the **Save** button. The model is saved with the name Tutorial 1 in the *Tutorial* folder of *Chapter 6*.

Tutorial 2

Create the multi-feature model shown in Figure 6.62. All dimensions are in mm.

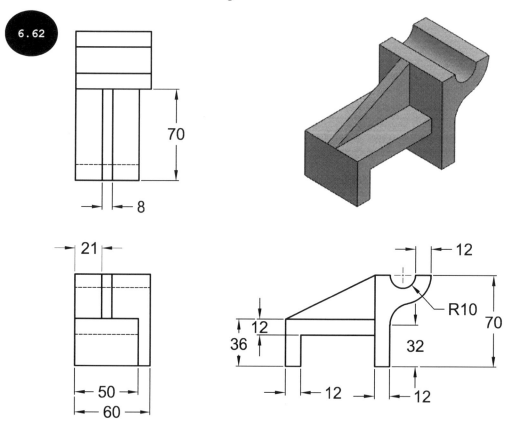

6.62

Section 1: Starting SOLIDWORKS
1. Double-click on the SOLIDWORKS icon on your desktop to start SOLIDWORKS.

Section 2: Invoking the Part Modeling Environment
1. Click on the **New** tool in the **Standard** toolbar. The **New SOLIDWORKS Document** dialog box appears.

2. In this dialog box, the **Part** button is activated by default. Click on the **OK** button in the dialog box. The Part modeling environment is invoked. Alternatively, double click on the **Part** button in the dialog box to invoke the Part modeling environment.

Section 3: Specifying Unit Settings
1. Move the cursor toward the lower right corner of the screen over the Status Bar and then click on the **Unit System** area. The **Unit System** flyout appears, see Figure 6.63.

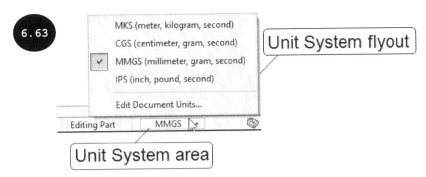

2. Make sure that the **MMGS (millimeter, gram, second)** option is tick-marked in the flyout, see Figure 6.63.

Section 4: Creating the Base/First Feature

1. Invoke the Sketching environment by selecting the Right plane as the sketching plane.

2. Create the sketch of the base feature and then apply the required relations and dimensions to the sketch, see Figure 6.64.

Tip: To make the sketch of the base feature fully defined, you need to apply the tangent relation between the line 2 and arc 3; arc 3 and arc 4 of the sketch, see Figure 6.65. Also, apply the concentric relation between the arc 4 and arc 6, see Figure 6.65. The sketch shown in the Figure 6.65 has been numbered for your reference only. The relations such as horizontal and vertical are applied automatically while drawing the horizontal and vertical line entities of the sketch.

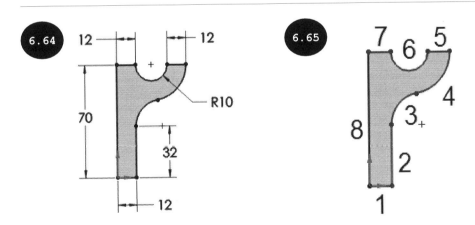

3. Click on the **Features** tab in the CommandManager and then click on the **Extruded Boss/Base** tool. The **Boss-Extrude PropertyManager** and the preview of the extruded feature appear, see Figure 6.66.

4. Invoke the **End Condition** drop-down list in the **Direction 1** rollout of the PropertyManager, see Figure 6.67.

268 Chapter 6 > Creating Reference Geometries

5. Click on the **Mid Plane** option in the **End Condition** drop-down list.

6. Enter **60** in the **Depth** field of the **Direction 1** rollout and then press ENTER. The depth of extrusion is added symmetrically on both sides of the sketching plane, see Figure 6.68.

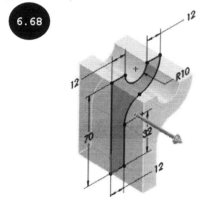

7. Click on the green tick mark ✓ in the PropertyManager. The extruded feature is created symmetrically about the sketching plane.

Section 5: Creating the Second Feature

To create the second feature of the model, you first need to create a reference plane at the offset distance of 10 mm from the right planar face of the base feature.

1. Invoke the **Reference Geometry** flyout in the **Features CommandManager**, see Figure 6.69.

2. Click on the **Plane** tool of this flyout. The **Plane PropertyManager** appears.

3. Select the right planar face of the base feature as the first reference. The preview of an offset reference plane appears in the graphics area, see Figure 6.70.

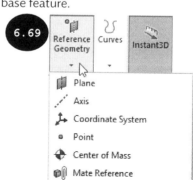

4. Enter **10** in the **Distance** field of the **First Reference** rollout of the PropertyManager and then select the **Flip offset** check box to flip the direction of the plane.

5. Click on the green tick mark ✓ in the PropertyManager. The offset reference plane is created, see Figure 6.71.

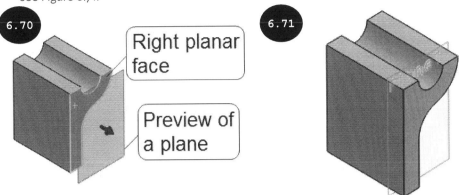

After creating the reference plane, create the second feature of the model.

6. Invoke the Sketching environment by selecting the newly created reference plane as the sketching plane.

7. Change the orientation of the model as normal to the viewing direction by clicking on the **Normal To** tool in the **View Orientation** flyout.

8. Create the sketch of the second feature and then apply required dimensions to the sketch, see Figure 6.72.

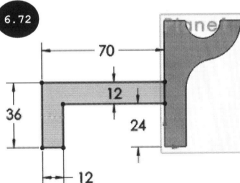

9. Click on the **Features** tab in the CommandManager to display the tools of the **Features** CommandManager.

10. Click on the **Extruded Boss/Base** tool in the **Features CommandManager**. The Boss-Extrude PropertyManager and the preview of the extruded feature appear. Next, change the orientation of the model to isometric by clicking on the **Isometric** tool in the **View Orientation** flyout of the **View (Heads-Up)** toolbar.

270 Chapter 6 > Creating Reference Geometries

11. Click on the **Reverse Direction** button in the **Direction 1** rollout to reverse the direction of extrusion similar to the one shown in Figure 6.73.

12. Enter **50** in the **Depth** field of the **Direction 1** rollout and then press ENTER.

13. Click on the green tick mark ✔ in the PropertyManager. The extruded feature is created, see Figure 6.74.

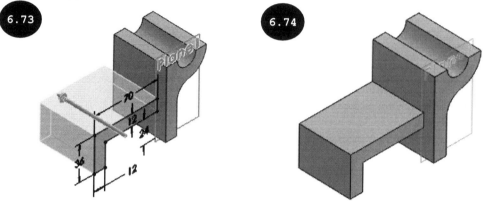

Section 6: Creating the Third Feature

To create the third feature of the model, you need to create a reference plane such that it passes through middle of the second feature.

1. Invoke the **Reference Geometry** flyout in the **Features CommandManager**, see Figure 6.75.

2. Click on the **Plane** tool in this flyout. The **Plane PropertyManager** appears.

3. Select the right planar face of the second feature as the first reference. The preview of an offset reference plane appears in the graphics area, see Figure 6.76.

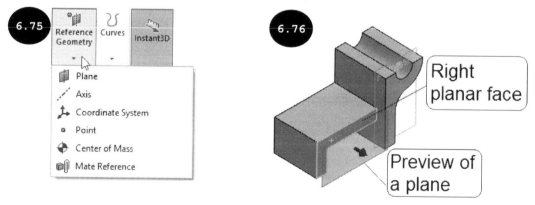

4. Rotate the model such that the left planar face of the second feature can be viewed in the graphics area, see Figure 6.77. To rotate the model, right-click in the graphics area and then click on the **Zoom/Pan/Rotate > Rotate View** in the shortcut menu appeared. Next, press and hold

the left mouse button and drag the cursor in the graphics area. Once the required rotated view of the model has been achieved, right-click in the graphics area and then click on the **Rotate View** tool in the shortcut menu appeared to exit the **Rotate View** tool. You can also rotate the model by dragging the cursor after pressing and holding the middle mouse button.

5. Click on the left planar face of the second feature as the second reference for creating the plane. The preview of a reference plane in the middle of the two selected planar faces appears in the graphics area, see Figure 6.78.

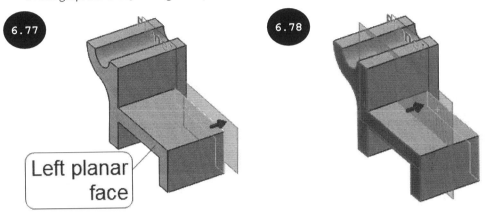

6. Change the view orientation of the model to isometric.

7. Click on the green tick mark  in the PropertyManager. The reference plane in the middle of two selected faces is created.

After creating the reference plane, create the third feature of the model.

8. Invoke the Sketching environment by selecting the newly created reference plane as the sketching plane.

9. Change the orientation of the model as normal to the viewing direction by clicking on the **Normal To** tool in the **View Orientation** flyout.

10. Create the closed sketch of the third feature (three line entities), see Figure 6.79. The sketch entities of the sketch shown in Figure 6.79 has been created by taking the reference of the vertices of the existing geometry.

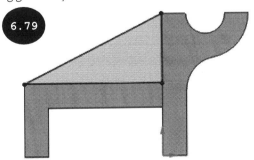

272 Chapter 6 > Creating Reference Geometries

11. Click on the **Features** tab in the CommandManager to display the tools of the **Features** CommandManager.

12. Click on the **Extruded Boss/Base** tool in the **Features** CommandManager. The **Boss-Extrude PropertyManager** and the preview of the extruded feature appear. Next, change the orientation of the model to isometric.

13. Invoke the **End Condition** drop-down list in the **Direction 1** rollout, see Figure 6.80.

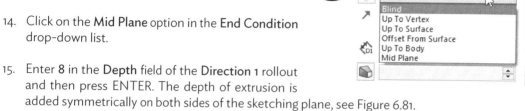

14. Click on the **Mid Plane** option in the **End Condition** drop-down list.

15. Enter **8** in the **Depth** field of the **Direction 1** rollout and then press ENTER. The depth of extrusion is added symmetrically on both sides of the sketching plane, see Figure 6.81.

16. Click on the green tick mark in the PropertyManager. The extruded feature is created symmetrically about the Sketching plane. Figure 6.82 shows the final model after creating all features of the model.

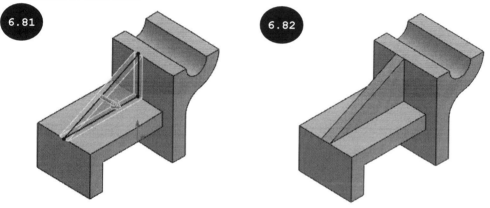

Section 7: Saving the Sketch
After creating the sketch, you need to save it.

1. Click on the **Save** tool of the **Standard** toolbar, the **Save As** dialog box appears.

2. Browse to the *Tutorial* folder of the *Chapter 6* and then save the model with the name Tutorial 2.

Tutorial 3

Create the model shown in Figure 6.83. All dimensions are in mm.

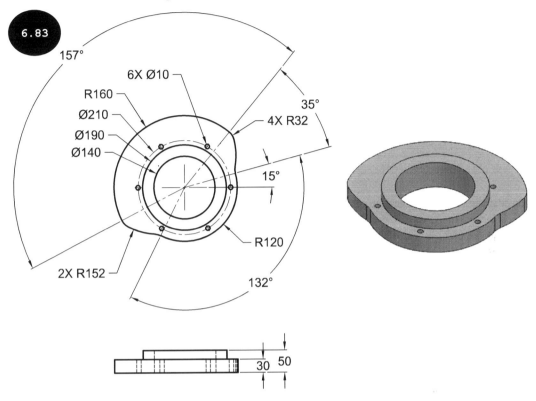

Section 1: Starting SOLIDWORKS
1. Double-click on the SOLIDWORKS icon on your desktop to start SOLIDWORKS.

Section 2: Invoking the Part Modeling Environment
1. Click on the **New** tool in the **Standard** toolbar and then double-click on the **Part** button in the **New SOLIDWORKS Document** dialog box to invoke the Part modeling environment.

Section 3: Specifying Unit Settings
1. Invoke the **Unit System** flyout in the Status Bar and then make sure that the **MMGS (millimeter, gram, second)** option is tick-marked in the flyout, see Figure 6.84.

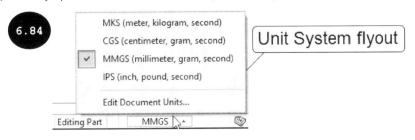

Section 4: Creating the Base/First Feature

1. Invoke the Sketching environment by selecting the Top plane as the sketching plane.

2. Create the sketch of the base feature and then apply the required relations and dimensions to the sketch, see Figure 6.85.

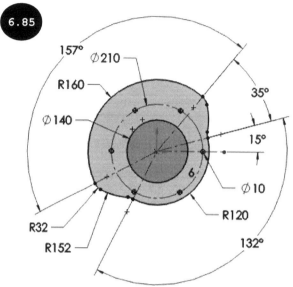

Tip: To make the sketch of the base feature fully defined as shown in Figure 6.85, you need to apply the tangent relation between all connecting arcs of the sketch. Also, you need to apply equal relations between the arcs having equal radius value. To create all circles of diameter 10 mm of the sketch, you can create a circle and then create a circular pattern to create the remaining circles of the sketch. After creating the sketch and applying the required relations, you need to apply the dimensions as shown in Figure 6.85.

3. Click on the **Features** tab in the CommandManager and then click on the **Extruded Boss/Base** tool. The preview of the extruded feature appear, see Figure 6.86.

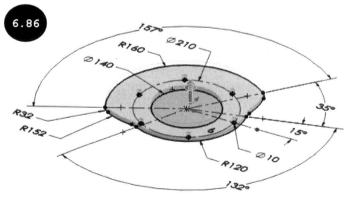

4. Enter 30 in the **Depth** field of the **Direction 1** rollout and then press ENTER.

5. Click on the green tick mark ✔ in the PropertyManager. The extruded feature is created, see Figure 6.87.

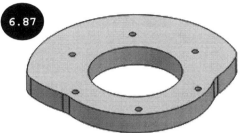

Section 5: Creating the Second Feature

1. Invoke the Sketching environment by selecting the top planar face of the base feature.

2. Change the orientation of the model as normal to the viewing direction by clicking on the **Normal To** tool in the **View Orientation** flyout.

3. Create the sketch (two circles) of the second feature and apply dimensions, see Figure 6.88.

4. Click on the **Features** tab and then click on the **Extruded Boss/Base** tool. The **Boss-Extrude PropertyManager** and the preview of the extruded feature appear. Next, change the orientation of the model to isometric.

5. Enter 20 in the **Depth** field of the **Direction 1** rollout and then press ENTER.

6. Click on the green tick mark ✔ in the PropertyManager. The extruded feature is created, see Figure 6.89.

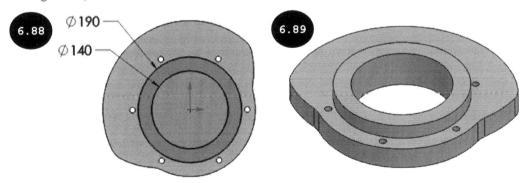

Section 6: Saving the Sketch

1. Click on the **Save** tool in the **Standard** toolbar. The **Save As** dialog box appears.

2. Browse to the *Tutorial* folder of the *Chapter 6* and then save the model with the name Tutorial 3.

Hands-on Test Drive 1

Create the model shown in Figure 6.90. All dimensions are in mm.

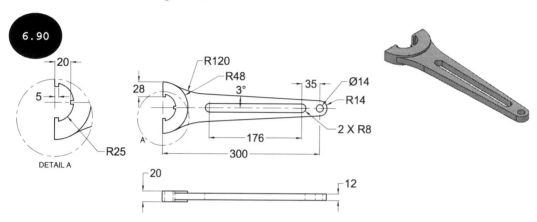

Summary

In this chapter, you have learned about three default planes: Front, Top, and Right. These three default planes may not be enough for creating models having multiple features. Therefore, you need to create additional reference planes. You have learned how to create additional reference planes. Also, you have learned about creating a reference axis, reference coordinates system and a reference point by using the respective tools.

Questions

- You can create reference planes by using the _____ tool.

- To create a reference plane parallel to a planar face of a model, you need to define two references: first reference can be a planar face and second reference can be a _____, _____, or _____ .

- To create a reference plane at an angle to a planar face/plane, you need to define two references: first reference can be a planar face/plane and second reference can be a _____, _____, or _____ .

- The _____ tool is used to create reference axis.

- The _____ tool is used to create coordinate systems.

- In SOLIDWORKS, you can create a reference point at the intersection of two entities. (True/False).

- You cannot select a planar face of existing features as the sketching plane for creating a feature. (True/False).

CHAPTER 7

Advanced Modeling - I

In this chapter, you will learn the following:

- Using Advanced Options of the Extruded Boss/Base Tool
- Using Advanced Options of the Revolved Boss/Base Tool
- Creating Cut Features
- Working with Different Types of Sketches
- Working with Contours of a Sketch
- Displaying Shaded Sketch Contours
- Projecting Edges onto the Sketching Plane
- Editing a Feature
- Measuring the Distance between Entities/Faces
- Assigning Appearance/Texture
- Applying Material
- Calculating Mass Properties

In the previous chapters, you have learned how to create features by using the **Extruded Boss/Base** and **Revolved Boss/Base** tools. In this chapter, you will learn how to use the advanced options of the **Extruded Boss/Base** and **Revolved Boss/Base** tools. Also, you will learn about creating cut features by using the **Extruded Cut** and **Revolved Cut** tools. Additionally, you will learn how to work with different types of sketches, measuring the distance between entities of a model, assigning appearance to a model, applying material properties, calculating mass properties of a model, and so on.

Using Advanced Options of the Extruded Boss/Base Tool

As discussed earlier, while extruding a sketch by using the **Extruded Boss/Base** tool, the **Boss-Extrude PropertyManager** appears on the left of the graphics area, see Figure 7.1. Some of the options of this PropertyManager have been discussed earlier while creating the base feature of a model. The remaining options of this PropertyManager are the advanced options and are used for creating real world multi-feature models. These options are discussed next.

From drop-down List

The options in the **From** drop-down list of the **From** rollout are used to define the start condition of extrusion, see Figure 7.2. The options such as **Sketch Plane** and **offset** of this drop-down list have been discussed earlier while creating base features and the remaining options are as follows:

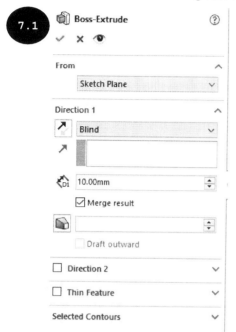

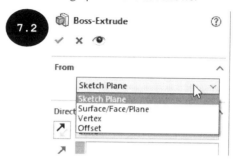

Surface/Face/Plane Updated

The **Surface/Face/Plane** option of the **From** drop-down list is used to select a surface, a face, or a plane as the start condition (from where extrusion starts) of extrusion. On selecting this option, the **Select A Surface/Face/Plane** field displays below the **From** drop-down list and is activated by default. As a result, you can select a surface, a face, or a plane as the start condition of extrusion. Figure 7.3 shows a sketch to be extruded and a face to be selected as the start condition of extrusion. Figure 7.4 shows the preview of the resultant extruded feature after selecting the face as the start condition.

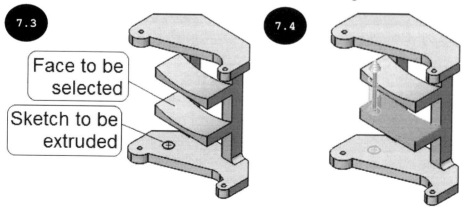

Note: In SOLIDWORKS 2017, you can select a surface, a face, or a plane of any size as the start condition of extrusion, even if the selected surface, face, or plane does not encapsulate the entire sketch.

Vertex

The **Vertex** option is used to select a vertex of a model as the start condition of extrusion. On selecting this option, the **Select A Vertex** field displays below the **From** drop-down list and is activated by default. As a result, you can select a vertex as the start condition of extrusion, see Figure 7.5.

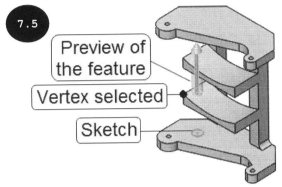

End Condition drop-down List

The **End Condition** drop-down list of the **Direction 1** rollout is used to define the end condition of extrusion, see Figure 7.6. The options such as **Blind** and **Mid Plane** of this drop-down list have been discussed earlier while creating base features and the remaining options are as follows:

Up To Vertex

The **Up To Vertex** option is used to define the end condition or termination of the extrusion by selecting a vertex. On selecting this option, the **Vertex** field becomes available in the rollout and is activated by default. As a result, you can select a vertex of the model up to which you want to extrude the feature. Figure 7.7 shows the preview of the feature whose end condition is defined by selecting a vertex of the model.

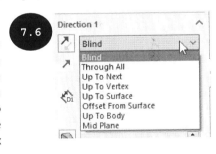

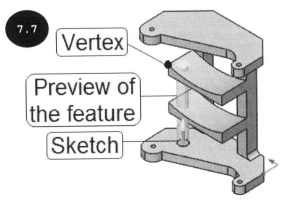

Up To Surface

The **Up To Surface** option is used to define the end condition or termination of extrusion up to a surface. When you select the **Up To Surface** option, the **Face/Plane** field becomes available in the **Direction 1** rollout and is activated by default. As a result, you can select a surface, a face, or a plane up to which you want to extrude the feature. Figure 7.8 shows the preview of a feature whose end condition is defined by selecting a face of the model.

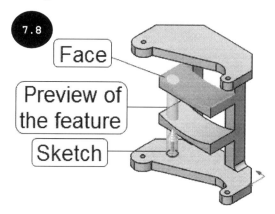

Offset From Surface

The **Offset From Surface** option is used to define the end condition or termination of extrusion at an offset distance from a surface, see Figure 7.9. When you select the **Offset From Surface** option, the **Face/Plane** and **Offset Distance** fields become available in the **Direction 1** rollout. Select an existing surface, a face, or a plane of the model as the end condition of extrusion and enter the offset distance value in the **Offset Distance** field. Once you enter the offset distance value, the resultant feature is terminated at an offset distance from the selected face. Figure 7.9 shows the preview of a feature whose end condition is defined at an offset distance from a face of the model.

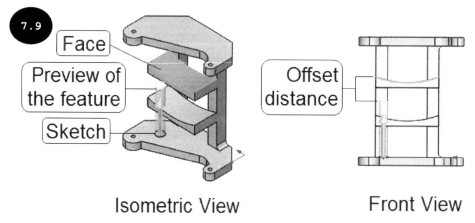

Up To Body

The **Up To Body** option is used to define the end condition or termination of extrusion up to a body. When you select this option, the **Solid/Surface Body** field becomes available in the **Direction 1** rollout of the PropertyManager and is activated by default. As a result, you can select a solid body or a surface body up to which you want to extrude the feature. Note that this option can be used when multiple bodies are available in the graphics area. You create bodies in the Part environment by unchecking the **Merge result** check box of the PropertyManager, which is discussed next.

Merge result

The **Merge result** check box of the **Direction 1** rollout is used to merge the feature with the existing features of the model. By default, this check box is selected. As a result, the feature of the model being created merges with the existing features of the model. If you uncheck this check box, the feature being created will not be merged with the existing features and a separate body will be created. Note that this check box is not available while creating the base/first feature of a model.

> **Note:** The options in the **Direction 2** rollout of the **Boss-Extrude PropertyManager** are the same as those of the **Direction 1** rollout with the only difference that the options of the **Direction 2** rollout are used to specify the end condition of extrusion in the second direction of the sketching plane.

Using Advanced Options of the Revolved Boss/Base Tool

As discussed earlier, while revolving a sketch by using the **Revolved Boss/Base** tool, the **Revolve PropertyManager** appears on the left of the graphics area, see Figure 7.10. Some of the options in the **Revolve Type** drop-down list of the PropertyManager have been discussed earlier while creating the base revolved feature of a model. The remaining options such as **Up To Vertex** and **Up To Surface** used to define the end condition of a revolved feature are same as the options used to define the end condition of an extruded feature. Figure 7.10 shows the **Revolve PropertyManager** with the expanded **Revolve Type** drop-down list.

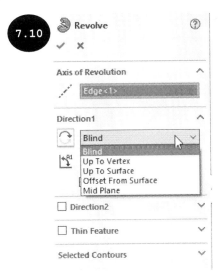

Creating Cut Features

Similar to adding material by extruding and revolving a sketch, you can remove material from a model by using the **Extruded Cut** and **Revolved Cut** tools. By using these tools, you can create an extruded cut feature and a revolved cut feature, as discussed next.

Creating Extruded Cut Features

You can create an extruded cut feature by using the **Extruded Cut** tool of the **Features CommandManager**. An extruded cut feature is created by removing the material of a model as normal to the sketching plane. Note that the geometry of the material removed is defined by the sketch of the cut feature. Figure 7.11 shows a sketch, which is created on the top planar face of the model and the resultant extruded cut feature.

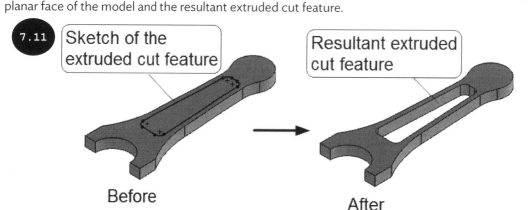

Figure 7.11

To create an extruded cut feature, click on the **Extruded Cut** tool in the **Features CommandManager**. The **Extrude PropertyManager** appears. Next, click on the sketch. The preview of the extruded cut feature appears in the graphics area with default parameters. Also, the **Cut-Extrude PropertyManager** appears on the left of the graphics area, see Figure 7.12. Note that if the sketch is selected before invoking the **Extruded Cut** tool, then as soon as you click on the **Extruded Cut** tool, the preview of the extruded cut feature and the **Cut-Extrude PropertyManager** appear. The options in the **Cut-Extrude PropertyManager** are used to define parameters of the extruded cut feature. These options are same as those discussed earlier, while creating the extruded feature with the only difference that these options are used to remove material from the model. You can also flip the side of the material to be removed by using the **Flip side to cut** check box of the PropertyManager, see Figure 7.13. After specifying parameters for creating the extruded cut feature, click on the green tick mark in the PropertyManager. The extruded cut feature is created.

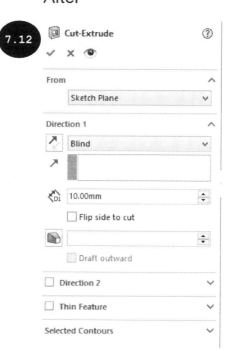

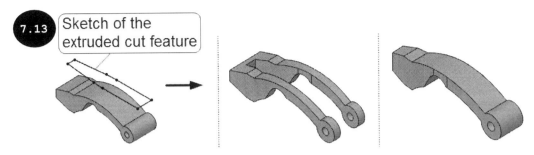

Figure 7.13 Sketch of the extruded cut feature / Flip side to cut check box is unchecked / Flip side to cut check box is selected

Procedure for Creating an Extruded Cut Feature

1. Create a sketch by using the sketching tools in the Sketching environment. After creating the sketch, do not exit the Sketching environment.
2. Click on the **Features** tab in the CommandManager and then click on the **Extruded Cut** tool. The preview of the cut feature appears in the graphics area. Also, the **Cut-Extrude** PropertyManager appears on the left of the graphics area.

Tip: If you exit the Sketching environment after creating the sketch and the sketch is not selected in the graphics area, then on clicking the **Extruded Cut** tool, the **Extrude** PropertyManager appears and you are prompted to select a sketch or create a sketch. Click on the sketch in the graphics area. The preview of the extruded cut feature and the **Cut-Extrude** PropertyManager appear.

3. Specify parameters required for removing the material in the PropertyManager.
4. Click on the green tick mark ✓ in the PropertyManager. The extruded cut feature is created.

Creating Revolved Cut Features

You can create a revolved cut feature by using the **Revolved Cut** tool. A revolved cut feature is created by removing the material of a model by revolving a sketch around an axis of revolution. Note that the sketch to be revolved should be on either side of the axis of revolution. Figure 7.14 shows a sketch to be revolved and Figure 7.15 shows the resultant revolved cut feature.

Revolved Cut

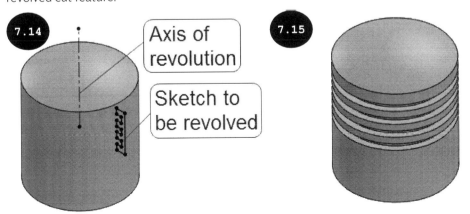

Figure 7.14 Axis of revolution / Sketch to be revolved — Figure 7.15

To create a revolved cut feature, click on the **Revolved Cut** tool in the **Features CommandManager**. The **Revolve PropertyManager** appears. Next, click on a centerline of the sketch as the axis of revolution. You can select a centerline, a linear sketch entity, a linear edge, or an axis as the axis of revolution. As soon as you select the axis of revolution, the preview of the revolved cut feature appears in the graphics area with default parameters. Also, the **Cut-Revolve PropertyManager** appears, see Figure 7.16. The options in this PropertyManager are used to define parameters of the revolved cut feature. These options are same as those discussed earlier, while creating the revolved feature with the only difference that these options are used to remove material. After specifying parameters for creating revolved cut feature, click on the green tick mark in the PropertyManager. The revolved cut feature is created.

7.16

Procedure for Creating a Revolved Cut Feature

1. Create a sketch of the revolved cut feature with a centerline as the axis of revolution. After creating the sketch, do not exit the Sketching environment.
2. Click on the **Features** tab in the CommandManager and then click on the **Revolved Cut** tool. The preview of the revolved cut feature appears in the graphics area. Also, the **Cut-Revolve PropertyManager** appears on the left of the graphics area.

> **Note:** If the sketch has two or more than two centerlines then on invoking the **Revolved Cut** tool, you are prompted to select a centerline as the axis of revolution. As soon as you select a centerline, the preview of the revolved cut feature appears.

> **Tip:** If you exit the Sketching environment after creating the sketch and the sketch is not selected in the graphics area, then on clicking the **Revolved Cut** tool, the **Revolve PropertyManager** appears. Also, you are prompted to select a sketch to be revolved or a sketching plane to create a sketch of the revolved cut feature. As soon as you select the sketch, the preview of the revolved cut feature appears in the graphics area. Also, the **Cut-Revolve PropertyManager** appears on the left of the graphics area.

3. Specify the required parameters of revolved cut feature in the PropertyManager.
4. Click on the green tick mark in the PropertyManager. The revolved cut feature is created.

Working with Different Types of Sketches

It is important to understand different types of sketches and their performance. Some of the important types of sketches are Closed sketches, Open sketches, Nested sketches, and Intersecting sketches. All these types of sketches are as follows:

Close Sketches

Closed sketches are those in which all entities are connected end to end with each other without any gap. On extruding a closed sketch, a solid extruded feature is created. Figure 7.17 shows a closed sketch having one closed region/area and its resultant extruded feature.

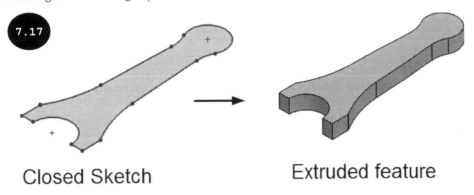

Closed Sketch   Extruded feature

Open Sketches

Open Sketches are those sketches that are open from one or more ends. On extruding an open sketch, a thin feature is created. Figure 7.18 shows an open sketch and its resultant thin extruded feature.

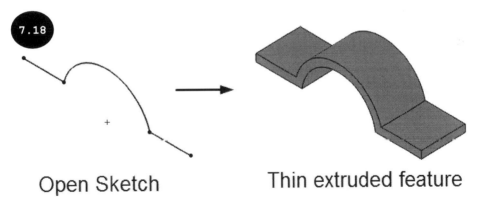

Open Sketch   Thin extruded feature

Nested Sketches

Nested sketches are similar to closed sketches with the only difference that the nested sketches have more than one closed regions/contours. On extruding a nested sketch having multiple closed regions/contours, a solid feature is created by adding the material to the most suitable closed contour of the sketch. Figure 7.19 shows a nested sketch having two closed contours and its resultant extruded feature. Figure 7.20 shows a nested sketch having three closed contours and its resultant extruded feature.

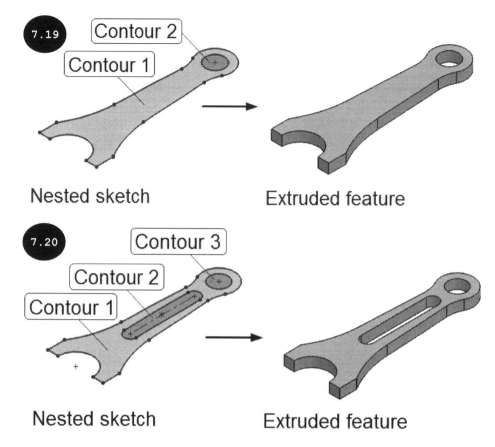

Nested sketch — Extruded feature

Nested sketch — Extruded feature

However, on extruding a nested sketch similar to the one shown in Figure 7.21, you will be prompted to select the contour of the sketch to be extruded. You can select the required closed contour of the sketch by using the **Selected Contours** rollout of the PropertyManager, as discussed in earlier chapters. Figure 7.22 shows the preview of an extruded feature by selecting a contour of a nested sketch. You will learn more about extruding different contours or closed regions of a nested sketch later in this chapter.

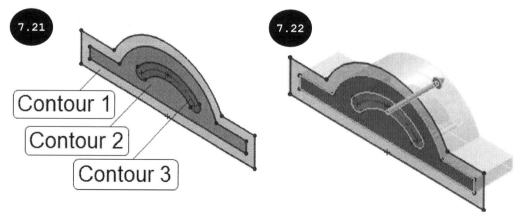

Intersecting Sketch

Intersecting sketches have intersecting entities in them, see Figure 7.23. On extruding an intersecting sketch, the automatic selection of a closed contour to add material does not take place and you are prompted to select a closed contour of the intersecting sketch to be extruded. You can select a required contour by using the **Selected Contours** rollout of the PropertyManager. Figure 7.23 shows an intersecting sketch and Figure 7.24 shows the preview of an extruded feature by extruding a closed region of the intersecting sketch. You will learn more about extruding closed contours of a sketch later in this chapter.

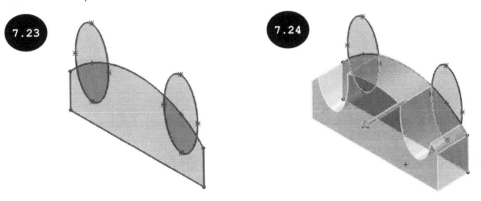

Note: Working with different types of sketches such as closed sketches, open sketches, nested sketches, and intersecting sketches are same for all tools such as **Extruded Base/Boss** and **Revolved Base/Boss**.

Working with Contours of a Sketch Updated

In SOLIDWORKS, you can create multiple features by using a single sketch that has multiple contours. Figure 7.25 shows a sketch having multiple contours and Figure 7.26 shows the resultant multi-feature model created by using this sketch.

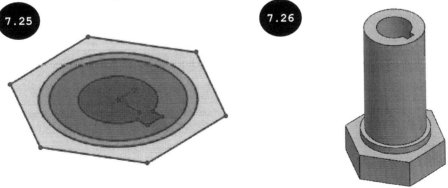

To extrude contours of a sketch for creating features, you can use the **Selected Contours** rollout of the PropertyManager or the **Contour Select Tool**. The procedures for creating features by extruding contours of a sketch are discussed next.

Procedure for Extruding Contours by using the Selected Contours Rollout

1. Create a sketch that has multiple contours in the Sketching environment, refer to Figure 7.27. Next, exit the Sketching environment.
2. Make sure that the sketch is selected in the graphics area. If not selected, click on the sketch name in the FeatureManager Design Tree to select it.
3. Invoke the tool such as the **Extruded Boss/Base** or **Revolved Boss/Base**, as required from the **Features CommandManager**. Depending upon the tool invoked, the PropertyManager of the respective tool appears with the expanded **Selected Contours** rollout. Also, the cursor changes to contour cursor .
4. Move the cursor over the contour of the sketch to be selected and then click when it highlights in the graphics area. The preview of the feature appears, see Figure 7.28.

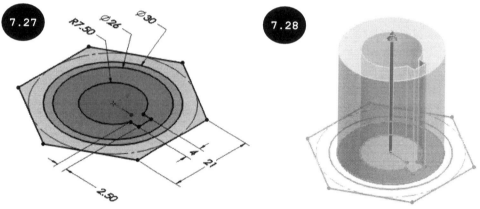

5. Specify parameters for creating the feature in the PropertyManager.
6. Click on the green tick mark in the PropertyManager. The feature is created and its name is added in the FeatureManager Design Tree. Also, the sketch disappears from the graphics area.
7. In the FeatureManager Design Tree, expand the node of the previously created feature by clicking on the arrow in its front, see Figure 7.29.
8. Click on the sketch of the previously created feature in the FeatureManager Design Tree. A Pop-up toolbar appears and then click on the **Show** tool in the Pop-up toolbar, see Figure 7.29.

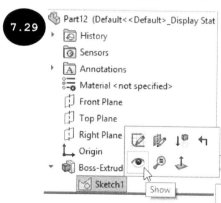

9. Repeat steps 2 to 8 for creating the remaining features by using another contours of the same sketch. Figure 7.30 shows a model created by extruding multi-contours of a sketch.

7.30

Note: In Figure 7.30, the sketch has been hidden. To hide the sketch, click on the sketch in the graphics area. A Pop-up toolbar appears. Next, click on the **Hide** tool.

Procedure for Extruding Contours by using the Contour Select Tool

1. Create a sketch that have multiple contours in the Sketching environment and then do not exit the Sketching environment.
2. Change the orientation of the model to isometric.
3. Press and hold the ALT key in the graphics area. The **Contour Select Tool** gets invoked and the cursor changes to the contour cursor.
4. Move the cursor over the contour to be extruded and then click the left mouse button when the contour highlights in the graphics area. The **Extruded Boss/Base** tool appears near the cursor, see Figure 7.31.

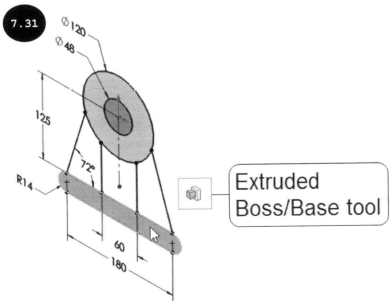

7.31

290 Chapter 7 > Advanced Modeling - I

5. Click on the **Extruded Boss/Base** tool appeared near the cursor in the graphics area. The preview of the feature appears in the graphics area with default parameters, see Figure 7.32. Also, the **Boss-Extrude PropertyManager** appears on the left of the graphics area.

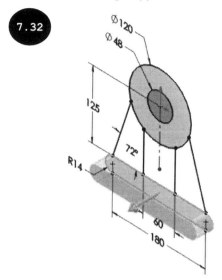

7.32

6. Specify parameters for creating the feature in the PropertyManager.
7. Click on the green tick mark ✓ in the PropertyManager. The feature is created and its name is added in the FeatureManager Design Tree. Also, the sketch disappears from the graphics area.

> **Note:** Alternatively, to invoke the **Contour Select Tool**, right-click in the graphics area. A shortcut menu appears. Expand the shortcut menu by clicking on the double arrows available at its bottom. Next, click on **Contour Select Tool** in the expanded shortcut menu. You can invoke the **Contour Select Tool** from the shortcut menu in the Sketching environment as well as in the Part modeling environment.

8. In the FeatureManager Design Tree, expand the node of the previously created feature by clicking on the arrow in its front, refer to Figure 7.33.
9. Click on the sketch of the previously created feature in the FeatureManager Design Tree. A Pop-up toolbar appears and then click on the **Show** tool in the Pop-up toolbar, see Figure 7.33.

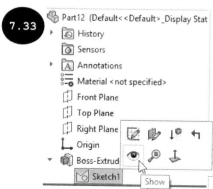

7.33

10. Right-click in the graphics area. A shortcut menu appears.
11. Expand the shortcut menu by clicking on the double arrows available at its bottom.
12. Click on **Contour Select Tool** in the expanded shortcut menu, see Figure 7.34. The **Contour Select Tool** gets invoked and the cursor is changed to contour cursor. Also, you are prompted to select a sketch, whose contour is to be extruded.
13. Move the cursor toward the sketch and then click on it.
14. Move the cursor over the required contour of the sketch and then click when it highlights in the graphics area.
15. Invoke the **Extruded Boss/Base** tool from the **Features CommandManager**. The preview of the feature appears in the graphics area.
16. Specify parameters for creating the feature in the PropertyManager.
17. Click on the green tick mark in the PropertyManager. The feature is created and its name is added in the FeatureManager Design Tree.
18. Repeat steps 10 to 17 for creating the remaining features by using another contours of the same sketch. Figure 7.35 shows a model created by using multi-contours of a sketch.

Figure 7.34

Figure 7.35

> **Note:** In Figure 7.35, the sketch has been hidden. To hide the sketch, click on the sketch in the graphics area. A Pop-up toolbar appears. Click on the **Hide** tool in the toolbar.

Displaying Shaded Sketch Contours New

In SOLIDWORKS 2017, the closed contours of a sketch are displayed in different blue shades (lightest to darkest blue shades), see Figure 7.36. In this figure, the outermost circle has the light blue shade and the innermost circle has the darkest blue shade. It helps to easily identify whether the geometry is fully closed or not. Note that if the geometry is not fully closed then it will not be displayed in blue shade. You can turn on or off the display of shaded sketch contours in the Sketching environment by using the **Shaded Sketch Contours** tool. By default, the **Shaded Sketch Contours** tool is activated. As a result, the display of shaded sketch contours is turned on in the Sketching environment. To turn off the display of shaded sketch contours, click on the **Shaded Sketch Contours** tool in the **Sketch CommandManager**, see Figure 7.37.

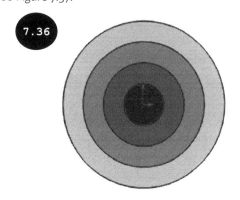

Projecting Edges onto the Sketching Plane

In SOLIDWORKS, while sketching, you can project edges of the existing features onto the current sketching plane as sketch entities by using the **Convert Entities** tool. Figure 7.38 shows a model in which the edges of the existing features have been projected as sketch entities on the current sketching plane in the Sketching environment.

To project edges of existing features onto the current sketching plane as sketch entities, click on the **Convert Entities** tool in the **Sketch CommandManager**. The **Convert Entities** **PropertyManager** appears, see Figure 7.39. The options in the PropertyManager are as follows:

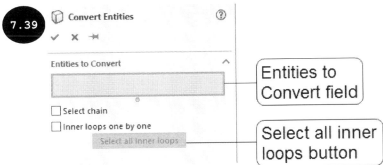

Entities to Convert

The **Entities to Convert** field is used to select edges, faces, or sketch entities to be projected onto the current sketching plane. By default, this field is activated. As a result, you can select edges, faces, or sketch entities by clicking the left mouse button.

> **Note:** On selecting a face, you can project all its outer or inner loops on to the current sketching plane. By default, the edges of the outer loop of the face will be projected on the current sketching plane. To project the edges of the inner loops of the face, you need to click on the **Select all inner loops** button in the PropertyManager.

Select chain

The **Select chain** check box is used to select all contiguous entities of a selected entity.

Inner loops one by one

The **Inner loops one by one** check box allows you to select inner loops of a face one by one.

Select all inner loops

The **Select all inner loops** button is used to select all inner loops of a face. Note that this button is enabled only after selecting a face of a model. As soon as you click on the **Select all inner loops** button, the edges of all inner loops of the face get selected for projection.

After selecting edges, faces, or sketch entities to be projected, click on the green tick mark in the PropertyManager. The selected edges are projected onto the current sketching plane as sketch entities.

> **Note:** You can select edges, faces, or sketch entities of existing features of a model before or after invoking the **Convert Entities** tool.

Procedure for Projecting Edges onto the Sketching Plane
1. Invoke the Sketching environment by selecting a plane or a planar face as the sketching plane.
2. Select existing edges, faces, or sketch entities of a model to be projected as sketch entities.
3. Click on the **Convert Entities** tool in the **Sketch CommandManager**. All the selected edges are projected as sketch entities onto the current sketching plane.

Tip: If you select a face of a model to be projected, then on invoking the **Convert Entities** tool, the edges of the outer loop of the selected face get projected onto the current sketching plane as sketch entities. To project edges of the inner loops of the face, you need to first invoke the **Convert Entities** tool and then select the face to be projected. Next, click on the **Select all inner loops** button in the **Convert Entities PropertyManager**. You can select edges, faces, or sketch entities to be projected before and after invoking the **Convert Entities** tool.

4. Once the edges have been projected as sketch entities onto the current sketching plane, you can convert the sketch into a feature by using the feature modeling tools such as **Extruded Boss/Base** and **Revolved Boss/Base**.

Editing a Feature
SOLIDWORKS allows you to edit features of a model as per the design change. As mentioned earlier, the FeatureManager Design Tree displays a list of all features created for a model, see Figure 7.40. In SOLIDWORKS, you can edit individual feature and its sketch. The procedure to edit a feature and its sketch is as follows:

Procedure for Editing a Feature
1. Click on the feature to be edited in the FeatureManager Design Tree. A Pop-up toolbar appears, see Figure 7.40.

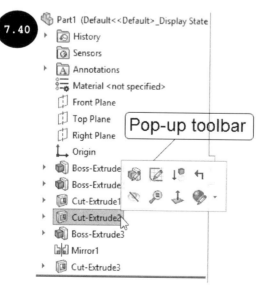

2. Click on the **Edit Feature** tool in the Pop-up toolbar, see Figure 7.41. The respective PropertyManager appears.

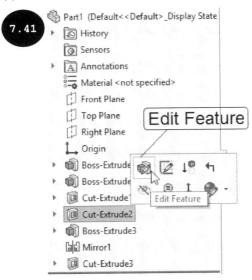

Figure 7.41

3. Change the parameters as per your requirement by entering the modified value in the PropertyManager.
4. Once you have edited the feature parameters, click on the green tick mark ✓ in the PropertyManager.

Procedure for Editing the Sketch of a Feature

1. Click on a feature in the FeatureManager Design Tree. A Pop-up toolbar appears, see Figure 7.42.
2. Click on the **Edit Sketch** tool in the Pop-up toolbar, see Figure 7.42. The Sketching environment is invoked.

Figure 7.42

3. By using the sketching tools in the Sketching environment, you can now modify the sketch of the feature as per your requirement.
4. Once you have edited the sketch of the feature, exit the Sketching environment.

Note: You can also select a sketch to be edited in the FeatureManager Design Tree and then click on the **Edit Sketch** tool in the Pop-up toolbar to invoke the Sketching environment for editing it.

Measuring the Distance between Entities/Faces

In SOLIDWORKS, you can measure the distance and angle between lines, points, faces, planes, and so on by using the **Measure** tool in the **Evaluate CommandManager**, see Figure 7.43. Also, you can measure radius and other parameters of different geometrical entities.

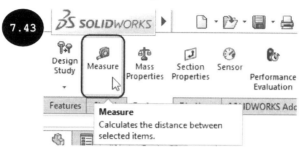

7.43

To measure the distance between entities, click on the **Evaluate** tab in the CommandManager to display the tools of the **Evaluate CommandManager**. Next, click on the **Measure** tool in the **Evaluate CommandManager**, see Figure 7.43. The **Measure** window appears, see Figure 7.44. Also, the cursor changes to measure cursor. You can expand the **Measure** window, if not expanded by default, by clicking on the down arrows available on the right of the window. Figure 7.45 shows the expanded **Measure** window. Some of the options of this window are as follows:

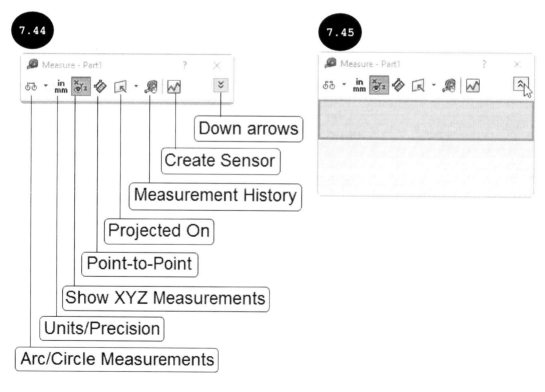

Arc/Circle Measurements

The options in the Arc/Circle Measurements flyout are used to specify the method of measuring arcs and circles, see Figure 7.46. To invoke this flyout, click on the down arrow available next to the Arc/Circle Measurements button in the window. The options in the Arc/Circle Measurements flyout are as follows:

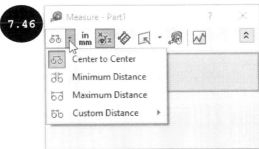

Center to Center

The Center to Center option of the Arc/Circle Measurements flyout is used to measure the center to center distance between two arc entities, circular entities, or cylindrical faces. On selecting the Center to Center option, the center to center distance between the selected entities is measured and appears in the graphics area as well as in the expanded Measure window, see Figure 7.47.

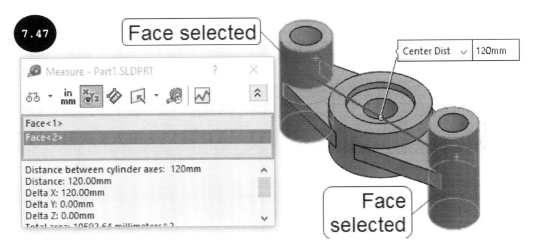

Minimum Distance

The Minimum Distance option is used to measure minimum distance between two selected arcs or circular entities. On selecting the Minimum Distance option, minimum distance between two selected entities is measured and appears in the graphics area, see Figure 7.48.

Maximum Distance

The Maximum Distance option is used to measure maximum distance between two selected arcs or circular entities, see Figure 7.49.

298 Chapter 7 > Advanced Modeling - I

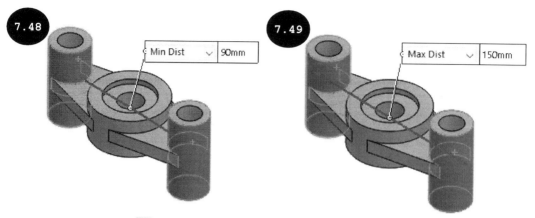

Custom Distance

The **Custom Distance** option is used to measure the distance between entities or faces, as per the requirement. When you move the cursor over the **Custom Distance** option of the flyout. A cascading menu appears, see Figure 7.50. By using this cascading menu, you can specify start and end conditions of measurement. Depending upon the start and end conditions specified, the respective distance between the selected entities is measured and appears in the graphics area.

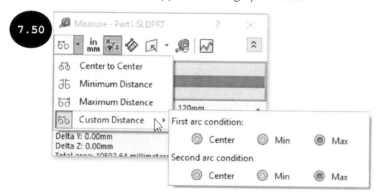

Units/Precision

The **Units/Precision** button is used to specify units and precision of measurement. When you click on this button, the **Measure Units/Precision** dialog box appears, see Figure 7.51. By default, the **Use document settings** radio button is selected in this dialog box. As a result, you can use the units and precision values specified in the current document of SOLIDWORKS for measurement. By selecting the **Use custom settings** radio button, you can customize the units and precision values of measurement.

Show XYZ Measurements

The **Show XYZ Measurements** button is used to measure the dX, dY, and dZ measurements between the selected entities, see Figure 7.52.

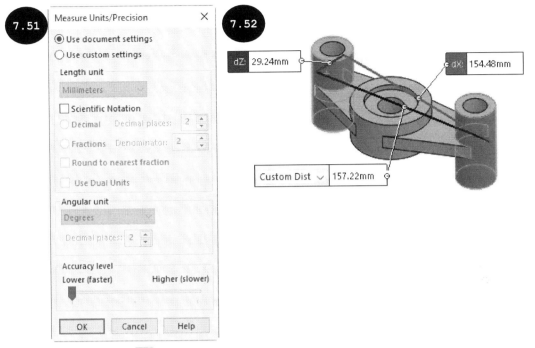

Point-to-Point

The Point-to-Point button is used to measure the distance between two points or vertices. When this button is activated, the point-to-point mode of measurement gets activated.

Measurement History

The **Measurement History** button is used to display the history of all measurements made in the current session of SOLIDWORKS. When you click on this button, the **Measurement History** dialog box appears with the details of measurement made so far in the current session, see Figure 7.53.

Procedure for Measuring Distance between Entities/Faces

1. Click on the **Measure** tool in the **Evaluate CommandManager**. The **Measure** window appears.
2. Specify the required option for the measurement in the **Measure** window.
3. Select entities or the faces of the model to be measured in the graphics area. The distance between the selected entities or faces appears in the graphics area.
4. After viewing the measurement, click anywhere in the graphics area to exit the selection.
5. Similarly, you can continue measuring the distance between other entities or faces.
6. Once you have done the measurement, press the ESC key to exit the tool.

Assigning Appearance/Texture

In SOLIDWORKS, you can change the default appearance/texture of a model by assigning predefined or customized appearance to the model, features, and faces. The methods of assigning predefined and customized appearance/texture are as follows:

Assigning Predefined Appearance/Texture

You can assign predefined appearance/texture to a model by using the **Appearances, Scenes, and Decals Task Pane**. To display this Task Pane, click on the **Appearances, Scenes, and Decals** tab available at the right of the graphics area, see Figure 7.54.

Procedure for Assigning Predefined Appearance/ Texture

1. Click on the **Appearances, Scenes, and Decals** tab in the Task Pane. The **Appearances, Scenes, and Decals Task Pane** appears, see Figure 7.54.

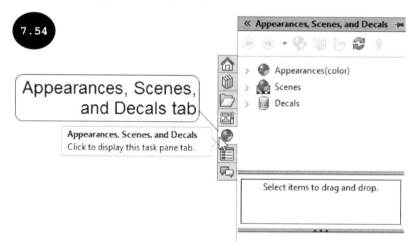

2. Expand the **Appearance(color)** node by clicking on the arrow available on its front. The predefined appearance categories appear.
3. Expand a required predefined category, such as **Plastic**, **Metal**, or **Glass**. The sub-categories of the selected category appear.
4. Select a required sub-category, see Figure 7.55. The thumbnails of the predefined appearance available in the selected sub-category appears in the lower half of the Task Pane, see Figure 7.55. In this figure, the **Textured** sub-category of the **Plastic** category is selected.

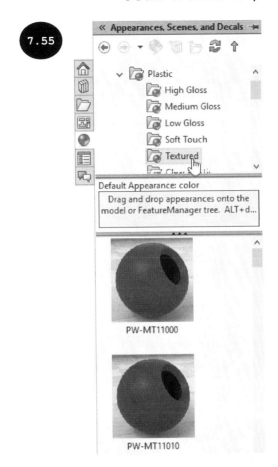

5. Drag and drop the required predefined appearance (thumbnail) from the lower half of the Task Pane over the face of the model by pressing and holding the left mouse button. A Pop-up toolbar appears, see Figure 7.56.

Note: The options in the Pop-up toolbar allow you to choose the required target for assigning the appearance. You can assign appearance to a face, a feature, a body, or a part by clicking on the respective tool in the Pop-up toolbar.

6. Click on the required tool in the Pop-up toolbar. The appearance is assigned to model depending upon the target selected in the Pop-up toolbar.

Note: If you drag and drop the appearance thumbnail in the graphics area (empty area), the appearance will be assigned to the entire model.

Assigning Customized Appearance

In addition to assigning predefined appearance to faces, features, bodies, you can also customize the appearance properties as required and then assign it. To assign the customized appearance, click on the **Edit Appearance** tool in the **View (Heads-up)** toolbar, see Figure 7.57. The **color PropertyManager** appears on the left side of the graphics area, see Figure 7.58. Also, the **Appearances, Scenes, and Decals Task Pane** appears on the right of the graphics area. The options in the **color PropertyManager** are used to assign colors, material appearances, and transparency to faces, features, or bodies.

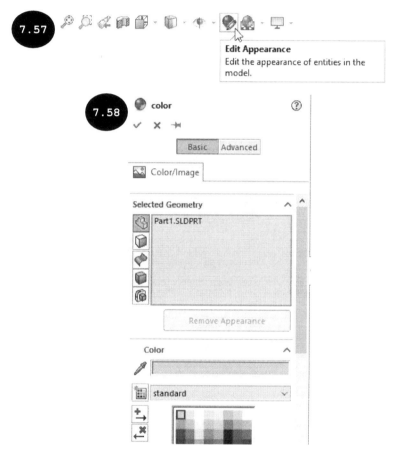

Note: If the model already has an appearance or texture assigned, then on clicking the **Edit Appearance** tool in the **View (Heads-up)** toolbar, the respective PropertyManager appears, which allows you to edit properties of the appearance or texture assigned.

You can also invoke the **color PropertyManager** by clicking on **Edit > Appearance > Appearance** from the SOLIDWORKS menus. Alternatively, select a face of the model. A Pop-up toolbar appears, see Figure 7.59. In this Pop-up toolbar, click on the down arrow next to the **Appearances** tool. A flyout appears, see Figure 7.59. Next, in this flyout, click on the field next to the *face name, feature name, body name,* or *Part name* to display the **color PropertyManager**.

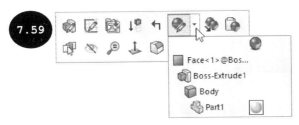

The options in the color PropertyManager are divided into two categories: Basic and Advanced. By default, on invoking the color PropertyManager, the Basic tab is activated. As a result, the PropertyManager displays basic and important options for customizing the appearance. To access advanced options, you need to activate the Advance tab of the PropertyManager. Some of the options of both these tabs are as follows:

Basic Tab
The Basic tab of the color PropertyManager displays the basic and important options for assigning appearance to faces, features, or bodies. Some of the options are as follows:

Selected Geometry
The Selected Geometry rollout is used to select geometry for applying appearance. You can select faces, features, bodies, or a part by clicking on their respective buttons (Select Part, Select Faces, Select Surfaces, Select Bodies, or Select Features) available on the left of this rollout, see Figure 7.60. For example, to assign color to the faces of the model, click on the Select Faces button and then select faces of the model from the graphics area. The name of the selected faces appears in the Selected Entities field of this rollout.

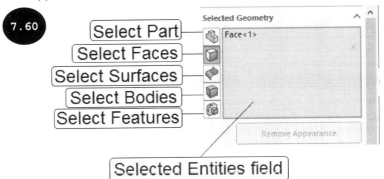

Note: To remove the already selected geometries in Selected Entities field, right-click on the Selected Entities field in the Selected Geometry rollout and then select the Clear Selection option from the shortcut menu, appeared. All selection geometries have been removed. You can also remove individual geometry. For doing so, select a geometry in the Selected Entities field of the rollout to be removed and then right-click. A shortcut menu appears. In this shortcut menu, click on the Delete option. The selected geometry has been removed from the selection.

Color

The **Color** rollout is used to select the required color to be assigned to the selected geometry or geometries, see Figure 7.61.

Advanced Tab

The **Advanced** tab of the **color PropertyManager** displays additional and advanced options for assigning appearance to selected faces, features, or bodies, see Figure 7.62. Some of the options of the **Advanced** tab are as follows:

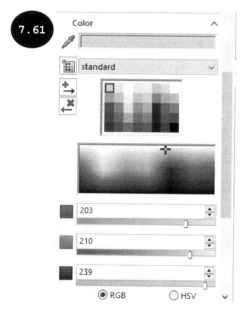

Color/Image

By default, the **Color/Image** button is activated in the **Advance** tab of the PropertyManager. As a result, the additional and advanced options for assigning appearance are available in the PropertyManager, see Figure 7.62. Some of these options are the same as those discussed earlier and the remaining options are as follows:

Appearance: The **Appearance** rollout is used to select an image file as the appearance for the selected geometries. By default, the **color.p2m** file is selected. You can also select any other file such as JPG and TIFF as the image file to be assigned. To assign an image file as the appearance, click on the **Browse** button of this rollout. The **Open** dialog box appears. Browse to the location where the image file has been saved and then select it. Next, click on the **Open** button of the dialog box. The **Save As** dialog box appears. Click on the **Save** button to save the file as .p2m for future use. The selected image file is assigned to the model. You can also save the current, customized appearance file for future use by using the **Save Appearance** button of the rollout.

Illumination
On clicking the **Illumination** button in the **Advance** tab, the options used to specify lighting properties for the selected appearance are displayed.

Mapping
On clicking the **Mapping** button in the **Advance** tab, the options used to map the selected image file on the selected geometry are displayed. By using these options, you can control the size, orientation, and location of the image file. Note that these options become available only when an image file or a predefined appearance has been applied to the geometry.

Surface Finish
On clicking the **Surface Finish** button in the **Advance** tab, the options used to specify the surface finishing for the appearance such as knurled, dimpled, or sandblasted are displayed.

Procedure for Assigning Customized Appearance
1. Invoke the **color PropertyManager** by clicking on the **Edit Appearance** tool in the **View (Heads-up)** toolbar.
2. Select required geometries (faces/features/surface/bodies/part) by using the respective button in the **Selected Geometry** rollout.
3. Select the required color by using the **Color** rollout. The preview appears in the graphics area.
4. Click on the green tick mark in the PropertyManager. The appearance is assigned.

Applying Material
In SOLIDWORKS, you can apply standard material properties such as density, elastic modulus, tensile strength to a model. Note that assigning standard material properties to a model is important in order to calculate its mass properties as well as to perform static and dynamic analysis. SOLIDWORKS contains almost all standard materials in its material library. You can directly apply the required standard material to a model from the material library. In addition to applying standard material, you can also customize the material properties and apply to a model. The procedure to apply standard material and custom material are as follows:

Procedure for Applying Standard Material
1. Right-click on the **Material <not specified>** option in the FeatureManager Design Tree. A shortcut menu appears, see Figure 7.63.

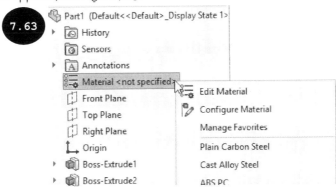

306 Chapter 7 > Advanced Modeling - I

2. Click on the **Edit Material** option in the shortcut menu, see Figure 7.63. The **Material** dialog box appears, see Figure 7.64.

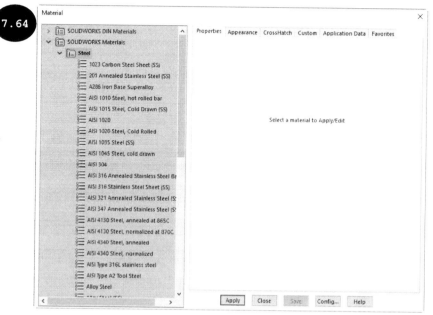

3. Expand the **SOLIDWORKS Materials** node (if not expanded by default). The different material categories such as Steel, Iron, and Aluminium Alloys appear in the dialog box.
4. Expand the required material category, such as Steel, Iron, or Aluminium Alloys. The materials available in the expanded material category appear, see Figure 7.65.
5. Select the required material from the list of available materials. The properties of the selected material appear on the right half of the dialog box, see Figure 7.65.

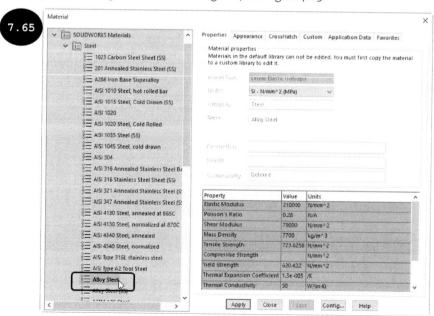

6. Click on the **Apply** button in the dialog box to apply the material properties of the selected material to the model. Next, click on the **Close** button to exit the dialog box.

Procedure for Applying Customized Material Properties

1. Invoke the **Material** dialog box and then right-click on the **Custom Materials** node in the dialog box. A shortcut menu appears, see Figure 7.66.
2. Click on the **New Category** option in the shortcut menu, see Figure 7.66. A new category is added under the **Custom Material** node. Also, its default name *New Category* appears in an edit field.

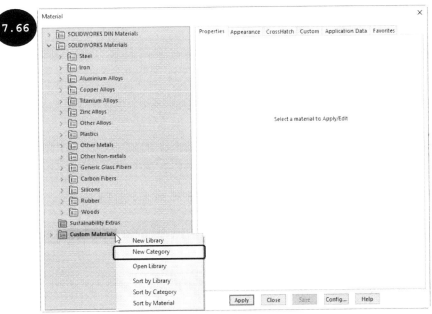

3. Enter a new name for the newly added category in the edit field and then click anywhere in the dialog box area.
4. Right-click on the newly added category in the dialog box to display a shortcut menu.
5. Click on the **New Material** option in the shortcut menu. A new material is added under the selected category. Also, its default name *Default* appears in an edit field.
6. Enter a new name for the newly added material in the edit field and then click anywhere in the drawing area.
7. Click on the newly added material. The default properties of the selected newly added material appeared on the right half of the dialog box, see Figure 7.67. In this figure, *SW CAD* material category and the *SW 1001* material are added in the **Custom Material** node.
8. Specify new material properties such as Poisson's ratio, Density, and Yield Strength as required in the respective fields of the dialog box. Next, click on the **Save** button to save the specified properties.
9. Click on the **Apply** button to apply the custom material to the model.
10. Click on the **Close** button to exit the dialog box.

Note: You can also copy material properties of a standard material and then customize it. For doing so, select a standard material and then right-click to display a shortcut menu. Next, click on the **Copy** option in the shortcut menu. After copying a standard material, select a custom material category in the **Custom Material** node of the dialog box and then right-click to display a shortcut menu. In the shortcut menu, click on the **Paste** option. The copied standard material is added in the selected custom material category. Now, select the newly added standard material in the custom material category to display its material properties on the right half of the dialog box. Now, you can customize the material properties of the standard material as required and then click on the **Apply** button of the dialog box.

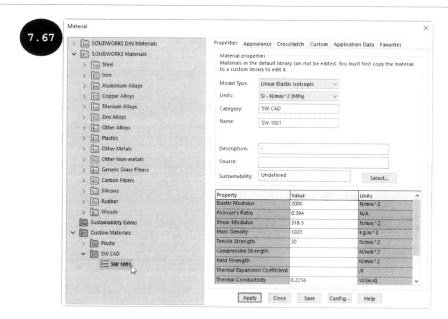

7.67

Calculating Mass Properties

In SOLIDWORKS, after assigning material properties to a model, you can calculate its mass properties such as mass and volume by using the **Mass Properties** tool in the **Evaluate CommandManager**, see Figure 7.68. To calculate the mass properties of a model, click on the **Mass Properties** tool. The **Mass Properties** dialog box appears and displays the mass properties of the model, see Figure 7.69. The options of the dialog box are as follows:

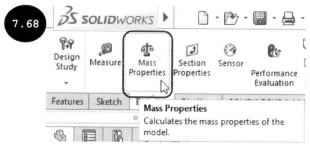

7.68

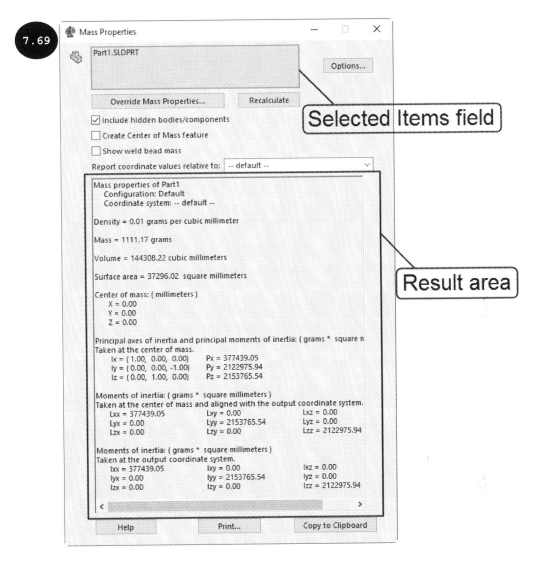

Figure 7.69

Selected Items
The **Selected Items** field in the dialog box is used to select a model for calculating its mass properties. By default, the model available in the graphics area gets selected and its name appears in this field, see Figure 7.69. As a result, the properties such as mass, volume, and center of mass of the model appear in the **Result** area of the dialog box, see Figure 7.69.

Options
The **Options** button is used to specify unit settings for mass properties. When you click on the **Options** button, the **Mass/Section Property Options** dialog box appears. By default, the **Use document settings** radio button is selected in this dialog box. As a result, the units and precision values specified for the current document of SOLIDWORKS are used for calculating mass properties. Also, the edit fields of this dialog box are not activated. To specify the custom unit settings for mass properties, select the **Use custom settings** radio button, see Figure 7.70. As soon as you select the

Use custom settings radio button, all the edit fields of the dialog box are activated which allow you to specify custom unit settings for mass properties, see Figure 7.70. After customizing the unit's settings, click on the OK button.

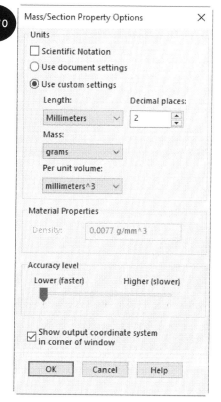

Figure 7.70

Recalculate

The **Recalculate** button is used to recalculate the mass properties of the model in case you have made any changes in the model or added/deleted any item in the selection set.

Override Mass Properties

The **Override Mass Properties** button is used to override the calculated mass properties of a model. On clicking this button, the **Override Mass Properties** dialog box appears. This dialog box is used to override the default calculated mass properties such as mass and center of mass of the model. Note that the edit fields of this dialog box are not enabled, by default. To enable these edit fields for overriding the mass properties, you need to select the respective check boxes: **Override mass, Override center of mass**, and **Override moments of inertia** of the dialog box, see Figure 7.71. In this figure, the **Override mass, Override center of mass**, and **Override moments of inertia** check boxes of the dialog box are selected. As a result, all the respective edit fields of the dialog box are enabled. In these edit fields, you can specify override values for mass, center of mass, and moments of inertia, respectively. After defining the override mass properties, click on the OK button in the dialog box.

Note: The override properties specified for a model are not the actual properties of the model.

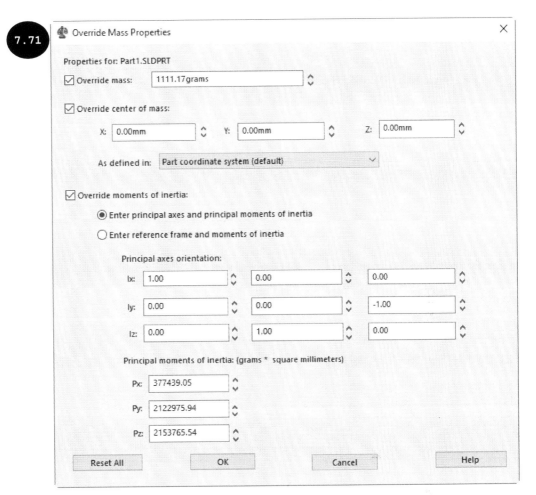

Figure 7.71

Include hidden bodies/components

By default, the **Include hidden bodies/components** check box of the **Mass Properties** dialog box is selected. As a result, all hidden bodies or components of the selected model are included while calculating the mass properties. However, on unchecking this check box, the hidden bodies/components are not included in the calculation.

Create Center of Mass feature

On selecting the **Create Center of Mass feature** check box, the center of mass of the model appears in the graphics area and its symbol is added in the FeatureManager Design Tree as soon as you exit **Mass Properties** dialog box.

> **Note:** The center of mass of a model is appeared in the graphics area either when it is selected in the FeatureManager Design Tree or its visibility is turned on in the graphics area. To turn on the visibility of the center of mass, click on the **Hide/Show Items** tool in the **View (Heads-Up)** toolbar to display a flyout, see Figure 7.72. Next, click on the **View Center of Mass** tool.

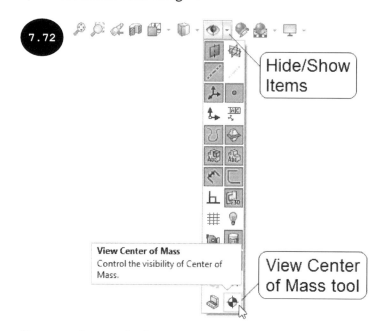

Report coordinate values relative to
The **Report coordinate values relative to** drop-down list of the **Mass Properties** dialog box is used to select a coordinate system with respect to which the mass properties are to be calculated. By default, the **default** option is selected in this drop-down list. As a result, the default coordinate system is used for calculating mass properties of the model.

Note: The **Report coordinate values relative to** drop-down list displays coordinate systems that are created in the current document of SOLIDWORKS. In case you have not created any coordinate system, then only the **default** option is displayed in this drop-down list.

Result
The **Result** area of the dialog box is used to display all calculated results of the model.

Print
The **Print** button is used to print the calculated results.

Copy to Clipboard
The **Copy to Clipboard** button is used to copy the results to the clipboard.

Procedure for Calculating Mass Properties
1. After specifying material properties to a model, click on the **Mass Properties** tool in the **Evaluate CommandManager**. The **Mass Properties** dialog box appears and displays mass properties of the current model.
2. Review the results of the mass properties and then exit the dialog box.

Tutorial 1

Create the model shown in Figure 7.73. You need to create the model by creating its all features one by one. All dimensions are in mm.

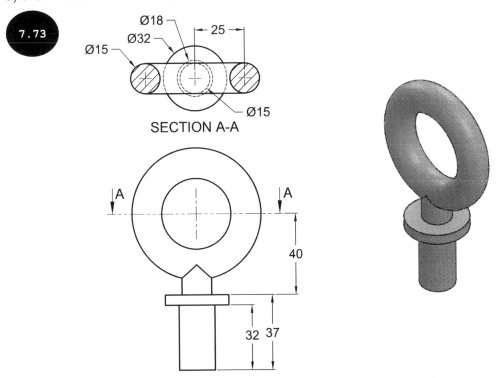

Section 1: Starting SOLIDWORKS
1. Double-click on the SOLIDWORKS icon on your desktop to start SOLIDWORKS.

Section 2: Invoking the Part Modeling Environment
1. Click on the **New** tool in the **Standard** toolbar. The **New SOLIDWORKS Document** dialog box appears.

2. Double-click on the **Part** button in the dialog box. The Part modeling environment is invoked.

Section 3: Specifying Unit Settings
1. Move the cursor toward the lower right corner of the screen over the Status Bar and then click on the **Unit System** area. The **Unit System** flyout appears, see Figure 7.74.

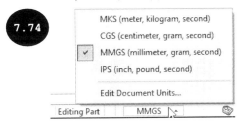

314 Chapter 7 > Advanced Modeling - I

2. Make sure that the **MMGS (millimeter, gram, second)** option is tick-marked in this flyout.

Tip: A tick mark in front of a unit system indicates that it has been selected as the unit system for the current document of SOLIDWORKS. You can also open the **Document Properties - Units** dialog box to specify unit system by selecting the **Edit Document Units** option of the **Unit System** flyout.

Section 4: Creating the Base/First Feature - Revolved Feature

1. Invoke the Sketching environment by selecting the Top plane as the sketching plane and then create the sketch of the base feature, see Figure 7.75. The base feature of the model is a revolved feature.

Tip: To make the sketch of the base feature fully defined as shown in Figure 7.75, you need to make sure that the centerpoint of the circle has coincident relation with the horizontal centerline. The vertical centerline in the figure will be used as the axis of revolution for creating the revolved feature.

2. Click on the **Features** tab in the CommandManager to display the tools of the **Features CommandManager**, see Figure 7.76.

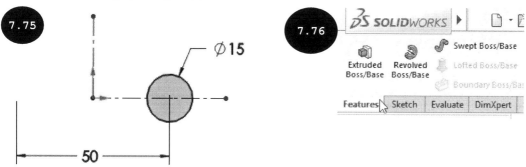

3. Click on the **Revolved Boss/Base** tool in the **Features CommandManager**. The **Revolve PropertyManager** appears. Also, the orientation of the sketch changes to trimetric orientation, see Figure 7.77.

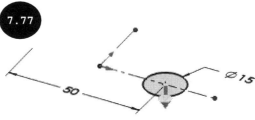

Note: If the sketch to be revolved has only one centerline, then on invoking the **Revolved Boss/Base** tool, the available centerline will automatically be selected as the axis of revolution and the preview of the revolved feature appears in the graphics area.

4. Click on the vertical centerline of the sketch as the axis of revolution. The preview of the revolved feature appears in the graphics area, see Figure 7.78.

5. Make sure that the 360-degree angle is specified in the **Direction 1 Angle** field of the PropertyManager.

6. Click on the green tick mark in the PropertyManager. The base/first revolved feature is created, see Figure 7.79.

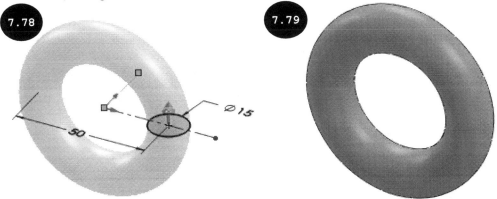

Section 5: Creating the Second Feature - Extruded Feature

To create the second feature of the model, you first need to create a reference plane at an offset distance of 40 mm from the Top plane.

1. Invoke the **Reference Geometry** flyout in the **Features CommandManager**, see Figure 7.80.

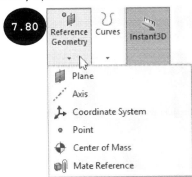

2. Click on the **Plane** tool in this flyout. The **Plane PropertyManager** appears.

3. Expand the FeatureManager Design Tree, which is now available at the top left corner of the graphics area by clicking on the arrow in its front, see Figure 7.81.

316 Chapter 7 > Advanced Modeling - I

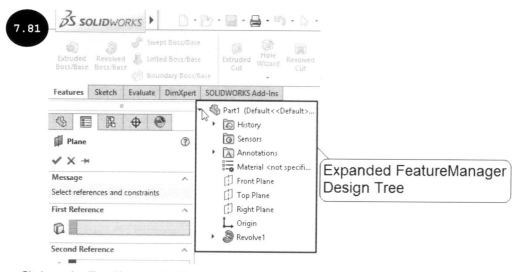

Figure 7.81

4. Click on the **Top Plane** in the FeatureManager Design Tree as the first reference. The preview of an offset plane appears in the graphics area, see Figure 7.82.

5. Select the **Flip offset** check box in the **First Reference** rollout of the PropertyManager to flip the direction of plane creation.

6. Enter **40** in the **Distance** field in the **First Reference** rollout of the PropertyManager.

7. Click on the green tick mark in the PropertyManager. The offset reference plane is created, see Figure 7.83.

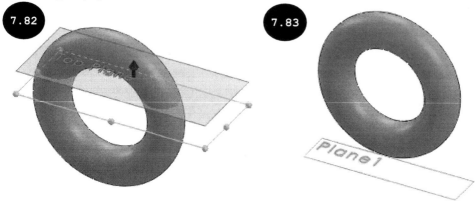

Figure 7.82   Figure 7.83

Now, you need to create the second feature of the model by selecting the newly created plane as the sketching plane.

8. Invoke the Sketching environment by selecting the newly created plane as the sketching plane.

9. Change the orientation of the model as normal to the viewing direction by using the **Normal To** tool of the **View Orientation** flyout, see Figure 7.84. Alternatively, press CTRL + 8.

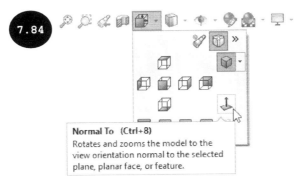

10. Create the sketch of the second feature (a circle of diameter 15 mm) and then apply diameter dimension, see Figure 7.85.

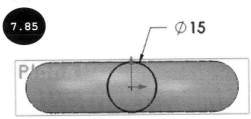

11. Click on the **Features** tab in the CommandManager to display the tools of the **Features CommandManager**.

12. Click on the **Extruded Boss/Base** tool. The **Boss-Extrude PropertyManager** and the preview of the extruded feature appear. Next, change the orientation of the model to isometric, see Figure 7.86.

13. Invoke the **End Condition** drop-down list in the **Direction 1** rollout, see Figure 7.87.

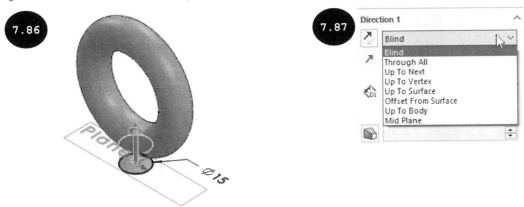

14. Click on the **Up To Next** option in the **End Condition** drop-down list. The preview of the feature gets modified in the graphics area such that it has been terminated at its next intersection, see Figure 7.88.

318 Chapter 7 > Advanced Modeling - I

15. Click on the green tick mark ✓ in the PropertyManager. The extruded feature is created, see Figure 7.89.

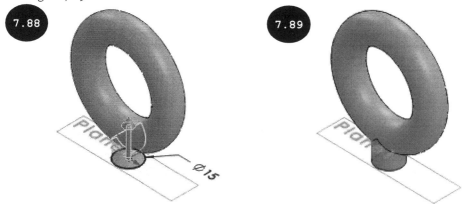

Section 6: Hiding the Reference Plane
1. Click on the reference plane in the graphics area. A Pop-up toolbar appears, see Figure 7.90.

2. Click on the **Hide** tool in the Pop-up toolbar, see Figure 7.90. The selected reference plane is hidden in the graphics area.

Section 7: Creating the Third Feature - Extruded Feature
1. Rotate the model such that the bottom planar face of the second feature is viewed, see Figure 7.91.

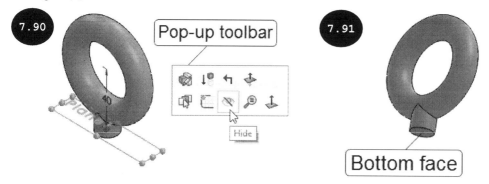

2. Invoke the Sketching environment by selecting the bottom planar face of the second feature as the sketching plane.

3. Change the orientation of the model as normal to the viewing direction by clicking on the **Normal To** tool in the **View Orientation** flyout. Alternatively, press CTRL + 8.

4. Create the sketch of the third feature (a circle of diameter 32 mm), see Figure 7.92.

5. Click on the **Features** tab and then click on the **Extruded Boss/Base** tool. The **Boss-Extrude PropertyManager** and the preview of the extruded feature appear. Next, change the orientation of the model to isometric.

6. Enter 5 in the Depth field of the Direction 1 rollout and then press ENTER.

7. Click on the green tick mark ✓ in the PropertyManager. The extruded feature is created, see Figure 7.93.

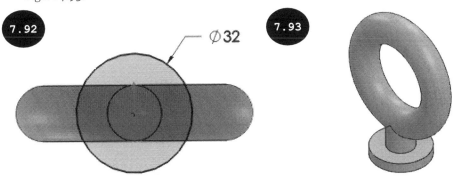

Section 8: Creating the Fourth Feature - Extruded Feature

1. Rotate the model such that the bottom planar face of the third feature is viewed. Next, invoke the Sketching environment by selecting the bottom planar face of the third feature as the sketching plane.

2. Change the orientation of the model as normal to the viewing direction by clicking on the Normal To tool in the View Orientation flyout. Alternatively, press CTRL + 8.

3. Create the sketch of the fourth feature (a circle of diameter 18 mm), see Figure 7.94.

4. Click on the Extruded Boss/Base tool in the Features CommandManager. The Boss-Extrude PropertyManager and the preview of the extruded feature appear. Next, change the orientation of the model to isometric.

5. Enter 32 in the Depth field of the Direction 1 rollout and then press ENTER.

6. Click on the green tick mark ✓ in the PropertyManager. The extruded feature is created, see Figure 7.95.

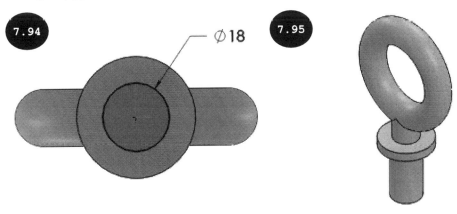

Section 9: Saving the Model

1. Click on the **Save** tool in the **Standard** toolbar. The **Save As** window appears.

2. Browse to the *SOLIDWORKS* folder and then create a folder with the name **Chapter 7**. Next, create another folder with the name **Tutorial** in the *Chapter 7* folder.

3. Enter **Tutorial 1** in the **File name** field of the dialog box as the name of the file and then click on the **Save** button. The model is saved as Tutorial 1 in the *Tutorial* folder of Chapter 7.

Tutorial 2

Create the model shown in Figure 7.96. You need to create the model by creating all its features one by one. After creating the model, assign the Alloy Steel material and calculate the mass properties of the model.

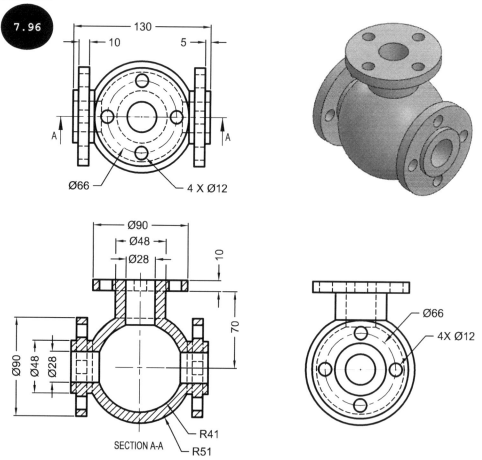

Section 1: Starting SOLIDWORKS
1. Double-click on the SOLIDWORKS icon on your desktop to start SOLIDWORKS.

Section 2: Invoking the Part Modeling Environment
1. Invoke the Part modeling environment by using the **New** tool of the **Standard** toolbar.

Section 3: Specifying Unit Settings
1. Move the cursor toward the lower right corner of the screen over the Status Bar and then click on the **Unit System** area. The **Unit System** flyout appears, see Figure 7.97.

2. Make sure that the **MMGS (millimeter, gram, second)** option is tick-marked in this flyout.

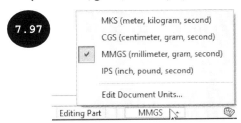

Section 4: Creating the Base/First Feature - Revolved Feature
1. Invoke the Sketching environment by selecting the Front plane as the sketching plane and then create the sketch of the base feature, see Figure 7.98. Do not exit the Sketching environment. Note that the base feature of the model is a revolved feature.

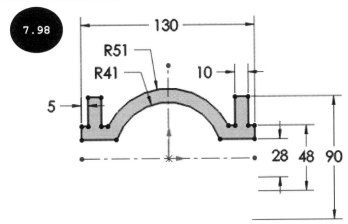

Tip: The sketch of the base feature shown in Figure 7.98 is symmetric about vertical centerline. As a result, you need to apply symmetric relations to the sketch entities with respect to the vertical centerline. Also, you need to apply equal relations between the entities of equal length, and collinear relations between the aligned entities of the sketch. You can also create line entities on one side of the vertical centerline and then mirror them to create entities on the other side of the vertical centerline.

2. Click on the **Features** tab in the CommandManager and then click on the **Revolved Boss/Base** tool. The **Revolve PropertyManager** appears. Also, the orientation of the sketch changes to trimetric, see Figure 7.99.

322 Chapter 7 > Advanced Modeling - I

> **Note:** If the sketch to be revolved has only one centerline than on invoking the **Revolved Boss/Base** tool, the available centerline is automatically selected as the axis of revolution and the preview of the revolved feature appears in the graphics area.

3. Click on the horizontal centerline of the sketch as the axis of revolution. The preview of the revolved feature appears in the graphics area.

4. Make sure that the 360-degree angle is specified in the **Direction 1 Angle** field of the PropertyManager.

5. Click on the green tick mark ✓ in the PropertyManager. The base/first revolved feature is created, see Figure 7.100.

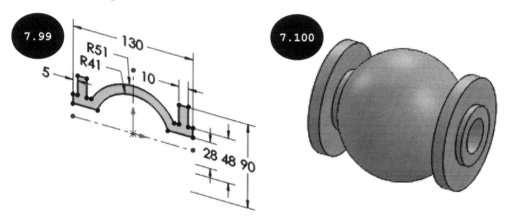

Section 5: Creating the Second Feature - Extruded Feature

To create the second feature of the model, you first need to create a reference plane at an offset distance of 70 mm from the Top plane.

1. Invoke the **Reference Geometry** flyout of the **Features CommandManager**, see Figure 7.101.

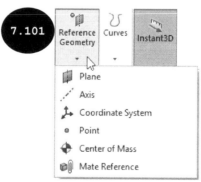

2. Click on the **Plane** tool of the **Reference Geometry** flyout. The **Plane** PropertyManager appears.

3. Expand the FeatureManager Design Tree which is now available at the top left corner of the graphics area by clicking on the arrow in its front.

4. Click on the **Top Plane** in the FeatureManager Design Tree as the first reference. The preview of an offset reference plane appears in the graphics area.

5. Enter **70** in the **Distance** field of the **First Reference** rollout in the PropertyManager.

6. Click on the green tick mark ✓ in the PropertyManager. The reference plane at the offset distance of 70 mm is created, see Figure 7.102.

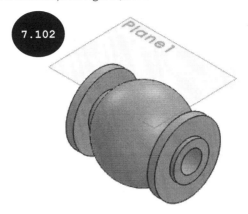

7.102

Now, you can create the second feature of the model by using the newly created plane.

7. Invoke the Sketching environment by selecting the newly created reference plane as the sketching plane.

8. Press CTRL + 8 to change the orientation of the model as normal to the viewing direction. Alternatively, click on the **Normal To** tool in the **View Orientation** flyout.

9. Create the sketch of the second feature (a circle of diameter 48 mm), see Figure 7.103. Do not exit the Sketching environment.

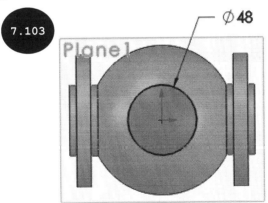

7.103

10. Click on the **Features** tab in the CommandManager. The tools of the **Features** CommandManager are displayed.

11. Click on the **Extruded Boss/Base** tool in the **Features CommandManager**. The Boss-Extrude PropertyManager and the preview of the extruded feature appear. Next, change the orientation of the model to isometric, see Figure 7.104.

324 Chapter 7 > Advanced Modeling - I

12. Click on the **Reverse Direction** button in the **Direction 1** rollout of the PropertyManager to reverse the direction of extrusion downward.

13. Invoke the **End Condition** drop-down list in the **Direction 1** rollout, see Figure 7.105.

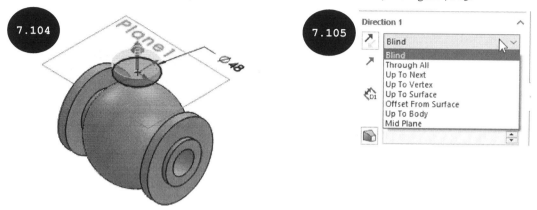

14. Click on the **Up To Next** option in the **End Condition** drop-down list. The preview of the feature is modified in the graphics area such that it has been terminated at its next intersection.

15. Click on the green tick mark in the PropertyManager. The extruded feature is created, see Figure 7.106.

Section 6: Hiding the Reference Plane
1. Click on the reference plane in the graphics area. A Pop-up toolbar appears, see Figure 7.107.

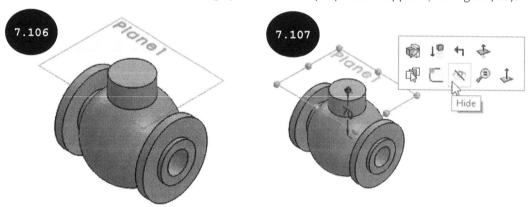

2. Click on the **Hide** tool in the Pop-up toolbar, see Figure 7.107. The selected reference plane is hidden in the graphics area.

Section 7: Creating the Third Feature - Extruded Feature
1. Invoke the Sketching environment by selecting the top planar face of the second feature as the sketching plane.

2. Press CTRL + 8 to change the orientation of the model as normal to the viewing direction.

3. Create the sketch of the third feature (a circle of diameter 90 mm), see Figure 7.108.

4. Click on the **Features** tab to display the tools of the **Features CommandManager**.

5. Click on the **Extruded Boss/Base** tool. The **Boss-Extrude PropertyManager** and the preview of the extruded feature appear. Change the orientation of the model to isometric.

6. Enter **10** in the **Depth** field in the **Direction 1** rollout and then press ENTER.

7. Click on the green tick mark ✓ in the PropertyManager. The extruded feature is created, see Figure 7.109.

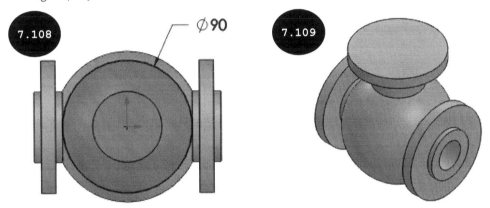

Section 8: Creating the Fourth Feature - Extruded Cut Feature

1. Invoke the Sketching environment by selecting the top planar face of the third feature as the sketching plane.

2. Press CTRL + 8 to change the orientation of the model as normal to the viewing direction.

3. Create the sketch of the fourth feature (a circle of diameter 28 mm), see Figure 7.110. Do not exit the Sketching environment.

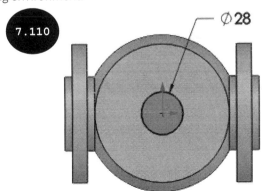

4. Click on the Features tab and then click on the **Extruded Cut** tool in the **Features CommandManager**. The **Cut-Extrude PropertyManager** and the preview of the extruded cut feature appear. Change the orientation of the model to isometric.

5. Invoke the **End Condition** drop-down list of the **Direction 1** rollout, see Figure 7.111.

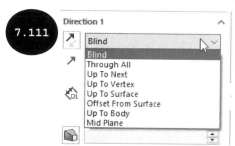

6. Click on the **Up To Surface** option in the **End Condition** drop-down list. The **Face/Plane** field is enabled in the **Direction 1** rollout and is activated by default.

7. Rotate the model such that the inner circular face of the base feature can be viewed, see Figure 7.112.

8. Click on the inner circular face of the base feature as the face to terminate the creation of extruded cut feature, see Figure 7.112. The preview of the extruded cut feature appears in the graphics area.

9. Click on the green tick mark ✓ in the PropertyManager. The extruded cut feature is created, see Figure 7.113.

Note: In Figure 7.113, the display style of the model has been changed to the 'hidden lines visible' display style by clicking on the **Hidden Lines Visible** tool in the **Display Style** flyout of the **View (Heads-Up)** toolbar. Also, the orientation of the model has been changed to the Front view for better understanding of the cut feature.

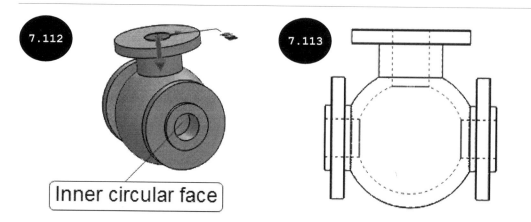

Section 9: Creating the Fifth Feature - Extruded Cut Feature

1. Invoke the Sketching environment by selecting the right planar face of the model as the sketching plane, see Figure 7.114.

2. Press CTRL + 8 to change the orientation of the model as normal to the viewing direction.

3. Create a circle of diameter 12 mm, see Figure 7.115. Note that you need to apply the vertical relation between the origin and the center point of the circle to make it fully defined.

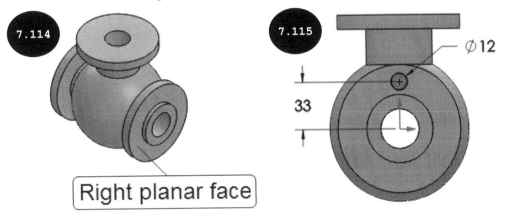

4. Invoke the **Circular Sketch Pattern** tool in the **Pattern** flyout of the **Sketch CommandManager**, see Figure 7.116 and then create a circular pattern of the circle for creating remaining circles of the same diameter and PCD, see Figure 7.117. Make sure that the center point of the circular pattern is at the origin. Next, exit the tool.

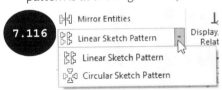
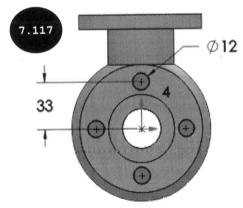

Note: Similar to pattern sketch entities in the Sketching environment, you can pattern features in the Part modeling environment. You will learn about how to pattern features in later chapters.

5. Click on the **Extruded Cut** tool in the **Features CommandManager**. The **Cut-Extrude PropertyManager** and the preview of the extruded cut feature appear. Next, change the orientation of the model to isometric, see Figure 7.118.

328   Chapter 7 > Advanced Modeling - I

6. Invoke the **End Condition** drop-down list of the **Direction 1** rollout and then click on the **Up To Next** option.

7. Click on the green tick mark ✓ in the PropertyManager. The extruded cut feature is created, see Figure 7.119.

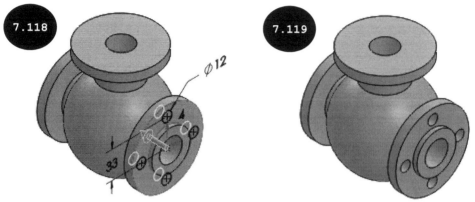

Section 10: Creating the Sixth Feature - Extruded Cut Feature
1. Similar to creating the extruded cut feature on the right planar face of the model, create the extruded cut feature on the left planar face of the model, see Figure 7.120. You can also mirror the extruded cut feature by selecting the Right plane as the mirroring plane to create the extruded cut feature on the left planar face.

Section 11: Creating the Seventh Feature - Extruded Cut Feature
1. Similar to creating the extruded cut feature on the right and left planar faces of the model, create the extruded cut feature on the top planar face of the model, see Figure 7.121.

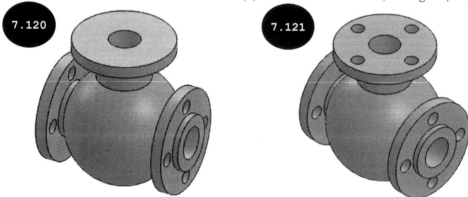

Section 12: Assigning the Material
1. Right-click on the **Material <not specified>** option in the FeatureManager Design Tree. A shortcut menu appears, see Figure 7.122.

2. Click on the **Edit Material** option in the shortcut menu. The **Material** dialog box appears, see Figure 7.123.

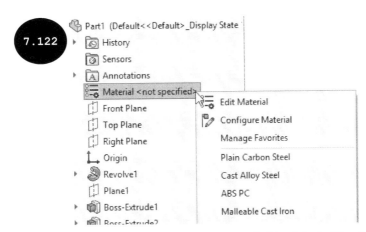

7.122

3. Expand the **SOLIDWORKS Materials** node, if not expanded by default. The different material categories such as Steel, Iron, and Aluminium Alloys appear in the dialog box.

4. Expand the **Steel** material category, see Figure 7.123. The list of materials available in the **Steel** category appears in the dialog box.

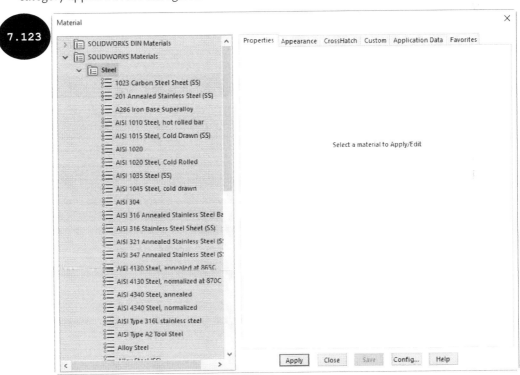

7.123

5. Click on the **Alloy Steel** material in the list of available materials. All material properties of the Alloy Steel material appear on the right side of the dialog box.

6. Click on the **Apply** button in the dialog box. The Alloy Steel material is applied to the model. Next, click on the **Close** button to exit the dialog box.

Section 13: Calculating Mass Properties

1. Click on the Evaluate tab in the CommandManager, see Figure 7.124.

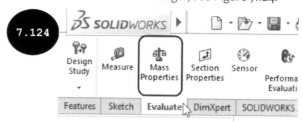

2. Click on the Mass Properties tool in the Evaluate CommandManager. The Mass Properties dialog box appears, which displays the mass properties of the model.

3. After reviewing the mass properties, exit the Mass Properties dialog box.

Section 14: Saving the Model

1. Click on the Save tool of the Standard toolbar. The Save As dialog box appears.

2. Browse to the *Tutorial* folder of *Chapter 7* and then save the file with the name Tutorial 2.

Tutorial 3

Create the model shown in Figure 7.125. After creating the model, assign the AISI 316 Stainless Steel Sheet (SS) material and calculate the mass properties of the model. All dimensions are in mm.

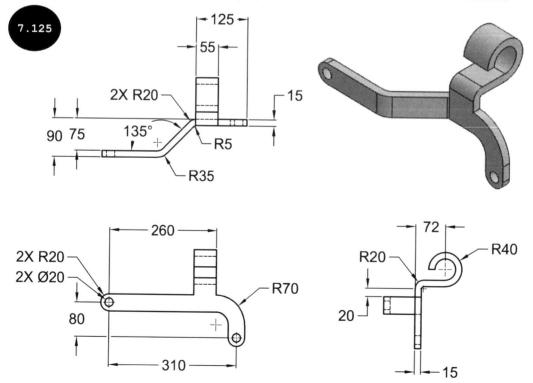

Section 1: Starting SOLIDWORKS
1. Double-click on the SOLIDWORKS icon on your desktop to start SOLIDWORKS.

Section 2: Invoking the Part Modeling Environment
1. Click on the **New** tool in the **Standard** toolbar. The **New SOLIDWORKS Document** dialog box appears.

2. Double-click on the **Part** button in the dialog box. The Part modeling environment is invoked.

Section 3: Specifying Unit Settings
1. Invoke the **Unit System** flyout, see Figure 7.126.

2. Make sure that the **MMGS (millimeter, gram, second)** option is tick-marked in the flyout.

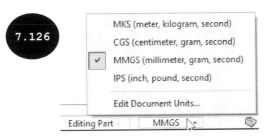

Section 4: Creating the Base/First Feature - Extruded Feature
1. Invoke the Sketching environment by selecting the Front plane as the sketching plane and then create the sketch of the base feature, see Figure 7.127. After creating the sketch, do not exit the Sketching environment.

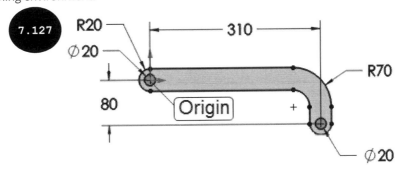

Tip: To make the sketch of the base feature fully defined as shown in Figure 7.127, you need to apply required relations such as tangent relations between tangent lines and arcs, equal relations between the entities having equal length, and the concentric relation between the arc entities sharing the same center point.

2. Click on the **Features** tab in the CommandManager and then click on the **Extruded Boss/Base** tool. The **Boss-Extrude PropertyManager** and the preview of the extruded feature appear, see Figure 7.128.

332 Chapter 7 > Advanced Modeling - I

3. Invoke the **End Condition** drop-down list in the **Direction 1** rollout, see Figure 7.129.

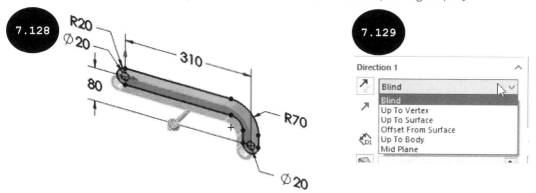

4. Click on the **Mid Plane** option in the **End Condition** drop-down list. The preview of the feature symmetric about the sketching plane appears in the graphics area.

5. Enter **90** in the **Depth** field in the **Direction 1** rollout of the PropertyManager.

6. Click on the green tick mark ✓ in the PropertyManager. The extruded feature is created, see Figure 7.130.

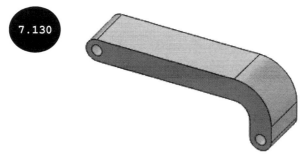

Section 5: Creating the Second Feature - Extruded Cut Feature

1. Invoke the Sketching environment by selecting the top planar face of the base feature as the sketching plane. Next, change the orientation of the model as normal to the viewing direction.

2. Create a sketch of the second feature, see Figure 7.131. Do not exit the Sketching environment.

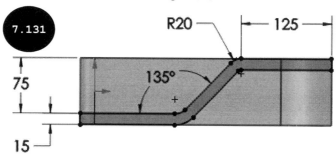

Tip: The sketch shown in Figure 7.131 is created by drawing one side of entities and then offset them at the offset distance of 15 mm, to create the other side of entities with closed caps, by using the **Offset Entities** tool.

3. Click on the **Extruded Cut** tool in the **Features CommandManager**. The **Cut-Extrude PropertyManager** and the preview of the extruded cut feature appear. Next, change the orientation of the model to isometric, see Figure 7.132.

4. Invoke the **End Condition** drop-down list in the **Direction 1** rollout, see Figure 7.133.

5. Click on the **Through All** option in the **End Condition** drop-down list to cut through the entire model.

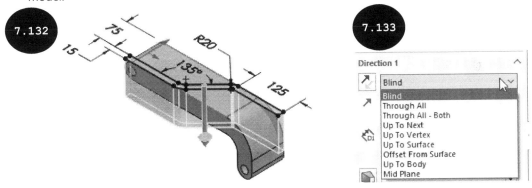

6. Click on the **Flip side to cut** check box in the **Direction 1** rollout of the PropertyManager. The side of cut material gets flipped.

7. Click on the green tick mark ✓ in the PropertyManager. The extruded cut feature is created, see Figure 7.134.

Section 6: Creating the Third Feature - Extruded Feature

To create the third feature of the model, you first need to create a reference plane at the offset distance of 205 mm from the Right plane.

1. Invoke the **Reference Geometry** flyout of the **Features CommandManager**, see Figure 7.135.

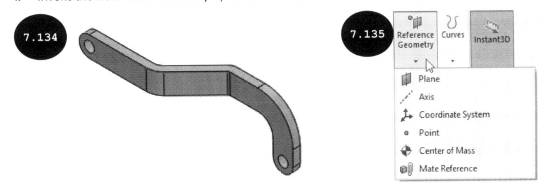

334   Chapter 7 > Advanced Modeling - I

2. Click on the **Plane** tool in the **Reference Geometry** flyout. The **Plane** PropertyManager appears.

3. Expand the FeatureManager Design Tree, which is now available on the top left corner of the graphics area, by clicking on the arrow in its front.

4. Click on the **Right Plane** as the first reference. The preview of an offset reference plane appears in the graphics area.

5. Enter **205** in the **Distance** field of the **First Reference** rollout in the PropertyManager.

6. Click on the green tick mark ✓ in the PropertyManager. The reference plane is created, see Figure 7.136.

   After creating the reference plane, you need to create the third feature of the model.

7. Invoke the Sketching environment by selecting the newly created reference plane as the sketching plane.

8. Press CTRL + 8 to change the orientation of the model as normal to the viewing direction.

9. Create the sketch of the third feature, see Figure 7.137. After creating the sketch, do not exit the Sketching environment.

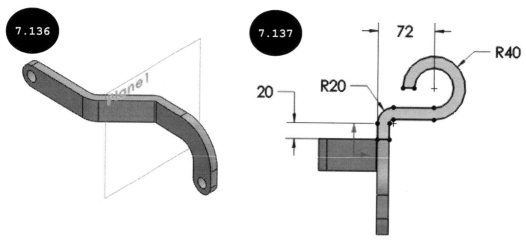

Tip: To make the sketch of the third feature fully defined as shown in Figure 7.137, you need to apply required relations such as tangent relations between tangent lines and arcs and concentric relation between the arc entities sharing the same center point.

10. Click on the **Features** tab in the CommandManager to display the tools of the **Features** CommandManager.

11. Click on the **Extruded Boss/Base** tool in the **Features CommandManager**. The Boss-Extrude PropertyManager and the preview of the extruded feature appear. Next, change the orientation of the model to isometric, see Figure 7.138.

12. Enter **55** in the **Depth** field in the **Direction 1** rollout of the PropertyManager. Next, press ENTER.

13. Click on the green tick mark ✓ in the PropertyManager. The extruded feature is created, see Figure 7.139. Next, hide the reference plane.

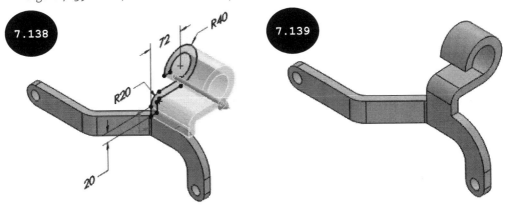

Section 7: Assigning the Material

1. Right-click on the **Material <not specified>** option in the FeatureManager Design Tree. A shortcut menu appears, see Figure 7.140.

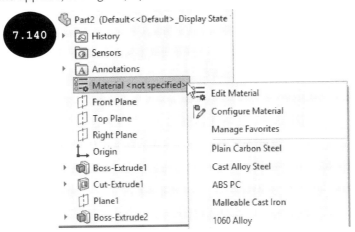

2. Click on the **Edit Material** option in the shortcut menu. The **Material** dialog box appears.

3. Expand the **SOLIDWORKS Materials** node, if not expanded by default. The different material categories such as Steel, Iron, and Aluminium Alloys appear in the dialog box.

4. Expand the **Steel** category. The materials in the **Steel** category appear, see Figure 7.141.

5. Click on the **AISI 316 Stainless Steel Sheet (SS)** material in the list of available materials, see Figure 7.141 The material properties of the selected material appear on the right panel of the dialog box, see Figure 7.141.

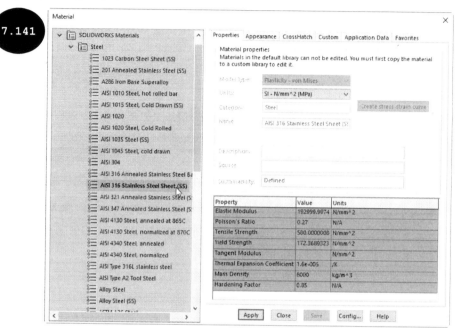

6. Click on the **Apply** button of the dialog box. The material is applied to the model. Next, click on the **Close** button to exit the dialog box.

Section 8: Calculating Mass Properties

1. Click on the **Evaluate** tab in the **CommandManager**. The tools of the **Evaluate CommandManager** are displayed.

2. Click on the **Mass Properties** tool in the **Evaluate CommandManager**. The **Mass Properties** dialog box appears, which displays the mass properties of the model.

3. After reviewing the mass properties, exit the **Mass Properties** dialog box.

Section 9: Saving the Model

1. Click on the **Save** tool of the **Standard** toolbar. The **Save As** dialog box appears.

2. Browse to the *Tutorial* folder of Chapter 7 and then save the model with the name Tutorial 3.

Hands-on Test Drive 1

Create the model shown in Figure 7.142. After creating the model, apply the Cast Alloy Steel material to the model and calculate its mass properties. All dimensions are in mm.

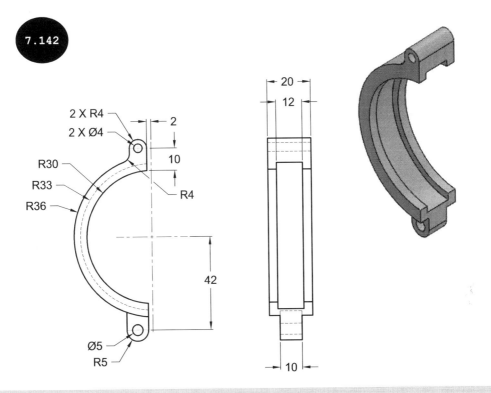

Hands-on Test Drive 2

Create the model shown in Figure 7.143. After creating the model, apply the Alloy Steel (SS) material to the model and calculate its mass properties. All dimensions are in mm.

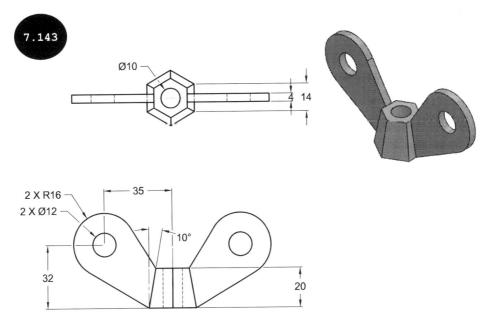

Summary

In this chapter, you have learned advanced options for creating extruded/revolved features. Also, you have learned how to create cut features by using the **Extruded Cut** and **Revolved Cut** tools as well as how to work with different types of sketches such as closed sketches, open sketches, and nested sketches. Additionally, you have learned how to create multiple features by using a single sketch having multiple contours/regions. After completing this chapter, you should be able to project the edges of existing features onto the current sketching plane by using the **Convert Entities** tool. Moreover, you have learned how to edit an existing feature and the sketch of a feature as per the design change.

You have also learned how to measure distance and angle between lines, points, faces, planes, and so on by using the **Measure** tool and how to assign an appearance/texture to a model, features, and faces. In addition, you can assign material properties and calculate the mass properties of a model.

Questions

- The options in the _____ drop-down list are used to define the start condition of extrusion.

- The _____ option is used to select a surface, a face, or a plane as the start condition of extrusion.

- The _____ option is used to define the end condition or termination of extrusion by selecting a vertex.

- You can create extruded cut features by using the _____ tool.

- The _____ sketches have all the entities connected end to end with each other without any gap.

- You can project the edges of existing features as sketch entities onto the current sketching plane by using the _____ tool.

- The _____ tool is used to calculate mass properties such as the mass and volume of a model.

- A revolved cut feature is created by removing material from the model by revolving a sketch around a centerline or an axis (True/False).

- You can edit individual features and their sketches as per your requirement. (True/False).

- In SOLIDWORKS, you cannot customize material properties. (True/False).

CHAPTER 8

Advanced Modeling - II

In this chapter, you will learn the following:

- Creating a Sweep Feature
- Creating a Sweep Cut Feature
- Creating a Lofted feature
- Creating a Lofted Cut Feature
- Creating a Boundary Feature
- Creating a Boundary Cut Feature
- Creating Curves
- Splitting Faces of a Model
- Creating 3D Sketches

In the previous chapters, you have learned about the primary modeling tools that are used to create 3D parametric models. Also, you have learned about the basic workflow of creating models, which is to first create the base feature of a model and then create the remaining features of the model one after another.

In this chapter, you will explore some of the advance tools such as **Swept Boss/Base**, **Lofted Boss/Base**, and **Boundary Boss/Base**. Also, you will learn how to split faces of a model and create different types of 3D curves and sketches.

Creating a Sweep Feature Updated

A sweep feature is created by adding material by sweeping a profile along a path. Figure 8.1 shows a profile and a path. Figure 8.2 shows the resultant sweep feature created by sweeping the profile along the path.

340 Chapter 8 > Advanced Modeling - II

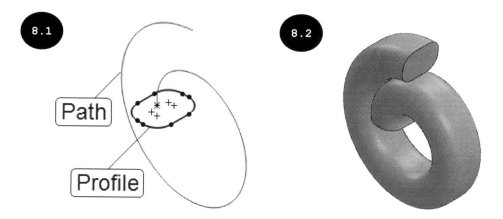

It is evident from the above figures that for creating a sweep feature, you first need to create a path and a profile where the profile follows the path and creates a sweep feature. To create a profile, you need to identify the cross-section of the feature to be created. To create a path, you need to identify the route/path taken by the profile for creating the feature. In SOLIDWORKS, you can create a sweep feature by using the **Swept Boss/Base** tool of the **Features CommandManager**. Note that for creating a sweep feature, you need to take care of the following points:

1. The profile must be a closed sketch. In SOLIDWORKS 2017, you can also select a face of a model as a profile. In addition to this, you can also select an edge or a group of edges of a model that form a closed loop as a profile.
2. The path can be an open or a closed sketch, which is made up of a set of end to end connected sketched entities, a curve, or a set of model edges.
3. The start point of the path must intersect the plane of the profile.
4. The profile and the path as well as the resultant sweep feature must not self-intersect.

After creating a path and a profile, click on the **Swept Boss/Base** tool in the **Features CommandManager**. The **Sweep PropertyManager** appears, see Figure 8.3. The options in the PropertyManager are as follows:

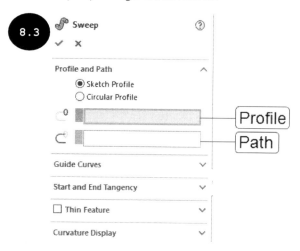

Profile and Path

The options in the **Profile and Path** rollout of the PropertyManager are used to select a profile and a path. The options are as follows:

Sketch Profile

The **Sketch Profile** radio button of the **Profile and Path** rollout is selected by default. As a result, the **Profile** and the **Path** fields are available in the PropertyManager, see Figure 8.3. The **Profile** field is used to select a profile of the sweep feature. You can select a closed sketch, a face, or an edge/a group of edges that form a closed loop as a profile, see Figure 8.4. The **Path** field is used to select a path of the sweep feature, see Figure 8.4. You can select an open or a closed sketch, an edge, or a curve as a path of the sweep feature.

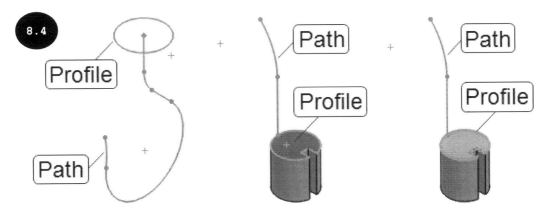

As soon as you select a profile and a path, the preview of the resultant sweep feature appears in the graphics area, see Figure 8.5.

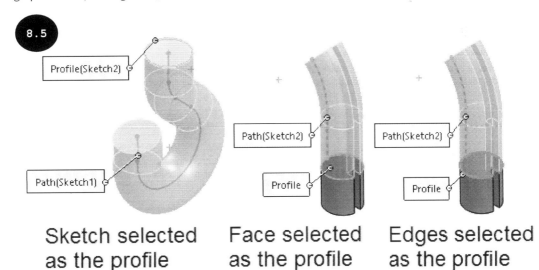

Note: If the profile is created in between the endpoints of the path, see Figure 8.6, then the preview of the sweep feature appears on either side of the profile, see Figure 8.7. Also, three buttons: **Direction 1**, **Bidirectional**, and **Direction 2** become available in the **Profile and Path** rollout, see Figure 8.8. The **Direction 1** and **Direction 2** buttons are used to sweep the profile on either direction of profile, whereas the **Bidirectional** button is used to sweep the profile on both the directions of the profile.

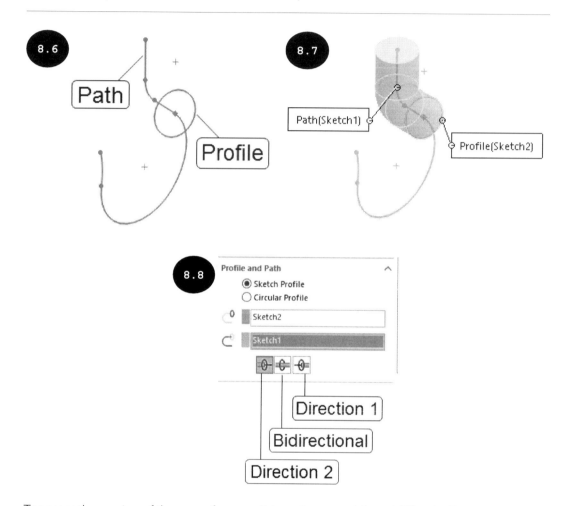

To accept the preview of the sweep feature, click on the green tick mark in the PropertyManager. The sweep feature is created.

Circular Profile

The **Circular Profile** radio button of the **Profile and Path** rollout is used to create a sweep feature having a circular section such as solid rod or hollow tube by specifying the diameter value. To create a sweep feature having a circular section by using this radio button, you do not need to select a profile. On selecting the **Circular Profile** radio button, the **Path** and **Diameter** fields become available in the rollout, see Figure 8.9.

The **Path** field is used to select a path of the sweep feature. By default, this field is activated. As a result, you can select an open or a closed sketch, an edge, or a curve as a path of the sweep feature. The **Diameter** field of the rollout is used to specify the diameter value of the circular profile. As soon as you select the path, the preview of the sweep feature having a circular profile of specified diameter appears in the graphics area, see Figure 8.10.

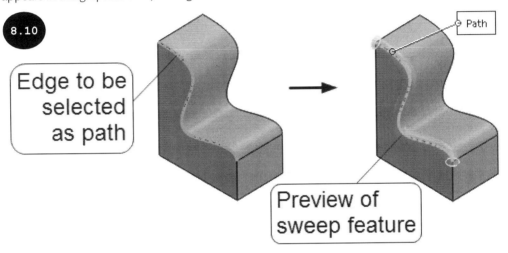

The options in the other rollouts of the **Sweep PropertyManager** are used to control the parameters of the sweep feature. These options are as follows:

Options

By default, the **Options** rollout of the PropertyManager is collapsed. To expand this rollout, click on the arrow available on its right, see Figure 8.11. Note that some of the options of the **Options** rollout are not available while creating a base/first feature. Also, the availability of options in this rollout depends upon the selection of **Sketch Profile** or **Circular Profile** radio button in the **Profile and Path** rollout of the PropertyManager. The options of the **Options** rollout are as follows:

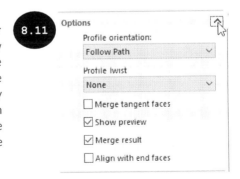

Profile orientation drop-down list

The options in the **Profile orientation** drop-down list are used to control the orientation of the profile along the path, see Figure 8.12. The options are as follows:

Follow Path

By default, the **Follow Path** option is selected in the drop-down list. As a result, the profile follows the path by maintaining the same angle of orientation from start to end. Also, aligns the profile normal to the path, see Figures 8.13 and 8.14.

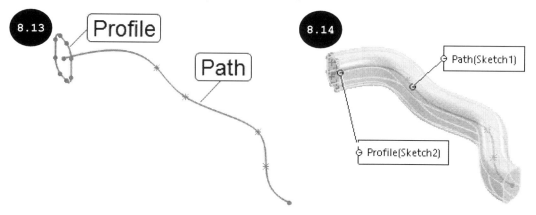

Keep Normal Constant

On selecting the **Keep Normal Constant** option, the profile follows the path such that it remains parallel throughout the path. In other words, the start and end sections of the resultant sweep feature will be parallel to each other. Figure 8.15 shows the preview of a sweep feature after selecting the **Follow Path** option and Figure 8.16 shows the preview of the sweep feature after selecting the **Keep Normal Constant** option.

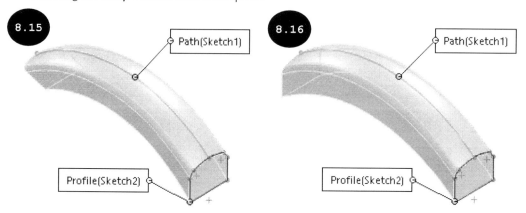

Profile Twist drop-down list

The options in the **Profile Twist** drop-down list are used to control the twisting or alignment of the profile along the path, see Figure 8.17. The options are as follows:

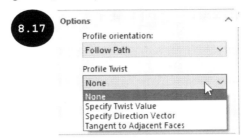

None
By default, the **None** option is selected in the **Profile Twist** drop-down list. As a result, the profile follows the path such that it maintains normal alignment with the path.

Specify Twist Value
By selecting the **Specify Twist Value** option, you can twist the profile along the path, see Figures 8.18 through 8.21. Figures 8.18 and 8.20 show the path and profile, respectively. Figures 8.19 and 8.21 show the preview of the resultant twisted sweep feature.

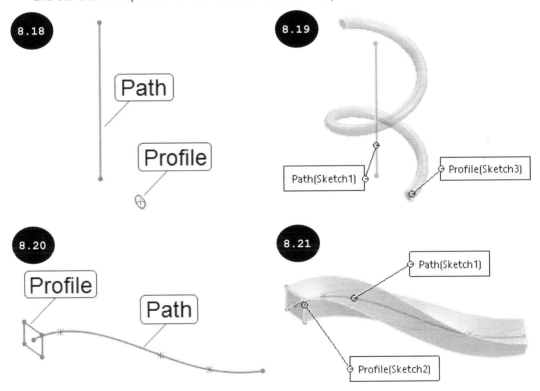

As soon as you select the **Specify Twist Value** option, the **Twist control** drop-down list and **Direction 1** field become available in the **Options** rollout, see Figure 8.22. The options in the **Twist control** drop-down list are used to control the twisting of the profile along the path. The options are as follows:

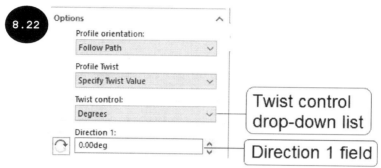

Figure 8.22

Degrees: By default, the **Degrees** option is selected in the **Twist control** drop-down list. As a result, you need to specify the twist angle in degrees in the **Direction 1** field of the rollout.

Radians: The **Radians** option is used to specify the twist angle in radians in the **Direction 1** field of the **Options** rollout.

Revolutions: By selecting the **Revolutions** option, you can specify the number of revolutions for the profile along the path in the **Direction 1** field. Figures 8.23 and 8.24 show the preview of a sweep feature after entering 3 in the **Direction 1** field as the number of revolutions.

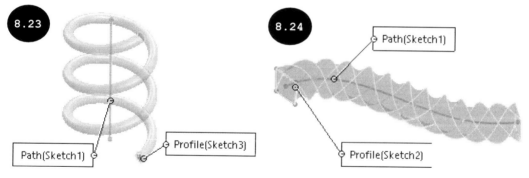

Figures 8.23 and 8.24

Note: If the profile is created in between the endpoints of the path, see Figure 8.25, and you are creating a bi-directional sweep feature, see Figure 8.26, then on selecting the **Specify Twist Value** option in the **Profile Twist** drop-down list, the **Direction 2** field also becomes available in the rollout along with the **Twist control** drop-down list and the **Direction 1** field. The **Direction 2** field is used to specify the twist angle in the second direction of the sweep feature, see Figure 8.27.

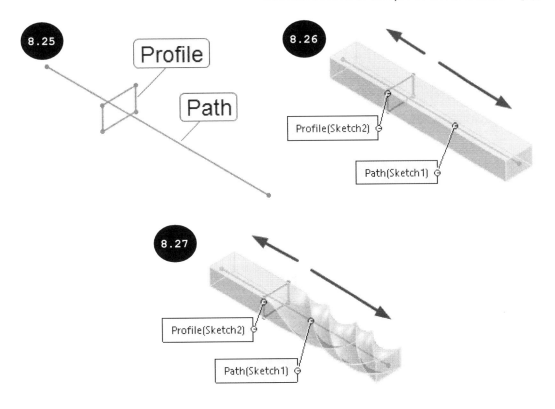

Specify Direction Vector

On selecting the **Specify Direction Vector** option in the **Profile Twist** drop-down list, the **Direction Vector** field becomes available. The **Direction Vector** field is used to select a direction vector for aligning the profile in its direction. You can select a plane, a planar face, a line, or a linear edge as a direction vector. Figure 8.28 shows a path, a profile, and a direction vector. Figure 8.29 shows the preview of the resultant sweep feature by selecting the Top plane as the direction vector.

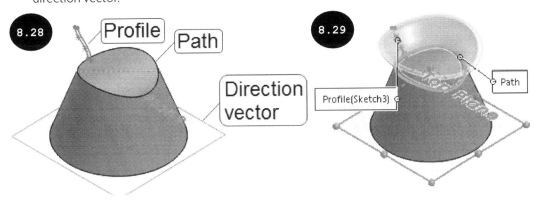

Tip: The path shown in the Figure 8.28 is a 3D closed edge of the model. You can select an open or closed edge of a model as a path for creating a sweep feature.

Minimum Twist

On selecting the **Minimum Twist** option in the **Profile Twist** drop-down list, the minimum twist is allowed to the profile while following the path in order to avoid the self-intersection, see Figure 8.30. Note that this option works better with 3D path and is available in the drop-down list only if a 3D sketch or a 3D edge is selected as the path of the sweep feature. You will learn more about creating 3D sketches later in this chapter. Figure 8.30 shows the preview of a sweep feature when the **Minimum Twist** option is selected.

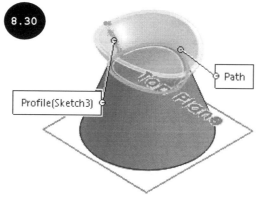

Tangent to Adjacent Faces

On selecting the **Tangent to Adjacent Faces** option, the profile maintains tangency with the adjacent face of the path, see Figure 8.31. This option works only if the path has adjacent face.

Natural

On selecting the **Natural** option in the **Profile Twist** drop-down list, the profile follows the path such that it maintains natural twist, see Figure 8.32. Note that this option works better with 3D path and is available in the drop-down list only if a 3D sketch or a 3D edge is selected as the path of the sweep feature. You will learn more about creating 3D sketches later in this chapter.

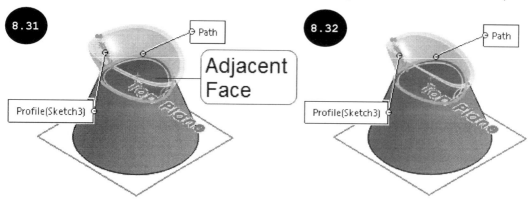

Follow Path and First Guide Curve

On selecting the **Follow Path and First Guide Curve** option, the profile follows the path as well as the 1st guide curve, see Figures 8.33 and 8.34. A guide curve is used to guide the profile (section) of a sweep feature. Note that this option is available in the drop-down list only after selecting a guide curve by using the **Guide Curves** rollout of the PropertyManager. To select a guide curve, expand the **Guide Curves** rollout by clicking on the arrow available on its front, see Figure 8.35. The field in this rollout is activated by default and is used to select guide curves from the graphics area. Make sure that the guide curve you select has pierce relation with the profile of the sweep feature. Figure 8.33 shows a path, a profile, and a guide curve. Figure 8.34 shows the preview of the resultant sweep feature.

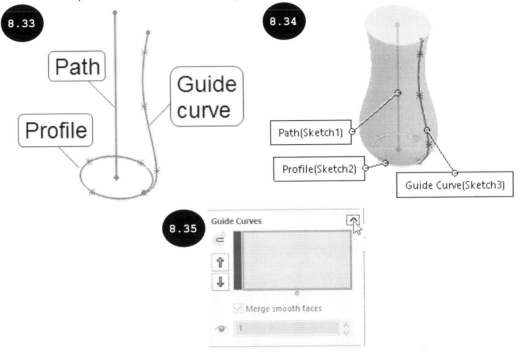

Note: In Figure 8.33, the path and the guide curve are created on the Front plane as individual sketches, and the profile is created on the Top plane. Also, the guide curve has pierce relation with the profile of the sweep feature.

Follow First and Second Guide Curve

On selecting the **Follow First and Second Guide Curve** option, the profile follows the path, and the first and second guide curves, see Figures 8.36 and 8.37. By using this option, you can guide the profile (section) of a sweep feature by using two guide curves. Note that this option is available in the drop-down list only after selecting two guide curves by using the **Guide Curves** rollout of the PropertyManager. To select guide curves, expand the **Guide Curves** rollout, see Figure 8.35. Next, select two guide curves one by one from the graphics area. Figure 8.36 shows a path, a profile, and two guide curves. Figure 8.37 shows the preview of the resultant sweep feature.

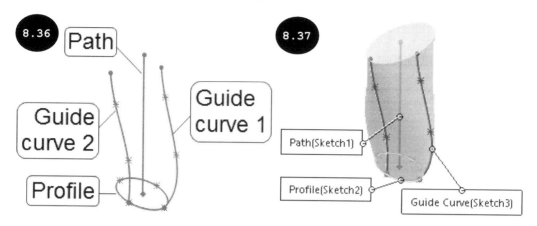

Note: In Figure 8.36, the path and the guide curve 1 are created on the Front plane as individual sketches, and the guide curve 2 is created on the Right plane. Also, the profile is created on the Top plane.

Tip: If the profile fails to follow both the guide curves, then you need to make sure that the resultant sweep feature does not have self intersection. Also, the guide curves must have pierce relation with the profile of the sweep feature.

Merge tangent faces
On selecting the **Merge tangent faces** check box in the **Options** rollout, the tangent faces of the resultant sweep feature merge into a single face. Figure 8.38 shows a sweep feature created by selecting the **Merge tangent faces** check box. Figure 8.39 shows a sweep feature created by unchecking the **Merge tangent faces** check box.

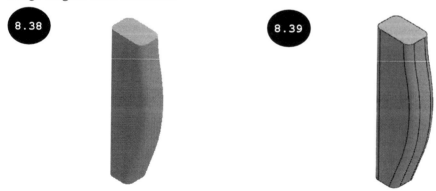

Merge result
By default, the **Merge result** check box is selected in the **Options** rollout, see Figure 8.40. As a result, the resultant sweep feature merges with the existing features of the model and forms a single body. On unchecking this check box, the sweep feature will not merge with the existing features of the model and make a separate body. Note that this check box is not available while creating the base/first feature of a model.

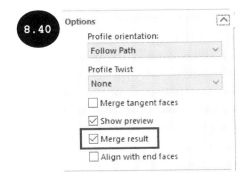

Align with end faces
On selecting the **Align with end faces** check box, the end section of the sweep feature gets aligned with the face of an existing feature, which is encountered by the path. Note that this check box is not available if the sweep feature being created is the base feature of a model. Figure 8.41 shows the preview of a sweep feature when the **Align with end faces** check box is selected and Figure 8.42 shows the preview of a sweep feature when the **Align with end faces** check box is unchecked.

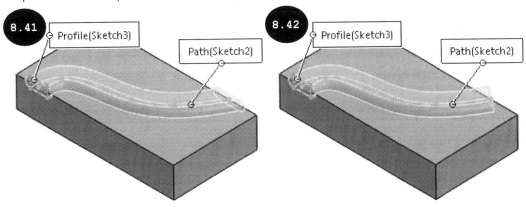

Show preview
By default, the **Show preview** check box is selected. As a result, while creating a sweep feature, its preview appears in the graphics area.

Guide Curves
The **Guide Curves** rollout of the **Sweep PropertyManager** is used to select guide curves of the sweep feature, see Figure 8.43. The options in the **Guide Curves** rollout are as follows:

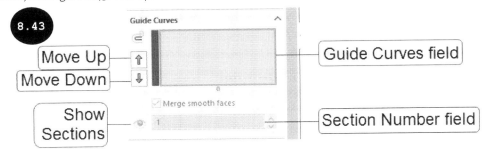

Guide Curves field

The **Guide Curves** field is used to select guide curves from the graphics area. Guide curves are used to guide the profile to follow the path. On selecting guide curves, their names are listed in this field in the sequence in which they are selected. You can select two guide curves. Note that the guide curves should have pierce relation with the profile of the sweep feature.

Move Up and Move Down

The **Move Up** and **Move Down** buttons are used to change the order or sequence of guide curves in the **Guide Curves** field. These buttons are on the left of the **Guide Curves** field.

Merge smooth faces

By default, the **Merge smooth faces** check box is selected. As a result, the smooth segments of the sweep feature get merged together. Figure 8.44 shows a sweep feature created by selecting the **Merge smooth faces** check box. Figure 8.45 shows a sweep feature created by unchecking the **Merge smooth faces** check box.

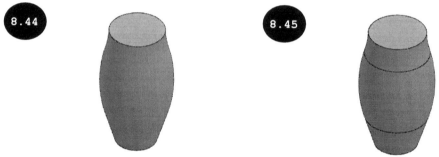

Show Sections

The **Show Sections** button of the rollout is used to view the intermediate sections of the sweep feature being created by using guide curves. By default, the **Show Sections** button is not activated. To activate this button, click on it. As soon as this button gets activated, the **Section Number** field is enabled in the rollout. On entering a section number in this field, the preview of the respective section is displayed in the graphics area, see Figure 8.46.

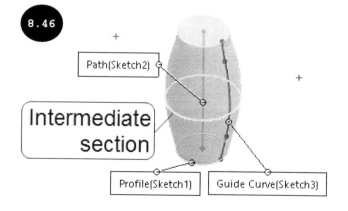

Start and End Tangency

The options in the **Start and End Tangency** rollout of the PropertyManager are used to specify the start and end tangency of the sweep feature. This rollout has two drop-down lists: **Start tangency type** and **End tangency type**, see Figure 8.47. The options in the drop-down lists are as follows:

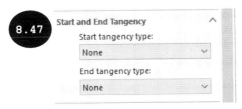

Start tangency type

The options in the **Start tangency type** drop-down list are used to specify the start tangency for a sweep feature. By default, the **None** option is selected in this drop-down list. As a result, tangency is not maintained at the start of the sweep feature. On selecting the **Path Tangent** option, the sweep feature maintains tangency with the path at its start. Figure 8.48 shows the preview of a sweep feature by selecting the **None** option and Figure 8.49 shows the preview of a sweep feature by selecting the **Path Tangent** option as the start tangency type.

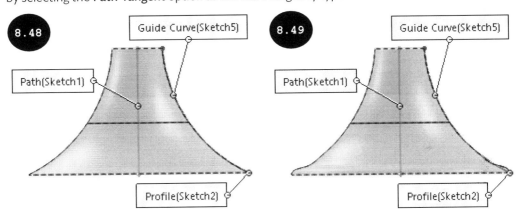

End tangency type

The options in the **End tangency type** drop-down list are used to specify the end tangency type for a sweep feature. By default, the **None** option is selected in this drop-down list. As a result, the tangency is not maintained at the end of the sweep feature. On selecting the **Path Tangent** option, the sweep feature maintains tangency with the path at its end.

Thin Feature

The **Thin Feature** rollout of the PropertyManager is used to create a thin sweep feature, see Figure 8.50. To create a thin sweep feature, expand this rollout by clicking on the check box on the title bar, see Figure 8.51. The options for creating the thin sweep feature are the same as those discussed earlier while creating the thin extruded and thin revolved features.

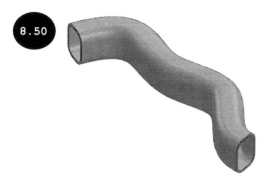
8.50

8.51

Procedure for Creating a Sweep Feature with Sketch Profile
1. Click on the **Swept Boss/Base** tool. The **Sweep PropertyManager** appears.
2. Make sure that the **Sketch Profile** radio button is selected in the **Profile and Path** rollout.
3. Select a closed sketch, a face, or an edge/edges that form a closed loop as the profile.
4. Select an open or a closed sketch, an edge, or a curve as the path of the sweep feature. The preview of the sweep feature appears.
5. Click on the green tick mark ✓ in the PropertyManager. The sweep feature is created.

Procedure for Creating a Sweep Feature with Circular Profile
1. Click on the **Swept Boss/Base** tool. The **Sweep PropertyManager** appears.
2. Click on the **Circular Profile** radio button in the **Profile and Path** rollout.
3. Select an open or a closed sketch, an edge, or a curve as the path of the sweep feature in the graphics area. The preview of the sweep feature appears with a default diameter of the profile.
4. Enter the diameter value for the circular profile in the **Diameter** field of the rollout.
5. Click on the green tick mark ✓ in the PropertyManager. The sweep feature is created.

Procedure for Creating a Sweep Feature with One Guide Curve
1. Create a path, a profile, and a guide curve as individual sketches.
2. Click on the **Swept Boss/Base** tool. The **Sweep PropertyManager** appears.
3. Make sure that the **Sketch Profile** radio button is selected in the **Profile and Path** rollout.
4. Select the profile of the sweep feature in the graphics area.
5. Select the path of the sweep feature. The preview of the sweep feature appears.
6. Expand the **Guide Curves** rollout of the PropertyManager.
7. Select the guide curve in the graphics area. The preview of the sweep feature appears such that the profile follows the path and its outer shape is maintained by the guide curve.
8. Click on the green tick mark ✓ in the PropertyManager. The sweep feature is created.

Procedure for Creating a Sweep Feature with Two Guide Curves
1. Create a path, a profile, and two guide curves as individual sketches.
2. Invoke the **Sweep PropertyManager**.
3. Make sure that the **Sketch Profile** radio button is selected in the **Profile and Path** rollout.
4. Select the profile and then select the path of the sweep feature in the graphics area.
5. Expand the **Guide Curves** rollout of the PropertyManager.
6. Select the first guide curve and then select the second guide curve. The preview of the sweep

feature appears such that the profile follows the path and its outer shape is maintained by guide curves.
7. Click on the green tick mark in the PropertyManager. The sweep feature is created.

Procedure for Creating a Twisted Sweep Feature
1. Invoke the **Sweep** PropertyManager.
2. Make sure that the **Sketch Profile** radio button is selected in the **Profile and Path** rollout.
3. Select a closed sketch, a face, or an edge/edges that form a closed loop as the profile.
4. Select an open or a closed sketch, an edge, or a curve as the path of the sweep feature. The preview of the sweep feature appears.
5. Expand the **Options** rollout of the PropertyManager.
6. Select the **Specify Twist Value** option in the **Profile Twist** drop-down list of the **Option** rollout.
7. Select the **Degrees**, **Radians**, or **Revolutions** option in the **Twist control** drop-down list.
8. Enter the twist value in the **Direction 1** field. The preview of the twist sweep feature appears.
9. Click on the green tick mark in the PropertyManager. The twisted sweep feature is created.

Creating a Sweep Cut Feature

The method of creating a sweep cut feature is same as creating a sweep feature with the only difference that sweep cut features are created by removing material from the model, see Figures 8.52 through 8.55. You can create sweep cut features by using the **Swept Cut** tool. Figures 8.52 and 8.54 show the profile and path, respectively. Figures 8.53 and 8.55 show the resultant sweep cut feature created such that the material is removed by sweeping the profile along the path.

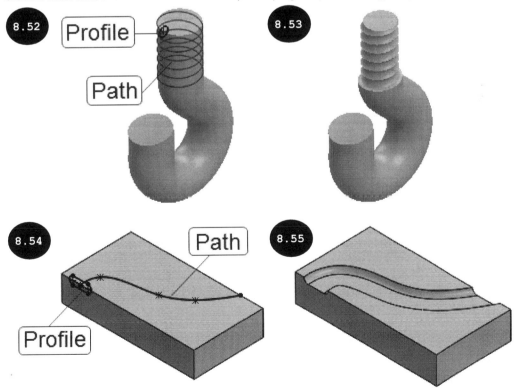

Note: In Figure 8.52, a helical curve has been created as a path and a circle has been created as a profile. You will learn about creating helical curves later in this chapter.

To create a sweep cut feature, click on the **Swept Cut** tool in the **Features CommandManager**. The **Cut-Sweep PropertyManager** appears, see Figure 8.56. In this PropertyManager, the **Sketch Profile** radio button is selected, by default. As a result, the **Profile** and **Path** fields are enabled in the PropertyManager. Select a profile of the sweep cut feature in the graphics area. You can select a closed sketch, a face, or an edge/a group of edges that forms a closed loop as a profile. Next, select a path of the sweep cut feature. You can select an open or a closed sketch, an edge, or a curve as the path of the sweep cut feature. As soon as you select the profile and path, the preview of the sweep cut feature appears in the graphics area.

On selecting the **Circular Profile** radio button of the PropertyManager, you can create a circular sweep cut feature similar to creating circular sweep feature without creating the sketch of the profile. On selecting the **Solid Profile** radio button, the **Tool body** and **Path** fields get enabled in the PropertyManager, see Figure 8.57. The **Tool body** field is activated, by default and is used to select a tool body that follows the path in order to create a sweep cut feature. Figure 8.58 shows a tool body and a helical path, and Figure 8.59 shows the resultant sweep cut feature. Also, refer to Figures 8.60 and 8.61 for a tool body, a path, and the resultant sweep cut feature. Note that the options for creating a sweep cut feature are the same as those discussed earlier while creating the sweep feature.

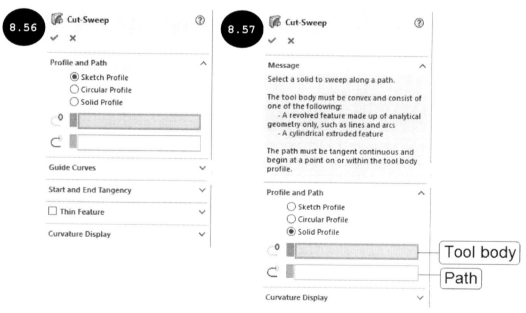

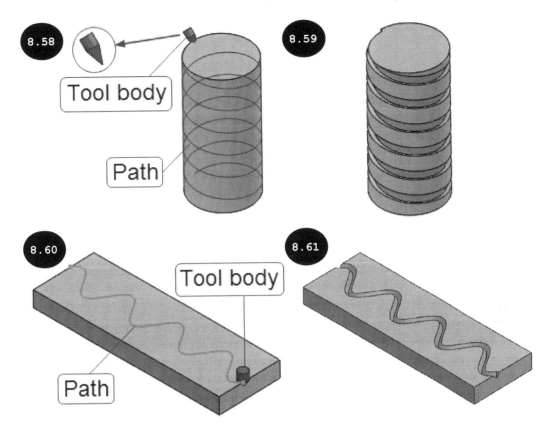

Note: In Figures 8.58 and 8.60, a solid body has been used as a tool body to follow the path. The tool body should be created as a separate body. To create a separate body, you need to uncheck the **Merge result** check box in the respective PropertyManager, which appeared on invoking the tool for creating a feature. On unchecking the **Merge result** check box, the resultant feature is treated as a separate body. Also, in Figure 8.58, a helical curve has been used as the path. You will learn about creating a helical curve later in this chapter.

Procedure for Creating a Sweep Cut Feature with Sketch Profile

1. Click on the **Swept Cut** tool. The **Cut-Sweep PropertyManager** appears.
2. Make sure that the **Sketch Profile** radio button is selected in the PropertyManager.
3. Select the profile of the sweep feature in the graphics area.
4. Select the path of the sweep feature. The preview of the sweep cut feature appears.
5. Click on the green tick mark ✓ in the PropertyManager. The sweep cut feature is created.

Procedure for Creating a Sweep Cut Feature with Circular Profile

1. Click on the **Swept Cut** tool. The **Cut-Sweep PropertyManager** appears.
2. Click on the **Circular Profile** radio button in the PropertyManager.
3. Select a sketch entity, a curve, or an edge of the model as the path of the sweep cut feature. The preview of the sweep cut feature appears having a circular profile of default diameter.

358 Chapter 8 > Advanced Modeling - II

4. Enter the diameter value for the circular profile in the **Diameter** field of the rollout.
5. Click on the green tick mark ✓ in the PropertyManager. The sweep cut feature is created.

Procedure for Creating a Sweep Cut Feature with Solid Profile
1. Create a path and a tool body (solid body).
2. Click on the **Swept Cut** tool. The **Cut-Sweep PropertyManager** appears.
3. Click on the **Solid Profile** radio button in the PropertyManager.
4. Select the tool body (solid body) in the graphics area.
5. Select the path of the sweep cut feature. The preview of the sweep cut feature appears.
6. Click on the green tick mark ✓ in the PropertyManager. The sweep cut feature is created.

Creating a Lofted feature

A lofted feature is created by lofting two or more than two profiles (sections) such that the cross-sectional shape of the lofted feature transits from one profile to another. Figure 8.62 shows two dissimilar profiles/sections created on different planes having offset distance between each other. Figure 8.63 shows the resultant lofted feature created.

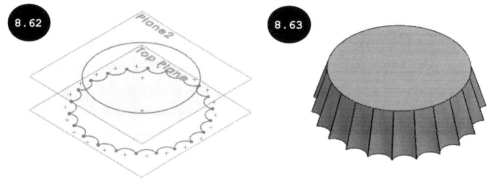

It is evident from the above figures that for creating a lofted feature, you first need to create all its sections that basically define the shape of the lofted feature. In SOLIDWORKS, you can create a lofted feature by using the **Lofted Boss/Base** tool of the **Features CommandManager**. Note that for creating a lofted feature, you need to take care of the following points:

1. Two or more than two profiles/sections (similar or dissimilar) must be available in the graphics area before invoking the **Lofted Boss/Base** tool.
2. Profiles must be closed. You can select closed sketches, faces, or edges as profiles.
3. All profiles must be created as different sketches.
4. The profiles and the resultant lofted feature must not self-intersect.

To create a lofted feature, click on the **Lofted Boss/Base** tool in the **Features CommandManager**. The **Loft PropertyManager** appears, see Figure 8.64. The options in this PropertyManager are as follows:

Figure 8.64

Profiles

The **Profiles** rollout of the PropertyManager is used to select profiles of the lofted feature. You can select two or more than two similar or dissimilar closed profiles for creating a lofted feature. As soon as you select profiles, the preview of the lofted feature appears in the graphics area with connectors, which are connecting the profiles, refer to Figure 8.65. Also, the names of the selected profiles appear in the **Profile** field of the rollout in an order in which they are selected. You can change the order of selection by using the **Move Up** and **Move Down** buttons on the left of the **Profile** field in the rollout, refer to Figure 8.64.

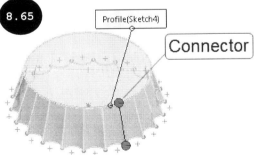

Figure 8.65

Note: By default, only one handle with its connectors appears in the graphics area. You can turn on the display of all handles in the graphics area. To turn on all handles, right-click in the graphics area and then select the **Show All Connectors** option from the shortcut menu appeared. Also, you can drag the connectors to create twist in the loft feature.

Start/End Constraints

The options in the **Start/End Constraint** rollout are used to define normal, tangent, or curvature continuity as the start and end constraints of a lofted feature. By default, this rollout is collapsed. To expand the rollout, click on the arrow in the title bar of the rollout, see Figure 8.66. The options in this rollout are as follows:

Start constraint

The options in the **Start constraint** drop-down list are used to define start constraint for a lofted feature, see Figure 8.67. The options in this drop-down list are as follows:

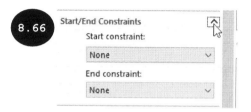
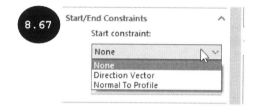

None

By default, the **None** option is selected in the **Start constraint** drop-down list. As a result, no constraint is applied and cross-sectional shape transits from one profile to another, linearly, see Figures 8.68 and 8.69. Figure 8.68 shows profiles and Figure 8.69 shows the preview of the resultant lofted feature.

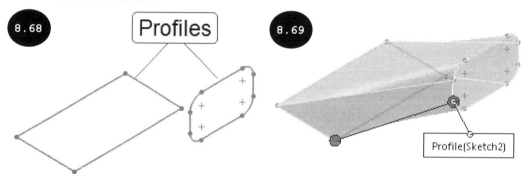

Direction Vector

On selecting the **Direction Vector** option, the **Direction Vector**, **Draft angle**, and **Start Tangent Length** fields become available, see Figure 8.70.

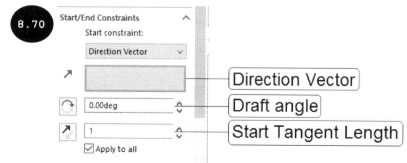

The **Direction Vector** field is used to select a direction vector that defines the start constraint for a lofted feature. You can select a plane, a linear edge, a linear sketch entity, or an axis as direction vector. Figure 8.71 shows the preview of the lofted feature after selecting the Top plane as a direction vector.

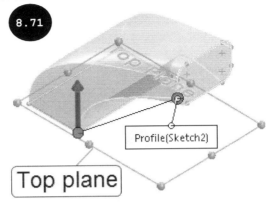

The **Draft angle** field is used to define the draft angle for start constraint. By default, the draft angle is set to 0 degrees. You can specify the draft angle as required. Figure 8.72 shows the front view of the preview of a lofted feature having a draft angle set to 0 degrees and Figure 8.73 shows the front view of the preview of a lofted feature having a draft angle set to 20 degrees.

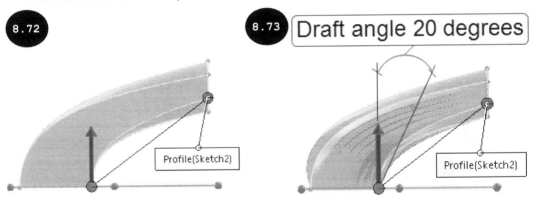

The **Start Tangent Length** field is used to define the start tangent length for start constraint. By default, the start tangent length is specified as 1. Figure 8.74 shows the preview of the lofted feature with a draft angle set to 0 degrees and the start tangent length is set to 2.

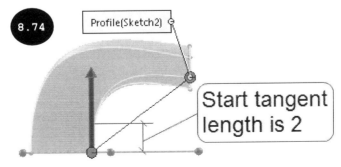

Normal To Profile
On selecting the **Normal To Profile** option in the **Start constraint** drop-down list, the tangency constraint is applied normal to the start section of the lofted feature. Also, the **Draft angle** and **Start Tangent Length** fields are enabled. The methods of specifying draft angle and start tangent length are the same as those discussed earlier.

Tangency To Face
On selecting the **Tangency To Face** option in the **Start constraint** drop-down list, the start section of the lofted feature maintains tangency with the adjacent face of existing geometry, see Figure 8.75. You can define the start tangent length of the feature in the **Start Tangent Length** field of the rollout.

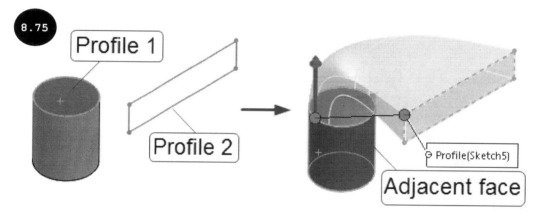

Note: The **Tangency To Face** option becomes available only when an existing feature is available in the graphics area. If the loft feature being created is the base/first feature, then this option will not be available in the drop-down list.

Curvature To Face
On selecting the **Curvature To Face** option, the start profile of a lofted feature maintains curvature continuity with the adjacent faces of existing geometry.

Note: If the loft feature being created is the base/first feature, then the **Curvature To Face** option will not be available in the drop-down list.

Reverse Direction and Reverse Tangent Direction
The **Reverse Direction** and **Reverse Tangent Direction** buttons of the **Start/End Constraint** rollout are used to reverse the direction of the applied constraints, see Figure 8.76. Note that the **Reverse Direction** button is available in the rollout after selecting the **Direction Vector** or **Normal To Profile** option in the **Start constraint** drop-down list. On the other hand, the **Reverse Tangent Direction** button is available in the rollout if the **Direction Vector**, **Normal To Profile**, **Tangency To Face**, or **Curvature To Face** option is selected.

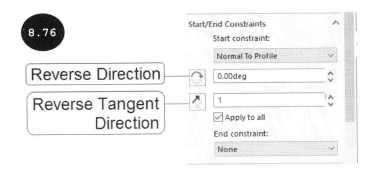

Apply to all

The **Apply to all** check box is selected in the rollout, by default. As a result, only one handle appears in the preview of a lofted feature, see Figure 8.77. The handle is used to control constraints of the entire profile. If you uncheck this check box, multiple handles appears in the preview of the lofted feature, see Figure 8.78. These handles are used to control the constraints of individual segments for the profile. Note that you can modify the constraints of a lofted feature by dragging the handles that appear in the preview of the lofted feature.

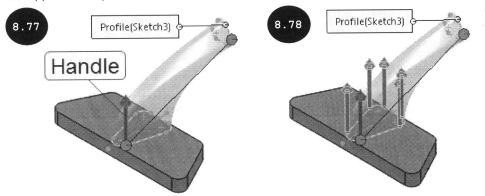

End constraint

The **End constraint** drop-down list is used to define the end constraint of a lofted feature. The options in this drop-down list are the same as those discussed earlier with the only difference that these options are used to define the end constraint. Figure 8.79 shows the preview of a lofted feature when the start and end constraints are not defined, whereas Figure 8.80 shows the preview of a lofted feature when the end constraint defined as normal to the profile.

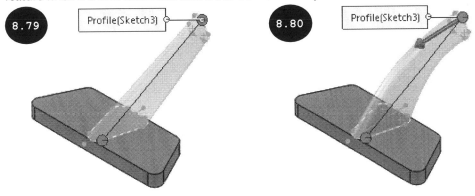

Guide Curves

Guide curves are used to guide the cross-sectional shape of a lofted feature. You can create multiple guide curves for controlling the shape of a lofted feature. The **Guide Curves** rollout of the PropertyManager is used to select guide curves of the lofted feature. Figure 8.81 shows two profiles and two guide curves, and Figure 8.82 shows the resultant lofted feature. Note that guide curves must have pierce relations with the profiles of the feature.

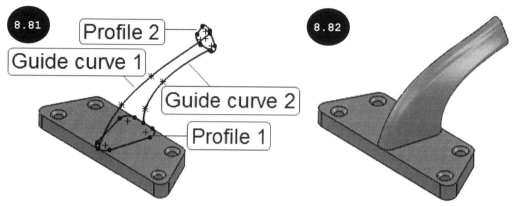

To select guide curves, click on the **Guide Curves** field in the **Guide Curves** rollout and then select the guide curves. The preview of the lofted feature appears such that its cross-sectional shape has been controlled by the guide curves. Also, the **Guide curves influence type** drop-down list appears, see Figure 8.83. The options in this drop-down list are used to control the influence of guide curves. The options are as follows:

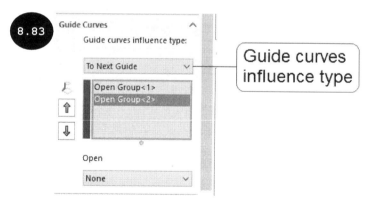

To Next Guide

The **To Next Guide** option in the **Guide curves influence type** drop-down list is used to extend the influence of the guide curve to the next guide curve only. Figure 8.84 shows two profiles and a guide curve. Figure 8.85 shows the preview of the resultant lofted feature when the **To Next Guide** option is selected.

To Next Sharp

The **To Next Sharp** option is used to extend the influence of the guide curve to the next sharp, see Figure 8.86. A sharp is a hard corner of the profile.

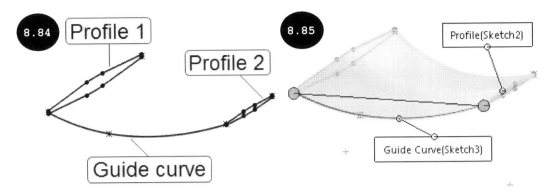

To Next Edge
The **To Next Edge** option is used to extend the influence of the guide curve to the next edge.

Global
The **Global** option is used to extend the influence of the guide curve to the entire lofted feature, see Figure 8.87.

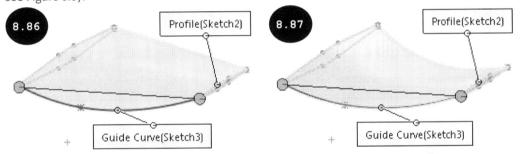

Centerline Parameters
The **Centerline Parameters** rollout in the PropertyManager is used to select a centerline for creating a lofted feature. Centerline is used to maintain the neutral axis of the lofted feature. To select a centerline, expand the **Centerline Parameters** rollout after selecting all profiles of the lofted feature. Next, select a centerline for a lofted feature. The preview of the resultant lofted feature appears in the graphics area. Note that in case of selecting a centerline, the intermediate sections of the resultant lofted feature become normal to the centerline. Figure 8.88 shows different profiles and a centerline, and Figure 8.89 shows the preview of the resultant lofted feature after selecting the centerline.

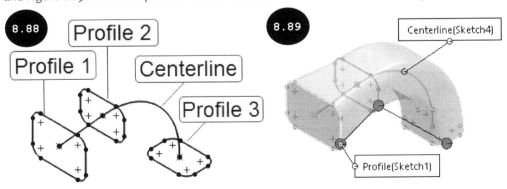

The **Show Sections** button of the **Centerline Parameters** rollout is used to show different sections of the lofted feature in the graphics area. On activating this button, the display of the different sections is turned on. Also, the **Section Number** field is enabled. In this field, you can enter section number to be displayed in the graphics area.

Sketch Tools

The **Sketch Tools** rollout is used to edit the 3D sketch sections/profiles of a lofted feature, see Figure 8.90. You can edit the 3D profiles of a lofted feature by dragging them in the graphics area by using the **Drag Sketch** button of this rollout. Note that the **Drag Sketch** button is enabled only when the profiles of the lofted feature being edited are drawn as 3D sketches. You will learn about drawing 3D sketches later in this chapter.

Options

The options in the **Options** rollout of the PropertyManager are used to merge tangent faces of the feature, create close lofted features, show preview, and merge result, see Figure 8.91. The options of this rollout are as follows:

Merge tangent faces

On selecting the **Merge tangent faces** check box, the tangent faces of the feature merge with each other. Figure 8.92 shows a lofted feature created when the **Merge tangent faces** check box is checked and Figure 8.93 shows a lofted feature created when the **Merge tangent faces** check box is unchecked.

Close Loft

The **Close loft** check box is used to create a lofted feature such that the start and end profiles of the lofted feature join automatically with each other and create a closed lofted feature. Figure 8.94 shows the preview of an open lofted feature when the **Close loft** check box is unchecked and Figure 8.95 shows the preview of a closed lofted feature when the **Close loft** check box is checked.

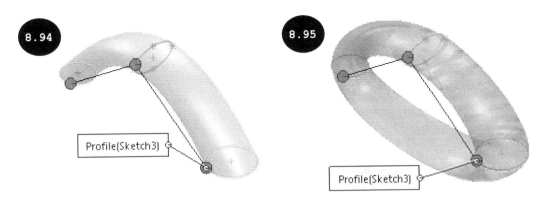

Note: To create a closed lofted feature, minimum three sections are required. Also, the total angle between the start and end sections should be more than 120 degrees.

Show preview
The **Show preview** check box is used to show the preview of the lofted feature in the graphics area. By default, this check box is selected. As a result, the preview of the lofted feature appears in the graphics area.

Thin Feature
The **Thin Feature** rollout is used to create a thin lofted feature, see Figure 8.96. The options in this rollout are same as those discussed earlier while creating thin extruded and revolved features.

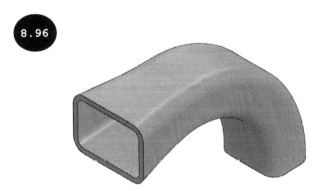

Procedure for Creating a Lofted Feature
1. Click on the **Lofted Boss/Base** tool. The **Loft PropertyManager** appears.
2. Select all profiles of the lofted feature one by one in the graphics area. You can select a closed sketch, a face, or an edge that forms a closed loop as a profile The preview of the lofted feature with connectors appears in the graphics area.
3. Make sure that the connectors are in one direction to avoid twisting. To twist a lofted feature, you can change the position of the connectors by dragging them.
4. Click on the green tick mark in the PropertyManager. The lofted feature is created.

Procedure for Creating a Lofted Feature by using Guide Curves

1. Create all the profiles and guide curves of the lofted feature as individual sketches.
2. Click on the **Lofted Boss/Base** tool. The **Loft PropertyManager** appears.
3. Select all profiles one by one from the graphics area. The preview of the lofted feature with connectors appears in the graphics area.
4. Make sure that the connectors are in one direction to avoid twisting.
5. Expand the **Guide Curves** rollout and then click on the **Guide Curves** field to activate it.
6. Select a guide curve in the graphics area. The preview of the lofted feature appears such that its shape is controlled by the guide curve. You can select two or more than two guide curves.
7. Click on the green tick mark ✓ in the PropertyManager. The lofted feature is created.

Procedure for Creating a Lofted Feature by using Centerline

1. Create all profiles and a centerline of the lofted feature.
2. Invoke the **Loft PropertyManager**.
3. Select all profiles of the lofted feature one by one from the graphics area.
4. Expand the **Centerline Parameters** rollout and then select the centerline from the graphics area. The preview of the lofted feature appears with respect to the centerline selected.
5. Click on the green tick mark ✓ in the PropertyManager. The lofted feature is created.

Creating a Lofted Cut Feature

The method of creating lofted cut features is same as creating lofted features with the only difference that the lofted cut features are created by removing material from the model. You can create a lofted cut feature by using the **Lofted Cut** tool in the **Features CommandManager**. Figure 8.97 shows profiles of a lofted cut feature and Figure 8.98 shows the preview of the resultant lofted cut feature. Figure 8.99 shows the resultant lofted cut feature created.

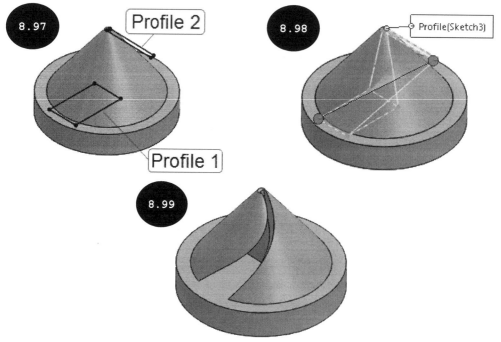

Creating a Boundary Feature

Boundary features are high quality, complex shaped, and accurate features. Boundary features are used to maintain high curvature continuity as well as to create complex shape features. You can create boundary features by using the **Boundary Boss/Base** tool, which is one of the powerful tools in the Part modeling environment. To create a boundary feature, you need to create all sections of a boundary feature as direction 1 guides and all curves as direction 2 guides. Figure 8.100 shows two sections as direction 1 guides and two curves as direction 2 guides of a boundary feature. Figure 8.101 shows the resultant boundary feature.

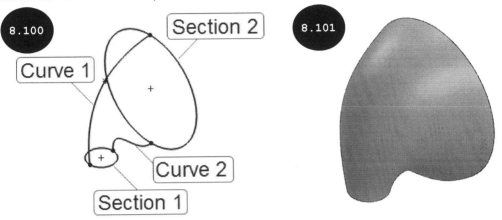

Figure 8.102 shows one section as direction 1 guide and three curves as direction 2 guides. Figure 8.103 shows the resultant boundary feature.

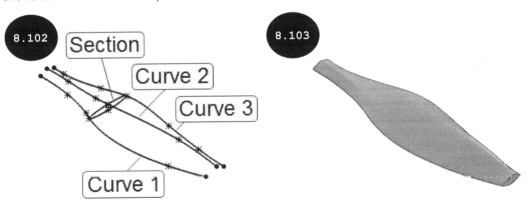

To create a boundary feature, create all sections and curves as direction 1 and direction 2 guides of the boundary feature, respectively, and then click on the **Boundary Boss/Base** tool in the **Features CommandManager**. The **Boundary PropertyManager** appears, see Figure 8.104. The options in this propertyManager are as follows:

370 Chapter 8 > Advanced Modeling - II

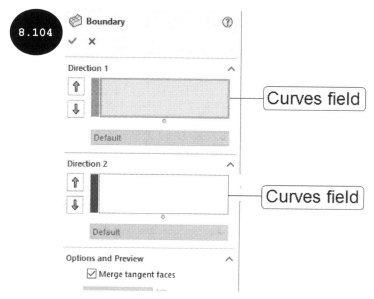

Direction 1

The **Curves** field in the **Direction 1** rollout is used to select the sections as direction 1 guides. By default, this field is activated. As a result, you are prompted to select sections. Select the sections as direction 1 guides from the graphics area one by one, see Figure 8.105. The preview of the boundary feature appears in the graphics area, see Figure 8.106. Also, the **Tangent Type** drop-down list and the **Draft angle** field get enabled in the **Direction 1** rollout, see Figure 8.107. You can select multiple sections or a single section as direction 1 guide curve. The options in the **Tangent Type** drop-down list, are same as those discussed earlier, while creating the lofted feature.

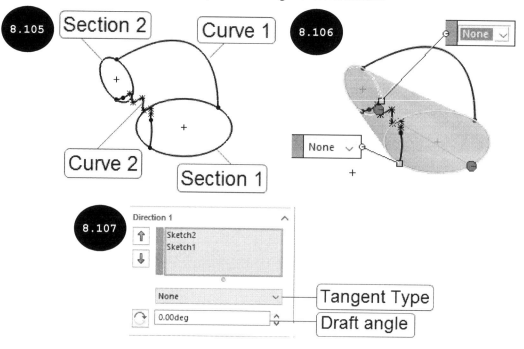

Tip: You can drag the connectors, which are connecting the sections of the feature with each other in order to create twist in the feature, as required.

Direction 2

The **Curves** field in the **Direction 2** rollout is used to select the curves as direction 2 guides. Click on this field and then select curves from the graphics area. The preview of the boundary feature is modified with respect to the curves selected, see Figure 8.108. You can select multiple curves to control the shape of the boundary feature as direction 2 guide curves. Additionally, you can specify the type of tangent continuity by using the options in the **Tangent Type** drop-down list of the **Direction 2** rollout. You can also control the influence of curves by using the options in the **Guide curves influence type** drop-down list of this rollout.

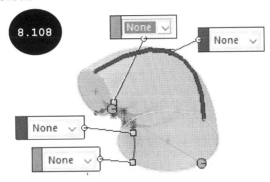

8.108

Tip: You can also flip the connectors in order to achieve the required shape. To flip the direction of connectors, select the curve/section whose connectors are to be flipped in the **Curves** field of the **Direction 1** or **Direction 2** rollout. Next, right-click to display a shortcut menu. In this shortcut menu, click on the **Flip Connectors** option. The direction of connectors gets flipped.

Options and Preview

The options in the **Options and Preview** rollout are the same as those discussed earlier, while creating the lofted feature except the **Trim by direction 1** check box, which is discussed next.

Trim by direction 1

The **Trim by direction 1** check box is used to trim the extended portion of the feature, which is beyond the direction 1 guides. To trim the extended portion of the feature by direction 1 curves, select this check box. Figure 8.109 shows two sections as direction 1 guides and one curve as a direction 2 guide. Figure 8.110 shows the preview of the resultant boundary feature when the **Trim by direction 1** check box is unchecked and Figure 8.111 shows the preview of the resultant boundary feature when the **Trim by direction 1** check box is checked.

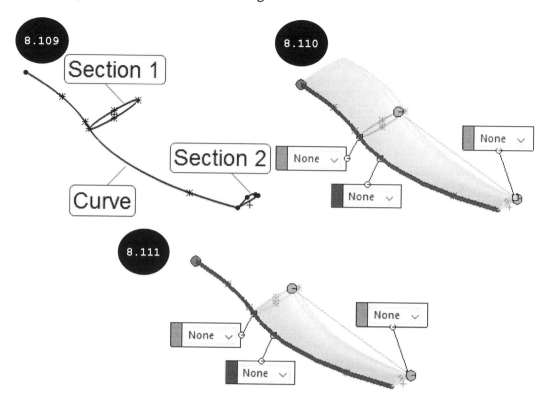

Thin Feature

The **Thin Feature** rollout is used to create a thin boundary feature, see Figure 8.112. The options in this rollout are the same as those discussed earlier while creating the thin extruded and revolved features.

Curvature Display

The options in the **Curvature Display** rollout are used to control the display style of the preview appeared in the graphics area, see Figure 8.113. The options are as follows:

Mesh preview

The **Mesh preview** check box is used to display the mesh preview in the graphics area, see Figure 8.114. On selecting this check box, the preview of the boundary feature appears with mesh in the graphics area, see Figure 8.114. You can control the number of lines in the mesh by increasing or decreasing the mesh density. To control the mesh density, you can use the **Mesh density** slider available below this check box.

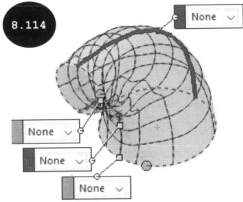

Zebra stripes

The **Zebra stripes** check box is used to turn on the appearance of zebra stripes in the preview of boundary features, see Figure 8.115. Zebra strips help you find small changes made in the feature by making them visible, which are hard to see in the standard display style.

Curvature combs

The **Curvature combs** check box is used to turn on the appearance of curvature combs in the preview of boundary features. On selecting this check box, the preview of the feature appears with curvature combs in the graphics area, see Figure 8.116. You can control the scale and density of the displayed curvature combs by using the **Scale** thumbwheel and the **Density** slider of the rollout.

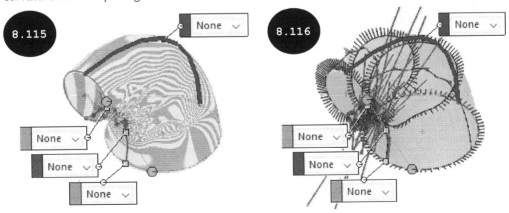

Procedure for Creating a Boundary Feature

1. Create profiles and curves of the boundary feature as direction 1 and direction 2 guide curves.
2. Click on the **Boundary Boss/Base** tool. The **Boundary PropertyManager** appears.
3. Select all profiles one by one from the graphics area as the direction 1 guides.

4. Click on the **Curves** field in the **Direction 2** rollout and then select curves as direction 2 guides.
5. Click on the green tick mark ✓ in the PropertyManager. The boundary feature is created.

Creating a Boundary Cut Feature

The method of creating a boundary cut feature is the same as creating a boundary feature with the only difference that the boundary cut feature is created by removing material from the model. You can create a boundary cut feature by using the **Boundary Cut** tool in the **Features CommandManager**.

Creating Curves

In SOLIDWORKS, you can create different types of curves. Curves are mainly used as the path, guide curves, and so on for creating features such as sweep, lofted, and boundary. The tools for creating different types of curves are grouped together in the **Curve** flyout, see Figure 8.117. The methods for creating different types of curves are as follows:

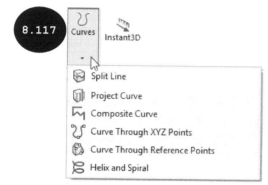

Creating Projected Curves

In SOLIDWORKS, you can create projected curves by using the **Project Curve** tool. The **Project Curve** tool is used to create projected curves by using two methods: Sketch on Faces and Sketch on Sketch. In Sketch on Faces method, the projected curve is created by projecting a sketch on to an existing face of a model, see Figure 8.118. You can select planar faces or curved faces to project sketch entities.

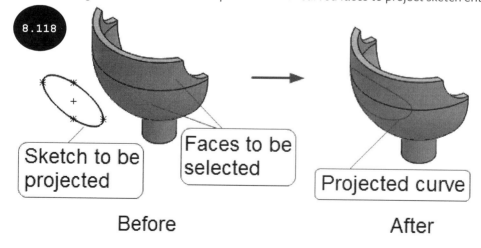

In the Sketch on Sketch method, the projected curve is created by projecting one sketch on to the other sketch such that the resultant projected curve represents the intersection of sketches, see Figure 8.119.

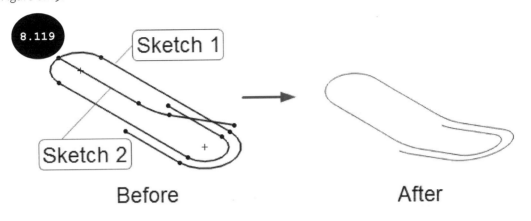

Before   After

Tip: In Figure 8.119, the sketch 1 is created on the Top plane and the sketch 2 is created on the Front plane.

To create a projected curve, invoke the **Curve** flyout by clicking on the down arrow in the **Curves** tool of the **Features CommandManager**, refer to Figure 8.117. Next, click on the **Project Curve** tool in the flyout. The **Projected Curve PropertyManager** appears, see Figure 8.120. The options in this PropertyManager are as follows:

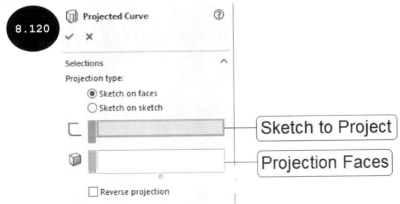

Selections

The options in the **Selections** rollout of the PropertyManager are used to select the projection method. Also, depending upon the projection method selected, the options of this rollout are used to select reference objects to create a projected curve. The options are as follows:

Sketch on faces

The **Sketch on faces** radio button is used to create projected curves by projecting a sketch on to an existing face of a model. On selecting this radio button, the **Sketch to Project** and the **Projection Faces** fields are enabled in the rollout, see Figure 8.120. By default, the **Sketch to**

Project field is activated. As a result, you can select a sketch to be projected. Click on the sketch to be projected in the graphics area, see Figure 8.121. The name of the sketch selected appears in the **Sketch to Project** field. Also, the **Projection Faces** field gets activated and you are prompted to select projection faces. Click on a face or faces in the graphics area, see Figure 8.121. The preview of the projected curve appears in the graphics area, see Figure 8.122. Make sure that the direction of projection is toward the selected projection face. You can reverse the direction of projection by using the **Reverse projection** check box. Next, click on the green tick mark ✓ in the PropertyManager. The projected curve is created.

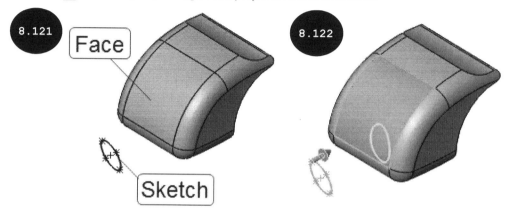

Sketch on sketch

The **Sketch on sketch** radio button is used to project one sketch onto another sketch such that the resultant projected curve represents the intersection of sketches. On selecting this radio button, the **Sketches to Project** field is enabled in the rollout. By default, this field is activated. As a result, you can select sketches to be projected. Select the sketches to be projected in the graphics area one by one by clicking the left mouse button, see Figure 8.123. The preview of the projected curve appears in the graphics area. Next, click on the green tick mark ✓ in the PropertyManager. The projected curve is created, see Figure 8.124.

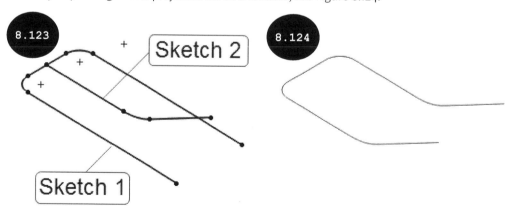

Tip: In Figure 8.123, the sketch 1 is created on the Top plane and the sketch 2 is created on the Front plane.

Procedure for Creating Curves by using the Sketch on Faces Method
1. Invoke the **Curves** flyout and then click on the **Project Curve** tool.
2. Click on the **Sketch on faces** radio button in the PropertyManager.
3. Click on the sketch to be projected.
4. Click on a face or faces of the model as the projection face/faces.
5. Select the **Reverse projection** check box to reverse the direction of projection, if needed.
6. Click on the green tick mark ✓ in the PropertyManager. The projected curve is created.

Procedure for Creating Curves by using the Sketch on Sketch Method
1. Invoke the **Curves** flyout and then click on the **Project Curve** tool.
2. Click on the **Sketch on sketch** radio button in the PropertyManager.
3. Select sketches to be projected in the graphics area one by one.
4. Click on the green tick mark ✓ in the PropertyManager. The projected curve is created.

Creating Helical and Spiral Curves
You can create helical and spiral curves by using the **Helix and Spiral** tool of the **Curves** flyout. You can use helical and spiral curves as path, guide curve, and so on for creating features like sweep and lofted. Figure 8.125 shows a helical curve and a circular profile, as well as the resultant sweep feature created by using them. To create a helical curve or a spiral curve in SOLIDWORKS, you first need to create a circle which defines the start diameter of the helical or the spiral curve.

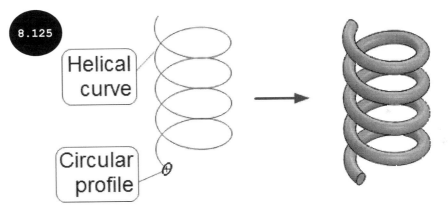

To create a helical or a spiral curve, create a circle and then invoke the **Curves** flyout. Next, click on the **Helix and Spiral** tool. The **Helix/Spiral PropertyManager** appears, see Figure 8.126. Also, you are prompted to select a circle or a sketching plane for creating a circle. Click on the circle in the graphics area as the start diameter of the curve. The **Helix/Spiral PropertyManager** gets modified, see Figure 8.127. Also, the preview of the curve appears in the graphics area, as per the default parameters, see Figure 8.128.

> **Note:** You can select a circle before or after invoking the **Helix and Spiral** tool. If the circle is selected before invoking the tool, then the modified **Helix/Spiral PropertyManager** and the preview of the curve appears directly in the graphics area.

378 Chapter 8 > Advanced Modeling - II

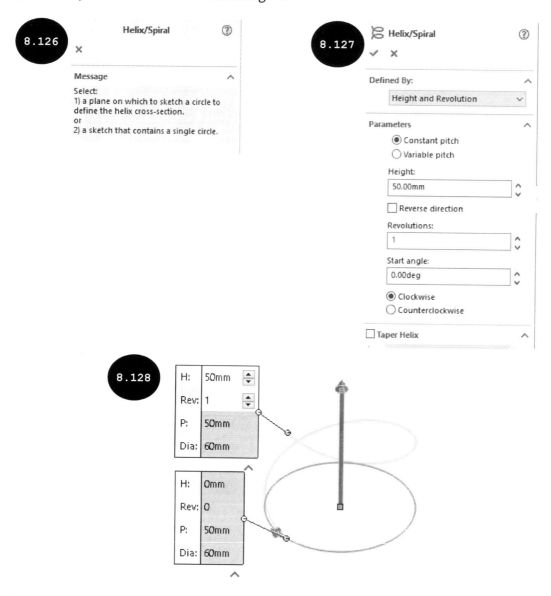

The options in the **Helix/Spiral PropertyManager** are used to create constant pitch helical curves, variable pitch helical curves, and spiral curves. The options are as follows:

Defined By
The **Defined By** rollout is used to define the type of curve (helical or spiral) to be created and the method to be adopted for creating it. The options in this rollout are available in a drop-down list, see Figure 8.129. The options are as follows:

Pitch and Revolution
The **Pitch and Revolution** option is used to create a helical curve by defining its pitch and number of revolutions. On selecting this option, the options for creating a helical curve by defining its pitch and revolutions are enabled in the **Parameters** rollout of the PropertyManager.

Height and Revolution
The **Height and Revolution** option is used to create a helical curve by defining its total height and number of revolutions. On selecting this option, the options for creating a helical curve by defining its height and revolutions are enabled in the **Parameters** rollout of the PropertyManager.

Height and Pitch
The **Height and Pitch** option is used to create a helical curve by defining its total height and pitch. On selecting this option, the options for creating a helical curve by defining its height and pitch are enabled in the **Parameters** rollout of the PropertyManager.

Spiral
The **Spiral** option is used to create a spiral curve by defining its pitch and number of revolutions. On selecting this option, the options for creating a spiral curve by defining its pitch and revolutions are enabled in the **Parameters** rollout. Figure 8.130 shows a spiral curve.

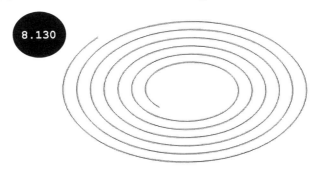

Parameters
The **Parameters** rollout of the PropertyManager is used to specify the parameters for creating a curve. The availability of most of the options in this rollout depends upon the option selected in the **Defined By** rollout. The options of this rollout are as follows:

Constant pitch
The **Constant pitch** radio button is used to create a helical curve with constant pitch through out the helix height, see Figure 8.131.

Pitch, Revolutions, Height, and Start angle
The **Pitch, Revolutions, Height,** and **Start angle** fields are used to specify pitch, revolutions, height, and start angle for the curve, respectively.

Reverse direction

The **Reverse direction** check box is used to reverse the direction of curve creation.

Clockwise and Counterclockwise

The **Clockwise** and **Counterclockwise** radio buttons are used to specify the direction of revolution clockwise or counterclockwise, respectively.

Variable pitch

The **Variable pitch** radio button is used to create a helical curve with variable pitch and variable diameter, see Figures 8.132 and 8.133. On selecting this radio button, the **Region parameters** table appears in the rollout, see Figure 8.134. In the **Region parameters** table, you can enter the variable pitch and diameter for creating a helical curve in the respective fields, see Figure 8.134. Note that the availability of options in this table depends upon the option selected in the **Defined By** rollout of the PropertyManager.

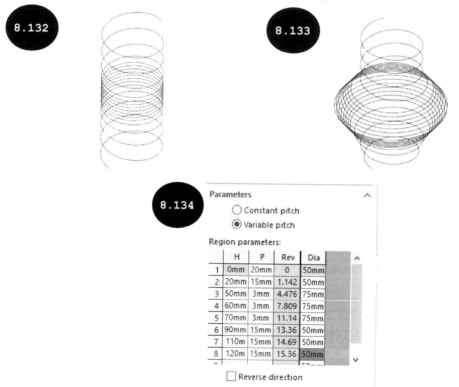

Note: If the **Height and Pitch** option is selected in the **Defined By** rollout then in the **Region parameters** table, you can enter the variable pitch at different heights as well as variable diameter at different heights, see Figure 8.134. If you select the **Height and Revolution** option, then the **Region parameters** table allows you to specify revolutions and variable diameter at different height. Also, the variable pitch of the curve will automatically be calculated based on the number of revolutions at different height. To enter values in the table, double-click on the respective fields of the table.

Taper Helix

The **Taper Helix** rollout of the PropertyManager is used to create tapered helical curves, see Figure 8.135. By default, the options of this rollout are not activated. To activate the options of this rollout, select the check box in the title bar of the **Taper Helix** rollout. The **Taper Angle** field of this rollout is used to specify the taper angle of the helical curve. Note that if the **Taper outward** check box is unchecked in this rollout, the helical curve tapers inward to the sketch. If you select the **Taper outward** check box, then the helical curve tapers outward to the sketch.

8.135

Procedure for Creating a Constant Pitch Helical Curve

1. Create a circle whose diameter defines the diameter of the helical curve in the Sketching environment. Next, exit the Sketching environment.
2. Select the circle either from the graphics area or from the FeatureManager Design Tree.
3. Invoke the **Curves** flyout and then click on the **Helix and Spiral** tool. The **Helix/Spiral PropertyManager** appears. Also, the preview of the curve appears in the graphics area.
4. Select the required option (**Pitch and Revolution**, **Height and Revolution**, or **Height and Pitch**) from the drop-down list of the **Defined By** rollout.
5. Make sure that the **Constant pitch** radio button is selected in the **Parameters** rollout.
6. Specify the parameters such as pitch, revolutions, and so on for the helical curve in the respective fields of the **Parameters** rollout.
7. Click on the green tick mark in the PropertyManager. The helical curve of constant pitch is created.

Procedure for Creating a Variable Pitch Helical Curve

1. Create a circle whose diameter defines the start diameter of the variable helical curve in the Sketching environment. Next, exit the Sketching environment.
2. Select the circle either from the graphics area or from the FeatureManager Design Tree.
3. Invoke the **Helix/Spiral PropertyManager**.
4. Select the required option (**Pitch and Revolution**, **Height and Revolution**, or **Height and Pitch**) in the drop-down list of the **Defined By** rollout.
5. Click on the **Variable pitch** radio button in the **Parameters** rollout.
6. Specify the variable parameters such as pitch, revolution, and diameter in the respective fields of the **Region parameters** table in the **Parameters** rollout. You can double-click on the fields of this table to enter values.
7. Click on the green tick mark in the PropertyManager. The variable helical curve is created.

Procedure for Creating a Taper Helical Curve
1. Create a circle and then exit the Sketching environment.
2. Invoke the **Helix/Spiral PropertyManager**.
3. Select the circle in the graphics area. The preview of the helical curve appears.
4. Select the required option (**Pitch and Revolution**, **Height and Revolution**, or **Height and Pitch**) in the drop-down list of the **Defined By** rollout to create the helical curve.
5. Click on the **Constant pitch** radio button in the **Parameters** rollout.
6. Specify the parameters such as pitch, revolutions, and so on for the helical curve in the respective fields of the **Parameters** rollout.
7. Expand the **Taper Helix** rollout by selecting the check box available on its title bar.
8. Enter the value of the taper angle in the **Taper Angle** field of the **Taper Helix** rollout.
9. Check or uncheck the **Taper outward** check box in the **Taper Helix** rollout, as required.
10. Click on the green tick mark ✓ in the PropertyManager. The taper helical curve is created.

Procedure for Creating a Spiral Curve
1. Create a circle whose diameter defines the start diameter of the spiral curve. Next, exit the Sketching environment.
2. Invoke the **Helix/Spiral PropertyManager**.
3. Select the circle in the graphics area.
4. Select the **Spiral** option from the drop-down list in the **Defined By** rollout.
5. Specify the parameters such as pitch and revolutions in the respective fields of the **Parameters** rollout.
6. Click on the green tick mark ✓ in the PropertyManager. The spiral curve is created.

Creating Curves by Specifying XYZ Points
You can create a curve by specifying coordinates (X, Y, Z), which define the shape of the curve. To create a curve by specifying points, invoke the **Curves** flyout and then click on the **Curve Through XYZ Points** tool. The **Curve File** dialog box appears, see Figure 8.136.

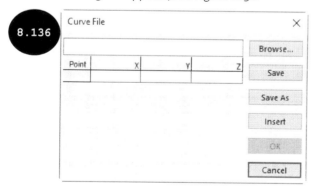

8.136

In the **Curve File** dialog box, you can specify the coordinates (X, Y, Z) of multiple points with respect to the origin (0, 0, 0) for creating a curve. Besides specifying coordinates of points, you can import .sldcrv or .txt (notepad) files containing the coordinates of a curve.

To specify coordinates in the dialog box, double-click on the field corresponding to the first row and the **X** column to activate it. Once this field has been activated, you can enter the X coordinate of the first point with respect to the origin. Similarly, you can activate the Y and Z fields and then enter the Y and Z coordinates of the first point. Note that, by default, only one row is available in this dialog box. However, the moment you activate a field of the first row, the second or next row is added automatically in the dialog box. Specify the coordinates of the second point in the second row of the dialog box. Similarly, you can specify the coordinates of the other points in the dialog box. Note that as you specify the coordinate in the dialog box, the preview of the curve appears in the graphics area. Figure 8.137 shows the **Curve File** dialog box with multiple coordinates of points specified and Figure 8.138 shows the preview of the resultant curve.

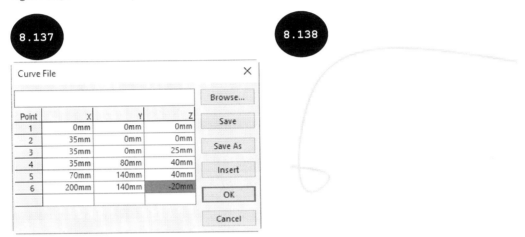

You can also save all coordinates of the points specified in the dialog box as *.sldcrv* file in your local drive for further use. To save the coordinates of the points as *.sldcrv* file, click on the **Save** button in the dialog box. The **Save As** dialog box appears. In this dialog box, browse the location where you want to save the file and then specify a name for the file in the **File name** edit box. Next, click on the **Save** button in the **Save As** dialog box. The file is saved as *.sldcrv* file. Once you have specified the coordinates of the points in the dialog box, click on the **OK** button. The curve is created.

If you have *.sldcrv* or *.txt* (notepad) file containing information about the coordinates of the points for creating a curve, click on the **Browse** button in the **Curve File** dialog box. The **Open** dialog box appears. In this dialog box, browse the location where the *.sldcrv* or *.txt* (notepad) file has been saved. Note that by default, the **Curves (*.sldcrv)** option is selected in the **File Type** drop-down list of the dialog box. As a result, you can only import *.sldcrv* file. To import a *.txt* (notepad) file, you need to select the **Text Files (*.txt)** option in the **File Type** drop-down list. After selecting the required file type in the drop-down list, select the file and then click on the **Open** button. The coordinate points of the selected file are filled in the dialog box. Also, the preview of the curve appears in the graphics area.

Tip: In *.txt* (notepad) file, the coordinates of all points should be written in separate lines. Also, the coordinates (X, Y, Z) of a point should be separated by a comma and a space like X, Y, Z.

Procedure for Creating a Curve by Specifying XYZ Points
1. Invoke the **Curves** flyout.
2. Click on the **Curve Through XYZ Points** tool. The **Curve File** dialog box appears.
3. Specify the coordinates (X, Y, Z) of the points with respect to the origin in the dialog box.
4. Once you have specified the coordinates (X, Y, Z) of all points, click on the **OK** button. The curve is created in the graphics area.

Procedure for Creating a Curve by Importing XYZ Points
1. Invoke the **Curves** flyout.
2. Click on the **Curve Through XYZ Points** tool. The **Curve File** dialog box appears.
3. Click on the **Browse** button. The **Open** dialog box appears.
4. Select the required file type **Curves (*.sldcrv)** or **Text Files (*.txt)** in the **File Type** drop-down list of the dialog box.
5. Select a file to be imported and then click on the **Open** button. All coordinate points of the selected file are filled in the **Curve File** dialog box and the preview of the respective curve appears in the graphics area.
6. Click on the **OK** button. The curve is created in the graphics area.

Creating Curves by Selecting Reference Points
In SOLIDWORKS, you can create 3D curves by selecting reference points from the graphics area. The reference points can be located in the same or different planes. You can also select the vertices of the features or sketch points as reference points for creating curve. To create a curve by selecting reference points, invoke the **Curves** flyout and then click on the **Curve Through Reference Points** tool. The **Curve Through Reference Points** PropertyManager appears, see Figure 8.139. Next, select sketch points or vertices in the graphics area one by one by clicking the left mouse button. The preview of the respective curve appears, see Figure 8.140. Also, the name of the selected points/vertices are listed in the **Thought Points** field of the PropertyManager.

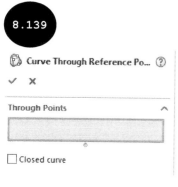

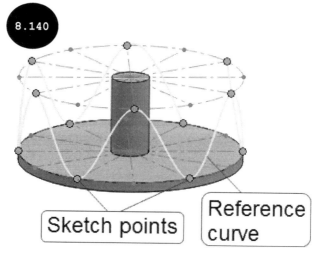

Note: On selecting the **Closed curve** check box of the PropertyManager, a closed curve is created by connecting the specified start point and end point of the curve.

Procedure for Creating a Curve by Selecting Reference Points

1. Click on the **Curve Through XYZ Points** tool in the **Curves** flyout.
2. Select reference points (sketch points and vertices) one by one from the graphics area.
3. Click on the green tick mark ✓ in the PropertyManager. The curve is created.

Creating a Composite Curve

A composite curve is created by joining two or more than two curves together. You can join curves or sketches together and form a composite curve by using the **Composite curve** tool of the **Curves** flyout.

To create a composite curve, click on the **Composite curve** tool in the **Curves** flyout. The **Composite Curve PropertyManager** appears, see Figure 8.141. Next, select curves, one by one in the graphics area by clicking the left mouse button and then click on the green tick mark ✓ in the PropertyManager. The composite curve is created. You can select sketch entities, curves, and edges for creating composite curves. Note that the curves to be joined must be connected end to end and have Pierce relations with each other. Figure 8.142 shows individual curves (five curves) and Figure 8.143 shows the resultant composite curve. Figure 8.144 shows a sweep feature created by sweeping a profile (circle) along the composite curve shown in Figure 8.143.

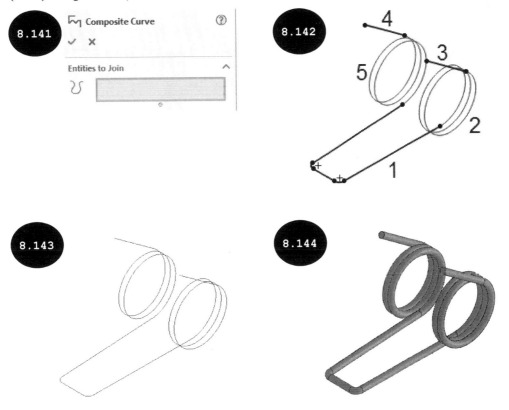

Procedure for Creating a Composite Curve
1. Invoke the **Curves** flyout.
2. Click on the **Composite Curve** tool in the **Curves** flyout. The **Composite Curve** PropertyManager appears.
3. Select curves one by one in the graphics area by clicking the left mouse button.
4. Click on the green tick mark ✓ in the PropertyManager. The composite curve is created.

> **Note:** In SOLIDWORKS, on creating a feature by using reference curves such as projected, composite, helical, and spiral curves; the used reference curves are not absorbed by the feature and appear separately in the FeatureManager Design Tree so that they can be used further for creating other features.

Splitting Faces of a Model
You can split faces of a model by creating split lines. In SOLIDWORKS, you can create split lines by using the **Split Line** tool. Click on the **Split Line** tool in the **Curves** flyout. The **Split Line** PropertyManager appears, see Figure 8.145. The options in this PropertyManager are as follows:

Type of Split
The options in the **Type of Split** rollout are used to select the type of split method to be used for splitting the faces of a model. The options are as follows:

Projection
The **Projection** radio button is used to split faces by projecting a sketch. Figure 8.146 shows a sketch to be projected and a face of a model to be split, and Figure 8.147 shows the resultant model after splitting the face by creating split lines. Note that split lines divide a face into different faces with respect to the projected sketch. After splitting a face into multiple faces, you can apply different textures or appearances on them.

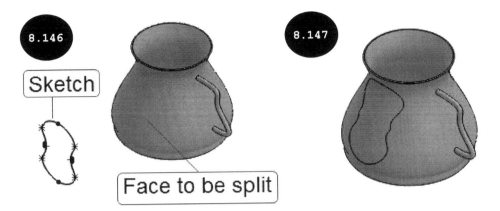

On selecting the **Projection** radio button, the **Sketch to Project** and **Faces to Split** fields are enabled in the **Selections** rollout of the PropertyManager, see Figure 8.148. By default, the **Sketch to Project** field is activated. As a result, you can select the sketch to be projected. As soon as you select the sketch to be projected, the **Faces to Split** field gets activated in the PropertyManager. Now, select the faces to be split. You can select curve faces or planar faces as the faces to be split. To project the split line in one direction, select the **Single direction** check box and to reverse the direction of projection, click on the **Reverse direction** check box in the PropertyManager. Next, click on the green tick mark ✓ in the PropertyManager. The selected faces are split.

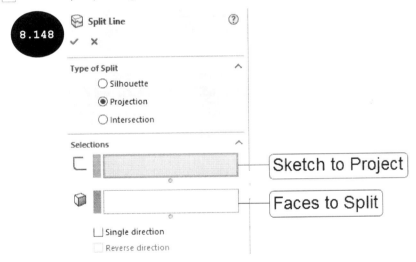

Intersection

The **Intersection** radio button is used to split faces by creating split lines at the intersection of two objects. The objects can be solid bodies, surfaces, faces, or combination with a plane. Figure 8.149 shows a face of a model and a plane. Figure 8.150 shows the resultant model after splitting the face at the intersection with the plane.

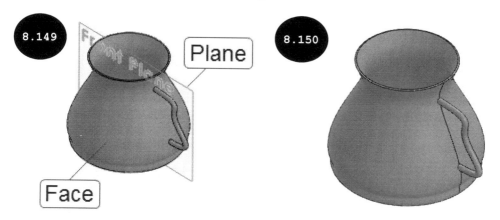

On selecting the **Intersection** radio button, the **Splitting Bodies/Faces/Planes** and **Faces/Bodies to Split** fields are enabled in the **Selections** rollout of the PropertyManager. By default, the **Splitting Bodies/Faces/Planes** field is activated. As a result, you can select bodies, faces, or planes as the splitting objects, see Figure 8.151. After selecting the splitting objects, click on the **Faces/Bodies to Split** field and then select faces or bodies to be split, see Figure 8.151. The preview of split lines appears in the graphics area, see Figure 8.152. Next, click on the green tick mark ✓ in the PropertyManager. The selected face gets split, see Figure 8.153. Note that in Figure 8.153, the visibility of splitting objects is turned off.

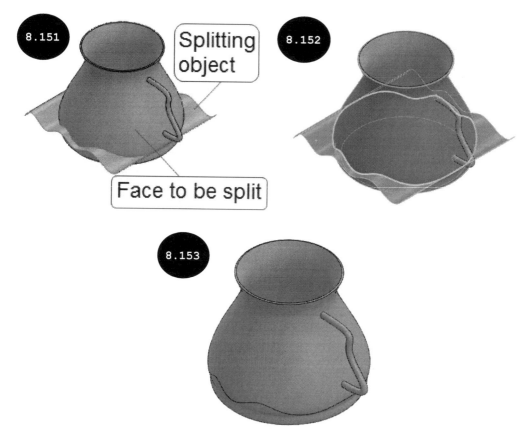

Note: The splitting object shown in Figure 8.151 is an extruded surface. An extruded surface is created by using the **Extruded Surface** tool in the **Surfaces CommandManager**. The options to create an extruded surface are same as those discussed earlier, while creating an extruded solid feature with the only difference that the extruded surface has zero thickness.

Silhouette

The **Silhouette** radio button is used to split faces at the intersection between a direction of projection and a curved face. Figure 8.154 shows a direction of projection and a curved face to be split. Figure 8.155 shows the split line created at the intersection of direction of projection and the curve face selected.

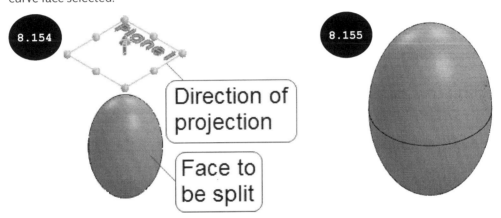

On selecting the **Silhouette** radio button, the **Direction of Pull** and **Faces to Split** fields are enabled in the **Selections** rollout of the PropertyManager. By default, the **Direction of Pull** field is activated. As a result, you can select a plane or a planar face as the direction of projection or pull. After selecting a plane or a planar face as the direction of projection, see Figure 8.154, the **Faces to Split** field gets activated. Now, you can select the curved faces to be split. Note that in case of creating the silhouette split line, you can only select curved faces as the faces to be split. After selecting the curved faces, specify the draft angle value in the **Angle** field of the PropertyManager. Next, click on the green tick mark in the PropertyManager. The split line is created. Figure 8.155 shows the split line created with the draft angle value set to 0 degrees in the **Angle** field. Figure 8.156 shows the split line created with the draft angle value set to 40 degrees.

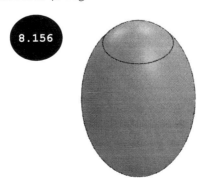

Procedure for Splitting Faces by using the Projection Method
1. Invoke the **Curves** flyout.
2. Click on the **Split Line** tool. The **Split Line PropertyManager** appears.
3. Make sure that the **Projection** radio button is selected in the **Type of Split** rollout.
4. Select a sketch to be projected and then select faces to be split in the graphics area.
5. Click on the green tick mark ✓ in the PropertyManager. The selected faces are split.

Procedure for Splitting Faces by using the Intersection Method
1. Invoke the **Curves** flyout.
2. Click on the **Split Line** tool. The **Split Line PropertyManager** appears.
3. Make sure that the **Intersection** radio button is selected in the **Type of Split** rollout.
4. Click on an object as the splitting object in the graphics area.
5. Click on the **Faces/Bodies to Split** field of the PropertyManager.
6. Click on an object or faces as the faces to split in the graphics area.
7. Click on the green tick mark ✓ in the PropertyManager. The selected faces are split at the intersection of the selected splitting object and the faces to split.

Procedure for Splitting Faces by using the Silhouette Method
1. Invoke the **Split Line PropertyManager**.
2. Click on the **Silhouette** radio button in the **Type of Split** rollout.
3. Click on a plane or a planar face as the direction of projection or pull.
4. Click on a curve face or faces of the object to be split in the graphics area.
5. Set the draft angle value in the **Angle** field of the PropertyManager, as required.
6. Click on the green tick mark ✓ in the PropertyManager. The selected faces are split.

Creating 3D Sketches

In SOLIDWORKS, in addition to creating 2D sketches and 3D curves, you can also create 3D sketches in the 3D Sketching environment. Most of the time, 3D sketches are used as 3D path and the guide curve for creating features like sweep, lofted, and boundary. To create 3D sketches, you need to invoke the 3D Sketching environment of SOLIDWORKS. To invoke the 3D Sketching environment, click on the down arrow below the **Sketch** tool in the **Sketch CommandManager**, see Figure 8.157. The **Sketch** flyout appears, see Figure 8.157. In this flyout, click on the **3D Sketch** tool. The 3D Sketching environment is invoked, see Figure 8.158. Now, you can create 3D sketches by using the tools of the **Sketch CommandManager**. Note that in the 3D Sketching environment, some of the tools such as **Polygon**, **Ellipse**, **Offset Entities**, and **Mirror Entities** are not enabled. This is because these tools are not used for creating 3D sketches. Some of the tools of the 3D Sketching environment are as follows:

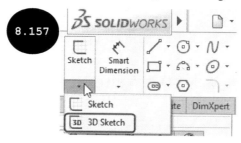

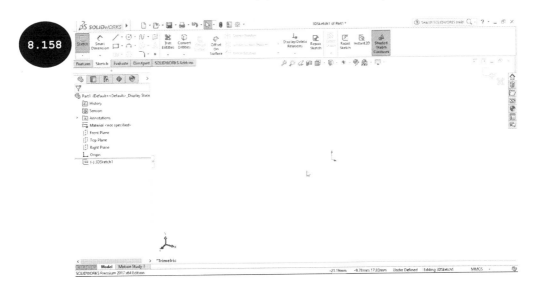

Using the Line Tool in the 3D Sketching Environment

1. Invoke the 3D Sketching environment by clicking on the **3D Sketch** tool in the **Sketch** flyout, which appears on clicking the down arrow in the **Sketch** tool of the **Sketch CommandManager**, refer to Figure 8.157.
2. Click on the **Line** tool in the **Sketch CommandManager**. The cursor changes to line cursor with the display of **XY** at its bottom, see Figure 8.159. The display of XY indicates that the XY plane (Front plane) is activated as the current sketching plane. You can press the **TAB** key to switch from one sketching plane to another for creating a 3D sketch.

3. Press the **TAB** key until the required sketching plane is activated.
4. Specify the start point of the line by clicking the left mouse button in the graphics area.
5. Move the cursor for a little distance from the start point. A rubber band line appears whose one end is fixed at the specified start point and the other end is attached to the cursor, see Figure 8.160.

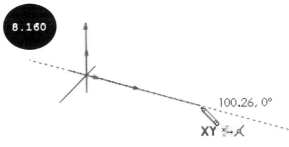

> **Tip:** You can toggle the sketching plane even after specifying the start point of the line by using the **TAB** key.

392 Chapter 8 > Advanced Modeling - II

6. Move the cursor to the required location in the drawing area and then click to specify the endpoint of the first line when the length of the line appears close to the required one near the cursor. Next, move the cursor to a little distance. The preview of the rubber band line appears.
7. Press the **TAB** key to switch the sketching plane, if required.
8. Move the cursor to the required location and then click to specify the endpoint of the next line, see Figure 8.161. In Figure 8.161, the sketching plane has been changed to YZ.
9. Similarly, create other line entities of the 3D sketch in different sketching planes, as required, see Figure 8.162.

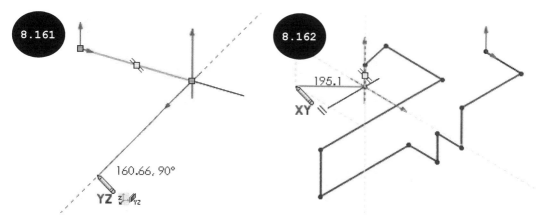

10. After creating all sketch entities of the 3D sketch, right-click in the graphics area, and then click on the **Select** option in the shortcut menu appeared to exit the **Line** tool.

Note: The procedure to apply dimensions to a 3D sketch in the 3D Sketching environment is same as applying dimensions to a 2D sketch by using the dimension tools.

11. Click on the **Sketch** tool in the **Sketch CommandManager** to exit the 3D Sketching environment. Alternatively, click on the **Exit Sketch** icon in the confirmation corner.

Figure 8.163 shows a 3D Sketch and Figure 8.164 shows a sweep feature created by sweeping a circular profile along the 3D sketch.

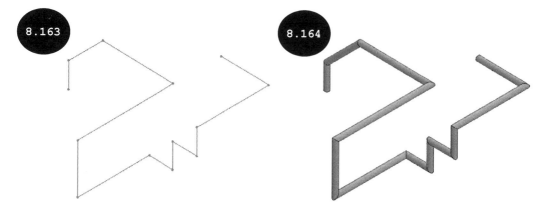

Using the Spline Tool in the 3D Sketching Environment

1. Invoke the 3D Sketching environment by clicking on the 3D Sketch tool in the Sketch flyout, which appears on clicking the down arrow in the Sketch tool of the Sketch CommandManager.
2. Press CTRL + 7 to change the current orientation of the sketch to isometric.
3. Click on the Spline tool in the Sketch CommandManager. The display of cursor changes such that the XY appears at its bottom, see Figure 8.165. The display of XY indicates that the XY plane (Front plane) is activated as the current sketching plane. You can press the TAB key to switch from one sketching plane to another for creating a 3D sketch.

4. Press the TAB key until the required sketching plane has been activated and its name appears below the cursor.
5. Click to specify the first control point of the spline in the graphics area. Next, move the cursor to a distance from the specified control point. A rubber band spline appears whose one end is fixed at the first control point and the other end is attached to the cursor, see Figure 8.166.
6. Press the TAB key to switch the sketching plane, as required.
7. Move the cursor to the required location and then click to specify the second control point of the spline, see Figure 8.167. Next, move the cursor for a little distance. The preview of another rubber band spline appears such that it passes through the specified control points.

Tip: In Figure 8.167, the second control point of the spline is specified on XY plane.

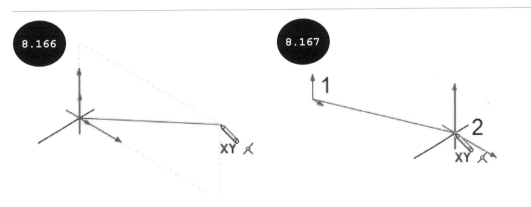

8. Press the TAB key to switch the sketching plane, if required. Next, move the cursor to the required location and then click to specify the third control point of the spline, see Figure 8.168.

Tip: In Figure 8.168, the third control point of the spline is specified on XY plane.

9. Press the TAB key to switch the sketching plane, as required. Next, move the cursor to the required location and then click to specify the fourth control point of the spline, see Figure 8.169. In Figure 8.169, the fourth control point of the spline is specified on YZ plane.

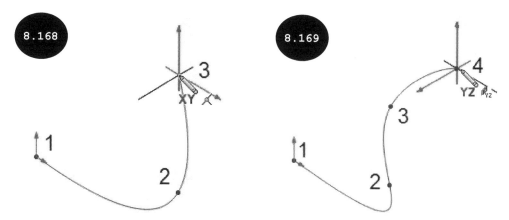

10. Similarly, specify remaining control points of the spline on different planes, as required. Once you have specified all control points of the spline, press the ESC key to exit the **Spline** tool. Figure 8.170 shows a spline created by specifying control points on different planes.

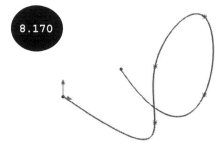

Tip: After creating the 3D spline, you can further control the shape of the spline by dragging its control points, as discussed while creating 2D spline. Once the 3D spline is created and required modification has been made, exit the 3D Sketching environment. Figure 8.171 shows a 3D spline and Figure 8.172 shows the resultant sweep feature created by sweeping a rectangular profile along the 3D spline.

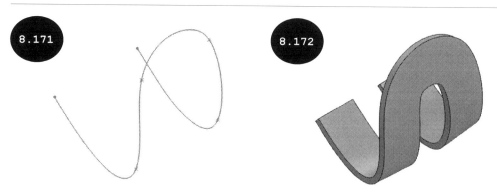

The use of the rectangle, arc, circle, point, and centerline tools in the 3D sketching environment are the same as those discussed earlier while creating 2D sketches.

Tutorial 1

Create the model shown in Figure 8.173. The different views and dimensions are given in the same figure. All dimensions are in mm.

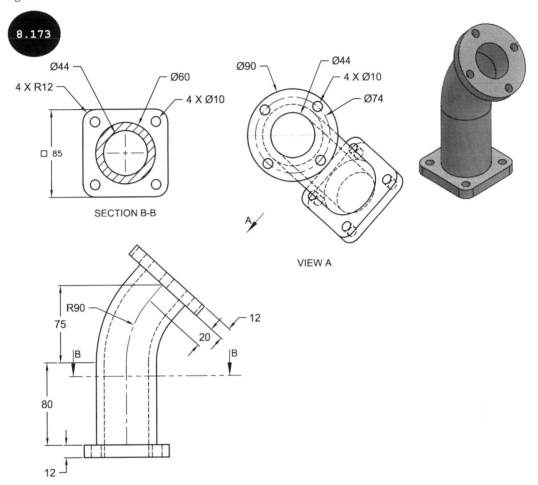

8.173

Section 1: Starting SOLIDWORKS
1. Double-click on the SOLIDWORKS icon on your desktop to start SOLIDWORKS.

Section 2: Invoking the Part Modeling Environment
1. Click on the **New** tool in the **Standard** toolbar. The **New SOLIDWORKS Document** dialog box appears.

2. In this dialog box, the **Part** button is activated by default. Click on the **OK** button to invoke the Part modeling environment.

   Once the Part modeling environment has been invoked, you can set the unit system and create the base/first feature of the model.

396 Chapter 8 > Advanced Modeling - II

Section 3: Specifying Unit Settings

1. Move the cursor toward the lower right corner of the screen over the Status Bar and then click on the **Unit System** area in the Status Bar. The **Unit System** flyout appears, see Figure 8.174.

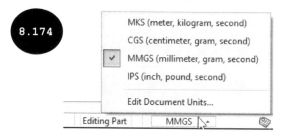

2. Make sure that the **MMGS (millimeter, gram, second)** option is tick-marked in this flyout.

Section 4: Creating the Base/First Feature - Sweep Feature

1. Invoke the Sketching environment by selecting the Front plane as the sketching plane and then create the path of the sweep feature and apply dimensions, see Figure 8.175.

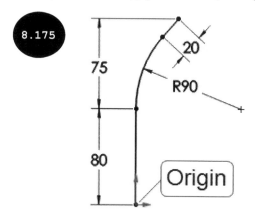

2. Exit the Sketching environment by clicking on the **Exit Sketch** tool in the **Sketch CommandManager**.

   After creating the path of the sweep feature, you need to create sweep feature having circular profile.

3. Click on the **Swept Boss/Base** tool in the **Features CommandManager**.  The **Sweep PropertyManager** appears.

4. Click on the **Circular Profile** radio button in the **Profile and Path** rollout of the PropertyManager.

5. Click on the path of the sweep feature in the graphics area. The preview of the sweep feature appears with the default diameter of circular profile.

6. Enter **60** in the **Diameter** field of the **Profile and Path** rollout and then press ENTER. The preview of the sweep feature appears, see Figure 8.176.

7. Expand the **Thin Feature** rollout of the PropertyManager by selecting the check box in the title bar of the rollout, see Figure 8.177.

8. Enter **8** in the **Thickness** field of the **Thin Feature** rollout.

9. Click on the **Reverse Direction** button in the **Thin Feature** rollout to reverse the direction of material addition such that the material is added inward to the profile, see Figure 8.178.

10. Click on the green tick mark ✓ in the PropertyManager. The thin sweep feature is created, see Figure 8.179.

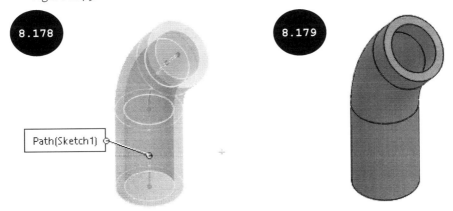

Section 5: Creating Second Feature - Extruded Feature

1. Rotate the model such that the bottom face of the base feature (sweep) can be viewed, see Figure 8.180. To rotate a model, right-click in the graphics area and then click on the **Rotate View** option in the shortcut menu appeared. Next, press and hold the left mouse button, and then drag the cursor. Alternatively, press and hold the middle mouse button and then drag the cursor in the graphics area.

398 Chapter 8 > Advanced Modeling - II

2. Invoke the Sketching environment by selecting the bottom face of the base feature (sweep) as the sketching plane.

3. Press CTRL + 8 to change the orientation of the model as normal to the viewing direction.

4. Create the sketch of the second feature, see Figure 8.181.

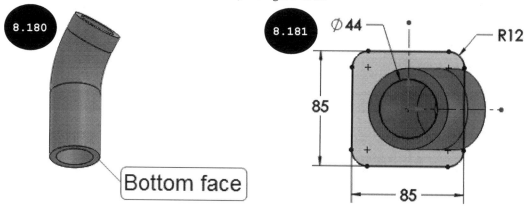

Tip: The sketch created in Figure 8.182 is symmetric about the vertical and horizontal centerlines. Also, the arcs of the sketch are of same radius and are created by using the **Fillet** tool.

5. Click on the **Features** tab in the CommandManager. The tools of the **Features CommandManager** are displayed.

6. Click on the **Extruded Boss/Base** tool in the Features CommandManager. The Boss-Extrude PropertyManager and the preview of the extruded feature appear. Next, change the orientation of the model to isometric, see Figure 8.182.

7. Enter **12** in the **Distance** field of the **Direction 1** rollout in the PropertyManager.

8. Click on the green tick mark ✓ in the PropertyManager. The extruded feature is created, see Figure 8.183.

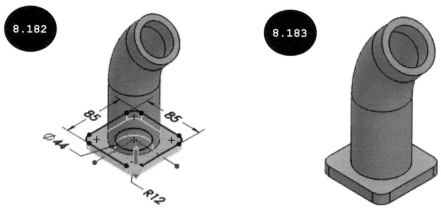

Section 6: Creating the Third Feature - Extruded Cut Feature

1. Invoke the Sketching environment by selecting the top planar face of the second feature as the sketching plane.

2. Press CTRL + 8 to change the orientation of the model as normal to the viewing direction.

3. Create the sketch (four circles of diameter 10 mm) of the third feature, see Figure 8.184.

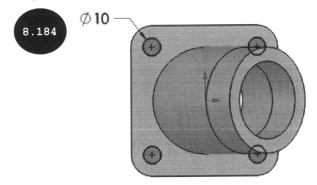

Tip: The sketch of the third feature shown in Figure 8.184 has four circles of the same diameter; therefore, the equal relation is applied among all circles. Also, the concentric relation is applied between the center point of circles and the respective semi-circular edge of the second feature. You can also create one circle and then pattern it circularly to create remaining circles.

4. Click on the **Features** tab of the CommandManager and then click on the **Extruded Cut** tool. The **Cut-Extrude PropertyManager** as well as the preview of the cut feature appear. Change the orientation of the model to isometric, see Figure 8.185.

5. Invoke the **End Condition** drop-down list in the **Direction 1** rollout of the PropertyManager and then click on the **Through All** option in it.

6. Click on the green tick mark in the PropertyManager. The extruded cut feature is created, see Figure 8.186.

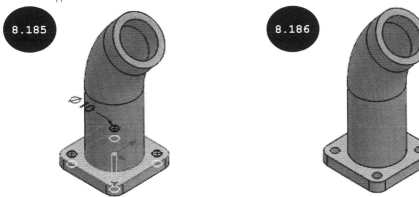

Section 7: Creating the Fourth Feature - Extruded Feature

1. Invoke the Sketching environment by selecting the top planar face of the sweep feature (first feature) as the sketching plane, see Figure 8.187.

2. Press CTRL + 8 to change the orientation of the model as normal to the viewing direction.

3. Create the sketch (two circles of diameter 90 mm and 44 mm) of the fourth feature, see Figure 8.188.

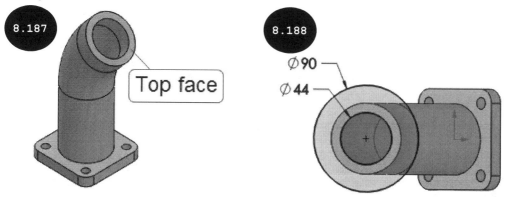

Tip: The sketch of the fourth feature shown in Figure 8.188 has two circles, which are concentric to the top circular edge of the sweep feature. You need to take the reference of the top circular edges of the sweep feature for specifying the center point of the circles.

4. Click on the **Features** tab in the CommandManager and then click on the **Extruded Boss/Base** tool. The **Boss-Extrude PropertyManager** and the preview of the extruded feature appear. Next, change the orientation of the model to isometric, see Figure 8.189.

5. Enter **12** in the **Distance** field of the **Direction 1** rollout in the PropertyManager.

6. Click on the green tick mark in the PropertyManager. The extruded feature is created, see Figure 8.190.

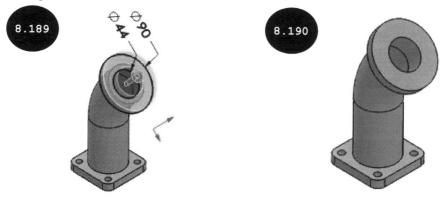

Section 8: Creating the Fifth Feature - Extruded Cut Feature

1. Invoke the Sketching environment by selecting the top planar face of the fourth feature as the sketching plane.

2. Press CTRL + 8 to change the orientation of the model as normal to the viewing direction.

3. Create a circle of diameter 10 mm, see Figure 8.191. Next, create a circular pattern of it to create the remaining circles of the same diameter and the same PCD by using the **Circular Sketch Pattern** tool, see Figure 8.192. Note that you need to change the position of the center point of the pattern to the center point of the circular edge of the fourth feature by dragging the dot appeared at the tip of the arrow in the pattern preview.

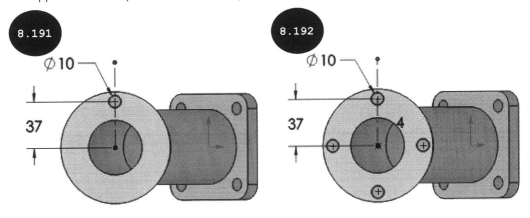

Tip: In Figure 8.191, the center point of the circle has coincident relation with the vertical centerline. Also, the start point of the vertical centerline is coincident with the center point of the circular edge of the fourth feature.

While specifying the start point of the vertical centerline shown in Figure 8.191, move the cursor over the outer circular edge of the fourth feature. The center point of the circular edge highlights. Next, move the cursor to the highlighted center point and then click to specify the start point of the vertical centerline when the cursor snaps to it.

4. Click on the **Extruded Cut** tool in the **Features CommandManager**. The **Cut-Extrude PropertyManager** as well as the preview of the extruded cut feature appear. Change the orientation of the model to isometric, see Figure 8.193.

5. Invoke the **End Condition** drop-down list in the **Direction 1** rollout of the PropertyManager and then click on the **Up to Next** option in it.

6. Click on the green tick mark ✓ in the PropertyManager. The extruded cut feature is created, see Figure 8.194.

402 Chapter 8 > Advanced Modeling - II

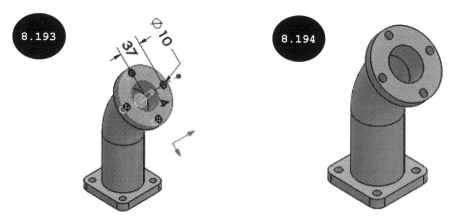

Section 9: Saving the Model

1. Click on the **Save** tool of the **Standard** toolbar. The **Save As** window appears.

2. Browse to the SOLIDWORKS folder and then create a folder with the name **Chapter 8**. Next, create another folder with the name **Tutorial** in the *Chapter 8* folder.

3. Enter **Tutorial 1** in the **File name** field of the dialog box as the name of the file and then click on the **Save** button. The model is saved with the name Tutorial 1 in the *Tutorial* folder of *Chapter 8*.

Tutorial 2

Create the model shown in Figure 8.195. The different views and dimensions are given in the same figure. All dimensions are in mm.

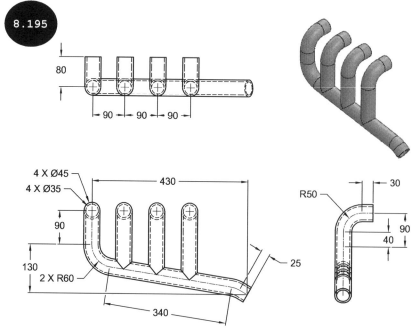

Section 1: Starting SOLIDWORKS

1. Double-click on the SOLIDWORKS icon on your desktop to start SOLIDWORKS.

Section 2: Invoking the Part Modeling Environment

1. Click on the **New** tool in the **Standard** toolbar. The **New SOLIDWORKS Document** dialog box appears.

2. Double-click on the **Part** button in the dialog box. The Part modeling environment is invoked.

   Once the Part modeling environment has been invoked, you can set the unit system and create the base/first feature of the model.

Section 3: Specifying Unit Settings

1. Move the cursor toward the lower right corner of the screen over the Status Bar and then click on the **Unit System** area. The **Unit System** flyout appears, see Figure 8.196.

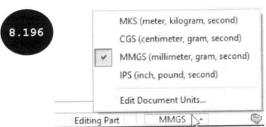

2. Make sure that the **MMGS (millimeter, gram, second)** option is tick-marked in this flyout.

Section 4: Creating the Base/First Feature - Sweep Feature

1. Invoke the Sketching environment by selecting the Right plane as the sketching plane and then create the path of the sweep feature, see Figure 8.197.

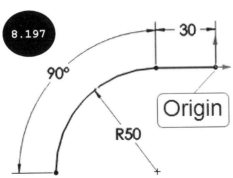

2. Exit the Sketching environment by clicking on the **Exit Sketch** button in the **Sketch CommandManager**.

404 Chapter 8 > Advanced Modeling - II

After creating the path of the sweep feature, you need to create the profile for the sweep feature.

3. Invoke the Sketching environment by selecting the Front plane as the sketching plane and then press CTRL + 8 to change the orientation as normal to the viewing direction.

4. Create the sketch of the profile (two circles of diameter 45 mm and 35 mm), see Figure 8.198.

5. Exit the Sketching environment by clicking on the **Exit Sketch** tool in the **Sketch CommandManager**.

6. Change the orientation of the model to isometric, see Figure 8.199.

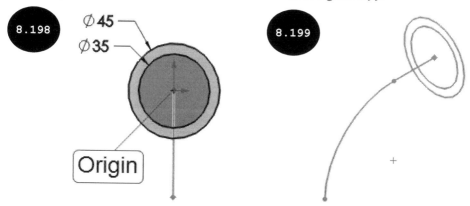

After creating the path and the profile, you need to create the sweep feature.

7. Click on the **Swept Boss/Base** tool. The **Sweep PropertyManager**  appears.

8. Make sure that the **Sketch Profile** radio button is selected in the **Profile and Path** rollout of the PropertyManager.

9. Click on the profile (two circles) of the sweep feature in the graphics area. The **Path** field in the **Sweep PropertyManager** gets activated.

10. Click on the path of the sweep feature in the graphics area. The preview of the sweep feature appears in the graphics area, see Figure 8.200.

> **Tip:** Instead of creating the sketch of the profile (two circles) for creating the sweep feature, you can also select the **Circular Profile** radio button in the **Sweep PropertyManager** and then specify the diameter of circular profile in the **Diameter** field of the PropertyManager. This is because the profile of the sweep feature is a circular profile.

11. Click on the green tick mark ✓ in the PropertyManager. The sweep feature is created, see Figure 8.201.

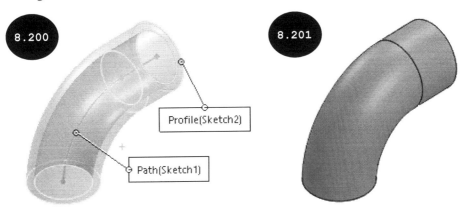

Section 5: Creating the Second Feature - Sweep Feature

To create the second feature of the model, you first need to create a reference plane at the offset distance of 80 mm from the Front plane.

1. Click on the down arrow in the **Reference Geometry** tool of the **Features CommandManager** to invoke the **Reference Geometry** flyout, see Figure 8.202.

2. Click on the **Plane** tool in the flyout. The **Plane PropertyManager** appears.

3. Expand the FeatureManager Design Tree, which is now available on the top left corner of the graphics area by clicking on the arrow in its front.

4. Click on the **Front Plane** in the FeatureManager Design Tree as the first reference. The preview of an offset reference plane appears in the graphics area.

5. Enter **80** in the **Distance** field of the **First Reference** rollout. Make sure that the direction of the plane creation is same as shown in the Figure 8.203. If needed, you can flip the direction of the plane creation.

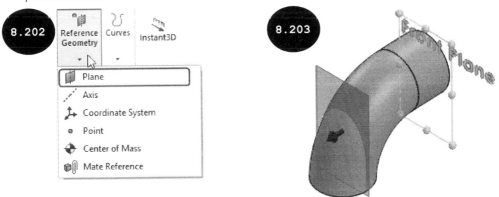

Chapter 8 > Advanced Modeling - II

6. Click on the green tick mark ✓ in the PropertyManager. The offset reference plane is created.

7. Invoke the Sketching environment by selecting the newly created reference plane as the sketching plane. Next, press CTRL + 8 to change the orientation of the model as normal to the viewing direction.

8. Create the path of the second sweep feature, see Figure 8.204.

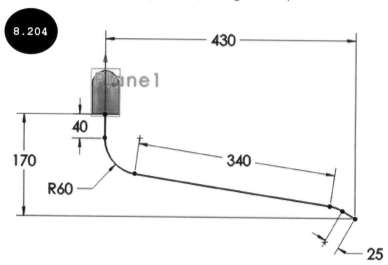

9. Exit the Sketching environment by clicking on the **Exit Sketch** tool in the **Sketch CommandManager**. Next, press CTRL + 7 to change the orientation to the model to isometric.

   After creating the path of the sweep feature, you need to create sweep feature.

10. Click on the **Swept Boss/Base** tool in the **Features CommandManager**. The **Sweep PropertyManager** appears.

11. Make sure that the **Sketch Profile** radio button is selected in the **Profile and Path** rollout of the PropertyManager.

12. Rotate the model such that the bottom face of the first feature (sweep) can be viewed, see Figure 8.205. To rotate the model, right-click in the graphics area and then click on the **Rotate View** option in the shortcut menu appeared. Next, press and hold the left mouse button, and then drag the cursor. Once the required orientation of the model has been achieved, press the ESC key to exit the **Rotate View** tool.

13. Select the bottom face of the first feature (sweep) as the profile of the second sweep feature, see Figure 8.205.

14. Click on the path of the sweep feature in the graphics area. The preview of the sweep feature appears, see Figure 8.206. Press CTRL + 7 to change the orientation of the model to isometric.

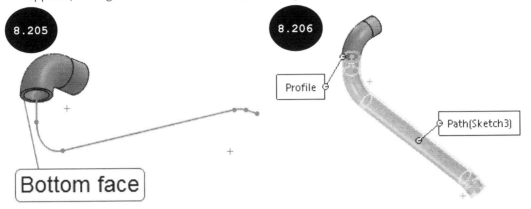

15. Click on the green tick mark ✓ in the PropertyManager. The sweep feature is created, see Figure 8.207. Hide the reference plane.

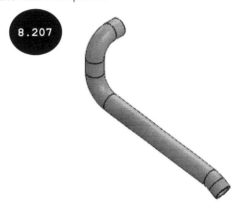

Section 6: Creating the Third Feature - Extruded Feature

To create the third feature of the model, you first need to create a reference plane at the offset distance of 50 mm from the Top plane.

1. Invoke the **Reference Geometry** flyout in the **Features CommandManager** and then click on the **Plane** tool to invoke the **Plane PropertyManager**.

2. Expand the FeatureManager Design Tree, which is now available on the top left corner of the graphics area, by clicking on the arrow in its front.

3. Click on the **Top Plane** in the FeatureManager Design Tree as the first reference. The preview of the offset reference plane appears in the graphics area.

4. Enter **50** in the **Distance** field of the **First Reference** rollout of the PropertyManager.

408 Chapter 8 > Advanced Modeling - II

5. Select the **Flip offset** check box in the **First Reference** rollout to reverse the direction of the plane creation downward.

6. Click on the green tick mark ✓ in the PropertyManager. The offset reference plane is created, see Figure 8.208.

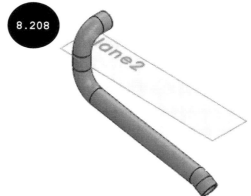

7. Invoke the Sketching environment by selecting the newly created reference plane as the sketching plane.

8. Press CTRL + 8 to change the orientation of the model as normal to the viewing direction.

9. Create the sketch of the third feature (three circles of same diameter), see Figure 8.209.

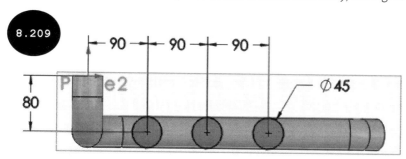

10. Click on the **Features** tab in the CommandManager to display the tools of the **Features** CommandManager.

11. Click on the **Extruded Boss/Base** tool in the Features CommandManager. The **Boss-Extrude** PropertyManager as well as the preview of the extruded feature appear. Next, change the orientation of the model to isometric, see Figure 8.210.

12. Click on the **Reverse Direction** button in the **Direction 1** rollout to reverse the direction of extrusion downward.

13. Invoke the **End Condition** drop-down list of the **Direction 1** rollout and then select the **Up To**

Next option in the drop-down list. The preview of the extruded feature appears in the graphics area such that it has been terminated at its next intersection.

14. Click on the green tick mark ✓ in the PropertyManager. The extruded feature is created, see Figure 8.211.

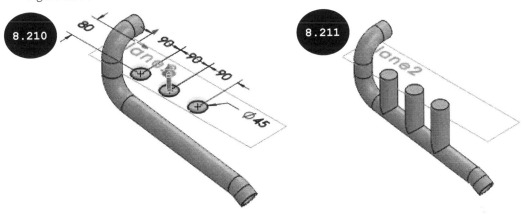

15. Hide the reference plane by clicking on the **Hide** option in the Pop-up toolbar that appears as soon as you select the plane to be hidden in the graphics area.

Section 7: Creating the Fourth Feature - Extruded Cut Feature

1. Invoke the Sketching environment by selecting the top planar face of the third feature as the sketching plane, see Figure 8.212.

2. Press CTRL + 8 to change the orientation of the model as normal to the viewing direction.

3. Create the sketch of the fourth feature (three circles of same diameter), see Figure 8.213.

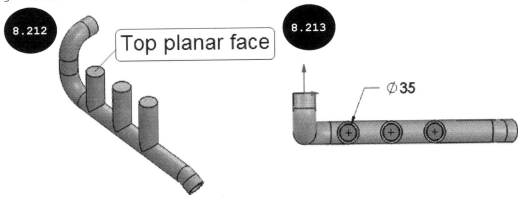

Tip: The sketch of the fourth feature shown in Figure 8.212 has three circles, which are concentric to the circular edges of the extruded feature. Also, the equal relation has been applied between all the circles.

410 Chapter 8 > Advanced Modeling - II

4. Click on the **Extruded Cut** tool in the **Features CommandManager**. The **Cut-Extrude PropertyManager** as well as the preview of the extruded cut feature appear. Next, change the orientation of the model to isometric.

5. Invoke the **End Condition** drop-down list in the **Direction 1** rollout of the PropertyManager.

6. Click on the **Up To Next** option in the **End Condition** drop-down list. The preview of the extruded cut feature appears in the graphics area such that it has been terminated at its next intersection.

7. Click on the green tick mark ✓ in the PropertyManager. The extruded cut feature is created, see Figure 8.214.

8.214

Section 8: Creating the Fifth Feature - Sweep Feature

To create the fifth feature of the model, you first need to create a reference plane at the offset distance of 90 mm from the Right plane.

1. Invoke the **Reference Geometry** flyout in the **Features CommandManager**, see Figure 8.215.

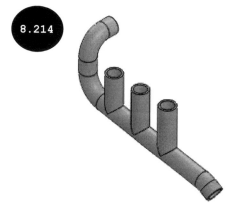

8.215

2. Click on the **Plane** tool in the flyout. The **Plane PropertyManager** appears.

3. Expand the FeatureManager Design Tree by clicking on the arrow in its front, which is now available on the top left corner of the graphics area.

4. Click on the **Right Plane** in the FeatureManager Design Tree as the first reference. The preview of the offset reference plane appears in the graphics area.

5. Enter **90** in the **Distance** field of the **First Reference** rollout of the **Plane PropertyManager**.

6. Click on the green tick mark ✓ in the PropertyManager. The offset reference plane is created, see Figure 8.216.

7. Invoke the Sketching environment by selecting the newly created reference plane as the sketching plane. Next, press CTRL + 8 to change the orientation of the model as normal to the viewing direction.

8. Create the path of the sweep feature, see Figure 8.217.

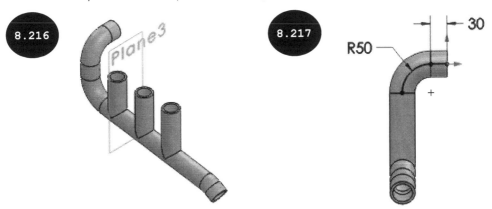

9. Exit the Sketching environment by clicking on the **Exit Sketch** tool in the **Sketch CommandManager**.

10. Change the current orientation of the model to isometric, see Figure 8.218. Hide the reference plane.

    After creating the path, you need to create the sweep feature.

11. Click on the **Swept Boss/Base** tool. The **Sweep PropertyManager** appears.

12. Make sure that the **Sketch Profile** radio button is selected in the **Profile and Path** rollout of the PropertyManager.

13. Select the top planar face of the extruded feature as the profile of the sweep feature, see Figure 8.219.

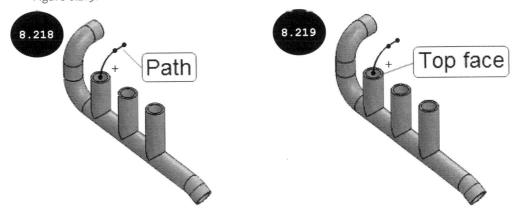

412 Chapter 8 > Advanced Modeling - II

14. Select the path of the sweep feature in the graphics area. The preview of the sweep feature appears, see Figure 8.220.

15. Click on the green tick mark ✓ in the PropertyManager. The sweep feature is created, see Figure 8.221.

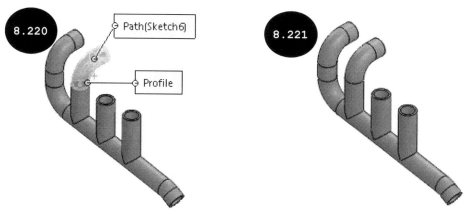

Section 9: Creating the Sixth and Seventh Features - Sweep Features

To create the sixth and seventh features (sweep), you can use the sketch of the fifth feature (sweep) of the model as the path.

1. Expand the node of the fifth feature (previously created sweep feature) in the FeatureManager Design Tree, see Figure 8.222.

2. Select the sketch (path) of the fifth feature (sweep feature) in the FeatureManager Design Tree, see Figure 8.222.

3. Click on the **Swept Boss/Base** tool in the **Features CommandManager**. The **Sweep PropertyManager** appears. Also, the selected sketch of the fifth feature is selected as the path of the sixth feature (sweep), see Figure 8.223.

4. Select the top planar face of the extruded feature as the profile of the sweep feature, see Figure 8.223. The preview of the sweep feature appears in the graphics area, see Figure 8.224.

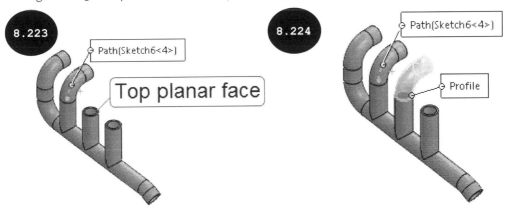

5. Click on the green tick mark ✓ in the PropertyManager. The sweep feature is created, see Figure 8.225.

6. Similarly, create the seventh feature, which is a sweep feature, by using the sketch of the fifth feature as the path. Figure 8.226 shows the final model.

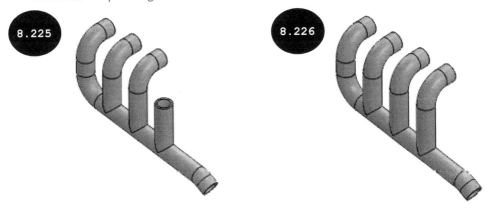

Section 10: Saving the Model

1. Click on the **Save** tool in the **Standard** toolbar. The **Save As** window appears.

2. Browse to the *Tutorial* folder of *Chapter 8* and then save the model with the name Tutorial 2.

414   Chapter 8 > Advanced Modeling - II

Tutorial 3

Create the model shown in Figure 8.227. All dimensions are in mm.

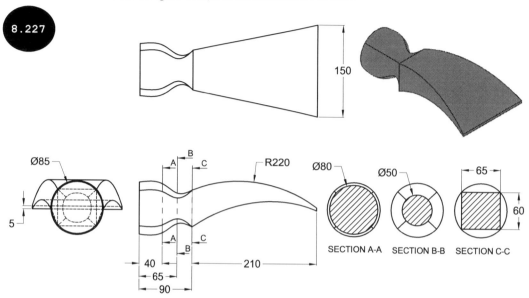

8.227

Section 1: Starting SOLIDWORKS
1. Double-click on the SOLIDWORKS icon on your desktop to start SOLIDWORKS, if not already started.

Section 2: Invoking the Part Modeling Environment
1. Invoke the Part modeling environment by using the **New** tool of the **Standard** toolbar.

   Once the Part modeling environment has been invoked, you need to set the unit system and create the base/first feature of the model.

Section 3: Specifying Unit Settings
1. Make sure that the **MMGS (millimeter, gram, second)** unit system is set as the current unit system for the opened part document.

Section 4: Creating the Base/First Feature - Lofted Feature
To create the base/first feature (lofted feature) of the model, you first need to create all its sections (profiles) on reference planes.

1. Invoke the Sketching environment by selecting the Right plane as the sketching plane.

2. Create the first section (profile) of the lofted feature, which is a circle of diameter 85 mm, see Figure 8.228.

3. Exit the Sketching environment and then press CTRL + 7 to change the orientation of the model to isometric.

   You have created the first section (profile) of the lofted feature, now you need to create the second section at the offset distance of 40 mm from the Right plane.

4. Create a reference plane at the offset distance of 40 mm from the Right plane by using the **Plane** tool of the **Reference Geometry** flyout, see Figure 8.229.

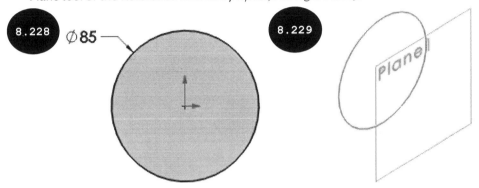

5. Invoke the Sketching environment by selecting the newly created reference plane as the sketching plane.

6. Press CTRL + 8 to change the orientation of the model as normal to the viewing direction.

7. Create the second section (a circle of diameter 80 mm) of the lofted feature, see Figure 8.230. Next, exit the Sketching environment.

8. Press CTRL + 7 to change the orientation of the model to isometric.

   You have created the second section (profile) of the lofted feature, now you need to create the third section of the feature at the offset distance of 65 mm from the Right plane.

9. Create a reference plane at the offset distance of 65 mm from the Right plane by using the **Plane** tool in the **Reference Geometry** flyout, see Figure 8.231.

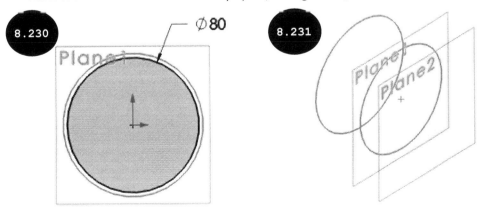

10. Invoke the Sketching environment by selecting the newly created reference plane as the sketching plane. Next, press CTRL + 8 to change the orientation of the model as normal to the viewing direction.

11. Create the third section (a circle of diameter 50 mm) of the lofted feature, see Figure 8.232. Next, exit the Sketching environment.

12. Press CTRL + 7 to change the current orientation of the model to isometric.

    You have created the third section (profile) of the lofted feature, now you need to create the fourth section of the feature at the offset distance of 90 mm from the Right plane.

13. Create a reference plane at the offset distance of 90 mm from the Right plane by using the Plane tool, see Figure 8.233.

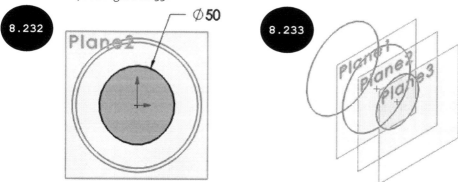

14. Invoke the Sketching environment by selecting the newly created reference plane as the sketching plane.

15. Press CTRL + 8 to change the orientation of the model as normal to the viewing direction.

16. Create the fourth section (rectangle of 65 X 60) of the lofted feature, see Figure 8.234.

17. Exit the Sketching environment and then press CTRL + 7 to change the current orientation to isometric, see Figure 8.235.

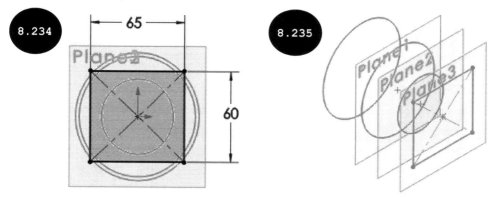

You have created all sections of the lofted feature, now you need to create the lofted feature.

18. Click on the **Lofted Boss/Base** tool in the **Features CommandManager**.  The **Loft PropertyManager** appears.

19. Select all the sections (profiles) of the lofted feature in the graphics area one by one by clicking the left mouse button. The preview of the lofted feature appears in the graphics area, see Figure 8.236. Make sure that the connectors appearing in the preview of the features are in one direction to avoid twisting, see Figure 8.236.

20. Click on the green tick mark ✓ in the PropertyManager. The lofted feature is created, see Figure 8.237. In Figure 8.237, the reference plane has been hidden.

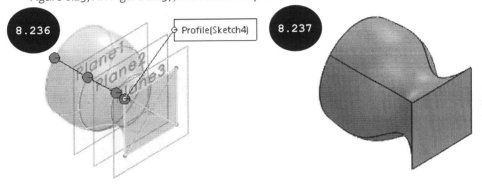

21. Hide the reference planes by clicking on the **Hide** tool in the Pop-up toolbar, which appears as soon as you select a plane to be hidden.

Section 5: Creating the Second Feature - Lofted Feature

Now, you need to create the second feature of the model, which is a lofted feature.

1. Create a reference plane at the offset distance of 210 mm from the right planar face of the base feature by using the **Plane** tool, see Figure 8.238.

2. Invoke the Sketching environment by selecting the newly created reference plane as the sketching plane. Next, change the orientation of the model as normal to the viewing direction.

3. Create the section (rectangle of 150 X 5) of the lofted feature, see Figure 8.239.

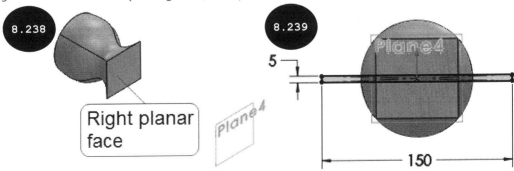

418 Chapter 8 > Advanced Modeling - II

4. Exit the Sketching environment and then change the current orientation to isometric.

   Now, you need to create a guide curve of the lofted feature on the Front plane.

5. Invoke the Sketching environment by selecting the Front plane as the sketching plane.

6. Press CTRL + 8 to change the orientation of the model as normal to the viewing direction.

7. Create the guide curve (an arc of radius 220 mm) of the lofted feature, see Figure 8.240.

> **Note:** The endpoints of the guide curve shown in the Figure 8.240 have Pierce relation with the rectangular section of the lofted feature and the top edge of the right planar face of the base feature.

8. Exit the Sketching environment and then change the current orientation to isometric.

   Now, you need to create the lofted feature.

9. Click on the **Lofted Boss/Base** tool in the **Features CommandManager**.  The **Loft PropertyManager** appears.

10. Select the right planar face of the base feature as the first section of the lofted feature and then select the rectangular section (rectangle of 150 X 5) as the second section of the loft feature. The preview of the lofted feature appears in the graphics area, see Figure 8.241.

11. Make sure that the connectors appearing in the preview of the feature are in one direction, see Figure 8.241. If needed, you can change the position of the connectors by dragging them.

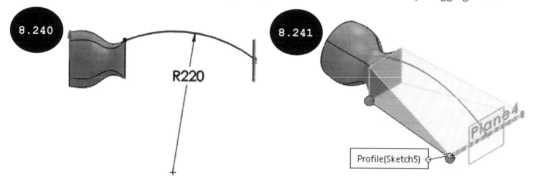

12. Click on the **Guide Curves** field in the **Guide Curves** rollout of the PropertyManager. The **Guide Curves** field is activated.

13. Click on the guide curve (arc of radius 220 mm) in the graphics area. The preview of the lofted feature appears such that it is guided by the guide curve, see Figure 8.242.

14. Click on the green tick mark ✓ in the PropertyManager. The lofted feature is created, see Figure 8.243.

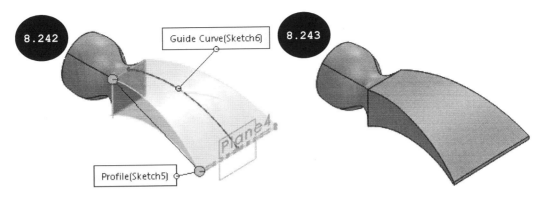

Section 6: Saving the Model

1. Click on the **Save** tool of the **Standard** toolbar. The **Save As** window appears.

2. Browse to the *Tutorial* folder of *Chapter 8* and then save the model with the name Tutorial 3.

Tutorial 4

Create the model shown in Figure 8.244. All dimensions are in mm.

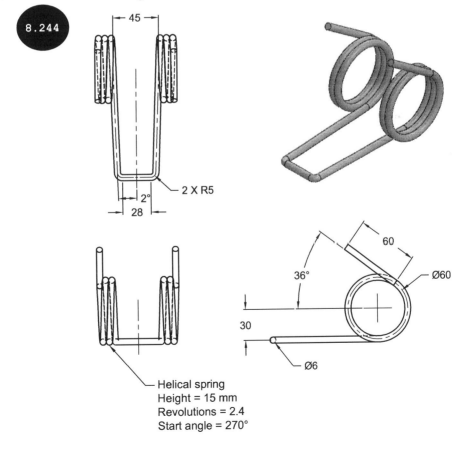

420 Chapter 8 > Advanced Modeling - II

Section 1: Starting SOLIDWORKS
1. Double-click on the SOLIDWORKS icon on your desktop to start SOLIDWORKS.

Section 2: Invoking the Part Modeling Environment
1. Invoke the Part modeling environment by using the **New** tool in the **Standard** toolbar.

   Once the Part modeling environment is invoked, you can set the unit system and create the base/first feature of the model.

Section 3: Specifying Unit Settings
1. Make sure that the **MMGS (millimeter, gram, second)** unit system is set for the currently opened part document.

Section 4: Creating the First Curve - Helical Curve
1. Invoke the Sketching environment by selecting the Right plane as the sketching plane and then create a circle of diameter 60 mm, which defines the diameter of helical curve, see Figure 8.245.

2. Exit the Sketching environment by clicking on the **Exit Sketch** button.

3. Invoke the **Curves** flyout in the **Features CommandManager** and then click on the **Helix and Spiral** tool. The **Helix/Spiral PropertyManager** appears.

   Note: If the circle has been selected before invoking the **Helix and Spiral** tool, then the **Helix/Spiral PropertyManager** as well as the preview of the helical curve appear. You can select the circle defining the diameter of the helical curve before or after invoking the **Helix and Spiral** tool.

4. Click on the circle in the graphics area. The preview of the helical curve appears, see Figure 8.246.

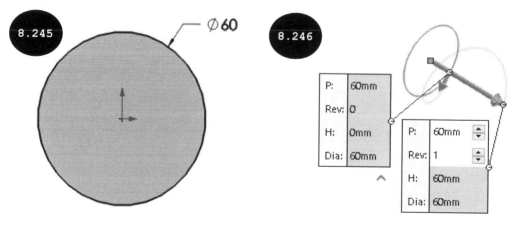

5. Invoke the **Type** drop-down list in the **Defined By** rollout of the PropertyManager, see Figure 8.247.

6. Select the **Height and Revolution** option in the **Type** drop-down list.

7. Enter **15** in the **Height** field, **2.4** in the **Revolutions** field, and **270** in the **Start angle** field of the **Parameters** rollout in the PropertyManager.

8. Select the **Reverse direction** check box in the **Parameters** rollout. The direction of the curve creation is reversed, see Figure 8.248.

9. Make sure that the **Counterclockwise** radio button is selected in the rollout.

10. Click on the green tick mark in the PropertyManager. The helical curve is created, see Figure 8.249.

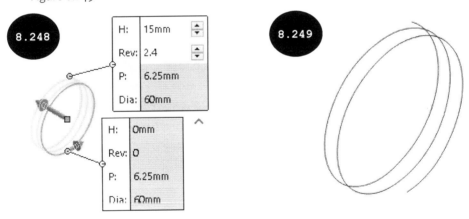

Section 5: Creating the Second Curve - Helical Curve

After creating the first helical curve, you need to create the second helical curve at the offset distance of 45 mm from the Right Plane.

1. Create a reference plane at the offset distance of 45 mm from the Right plane by using the **Plane** tool, see Figure 8.250.

2. Invoke the Sketching environment by selecting the newly created reference plane as the sketching plane.

3. Press CTRL + 8 to change the orientation of the model as normal to the viewing direction.

4. Create a circle of diameter 60 mm as the diameter of the second helical curve, see Figure 8.251.

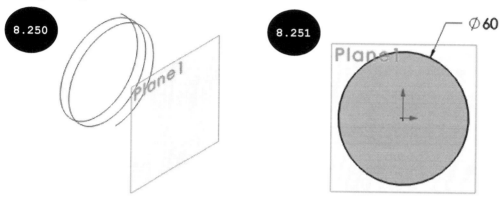

5. Invoke the **Curves** flyout in the **Features CommandManager** and then click on the **Helix and Spiral** tool. The preview of the helical curve as well as the **Helix/Spiral PropertyManager** appear.

6. Press CTRL + 7 to change the current orientation of the model to isometric.

7. Select the **Height and Revolution** option in the **Type** drop-down list of the **Defined By** rollout.

8. Enter **15** in the **Height** field, **2.4** in the **Revolutions** field, and **270** in the **Start angle** field of the **Parameters** rollout of the PropertyManager.

9. Make sure that the **Reverse direction** check box is unchecked in the rollout.

10. Make sure that the **Counterclockwise** radio button is selected in the rollout.

11. Click on the green tick mark ✓ in the PropertyManager. The helical curve is created, see Figure 8.252.

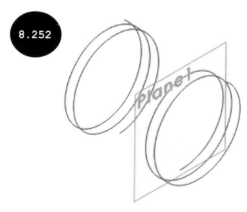

12. Hide the reference plane by selecting the **Hide** option in the Pop-up toolbar, which appeared on selecting the plane to be hidden.

Section 6: Creating the Third Curve - Sketch

After creating the helical curves, you need to create a sketch on a reference plane, which is parallel to the Top Plane and passes through the start point of the first helical curve.

1. Create a reference plane parallel to the Top Plane and passes through the start point of the first helical curve, see Figures 8.253 and 8.254. Figure 8.253 shows the preview of the reference plane.

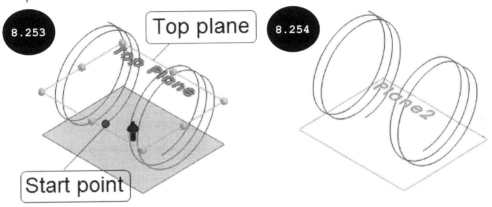

Note: To create a reference plane parallel to the Top plane and passes through the start point of the first helical curve, you need to select the Top plane as the first reference and the start point of the first helical curve as the second reference.

2. Invoke the Sketching environment by selecting the newly created reference plane as the sketching plane.

3. Press CTRL + 8 to change the orientation of the model as normal to the viewing direction.

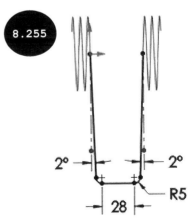

4. Create a sketch as the third curve in the drawing area, see Figure 8.255. Note that the both the endpoints of the sketch shown in Figure 8.255 have Pierce relation with the respective helical curves.

5. Exit the Sketching environment by clicking on the **Exit Sketch** button.

6. Press CTRL + 7 to change the orientation of the model to isometric, see Figure 8.256.

424 Chapter 8 > Advanced Modeling - II

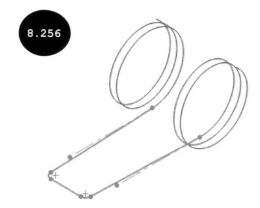

Section 7: Creating the Fourth Curve - Sketch

You need to create the fourth sketch on a reference plane, which is parallel to the Right plane and passes through the endpoint of the first helical curve.

1. Create a reference plane parallel to the Right plane and passes through the endpoint of the first helical curve, see Figures 8.257 and 8.258. Figure 8.257 shows the preview of the reference plane.

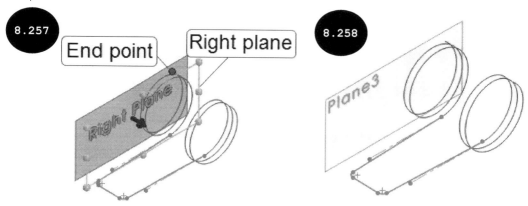

Note: To create a reference plane parallel to the Right plane and passes through the endpoint of the first helical curve, you need to select the Right plane as the first reference and the endpoint of the first helical curve as the second reference for creating the plane.

2. Invoke the Sketching environment by selecting the newly created reference plane as the sketching plane.

3. Press CTRL + 8 to change the orientation of the model as normal to the viewing direction.

4. Create the fourth sketch (an inclined line of length 60 mm), see Figure 8.259.

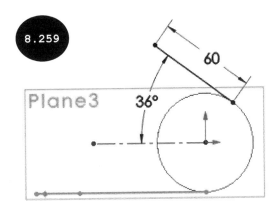

Figure 8.259

Note: The start point of the inclined line shown in Figure 8.259 has Pierce relation with the first helical curve. To apply the Pierce relation, select the start point of the line and then select the first helical curve. A Pop-up toolbar appears. In this Pop-up toolbar, click on the **Pierce** tool. You may need to rotate the model to select the first helical curve.

5. Exit the Sketching environment by clicking on the **Exit Sketch** button and then hide the reference plane.

6. Press CTRL + 7 to change the current orientation of the model to isometric, see Figure 8.260.

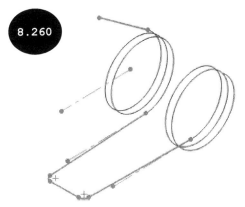

Figure 8.260

Section 8: Creating the Fifth Curve - Sketch

You need to create the fifth curve on a reference plane, which is parallel to the Right plane and passes through the endpoint of the second helical curve.

1. Create a reference plane parallel to the Right plane and passes through the endpoint of the second helical curve, see Figures 8.261 and 8.262. Figure 8.261 shows the preview of the reference plane.

426 Chapter 8 > Advanced Modeling - II

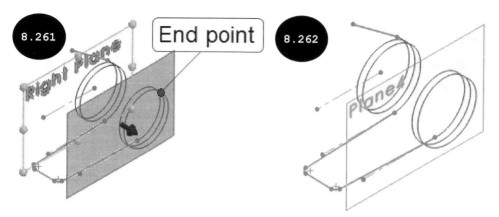

2. Invoke the Sketching environment by selecting the newly created reference plane as the sketching plane.

3. Press CTRL + 8 to change the orientation of the model as normal to the viewing direction.

4. Create the sketch (an inclined line of length 60 mm), see Figure 8.263. Note that the inclined line shown in Figure 8.263 has been created by specifying its start point and endpoint on the start point and endpoint of the existing inclined line, respectively.

5. Exit the Sketching environment by clicking on the **Exit Sketch** button and then hide the reference plane.

6. Press CTRL + 7 to change the current orientation of the model to isometric, see Figure 8.264.

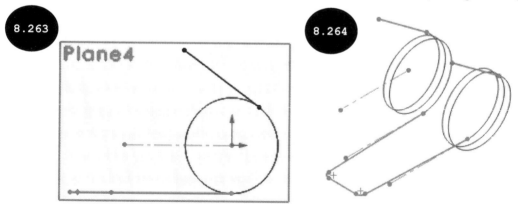

Section 9: Creating the Composite Curve - Sweep Path

After creating all curves (helical and sketch), you need to create composite curve as the path of the sweep feature by combining all the curves together.

1. Invoke the **Curves** flyout in the **Features CommandManager** and then click on the **Composite Curve** tool. The **Composite Curve PropertyManager** appears.

2. Select all the curves (two helical curves and three sketches), one by one in the graphics area by clicking the left mouse button.

3. Click on the green tick mark ✓ in the PropertyManager. The composite curve is created, see Figure 8.265.

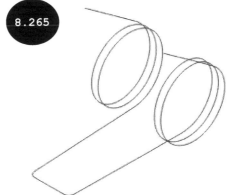

Section 10: Creating the Sweep Feature

After creating the path, you need to create sweep feature with circular profile.

1. Click on the **Swept Boss/Base** tool in the **Features CommandManager**.  The **Sweep PropertyManager** appears.

2. Click on the **Circular Profile** radio button in the **Profile and Path** rollout of the PropertyManager.

3. Click on the path (composite curve) of the sweep feature in the graphics area. The preview of the sweep feature appears with default diameter of the circular profile.

4. Enter **6** in the **Diameter** field of the **Profile and Path** rollout and then press ENTER. The preview of the sweep feature appears, see Figure 8.266.

5. Click on the green tick mark ✓ in the PropertyManager. The sweep feature is created, see Figure 8.267.

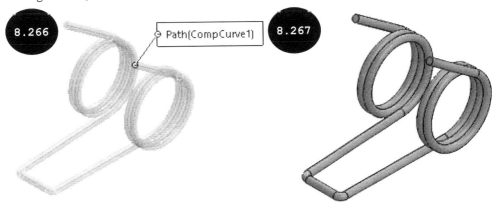

428　Chapter 8 > Advanced Modeling - II

> **Note:** In Figure 8.267, the display of the composite curve (path) has been turned off. To turn off the display of the composite curve, click on the composite curve in the FeatureManager Design Tree. A Pop-up toolbar appears. In the Pop-up toolbar, click on the **Hide** tool.

Section 11: Saving the Model

1. Click on the **Save** tool of the **Standard** toolbar. The **Save As** window appears.

2. Browse to the *Tutorial* folder of *Chapter 8* and then save the model with the name Tutorial 4.

Hands-on Test Drive 1

Create the model shown in Figure 8.268, apply the Cast Alloy Steel material, and calculate the mass properties of the model. All dimensions are in mm.

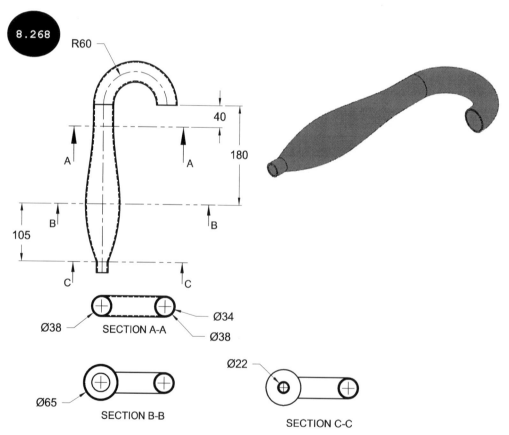

Hands-on Test Drive 2

Create the model shown in Figure 8.269, apply the Alloy Steel material, and calculate the mass properties of the model. All dimensions are in mm.

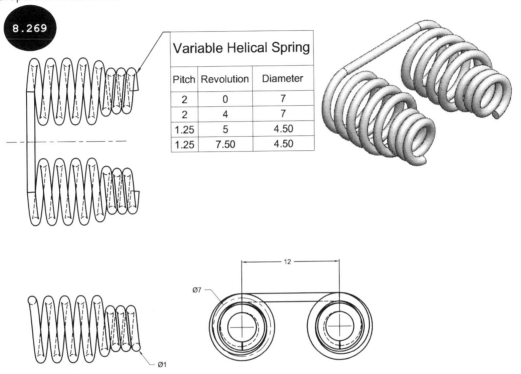

8.269

Variable Helical Spring

Pitch	Revolution	Diameter
2	0	7
2	4	7
1.25	5	4.50
1.25	7.50	4.50

Summary

In this chapter, you have learned how to create sweep features, sweep cut features, lofted features, lofted cut features, boundary features, boundary cut features, curves, split face, and 3D Sketches.

A sweep feature is created by sweeping a profile along a path. The profile of the sweep feature can be a closed sketch, whereas a path can be an open or a closed sketch. You can also use guide curves to guide the profile (section) of the sweep feature. Additionally, you can twist the profile along the path. You can also create thin sweep feature. You have also learned that while creating the sweep cut feature, you can use a closed sketch and a solid body as the profile to sweep along the path.

A lofted feature is created by lofting two or more than two profiles (sections) such that its cross-sectional shape transits from one profile to another. You can also use guide curves to control the cross-sectional shape of the lofted feature. You can also create closed lofted feature. Similar to creating lofted features, you can also create boundary features, which are high quality and complex shaped features.

You have also learned about creating projected curves, helical and spiral curves, curves by specifying XYZ points, curves by selecting reference points, and composite curves. In addition, you have learned how to split the faces of a model and create 3D sketches.

Questions

- The _____ tool is used to create sweep features.

- While creating a sweep feature, the _____ option is selected by default. As a result, the profile follows the path.

- Selecting the _____ option creates a sweep feature such that the profile twists along a path.

- By selecting the _____ option, you can select a tool body following the path to create a sweep cut feature.

- You can create projected curves by using two methods: _____ and _____.

- The _____ radio button is used to create helical curve with a variable pitch.

- By selecting the _____ option, you can create a helical curve by defining its pitch and number of revolutions.

- The _____ tool is used to create curve by specifying coordinate points.

- The profiles/sections of a lofted feature must be closed (True/False).

- In SOLIDWORKS, you cannot create tapered helical curves. (True/False).

- For creating sweep feature, the start point of the path must lie on the plane of the profile created. (True/False).

CHAPTER 9

Patterning and Mirroring

In this chapter, you will learn the following:

- Patterning Features/Faces/Bodies
- Creating a Linear Pattern
- Creating a Circular Pattern
- Creating a Curve Driven Pattern
- Creating a Sketch Driven Pattern
- Creating a Table Driven Pattern
- Creating a Fill Pattern
- Creating a Variable Pattern
- Mirroring a Feature

Patterning and mirroring tools are very powerful tools that help the designers to speed up the creation of a design, increase efficiency, and save time. For example, if a plate has 1000 holes of the same diameter, instead of creating all the holes one by one, you can create one hole and then pattern it to create all the remaining holes. Similarly, if the geometry is symmetric, you can create its one side and mirror it to create the other side of geometry. The various methods used for patterning and mirroring features, faces, or bodies are discussed next.

Patterning Features/Faces/Bodies

In SOLIDWORKS, you can create different types of patterns, such as linear pattern, circular pattern, curve driven pattern, sketch driven pattern, table driven pattern, and variable pattern. The tools used to create different types of patterns are grouped together in the **Pattern** flyout of the **Features CommandManager**, see Figure 9.1.

432 Chapter 9 > Patterning and Mirroring

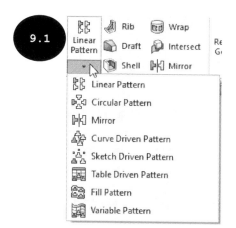

Different types of patterns that can be created by using the pattern tools are as follows:

1. Linear Pattern
2. Circular pattern
3. Curve Driven Pattern
4. Sketch Driven Pattern
5. Table Driven Pattern
6. Fill Pattern
7. Variable Pattern

Creating a Linear Pattern

Linear pattern is created by making multiple instances of features, faces, or bodies, linearly in one or two linear directions, see Figure 9.2.

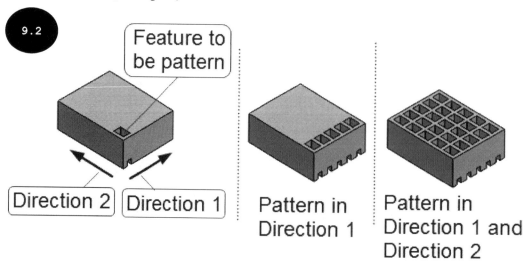

To create a linear pattern, click on the **Linear Pattern** tool in the **Features CommandManager**. The **Linear Pattern PropertyManager** appears, see Figure 9.3. The options in this PropertyManager are as follows:

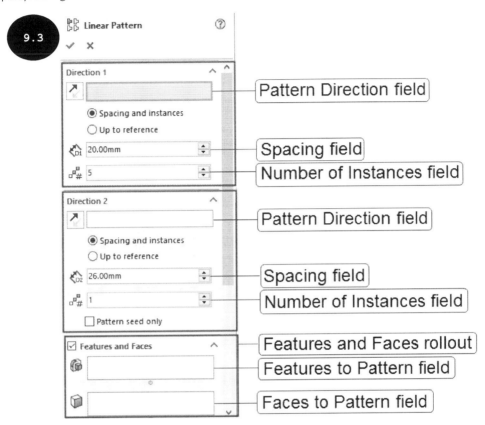

Features and Faces

The **Features and Faces** rollout of the PropertyManager is used to select features and faces to be patterned, see Figure 9.4. To select features to be patterned, click on the **Features to Pattern** field in this rollout and then select features from the graphics area or from the FeatureManager Design Tree. On selecting features to be patterned, the names of the selected features appear in the **Features to Pattern** field. The features selected to be patterned are known as seed or parent features.

You can also pattern faces of a model that form a closed volume. To pattern faces of a model, click on the **Faces to Pattern** field in the rollout and then select faces to be patterned from the graphics area. Note that faces to be patterned should form a closed volume and make up a feature.

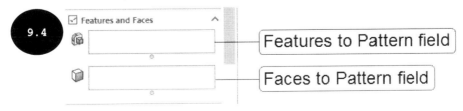

434 Chapter 9 > Patterning and Mirroring

Bodies
The **Bodies** rollout is used to select bodies to be patterned. To select bodies, you need to expand the **Bodies** rollout by clicking on the check box in the title bar of this rollout and then select the bodies to be patterned from the graphics area or from the FeatureManager Design Tree.

> **Tip:** You can select features, faces, or bodies to be patterned before and after invoking the **Linear Pattern PropertyManager**.

After selecting features, faces, or bodies to be patterned, you need to define the directions of pattern by using the **Direction 1** and **Direction 2** rollouts of the PropertyManager, which are as follows:

Direction 1
The options in the **Direction 1** rollout of the PropertyManager are used to create multiple instances or copies of selected features, faces, or bodies in Direction 1, see Figure 9.5. The options are as follows:

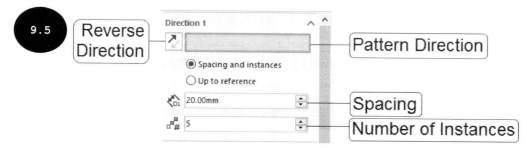

Pattern Direction
The **Pattern Direction** field is used to specify the direction of the pattern. To specify the direction of pattern, click on the **Pattern Direction** field and then specify the direction of the pattern. You can select a linear edge, a linear sketch entity, an axis, a planar face, a conical/circular face, a circular edge, a reference plane, or a dimension as the direction of the pattern. As soon as you specify the direction of the pattern, the preview of the linear pattern appears in the graphics area with a callout attached to the specified direction of the pattern and an arrow appears pointing toward the direction of pattern, see Figures 9.6 and 9.7. In Figure 9.6, a linear edge is selected as the pattern direction and in Figure 9.7, a circular face is selected as the pattern direction.

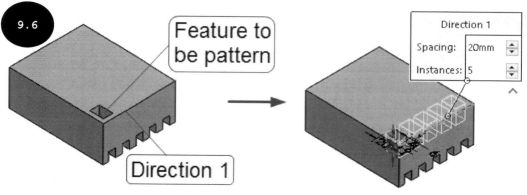

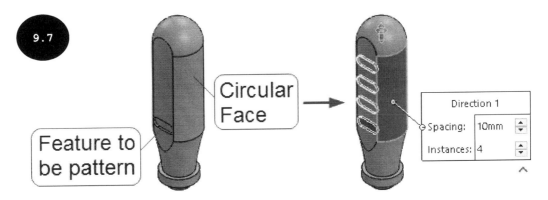

Spacing and instances
The **Spacing and instances** radio button is selected by default. As a result, the **Spacing** and **Number of Instances** fields become available in the rollout. These fields are discussed next.

Spacing. The **Spacing** field is used to specify spacing between two pattern instances. You can also specify the spacing between pattern instances by using the callout, which appeared in the preview of a linear pattern in the graphics area. To do so, click on the **Spacing** field in the callout and then enter the required spacing value between the pattern instances in it.

Number of Instances. The **Number of Instances** field is used to specify the number of instances to be created in the direction of the pattern. Note that the number of instances specified in the **Number of Instances** field also includes the parent feature. You can also specify the number of instances in the callout, which appeared in the preview of the linear pattern in the graphics area.

Reverse Direction
The **Reverse Direction** button is used to reverse the direction of pattern.

Up to reference
On selecting the **Up to reference** radio button, the options of the **Direction 1** rollout appear as shown in Figure 9.8. These options are used to create a linear pattern by specifying a reference geometry up to which the linear pattern is to be created based on the number of instances or spacing between the instances specified in the respective fields. The options are as follows:

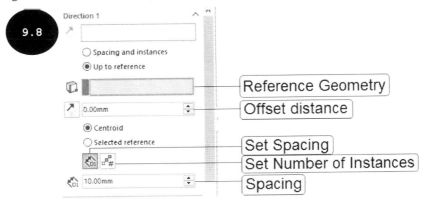

Reference Geometry. The **Reference Geometry** field is used to select a reference geometry, which controls the pattern based on the number of pattern instances or spacing specified. Note that on modifying the reference geometry, the respective pattern also gets modified automatically by adjusting the number of instances or spacing between instances. Figure 9.9 shows a preview as well as the resultant linear pattern with a vertex selected as the reference geometry and the spacing between pattern instances defined as 15 mm. Figure 9.10 shows the linear pattern after increasing the length of the model. Note that on modifying the length of the model, the linear pattern also gets modified by adjusting the number of pattern instances such that the specified spacing between the pattern instances remains same.

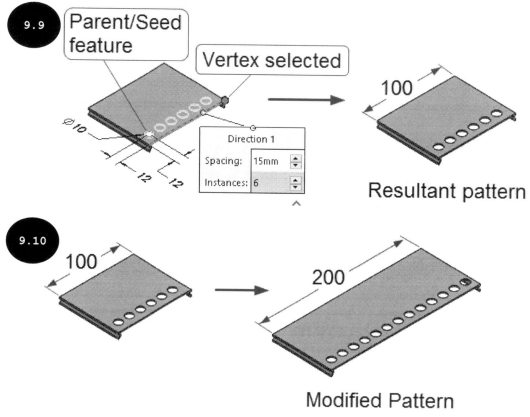

Offset distance. The **Offset distance** field is used to specify the offset distance between the last pattern instance and the reference geometry.

Centroid. On selecting the **Centroid** radio button, the offset distance specified in the **Offset distance** field is measured from the centroid of the patterned feature to the reference geometry.

Selected reference. On selecting the **Selected reference** radio button, the **Seed Reference** field becomes available in the rollout. By using this field, you can select a reference of the parent feature to measure the offset distance from the reference geometry.

Set Spacing. The **Set Spacing** button is used to specify the spacing between the pattern instances in the **Spacing** field, which is enabled below this button in the rollout.

Set Number of Instances. The **Set Number of Instances** button is used to specify the number of pattern instances in the **Number of Instances** field, which is enabled below this button.

Direction 2

The options in the **Direction 2** rollout are used to create multiple instances of the selected feature in Direction 2. Figure 9.11 shows the preview of a linear pattern with 9 instances in Direction 1 and 4 instances in Direction 2.

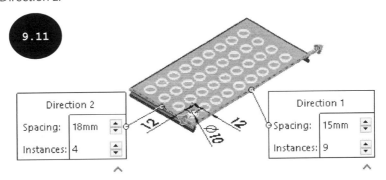

The options in the **Direction 2** rollout are the same as the **Direction 1** rollout, except the **Pattern seed only** check box, which is as follows:

Pattern seed only

On selecting the **Pattern seed only** check box, a pattern is created such that only the seed/parent feature is patterned and the replication the pattern instances of the Direction 1 is not created, see Figure 9.12.

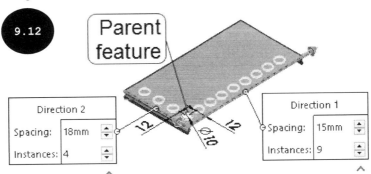

Instances to Skip

The **Instances to Skip** rollout is used to skip some of the instances of the pattern. To skip pattern instances, expand the **Instances to Skip** rollout by clicking on the arrow in the title bar of this rollout, see Figure 9.13. As soon as you

expand the **Instances to Skip** rollout, the pink dots are displayed at the center of all pattern instances in the graphics area, see Figure 9.14. Move the cursor over the pink dot, of a pattern instance to be skipped and then click the left mouse button when the appearance of the cursor changes to the hand cursor, see Figure 9.14. As soon as you click on the pink dot, of a pattern instance, the selected pattern instance disappears or skips and the pink dot is changed to white, see Figure 9.15. Also, the pattern instance number appears in the **Instances to Skip** field of the rollout. Similarly, you can skip multiple instances of the pattern, as required. In SOLIDWORKS 2017, you can also use Window selection and Lasso selection methods to skip pattern instances. To skip pattern instances by using the Window selection method, draw a window around the instances by dragging the cursor after pressing and holding the left mouse button. Similarly, to skip pattern instances by using the Lasso selection method, right-click in the graphics area and then click on the **Lasso Selection** option in the shortcut menu appeared. Next, drag the cursor by pressing and holding the left mouse button around the pattern instances to be skipped. You can also restore the skipped instances by clicking on the white dot of the instance to be restored in the graphics area or by using the Window and Lasso selection methods.

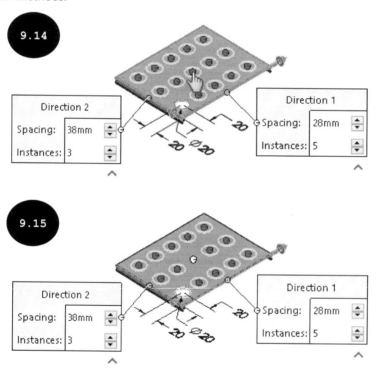

Options
The options in the **Options** rollout are as follows:

Vary sketch
The **Vary sketch** check box is used to vary pattern instances of a pattern with respect to a path. Figure 9.16 shows a feature to be patterned and Figure 9.17 shows the resultant variable linear pattern created by selecting the **Vary sketch** check box. Note that the **Vary sketch** check box is enabled only on selecting a dimension as the pattern direction, see Figure 9.16.

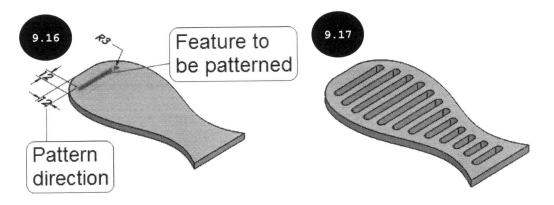

Note: The sketch of the feature to vary must contain a reference sketch/curve, which used as the path to follow by the feature, see Figure 9.18. Also, the varying length of the sketch must not be restricted by dimensions, see Figure 9.18. In this figure, the sketch of the cut feature to be varied has been fully defined by applying dimensions with respect to the reference curve (path) and the length of the feature has not been dimensioned.

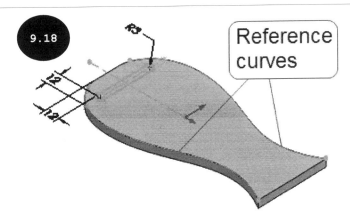

Geometry pattern

By default, the **Geometry pattern** check box is unchecked. As a result, all the pattern instances maintained the same geometrical relations as those of the parent feature. For example, Figure 9.19 shows the front view of a model in 'hidden lines visible' display style, in which the cut feature is created by defining the end condition as 4 mm offset from the bottom face of the model. Figure 9.20 shows the resultant pattern of the cut feature created by unchecking the **Geometry pattern** check box and Figure 9.21 shows the resultant pattern of the cut feature with the **Geometry pattern** check box selected.

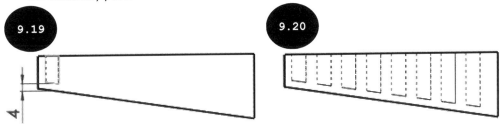

440 Chapter 9 > Patterning and Mirroring

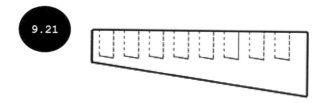
9.21

Propagate visual properties
By default, this check box is selected. As a result, all the visual properties such as colors, textures, and cosmetic thread of the parent feature are propagated to all the instances of the pattern.

Full preview and Partial preview
The Full preview and Partial preview radio buttons are used to display full and partial previews of the pattern in the graphics area, respectively.

Instances to Vary

The **Instances to Vary** rollout is used to create a pattern with incremental spacing between pattern instances in Direction 1 and Direction 2. Besides creating a pattern with incremental spacing between instances, you can also vary the geometry of instances. Note that this rollout is enabled only after selecting a feature to be patterned and a direction of the pattern. Once this rollout is enabled, you need to expand it by selecting the check box in its title bar, see Figure 9.22. The options in this rollout are as follows:

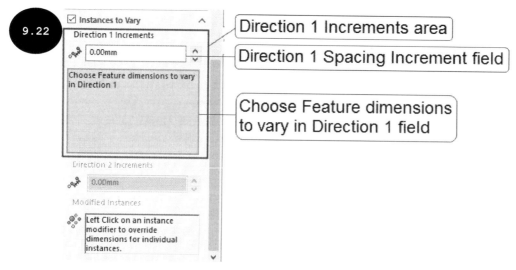
9.22

Direction 1 Increments
The **Direction 1 Increments** area of this rollout is used to specify incremental spacing between pattern instances and incremental dimensions such as diameter and height of the pattern feature in Direction 1. The options in this area are as follows:

Direction 1 Spacing Increment: This field is used to specify the incremental spacing between pattern instances. Figure 9.23 shows the preview of a pattern with incremental spacing of 5 mm specified in this field.

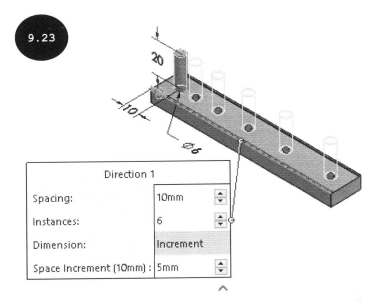

9.23

Choose Feature dimensions to vary in Direction 1: This field is used to select the dimensions of the parent feature such as diameter and height to be varied in the pattern instances. Click on the dimensions in the graphics area to be varied. A table with dimension name, dimension value, and increment value columns appear in this field, see Figure 9.24. Now, you can double-click on the field corresponding to the increment value column to activate its editing mode and then enter the increment value for the selected dimension. Figure 9.25 shows the linear pattern created with incremental spacing of 5 mm, incremental diameter of 2 mm, and increment height of 4 mm.

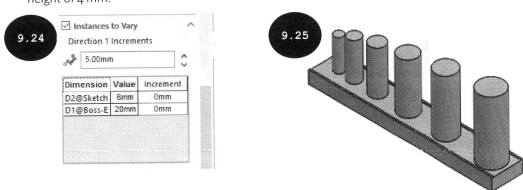

Direction 2 Increments

The **Direction 2 Increments** area is used to specify the incremental spacing between pattern instances and incremental dimensions in Direction 2. The options in this area the same as those discussed in the **Direction 1 Increments** area. Note that the options in this area are enabled when you pattern features in Direction 2 as well.

Procedure for Creating a Linear Pattern in Direction 1 and Direction 2

1. Click on the **Linear Pattern** tool. The **Linear Pattern PropertyManager** appears.
2. Click on the **Features to Pattern** field in the **Features and Faces** rollout and then select the features to be patterned from the graphics area.
3. Click on the **Pattern Direction** field in the **Direction 1** rollout.
4. Specify a direction of the pattern. You can select a linear edge, a linear sketch entity, an axis, a planar face, a conical/circular face, a circular edge, a reference plane, or a dimension as the direction of the pattern. The preview of the linear pattern in Direction 1 appears.
5. If needed, flip the direction of pattern by clicking on the **Reverse Direction** button.
6. Make sure that the **Spacing and instances** radio button is selected in the **Direction 1** rollout.
7. Specify the spacing between pattern instances in the **Spacing** field of the **Direction 1** rollout.
8. Specify pattern instances in the **Number of Instances** field of the **Direction 1** rollout.
9. Specify the direction of the pattern for Direction 2 by selecting a linear edge, a linear sketch entity, an axis, a planar face, a conical/circular face, a circular edge, a reference plane, or a dimension. The preview of the linear pattern in Direction 2 appears.
10. Make sure that the **Spacing and instances** radio button is selected in the **Direction 2** rollout.
11. Specify pattern instances in the **Number of Instances** field of the **Direction 2** rollout.
12. Specify the spacing between pattern instances in the **Spacing** field of the **Direction 2** rollout.
13. Flip the direction of the pattern, if needed, by clicking on the **Reverse Direction** button.
14. Click on the green tick mark in the PropertyManager. The linear pattern in Direction 1 and Direction 2 is created.

Procedure for Creating a Linear Pattern up to a Reference Geometry

1. Click on the **Linear Pattern** tool. The **Linear Pattern PropertyManager** appears.
2. Click on the **Features to Pattern** field in the **Features and Faces** rollout and then select the features to be patterned from the graphics area.
3. Click on the **Pattern Direction** field in the **Direction 1** rollout of the PropertyManager.
4. Specify a direction of the pattern. You can select a linear edge, a linear sketch entity, an axis, a planar face, a conical/circular face, a circular edge, a reference plane, or a dimension as the direction of the pattern. The preview of the linear pattern in Direction 1 appears.
5. If needed, flip the direction of pattern by clicking on the **Reverse Direction** button.
6. Click on the **Up to reference** radio button in the **Direction 1** rollout.
7. Select a reference geometry for controlling the pattern instances. You can select a vertex, a face, or an edge as the reference geometry.
8. Select the **Centroid** radio button in the **Direction 1** rollout to specify the offset distance from the center of the last pattern instance to the reference geometry.
9. Specify the offset distance between the last pattern instance and the reference geometry in the **Offset distance** field of the **Direction 1** rollout.
10. Click on the **Set Spacing** or **Set Number of Instances** button in the **Direction 1** rollout to define the spacing between instances or number of pattern instances, respectively.
11. Specify the spacing between instances or number of pattern instances in the respective field that appears below the **Set Spacing** or **Set Number of Instances** button.
12. Similarly, define parameters for creating the pattern in the Direction 2, if needed.
13. Click on the green tick mark in the PropertyManager. The linear pattern is created up to the selected reference geometry. Note that on modifying the reference geometry, the linear pattern will also be modified accordingly.

Procedure for Creating a Linear Pattern by Skipping Pattern Instances

1. Click on the **Linear Pattern** tool. The **Linear Pattern PropertyManager** appears.
2. Click on the **Features to Pattern** field in the **Features and Faces** rollout and then select the features to be patterned from the graphics area.
3. Specify parameters for creating linear pattern in Direction 1 and Direction 2, as discussed.
4. Expand the **Instances to Skip** rollout in the PropertyManager. A pink dot appears at the center of all instances in the graphics area.
5. Click on the pink dots of the instances to be skipped in the graphics area.
6. Click on the green tick mark ✓ in the PropertyManager. The linear pattern after skipping pattern instances is created.

Procedure for Creating a Linear Pattern with Vary Sketch

1. Invoke the **Linear Pattern PropertyManager**.
2. Click on the **Features to Pattern** field in the **Features and Faces** rollout and then select a feature to be patterned.

   Note: The sketch of the feature to be patterned with vary sketch must contain a reference curve as the path to be followed by pattern instances. Also, the varying length of sketch must not be restricted by the dimensions.

3. Click on the **Pattern Direction** field in the **Direction 1** rollout and then select a linear dimension as the direction of the pattern.
4. Click on the **Vary sketch** check box in the **Option** rollout of the PropertyManager.
5. Specify other parameters such as spacing between the instances and the number of instances in the respective fields of the PropertyManager.
6. Click on the green tick mark ✓ in the PropertyManager. The linear pattern with variable instances is created.

Procedure for Creating a Linear Pattern with Instance to Vary

1. Invoke the **Linear Pattern PropertyManager**.
2. Click on the **Features to Pattern** field in the **Features and Faces** rollout and then select a feature to be patterned from the graphics area.
3. Specify parameters for creating linear pattern in Direction 1 and Direction 2.
4. Expand the **Instance to Vary** rollout of the PropertyManager.
5. Specify the incremental spacing value between pattern instances in the **Direction 1 Spacing Increments** field and **Direction 2 Spacing Increments** field of the **Instance to Vary** rollout.
6. Select the dimensions of the feature to be varied in the pattern instances.
7. Double-click on the field corresponding to the **Increment value** column in the table of the **Instance to Vary** rollout and then specify the increment value for the dimension selected.
8. Click on the green tick mark ✓ in the PropertyManager. The linear pattern with specified incremental spacing and dimension is created.

Creating a Circular Pattern Updated

A circular pattern is created by making multiple instances of features, faces, or bodies, circularly around an axis, see Figure 9.26. To create a circular pattern, click on the down arrow in the **Linear Pattern** tool. The **Pattern** flyout appears, see Figure 9.27. In this flyout, click on the **Circular Pattern** tool. The **CirPattern PropertyManager** appears, see Figure 9.28. The options in the **CirPattern PropertyManager** are as follows:

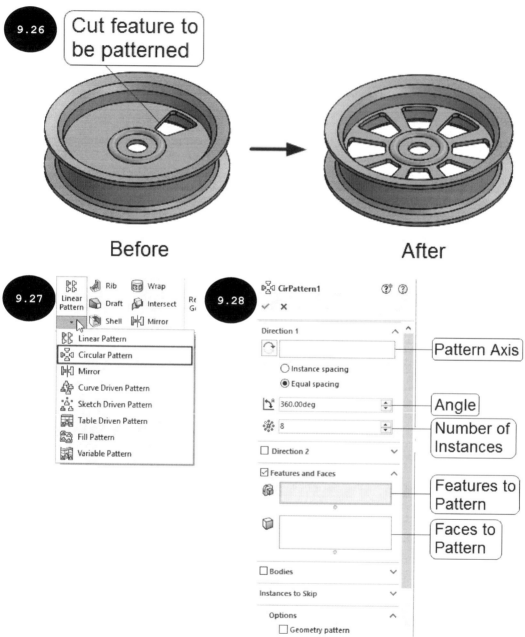

Features and Faces

The **Features and Faces** rollout is used to select the features or faces to be patterned, circularly around an axis. By default, the **Features to Pattern** field is activated in this rollout. As a result, you can select features to be patterned from the graphics area or from the FeatureManager Design Tree. As soon as you select the features to be patterned, the names of the selected features get listed in the **Features to Pattern** field. You can select features to be patterned before and after invoking the PropertyManager.

To select the faces to be patterned, click on the **Faces to Pattern** field in the rollout and then select faces of the model to be patterned. Note that the faces to be patterned should form a closed volume.

Direction 1

The options in the **Direction 1** rollout are used to specify parameters for creating circular pattern in Direction 1 around a pattern axis. The options are as follows:

Pattern Axis

The **Pattern Axis** field is used to select an axis around which you want to create a circular pattern. To select a pattern axis, click on the **Pattern Axis** field and then select an axis, a circular face, a circular edge, a linear edge, a linear sketch, or an angular dimension as the pattern axis, see Figure 9.29. This figure shows the preview of a circular pattern when a circular face is selected as the pattern axis. Note that in case of selecting a circular face, a circular edge, or an angular dimension as the pattern axis, the respective center axis is automatically determined and used as the axis of circular pattern. As soon as you select a pattern axis, the preview of the circular feature appears in the graphics area with a callout attached to the pattern axis, see Figure 9.29.

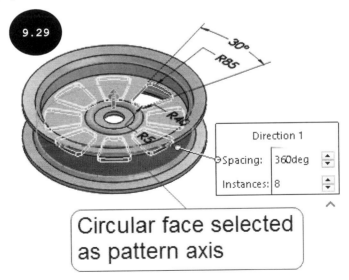

Angle

The **Angle** field is used to specify the angle value between pattern instances. You can also specify the angle between pattern instances by using the callout appeared in the graphics area. Note

446 Chapter 9 > Patterning and Mirroring

that if the **Equal spacing** radio button is selected in the rollout then the angle value specified in the **Angle** field is considered as the total angle of the pattern and all pattern instances are arranged within the specified angle value with equal angular spacing among all instances. If the **Instance spacing** radio button is selected in the rollout then the angle value specified in the **Angle** field is used as the angle between two pattern instances.

Number of Instances
The **Number of Instances** field is used to specify the number of instances to be created in the pattern. Figure 9.30 shows the preview of a circular pattern with 5 pattern instances. Note that the number of instances specified in this field also includes the parent or seed feature. You can also specify the number of instances in the callout appeared in the graphics area.

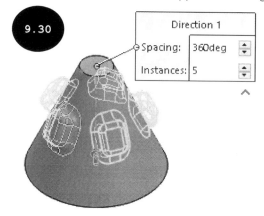

Reverse Direction
The **Reverse Direction** button is used to reverse the angle of rotation.

Direction 2
The options in the **Direction 2** rollout are used to specify parameters for creating a circular pattern in Direction 2 around the pattern axis, see Figure 9.31. This figure shows the preview of a circular pattern with 5 instances in Direction 1 and 2 instances in Direction 2.

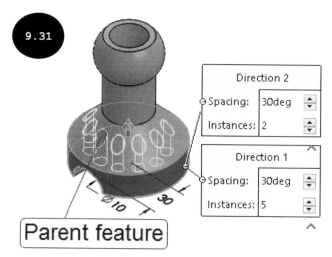

The options in the **Direction 2** rollout are the same as the options discussed in the **Direction 1** rollout of the PropertyManager except the **Symmetric** check box. The **Symmetric** check box is used to create a circular pattern, symmetrically in both directions from the parent or seed feature.

The options in the remaining rollouts of the PropertyManager such as **Instances to Skip** and **Instances to Vary** are the same as those of the **Linear Pattern PropertyManager**.

Procedure for Creating a Circular Pattern
1. Invoke the **Pattern** flyout and then click on the **Circular Pattern** tool.
2. Select a feature to be patterned.
3. Click on the **Pattern Axis** field in the **Direction 1** rollout of the PropertyManager and then select an axis, a circular face, a circular edge, a linear edge, a linear sketch entity, or an angular dimension as the axis of the pattern.
4. Select either the **Instance spacing** or **Equal spacing** radio button, as required.
5. Specify the angle value for the pattern instances in the **Angle** field.
6. Specify the pattern instances in the **Number of Instances** field.
7. Similarly, specify parameters such as angle value and number of pattern instances in the **Direction 2** rollout, if required.
8. Click on the green tick mark ✓ in the PropertyManager. The circular pattern is created.

Creating a Curve Driven Pattern
A curve driven pattern is created by making multiple instances of features, faces, or bodies along a curve, see Figure 9.32. This figure shows a feature to be patterned, a closed sketch as the curve, and the resultant curve driven pattern. You can select a 2D/3D open or close sketch, or an edge as the curve to drive the pattern instances.

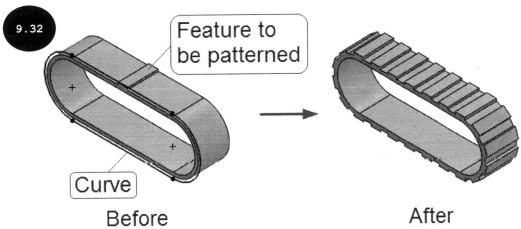

To create a curve driven pattern, click on the down arrow in the **Linear Pattern** tool. The **Pattern** flyout appears, see Figure 9.33. In this flyout, click on the **Curve Driven Pattern** tool. The **Curve Driven Pattern PropertyManager** appears, see Figure 9.34. The options in this PropertyManager are as follows:

448 Chapter 9 > Patterning and Mirroring

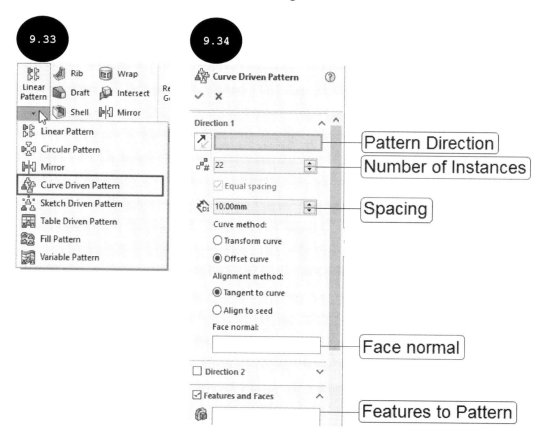

9.33

9.34

Features and Faces
The **Features and Faces** rollout of the PropertyManager is used to select features or faces to be patterned. To select the features to be patterned, click on the **Features to Pattern** field in this rollout and then select the features either from the graphics area or from the FeatureManager Design Tree. You can select features to be patterned before and after invoking the PropertyManager.

To select faces to be patterned, click on the **Faces to Pattern** field in the rollout and then select the faces from the graphics area. Note that faces to be patterned should form a closed volume.

Direction 1
The options in the **Direction 1** rollout are used to select a driving curve and specify parameters for creating a curve driven pattern in the Direction 1. The options of this rollout are as follows:

Pattern Direction
The **Pattern Direction** field is used to select a curve as the path for driving pattern instances. You can select a 2D/3D open or close sketch, or an edge as the path for driving pattern instances. To select a curve, click on the **Pattern Direction** field and then select a curve from the graphics area. As soon as you select a curve, the preview of the curve driven pattern appears in the graphics

area with default parameters, see Figures 9.35 and 9.36. Figure 9.35 shows the preview of a curve driven pattern in which a closed sketch is selected as the path for driving pattern instances and in Figure 9.36, an open sketch is selected as the path for driving pattern instances.

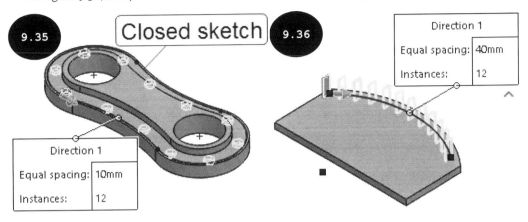

Note: If the sketch to be selected as the curve to drive pattern instances has multiple entities/segments, then it is recommended to select the sketch from the FeatureManager Design Tree.

Number of Instances
The **Number of Instances** field is used to specify number of instances in a pattern.

Equal spacing
When the **Equal spacing** check box is selected, the spacing among all pattern instances is equally arranged in accordance with the total length of the curve selected. If you uncheck this check box, the **Spacing** field gets enabled, which is used to specify the spacing between pattern instances.

Reverse Direction
The **Reverse Direction** button is used to reverse the direction of pattern.

Curve method
The **Curve method** area is used to select a method for transforming pattern instances along the curve, see Figure 9.37. The options in this area are as follows:

Transform curve: When the **Transform curve** radio button is selected, the delta X and delta Y distances between the parent feature and the origin of the curve are maintained by pattern instances, see Figure 9.38.

Offset curve: When the **Offset curve** radio button is selected, the normal distance between the parent feature and the origin of the curve is maintained by pattern instances, see Figure 9.39.

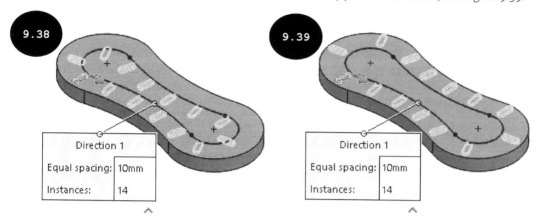

Note: The Transform curve method and the Offset curve method discussed above work in combination with the Alignment method (**Tangent to curve** or **Align to seed**), which is discussed next. In Figures 9.38 and 9.39, the **Tangent to curve** alignment method is selected.

Alignment method

The **Alignment method** area is used to specify an alignment method for aligning pattern instances along the curve, see Figure 9.40. The options in this area are as follows:

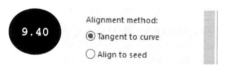

Tangent to curve: On selecting the **Tangent to curve** radio button, each pattern instance is aligned tangent to the selected curve, see Figures 9.38 and 9.39. In both these figures, the pattern instances are aligned tangent to the curve.

Note: Figure 9.38 shows the preview of a curve driven pattern when the **Transform curve** and **Tangent to curve** radio buttons are selected and in Figure 9.39, the **Offset curve** and **Tangent to curve** radio buttons are selected.

Align to seed: On selecting the **Align to seed** radio button, each pattern instance is aligned to match the parent feature, see Figures 9.41 and 9.42. In both these figures, the pattern instances are aligned to match the parent feature.

Note: Figure 9.41 shows the preview of a curve driven pattern when the **Transform curve** and **Align to seed** radio buttons are selected and in Figure 9.42, the **Offset curve** and **Align to seed** radio buttons are selected.

SOLIDWORKS 2017: A Power Guide > 451

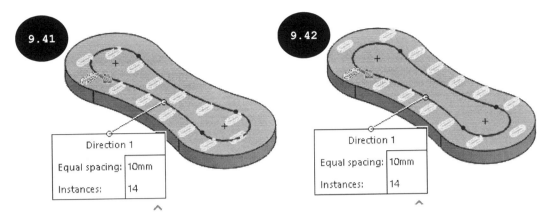

Face normal

The **Face normal** field of the **Direction 1** rollout is used to select a face, which is normal to the 3D curve selected as the path for driving instances, see Figure 9.43. Note that while creating a curve driven patter by selecting a 3D curve as the path for driving pattern instances, you may need to select a face which is normal to the 3D curve. Figure 9.43 shows a feature to be patterned, a 3D curve (helix curve), a face, and the resultant curve driven pattern.

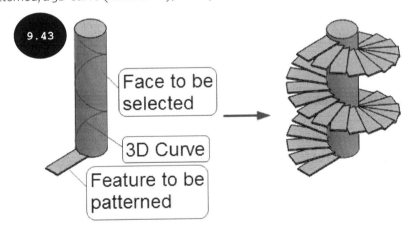

Direction 2

The options in the **Direction 2** rollout are used to create pattern instances in the Direction 2. The options in this rollout are the same as those of the **Direction 1** rollout. Figure 9.44 shows the preview of a curve driven pattern in Direction 1 and Direction 2.

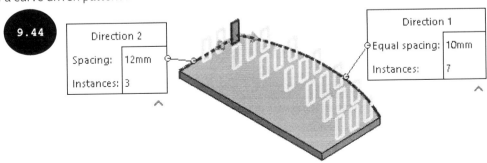

452 Chapter 9 > Patterning and Mirroring

The options in the remaining rollouts such as **Bodies**, **Instances to Skip**, and **Options** of the PropertyManager are the same as those discussed earlier.

Procedure for Creating a Curve Driven Pattern

1. Invoke the **Pattern** flyout and then click on the **Curve Driven Pattern** tool. The **Curve Driven Pattern PropertyManager** appears.
2. Click on the **Features to Pattern** field in the **Features and Faces** rollout and then select the features to be patterned from the graphics area.
3. Click on the **Pattern Direction** field in the **Direction 1** rollout and then select a sketch entity, a closed/open sketch, an edge, or a 3D curve as the curve for driving pattern instances.
4. Enter the number of pattern instances in the **Number of Instances** field.
5. Select the **Equal spacing** check box or enter the spacing between pattern instances in the **Spacing** field.
6. Select the curve method (**Transform curve** or **Offset curve**) in the **Curve method** area.
7. Select the alignment method (**Tangent to curve** or **Align to seed**) in the **Alignment method** area.
8. Click on the green tick mark in the PropertyManager. The curve driven pattern is created.

Creating a Sketch Driven Pattern

A sketch driven pattern is created by making multiple instances of features, faces, or bodies using sketch points of a sketch. In a sketch driven pattern, the parent/seed feature gets propagated to each sketch point of the sketch, see Figure 9.45. Figure 9.45 shows a sketch having multiple points, a feature to be patterned, and the resultant sketch driven pattern.

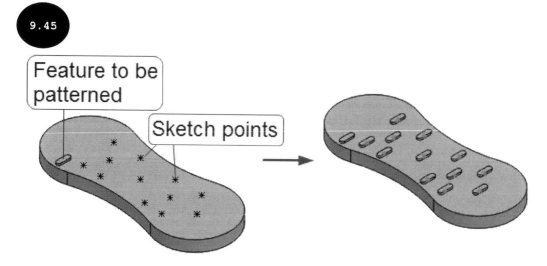

9.45

To create a sketch driven pattern, invoke the **Pattern** flyout and then click on the **Sketch Driven Pattern** tool. The **Sketch Driven Pattern PropertyManager** appears, see Figure 9.46. The options in the PropertyManager are as follows:

Features and Faces

The **Features and Faces** rollout of the PropertyManager is used to select the features or faces to be patterned. To select features to be patterned, click on the **Features to Pattern** field in this rollout and then the select features either from the graphics area or from the FeatureManager Design Tree. You can select the features to be patterned before and after invoking the PropertyManager. To select the faces to be patterned, click on the **Faces to Pattern** field in the rollout and then select faces of a model that form a closed volume.

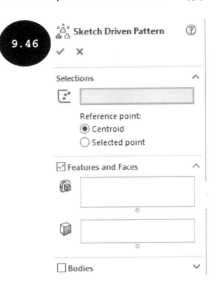

Selections

The options in the **Selections** rollout are used to select sketch points. The options are as follows:

Reference Sketch

The **Reference Sketch** field is used to select a sketch having multiple points for driving the pattern instances. To select a sketch, click on the **Reference Sketch** field to activate it and then select a sketch from the graphics area.

Centroid

By default, the **Centroid** radio button is selected. As a result, the centroid of the parent feature can be used as the base point for creating pattern instances and the center point of each pattern instance is coincident with the sketch point, see Figure 9.47.

Selected point

On selecting the **Selected point** radio button, the **Reference Vertex** field appears in the rollout, which allows you to select a reference point as the base point for the pattern, see Figure 9.48.

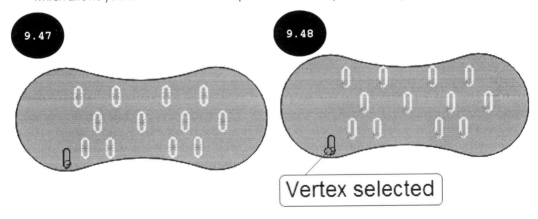

The options in the remaining rollouts such as **Bodies** and **Options** of the PropertyManager are the same as those discussed earlier.

454   Chapter 9 > Patterning and Mirroring

Procedure for Creating a Sketch Driven Pattern
1. Select the feature to be patterned from the graphics area.
2. Invoke the **Pattern** flyout and then click on the **Sketch Driven Pattern** tool.
3. Select a sketch as the reference sketch having multiple sketch points.
4. Select the **Centroid** or **Selected point** radio button, as required. Note that on selecting the **Selected point** radio button, you need to select a reference point as the base point for the pattern.
5. Click on the green tick mark ✓ in the PropertyManager. The sketch driven pattern is created.

Creating a Table Driven Pattern
A table driven pattern is created by specifying coordinates (X, Y) for each pattern instance with respect to a coordinate system. To create a table driven pattern, you need to have a coordinate system created in the graphics area. You can create a coordinate system by using the **Coordinate System** tool available in the **Reference Geometry** flyout, as discussed in chapter 6. After creating a coordinate system, click on the **Table Driven Pattern** tool in the **Pattern** flyout. The **Table Driven Pattern** dialog box appears, see Figure 9.49. Most of the options in this dialog box are the same as those discussed earlier and the remaining options are as follows:

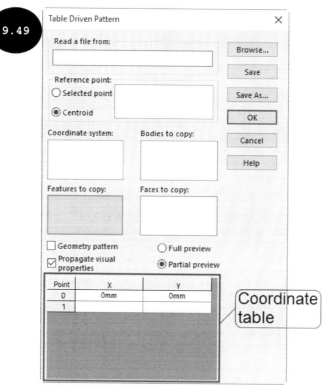

9.49

Features to copy
The **Features to copy** field is used to select features to be patterned. To select features to be patterned, click on this **Features to copy** field in the dialog box and then select features either from the graphics area or from the FeatureManager Design Tree.

Coordinate system

The **Coordinate system** field of the dialog box is used to select a coordinate system from the graphics area. Note that the origin of the selected coordinate system is used as the origin for the table driven pattern. Figure 9.50 shows a feature to be patterned and a coordinate system.

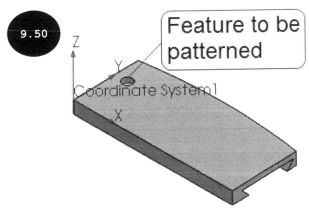

9.50

Coordinate table

The **Coordinate table** is available at the bottom of the **Table Driven Pattern** dialog box and is used to specify X and Y coordinates for each pattern instance with respect to the selected coordinate system, see Figure 9.51. To specify the X coordinate of point 1 (first pattern instance), double-click on the X field corresponding to the **Point 1** field in the table. Similarly, specify the Y coordinate of point 1 (first pattern instance). Note that each row of this table represents a pattern instance and its X and Y fields represent the coordinates of the pattern instance. You can add multiple rows in the table to specify coordinates of multiple pattern instances. Note that a new row is added automatically in the table as soon as you double-click on a field of the last row in the table. Figure 9.51 shows the **Coordinate table** of the dialog box, in which coordinates of 5 pattern instances, including the coordinates of the parent feature are specified.

9.51

Point	X	Y
0	10mm	35mm
1	30mm	40mm
2	60mm	45mm
3	90mm	40mm
4	120mm	35mm
5		

Note: To delete a row in the table, select the row to be deleted and then press DELETE.

Save/Save As

The **Save/Save As** button is used to save the coordinates of the pattern instances specified in the table as external *Pattern Table* file (*.sldptab) for later use.

Read a file from

The **Read a file from** field is used to read an existing *Pattern Table (*.sldptab)* or *.txt (notepad)* file containing coordinate points for creating the pattern. To create the pattern by using an existing file, click on the **Browse** button. The **Open** dialog box appears. Select the *Pattern Table (*.sldptab)* or *.txt (notepad)* file and then click on the **Open** button. The coordinate points specified in the imported file are filled automatically in the **Coordinate table** of the dialog box.

OK

After specifying parameters for creating the table driven pattern, click on the **OK** button in the dialog box. Figure 9.52 shows the table driven pattern created by specifying coordinates of the instances shown in Figure 9.51.

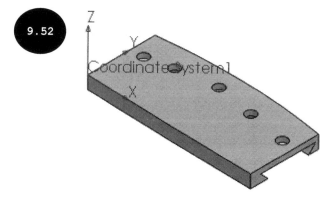

9.52

Procedure for Creating a Table Driven Pattern

1. Create a coordinate system in the graphics area with respect to which coordinates of the pattern instances are to be measured.
2. Invoke the **Pattern** flyout and then click on the **Table Driven Pattern** tool. The **Table Driven Pattern** dialog box appears.
3. Select a feature to be patterned from the graphics area.
4. Click on the **Coordinate system** field in the dialog box and then select a coordinate system.
5. Double-click on the field corresponding to the **Point 1** row and the **X** column in the **Coordinate table** of the dialog box to activate its edit mode. Next, enter the **X** coordinate of the point 1 (first pattern instance).
6. Similarly, specify the **Y** coordinate of the point 1 (first pattern instance).
7. Similarly, specify X and Y coordinates for the remaining points (other instances) in the table.
8. Click on the **OK** button. The table driven pattern is created.

Creating a Fill Pattern

A fill pattern is created by populating an area with pattern instances. In the fill pattern, you can create multiple instances of features, faces, bodies, or a predefined cut shape by filling in a particular area of a model. To define an area to be filled in with pattern instances, you can select a face of a model or a closed sketch, see Figures 9.53 and 9.54. Figure 9.53 shows a feature to be patterned, a face to be filled in, and the resultant fill pattern. Figure 9.54 shows the feature to be patterned, a closed sketch to be filled in, and the resultant fill pattern.

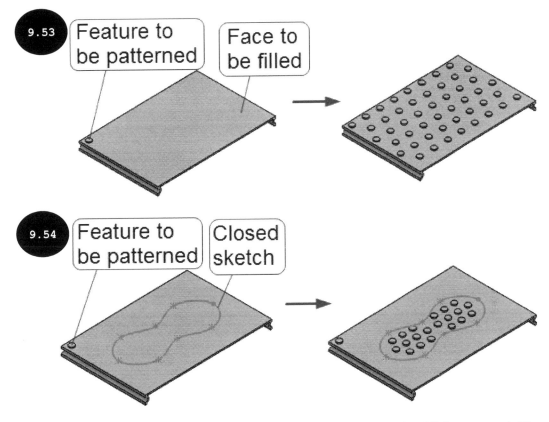

To create fill pattern, invoke the **Pattern** flyout and then click on the **Fill Pattern** tool. The **Fill Pattern PropertyManager** appears, see Figure 9.55. The options in the PropertyManager are as follows:

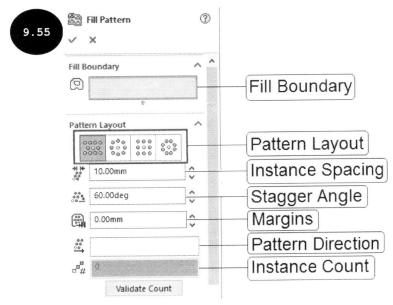

Fill Boundary

By default, the **Fill Boundary** field is activated in the **Fill Boundary** rollout of the PropertyManager. As a result, you are prompted to select a boundary to be filled in with pattern instances. You can select a face or a closed sketch as the boundary to be filled in.

Features and Faces

The **Features and Faces** rollout of the PropertyManager is used to select features, faces, or a predefined cut shape to be patterned. By default, the **Selected features** radio button is selected in the rollout, see Figure 9.56. As a result, the **Features to Pattern** field is enabled, which is used to select features to be patterned. Click on the **Features to Pattern** field and then select the features to be patterned. After specifying a boundary to be filled in and a feature to be patterned, the preview of the filled patterned appears in the graphics area, see Figure 9.57. In this figure, a face is selected as the boundary.

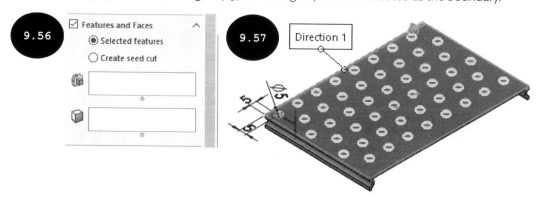

To select the faces to be patterned, click on the **Faces to Pattern** field of the rollout and then select faces to be patterned. Note that the faces to be patterned should form a closed volume.

On selecting the **Create seed cut** radio button in the **Features and Faces** rollout, different types of predefined cut shape buttons appear in the rollout, see Figure 9.58. By default, the **Circle** button is selected. As a result, the selected boundary is filled in with predefined circular cut features, see Figure 9.59. You can specify the required diameter for the predefined circular cut feature by using the **Diameter** field of the rollout. The **Vertex or Sketch Point** field is used to define the center of the parent or seed feature. You can select a vertex or a sketch point to define the center of the parent feature. On defining it, the pattern starts from the defined center of the parent feature. Note that if you do not define the center of the parent feature, then the pattern will start from the center of the boundary face selected to be filled in.

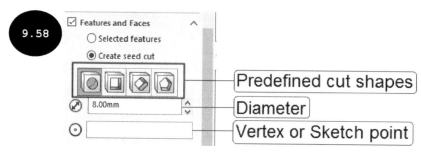

You can select circular, square, diamond, and polygon predefined cut shape by clicking on the respective button in the rollout, see Figures 9.59 through 9.62.

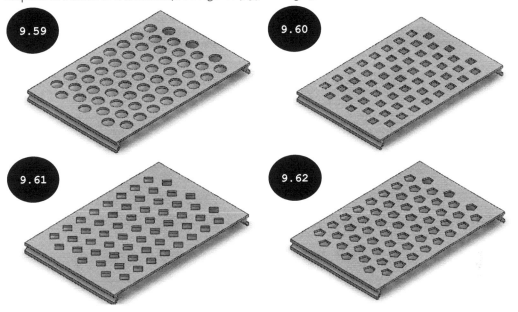

Pattern Layout

The options in the **Pattern Layout** rollout are used to select type of layout for the fill pattern. You can select the **Perforation**, **Circular**, **Square**, or **Polygon** button for defining the type of layout to be used for the fill pattern, see Figures 9.63 through 9.66.

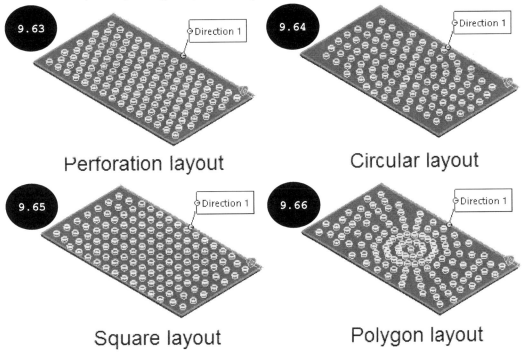

You can use the remaining options of the **Pattern Layout** rollout to control the parameters of the pattern layout such as spacing between pattern instances, margin between the fill boundary and the outermost instance, and pattern direction. These options are the same as those discussed earlier.

> **Note:** On selecting a face as the boundary of the fill pattern, the pattern direction is automatically selected and the preview of the pattern appears in the graphics area. However, on selecting a closed sketch as the boundary of the fill pattern, you may need to select a pattern direction. You can select a linear edge or a sketch entity as the pattern direction.

Procedure for Creating a Fill Pattern
1. Select the feature to be patterned.
2. Invoke the **Pattern** flyout and then click on the **Fill Pattern** tool. The **Fill Pattern PropertyManager** appears.
3. Select a face or a closed sketch as the boundary to be filled in with pattern instances.
4. Select the type of the pattern layout: **Perforation**, **Circular**, **Square**, or **Polygon**.
5. Specify parameters for the pattern layout in the respective fields of the **Pattern Layout** rollout.
6. Click on the green tick mark ✓ in the PropertyManager. The fill pattern is created.

Procedure for Creating a Fill Pattern with Predefined Cut Feature
1. Invoke the **Pattern** flyout and then click on the **Fill Pattern** tool. The **Fill Pattern PropertyManager** appears.
2. Select a face or a closed sketch as the boundary to be filled in with a predefined cut shape.
3. Click on the **Create seed cut** radio button in the **Features to Pattern** rollout.
4. Select the required predefined cut shape: **Circle**, **Square**, **Diamond**, or **Polygon**.
5. Specify parameters for the predefined cut shape, in the respective fields of the **Features to Pattern** rollout.
6. Select the type of the pattern layout: **Perforation**, **Circular**, **Square**, or **Polygon** in the **Pattern Layout** rollout.
7. Specify parameters for the pattern layout in the respective fields of the **Pattern Layout** rollout.
8. Click on the green tick mark ✓ in the PropertyManager. The fill pattern with predefined cut shape is created.

Creating a Variable Pattern
In SOLIDWORKS, you can create a variable pattern by using the **Variable Pattern** tool of the **Pattern** flyout. This tool is used to create a variable pattern such that you can vary dimensions and reference geometries of a feature, see Figure 9.67. In this figure, the variable pattern has been created by varying the length and angle of the slot feature.

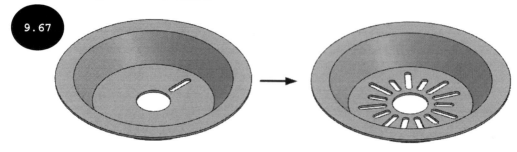

9.67

To create a variable pattern, invoke the **Pattern** flyout and then click on the **Variable Pattern** tool. The **Variable Pattern PropertyManager** appears, see Figure 9.68. The options in this PropertyManager are as follows:

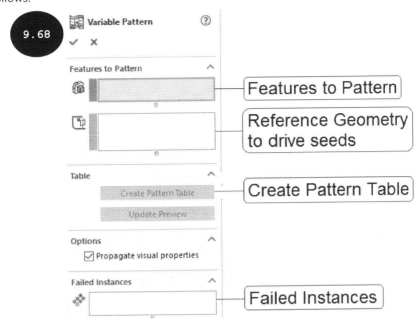

9.68

Features to Pattern

The **Features to Pattern** field is used to select features to be patterned. By default, this field is activated. As a result, you can select features to be patterned either from the graphics area or from the FeatureManager Design Tree. You can select extruded, cut extruded, revolved, cut revolved, sweep, cut sweep, lofted, cut lofted, fillet, chamfer, dome, and draft features as the features to be patterned for creating the variable pattern. Once you select a feature to be patterned, the respective dimensions appear in the graphics area so that you can select its dimensions to be varied in the pattern, see Figure 9.69.

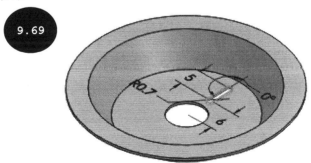

9.69

Reference Geometry to drive seeds

The **Reference Geometry to drive seeds** field is used to select reference geometries on which the selected seed or parent feature is dependent. To select reference geometries from the graphics area, click on the **Reference Geometry to drive seeds** field in the **Features to Pattern** rollout and then select them. Once you select reference geometries, respective dimensions of the selected geometries appear in the graphics area so that you can select them as the dimensions to be varied. You can select axis, plane, point, curve, 2D sketch, or 3D sketch as reference geometries. Figure 9.70 shows an extruded feature selected as the feature to be patterned as well as the respective reference geometries (a plane and a 3D point) selected on which the extruded feature depends. Note that the extruded feature shown in the figure has been created on a non planar face of the model with the help of a reference plane and a 3D point.

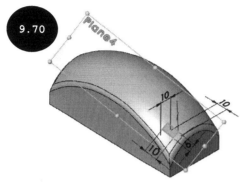

9.70

Create Pattern Table

The **Create Pattern Table** button of the PropertyManager is used to invoke the **Pattern Table** dialog box. The **Pattern Table** dialog box is used to select the dimensions of the features and reference geometries to be varied. Once the **Pattern Table** dialog box has been invoked, you can select dimensions to be varied. Once you select the dimensions to be varied, the selected dimensions get listed in the **Pattern Table** dialog box, see Figure 9.71. The dialog box shown in Figure 9.71, the slot angle and the slot length dimensions of the model are selected as the dimensions to be varied.

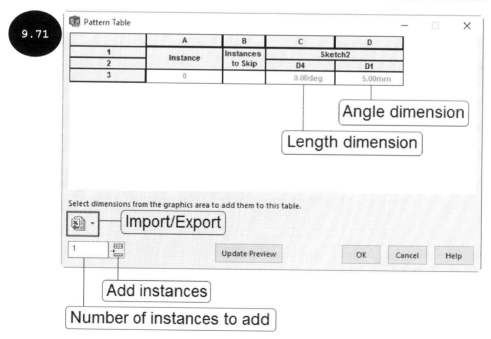

9.71

The **Number of instances to add** field of the **Pattern Table** dialog box is used to enter the number of instances to be created. After specifying the number of instances in this field, click on the **Add instances** button in the dialog box. The multiple rows equivalent to the number of instances specified are added in the **Pattern Table** dialog box, see Figure 9.72. Note that each row of this dialog box represents a pattern instance. You can modify the dimensions for each pattern instance by entering the required dimension values in the respective fields of the dialog box, see Figure 9.72. This dialog box works in the same way as that of the *Microsoft Office Excel*.

9.72

	A	B	C	D
1	Instance	Instances to Skip	Sketch2	
2			D4	D1
3	0		0.00deg	5.00mm
4	1	☐	24.00deg	3.00mm
5	2	☐	48.00deg	5.00mm
6	3	☐	72.00deg	3.00mm
7	4	☐	96.00deg	5.00mm
8	5	☐	120.00deg	3.00mm
9	6	☐	144.00deg	5.00mm
10	7	☐	168.00deg	3.00mm
11	8	☐	192.00deg	5.00mm
12	9	☐	216.00deg	3.00mm
13	10	☐	240.00deg	5.00mm
14	11	☐	264.00deg	3.00mm
15	12	☐	288.00deg	5.00mm
16	13	☐	312.00deg	3.00mm
17	14	☐	336.00deg	5.00mm

Select dimensions from the graphics area to add them to this table.

After modifying the dimension values in the dialog box for each pattern instance, click on the **Update Preview** button. This button is used to update the preview of pattern instances in the graphics area. You can also import an excel file (*.xlsx) containing variable dimensions of pattern instances by using the **Import from Excel** option of the dialog box. The **Export to Excel** option of the dialog box is used to save the variable dimensions as an external excel file for later use. Once you have specified variable dimensions for all pattern instances, click on the **OK** button. The variable pattern is created, see Figure 9.73.

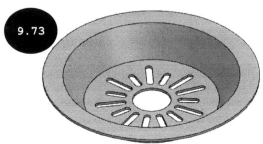

9.73

Procedure for Creating a Variable Pattern

1. Invoke the **Pattern** flyout and then click on the **Variable Pattern** tool. The **Variable Pattern** **PropertyManager** appears.
2. Select a feature to be patterned from the graphics area.
3. Click on the **Reference Geometry to drive seeds** field in the PropertyManager and then select the reference geometries on which the selected feature is dependent. If the feature to be patterned does not depend on any reference geometry, then you can skip this step.
4. Click on the **Create Pattern Table** button. The **Pattern Table** dialog box appears.
5. Click on the dimensions of the feature to be varied in the graphics area. The selected dimensions get listed in the **Pattern Table** dialog box.
6. Enter the number of pattern instances to be created in the **Number of instances to add** field.
7. Click on the **Add instances** button in the dialog box. The rows equivalent to the number of instances specified are added in the dialog box.
8. Modify the dimensions of each pattern instance, in the respective fields of the dialog box.
9. Click on the **OK** button in the dialog box.
10. Click on the green tick mark ✓ in the PropertyManager. The variable pattern is created.

Mirroring a Feature

Mirror features are created by mirroring features, faces, or bodies about a mirroring plane. Figure 9.74 shows features to be mirrored, mirroring plane, and the resultant mirror feature created.

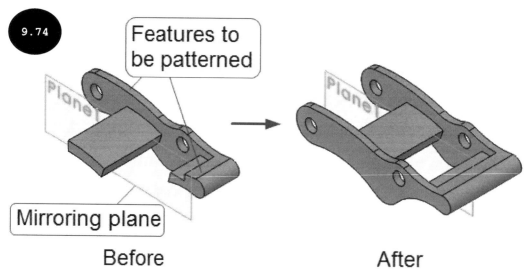

To create a mirror feature, click on the **Mirror** tool in the **Features CommandManager**. The **Mirror PropertyManager** appears, see Figure 9.75. You can also invoke the **Mirror** tool from the **Pattern** flyout. The options in the **Mirror PropertyManager** are as follows:

Mirror Face/Plane

The **Mirror Face/Plane** field is used to select mirroring plane. By default, this field is activated. As a result, you can select a mirroring plane from the graphics area. You can select a plane or a planar face of the model as the mirroring plane either from the graphics area or from the FeatureManager Design Tree.

Features to Mirror

The **Features to Mirror** field is used to select features to be mirrored about the mirroring plane. To select the features to be mirrored, click on this field and then select features either from the graphics area or from the FeatureManager Design Tree. After selecting the mirroring plane and the features to be mirrored, the preview of the mirror feature appears in the graphics area.

Faces to Mirror and Bodies to Mirror

The **Faces to Mirror** and **Bodies to Mirror** rollouts of the PropertyManager are used to select faces and bodies to be mirrored, respectively. Note that faces to be mirrored should form a closed volume and make up a feature.

Options

The options in the **Options** rollout are the same as those discussed while creating patterns. By default the **Geometry Pattern** check box is unchecked in the rollout. As a result, the resultant mirror feature maintains the same geometrical relations as the parent feature. Figure 9.76 shows the front view of a model having cut feature in the 'hidden lines visible' display style. This cut feature is created by defining its end condition as 4 mm offset from the bottom face of the model by using the **Offset from Surface** option. Figure 9.77 shows the resultant mirror feature created by unchecking the **Geometry Pattern** check box and Figure 9.78 shows the resultant mirror feature created by selecting the **Geometry Pattern** check box.

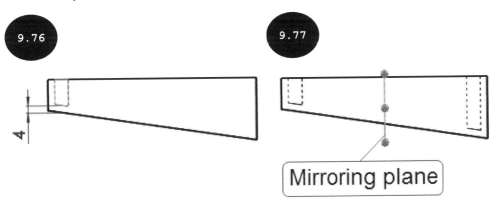

466 Chapter 9 > Patterning and Mirroring

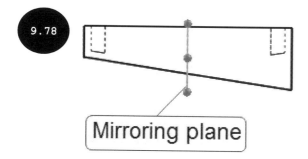

By default, the **Propagate visual properties** check box is selected in the **Options** rollout. As a result, all the visual properties such as colors, textures, and cosmetic thread of the parent feature are propagated to the resultant mirror feature.

Procedure for Creating a Mirror Feature

1. Click on the **Mirror** tool. The **Mirror PropertyManager** appears.
2. Select a plane or a planar face as the mirroring plane.
3. Click on the **Features to Mirror** field in the PropertyManager and then select a feature or features to be mirrored.
4. Click on the green tick mark ✓ in the PropertyManager. The mirror feature is created.

Tutorial 1

Create the model shown in Figure 9.79. All dimensions are in mm.

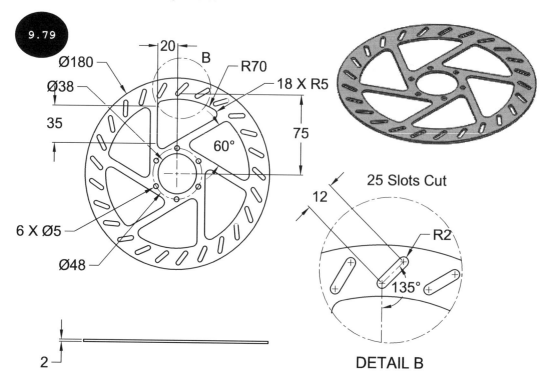

Section 1: Starting SOLIDWORKS
1. Double-click on the SOLIDWORKS icon on your desktop to start SOLIDWORKS.

Section 2: Invoking the Part Modeling Environment
1. Click on the **New** tool in the **Standard** toolbar. The **New SOLIDWORKS Document** dialog box appears.

2. In this dialog box, the **Part** button is activated by default. Click on the **OK** button to invoke the Part modeling environment.

   Once the Part modeling environment has been invoked, you need to set the unit system and create the base feature of the model.

Section 3: Specifying Unit Settings
1. Move the cursor toward the lower right corner of the screen over the Status Bar and then click on the **Unit System** area in the Status Bar. The **Unit System** flyout appears, see Figure 9.80.

2. In this flyout, make sure that the **MMGS (millimeter, gram, second)** option is tick-marked.

Section 4: Creating the Base Feature - Extruded Feature
1. Invoke the Sketching environment by selecting the Top plane as the sketching plane.

2. Create the sketch of the base feature of the model, see Figure 9.81. After creating the sketch, do not exit the Sketching environment.

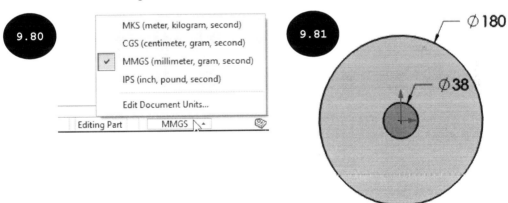

3. Click on the **Features** tab in the CommandManager to display the tools of the **Features** CommandManager.

4. Click on the **Extruded Boss/Base** tool. The **Boss-Extrude PropertyManager** and the preview of the extruded feature appear.

5. Enter **2** in the **Depth** field of the **Direction 1** rollout and then press ENTER.

468 Chapter 9 > Patterning and Mirroring

6. Click on the green tick mark ✓ in the PropertyManager. The extruded feature is created, see Figure 9.82.

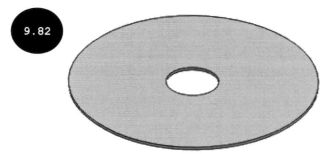
9.82

Section 5: Creating the Second Feature - Extruded Cut Feature

1. Invoke the Sketching environment by selecting the top planar face of the base feature as the sketching plane.

2. Press CTRL + 8 to change the orientation of the model as normal to the viewing direction.

3. Create the sketch of the second feature, see Figure 9.83. After creating the sketch, do not exit the Sketching environment.

4. Click on the **Features** tab in the CommandManager to display the tools of the **Features CommandManager**.

5. Click on the **Extruded Cut** tool in the Features CommandManager. The **Cut-Extrude PropertyManager** and the preview of the extruded cut feature appear. Next, change the orientation of the model to isometric.

6. Invoke the **End Condition** drop-down list in the **Direction 1** rollout and then select the **Through All** option in it.

7. Click on the green tick mark ✓ in the PropertyManager. The extruded cut feature is created, see Figure 9.84.

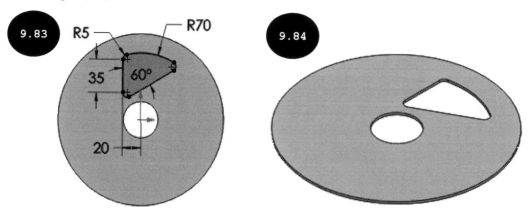
9.83
9.84

Section 6: Creating the Third Feature - Circular Pattern

1. Click on the down arrow at the bottom of the **Linear Pattern** tool. The **Pattern** flyout appears, see Figure 9.85.

2. Click on the **Circular Pattern** tool in the **Pattern** flyout, see Figure 9.85. The **CirPattern PropertyManager** appears.

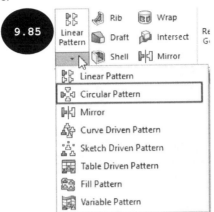

3. Expand the FeatureManager Design Tree, which is now available on the top left corner of the graphics area, by clicking on the arrow in its front.

4. Click on the second feature (extruded cut) in the FeatureManager Design Tree as the feature to be patterned.

5. Click on the **Pattern Axis** field in the **Direction 1** rollout of the PropertyManager to activate it.

6. Click on the circular edge of the base feature to define the pattern axis, see Figure 9.86. The preview of the circular pattern appears, see Figure 9.86.

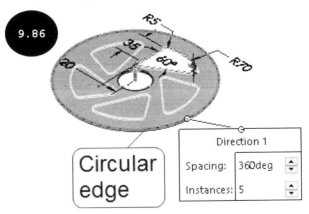

7. Make sure that the **Equal spacing** radio button is selected in the **Direction 1** rollout of the PropertyManager.

470 Chapter 9 > Patterning and Mirroring

8. Enter **6** in the **Number of Instances** field of the **Direction 1** rollout.

9. Click on the green tick mark ✓ in the PropertyManager. The circular pattern is created, see Figure 9.87.

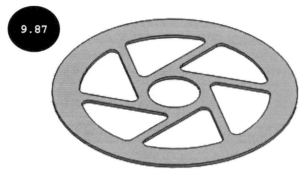
9.87

Section 7: Creating the Fourth Feature - Extruded Cut Feature

1. Invoke the Sketching environment by selecting the top planar face of the base feature as the sketching plane.

2. Press CTRL + 8 to change the orientation of the model as normal to the viewing direction.

3. Create the sketch of the fourth feature of the model, see Figure 9.88. Do not exit the Sketching environment.

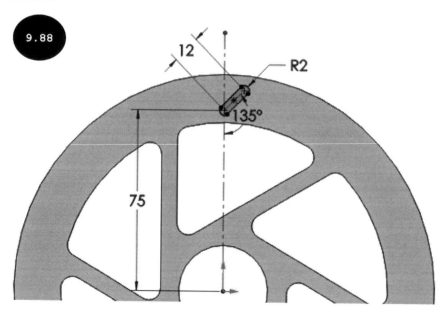
9.88

4. Click on the **Features** tab in the CommandManager and then click on the **Extruded Cut** tool. The **Cut-Extrude** PropertyManager and the preview of the extruded cut feature appear. Next, change the orientation of the model to isometric.

Extruded Cut

5. Invoke the **End Condition** drop-down list in the **Direction 1** rollout of the PropertyManager and then select the **Through All** option in it.

6. Click on the green tick mark ✓ in the PropertyManager. The extruded cut feature is created, see Figure 9.89.

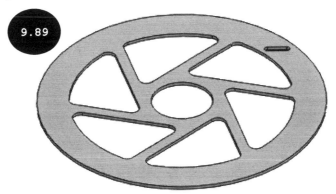

9.89

Section 8: Creating the Fifth Feature - Circular Pattern

1. Click on the down arrow at the bottom of the **Linear Pattern** tool. The **Pattern** flyout appears, see Figure 9.90.

2. Click on the **Circular Pattern** tool in the **Pattern** flyout. The **CirPattern PropertyManager** appears.

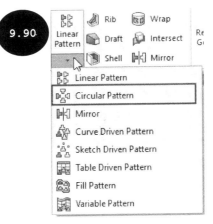

9.90

3. Expand the FeatureManager Design Tree, which is now available on the top left corner of the graphics area, by clicking on the arrow in its front.

4. Click on the fourth feature (previously created extruded cut feature) from the FeatureManager Design Tree as the feature to be patterned.

5. Click on the **Pattern Axis** field in the **Direction 1** rollout of the PropertyManager to activate it.

6. Click on the circular edge of the base feature to define the pattern axis. The preview of the circular pattern appears, see Figure 9.91.

7. Make sure that the **Equal spacing** radio button is selected in the **Direction 1** rollout of the PropertyManager.

8. Enter **25** in the **Number of Instances** field of the **Direction 1** rollout.

9. Click on the green tick mark ✓ in the PropertyManager. The circular pattern is created, see Figure 9.92.

472 Chapter 9 > Patterning and Mirroring

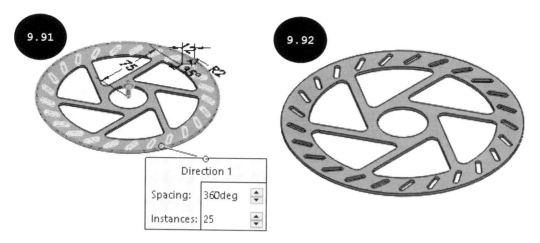

Section 9: Creating the Sixth Feature - Extruded Cut Feature

1. Invoke the Sketching environment by selecting the top planar face of the base feature as the sketching plane.

2. Press CTRL + 8 to change the orientation of the model as normal to the viewing direction.

3. Create the sketch of the sixth feature (circle of diameter 5 mm), see Figure 9.93. Do not exit the Sketching environment.

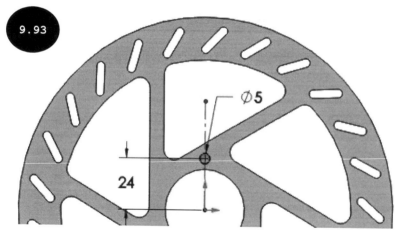

4. Click on the **Features** tab in the CommandManager and then click on the **Extruded Cut** tool. The **Cut-Extrude PropertyManager** and the preview of the extruded cut feature appear. Next, change the orientation of the model to isometric.

5. Select the **Through All** option in the **End Condition** drop-down list of the **Direction 1** rollout.

6. Click on the green tick mark ✓ in the PropertyManager. The extruded cut feature is created, see Figure 9.94.

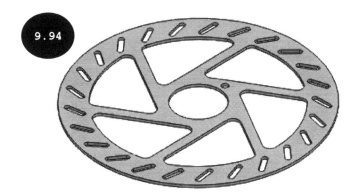

9.94

Section 10: Creating the Seventh Feature - Circular Pattern

1. Invoke the **Pattern** flyout and then click on the **Circular Pattern** tool. The **CirPattern** PropertyManager appears.

2. Expand the FeatureManager Design Tree, which is now available on the top left corner of the graphics area, by clicking on the arrow in its front.

3. Click on the sixth feature (previously created extruded cut feature) from the FeatureManager Design Tree as the feature to be patterned.

4. Click on the **Pattern Axis** field in the **Direction 1** rollout of the PropertyManager.

5. Click on the circular edge of the base feature to define the pattern axis. The preview of the circular pattern appears, see Figure 9.95.

6. Make sure that the **Equal spacing** radio button is selected in the **Direction 1** rollout.

7. Enter **6** in the **Number of Instances** field of the **Direction 1** rollout.

8. Click on the green tick mark in the PropertyManager. The circular pattern is created, see Figure 9.96.

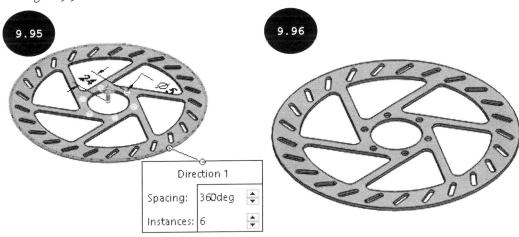

9.95   9.96

474 Chapter 9 > Patterning and Mirroring

Section 11: Saving the Model

1. Click on the **Save** tool in the **Standard** toolbar. The **Save As** window appears.

2. Browse to the *SOLIDWORKS* folder and then create a folder with the name **Chapter 9**. Next, create another folder with the name **Tutorial** in the *Chapter 9* folder.

3. Enter **Tutorial 1** in the **File name** field of the dialog box and then click on the **Save** button. The model is saved with the name Tutorial 1 in the *Tutorial* folder of *Chapter 9*.

Tutorial 2

Create the model shown in Figure 9.97. The different views and dimensions are given in the same figure. All dimensions are in mm.

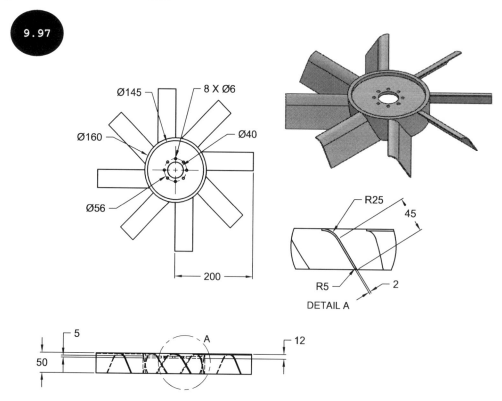

9.97

Section 1: Starting SOLIDWORKS

1. Double-click on the SOLIDWORKS icon on your desktop to start SOLIDWORKS.

Section 2: Invoking the Part Modeling Environment

1. Click on the **New** tool in the **Standard** toolbar. The **New SOLIDWORKS Document** dialog box appears.

2. In this dialog box, the **Part** button is activated by default. Click on the **OK** button to invoke the Part modeling environment.

   Once the Part modeling environment has been invoked, you need to set the unit system and create the base/first feature of the model.

Section 3: Specifying Unit Settings

1. Make sure that the **MMGS (millimeter, gram, second)** unit system is set for the currently opened part document.

Section 4: Creating the Base Feature - Extruded Feature

1. Invoke the Sketching environment by selecting the Top plane as the sketching plane.

2. Create the sketch of the base feature of the model, see Figure 9.98. After creating the sketch, do not exit the Sketching environment.

3. Click on the **Features** tab in the CommandManager. The tools of the **Features** CommandManager are displayed.

4. Click on the **Extruded Boss/Base** tool. The **Boss-Extrude PropertyManager** and the preview of the extruded feature appear.

5. Invoke the **End Condition** drop-down list in the **Direction 1** rollout of the PropertyManager.

6. Select the **Mid Plane** option in the **End Condition** drop-down list.

7. Enter **50** in the **Depth** field of the **Direction 1** rollout and then press ENTER.

8. Click on the green tick mark in the PropertyManager. The extruded feature is created, see Figure 9.99.

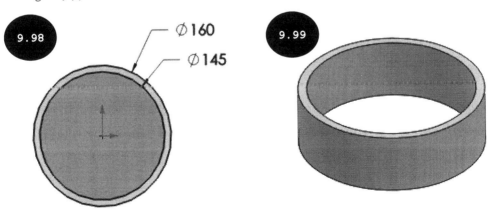

Section 5: Creating the Second Feature - Extruded Feature

1. Invoke the Sketching environment by selecting the top planar face of the base feature as the sketching plane.

2. Press CTRL + 8 to change the orientation of the model as normal to the viewing direction.

3. Create the sketch (two circles of diameter 145 mm and 40 mm) of the second feature, see Figure 9.100. After creating the sketch, do not exit the Sketching environment.

4. Click on the **Extruded Boss/Base** tool in the **Features CommandManager**. The **Boss-Extrude PropertyManager** and the preview of the extruded feature appear. Next, change the orientation of the model to isometric.

5. Invoke the **Start Condition** drop-down list in the **From** rollout of the PropertyManager, see Figure 9.101.

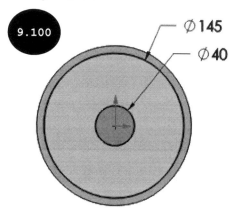

6. Select the **Offset** option in the **Start Condition** drop-down list of the **From** rollout.

7. Enter **12** in the **Enter Offset Value** field of the **From** rollout in the PropertyManager.

8. Click on the **Reverse Direction** button in the **From** rollout to reverse the direction of material addition.

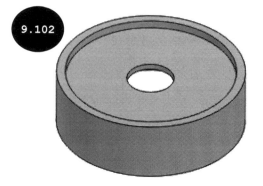

9. Enter **5** in the **Depth** field of the **Direction 1** rollout in the PropertyManager.

10. Click on the green tick mark ✓ in the PropertyManager. The extruded feature is created, see Figure 9.102.

Section 6: Creating the Third Feature - Extruded Cut Feature

1. Invoke the Sketching environment by selecting the top planar face of the second feature (previously created extruded feature) as the sketching plane.

2. Press CTRL + 8 to change the orientation of the model as normal to the viewing direction.

3. Create a circle of diameter 6 mm as the sketch of the third feature, see Figure 9.103. Do not exit the Sketching environment.

4. Click on the **Features** tab in the CommandManager and then click on the **Extruded Cut** tool. The **Cut-Extrude PropertyManager** and the preview of the extruded cut feature appear. Next, change the orientation of the model to isometric.

5. Invoke the **End Condition** drop-down list of the **Direction 1** rollout and then select the **Through All** option in it.

6. Click on the green tick mark in the PropertyManager. The extruded cut feature is created, see Figure 9.104.

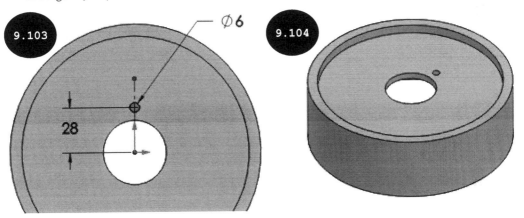

Section 7: Creating the Fourth Feature - Circular Pattern

1. Invoke the **Pattern** flyout by clicking on the down arrow at the bottom of the **Linear Pattern** tool.

2. Click on the **Circular Pattern** tool in the **Pattern** flyout. The **CirPattern PropertyManager** appears.

3. Expand the FeatureManager Design Tree, which is now available on the top left corner of the graphics area, by clicking on the arrow in its front.

4. Click on the third feature (previously created extruded cut) in the FeatureManager Design Tree as the feature to be patterned.

5. Click on the **Pattern Axis** field in the **Direction 1** rollout of the PropertyManager to activate it.

478 Chapter 9 > Patterning and Mirroring

6. Click on the outer circular face of the base feature in the graphics area to define the pattern axis, see Figure 9.105. The preview of the circular pattern appears, see Figure 9.105.

7. Make sure that the **Equal spacing** radio button is selected in the **Direction 1** rollout of the PropertyManager.

8. Enter **8** in the **Number of Instances** field of the **Direction 1** rollout.

9. Click on the green tick mark ✓ in the PropertyManager. The circular pattern is created, see Figure 9.106.

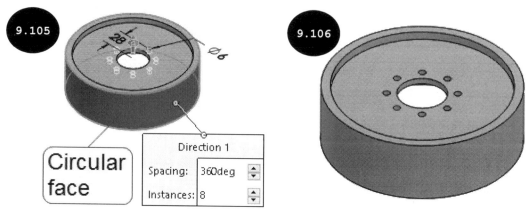

Section 8: Creating the Fifth Feature - Extruded Feature

The fifth feature of the model is an extruded feature and its sketch is to be created on a reference plane, which is at the offset distance of 200 mm from the Right plane.

1. Invoke the **Plane PropertyManager** by clicking on the **Plane** tool in the **Reference Geometry** flyout and then create a reference plane at the offset distance of 200 mm from the Right plane, see Figure 9.107.

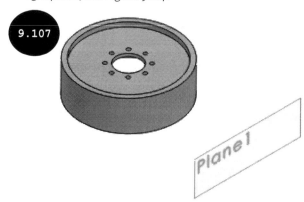

2. Invoke the Sketching environment by selecting the newly created reference plane as the sketching plane.

3. Press CTRL + 8 to change the orientation of the model as normal to the viewing direction.

4. Create the sketch of the extruded feature, see Figure 9.108. After creating the sketch, do not exit the Sketching environment.

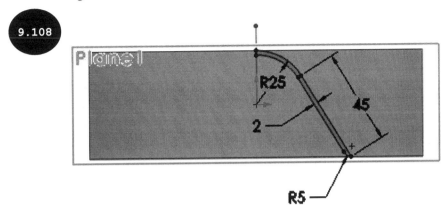

9.108

Note: In the sketch shown in Figure 9.108, the tangent relation has been applied between the connecting arcs and lines of the sketch. Also, the center point of the arc having the radius of 25 mm is coincident with the origin.

5. Click on the **Features** tab in the CommandManager and then click on the **Extruded Boss/Base** tool. The **Boss-Extrude PropertyManager** and the preview of the extruded feature appear. Next, change the orientation of the model to isometric.

6. Invoke the **End Condition** drop-down list in the **Direction 1** rollout of the PropertyManager.

7. Select the **Up To Surface** option in the **End Condition** drop-down list. The **Face/Plane** field becomes available in the **Direction 1** rollout and is activated by default.

8. Click on the outer circular face of the base feature. The preview of the extruded feature appears in the graphics area such that it is extruded up to the selected face, see Figure 9.109.

9.109

480 Chapter 9 > Patterning and Mirroring

9. Click on the green tick mark ✓ in the PropertyManager. The extruded feature is created, see Figure 9.110.

9.110

Section 9: Creating the Six Feature - Circular Pattern

1. Invoke the **Pattern** flyout by clicking on the down arrow at the bottom of the **Linear Pattern** tool.

2. Click on the **Circular Pattern** tool in the **Pattern** flyout. The **CirPattern**  **PropertyManager** appears.

3. Select the fifth feature (previously created extruded feature) as the feature to be patterned from the graphics area.

4. Click on the **Pattern Axis** field in the **Direction 1** rollout of the PropertyManager.

5. Click on the outer circular face of the base feature in the graphics area to define the pattern axis. The preview of the circular pattern appears.

6. Make sure that the **Equal spacing** radio button is selected in the **Direction 1** rollout.

7. Enter **8** in the **Number of Instances** field of the **Direction 1** rollout.

8. Click on the green tick mark ✓ in the PropertyManager. The circular pattern is created, see Figure 9.111.

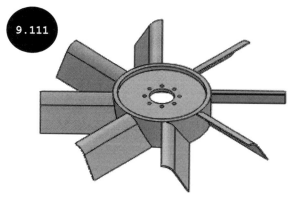

9.111

Section 10: Saving the Model

1. Click on the **Save** tool in the **Standard** toolbar. The **Save As** dialog box appears.

2. Browse to the *Tutorial* folder of *Chapter 9* and then save the model with the name Tutorial 2.

Hands-on Test Drive 1

Create the model shown in Figure 9.112. The different views and dimensions are given in the same figure for your reference.

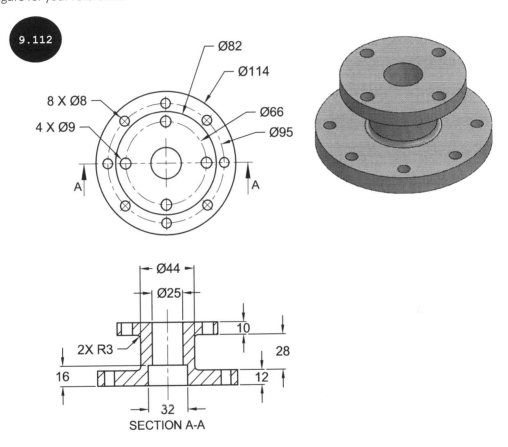

482 Chapter 9 > Patterning and Mirroring

Hands-on Test Drive 2

Create the model shown in Figure 9.113. The different views and dimensions are given in the same figure for your reference.

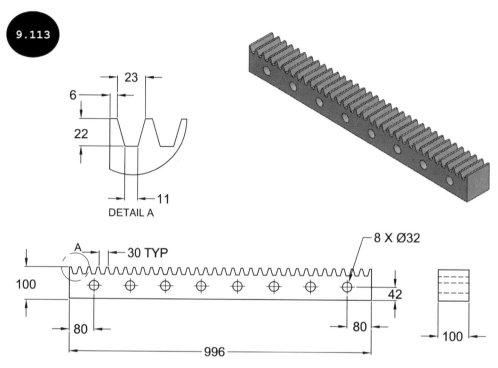

9.113

Summary

In this chapter, you have learned how to use various patterning and mirroring tools. Once you have read the chapter thoroughly, you can create different types of patterns such as linear pattern, circular pattern, curve driven pattern, and sketch driven pattern.

The linear pattern is created by making multiple instances of features, faces, or bodies, linearly in Direction 1 and Direction 2. You can also skip pattern instances which are not required in the pattern. The circular pattern is created by making multiple instances of features, faces, or bodies in a circular manner about an axis. You can select an axis, a circular face, a circular edge, a linear edge, a linear sketch or an angular dimension to define the axis of circular pattern. The curve driven pattern is created by making multiple instances of features, faces, or bodies along a curve. You can select a 2D/3D sketch/curve or an edge as curve to drive pattern instances.

The sketch driven pattern is created by using sketch points of a sketch. The table driven pattern is created by specifying coordinate points for each pattern instance with respect to a coordinate system. The fill Pattern is created by filling in an area with pattern instances of the selected feature.

You can also use the predefined cut shapes to fill in the defined area or boundary in the fill pattern. The variable pattern is created by varying the dimensions and reference geometries of the features to be patterned. In this chapter, you have learned how to mirror features, faces, or bodies about a mirroring plane.

Questions

- The _____ tool is used to create multiple instances of features, faces, or bodies, linearly in Direction 1 and Direction 2.

- The _____ tool is used to create multiple instances of features, faces, or bodies along a curve.

- You can create a variable pattern by using the _____ tool.

- In a variable pattern, you can vary _____ and _____ of the features to be patterned.

- When the _____ check box is unchecked, all the instances of the linear pattern maintain same geometrical relations as the original or parent feature.

- The _____ pattern is created by specifying coordinate points for each pattern instance with respect to a coordinate system.

- While creating a linear pattern, you cannot vary pattern instances with respect to a path. (True/False).

- In SOLIDWORKS, you can mirror features as well as faces of a model. (True/False).

CHAPTER 10

Advanced Modeling - III

In this chapter, you will learn the following:

- Working with Hole Wizard
- Creating Advanced Holes
- Adding Cosmetic Threads
- Creating Threads
- Creating Fillets
- Creating Chamfers
- Creating Rib Features
- Creating Shell Features
- Creating Wrap Features

In earlier chapters, you have learned about creating circular cut features representing holes by using the **Extruded Cut** tool. In this chapter, you will learn about creating standard or customized holes such as counterbore, countersink, straight tap, and tapered tap as per the standard specifications by using the **Hole Wizard** tool and the **Advanced Hole** tool. Moreover, you will learn about other advanced modeling tools such as **Cosmetic Thread**, **Thread**, **Rib**, **Shell**, **Wrap**, **Fillet**, and **Chamfer**.

Working with Hole Wizard

The **Hole Wizard** tool is used to create standard holes such as counterbore, countersink, and straight tap as per the standard specifications. To create standard holes by using the **Hole Wizard** tool, click on the **Hole Wizard** tool in the **Features CommandManager**. The **Hole Specification PropertyManager** appears, see Figure 10.1. The options in this PropertyManager are as follows:

Type Tab

The **Hole Specification** PropertyManager has two tabs: **Type** and **Positions**. By default, the **Type** tab is activated. As a result, the options to specify the type of hole and hole specifications are displayed in different rollouts of the PropertyManager. The options are as follows:

Hole Type

The **Hole Type** rollout of the PropertyManager is used to select the type of hole such as counterbore, countersink, or straight tap. Depending upon the type of hole to be created, you can click on the **Counterbore**, **Countersink**, **Hole**, **Straight Tap**, **Tapered Tap**, or **Legacy** button in this rollout. Figure 10.2 shows counterbore holes and Figure 10.3 shows countersink holes created on the top face of the model.

Using this rollout, you can not only create standard holes, but also create slot holes by selecting the **Counterbore Slot**, **Countersink Slot**, and **Slot** buttons. Figure 10.4 shows counterbore slots and Figure 10.5 shows countersink slots created on the top face of the model. The remaining options of this rollout are as follows:

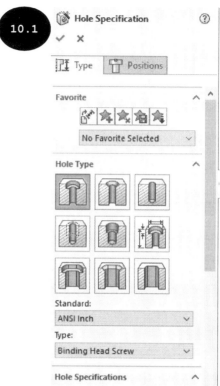

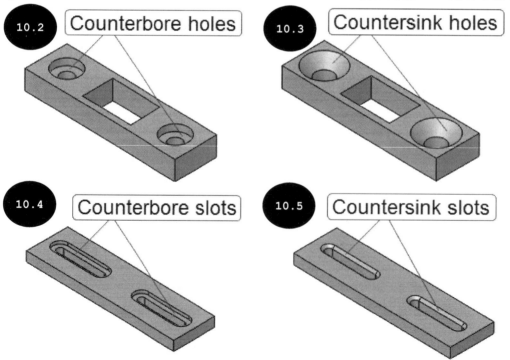

Standard
The **Standard** drop-down list is used to select the type of standard such as ANSI Metric, ANSI Inch, BSI, IS, JIS, and ISO for creating hole, see Figure 10.6.

Type
The **Type** drop-down list is used to specify the type of fastener to be inserted into the hole. The availability of options in this drop-down list depends upon the type of hole and standard selected. Figure 10.7 shows the **Type** drop-down list when the **Counterbore** hole type and the **ANSI Metric** standard are selected.

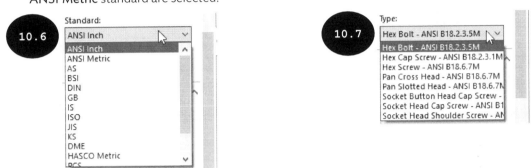

Hole Specifications
The **Hole Specifications** rollout of the PropertyManager is used to define specifications for the fastener to be inserted into the hole. The options of this rollout are as follows:

Size
The **Size** drop-down list is used to select the size of the fastener to be inserted. The availability of options in this drop-down list depends upon the type of hole and standard selected.

Fit
The **Fit** drop-down list is used to select the type of fit between the fastener and hole. You can specify close, normal, or loose fastener fit.

Note: The size of the hole depends upon the size of the fastener and the type of fit. In SOLIDWORKS, the size of the hole is automatically adjusted depending upon the specification of the fastener and type of fit selected.

Show custom sizing
The **Show custom sizing** check box is used to display and customize the standard size of the hole. On selecting the **Show custom sizing** check box, the standard size of the hole as per the specified specifications appears in the respective fields of the rollout, see Figure 10.8.

You can modify the standard specifications of the hole by entering the required values in the respective fields. Note that the background color of the fields, whose values are edited or customized, are changed to yellow color. After editing the specifications, if you want to restore the default standard specifications, click on the **Restore Default Values** button of this rollout.

End Condition

The options in the **End Condition** rollout are used to define the end condition or termination method for a hole. The options to define the end condition of the hole are the same as those discussed earlier while creating the extruded feature.

Options

The availability of the options in the **Options** rollout depends upon the type of hole selected. Figure 10.9 shows the **Options** rollout when the **Counterbore** hole type is selected. The options are as follows:

Head clearance
On selecting the **Head clearance** check box, the
Head Clearance field appears below it. In this field, you can specify the head clearance value for the counterbore or countersink hole. In other words, the value entered in the **Head Clearance** field is used to define the clearance between the top face of the fastener head and the hole.

Near side countersink
The **Near side countersink** check box is used to create the countersink shape in the near side of the placement face of the hole, see Figure 10.10. On selecting the **Near side countersink** check box, the **Near Side Countersink Diameter** and **Near Side Countersink Angle** fields appear in the rollout. These fields are used to specify the diameter and angle of the countersink shape to be created in the near side of the placement face of the hole. Figure 10.10 shows a counterbore hole with countersink shape created in its near side of the placement face.

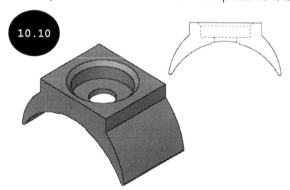

Far side countersink
The **Far side countersink** check box is used to create countersink shape in the far side of the placement face of the hole, see Figure 10.11. On selecting the **Far side countersink** check box, the **Far Side Countersink Diameter** and **Far Side Countersink Angle** fields appear in the rollout. These fields are used to specify countersink diameter and angle for the countersink shape to be

created in the far side of the placement face of the hole. Figure 10.11 shows a counterbore hole with countersink shape created at the far side of the placement face.

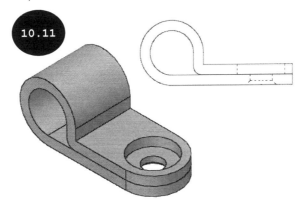

Under head countersink
The **Under head countersink** check box is used to create countersink shape under the hole head, see Figure 10.12. On selecting the **Under head countersink** check box, the **Under Head Side Countersink Diameter** and **Under Head Side Countersink Angle** fields appear. These fields are used to specify the countersink diameter and angle for the countersink shape to be created under the hole head diameter. Figure 10.12 shows a counterbore hole with countersink shape created under the head diameter.

In case of Straight tap hole type, the options in the **Options** rollout appear as shown in Figure 10.13. These options are as follows:

Tap drill diameter, Cosmetic thread, and Remove thread

The **Tap drill diameter** button is used to create a Straight tap hole having the same diameter as the tapped diameter of the hole with no thread representation, see Figure 10.14. The **Cosmetic thread** button is used to create a Straight tap hole having the same diameter as the tapped hole with the cosmetic representation of thread, see Figure 10.15. The **Remove thread** button is used to create a Straight tap hole having a diameter equal to the thread diameter of the taped hole, see Figure 10.16.

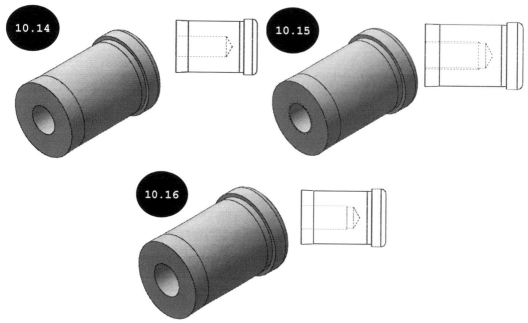

Thread class

On selecting the **Thread class** check box, the **Thread class** drop-down list becomes available in front of it. By using this drop-down list, you can select a class for the threaded or tapped holes.

After specifying all specifications in the **Type** tab of the PropertyManager, you need to define the placement point for the hole in the model by using the **Position** tab of the PropertyManager.

Positions Tab

The **Positions** tab of the PropertyManager is used to define the position of the hole. After specifying all specifications for the hole in the **Type** tab, click on the **Positions** tab in the PropertyManager. The name of the PropertyManager changes to **Hole Position PropertyManager**, see Figure 10.17. Also, you are promoted to specify the placement face for the hole. You can select a planar face, a plane, or a curved face as the placement face for the hole. Click on a face of the model as the placement face for the hole. The preview of the hole appears, which

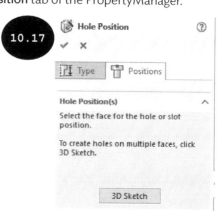

follows the cursor as you move it over the placement face. Now, you need to define the placement point for the hole. Click the left mouse button arbitrarily to specify the placement point for the hole. The center point of the hole is placed at the defined placement point. Similarly, you can specify multiple placement points for creating multiple holes of similar parameters. After specifying the placement points arbitrarily, you can use the dimension tools of the **Sketch CommandManager** to position the placement points of the hole, as required, see Figure 10.18. You can also apply relations such as horizontal and vertical to position the placement point of the hole. Once the position of the hole is defined by applying dimensions, click on the green tick mark ✓ in the PropertyManager. The hole is created.

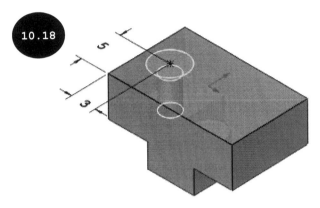

Note: On selecting the planar face as the placement face for the hole, the 2D sketch environment is invoked. As a result, you can create multiple holes on the selected placement face only. However, on selecting a curved face as the placement face, the 3D sketch environment is invoked. As a result, you can create multiple holes on different placement faces. You can also invoke the 3D sketch environment by clicking on the **3D Sketch** button in the PropertyManager for creating holes on different faces.

Procedure for Creating a Hole by using Hole Wizard

1. Click on the **Hole Wizard** tool. The **Hole Specification PropertyManager** appears.
2. Specify the type of hole and other hole specifications, as required, in the **Type** tab of the PropertyManager.
3. After specifying the hole specifications, click on the **Position** tab in the PropertyManager.
4. Click on a planar face, a plane, or a curved face as the placement face of the hole.
5. Click to specify the placement point of the hole on the placement face.
6. Apply dimensions and relations to position the placement point of the hole, as required.
7. Click on the green tick mark ✓ in the PropertyManager. The hole is created.

Tip: In SOLIDWORKS, the settings specified in the **Hole Specification PropertyManager** are retained and appear while editing the hole.

Creating Advanced Holes (New)

In SOLIDWORKS 2017, you can create advanced holes such as manifolds and multi-stepped by using the **Advanced Hole** tool. You can also define customized hole types with the combinations of different standard holes such as counterbore, countersink, straight tap, and tapered by using this tool. This is a very powerful tool for creating complex multi-stepped holes in a single command. To invoke the **Advanced Hole** tool, click on the down arrow at the bottom of the **Hole Wizard** tool. A flyout appears, see Figure 10.19. In this flyout, click on the **Advanced Hole** tool. The **Advanced Hole PropertyManager** and the **Near Side** flyout appear, see Figure 10.20. The options in the PropertyManager and the flyout are as follows:

Near And Far Side Faces

The **Near And Far Side Faces** rollout of the PropertyManager is used to select near and far side faces of a hole. By default, the **Near Side Faces** field is available in this rollout. As a result, you can select one or more faces as the near side faces of the hole. Select a face of the model as the near side face of the hole, see Figure 10.21. The preview of the hole with default specifications appears on the selected face, see Figure 10.21.

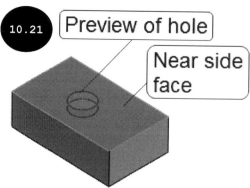

After selecting the near side face of the hole, you can define the near side hole elements by using the **Near Side** flyout. By default, the Counterbore is selected as the first near side element in this flyout. Invoke the **Near Side** flyout by clicking on its down arrow, see Figure 10.22. In this flyout, you can click on the required button: **Near Side Counterbore**, **Near Side Countersink**, **Near Side Tapered Tap**, **Hole**, or **Straight Tap** as the near side element. Once you have defined the first near side hole element by using the **Near Side** flyout, you need to define the hole element specifications such as type of hole, standard, and size by using the options of the **Element Specification** rollout of the PropertyManager. The options in this rollout of the PropertyManager are same as discussed earlier. After defining the first near side hole element and its specifications, you can add second near side hole element. To add the second near side hole element, click on the **Insert Element Below Active Element** button in the flyout, see Figure 10.22. The default second hole element is added below the first hole element in the flyout, see Figure 10.23. Also, the preview of the hole in the graphics area is modified such that the second hole element with its default specifications is added. Now, you need to define the required type of the second hole element, such as Counterbore, Countersink, and Straight Tap by using the **Near Side** flyout and the required hole specification by using the **Element Specification** rollout of the PropertyManager. Similarly, you can add multiple near side hole elements by using the **Near Side** flyout. Note that you can also add a hole element above an active hole element by using the **Insert Element Above Active Element** button of the flyout. To delete a hole element, click on the element to activate it and then click on the **Delete Active Element** button of the flyout. You can also reverse the direction of a hole by using the **Reverse Stack Direction** button of the flyout.

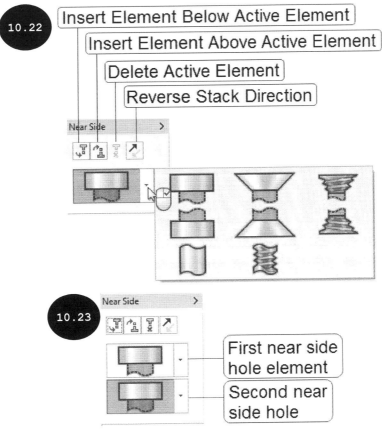

494 Chapter 10 > Advanced Modeling - III

To define the far side face of the hole, select the **Far Side** check box in the **Near And Far Side Faces** rollout of the PropertyManager, see Figure 10.24. The **Far Side Face** field and the **Far Side** flyout appears, see Figure 10.24. By default, the **Far Side Face** field is activated in the rollout. As a result, you can select a face of the model as the far side face of the hole. Select a face of the model as the far side face of the hole, see Figure 10.25. The preview of the hole is modified in the graphics area such that the default far side hole element is added, see Figure 10.25.

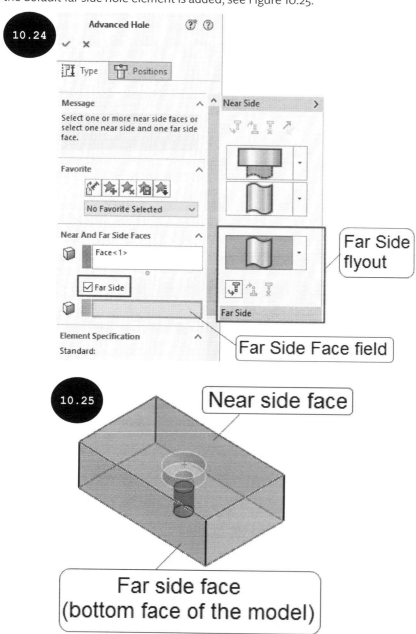

You can select a required far side hole element by using the **Far Side** flyout. To select a far side hole element, invoke the **Far Side** flyout, see Figure 10.26 and then click on the **Far Side Counterbore, Far Side Countersink, Far Side Tapered Tap, Hole,** or **Straight Tap** button.

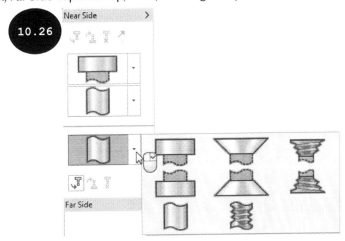

10.26

After selecting the required first far side hole element, you need to define its specifications by using the options of the **Element Specification** rollout in the PropertyManager. You can also add multiple far side elements by using the **Insert Element Below Active Element** and **Insert Element Above Active Element** buttons of the **Far Side** flyout. Figure 10.27 shows the preview of a multi-stepped hole having multiple near and far side elements. After defining the required near and far side elements of the hole with the required specifications, you need to define the placement point of the hole. To define the placement of the hole, click on the **Positions** tab in the PropertyManager. The name of PropertyManager changes to **Hole Position PropertyManager**, see Figure 10.28. Also, you are promoted to specify the placement point for the hole. Click the left mouse button arbitrarily on the near side face of the hole to specify its placement point. The center point of the hole is placed at the defined placement point. Similarly, you can create multiple instances of the hole by specifying the placement points. After specifying the placement points arbitrarily, you can use the dimension tools of the **Sketch CommandManager** to position the placement point of the hole, as required. You can also skip the instances of the hole by using the **Instances To Skip** rollout of the PropertyManager. Once the position of the hole is defined by applying dimensions, click on the green tick mark in the PropertyManager. The hole is created.

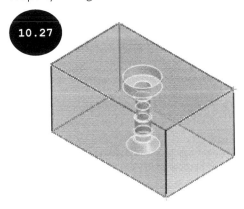

10.27

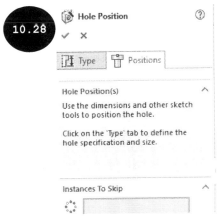

10.28

496 Chapter 10 > Advanced Modeling - III

Note: The appearance of the model shown in Figure 10.27 has been changed to clear glass for clarity. The method of changing the appearance of a model has been discussed in earlier chapters.

Adding Cosmetic Threads

A Cosmetic thread represents the real thread of a feature. It is recommended to add cosmetic threads to holes, fasteners, or cylindrical features of a model, because adding cosmetic threads help in reducing the complexity of the model and improves overall performance of the system. Figure 10.29 shows a cosmetic thread added to a cylindrical feature and Figure 10.30 shows a cosmetic thread added to a hole/cut extruded feature.

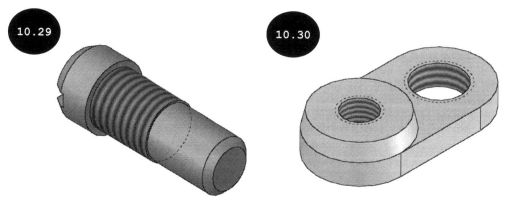

To add a cosmetic thread, click on the **Insert > Annotations > Cosmetic Thread** in the SOLIDWORKS menus. The **Cosmetic Thread PropertyManager** appears, see Figure 10.31. The options in this PropertyManager are as follows:

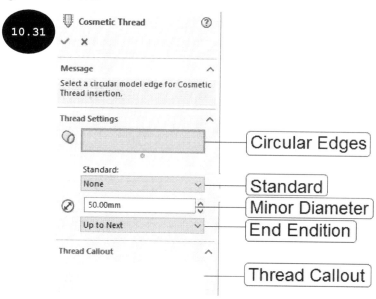

Message Rollout

The **Message** rollout displays a message that you need to select a circular edge of a model for adding the cosmetic thread.

Thread Settings

The **Circular Edges** field of the **Thread Settings** rollout is activated by default. As a result, you can select a circular edge of a feature for adding the cosmetic thread. Click on a circular edge of a feature for adding cosmetic thread. A dotted circle appears in the graphics area, represents the minor or major diameter of the thread, see Figures 10.32 and 10.33. Also, the name of the selected circular edge appears in the **Circular Edges** field. The other options in the **Thread Settings** rollout are as follows:

Note: On selecting the circular edge of a cylindrical feature, the dotted circle represents the minor (inner) diameter of the thread, see Figure 10.32 whereas, on selecting the circular edge of a cut/hole feature, the dotted circle represents the major (outer) diameter of the thread, see Figure 10.33.

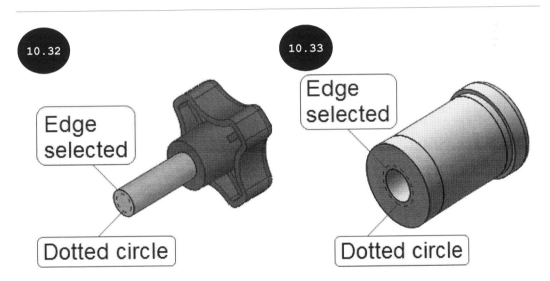

Standard

The **Standard** drop-down list is used to select the type of standard such as ANSI Inch or ANSI Metric to be followed for creating the cosmetic thread.

Type

The **Type** drop-down list is used to select the type of thread to be added. Note that this drop-down list will not be available if the **None** option is selected in the **Standard** drop-down list.

Size

The **Size** drop-down list is used to select the standard size of the thread. Note that this drop-down list will not be available if the **None** option is selected in the **Standard** drop-down list.

Minor Diameter / Major Diameter

The **Minor Diameter / Major Diameter** field is used to specify the minor/major diameter of the thread, respectively. Note that this field is enabled only if the **None** option is selected in the **Standard** drop-down list. Also, the field (**Minor Diameter** or **Major Diameter**) appears, depending upon the circular edge selected for applying the thread. If the circular edge of a cylindrical feature is selected, the **Minor Diameter** field appears and if the circular edge of a hole feature is selected, the **Major Diameter** field appears.

End Condition

The **End Condition** drop-down list is used to specify the end condition or termination for the cosmetic thread. Note that the circular edge selected for adding the cosmetic thread is the start condition of the cosmetic thread.

Thread Callout

The **Thread Callout** field is used to enter text or comment for a thread, which appears in the thread callout of the drawing view. You can create drawing views in the Drawing environment of SOLIDWORKS. You will learn about creating drawing views in later chapters.

Note: The **Thread Callout** field of the **Thread Callout** rollout is activated only if the **None** option is selected in the **Standard** drop-down list. If you select a standard such as ANSI Inch or ANSI Metric then this field is not activated. However, the default text appears in this field, depending upon the type of standard and thread selected.

After specifying all parameters for adding cosmetic thread in the PropertyManager, click on the green tick mark ✓ in the PropertyManager. The respective cosmetic thread is added and appears in the graphics area, see Figure 10.34. Also, a cosmetic thread feature is added under the node of the feature in the FeatureManager Design Tree, see Figure 10.35.

Note: In Figure 10.34, the shaded display style of cosmetic thread is turned off. As a result, only the dotted circle representing the thread diameter appears in the graphics area. To turn on the shaded display style, click on the **Annotations** node in the FeatureManager Design Tree and then right-click. A shortcut menu appears, see Figure 10.36. In this shortcut menu, click on the **Details** option. The **Annotation Properties** dialog box appears. Next, select the **Shaded cosmetic threads** check box in this dialog box to turn on the shaded display style of the cosmetic thread. Figure 10.37 shows a cosmetic thread in shaded display style.

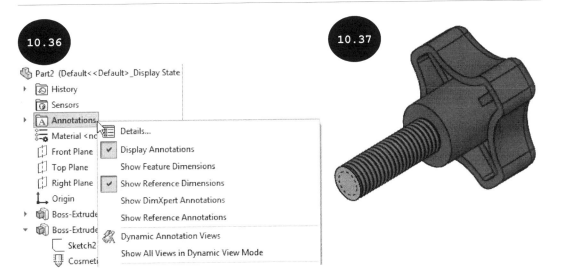

Procedure for Adding a Cosmetic Thread

1. Click on **Insert > Annotations > Cosmetic Thread** in the SOLIDWORKS menus.
2. Select a circular edge of a model to add the cosmetic thread.
3. Specify parameters such as standard, size, and end condition for the cosmetic thread.
4. Click on the green tick mark ✓ in the PropertyManager. The cosmetic thread is added.

Creating Threads Updated

In SOLIDWORKS, in addition to adding cosmetic threads, you can create real threads on cylindrical or circular cut features by removing material from the model, see Figure 10.38.

You can create a real thread on a cylindrical or a circular cut feature by using the **Thread** tool. To invoke the **Thread** tool, click on the down arrow at the bottom of the **Hole Wizard** tool of the **Features CommandManager**. A flyout appears, see Figure 10.39. In this flyout, click on the **Thread** tool. The **Thread PropertyManager** appears, see Figure 10.40. The options in this PropertyManager are as follows:

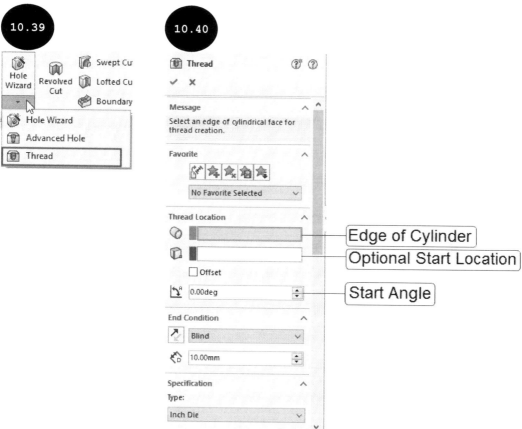

Thread Location
By default, the **Edge of Cylinder** field in the **Thread Location** rollout is activated. As a result, you can select the circular edge of a cylindrical feature or a hole feature for creating a thread. Click on the circular edge of a cylindrical or a hole feature. The preview of the thread appears with default parameters in the graphics area, see Figure 10.41. Note that by default, the selected circular edge is used as the start location of the thread. You can define the start location of the thread other than the selected circular edge. To do so, click on the **Optional Start Location** field in the **Thread Location** rollout and then select a vertex, an edge, a plane, or a planar face as the start location of the thread.

The **Offset** check box is used to create the thread at an offset distance from the start location, see Figure 10.42. To create the thread at an offset distance from the start location, select the **Offset** check box. The **Offset Distance** field becomes available below the check box. In this field, enter the offset distance. The **Start Angle** field is used to define the start angle for the helix of the thread. Note that the start angle must be positive.

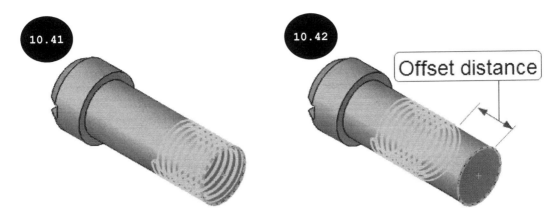

End Condition

The **End Condition** rollout of the PropertyManager is used to specify the end condition or termination for the thread. By default, the **Blind** option is selected in the **End condition** drop-down list of the rollout. As a result, you can enter the depth value for the thread in the **Depth** field. On selecting the **Revolutions** option in the **End Condition** drop-down list, you can specify the number of revolutions for the thread in the **Revolutions** field. On selecting the **Up To Selection** option, the **End Location** field becomes available in the rollout. As a result, you can select a vertex, an edge, a plane, or a planar face as the end condition for the thread.

The **Maintain thread length** check box is used to maintain the constant length of the thread from its starting location. Note that this check box is enabled only if the **Blind** or the **Revolutions** option is selected in the **End Condition** drop-down list.

Specification

The **Specification** rollout is used to define specifications for the thread such as type and size. The **Type** drop-down list of this rollout is used to select the type of the thread and the **Size** drop-down list is used to select the standard size of the thread.

The **Diameter** field of the **Specification** rollout is used to display the helix diameter of the thread, which depends on the cylindrical edge selected for creating the thread, see Figure 10.43. You can override the helix diameter of the thread by using the **Override Diameter** button. On clicking the **Override Diameter** button, the **Diameter** field is enabled. In this field, you can enter the override value for the helical diameter of the thread. Similarly, on clicking the **Override Pitch** button, the **Pitch** field is enabled for entering the override value for the helix pitch of the thread.

By default, the **Cut Thread** radio button is selected as the thread method in the **Specification** rollout. As a result, the thread is created by removing the material from the model, see Figure 10.44. On selecting the **Extrude Thread** radio button, you can create a thread by adding the material in the features, see Figure 10.45.

> **Note:** While creating a thread on a cylindrical feature by adding material using the **Extrude Thread** radio button, you need to flip the thread profile by selecting the **Mirror Profile** check box. Similarly, while creating a thread on a hole feature by removing the material using the **Cut Thread** radio button, you need to flip the thread profile by selecting the **Mirror Profile** check box.

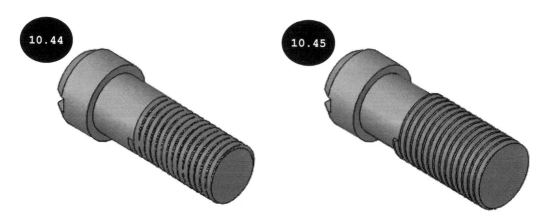

The **Mirror Profile** check box is used to flip the thread profile about its horizontal or vertical axis by using the **Mirror horizontally** or **Mirror vertically** radio button, respectively. Note that these buttons become available as soon as you select the **Mirror Profile** check box. The **Rotation Angle** field is used to specify the rotation angle for the thread helix. On clicking the **Locate Profile** button, the profile of the thread is zoomed such that you can change the sketch points or vertices of the thread profile.

Thread Options

The **Thread Options** rollout is used to select the thread direction (clockwise or counter-clockwise) and align the thread to the start and end faces of the feature, see Figure 10.46. By default, the **Right-hand thread** radio button is selected. As a result, the resultant thread is created in the clockwise direction. On selecting the **Left-hand thread** radio button, the resultant thread is created in counter clockwise direction.

In SOLIDWORKS 2017, you can align the thread to start and end faces of the feature by using the **Trim with start face** and **Trim with end face** check boxes of the **Thread Options** rollout, respectively. Figure 10.47 shows the start edge and the end face of the cylindrical feature to be selected for creating the thread by adding the material using the **Extrude Thread** radio button. Figure 10.48 shows the resultant thread feature created when the **Trim with end face** check box is unchecked and Figure 10.49 shows the resultant thread feature created when the **Trim with end face** check box is selected.

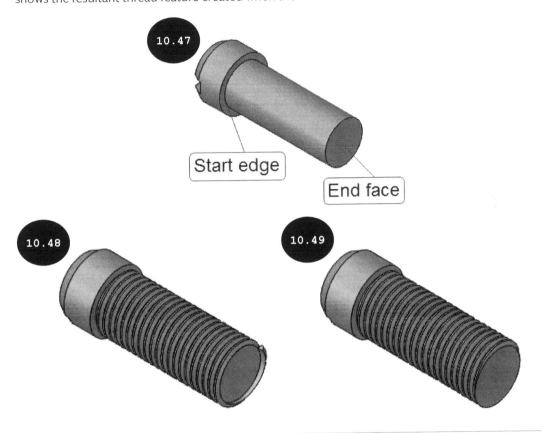

Note: To define the end face of a thread, you need to select the **Up To Selection** option in the **End Condition** drop-down list of the **End Condition** rollout and then select a face as the end face of the thread.

In SOLIDWORKS 2017, you can specify the number of starts for a thread by selecting the **Multiple Start** check box. On selecting this check box, the **Number of Starts** field becomes available in the rollout, which allows you to specify the number of starts for the thread. Note that the number of starts specified in this field define the number of times the thread is created in an equally spaced circular pattern around the feature, see Figure 10.50. In this figure, the thread has been created by specifying 5 as the number of starts for the thread. Note that the pitch of the thread must allow multiple starts for the thread. If the pitch of the thread does not allow multiple starts then the self-intersection between the threads occur which does not allow you to create thread with multiple starts.

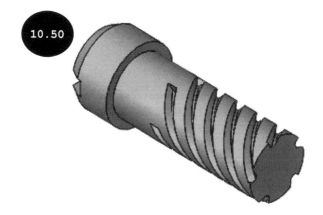

Preview Options
The options in the **Preview Options** rollout is used to specify the type of preview to be appeared in the graphics area.

Procedure for Creating a Thread
1. Click on the down arrow in the **Hole Wizard** tool. A flyout appears.
2. Click on the **Thread** tool in the flyout. The **Thread PropertyManager** appears.
3. Select a circular edge to create the thread.
4. Specify parameters such as end condition, type, and size of the thread.
5. Select the thread method: **Cut thread** or **Extrude thread** radio button in the **Specification** rollout.
6. Select the **Mirror Profile** check box to flip the direction of thread profile, if needed.
7. Click on the green tick mark ✓ in the PropertyManager. The thread is created.

Creating Fillets Updated
A fillet is a curved face of a constant or variable radii and is used to remove sharp edges of a model that may cause injury while handling the model. Figure 10.51 shows a model before and after applying constant radius fillets.

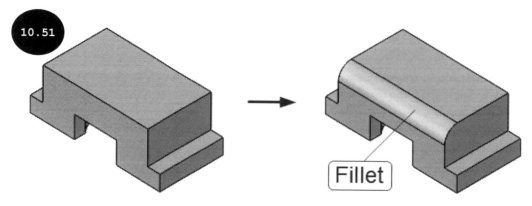

In SOLIDWORKS, you can create fillets by using two methods: Manual and FilletXpert. The Manual method is used to create fillets manually. By using this method, you can create four types of fillets: constant radius fillet, variable radius fillet, face fillet, and full round fillet. On the other hand, the FilletXpert method is used to create fillets automatically. By using this method, you can only create constant radius fillets in a model. The methods of creating different types of fillets manually are as follows:

To create fillets by using the Manual method, click on the **Fillet** tool in the **Features CommandManager**. The **Fillet PropertyManager** appears, see Figure 10.52. If the **FilletXpert PropertyManager** appears on clicking the **Fillet** tool, then click on the **Manual** tab in the PropertyManager to invoke the **Fillet PropertyManager**.

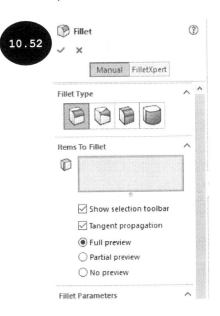

Creating a Constant Radius Fillet

A constant radius fillet is a fillet that has a constant radius throughout the selected edge, see Figure 10.53. You can create a constant radius fillet by clicking on the **Constant Size Fillet** button in the **Fillet Type** rollout of the PropertyManager, see Figure 10.54. The options that become available in different rollouts of the PropertyManager after selecting this button are as follows:

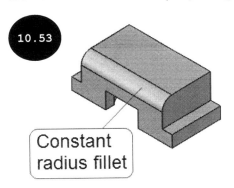

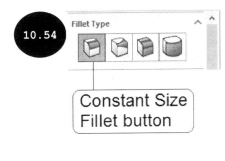

Items To Fillet

The options in the **Items To Fillet** rollout are used to select entities such as edges, faces, and features to create fillet. The options are as follows:

Edges, Faces, Features and Loops

The **Edges, Faces, Features and Loops** field of this rollout is activated by default. As a result, you can select edges, faces, features, or loops for creating a constant radius fillet. As soon as you select edges, faces, features, or loops to create a constant radius fillet, the preview of the constant radius fillet appears in the graphics area with the default radius value.

Note: If you select a face to create a fillet, all the edges of the selected face are filleted, see Figure 10.55 and if you select a feature, all the edges of the selected feature are filleted, see Figure 10.56. Both these figures show the fillet preview.

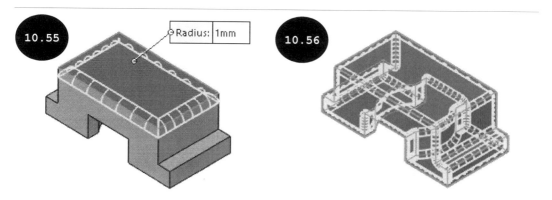

Tangent propagation

The **Tangent propagation** check box is used to apply fillet to all the edges that are tangent to the selected edge. Figure 10.57 shows an edge to be selected for applying fillet. Figures 10.58 and 10.59 show the preview of the resultant fillet when the **Tangent propagation** check box is unchecked and selected, respectively.

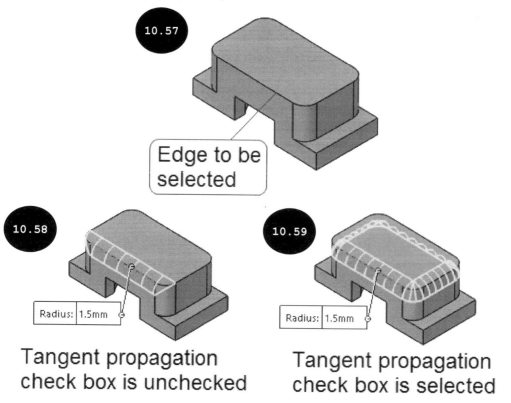

Show selection toolbar

The **Show selection toolbar** check box of the **Items To Fillet** rollout is selected by default. As a result, the **Selection** toolbar appears on selecting an entity for creating a fillet, see Figure 10.60. The tools of the **Selection** toolbar help you in selecting multiple edges of the feature.

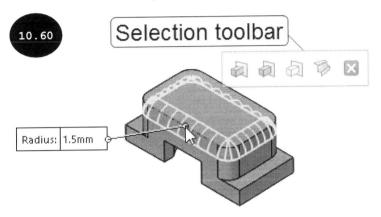

Full preview, Partial preview, and No preview

The **Full preview** radio button is used to display full preview of the fillet, which includes the preview of all fillet edges. On selecting the **Partial preview** radio button, the partial view of the fillet appears. Note that in case of partial preview, the preview appears only in one fillet edge. On selecting the **No preview** radio button, the display of preview is turned off.

Fillet Parameters

The options in the **Fillet Parameters** rollout are used to specify fillet parameters, see Figure 10.61. The options are as follows:

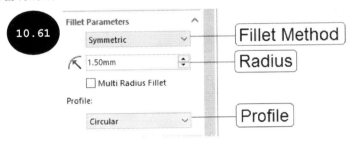

Fillet Method

The **Fillet Method** drop-down list is used to select the type of method to be used for creating the fillet. By selecting the **Symmetric** option, you can create a fillet, which is symmetric on both sides of the edge selected for creating the fillet, see Figure 10.62. When this option is selected, the **Radius** field becomes available in the rollout, which is used to enter symmetric radius of the fillet. On selecting the **Asymmetric** option, the **Distance 1** and **Distance 2** fields become available in the rollout, which are used to specify two different radii for both the sides of the edge, see Figure 10.63.

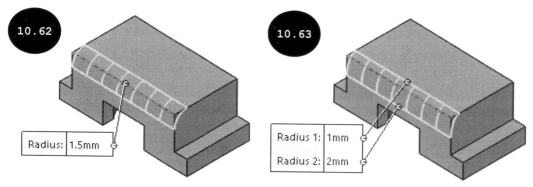

Multiple radius fillet

By selecting the **Multiple radius fillet** check box, you can assign different radius values for the selected edges. For example, if you have selected two edges for applying fillet, then on selecting this check box, you can assign different radius values or control the radius of both the edges, individually. By default, this check box is unchecked. As a result, all edges selected for applying the fillet have the same radius value.

Profile

The **Profile** drop-down list is used to select the type of fillet profile. Note that the fillet profile defines the cross sectional shape of the fillet. You can select the **Circular**, **Conic Rho**, **Conic Radius**, or **Curvature Continuous** option from this drop-down list to define the fillet profile. On selecting the **Circular** option, a fillet of circular shape is created, see Figure 10.64. If you select the **Conic Rho** option, the **Rho** field becomes available below this drop-down list. In this field, you can specify the Rho value for the fillet. Note that the Rho value is between 0 and 1, see Figures 10.65 through 10.67.

Tip: If the Rho value is less than 0.5 then the fillet profile is of elliptical shape. If the Rho value is 0.5 then the fillet profile is of parabola shape. If the Rho value is greater than 0.5 then the fillet profile is of hyperbola shape.

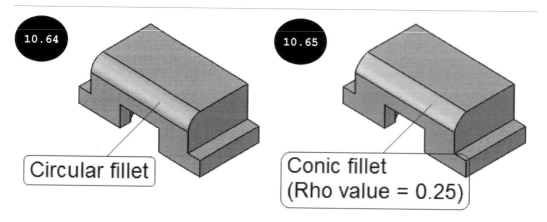

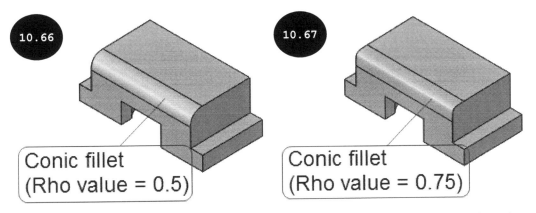

By selecting the **Conic Radius** option, the **Conic radius** field appears below the drop-down list, which is used to specify the radius of curvature at the corner of the fillet. By selecting the **Curvature Continuous** option, a fillet is created such that it maintains a smoother curvature between the adjacent faces of the edge selected for creating the fillet.

Setback Parameters

The options in the **Setback Parameters** rollout are used to define parameters for creating a setback fillet. A setback fillet is a fillet that has a smooth transition from fillet edges to a common intersecting vertex. You can create a setback fillet on three or more than three edges that are intersecting at a common vertex, see Figure 10.68. This figure shows the preview of a setback fillet. To create a setback fillet, expand the **Setback Parameters** rollout by clicking on the arrow, which is available at its title bar, see Figure 10.69. The options in the **Setback Parameters** rollout are as follows:

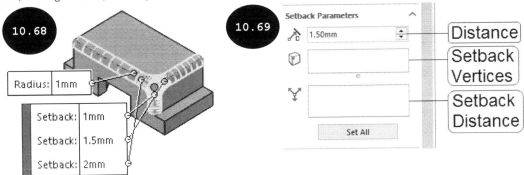

Setback Vertices
The **Setback Vertices** field is used to select a vertex where the fillet edges intersect each other.

Distance
The **Distance** field is used to specify the fillet setback distance, which is calculated from the selected setback vertex.

Setback Distances
The **Setback Distances** field is used to specify the setback distance for the individual edge of the fillet from the setback vertex. Note that as soon as you select the setback vertex, a list of corresponding edges appears in this field. To assign the setback distance to an edge, select

an edge from this field and then enter the setback distance in the **Distance** field. Next, press ENTER. Similarly, you can assign the setback distance to other edges of the setback fillet. Figure 10.68 shows the preview of a setback fillet with different setback distances assigned with respect to a setback vertex.

Set All
The **Set All** button is used to assign the current setback distance to all the edges listed under the **Setback Distance** field.

Fillet Options
The **Fillet Options** rollout is shown in Figure 10.70. The options in this rollout are as follows:

Select through faces
By selecting the **Select through faces** check box, you can select the invisible edges of the model for applying fillets, see Figure 10.71. In this figure, three edges are visible and the fourth edge is not visible from the front. You can select the invisible edges of the model from the front when the **Select through faces** check box is selected.

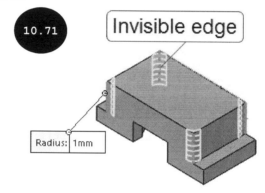

Keep features
After selecting the **Keep features** check box, if you apply a fillet of large radius which covers the other feature (extruded boss or cut) of a model, then the fillet is created such that the covered feature remains available in the model. However, if you uncheck this check box, then the fillet is created such that the covered feature is no longer available in the model. Figure 10.72 shows the preview of a fillet with large radius, which covers a cylindrical feature of the model. Figures 10.73 and 10.74 show the resultant model after creating the fillet when the **Keep features** check box is selected and unchecked, respectively.

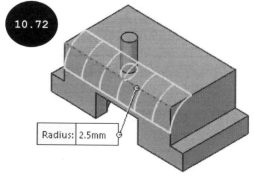

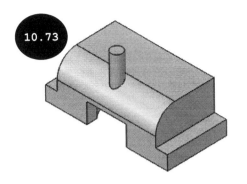
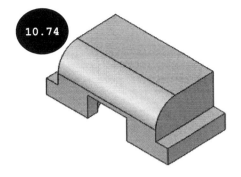

Note: In SOLIDWORKS 2017, after creating a constant radius fillet, you can convert it into a chamfer and vice-versa. To convert a constant radius fillet into a chamfer, select the constant radius fillet in the FeatureManager Design Tree or in the graphics area. A Pop-up toolbar appears near the cursor. In this Pop-up toolbar, click on the **Edit Feature** tool. The **Fillet PropertyManager** appears. In this PropertyManager, click on the **Chamfer Type** button to convert the selected fillet into the chamfer. Next, click on the green tick mark button.

Procedure for Creating a Constant Radius Fillet
1. Click on the **Fillet** tool. The **Fillet PropertyManager** appears.
2. Make sure that the **Constant Size Fillet** button is selected in the **Fillet Type** rollout.
3. Select edges, faces, features, or loops to create constant radius fillet.
4. Specify the radius value of the fillet in the **Radius** field of the **Fillet Parameters** rollout.
5. Click on the green tick mark in the PropertyManager. The constant radius fillet is created.

Creating a Variable Radius Fillet
A variable radius fillet is a fillet that has variable radii, see Figure 10.75. You can create a variable radius fillet by using the **Variable Size Fillet** button of the **Fillet Type** rollout. When this button is activated, the options in the PropertyManager appear as shown in Figure 10.76. The options are as follows:

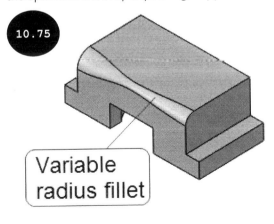
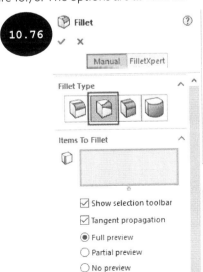

Items To Fillet

The **Edges, Faces, Features and Loops** field of the **Items To Fillet** rollout is activated by default. As a result, you can select edges, faces, features, or loops for creating variable radius fillet. The other options of the **Items To Fillet** rollout are the same as those discussed earlier, while creating the constant radius fillet.

Variable Radius Parameters

The options in the **Variable Radius Parameters** rollout are used to define variable radius fillet, see Figure 10.77. The options are as follows:

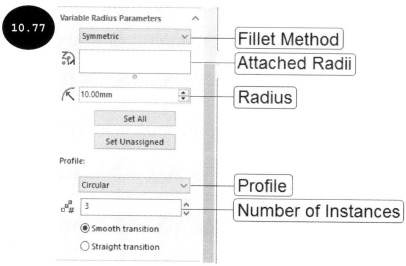

Attached Radii

The **Attached Radii** field displays a list of all vertices and control points of the selected edge or edges for defining a variable radii.

Number of Instances

The **Number of Instances** field is used to specify the number of control points on the selected edge for defining variable radii. After specifying the number of control points, press ENTER. The pink dots representing control points appear along the edge selected for applying the fillet, see Figure 10.78. You can specify a different fillet radius for each control point.

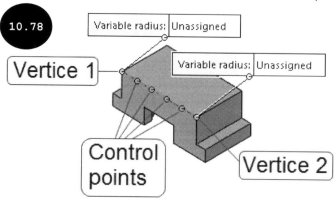

To specify a different radius value for each control point, click on the control points appeared in the graphics area one by one. The callouts having **R** and **P** fields appear attached to the control points in the graphics area, see Figure 10.79. By using the **R** field of a callout, you can specify the radius value for the control point and by using the **P** field, you can specify the location of the control point on the edge in terms of percentage value. Note that by default, the editing mode of the callout fields (R and P) is not enabled. To enable the editing mode, you need to click on the field to be edited.

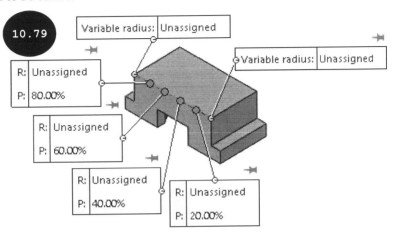

In addition to the display callouts in the graphics area, the name of the selected control points appears in the **Attached Radii** field of the PropertyManager. You can also specify the radius value for a control point by selecting its name in the **Attached Radii** field and then entering the radius value in the **Radius** field of the PropertyManager.

Set All
The **Set All** button is used to assign the radius value specified in the **Radius** field to all the control points and vertices of the edge.

Set Unassigned
The **Set Unassigned** button is used to assign the specified radius value to all control points and vertices whose radius value is not assigned.

Smooth transition
The **Smooth transition** radio button is selected by default. As a result, the variable fillet is created such that the smooth transition is carried out from one radius value to another, see Figure 10.80.

Straight transition
On selecting the **Straight transition** radio button, the linear/straight transition is carried out from one radius value to another, see Figure 10.81.

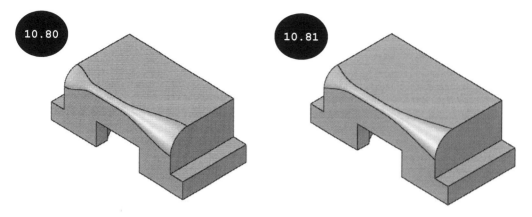

The other options of this rollout and the options of the other rollouts of the PropertyManager are the same as those discussed earlier while creating the constant radius fillet.

Procedure for Creating a Variable Radius Fillet
1. Click on the **Fillet** tool. The **Fillet PropertyManager** appears.
2. Click on the **Variable Size Fillet** button in the **Fillet Type** rollout of the PropertyManager.
3. Select edges, faces, features, or loops to create a variable radius fillet.
4. Specify the number of control points in the **Number of Instances** field of the **Variable Radius Parameters** rollout in the PropertyManager.
5. Click on the control points appeared in the graphics area, one by one.
6. Specify the radius value and location for each control point by using the respective callouts.
7. Click on the green tick mark ✓ in the PropertyManager. The variable radius fillet is created.

Creating a Face Fillet
A face fillet is created between two non-adjacent or non-continuous faces of a model, see Figure 10.82.

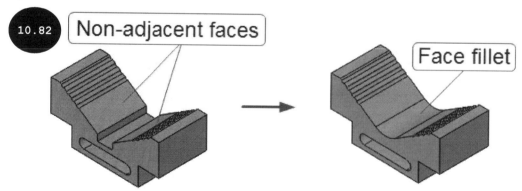

To create a face fillet, invoke the **Fillet PropertyManager**. Next, click on the **Face Fillet** button in the **Fillet Type** rollout of the PropertyManager, see Figure 10.83. When the **Face Fillet** button is activated, the options in the PropertyManager appear, as shown in Figure 10.83. The options are as follows:

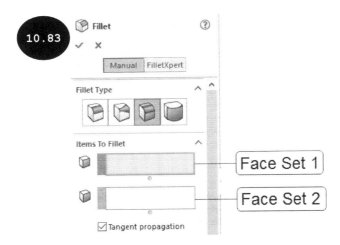

10.83

Items To Fillet

The options of the **Items To Fillet** rollout are used to select non-adjacent faces and are as follows:

Face Set 1
The **Face Set 1** field is used to select the first set of non-continuous faces, see Figure 10.84.

Face Set 2
The **Face Set 2** field is used to select the second set of non-continuous faces of a model, see Figure 10.84. On selecting two non-continuous set of faces, the preview of the face fillet appears, see Figure 10.85. In case the preview of the face fillet does not appear, you need to adjust its radius value.

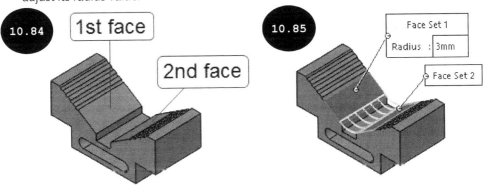

The other options in the PropertyManager are the same as those discussed earlier while creating the constant radius fillet. Once you have specified all the parameters for creating the face fillet, click on the green tick mark in the PropertyManager. The face fillet is created.

Note: In SOLIDWORKS 2017, after creating a face fillet, you can convert it into a chamfer and vice-versa. To convert a face fillet into a chamfer, select the face fillet in the graphics area. A Pop-up toolbar appears. In this Pop-up toolbar, click on the **Edit Feature** tool. The Fillet PropertyManager appears. In this PropertyManager, click on the **Chamfer Type** button to convert the fillet into the chamfer. Next, click on the green tick mark button.

Procedure for Creating a Face Fillet

1. Click on the **Fillet** tool. The **Fillet PropertyManager** appears.
2. Click on the **Face Fillet** button in the **Fillet Type** rollout of the PropertyManager.
3. Select the first non-continuous face of a model.
4. Click on the **Face Set 2** field in the **Items To Fillet** rollout to activate it.
5. Select the second non-continuous face of the model.
6. Specify the fillet radius value in the **Radius** field of the **Fillet Parameters** rollout.
7. Click on the green tick mark ✓ in the PropertyManager. The face fillet is created.

Creating a Full Round Fillet

A full round fillet is created tangent to three adjacent faces of a model, see Figure 10.86.

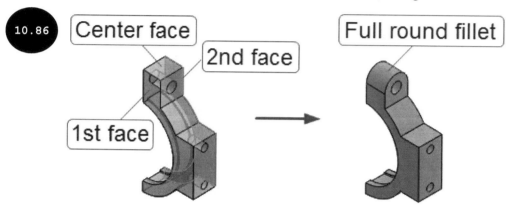

To create a full round fillet, invoke the **Fillet PropertyManager** and then click on the **Full Round Fillet** button in the **Fillet Type** rollout of the PropertyManager, see Figure 10.87. When the **Full Round Fillet** button is activated, the options in the PropertyManager appear as shown in Figure 10.87. The options are as follows:

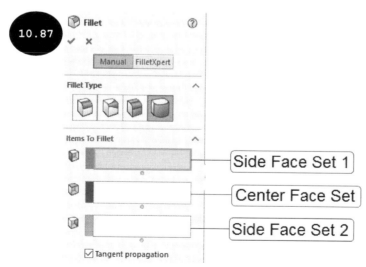

Items To Fillet

The options in the **Items To Fillet** rollout are used to select three adjacent faces for creating the full round fillet. The options are as follows:

Side Face Set 1
The **Side Face Set 1** field is used to select the first or start adjacent face of a model for creating the full round fillet in the graphics area, see Figure 10.88.

Center Face Set
The **Center Face Set** field is used to select the center adjacent face of the model for creating the full round fillet, see Figure 10.88.

Side Face Set 2
The **Side Face Set 2** field is used to select the end adjacent face of the model for creating the full round fillet, see Figure 10.88.

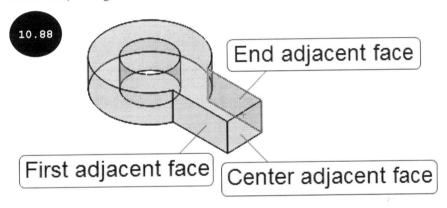

On selecting the three adjacent faces of a model, the preview of the full round fillet appears in the graphics area, see Figure 10.89.

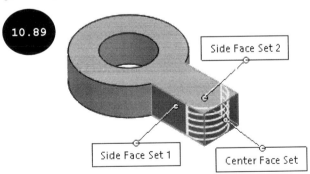

The other options in the PropertyManager are the same as those discussed earlier while creating the constant radius fillet. Once you have specified all the parameters for creating the full round fillet, click on the green tick mark ✓ in the PropertyManager. The full round fillet is created.

518 Chapter 10 > Advanced Modeling - III

Procedure for Creating a Full Round Fillet
1. Click on the **Fillet** tool. The **Fillet PropertyManager** appears.
2. Click on the **Full Round Fillet** button in the **Fillet Type** rollout of the PropertyManager.
3. Select the first adjacent face of a model in the graphics area.
4. Click on the **Center Face Set** field in the **Items To Fillet** rollout to activate it.
5. Select the center adjacent face of the model.
6. Click on the **Side Face Set 2** field in the **Items To Fillet** rollout to activate it.
7. Select the end adjacent face of the model.
8. Click on the green tick mark ✓ in the PropertyManager. The full round fillet is created.

Creating Chamfers Updated

A chamfer is a bevel face that is non perpendicular to its adjacent faces, see Figure 10.90. You can create different types of chamfer: Angle Distance chamfer, Distance Distance chamfer, Vertex chamfer, Offset Face chamfer, and Face Face chamfer.

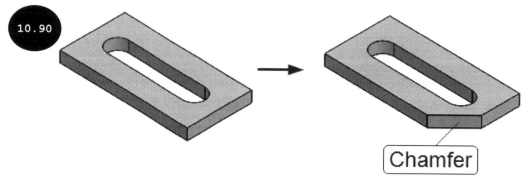

To create a chamfer, click on the down arrow below the **Fillet** tool in the CommandManager. A flyout appears, see Figure 10.91. Next, click on the **Chamfer** tool of the flyout. The **Chamfer PropertyManager** appears, see Figure 10.92. The options in this PropertyManager are as follows:

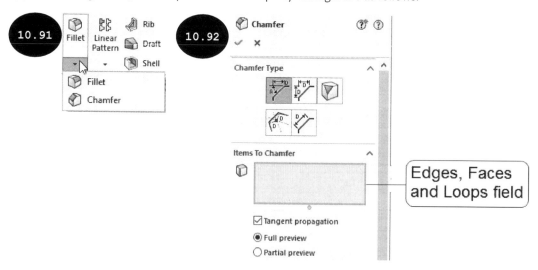

Chamfer Type

The **Chamfer Type** rollout of the PropertyManager is used to select the type of chamfer to be created by clicking on the respective button in this rollout, see Figure 10.93. The different types of chamfer are as follows:

Figure 10.93

Angle Distance Chamfer

The **Angle Distance** button of the **Chamfer Type** rollout is used to create an Angle Distance chamfer by specifying its angle and distance values. To create a chamfer by specifying its angle and distance values, click on the **Angle Distance** button and then select edges, faces, or loops as the entities to create chamfer. As soon as you select an entity, the preview of the chamfer with a default angle and distance values appears in the graphics area, see Figure 10.94. You can specify the required angle and distance values of the chamfer by using the **Angle** and **Distance** fields of the **Chamfer Parameters** rollout in the PropertyManager, see Figure 10.95. You can also specify the distance and angle values of the chamfer by using the callout that appears in the preview of the chamfer. Note that in the preview of a chamfer, an arrow appears that points to the direction of the distance value measured. You can flip the direction of the distance value by selecting the **Flip direction** check box in the **Chamfer Parameters** rollout.

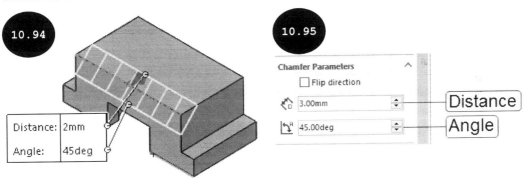

Figure 10.94, Figure 10.95

Note: On selecting a face as the entity to chamfer, all the edges of the selected face get selected to apply chamfer.

Distance Distance Chamfer

The **Distance Distance** button is used to create a Distance Distance chamfer by specifying symmetric or asymmetric distance values on both sides of the chamfer edge. To create a chamfer by specifying symmetric or asymmetric distance values, click on the **Distance Distance** button in the **Chamfer Type** rollout of the PropertyManager and then select edges, faces, or loops as the entities to create chamfer. As soon as you select an entity, the preview of the chamfer with default parameters appears in the graphics area, see Figure 10.96. Note that if the **Symmetric** option is selected in the **Chamfer**

Method drop-down list of the **Chamfer Parameters** rollout then the **Distance** field is available in the **Chamfer Parameters** rollout, see Figure 10.97. Also, the preview of the chamfer appears such that the value specified in the **Distance** field is symmetric on both sides of the selected entity, see Figure 10.96.

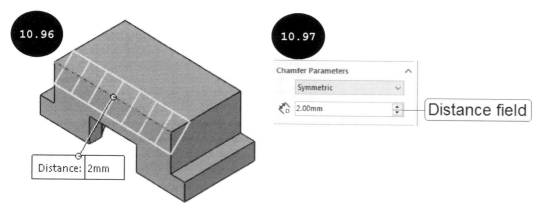

By selecting the **Asymmetric** option in the **Chamfer Method** drop-down list of the **Chamfer Parameters** rollout, the **Distance 1** and **Distance 2** fields become available in the rollout, see Figure 10.98. In these fields, you can specify different distance values on both sides of the selected entity, see Figure 10.99. You can also specify the required distance values of the chamfer by using the callout, which appears in the preview of the chamfer.

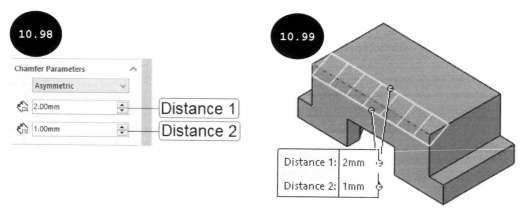

Vertex Chamfer

The **Vertex** button of the **Chamfer Type** rollout is used to create a Vertex chamfer on a vertex of a model. To create a chamfer on a vertex, click on the **Vertex** button in the **Chamfer Type** rollout of the PropertyManager and then select a vertex of the model. The preview of a chamfer with default parameters appears in the graphics area, see Figure 10.100. Also, the **Distance 1**, **Distance 2**, and **Distance 3** fields appear in the **Chamfer Parameters** rollout, see Figure 10.101. These fields are used to specify different distance values on all sides of the selected vertex. If you select the **Equal distance** check box in the rollout, only the **Distance** field becomes available and the distance specified in this field is equally applied on all sides of the vertex.

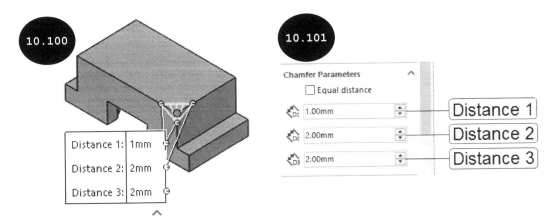

Offset Face Chamfer

The **Offset Face** button of the **Chamfer Type** rollout is used to create multiple chamfers of different sizes. To create multiple chamfers of different sizes, click on the **Offset Face** button and then select multiple edges of a model one by one. The preview of multiple chamfers with default parameters appears in the graphics area. Select the **Symmetric** option in the **Chamfer Parameters** rollout and then select the **Multi Distance Chamfer** check box. A callout attached to each selected edge of the model appears in the preview, see Figure 10.102. By using these callout, you can specify different distance values for each chamfer edge. Note that to specify a distance value in a callout, click on the default value specified in the callout and then specify the new distance value. In addition to selecting edges for creating the Offset Face chamfer, you can also select faces, features, and loops. The other options of the PropertyManager for creating the Offset Face chamfer are same as those discussed earlier. Next, click on the green tick mark in the PropertyManager. The multiple chamfers of different sizes are created as a single feature.

Note: The chamfer created by using the **Offset Face** button can be converted to a fillet and vice-versa. To convert an Offset Face chamfer into a fillet, select an Offset Face chamfer in the FeatureManager Design Tree or in the graphics area and then right-click to display a shortcut menu. In this shortcut menu, click on the **Convert Chamfer to Fillet** option, see Figure 10.103. The Offset Face chamfer gets converted to a fillet. Similarly, you can convert the fillet back to the chamfer.

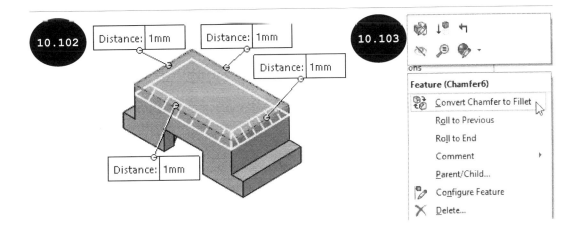

Face Face Chamfer

The **Face Face** button of the **Chamfer Type** rollout is used to create a Face Face chamfer between non-adjacent or non-continuous faces of a model. To create a chamfer between non-adjacent or non-continuous faces of a model, click on the **Face Face** button in the **Chamfer Type** rollout of the **Chamfer PropertyManager**. The **Face Set 1** and **Face Set 2** fields become available in the **Items To Chamfer** rollout, see Figure 10.104. The **Face Set 1** field is activated, by default. As a result, you can select the first set of non-adjacent faces. After selecting the first set of non-adjacent faces, click on the **Face Set 2** field to activate it. Next, select the second set of non-adjacent faces. The preview of the chamfer appears in the graphics area with default parameters, see Figure 10.105. In this figure, two non-adjacent faces are selected for creating the chamfer. In case, the preview of the chamfer does not appear, you need to adjust its distance value in the **Offset Distance** field of the **Chamfer Parameters** rollout.

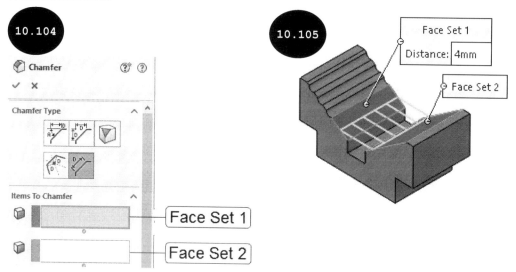

The remaining options in the PropertyManager are the same as those discussed earlier. Next, click on the green tick mark button in the PropertyManager. The chamfer is created.

> **Note:** The chamfer created by using the **Face Face** button can be converted to a fillet and vice-versa. To convert a chamfer into a fillet, select the chamfer in the FeatureManager Design Tree or in the graphics and then right-click to display a shortcut menu. In this shortcut menu, click on the **Convert Chamfer to Fillet** option. The selected chamfer gets converted to a fillet. Similarly, you can convert the fillet back to the chamfer.

Procedure for Creating a Chamfer

1. Click on the **Chamfer** tool. The **Chamfer PropertyManager** appears.
2. Select the required type of chamfer to be created by clicking on the respective button in the **Chamfer Type** rollout of the PropertyManager.
3. Select the entities to be chamfered. Note that the selection of entities depends upon the type of chamfer selected. The preview of the chamfer with default parameters appears.
4. Specify the required chamfer parameters in the **Chamfer Parameters** rollout of the

PropertyManager. Note that the availability of chamfer parameters depends upon the type of chamfer selected.

5. Click on the green tick mark ✓ in the PropertyManager. The chamfer is created.

Creating Rib Features

Rib features act as supporting features and are generally used to increase the strength of a model. You can create a rib feature from an open or closed sketch by adding thickness in a specified direction. Figure 10.106 shows a model with an open sketch as well as the resultant rib feature created.

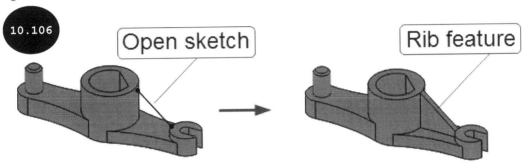

10.106

To create a rib feature, create an open sketch on a plane that intersects with the model, see Figure 10.107. Note that the projection of both the ends of the sketch should lie on the geometry of the model. After creating the sketch of the rib feature, click on the **Rib** tool in the **Features CommandManager**. The **Rib PropertyManager** appears and you are promoted to select either a sketching plane for creating the sketch of the rib feature or an existing sketch of the rib feature. If you have already created a sketch for the rib feature, then select it from the graphics area. The modified **Rib PropertyManager** appears as shown in Figure 10.108. Also, the preview of the rib feature appears in the graphics area, see Figure 10.109. The options in the PropertyManager are as follows:

Note: If the sketch of the rib feature has been selected before invoking the **Rib** tool, then on invoking the tool, the modified **Rib PropertyManager** appears as shown in Figure 10.108. Also, the preview of the rib feature appears in the graphics area.

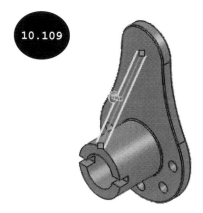

Figure 10.109

Parameters

The options in the **Parameters** rollout of the PropertyManager are used to specify parameters of the rib feature. The options are as follows:

Thickness

The **Thickness** area of the **Parameters** rollout has three buttons: **First Side**, **Both Sides**, and **Second Side**. On selecting the **First Side** button, thickness is added to one side of the rib sketch. On selecting the **Both Sides** button, thickness is equally added to both sides of the rib sketch. On selecting the **Second Side** button, thickness is added to the second or the other side of the sketch.

Rib Thickness

The **Rib Thickness** field is used to specify the thickness value of the rib feature.

Extrusion direction

The **Extrusion direction** area has two buttons: **Parallel to Sketch** and **Normal to Sketch**. On selecting the **Parallel to Sketch** button, the rib feature is created by adding material parallel to the sketch. On selecting the **Normal to Sketch** button, the rib feature is created by adding material normal to the sketch. Figure 10.110 shows a sketch of a rib feature. Figures 10.111 and 10.112 show the resultant rib feature created by selecting the **Parallel to Sketch** and **Normal to Sketch** buttons, respectively.

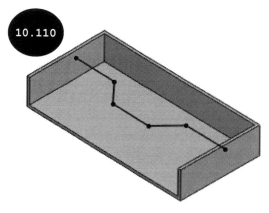

Figure 10.110

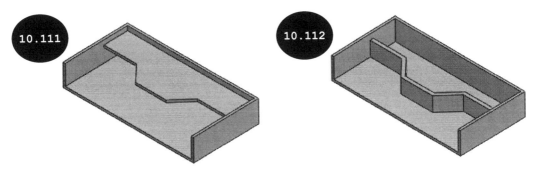

Flip material side
The **Flip material side** check box is used to flip the direction of extrusion of the rib feature.

Draft On/Off
The **Draft On/Off** button is used to add draft to the rib feature. On activating this button, the **Draft Angle** field and the **Draft outward** check box become available in the PropertyManager. By using the **Draft Angle** field, you can specify the draft angle value of the rib feature. Note that by default, the draft angle is added inward to the sketch of the rib feature. To add the draft angle outward to the sketch, select the **Draft outward** check box.

Selected Contours
The **Selected Contours** rollout is used to select the required contour of the sketch for creating the rib feature.

Procedure for Creating a Rib Feature
1. Click on the **Rib** tool in the **Features CommandManager**. The **Rib PropertyManager** appears.
2. Select the sketch of the rib feature in the graphics area.
3. Specify the thickness of rib feature in the **Rib Thickness** field of the PropertyManager.
4. Specify the direction of extrusion of the rib feature by clicking on the **Parallel to Sketch** button or the **Normal to Sketch** button in the PropertyManager.
5. Select the **Flip material side** check box to flip the direction of material side, if required.
6. Click on the green tick mark in the PropertyManager. The rib feature is created.

Creating Shell Features
A shell feature is a thin walled feature, which is created by making a model hollow from inside, see Figure 10.113. In this figure, the models are shown in 'hidden line visible' display style for clarity.

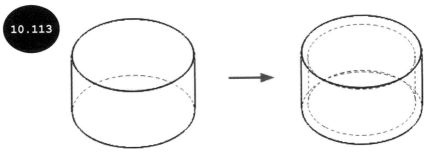

Chapter 10 > Advanced Modeling - III

To create a shell feature, click on the **Shell** tool in the **Features CommandManager**. The **Shell PropertyManager** appears, see Figure 10.114. The options in this PropertyManager are as follows:

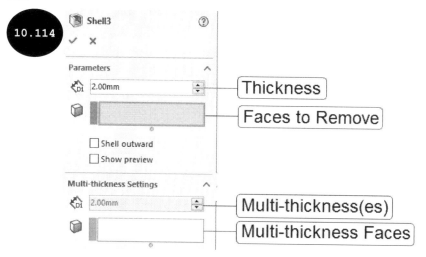

Parameters
The options in the **Parameters** rollout are used to specify parameters for creating the shell feature. The options are as follows:

Thickness
The **Thickness** field is used to specify wall thickness for the shell feature. Note that the thickness specified in this field is applied to all walls of the feature, such that a shell feature with uniform thickness is created.

Faces to Remove
The **Faces to Remove** field is used to select faces of the model to be removed. Figure 10.115 shows a face of a model to be removed and Figure 10.116 shows the resultant model after creating the shell feature. Note that if you do not select any face to be removed then a closed hollow model is created.

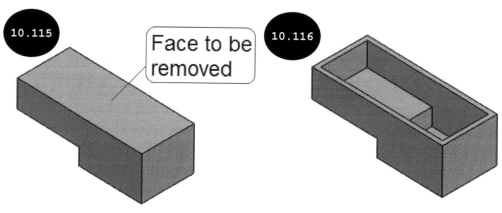

Shell outward
On selecting the **Shell outward** check box, thickness is added outward to the model.

Show preview
On selecting the **Show preview** check box, the preview of the shell feature appears in the graphics area.

Multi-thickness Settings
The options in the **Multi-thickness Settings** rollout of the PropertyManager are used to create multi-thickness shell feature. The option are as follows:

Multi-thickness Faces
The **Multi-thickness Faces** field is used to select faces of a model on which thickness is to be applied other than the one specified in the **Thickness** field of the **Parameters** rollout. As soon as you select a face, the **Multi-thickness(es)** field gets enabled, which allows you to specify thickness value for the selected face of the model. You can select multiple faces of the model and apply different thickness values to them. Figure 10.117 shows a shell model with multi-thickness walls.

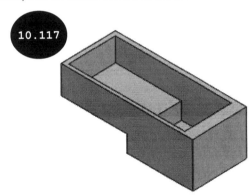

Procedure for Creating a Shell Feature with Uniform Thickness
1. Click on the **Shell** tool in the **Features CommandManager**. The **Shell PropertyManager** appears.
2. Enter wall thickness for the shell feature in the **Thickness** field.
3. Select a face or faces to be removed from the model, if needed.
4. Click on the green tick mark ✓ in the PropertyManager. The shell feature is created.

Procedure for Creating a Shell Feature with Multi-Thickness
1. Click on the **Shell** tool. The **Shell PropertyManager** appears.
2. Enter wall thickness for the shell feature in the **Thickness** field.
3. Select a face or faces to be removed from the model, if needed.
4. Click on the **Multi-thickness Faces** field in the **Multi-thickness Settings** rollout.
5. Select a face or faces of the model to apply different thickness values. The names of the selected faces appear in the **Multi-thickness Faces** field of the PropertyManager.

528 Chapter 10 > Advanced Modeling - III

6. Specify thickness value for each selected face in the **Multi-thickness(es)** field one by one. Note that the thickness value specified in the **Multi-thickness(es)** field is applied to the face currently selected in **Multi-thickness Faces** field.
7. Click on the green tick mark ✓ in the PropertyManager. The multi-thickness shell feature is created.

Creating Wrap Features Updated

A Wrap feature is created by wrapping a sketch onto a face or faces of a model, see Figure 10.118. This figure shows a sketch to be wrapped, a face, and the resultant model after wrapping the sketch onto the face of the model.

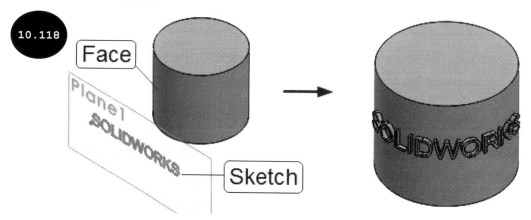

10.118

To wrap a sketch onto a face, select a sketch to be wrapped either from the FeatureManager Design Tree or from the graphics area and then click on the **Wrap** tool in the **Features CommandManager**. The **Wrap PropertyManager** appears, see Figure 10.119. The options in the PropertyManager are as follows:

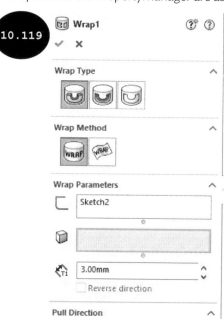

10.119

Wrap Type
The options in the **Wrap Type** rollout of the PropertyManager are used to select the type of wrap: emboss, deboss, or scribe to be created. The options are as follows:

Emboss
The **Emboss** button in the **Wrap Type** rollout is used to create a wrap feature by adding the material on the face, refer to Figure 10.118.

Deboss
The **Deboss** button is used to create a wrap feature by removing the material from the face of the model, see Figure 10.120.

Scribe
The **Scribe** button is used to create a wrap feature by splitting the face of the model such that an imprint of the sketch is created on the face, see Figure 10.121.

Wrap Method
The options in the **Wrap Method** rollout of the PropertyManager are used to select a method for creating the wrap feature. You can create a wrap feature by using two methods: Analytical or Spline Surface. The options are as follows:

Analytical
The **Analytical** button of the **Wrap Method** rollout is used to wrap a sketch completely around a cylindrical or a conical face of a model. Note that by using this button, you can wrap a sketch only onto planar or non-planar faces of cylindrical, conical, extruded, or revolved features of a model.

Spline Surface
The **Spline Surface** button of the **Wrap Method** rollout is used to create a wrap feature by wrapping a sketch onto any face of a model. However, by using this method, you cannot wrap a sketch completely around a cylindrical or conical face of a model.

Wrap Parameters
The options in the **Wrap Parameters** rollout are used to specify parameters for creating the wrap feature, see Figure 10.122. The options are as follows:

Source Sketch
The **Source Sketch** field of the PropertyManager is used to select a sketch to be wrapped. Note that if you select a sketch before invoking the **Wrap PropertyManager** then the name of the selected sketch appears in this field, which indicates that the sketch is selected, see Figure 10.122.

Face for Wrap Sketch
The **Face for Wrap Sketch** field is used to select a face or faces of a model for wrapping the sketch. Note that if the **Analytical** button is selected in the **Wrap Method** rollout then you can only select planar or non planar faces of cylindrical, conical, extruded, or revolved features of a model.

Thickness
The **Thickness** field is used to specify thickness of the wrap feature. Note that this field becomes available only if the **Emboss** button is selected in the **Wrap Type** rollout, which is used to create a wrap feature by adding the material on the face.

Depth
The **Depth** field is used to specify the depth of the wrap feature. Note that this field becomes available only if the **Deboss** button is selected in the **Wrap Type** rollout, which is used to create a wrap feature by removing the material on the face.

Reverse Direction
The **Reverse Direction** check box is used to reverse the direction of projection, see Figures 10.123 and 10.124.

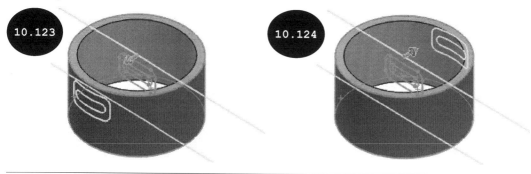

Tutorial 1

Create the model shown in Figure 10.125. All dimension are in mm.

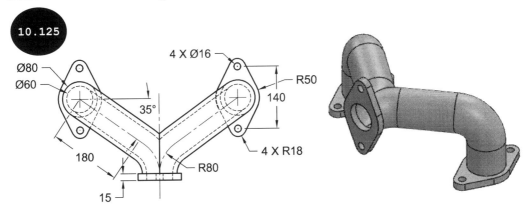

Section 1: Starting SOLIDWORKS
1. Double-click on the SOLIDWORKS icon on your desktop to start SOLIDWORKS.

Section 2: Invoking the Part Modeling Environment
1. Invoke the Part modeling environment by using the **New** tool in the **Standard** toolbar.

Section 3: Specifying Unit Settings
1. Make sure that the **MMGS** (millimeter, gram, second) unit system is set for the currently opened part document.

Section 4: Creating the 3D Path - Sweep Feature
The base feature of the model is a sweep feature. To create this sweep feature, you need to create a 3D sketch as the path of the sweep feature.

1. Click on the **Sketch** tab in the CommandManager to display the tools of the **Sketch** CommandManager.

2. Click on the down arrow below the **Sketch** button in the **Sketch** CommandManager. The **Sketch** flyout appears, see Figure 10.126.

3. Click on the **3D Sketch** tool in the **Sketch** flyout. The 3D Sketching environment is invoked.

4. Click on the **Line** tool in the **Sketch CommandManager**. The **Line** tool is invoked and the display of **XY** appears near the cursor, see Figure 10.127.

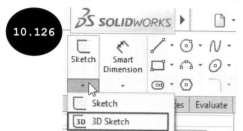

Note: The display of XY near the cursor indicates that the XY (Front) plane is the current sketching plane. You can press the TAB key to switch between the sketching planes for creating a 3D sketch.

5. Move the cursor to the origin and then click to specify the start point of the line when the cursor snaps to the origin.

6. Move the cursor vertically upward and click to specify the endpoint of the line when the length of the line appears close to 120 mm near the cursor, see Figure 10.128.

7. Press the TAB key twice to activate the ZX plane (Top plane) as the sketching plane, see Figure 10.129.

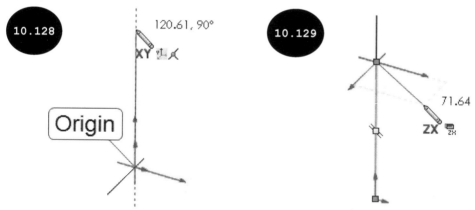

8. Move the cursor toward right at an angle to the X axis, see Figure 10.130. Next, click to specify the endpoint of the second line when the length of the line appears close to 180 mm near the cursor, see Figure 10.130.

9. Move the cursor away from the last specified point and then move it back to the last specified point. A dot appears at the endpoint in the graphics area, see Figure 10.131.

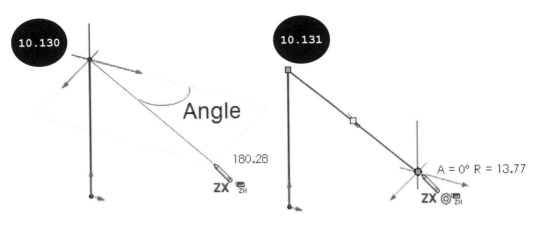

10. Move the cursor for a little distance toward the right. The arc mode gets activated and the preview of a tangent arc appears in the graphics area, see Figure 10.132.

11. Click to specify the endpoint of the arc when the radius of the arc appears close to 80 mm, see Figure 10.132.

12. Right-click in the graphics area. A shortcut menu appears. Next, click on the **Select** option in the shortcut menu to exit the **Line** tool.

13. Invoke the **Centerline** tool and then create a horizontal centerline along the X axis direction of any length by specifying its start point at the endpoint of the first line entity, see Figure 10.133. Next, exit the **Centerline** tool.

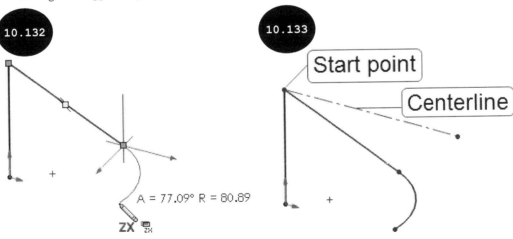

Section 5: Applying Dimensions

1. Click on the **Smart Dimension** tool and then click on the vertical line (first line entity) in the graphics area. The linear dimension is attached to the cursor.

2. Click in the graphics area to specify the placement point for the attached dimension. The **Modify** dialog box appears.

534 Chapter 10 > Advanced Modeling - III

3. Enter **120** in the **Modify** dialog box and then click on the green tick mark ✓ button. The length of the line changes to 120 mm and the dimension is applied to the line, see Figure 10.134.

4. Click on the inclined line (second line entity) in the graphics area to apply dimension. The dimension is attached to the cursor.

5. Click in the graphics area to specify the placement point for the dimension attached to the cursor. The **Modify** dialog box appears.

6. Enter **180** in the **Modify** dialog box and then click on the green tick mark ✓ button. The length of the line changes to 180 mm and the dimension is applied to the line, see Figure 10.135.

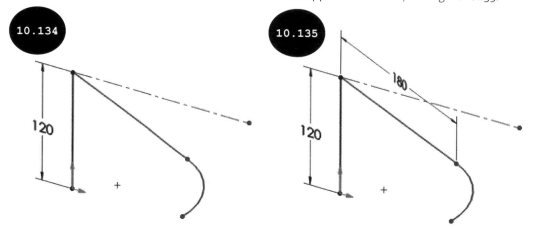

7. Click on the inclined line (second line entity) and then the horizontal centerline. The angular dimension is attached to the cursor.

8. Click in the graphics area to specify the placement point for the attached dimension. The **Modify** dialog box appears.

9. Enter **35** in the **Modify** dialog box and then click on the green tick mark ✓. The angular dimension is applied between the second line entity and the centerline, see Figure 10.136.

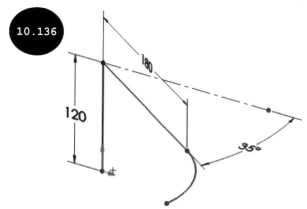

10. Click on the arc sketch entity to apply radius dimension. The radius dimension is attached to the cursor.

11. Click in the graphics area to specify the placement point for the attached dimension. The **Modify** dialog box appears.

12. Enter **80** in the **Modify** dialog box and then click on the green tick mark ✓. The radius of the arc changes to 80 mm and the dimension is applied to the arc, see Figure 10.137.

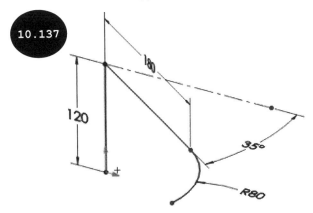

13. Change the current orientation of the sketch to the front view by clicking on the **Front** tool in the **View Orientation** flyout, see Figure 10.138. Alternatively, press CTRL + 1 to change the orientation of the sketch to the front view.

14. Click on the vertical line (first line entity) and then click on the second line entity in the graphics area. The angular dimension appears attached to the cursor.

15. Click in the graphics area to specify the placement point for the angular dimension. The **Modify** dialog box appears.

16. Enter **90** in the **Modify** dialog box and then click on its green tick mark ✓ button. The angular dimension is applied, see Figure 10.139. Next, exit the **Smart Dimension** tool.

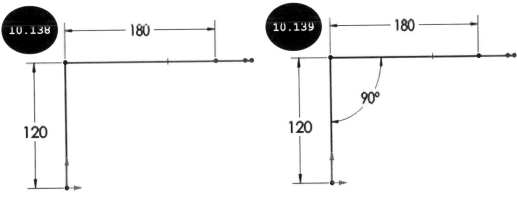

536 Chapter 10 > Advanced Modeling - III

Section 6: Applying Relation
1. Press CTRL + 5 to change the current orientation of the sketch to the top view.

2. Press the CTRL key and then select the center point of the arc as well as the endpoint of the arc in the graphics area, see Figure 10.140. Next, release the CTRL key. A Pop-up toolbar appears near the cursor, see Figure 10.140.

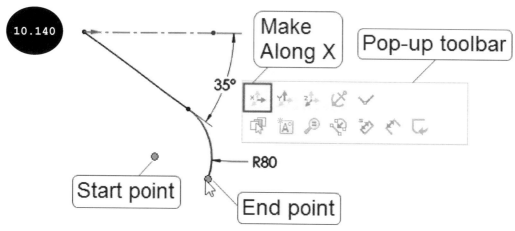

3. Click on the **Make Along X** tool in the Pop-up toolbar. The Along X relation is applied between the center point and the endpoint of the arc.

4. Similarly, apply the Along X relation to the horizontal centerline, if not applied by default.

5. Press CTRL + 7 to change the current orientation of the sketch to isometric.

Section 7: Creating Fillet
1. Click on the **Sketch Fillet** tool in the **Sketch CommandManager**. The **Sketch Fillet** PropertyManager appears.

2. Enter **60** in the **Fillet Radius** field of the **Fillet Parameters** rollout in the PropertyManager.

3. Click on the vertex of the sketch. The preview of the fillet appears, see Figure 10.141.

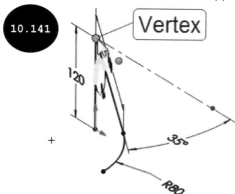

4. Click on the green tick mark ✓ in the PropertyManager. The fillet of radius 60 mm is created on the selected vertex of the sketch. Next, exit the PropertyManager.

5. Exit the 3D Sketching environment by clicking on the **Exit Sketch** tool in the Confirmation Corner, which is available at the top right corner of the graphics area.

Section 8: Creating the Base Feature - Sweep Feature

After creating the path of the sweep feature, you need to create the sweep feature with circular profile.

1. Click on the **Swept Boss/Base** tool in the **Features CommandManager**.  The **Sweep PropertyManager** appears.

2. Click on the **Circular Profile** radio button in the **Profile and Path** rollout.

3. Click on the 3D sketch as the path of the sweep feature in the graphics area. The preview of the sweep feature appears with the default diameter of the circular profile.

4. Enter **80** in the **Diameter** field of the **Profile and Path** rollout and then press ENTER. The preview of the sweep feature appears as shown in Figure 10.142.

5. Click on the green tick mark ✓ in the PropertyManager. The sweep feature is created, see Figure 10.143.

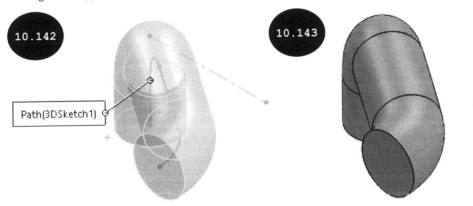

Section 9: Creating the Second Feature - Mirror Feature

The second feature of the model can be created by mirroring the first feature about a reference plane, which passes through the center of the end circular face of the first feature and parallel to the Right plane. To create the reference plane, you need to first create a reference point at the center of the end circular face of the first feature.

1. Invoke the **Reference Geometry** flyout in the **Features CommandManager** and then click on the **Point** tool, see Figure 10.144. The **Point PropertyManager** appears.

538 Chapter 10 > Advanced Modeling - III

2. Click on the end circular face of the first feature (sweep), see Figure 10.145. The preview of the reference point appears at the center of the circular face selected, see Figure 10.145.

3. Click on the green tick mark ✓ in the PropertyManager. The reference point is created.

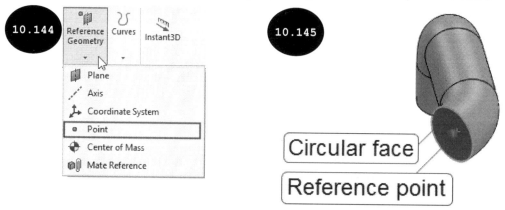

4. Invoke the **Reference Geometry** flyout, refer to Figure 10.144 and then click on the **Plane** tool. The **Plane PropertyManager** appears.

5. Expand the FeatureManager Design Tree, which is now available at the top left corner of the graphics area, by clicking on the arrow in its front.

6. Click on the **Right Plane** in the FeatureManager Design Tree as the first reference. The preview of an offset reference plane appears in the graphics area.

7. Click on the reference point in the graphics area as the second reference. The preview of a reference plane, which is parallel to the Right plane and passes through the reference point appears in the graphics area, see Figure 10.146.

8. Click on the green tick mark ✓ of the PropertyManager. The reference plane is created, see Figure 10.147.

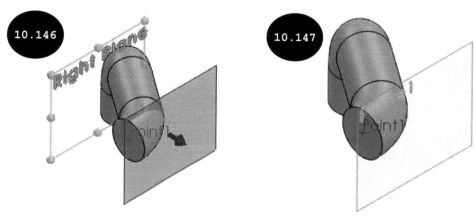

After creating the reference plane, you need to mirror the first feature (sweep).

9. Click on the **Mirror** tool in the **Features CommandManager**. The **Mirror PropertyManager** appears.

10. Click on the newly created reference plane as the mirroring plane.

11. Click on the base feature (sweep feature) as the feature to be mirrored in the graphics area. The preview of the mirror feature appears.

12. Click on the green tick mark in the PropertyManager. The mirror feature is created, see Figure 10.148. Next, hide the reference plane and the reference point in the graphics area.

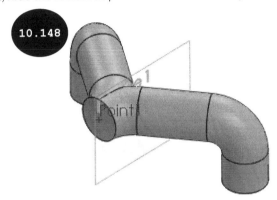

Section 10: Creating the Third Feature - Shell Feature

1. Click on the **Shell** tool in the **Features CommandManager**. The **Shell PropertyManager** appears.

2. Enter **10** in the **Thickness** field of the **Parameters** rollout in the PropertyManager.

3. Click on the three circular faces of the model as the faces to be removed, see Figure 10.149.

4. Click on the green tick mark button. The shell feature is created, see Figure 10.150.

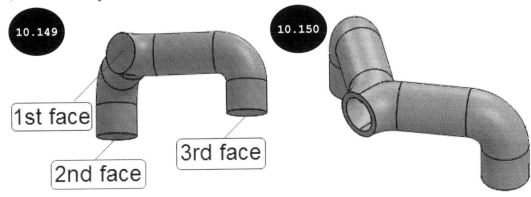

540 Chapter 10 > Advanced Modeling - III

Section 11: Creating the Fourth Feature - Extruded Feature

1. Invoke the Sketching environment by selecting the Top plane as the sketching plane.

2. Press CTRL + 8 to change the orientation of the model as normal to the viewing direction.

3. Create the sketch of the fourth feature (extruded), see Figure 10.151. After creating the sketch, do not exit the Sketching environment.

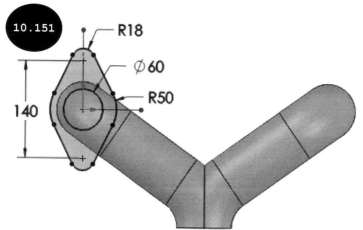

Note: The sketch of the fourth feature shown in Figure 10.151 has been fully defined by applying the required dimensions and relations. You need to apply the tangent relation between each connected line and arc entities of the sketch; symmetric relation between the center points of the upper and lower arcs of the sketch with respect to the horizontal centerline; and equal relation between the upper and lower arcs of the sketch.

4. Click on the **Features** tab in the CommandManager to display the tools of the **Features** CommandManager.

5. Click on the **Extruded Boss/Base** tool in the Features CommandManager. The Boss-Extrude PropertyManager and the preview of the extruded feature appear. Next, change the orientation of the model to isometric.

6. Click on the **Reverse Direction** button in the **Direction 1** rollout of the PropertyManager to reverse the direction of extrusion downward.

7. Enter **15** in the **Depth** field of the **Direction 1** rollout in the PropertyManager.

8. Click on the green tick mark of the PropertyManager. The extruded feature is created, see Figure 10.152.

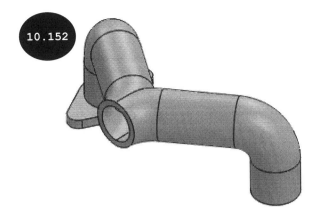

Section 12: Creating the Fifth Feature - Mirror Feature

1. Click on the **Mirror** tool in the **Features CommandManager**. The **Mirror PropertyManager** appears.

2. Expand the FeatureManager Design Tree, which is now available at the top left corner of the graphics area, by clicking on the arrow in its front.

3. Click on the reference plane (Plane 1) created earlier in the FeatureManager Design Tree as the mirroring plane, see Figure 10.153.

4. Click on the fourth feature (previously created extruded feature) as the feature to be mirrored in the graphics area. The preview of the mirror feature appears, see Figure 10.153.

5. Click on the green tick mark ✓ in the PropertyManager. The mirror feature is created.

Section 13: Creating the Sixth Feature - Extruded Feature

1. Invoke the Sketching environment by selecting the front planar face of the model as the sketching plane, see Figure 10.154.

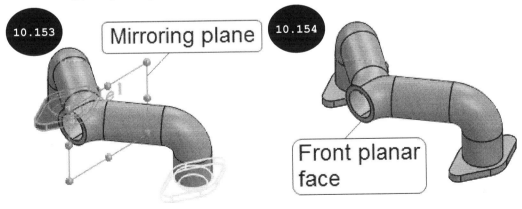

542 Chapter 10 > Advanced Modeling - III

2. Press CTRL + 8 to change the orientation of the model as normal to the viewing direction.

3. Create the sketch of the sixth feature (extruded), see Figure 10.155. After creating the sketch, do not exit the Sketching environment.

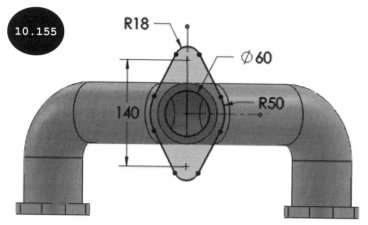

4. Click on the **Features** tab in the CommandManager to display the tools of the **Features CommandManager**.

5. Click on the **Extruded Boss/Base** tool in the **Features CommandManager**. The **Boss-Extrude PropertyManager** and the preview of the extruded feature appear. Next, change the orientation of the model to isometric.

6. Enter **15** in the **Depth** field of the **Direction 1** rollout.

7. Click on the green tick mark ✓ in the PropertyManager. The extruded feature is created, see Figure 10.156.

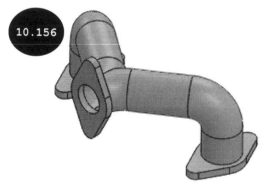

Section 14: Creating the Seventh Feature - Hole Feature

In this section, you need to create holes by using the **Hole Wizard** tool.

1. Click on the **Hole Wizard** tool in the **Features CommandManager**. The **Hole Specification PropertyManager** appears, see Figure 10.157.

2. Click on the **Hole** tool in the **Hole Type** rollout of the PropertyManager.

3. Select the **ANSI Metric** option in the **Standard** drop-down list of the **Hole Type** rollout.

4. Select the **Drill sizes** option in the **Type** drop-down list.

5. Select the **ø16.0** option in the **Size** drop-down list of the **Hole Specifications** rollout.

6. Select the **Up To Next** option in the **End Condition** drop-down list.

7. Make sure that the **Near side countersink** and the **Far side countersink** check boxes are unchecked in the **Options** rollout of the PropertyManager.

   After specifying the hole type as well as the hole specifications, you need to define the placement of the hole.

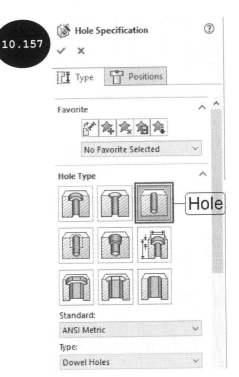

8. Click on the **Positions** tab in the **Hole Specification PropertyManager**. The name of the PropertyManager changes to the **Hole Position PropertyManager**.

9. Move the cursor over the top planar face of the right extruded feature, see Figure 10.158 and then click on the top planar face of the extruded feature as the placement face.

10. Move the cursor over the front semi-circular edge of the right extruded feature, see Figure 10.159. The center point of the semi-circular edge gets highlighted, see Figure 10.159.

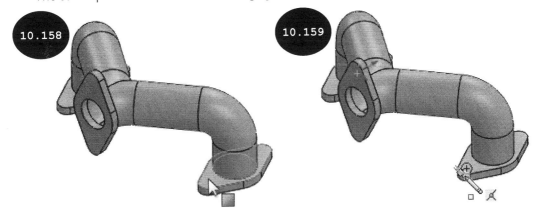

544 Chapter 10 > Advanced Modeling - III

11. Move the cursor over the highlighted center point of the semi-circular edge and then click to specify the center point of the hole when the cursor snaps to it. The preview of the hole appears at the specified location in the graphics area.

12. Similarly, move the cursor over the back semi-circular edge of the right extruded feature, see Figure 10.160. The center point of the semi-circular edge gets highlighted, see Figure 10.160.

13. Move the cursor over the highlighted center point of the semi-circular edge and then click to specify the center point of the hole when the cursor snaps to it. The preview of the hole appears at the specified location in the graphics area.

14. Similarly, move the cursor over the semi-circular edges of the left extruded feature and then specify the center points of the holes on its top planar face, see Figure 10.161.

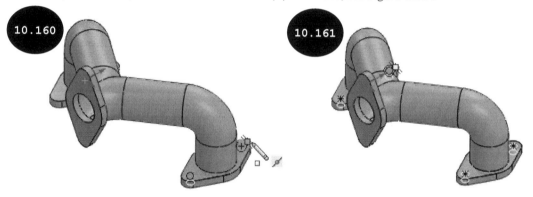

15. Click on the green tick mark ✓ in the PropertyManager. The holes are created, see Figure 10.162. Also, the PropertyManager is closed.

16. Similarly, create holes on the front planar face of the middle extruded feature by using the **Hole Wizard** tool, see Figure 10.163.

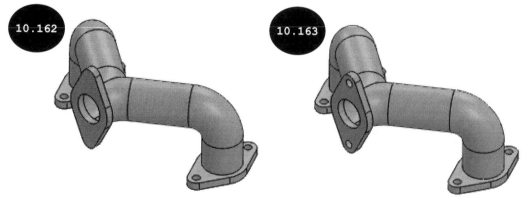

Section 15: Saving the Model

1. Click on the **Save** tool in the **Standard** toolbar. The **Save As** dialog box appears.

2. Browse to the *SOLIDWORKS* folder and then create a folder with the name **Chapter 10**. Next, create another folder with the name **Tutorial** in the *Chapter 10* folder.

3. Enter **Tutorial 1** in the **File name** field of the dialog box as the name of the file and then click on the **Save** button, the model is saved with the name Tutorial 1 in the *Tutorial* folder of *Chapter 10*.

Tutorial 2

Create the model shown in Figure 10.164. All dimensions are in mm.

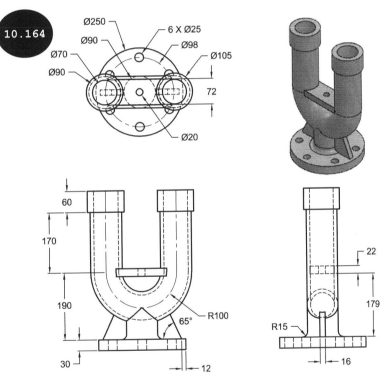

Section 1: Starting SOLIDWORKS
1. Start SOLIDWORKS, if not already started.

Section 2: Invoking the Part Modeling Environment
1. Invoke the Part modeling environment by using the **New** tool in the **Standard** toolbar.

Section 3: Specifying Unit Settings
1. Make sure that the MMGS (millimeter, gram, second) unit system is set for the currently opened part document.

Section 4: Creating the Base Feature - Sweep Feature

The base feature of the model is a sweep feature having circular profile. To create a sweep feature having circular profile, you need to first create its path.

1. Invoke the Sketching environment by selecting the Front plane as the sketching plane.

2. Create the sketch of the path of the sweep feature, see Figure 10.165.

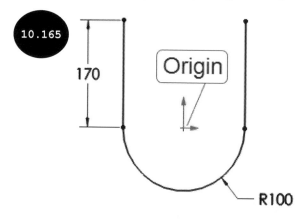

> **Note:** In Figure 10.165, the center point of the arc has coincident relation with the origin. Also, the connecting line and arc entities of the sketch have tangent relations with each other. In addition, the equal relation has been applied between the vertical lines of the sketch.

3. Exit the Sketching environment by clicking on the **Exit Sketch** tool in the **Sketch CommandManager**. Next, press CTRL + 7 to change the orientation of the sketch to isometric.

    After creating the path of the sweep feature, you need to create the sweep feature.

4. Click on the **Swept Boss/Base** tool in the **Features CommandManager**.  The **Sweep PropertyManager** appears.

5. Click on the **Circular Profile** radio button in the **Profile and Path** rollout.

6. Click on the path of the sweep feature in the graphics area. The preview of the sweep feature appears with the default diameter.

7. Enter **90** in the **Diameter** field of the **Profile and Path** rollout and then press ENTER. The preview of the sweep feature appears as shown in Figure 10.166.

8. Expand the **Thin Feature** rollout of the PropertyManager by clicking on the check box available in its title bar, see Figure 10.167.

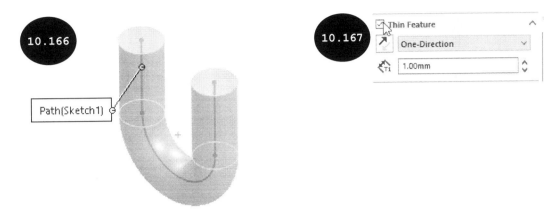

9. Enter 10 in the **Thickness** field of the **Thin Feature** rollout.

10. Click on the **Reverse Direction** button in the **Thin Feature** rollout to reverse the direction of material inward.

11. Click on the green tick mark in the PropertyManager. The sweep feature is created.

Section 5: Creating the Second Feature - Extruded Feature

1. Invoke the Sketching environment by selecting the top planar face of the base feature (sweep) as the sketching plane, see Figure 10.168.

2. Press CTRL + 8 to change the orientation of the model as normal to the viewing direction.

3. Create two circles as the sketch of the second feature, see Figure 10.169. After creating the sketch, do not exit the Sketching environment.

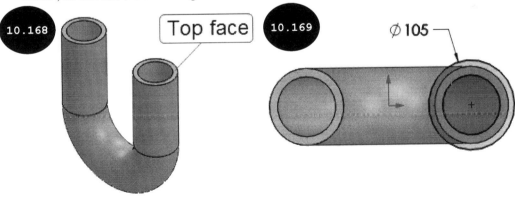

Note: The sketch of the second feature shown in the Figure 10.169 has two circles: outer circle is of diameter 105 mm and the inner circle has coradial relation with the inner circular edge of the sweep feature. This is because the inner circle of the sketch has the same diameter as the inner circular edge of the feature as well as sharing the same center point.

548 Chapter 10 > Advanced Modeling - III

4. Click on the **Features** tab in the CommandManager to display the tools of the **Features** CommandManager.

5. Click on the **Extruded Boss/Base** tool in the **Features** CommandManager. The **Boss-Extrude** PropertyManager and the preview of the extruded feature appear. Next, change the orientation of the model to isometric.

6. Enter **60** in the **Depth** field of the **Direction 1** rollout in the PropertyManager.

7. Click on the green tick mark ✓ in the PropertyManager. The extruded feature is created, see Figure 10.170.

Section 6: Creating the Third Feature - Mirror Feature

1. Click on the **Mirror** tool in the **Features** CommandManager. The **Mirror** PropertyManager appears.

2. Expand the FeatureManager Design Tree, which is now available at the top left corner of the graphics area and then click on the **Right Plane** as the mirroring plane.

3. Click on the second feature (previously created extruded feature) as the feature to be mirrored in the graphics area. The preview of the mirror feature appears in the graphics area.

4. Click on the green tick mark ✓ in the PropertyManager. The mirror feature is created, see Figure 10.171.

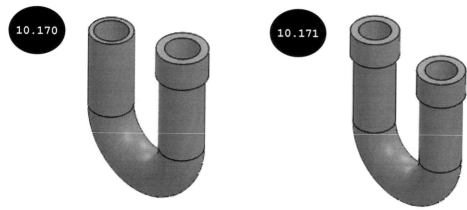

10.170 10.171

Section 7: Creating the Fourth Feature - Extruded Feature

To create the sketch of the fourth extruded feature, you need to create a reference plane at an offset distance from the Top plane.

1. Click on the **Plane** tool in the **Reference Geometry** flyout. The **Plane** PropertyManager appears.

2. Click on the **Top Plane** in the FeatureManager Design Tree as the first reference. The preview of an offset reference plane appears.

3. Enter **190** in the **Distance** field of the **First Reference** rollout in the PropertyManager.

4. Click on the **Flip offset** check box in the rollout to reverse the direction of plane downward.

5. Click on the green tick mark ✓ in the PropertyManager. The reference plane is created, see Figure 10.172.

6. Invoke the Sketching environment by selecting the newly created reference plane as the sketching plane.

7. Press CTRL + 8 to change the orientation of the model as normal to the viewing direction.

8. Create a circle of diameter 90 mm as the sketch of the fourth feature, see Figure 10.173. Note that the center point of the circle is at the origin.

9. Click on the **Features** tab in the CommandManager and then click on the **Extruded Boss/Base** tool. The **Boss-Extrude PropertyManager** and the preview of the extruded feature appear. Next, change the orientation of the model to isometric.

10. Select the **Up To Next** option in the **End Condition** drop-down list of the **Direction 1** rollout.

11. Click on the green tick mark ✓ in the PropertyManager. The extruded feature is created, see Figure 10.174.

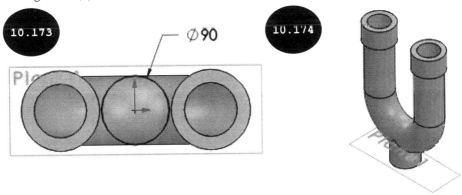

550 Chapter 10 > Advanced Modeling - III

Section 8: Creating the Fifth Feature - Extruded Feature

1. Click on the **Extruded Boss/Base** tool in the **Features CommandManager**. The **Extrude PropertyManager** appears. Also, you are prompted to either select a sketch to be extruded or a sketching plane.

2. Click on the reference plane (Plane 1), which is created at the offset distance of 190 mm from the Top plane as the sketching plane. Next, press CTRL + 8 to change the orientation of the model as normal to the viewing direction.

3. Create a circle of diameter 250 mm as the sketch of the fifth feature, see Figure 10.175.

4. Click on the **Exit Sketch** tool in the **Sketch CommandManager** to exit the Sketching environment. The **Boss-Extrude PropertyManager** and the preview of the extruded feature appear. Next, change the orientation of the model to isometric.

5. Enter 30 in the **Depth** field of the **Direction 1** rollout in the PropertyManager.

6. Click on the **Reverse Direction** button in the **Direction 1** rollout of the PropertyManager to reverse the direction of material downward.

7. Click on the green tick mark ✓ in the PropertyManager. The extruded feature is created, see Figure 10.176.

8. Hide the reference plane. To hide the reference plane, click on the plane. A Pop-up toolbar appears. In this Pop-up toolbar, click on the **Hide** tool.

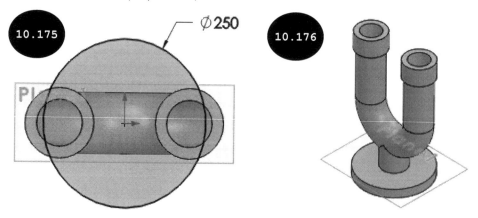

Section 9: Creating the Sixth Feature - Extruded Cut Feature

1. Click on the **Extruded Cut** tool in the **Features CommandManager**. The **Extrude PropertyManager** appears.

2. Click on the top planar face of the fifth feature (previously created extruded feature) as the sketching plane.

3. Press CTRL + 8 to change the orientation of the model as normal to the viewing direction.

4. Create a circle of diameter 25 mm as the sketch of the sixth feature, see Figure 10.177.

Note: In Figure 10.177, the vertical relation has been applied between the center point of the circle and the origin to make the sketch fully defined.

5. Click on the **Exit Sketch** tool in the **Sketch CommandManager** to exit the Sketching environment. The **Cut-Extrude PropertyManager** appears. Next, change the orientation of the model to isometric.

6. Select the **Through All** option in the **End Condition** drop-down list of the **Direction 1** rollout.

7. Click on the green tick mark ✓ in the PropertyManager. The extruded cut feature is created, see Figure 10.178.

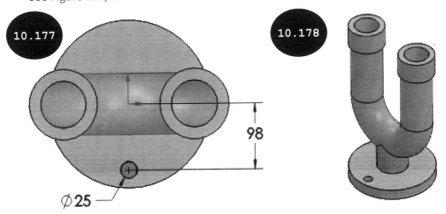

Section 10: Creating the Seventh Feature - Circular Pattern

1. Invoke the **Pattern** flyout by clicking on the down arrow at the bottom of the **Linear Pattern** tool, see Figure 10.179.

2. Click on the **Circular Pattern** tool in the **Pattern** flyout. The **CirPattern PropertyManager** appears.

3. Click on the sixth feature (previously created extruded cut feature) as the feature to be patterned in the FeatureManager Design Tree or in the graphics area.

4. Click on the **Pattern Axis** field in the **Direction 1** rollout of the PropertyManager.

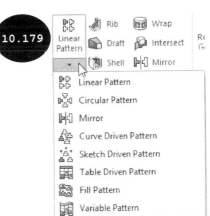

5. Click on the outer circular face of the fifth feature to define the pattern axis, see Figure 10.180. The preview of the circular pattern appears with default parameters, see Figure 10.180.

6. Make sure that the **Equal spacing** radio button is selected in the **Direction 1** rollout.

7. Enter **6** in the **Number of Instances** field of the **Direction 1** rollout.

8. Click on the green tick mark ✓ in the PropertyManager. The circular pattern is created, see Figure 10.181.

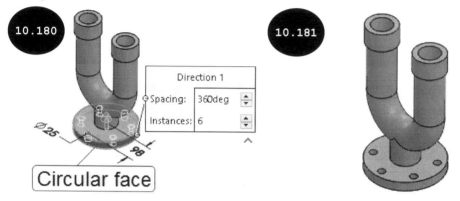

Section 11: Creating the Eighth Feature - Fillet

1. Click on the **Fillet** tool in the **Features** CommandManager. The **Fillet** PropertyManager appears.

2. Make sure that the **Constant Size Fillet** button is activated in the **Fillet Type** rollout.

3. Click on the circular edge of the model to apply the fillet as shown in Figure 10.182. The preview of the fillet appears in the graphics area with default radius.

4. Enter **15** in the **Radius** field of the **Fillet Parameters** rollout in the PropertyManager. Next, make sure that the **Symmetric** option is selected in the **Fillet Method** drop-down list.

5. Click on the green tick mark ✓ in the PropertyManager. The fillet of radius 15 mm is created, see Figure 10.183.

Section 12: Creating the Ninth Feature - Rib Feature

1. Click on the **Rib** tool in the **Features CommandManager**. The **Rib PropertyManager** appears.

2. Expand the FeatureManager Design Tree, which is now available at the top left corner of the graphics area. Next, click on the **Front Plane** in it as the sketching plane.

3. Press CTRL + 8 to change the orientation of the model as normal to the viewing direction.

4. Create an inclined line as the sketch of the rib feature, see Figure 10.184.

5. Click on the **Exit Sketch** tool in the **Sketch CommandManager** to exit the Sketching environment. The **Rib PropertyManager** appears. Next, press CTRL + 7 to change the orientation of the model to isometric.

6. Make sure that the **Both Sides** button is activated in the **Thickness** area of the **Parameters** rollout.

7. Enter **16** in the **Rib Thickness** field of the **Parameters** rollout.

8. Make sure that the **Parallel to Sketch** button is activated in the **Extrusion direction** area of the **Parameters** rollout.

9. Select the **Flip material side** check box in the **Parameters** rollout to flip the direction of extrusion inward, if needed.

10. Click on the green tick mark in the PropertyManager. The rib feature is created, see Figure 10.185.

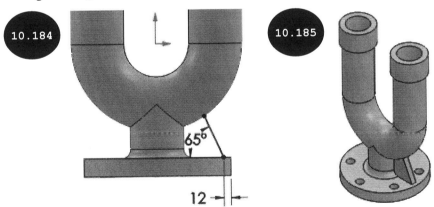

Section 13: Creating the Tenth Feature - Mirror Feature

1. Click on the **Mirror** tool. The **Mirror PropertyManager** appears.

2. Expand the FeatureManager Design Tree and then click on the **Right Plane** in the FeatureManager Design Tree as the mirroring plane.

554 Chapter 10 > Advanced Modeling - III

3. Click on the rib feature as the feature to be mirrored in the graphics area. The preview of the mirror feature appears.

4. Click on the green tick mark ✓ in the PropertyManager. The mirror feature is created, see Figure 10.186.

Section 14: Creating the Eleventh Feature - Extruded Feature

1. Click on the **Extruded Boss/Base** tool. The **Extrude PropertyManager** appears.

2. Expand the FeatureManager Design Tree and then click on the **Right Plane** as the sketching plane. Next, press CTRL + 8 to change the orientation of the model as normal to the viewing direction.

3. Create a rectangle as the sketch of the eleventh feature, see Figure 10.187.

10.186

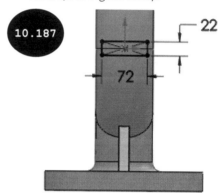
10.187

4. Click on the **Exit Sketch** tool in the **Sketch CommandManager** to exit the Sketching environment. The **Boss-Extrude PropertyManager** and the preview of the extruded feature appear. Next, change the orientation of the model to isometric.

5. Select the **Up To Next** option in the **End Condition** drop-down list of the **Direction 1** rollout.

10.188

6. Expand the **Direction 2** rollout of the PropertyManager and then select the **Up To Next** option in the **End Condition** drop-down list of the **Direction 2** rollout.

7. Click on the green tick mark ✓ in the PropertyManager. The extruded feature is created, see Figure 10.188.

Section 15: Creating the Twelfth Feature - Extruded Cut Feature

1. Click on the **Extruded Cut** tool in the **Features CommandManager**. The **Extrude PropertyManager** appears.

2. Click on the top planar face of the eleventh feature (previously created extruded feature) as the sketching plane.

3. Press CTRL + 8 to change the orientation of the model as normal to the viewing direction.

4. Create a circle of diameter 20 mm, whose center point is at the origin, as the sketch of the twelfth feature, see Figure 10.189.

5. Click on the **Exit Sketch** tool in the **Sketch CommandManager** to exit the Sketching environment. The **Cut-Extrude PropertyManager** appears. Next, change the orientation of the model to isometric.

6. Select the **Up To Next** option in the **End Condition** drop-down list of the **Direction 1** rollout.

7. Click on the green tick mark in the PropertyManager. The extruded cut feature is created, see Figure 10.190.

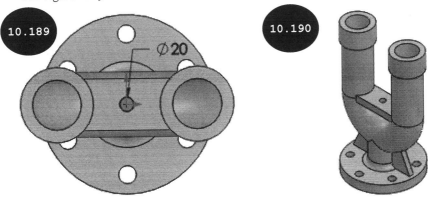

Section 16: Saving the Model

1. Click on the **Save** tool of the **Standard** toolbar. The **Save As** dialog box appears.

2. Browse to the *Tutorial* folder of *Chapter 10* and then save the model with the name Tutorial 2.

Hands-on Test Drive 1

Create the model shown in Figure 10.191. All dimensions are in mm.

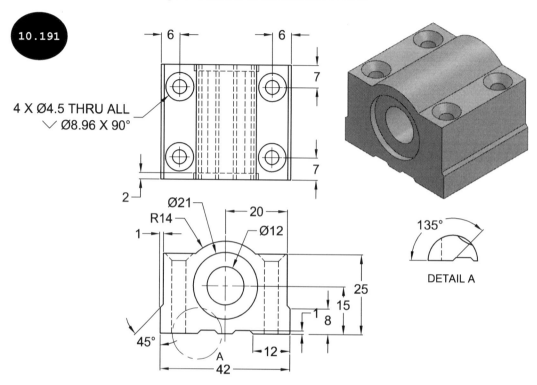

Hands-on Test Drive 2

Create the model shown in Figure 10.192. All dimensions are in mm.

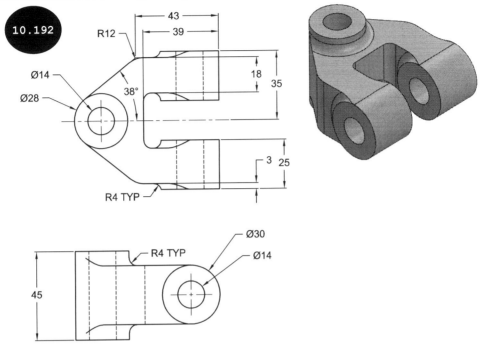

Summary

In this chapter, you have learned how to create standard or customized holes such as counterbore, countersink, straight tap, tapered tap, and multi-stepped holes as per standard specifications. Also, you have learned that cosmetic threads can be used to represent real threads on the holes, fasteners, and cylindrical features to reducing the complexity of a model and improve the overall performance of the system. In addition to the cosmetic threads, you have also learned how to create the realistic threads on a cylindrical feature or cut/hole feature of a model. You can add constant and variable radius fillets to remove the sharp edges of a model. In addition, you have learned about various methods of adding chamfer on the edges of a model. You can create a rib feature by using the open or closed sketch. At last, you have learned about creating the shell and wrap features.

Questions

- The _____ tool is used to create standard holes such as counterbore and countersink.

- The _____ tool is used to add cosmetic threads to holes, fasteners, and cylindrical features.

- Using the **Fillet** tool, you can create _____, _____, _____, and _____ fillets.

Chapter 10 > Advanced Modeling - III

- If the Rho value is less than _____ then the resultant fillet profile becomes elliptical in shape.

- The _____ fillet is created tangent to three adjacent faces of a model.

- The _____ fillet is created between the two non-continuous faces of a model.

- You can create a rib feature by using the open or closed sketch. (True/False).

- You cannot create a rib feature with a draft angle. (True/False).

- While creating a hole by using the **Hole Wizard** tool, you cannot customize the size of hole. (True/False).

- Using the **Hole Wizard** tool, you can create counterbore slot, countersink slot, or slot holes. (True/False).

CHAPTER 11

Working with Configurations

In this chapter, you will learn the following:

- Creating Configurations by using the Manual Method
- Creating Configurations by using the Design Table
- Suppressing and Unsuppressing Features

Configurations is one of the most powerful feature of SOLIDWORKS, which allows you to create multiple variations of a model within a single file. It helps you quickly and easily manage multiple design alternates based on different dimensions, features, materials, and so on within a single file. For example, if you have to create ten hexagonal bolts with different diameters and heights then instead of creating ten hexagonal bolts as separate files, you can create one single bolt with ten different configurations. In SOLIDWORKS, you can create configurations by using the Manual method and Design Table method. Both these methods of creating configurations are as follows:

Creating Configurations by using the Manual Method

In the Manual method, after creating the parent model in the Part modeling environment, you can create its configurations. You can create multiple configurations of a model and modify the model parameters for each configuration, as required. Consider a case of a plate shown in Figure 11.1, in which you need to create three different designs. In the first design, you need to create four counterbore holes at each corner and one countersink hole at the center of the plate, see Figure 11.1. In the second design of the plate, you need to have only four counterbore holes at each corner, see Figure 11.2. In the third design of the plate, you need to have only one countersink hole at the center of the plate, see Figure 11.3.

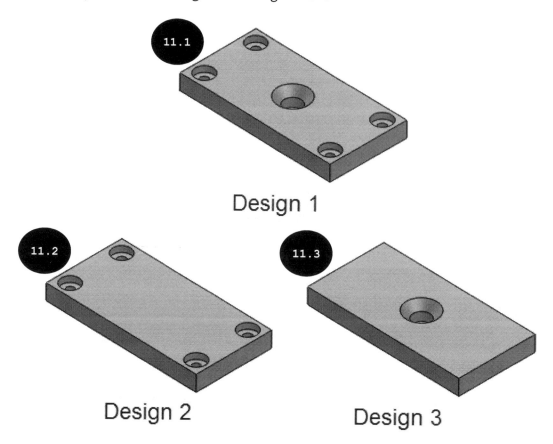

To create multiple configurations of a model, click on the **ConfigurationManager** tab, see Figure 11.4. The ConfigurationManager appears, which displays a list of all the available configurations of the current model. By default, the Default configuration of the current model is saved and is activated, see Figure 11.4. A green tick-mark in front of a configuration indicates that it is activated. Note that the model appears in the graphics area as per its active configuration.

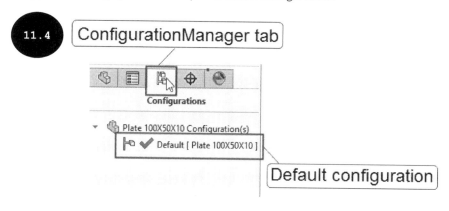

After invoking the ConfigurationManager, right-click on the name of the model. A shortcut menu appears, see Figure 11.5. In this shortcut menu, click on the **Add Configuration** option. The **Add Configuration PropertyManager** appears at the left of the graphics area, see Figure 11.6. The options in the **Add Configuration PropertyManager** are as follows:

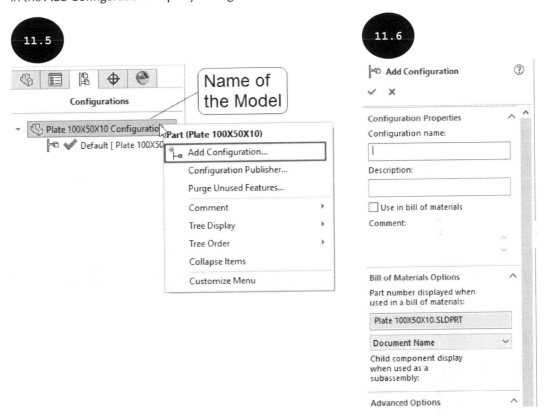

Configuration Properties

The **Configuration name** field of the **Configuration Properties** rollout in the PropertyManager is used to specify the name of the configuration. It is recommended to specify some logical name for the configuration so that you can easily identify it in later use. The **Description** field of the **Configuration Properties** rollout is used to specify description for the configuration. On selecting the **Use in bill of material** check box, the description specified in the **Description** field will be displayed in the BOM (Bill of Material). The **Comment** field of this rollout is used to specify a comment about the configuration.

Bill of Materials Options

The **Part number displayed when used in a bill of materials** drop-down list of the **Bill of Materials Options** rollout is used to select an option to display the name of the model in the Bill of Materials (BOM) when this configuration is used in the assembly. By default, the **Document Name** option is selected in this drop-down list. As a result, the name of the model is displayed in the BOM, when this configuration is used. On selecting the **Configuration Name** option in the drop-down list, the name of the configuration specified in the **Configuration name** field of the **Configuration Properties** rollout is display in the BOM, when this configuration is used. On selecting the **User Specified Name** option, you can specify a new name for the configuration, to be displayed in the BOM, in the field enabled above the drop-down list in the rollout.

Advanced Options

The **Suppress features** check box is selected by default in the **Advanced Options** rollout, see Figure 11.7. As a result, new features added to other configurations of the model are automatically suppressed in this configuration. If you clear the **Suppress features** check box then the new features added in other configurations of the model are also included in this configuration. The **Use configuration specific color** check box is used to specify a color for this configuration. To specify a color for this configuration, select this check box. The **Color** button is enabled below the check box in this rollout. Click on the **Color** button to display the **Color** window. By using the **Color** window, you can specify a color for this configuration.

After specifying the configuration properties such as name and description, click on the green tick mark in the **Add Configuration PropertyManager**. The configuration with specified properties is created and displayed in the ConfigurationManager, see Figure 11.8. In this figure, the **Design 1** configuration is added. Note that the newly created configuration becomes the active configuration of the model.

After creating a configuration, you can make the required modifications in the model such as suppress or unsuppress existing features, add new features, and edit other properties. You will learn about suppressing and unsuppressing features later in this chapter. Note that the modifications made in the model are limited to the current active configuration only and will not affect the default or other configurations of the model. However, if you modify feature parameters such as extruded depth and dimensions of sketches then you need to specify whether the modification is for the current active configuration only or for all configurations of the model. For example, while modifying the depth of an extruded feature, you need to select the required radio button: **This configuration**, **All configurations**, or **Specify configuration** in the **Configurations** rollout of the respective PropertyManager, see Figure 11.9. If you select the **This configuration** radio button, then the modification is made in the current active configuration of the model only, whereas if you select the **All configuration** radio button, then the modification is made in all configurations of the model including the default configuration. Similarly, while modifying a dimension of a sketch, you need to specify whether the modification is for the current active configuration only or for all the configurations of the model by using the **Configuration** flyout of the **Modify** dialog box, which appears while modifying a dimension, see Figure 11.10.

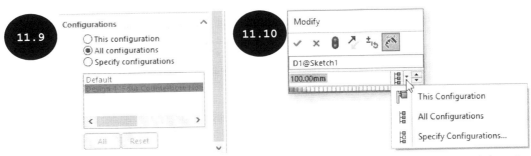

To create the second configuration of a model, right-click on the name of the model in the ConfigurationManager to display a shortcut menu, see Figure 11.11. In this shortcut menu, click on the **Add Configuration** option. The **Add Configuration PropertyManager** appears. In this PropertyManager, specify the configuration properties such as name and description and then click on the green tick mark. A new configuration is created and its name appears in the ConfigurationManager, see Figure 11.12. In this figure, the **Design 1** and **Design 2** configuration are added. Note that the newly created configuration (**Design 2**) is the active configuration of the model. After creating the second configuration of a model, you can make the required modifications in the model. Similarly, you can create multiple configurations of a model. Figure 11.13 shows a model with three different configurations (Design 1, Design 2, and Design 3).

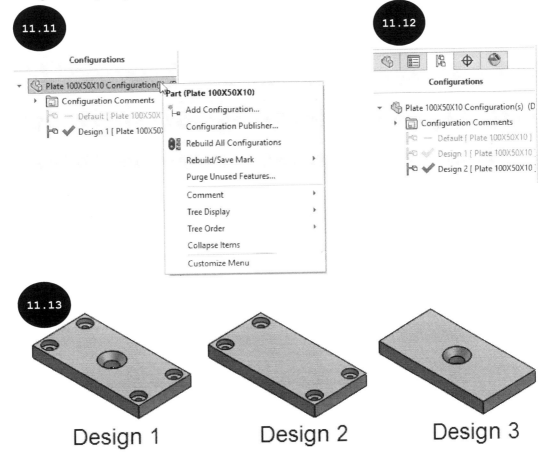

Note: You can activate any existing configuration of a model by double-clicking on its name in the ConfigurationManager. Alternatively, right-click on the name of the configuration to be activated in the ConfigurationManager to display a shortcut menu and then click on the **Show Configuration** option. Once the required configuration is activated, you can make necessary modifications in the model for the active configuration.

Procedure for Creating Configurations by using the Manual Method

1. Invoke the ConfigurationManager by clicking on the **ConfigurationManager** tab.
2. Right-click on the name of the model in the ConfigurationManager. A shortcut menu appears.
3. In the shortcut menu, click on the **Add Configuration** option. The **Add Configuration PropertyManager** appears.
4. Specify configuration properties such as configuration name and description in the PropertyManager and then click on the green tick mark. The configuration with specified properties is created and its name is displayed in the ConfigurationManager. Also, the newly created configuration becomes the current active configuration of the model.
5. Modify the model such as suppress or unsuppress existing features or add new features in the model. The modifications made in the model are part of the active configuration only and do not affect the Default or other configurations of the model. However, if you modify feature parameters such as extruded depth and dimensions, then you need to specify whether the modification is for the active configuration only or for all configurations.
6. Similarly, you can add multiple configurations and modify the model for each configuration.

Creating Configurations by using the Design Table

The Design Table method is very easy and convenient way of creating configurations of a model. It provides you embedded Microsoft excel worksheet, where you can easily create or manage multiple configurations by specifying parameters. To create configurations by using the Design Table, click on the **Insert > Tables > Design Table** in the SOLIDWORKS menus, see Figure 11.14. The **Design Table PropertyManager** appears, see Figure 11.15. The options of the PropertyManager are as follows:

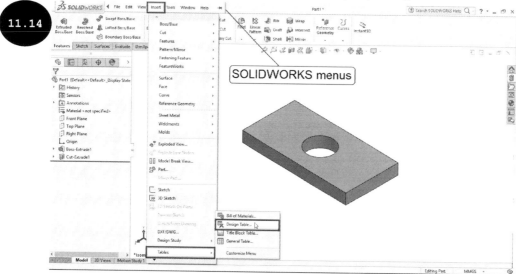

Note: To create configurations by using the Design Table, you need to make sure that the Microsoft Excel is installed on your computer.

Source

By default the **Auto-create** radio button is selected in the **Source** rollout of the **Design Table PropertyManager**, see Figure 11.15. As a result, all parameters of the source model are automatically loaded in the design table. On selecting the **Blank** radio button, you are provided with a blank design table where you need to fill in the parameters for each configuration. On selecting the **From file** radio button, you can import an existing design table or a Microsoft excel file containing different configurations of the model with their parameters. As soon as you select the **From file** radio button, the **Browse** button is enabled in the rollout. Click on the **Browse** button. The **Open** dialog box appears. In this dialog box, browse to the location where the existing design table or the Microsoft excel file is saved and then select it. Next, click on the **Open** button. The name and path of the selected design table or Microsoft excel file appears in the field below the **From file** radio button. If you select the **Link to file** check box in the rollout then the

Figure 11.15

imported Microsoft excel file is linked with the model. As a result, if you make any modifications in the excel file the same modifications are reflected in the model and vice-versa.

Edit Control

The **Allow model edits to update the design table** radio button is selected in the **Edit Control** rollout, by default, see Figure 11.15. As a result, if you make any modifications in the model, the same modifications are reflected in the design table as well. On selecting the **Block model edits that would update the design table** radio button, you are not allowed to make modifications in the model, which would update the parameters of the design table.

Options

The **New parameters** check box is selected in the **Options** rollout, by default. As a result, on adding a new parameter in the model, a new column for the parameter is added automatically in the design table. If the **New configurations** check box is selected in the rollout then on adding a new configuration in the model, a new row for the configuration is added automatically in the design table. If the **Warn when updating design table** check box is selected, then a warning message appears on updating the design table. If the **Enable cell drop-down lists** check box is selected, the cells of the design table contain drop-down lists for multiple entries.

566 Chapter 11 > Working with Configurations

In the **Design Table PropertyManager**, accept the default selected options and then click on the green tick mark in it. The process of creating the design table starts. Also, the **Dimensions** window and an embedded Microsoft excel worksheet appear on the screen, see Figure 11.16. The **Dimensions** window displays a list of all dimensions of the model available in the graphics area.

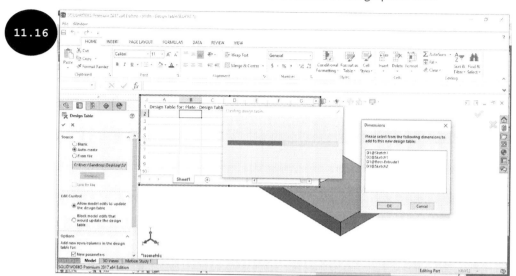

In the **Dimensions** window, select the dimensions of the model to be added in the design table by pressing and holding the CTRL key. After selecting the dimensions in the **Dimensions** window, click on the **OK** button. The design table appears as a Microsoft excel worksheet with the Default configuration of the model, see Figure 11.17. In the design table, the name of the selected dimensions of the model are added in separate columns and the Default configuration is added in a row. Also, the dimension values of the selected dimensions are added in cells, corresponding to the dimension name column and the Default configuration row, see Figure 11.17.

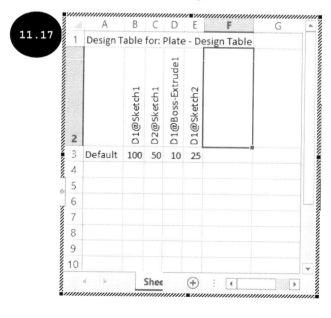

You can add multiple configurations of a model by entering their names in different rows of the table, see Figure 11.18. Note that for each configuration, you can specify different dimension values in the respective cells, see Figure 11.18. In this figure, in addition to the Default configuration, three more configurations (Plate 50X25X5, Plate 30X15X5, and Plate 200X100X10) of the model have been created with different dimension values.

In addition to specifying different dimension values for each configuration in the design table, you can also specify suppress or unsuppress state for the features of the model in each configuration. Consider a case of a plate having one circular cut feature at the center, see Figure 11.19. If you do not want the circular cut feature of the model to become a part of a configuration then you can specify its state as suppressed in the design table. To specify suppress or unsuppress state of a feature in the design table, click on the column, next to the last dimension name in the design table, refer to Figure 11.18. Next, double-click on the name of the feature in the FeatureManager Design Tree. The name of the selected feature is added in the selected column of the design table, see Figure 11.20. Also, notice that the unsuppressed state is specified for the Default configuration, by default. You can specify suppress or unsuppress state for the feature in each configuration of the design table. To specify suppress state for a feature, enter S, 1, or SUPPRESSED in the cell corresponding to the feature and the configuration. Similarly, to specify unsuppress state, enter U, 0, or UNSUPPRESSED. After creating different configurations and specifying parameters for each configuration, click anywhere in the graphics area. The SOLIDWORKS message window appears which informs you that the design table is generated with the specified configurations. Click on the OK button in the SOLIDWORKS message window. The configurations are created and are listed in the ConfigurationManager, see Figure 11.21.

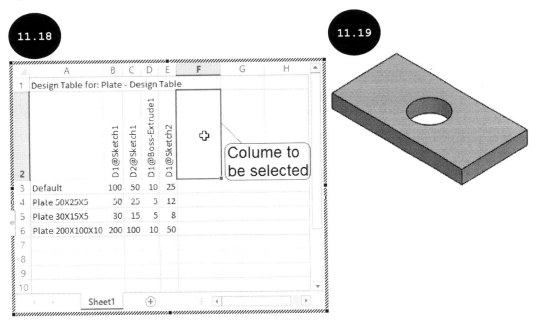

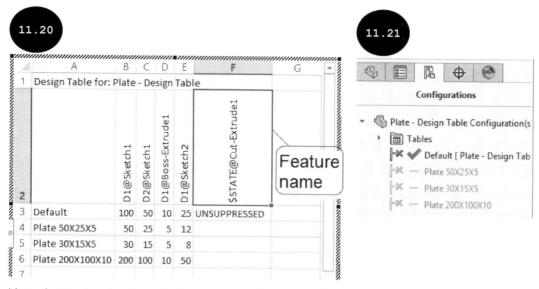

Note that in the ConfigurationManager, the Default configuration is activated. As a result, the model that appears in the graphics area is based on the parameters of the Default configuration. To activate a configuration, double-click on the name of the configuration to be activated in the ConfigurationManager. Alternatively, right-click on the name of the configuration and then click on the **Show Configuration** option in the shortcut menu appeared. The selected configuration gets activated and the model is updated in the graphics area, accordingly.

Note: After generating a design table with multiple configurations, you can further edit its parameters. To edit a design table, expand the **Tables** node in the ConfigurationManager and then right-click on the **Design Table** appeared. A shortcut menu appears, see Figure 11.22. In this shortcut menu, click on the **Edit Table** option. The **Add Rows and Columns** window appears. Click on the **OK** button in this window. The design table as Microsoft excel worksheet appear in the graphics area. Now, you can make the necessary modifications in the parameters of the existing configurations and add new configurations as well. After editing the design table, click anywhere in the graphics area.

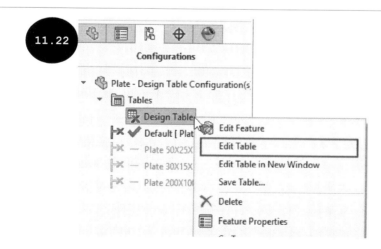

Procedure for Creating Configurations by using the Design Table

1. Click on the **Insert > Tables > Design Table** in the SOLIDWORKS menus. The **Design Table** PropertyManager appears.
2. Accept the default selected options in the PropertyManager and then click on the green tick mark. The **Dimensions** window appears in the graphics area.
3. Press and hold the CTRL key and then select the dimensions in the **Dimensions** window. Next, click on the **OK** button. The design table appears as a microsoft excel worksheet with a Default configuration.
4. Enter the names of the configurations to be created in different rows of the table and then specify the respective parameters for each configuration.
5. After creating different configurations and specifying parameters for each configuration, click anywhere in the graphics area. The **SOLIDWORKS** message window appears.
6. Click on the **OK** button in the window. The configurations are created and are listed in the ConfigurationManager. Now, you can double-click on a configuration to activate it.

Suppressing and Unsuppressing Features

In SOLIDWORKS, you can suppress or unsuppress the features of a model. A suppressed feature is removed from the model and does not appear in the graphics area. Also, the name of the suppressed feature appears in gray color in the FeatureManager Design Tree. Note that a suppressed feature is not deleted from the model; it is only removed or disappeared such that it does not load into the RAM (random access memory) while rebuilding the model. This helps you speed up the overall performance of the system when you are working with complex models.

To suppress a feature of a model, select the feature to be suppressed either from the graphics area or from the FeatureManager Design Tree. A Pop-up toolbar appears, see Figure 11.23. In this Pop-up toolbar, click on the **Suppress** tool. The selected feature is suppressed.

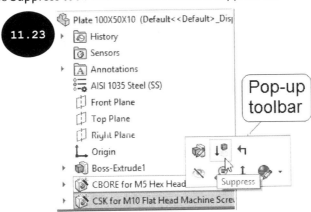

To unsuppress a suppressed feature, select the suppressed feature from the FeatureManager Design Tree. A Pop-up toolbar appears. In this Pop-up toolbar, click on the **Unsuppress** tool. The feature is unsuppressed and appears in the model.

Chapter 11 > Working with Configurations

Tutorial 1

Create the model (Weld Neck Flange) shown in Figure 11.24. After creating the model, create its three different configurations by using the Design Table method. The details of the configurations to be created are given in the below table. All dimensions are in mm.

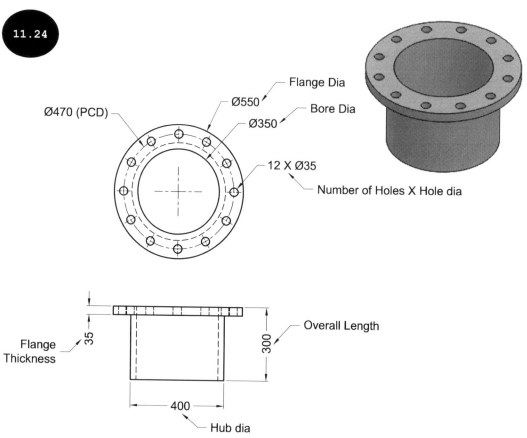

11.24

	Bore Dia	Hub Dia	Overall Length	Flange Dia	Flange Thickness	Hole Dia	Hole PCD	No. of Holes
350 Bore Dia	350	400	300	550	35	35	470	12
400 Bore Dia	400	450	300	600	35	35	520	16
450 Bore Dia	450	500	300	650	35	35	570	20

Section 1: Starting SOLIDWORKS
1. Start SOLIDWORKS, if not already started.

Section 2: Invoking the Part Modeling Environment
1. Invoke the Part modeling environment by using the **New** tool in the **Standard** toolbar.

Section 3: Specifying Unit Settings

1. Make sure that the **MMGS** (millimeter, gram, second) unit system is set for the currently opened part document.

Section 4: Creating the Base Feature - Extruded Feature

1. Invoke the Sketching environment by selecting the Top plane as the sketching plane.

2. Create a circle by specifying its center point at the origin, see Figure 11.25.

3. Click on the **Smart Dimension** tool in the **Sketch CommandManager**. Next, click on the circle in the drawing area. The diameter dimension of the circle is attached to the cursor.

4. Click to specify the placement point for the attached diameter dimension of the circle in the drawing area. The **Modify** dialog box appears, see Figure 11.26.

5. Enter **350** as the diameter of the circle in the **Dimension** field of the **Modify** dialog box, see Figure 11.26.

6. Enter **Bore Dia** as the name of the dimension in the **Name** field, see Figure 11.26.

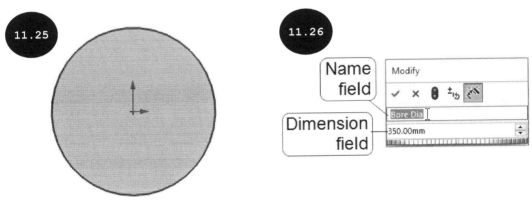

7. Click on the green tick mark button in the **Modify** dialog box. The diameter dimension with specified diameter value and name is applied to the circle.

8. Similarly, create another circle and specify its diameter value as 400 mm and name as Hub Dia, see Figure 11.27.

9. Click on the **Extruded Boss/Base** tool in the **Features CommandManager**. The preview of the extruded feature and the **Boss-Extrude PropertyManager** appear. Also the orientation of the model changes to Trimetric.

10. Enter **300** in the **Depth** field of the PropertyManager and then click on its green tick mark. The extruded feature is created, see Figure 11.28.

572 Chapter 11 > Working with Configurations

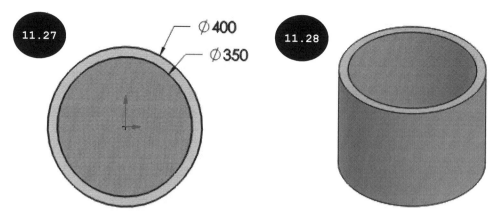

Section 5: Creating the Second Feature - Extruded Feature

1. Invoke the Sketching environment by selecting the top planar face of the base feature as the sketching plane.

2. Press CTRL + 8 to change the orientation of the model as normal to the viewing direction.

3. Create two circles by specifying their center points at the origin.

4. Apply the coradial relation between a circle and the inner circular edge of the base feature.

5. Apply the diameter dimension to the second circle by specifying its diameter value as 550 mm and name as Flange Dia in the **Modify** dialog box, see Figure 11.29.

6. Click on the **Extruded Boss/Base** tool in the **Features CommandManager**. The preview of the extruded feature and the **Boss-Extrude PropertyManager** appear. Next, change the orientation of the model to Isometric.

7. Enter **35** in the **Depth** field of the PropertyManager and then Press ENTER.

8. Click on the **Reverse Direction** button in the **Direction 1** rollout of the PropertyManager to reverse the direction of extrusion downward. Next, click on the green tick mark in the PropertyManager. The extruded feature is created., see Figure 11.30.

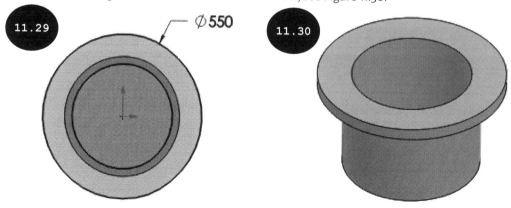

Section 6: Creating the Third Feature - Cut Feature

1. Invoke the Sketching environment by selecting the top planar face of the model as the sketching plane.

2. Create the sketch of the third feature (cut feature) and then apply required dimensions and relations, see Figure 11.31. Note that you need to specify the Hole Dia as the name of the diameter dimension 35 mm and PCD as the name of the diameter dimension 470 mm.

Tip: Specifying name to each sketch dimension will help you in identifying them while specifying parameters for creating configurations in the design table.

3. Click on the **Extruded Cut** tool in the **Features CommandManager**. The **Cut-Extrude PropertyManager** appears. Next, change the orientation of the model to isometric.

4. Select the **Up to Next** option in the **End Condition** drop-down list of the **Direction 1** rollout and then click on the green tick mark in the PropertyManager. The cut feature is created, see Figure 11.32.

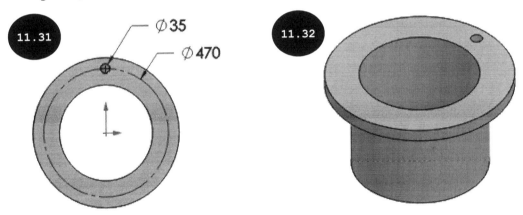

Section 7: Creating the Fourth Feature - Circular Pattern

1. Create the circular pattern of the previously created cut feature by specifying 12 as the number of instances, see Figure 11.33.

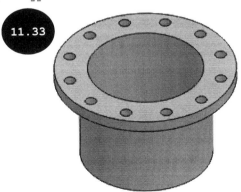

574 Chapter 11 > Working with Configurations

Section 8: Creating Configurations - Design Table

1. Click on the **Insert > Tables > Design Table** in the SOLIDWORKS menus. The **Design Table PropertyManager** appears.

2. Accept the default selected options in the PropertyManager and click on the green tick mark in the PropertyManager. The process of creating the design table gets started and the **Dimensions** window appears, see Figure 11.34.

3. Press and hold the CTRL key and then select all the dimensions listed in the **Dimensions** dialog box. Next, click on the **OK** button in the dialog box. The design table appears as a Microsoft excel worksheet with the Default configuration of the model, see Figure 11.35.

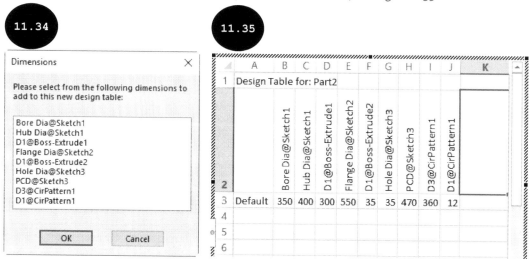

4. Enter three new configuration names: **350 Bore Dia**, **400 Bore Dia**, and **450 Bore Dia** below the Default configuration in the design table and then specify their parameters, see Figure 11.36. Note that the working with design table is the same as an excel file.

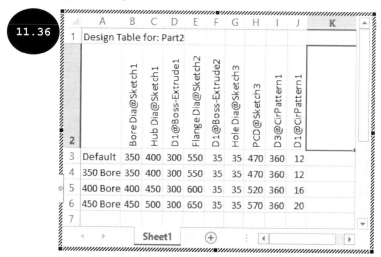

5. After specifying parameters for each configuration in the design table, click anywhere in the graphics area. The **SOLIDWORKS** message window appears, see Figure 11.37.

6. Click on the **OK** button in the **SOLIDWORKS** message window. Three new configurations are created in addition to the Default configuration. Notice that the names of all the configurations are listed in the ConfigurationManager, see Figure 11.38. In this figure, the Default configuration is activated.

7. Double-click on the name of each configuration in the ConfigurationManager one by one to review the respective design of the model. Note that the model appears in the graphics area as per the activated configuration.

Section 9: Saving the Model

1. Click on the **Save** tool in the **Standard** toolbar. The **Save As** dialog box appears.

2. Browse to the SOLIDWORKS folder and then create a folder with the name **Chapter 11**. Next, create another folder with the name **Tutorial** in the *Chapter 11* folder.

3. Enter **Tutorial 1** in the **File name** field of the dialog box as the name of the file and then click on the **Save** button, the model is saved with the name Tutorial 1 in the *Tutorial* folder of *Chapter 11*.

Hands-on Test Drive 1

Create the model shown in Figure 11.39. After creating the model, create its two configurations: With Slot Cut and Without Slot Cut by using the Manual method. All dimensions are in mm.

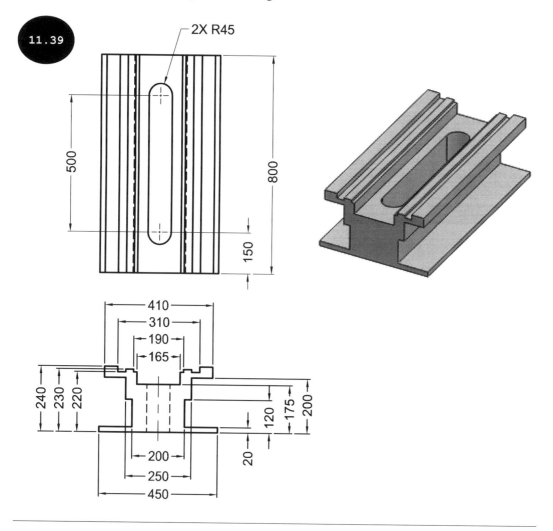

Summary

In this chapter, you have learned how to create configurations of a model by using the Manual and Design Table methods. You have also learned about suppressing and unsuppressing features of a model.

Questions

- You can create configurations of a model by using two methods: _____ and _____.

- By default, the _____ configuration is created for a model.

- You can suppress a feature by using the _____ tool.

- You cannot suppress features of a model by using the Design Table. (True/False)

CHAPTER 12

Working with Assemblies - I

In this chapter, you will learn the following:

- Bottom-up Assembly Approach
- Top-down Assembly Approach
- Creating Assembly by using Bottom-up Approach
- Working with Degrees of Freedom
- Applying Relations or Mates
- Working with Standard Mates
- Working with Advanced Mates
- Working with Mechanical Mates
- Moving and Rotating Individual Components
- Working with SmartMates

In the earlier chapters, you have learned about the basic and advance techniques of creating real world mechanical components. In this chapter, you will learn about different techniques of creating mechanical assemblies. An assembly is made up of two or more than two components joined together by applying relations/mates. You will learn about applying relations/mates later in this chapter. Figure 12.1 shows an assembly, in which multiple components are assembled with respect to each other by applying required mates.

12.1

In SOLIDWORKS, you can create assemblies in the Assembly environment by using two approaches: Bottom-up Assembly Approach and Top-down Assembly Approach. Moreover, you can use the combination of both the approaches for creating an assembly. Both the approaches are as follows:

Bottom-up Assembly Approach

The Bottom-up Assembly Approach is most widely used approach for assembling components. In this approach, first all the components of an assembly have created one by one in the Part modeling environment and then saved in a common location. Later, all the components are inserted one by one in the Assembly environment and then assembled with respect to each other by applying the required mates.

Tip: SOLIDWORKS has the bidirectional association between all its environments. As a result, if any, change or modification is made into a component in the Part modeling environment, the same change automatically replicates or reflects in the Assembly and Drawing environments as well, and vice-versa.

Top-down Assembly Approach

The Top-down Assembly Approach is mainly used for creating concept-based design, in which new components of an assembly are created by taking reference from the existing components of the assembly in the Assembly environment and maintain the relationships between them.

In the Top-down Assembly Approach, all the components of an assembly are created in the Assembly environment. Creating all components of an assembly in the Assembly environment helps you create components by taking reference from existing components of the assembly.

Creating Assembly by using Bottom-up Approach

After creating all components of an assembly in the Part modeling environment and saving them in a common location, you need to invoke the Assembly environment of SOLIDWORKS for assembling them. To invoke the Assembly environment, click on the **New** tool in the **Standard** toolbar. The **New SOLIDWORKS Document** dialog box appears, see Figure 12.2. In this dialog box, click on the **Assembly** button and then click on the **OK** button. The Assembly environment is invoked with the **Begin Assembly PropertyManager** on its left. Also, the **Open** dialog box appears on the screen, see Figure 12.3. Note that along with the **Begin Assembly PropertyManager**, the **Open** dialog box appears every time on invoking the Assembly environment. This is because, in the **Options** rollout of the **Begin Assembly PropertyManager**, the **Automatic Browse when creating new assembly** check box is selected, by default. It is used to invoke the **Open** dialog box automatically, if no components are opened in the current session of SOLIDWORKS. By using the **Open** dialog box, you can insert a component in the Assembly environment. The methods for inserting components in the Assembly environment are discussed next.

12.2

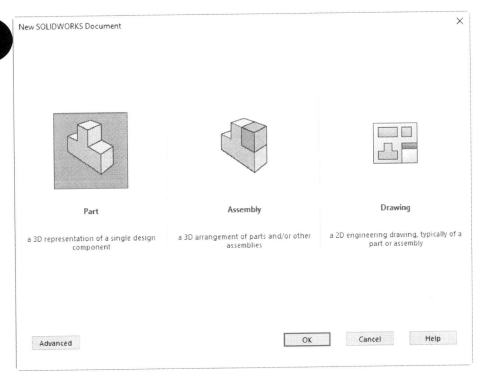

12.3

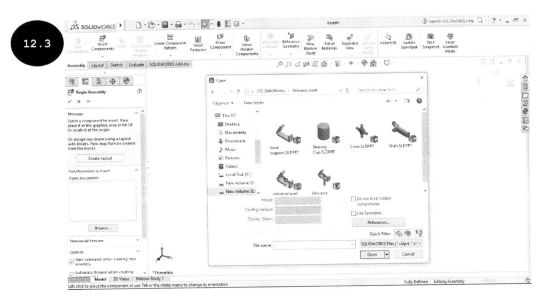

580   Chapter 12 > Working with Assemblies - I

Note: The **Begin Assembly PropertyManager** appears every time on invoking the Assembly environment for inserting components in the Assembly environment. This is because, in the **Options** rollout of the **Begin Assembly PropertyManager**, the **Start command when creating new assembly** check box is selected, by default, refer to Figure 12.3. If you uncheck this check box, next time when you invoke the Assembly environment, the **Begin Assembly PropertyManager** as well as the **Open** dialog box do not appear. In such a case, you can insert components in the Assembly environment by using the **Insert Components** tool of the **Assembly CommandManager**. You will learn about inserting components by using the **Insert Components** tool later in this chapter.

Inserting Components in the Assembly Environment Updated

As discussed, on invoking the Assembly environment, if no components are opened in the current session of SOLIDWORKS, the **Open** dialog box appears, automatically along with the **Begin Assembly PropertyManager**. If the **Open** dialog box does not appear then click on the **Browse** button in the **Begin Assembly PropertyManager** to invoke the **Open** dialog box. In the **Open** dialog box, browse to the location where all components of the assembly are saved and then select a component to be inserted. Next, click on the **Open** button in the dialog box. The selected component gets attached to the cursor and the **Rotate Context** toolbar appears in the graphics area, see Figure 12.4. If needed, you can change the orientation of the attached component by using the tools of the **Rotate Context** toolbar. By default, **90 degrees** is entered in the **Angle** field of the **Rotate Context** toolbar. As a result, when you click on the **X, Y,** or **Z** tool in this toolbar; the component rotates 90 degrees about the X, Y, or Z axis, respectively. You can enter any required value for the angle of rotation in the **Angle** field and rotate the component about X, Y, or Z axis by using this toolbar.

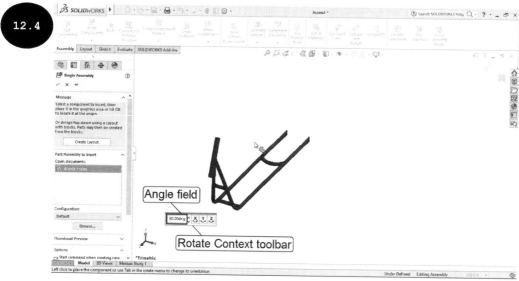

Note: By default, the **Rotate Context** toolbar appears ever time when you insert a component in the Assembly environment because the **Show Rotate context toolbar** check box is selected in the **Options** rollout of the **Begin Assembly PropertyManager**.

Once the orientation of the component has been set by using the **Rotate Context** toolbar, click anywhere in the graphics area. The component moves toward the origin of the assembly and becomes a fixed component with respect to the origin of the assembly. Notice that the name of the inserted component gets listed in the **FeatureManager Design Tree** with '(f)' sign in front of its name, see Figure 12.5. The '(f)' sign indicates that all degrees of freedom of the component are fixed and the component cannot move or rotate in any direction. In SOLIDWORKS, the first component you insert in the Assembly environment becomes a fixed component automatically and does not allow any translational or rotational movement. You can also change the fixed component to a floating component, whose all degrees of freedom are free. Means the floating component is free to move or rotate in the graphics area. To change a fixed component to a floating component, right-click on the name of the fixed component in the FeatureManager Design Tree and then click on the **Float** option in the shortcut menu appeared. In addition, notice that as soon as the first component is inserted in the Assembly environment, the **Begin Assembly PropertyManager** gets closed. Therefore, to insert the remaining components of the assembly in the Assembly environment, you need to use the **Insert Components** tool of the **Assembly CommandManager**. The method of inserting components by using the **Insert Components** tool is as follows:

Note: If any component is opened in the current session of SOLIDWORKS then on invoking the Assembly environment; the **Open** dialog box will not be opened, automatically and the name of the opened component is listed in the **Open documents** field of the **Begin Assembly PropertyManager**, see Figure 12.6. In this figure, four components are listed in the **Open documents** field. You can select a component to be inserted in the Assembly environment from the **Open documents** field or click on the **Browse** button to open the **Open** dialog box.

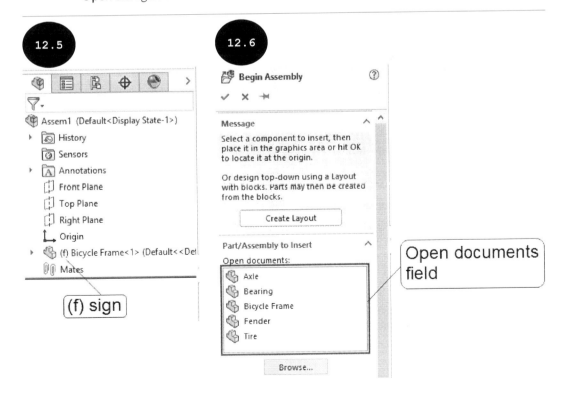

Tip: If you pin the **Begin Assembly PropertyManager** by clicking on the **Keep Visible** icon available at the upper right corner of the PropertyManager then the display of the PropertyManager will not be closed after inserting the component and you can continue inserting the components by using the **Begin Assembly PropertyManager**.

Inserting Components by using the Insert Components Tool

To insert a component in the Assembly environment by using the **Insert Components** tool, click on the **Insert Components** tool in the **Assembly CommandManager**, see Figure 12.7. The **Insert Component PropertyManager** and the **Open** dialog box appear. Figure 12.8 shows the **Insert Component PropertyManager**.

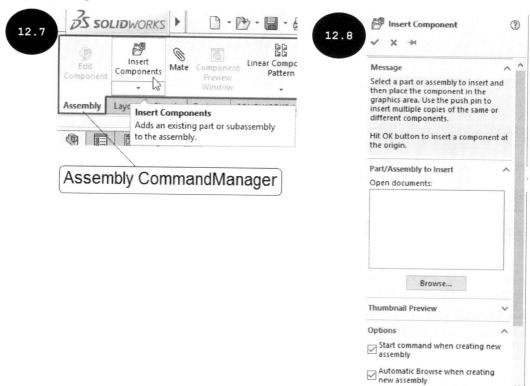

Note that in the **Insert Component PropertyManager**, the **Automatic Browse when creating new assembly** check box is selected, by default. As a result, the **Open** dialog box appears, automatically if no components are opened in the current session of SOLIDWORKS. If the **Open** dialog box does not appear, then click on the **Browse** button in the **Insert Component PropertyManager** to invoke the **Open** dialog box. In the **Open** dialog box, browse to the location where all components of the assembly are saved and then select a component. Next, click on the **Open** button in the dialog box. The selected component is attached to the cursor. Also, the **Rotate Context** toolbar appears in the graphics area, see Figure 12.9.

Note: The **Start command when creating new assembly** check box of the **Insert Component PropertyManager** is used to turn on or off the display of the **Begin Assembly PropertyManager** on invoking the Assembly environment.

Change the current orientation of the component by using the **Rotate Context** toolbar, as needed. Once the orientation of the component has been set, as required then click the left mouse button anywhere in the graphics area to define the placement point for the attached component. The attached component is placed on the location defined and the PropertyManager is closed. Also, the name of the inserted component is added in the FeatureManager Design Tree with '(-)' sign in front of its name, see Figure 12.10. The '(-)' sign indicates that all degrees of freedom of the component are not defined. Means the component is free to move or rotate in the graphics area. You need to assemble the free component with the existing components of the assembly by applying the required relations or mates. You will learn about applying relations or mates later in this chapter. Similarly, you can insert multiple components in the Assembly environment one by one by using the **Insert Component PropertyManager**.

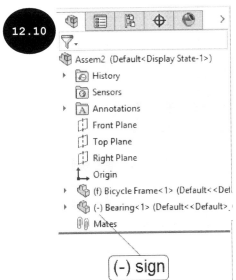

Tip: While defining the placement point for a component in the graphics area, make sure that the component does not intersect with any existing component of the assembly.

Note: If you pin the **Insert Component PropertyManager** by clicking on the **Keep Visible** icon available at its upper right corner then the display of the PropertyManager will not be closed after inserting the component and notice that the second instance of the inserted component is attached to the cursor. Click in the graphics area to insert the second instance of the same component. Similarly, you can insert multiple instances of a component in the Assembly environment by clicking the left mouse button.

After inserting the second component, it is recommended that you first assemble the second component with the first component by applying required mates before inserting the third or next component in the Assembly environment. However, before you learn applying mates between assembly components, first it is important to understand the concept of degrees of freedom, which is as follows:

Working with Degrees of Freedom

A free component within the Assembly environment has six degrees of freedom: three translational and three rotational. It means a free component in the Assembly environment can move along the X, Y, and Z axes and rotate about the X, Y, and Z axes. As discussed earlier, the first component inserted in the Assembly environment becomes the fixed component automatically and does not allow any translational or rotational movement. It means all its degrees of freedom are fixed. However, the second or further components inserted in the Assembly environment of SOLIDWORKS are free for all movements, which means degrees of freedom of components are not restricted. In such cases, a designer needs to fix the degrees of freedom of components by applying mates. It is not about fixing the degrees of freedom of components, you need to maintain actual relationships between them as exactly it is in the real world assembly. You need to allow movable components of an assembly to move freely in the respective movable directions. For example, the working of a shaft in an assembly is to rotate about its axis therefore, you need to retain its rotation degree of freedom free to rotate.

Note: To check the degrees of freedom of a component, you can move or rotate the component along or about its degrees of freedom by using the **Move Component** tool or **Rotate Component** tool, respectively. You can also move or rotate components along or about their free degrees of freedom by dragging them in the graphics area. You will learn about moving or rotating individual component of an assembly later in this chapter.

Applying Relations or Mates Updated

In SOLIDWORKS, you can assemble components together by using three types of mates: Standard, Advanced, and Mechanical. All these types of mates can be applied by using the **Mate PropertyManager** that appears after clicking on the **Mate** tool in the **Assembly CommandManager**.

To apply a mate between components, click on the **Mate** tool in the **Assembly CommandManager**. The **Mate PropertyManager** appears, see Figure 12.11. Note that the **Entities to Mate** field in the **Mate Selections** rollout of the PropertyManager is activated by default. As a result, you can select entities of two different components to mate. Select the required entities such as faces, edges, planes, or a combination of these to apply a mate. Note that the first selected component for applying a mate becomes transparent in the graphics area, see Figure 12.12. It helps you easily select the second component, especially when the second component is not visible or behind the first component in the graphics area. This is because the **Make first selection transparent** check box is selected in the **Options** rollout of the **Mate PropertyManager**. Notice that as soon as you select entities for applying a mate, the **Mate** Pop-up toolbar appears in the graphics area, see Figure 12.12. The availability of tools in the **Mate** Pop-up toolbar depends on the entities selected for applying the mate. Also, in **Mate** Pop-up toolbar, the best suitable mate that can be applied between the selected entities is activated, by default and the preview of components appears after applying the best suitable mate, see Figure 12.12. In this figure, two cylindrical faces of the components are selected for applying a mate. As a result, the Concentric mate is activated, by default and the preview of selected entities appears concentric to each other. To accept the default selected mate, click on the green tick mark ✓ in the **Mate** Pop-up toolbar. You can also apply a mate other than the mate selected by default in the **Mate** Pop-up toolbar. To apply a mate other than the default selected mate, click on the required mate tool to be applied between the entities in the **Mate** Pop-up toolbar. In addition to applying a mate by using the **Mate** Pop-up toolbar, you can also apply a mate between the entities by using the **Mate PropertyManager**. Different types of mates are as follows:

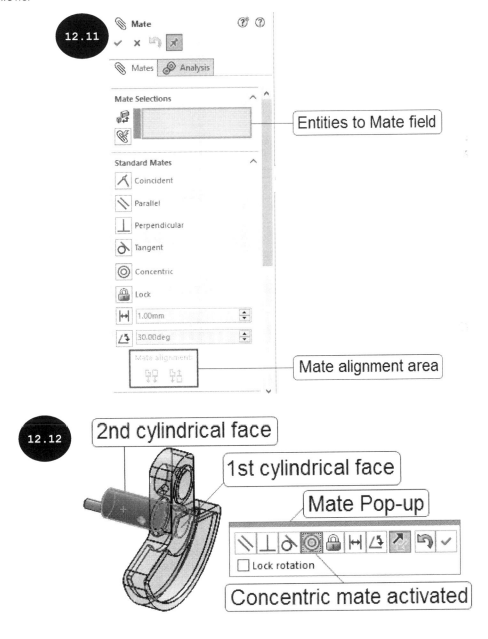

Note: The **Flip Mate Alignment** tool of the **Mate** Pop-up toolbar is used to flip the mate alignment between the selected entities. You can also flip the mate alignment between the entities by using the **Aligned** and **Anti-Aligned** buttons of the **Mate alignment** area in the **Mate PropertyManager**, refer to Figure 12.11. Note that these buttons are enabled only after selecting the entities. You will learn more about mate alignment between the entities later in this chapter.

Working with Standard Mates Updated

Standard mates are used for positioning components of an assembly by restricting or reducing the degrees of freedom of the components. You can apply standard mates such as coincident, parallel, perpendicular, concentric, and tangent between entities of the components to position them in the assembly. The standard mates are as follows:

Coincident

Coincident mate is used to make the selected entities of two different components coincident to each other, see Figure 12.13. You can select faces, edges, planes, vertices, or a combination of these as entities for applying the coincident mate. On applying the coincident mate, the selected entities get aligned or share the same plane. Figure 12.13 shows two planar faces for applying coincident mate and the resultant model after applying the coincident mate.

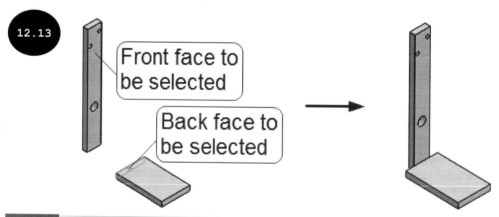

12.13

Note: If you click on the **Flip Mate Alignment** tool in the **Mate** Pop-up toolbar, the alignment of the selected entities changes from Anti-Aligned to Aligned or vice versa, see Figure 12.14. You can also flip the alignment by using the **Aligned** and **Anti-Aligned** buttons of the **Mate alignment** area in the **Mate PropertyManager**.

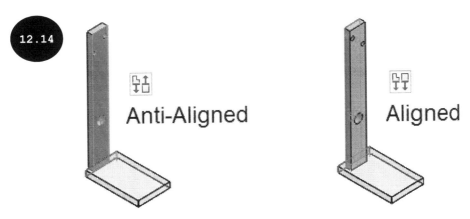

Parallel

The parallel mate is used to make the selected entities parallel to each other, see Figure 12.15. You can select planar faces, edges, planes, or a combination of these as entities for applying parallel mate. Figure 12.15 shows two planar faces and the resultant model after applying the parallel mate.

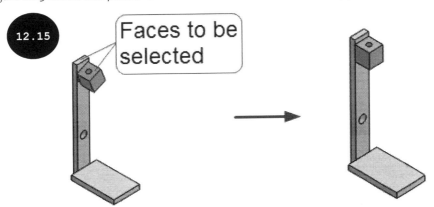

Perpendicular

The perpendicular mate is used to make the selected entities perpendicular to each other, see Figure 12.16. You can select planar faces, edges, planes, or a combination of these as entities for applying perpendicular mate.

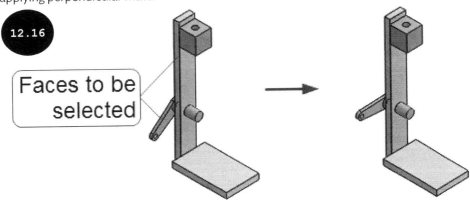

Concentric

The concentric mate is used to make the selected circular entities concentric to each other, see Figure 12.17. You can apply concentric mate between two circular or semi-circular faces and edges. On applying concentric mate, both the selected circular entities share a common axis.

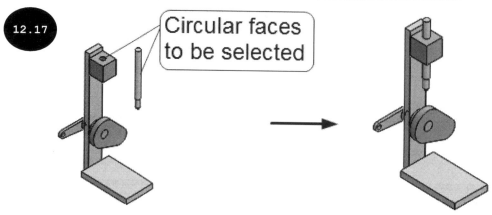

Tangent

The tangent mate is used to make the selected entities tangent to each other. You can select a planar face, a curved face, an edge, or a plane as the first entity and a cylindrical, conical, or spherical face as the second entity for applying the tangent mate. Figure 12.18 shows two faces for applying tangent mate and the resultant model after applying the tangent mate.

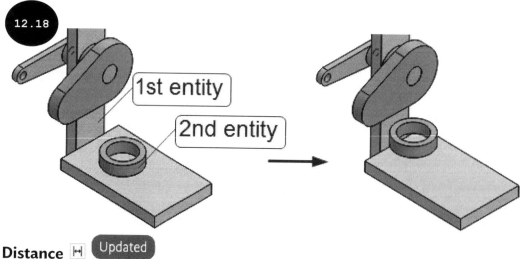

Distance **Updated**

The distance mate is used to keep distance between two entities. You can select planar faces, cylindrical faces, and planes as the entities to apply the distance mate. To apply the distance mate, after selecting the entities, click on the **Distance** button in the **Standard Mates** rollout of the PropertyManager or in the **Mate** Pop-up toolbar. Next, enter the required distance value in the **Distance** field. Figure 12.19 shows planar faces and the resultant model after applying the distance mate. In SOLIDWORKS 2017, while applying the distance mate between two cylindrical faces: **Center to Center, Minimum Distance, Maximum Distance,** and **Custom Distance** buttons become available in the **Standard Mates** rollout of the PropertyManager, see Figure 12.20. By using these buttons, you specify the type of distance measurement between the selected cylindrical faces, see Figure 12.21. In this figure, the distance mate is applied by measuring the center to center distance between the entities.

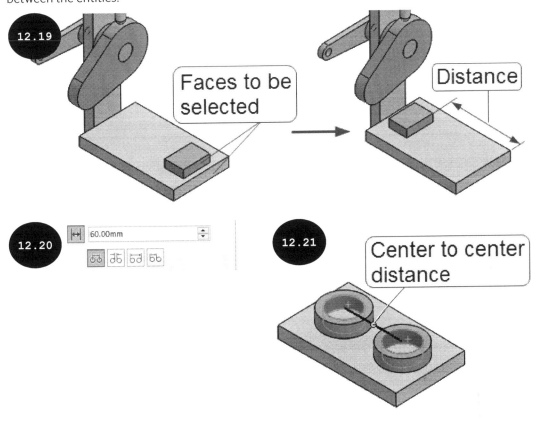

Angle
The angle mate is used to make angle between two selected entities. Figure 12.22 shows faces to be selected and the resultant model after applying the angle mate.

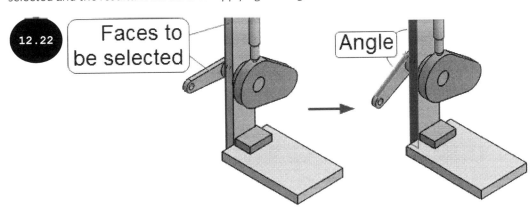

Note: In case of the coincident, parallel, distance, and angle mates, you can flip the mate alignment between the selected entities from aligned to anti-aligned or vice versa.

Lock
The lock mate is used to lock the selected entities at a desired position in the graphics area. On applying the lock mate, all degrees of freedom of the selected entities get fixed.

Working with Advanced Mates
Advanced mates are special types of mates and work one step forward above the standard mates for restricting or reducing degrees of freedom of components. You can apply advanced mates such as profile center, symmetric, width, path, and linear/linear coupler between components by using the **Mate** tool.

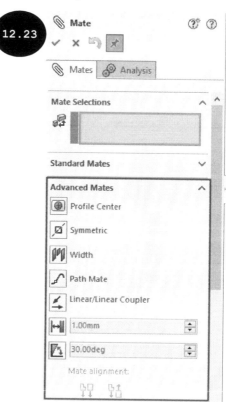

To apply advanced mates, click on the **Mate** tool in the **Assembly CommandManager**. The **Mate PropertyManager** appears. In this PropertyManager, expand the **Advanced Mates** rollout, see Figure 12.23. By using the buttons such as **Profile Center**, **Symmetric**, **Width**, and **Path Mate** in the **Advanced Mates** rollout, you can apply the respective advanced mates between components. The different advanced mates are as follows:

Profile Center Mate
The profile center mate is used to center-align two rectangular profiles, two circular profiles, or a rectangular and a circular profiles of two different components with each other, see Figures 12.24 through 12.26.

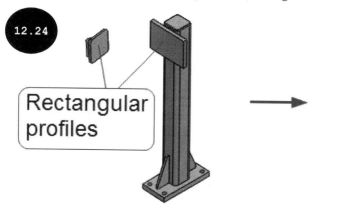
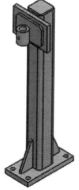

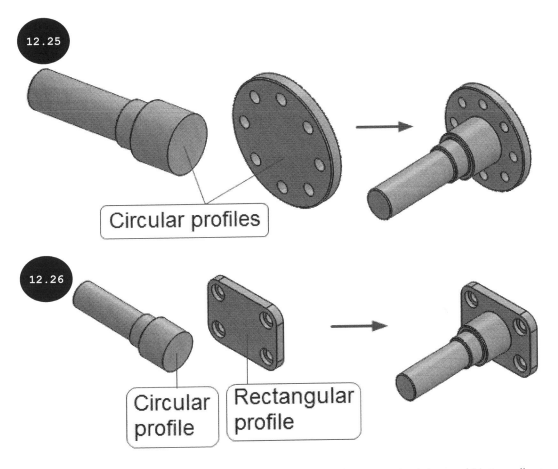

To apply the profile center mate, click on the **Profile Center** button in the **Advanced Mates** rollout of the **Mate PropertyManager**. The **Offset Distance** field is enabled in the **Advanced Mates** rollout, see Figure 12.27.

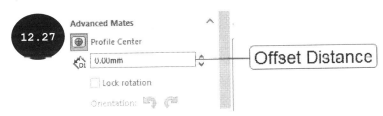

Select entities for applying the profile center mate in the graphics area. You can select two rectangular profiles, two circular profiles (circular faces or circular edges), or a rectangular profile and a circular profile as the entities for applying the profile center mate, refer to Figures 12.24 through 12.26. As soon as you select entities, the preview appears such that the selected entities get centrally aligned to each other. You can also specify offset distance between the selected entities/profiles by using the **Offset Distance** field of the **Advanced Mates** rollout. By default, **0** (zero) is entered in this field. You can enter an offset distance between the selected profiles, as required. The **Flip dimension** check box of the **Advanced Mates** rollout is used to flip the direction of offset dimension between the entities.

The **Lock rotation** check box is used to restrict the rotation movement of the circular profile. Note that the **Lock rotation** check box is enabled if any of the selected entity is a circular profile.

Symmetric Mate

The symmetry mate is used to make two entities of different components symmetric about a plane or a planar face. You can select two vertices, sketch points, edges, axes, sketch lines, planes, planar faces, curved faces of same radii, and so on as the entities to be symmetric.

To apply the symmetric mate, click on the **Symmetric** button in the **Advanced Mates** rollout. The **Entities to Mate** and **Symmetry Plane** fields are enabled in the **Mate Selections** rollout of the PropertyManager. By default, the **Symmetry Plane** field is activated. As a result, you can select a plane or a planar face as the symmetric plane. Select a plane or a planar face as the symmetric plane in the graphics area. The **Entities to Mate** field gets activated, automatically. Select two entities of different components to be symmetric about the symmetric plane in the graphics area. Next, click on the green tick mark ✓ in the PropertyManager. The symmetric mate is applied between the entities with respect to the symmetric plane. Figure 12.28 shows two planar faces as the entities to be symmetric about a symmetric plane and the resultant model after applying the symmetric mate.

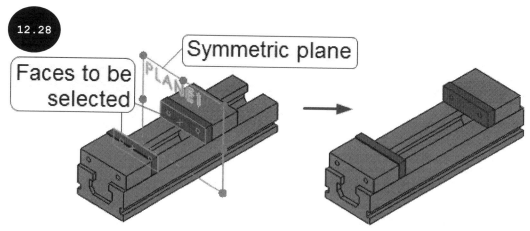

12.28

Width Mate

The width mate is used to make two planar faces, a cylindrical face, or an axis of a component centered between two planar faces of another component, see Figure 12.29. The width mate needs two pairs of selections: one pair of selection is known as width selection and the other pair of selection is known as tab selection, see Figure 12.29. After applying the width mate, the tab selection set is aligned centrally between the width selection set, by default. You can select two planar faces (parallel or non parallel), a cylindrical face, or an axis as the tab selection set. For a width selection set, you can select two parallel or non parallel faces. Figure 12.29 shows planar faces selected as the width selection set and the tab selection set, and the resultant model after applying the width mate.

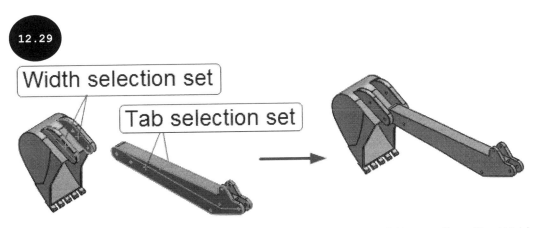

Figure 12.29

To apply the width mate, click on the **Width** button in the **Advanced Mates** rollout. The **Width selections** and **Tab selections** fields are enabled in the **Mate Selections** rollout of the PropertyManager. Also, the **Constraint** drop-down list becomes available in the **Advanced Mates** rollout, see Figure 12.30.

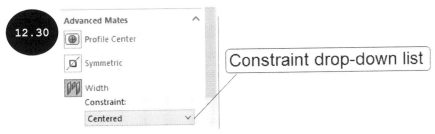

Figure 12.30

By default, the **Width selections** field is activated in the **Mate Selections** rollout. As a result, you can select width selection set in the graphics area. Select two entities (parallel or non parallel faces) as the width selection set. As soon as you select the width selection set, the **Tab selections** field gets activated. Select two planar faces or a cylindrical face as the tab selection set. The preview of the width mate appears. Figure 12.31 shows the two planar faces as the width selection, a cylindrical face as the tab selection, and the preview of the resultant width mate.

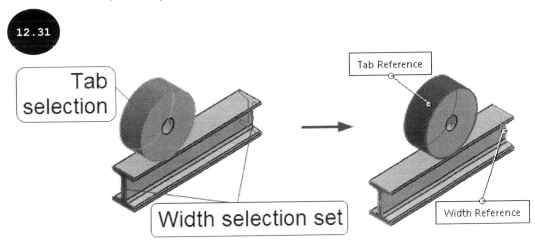

Figure 12.31

Note that the **Centered** option is selected in the **Constraint** drop-down list of the **Advanced Mates** rollout, refer to Figure 12.30. As a result, the tab selection set is centered between the width selection set. You can also select the **Free**, **Dimension**, or **Percent** option from the **Constraint** drop-down list, as required. On selecting the **Free** option, the tab selection set can move freely within the limit of the width selection set. On selecting the **Dimension** option, you can control the position of the tab selection set by specifying a distance value in the **Distance from the End** field of the rollout. On selecting the **Percent** option, you can control the position of the tab selection set by specifying a percentage value in the **Percentage of Distance from the End** field of the rollout. After selecting the required option in the **Constraint** drop-down list, click on the green tick mark in the PropertyManager. The width mate is applied between the selected entities.

Path Mate ⌒ Updated

The path mate is used to constraint a point or a vertex of a component with a path such that the component can move along the defined path, see Figure 12.32.

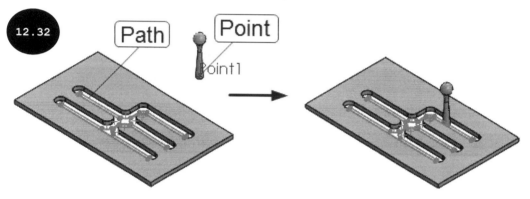

To apply the path mate, click on the **Path Mate** button in the **Advanced Mates** rollout. The **Component Vertex** and **Path Selection** fields are enabled in the **Mate Selections** rollout of the PropertyManager. By default, the **Component Vertex** field is activated. As a result, you can select a point or a vertex of a component for applying the path mate, refer to Figure 12.32. As soon as you select a point or a vertex, the **Path Selection** field gets activated. Select a sketch (open or close) or an edge as the path from the graphics area by clicking the left mouse button. You can use the **SelectionManager** button of the **Mate Selections** rollout to select a sketch having multiple entities. On clicking this button, the **Selection** Pop-up toolbar appears, see Figure 12.33. By using the **Select Closed Loop** and the **Select Open Loop** tools of this Pop-up toolbar, you can select a closed loop and an open loop sketch as the path, respectively. After selecting the path by using the **Selection** Pop-up toolbar, click on the green tick mark in the Pop-up toolbar.

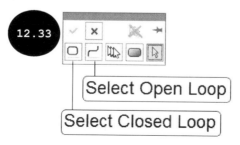

Note that the **Free** option is selected in the **Path Constraint** drop-down list in the **Advanced Mates** rollout, see Figure 12.34. As a result, the component moves freely along the selected path. You can also select the **Distance Along Path** or **Percent Along Path** option from the **Path Constraint** drop-down list, as required. On selecting the **Distance Along Path** option, you can control the position of the component along the path by specifying a distance value in the **Distance from the End** field of the rollout. On selecting the **Percent Along Path** option, you can control the position of the component along the path by specifying a percentage value in the **Percentage of Distance from the End** field of the rollout. Also, in the **Pitch/Yaw Control** and **Roll Control** drop-down lists in the rollout, the **Free** option is selected, by default. As a result, the pitch, yaw, and roll of the component are not constrained and the component is allowed to move freely along the path. On selecting the **Follow Path** option in the **Pitch/Yaw Control** drop-down list, you make an axis (X, Y, or Z) of the component tangent to the path by selecting the respective radio button which appeared on selecting the **Follow Path** option. On selecting the **Up Vector** option in the **Roll Control** drop-down list, you can align an axis (X, Y, or Z) of the component to a vector. You can select a linear edge or a planar face as the vector by using the field which appeared on selecting the **Up Vector** option. After selecting the required option in the **Path Constraint**, **Pitch/Yaw Control**, and **Roll Control** drop-down lists, click on the green tick mark in the PropertyManager. The path mate is applied.

12.34

Tip: To review the movement of the component along the path after applying the path mate, select the moveable component and then drag it such that it travels along the defined path.

Note: To achieve the correct path motion, you need to define the degrees of freedom of the component to be moved such that the component can only move along the path.

Linear/Linear Coupler Mate

The linear/linear coupler mate is used to translate the motion of components with respect to each other. After applying the linear/linear coupler mate between two components, when you move a component, the other component also moves accordingly, see Figure 12.35.

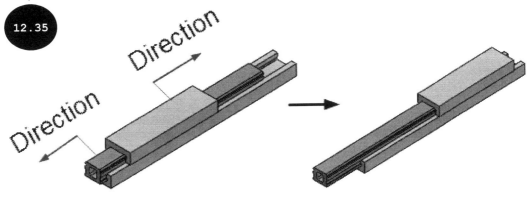

12.35

596 Chapter 12 > Working with Assemblies - I

You can specify the translation ratio between the components by using the **Ratio** fields of the PropertyManager, see Figure 12.36. If the translation ratio is 1: 2 in mm unit, on translating one component to a distance of 1 mm in a direction; the second component is translated automatically to a distance of 2 mm. You can reverse the translation direction of components by using the **Reverse** check box.

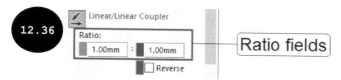

12.36

To apply the linear/linear coupler mate, click on the **Linear/Linear Coupler** button in the **Advanced Mates** rollout. Next, select linear edges of two components one by one as the direction to move the components with respect to each other. Next, specify the translation ratio in the **Ratio** fields of the PropertyManager and then click on the green tick mark ✓ in the PropertyManager. The linear/linear coupler mate is applied.

Tip: To review the translation motion between two components after applying the linear/linear coupler mate, select a component and then drag it.

Distance Mate

The advanced distance mate of the **Advance Mates** rollout is used to specify the minimum and maximum distance limit between two components. After applying this mate, the components can move or translate within the specified distance limit, see Figure 12.37.

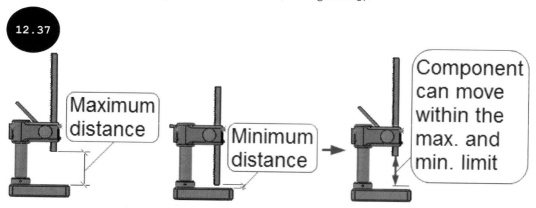

12.37

To apply the advanced distance mate, click on the **Distance** button in the **Advanced Mates** rollout. The **Distance, Maximum Value,** and **Minimum Value** fields get enabled in the PropertyManager, see Figure 12.38. Specify the maximum distance value in the **Maximum Value** field. Next, specify the minimum distance value in the **Minimum Value** field. After specifying the maximum and minimum distance values, select two entities (faces, planes, edges, points, vertices, or a combination of these) of two different components and then click on the green tick mark ✓ in the PropertyManager. The advanced distance mate is applied between the selected entities of the components such that the moveable component can move within the specified maximum and minimum distance limit, refer to Figure 12.37.

SOLIDWORKS 2017: A Power Guide > 597

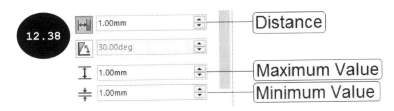

Tip: To review the distance motion between components, select the moveable component and then drag it.

Angle mate

The advanced angle mate of the **Advance Mates** rollout is used to specify the minimum and maximum angle limit between two components. After applying this mate, the components can rotate within the specified angle limit, see Figure 12.39.

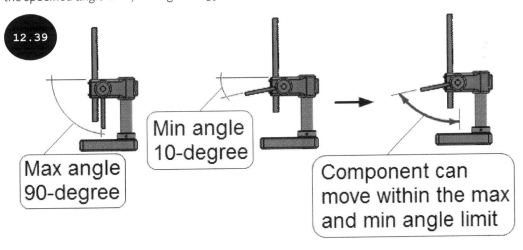

To apply the advanced angle mate, click on the **Angle** button in the **Advanced Mates** rollout. The **Angle**, **Maximum Value**, and **Minimum Value** fields are enabled in the PropertyManager, see Figure 12.40. Specify the maximum angle value in the **Maximum Value** field. Next, specify the minimum angle value in the **Minimum Value** field of the rollout. After specifying the maximum and minimum angle values, select two faces of two different components and then click on the green tick mark in the PropertyManager. The advanced angle mate is applied between the selected faces of the components such that the moveable component can rotate within the specified maximum and minimum angle limit, see Figure 12.39.

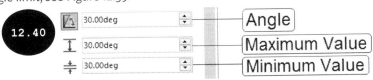

Tip: To review the angle motion between components, select the moveable component and then drag it.

Working with Mechanical Mates

Mechanical mates are used to create mechanism between components of an assembly. You can create cam and follower, gear, hinge, rack and pinion, screw, and universal joint mechanisms between components of an assembly by using mechanical mates. Different types of mechanical mates are available in the **Mechanical Mates** rollout of the **Mate PropertyManager**.

> **Note:** To create a mechanism between components of an assembly by applying mechanical mates, it is necessary to have required degrees of freedom of components such that the components can only be moved or rotated in the desired directions. For example, to create a gear mechanism between two gear components, you need to first constraint the gear components such that they can only rotate about their axes. You can constraint degrees of freedom of a component by using the standard and advanced mates.

To apply a mechanical mate, expand the **Mechanical Mates** rollout of the **Mate PropertyManager**, see Figure 12.41. Different types of mechanical mates are as follows:

Figure 12.41

Cam Mate
The cam mate is used to create cam and follower mechanism between two components of an assembly.

To apply the cam mate, click on the **Cam** button in the **Mechanical Mates** rollout. The **Cam Path** and **Cam Follower** fields appear in the **Mate Selections** rollout of the PropertyManager. By default, the **Cam Path** field is activated. As a result, you can select a face of the cam component. Select a face of the cam component, which is tangent to the series of other faces of the cam component and forms a closed loop, see Figure 12.42. As soon as you have selected a face of the cam component, all faces that are tangent to the selected face get selected automatically and the cam component becomes transparent in the graphics area, see Figure 12.42. Also, the **Cam Follower** field gets activated in the **Mate Selections** rollout. As a result, you can select a face of the follower component. Select a cylindrical, a semi-cylindrical, or a planar face of the follower component, see Figure 12.43. The selected face of the follower component is placed over the cam component, see Figure 12.44. Next, click on the green tick mark in the PropertyManager. The cam mate is applied between the cam and follower components. Now, on rotating the cam component, the follower component moves up and down with respect to the cam profile such that it follows the cam and follower mechanism.

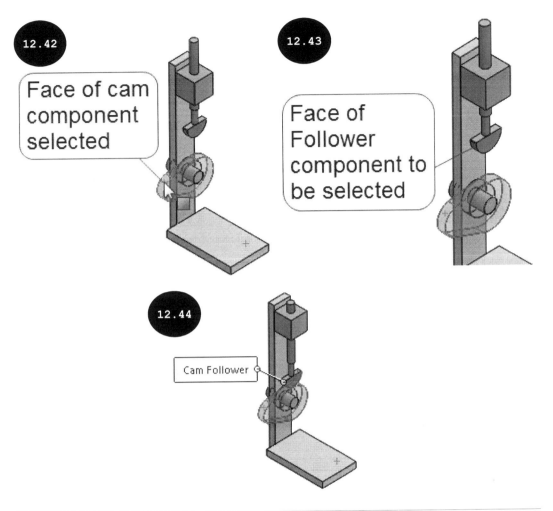

Tip: To review the cam and follower mechanisms between the components, select the cam component and then drag it such that it rotates around its axis of rotation.

Note: To select faces of components for applying mates, you may need to move or rotate the assembly or its individual components. To rotate an assembly, drag the cursor by pressing and holding the middle mouse button. To pan the assembly, drag the cursor by pressing and holding the CTRL key pulse middle mouse button. Alternatively, you can use the **Rotate** and **Pan** tools to rotate and pan the assembly, respectively. You will learn about moving or rotating individual components of an assembly later in this chapter.

Slot Mate

The slot mate is used to drive a bolt, a pin, or a cylindrical feature of a component along the slot of another component in an assembly, see Figure 12.45. You can also apply the slot mate mechanism between two slots of the components.

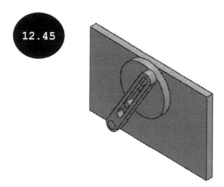

To apply the slot mate, click on the **Slot** button in the **Mechanical Mates** rollout. Next, select a face of the slot of a component, see Figure 12.46. All the remaining tangent faces of the slot are selected, automatically and the component becomes transparent in the graphics area, see Figure 12.46. Next, select a cylindrical face of another component (a bolt, a pin, or a cylindrical feature), see Figure 12.47. The cylindrical face is placed between the slot, see Figure 12.47. Next, click on the green tick mark ✓ in the PropertyManager. The slot mate is applied between the components and now you can review the slot mechanism by dragging the components.

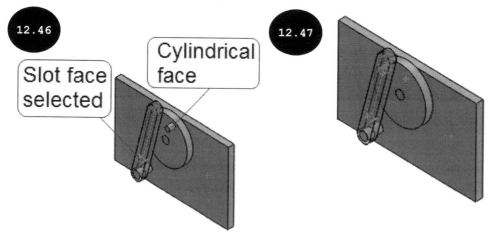

Note: When you click on the **Slot** button, the **Constraint** drop-down list appears in the rollout, see Figure 12.48. By default, the **Free** option is selected in this drop-down list. As a result, the component having the bolt, pin, or cylindrical feature can move freely within the slot of the other component. You can constrain the movement of components by using the **Center in Slot**, **Distance Along Slot**, or **Percentage Along Slot** option of the **Constraint** drop-down list.

Hinge Mate

The hinge mate is used to create hinge mechanism between two components by fixing all degrees of freedom of the components except the rotational degree of freedom, see Figure 12.49. You can also limit the rotational degree of freedom by specifying the minimum and maximum angle of rotation.

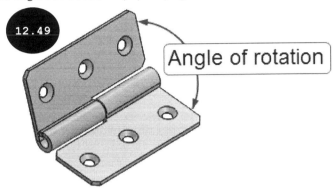

To apply the hinge mate, click on the **Hinge** button, the **Concentric Selections** and **Coincident Selections** fields are enabled in the **Mate Selections** rollout of the PropertyManager. Select two circular faces or circular edges of two different components to be concentric with each other, see Figure 12.50. Next, select two planar faces of the components to be coincident with each other, see Figure 12.51. The concentric and coincident mates are applied between the selected faces of the components, see Figure 12.52. Next, click on the green tick mark ✓ in the PropertyManager. The hinge mate is applied and now you can review the hinge mechanism by dragging the components.

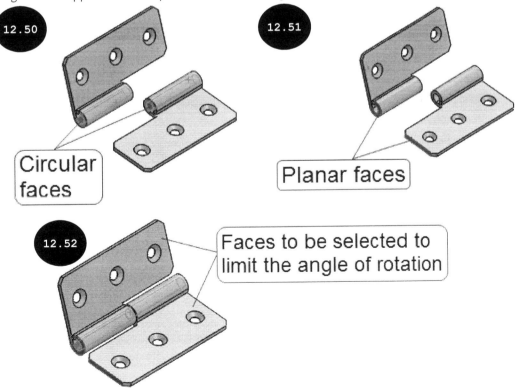

Note: By default, the angle of rotation for the hinge mechanism is 360 degrees. To limit the angle of rotation for the hinge mechanism between the components, click on the **Specify angle limits** check box in the **Mate Selections** rollout of the PropertyManager. The **Angle Selections, Angle, Maximum Value**, and **Minimum Value** fields are enabled in the rollout. By default, the **Angle Selections** field is activated. As a result, you can select faces of the components to limit the angle of rotation between them. Select two planar faces of components, see Figure 12.52. Next, specify the maximum and minimum angle values in the **Maximum Value** and **Minimum Value** fields, respectively and then click on the green tick mark in the PropertyManager.

Gear Mate

The gear mate is used to create gear mechanism between components such that the components can rotate relative to each other, see Figure 12.53.

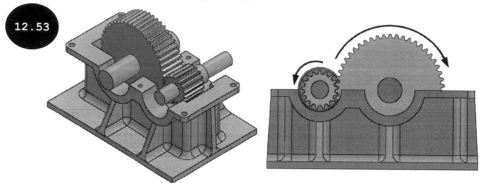

To apply the gear mate, click on the **Gear** button in the **Mechanical Mates** rollout. Next, select a circular face of a gear teeth of the first gear component and then select a circular face of a gear teeth of the second gear component, see Figure 12.54. On selecting the circular faces of the gear components, the axis of rotations of the gears are defined automatically. You can select circular faces, conical faces, axes, or linear edges of the gear components to define the axes of rotation. Next, specify the gear ratio in the **Ratio** fields of the **Mechanical Mates** rollout. Notice that based on the relative size of the faces selected for defining the axis of rotation, the gear ratio is automatically calculated. After defining the gear ratio, click on the green tick mark in the PropertyManager. The gear mate is applied and now you can review the gear mechanism by dragging the gears.

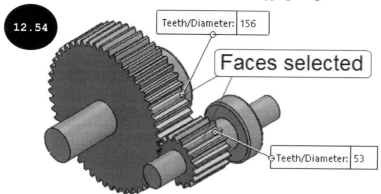

Rack Pinion Mate

The rack pinion mate is used to translate linear motion of one component to the rotational motion of another component and vice versa. This mate creates the rack and pinion mechanism, see Figure 12.55, where the linear motion of the rack component creates rotary motion in the pinion component and vice versa.

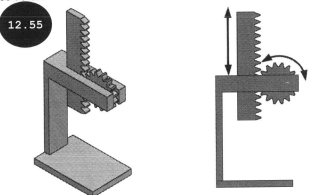

To apply the rack pinion mate, click on the **Rack Pinion** button, the **Rack** and **Pinion/Gear** fields are enabled in the **Mate Selections** rollout of the PropertyManager. Select a linear edge of the rack component, which defines the direction of movement of the rack component, see Figure 12.56. As soon as you select a linear edge of the rack component, the **Pinion/Gear** field gets activated. Select a circular face of the pinion/gear component, which defines the axis of rotation of the pinion component, see Figure 12.56. Next, click on the green tick mark in the PropertyManager. The rack pinion mate is applied between the components and now you can review the rack and pinion mechanism by dragging the components.

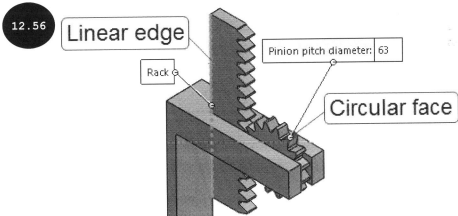

Screw Mate

The screw mate applies the pitch relationship between the rotation of one component and the translation of the other component such that it forms a screw mechanism, see Figure 12.57. On applying the screw mate, the translational motion of one component causes rotational motion in other component based on the specified pitch relationship. You can specify the pitch relationship between two components either by defining the number of revolutions of one component with respect to the per millimeter translation of another component or by defining the distance travelled by one component with respect to the per revolution of the other component.

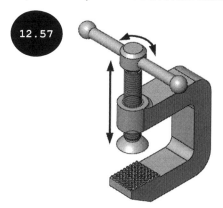

To apply the screw mate, click on the **Screw** button in the **Mechanical Mates** rollout. Next, select a circular face of the first component and then select a circular face of the second component to define their axes of rotation, see Figure 12.58. On selecting the circular faces of both the components, an arrow appears in the graphics area which indicates the direction of revolution, see Figure 12.58. You can reverse the direction of revolution by using the **Reverse** check box of the **Mechanical Mates** rollout, see Figure 12.59. By default, the **Revolutions/mm** radio button is selected in the **Mechanical Mates** rollout, see Figure 12.59. As a result, you can specify the number of revolutions of one component with respect to the per millimeter translation of the other component in the **Revolutions/Distance** field. If you select the **Distance/revolution** radio button then you can specify the distance travelled by one component with respect to the per revolution of other component in the **Revolutions/Distance** field. Next, click on the green tick mark ✓ in the PropertyManager. The screw mate is applied between the components and now you can review the screw mechanism by dragging the components.

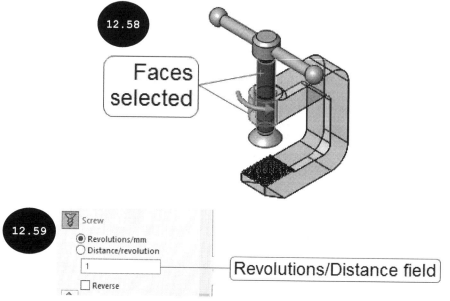

Universal Joint

The universal joint mate is used to translate the rotational movement of one component to the rotational movement of another component about their axes of rotation, see Figure 12.60.

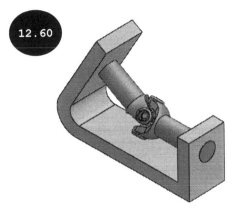

To apply the universal joint mate, click on the **Universal Joint** button in the **Mechanical Mates** rollout. Next, select two cylindrical faces of different components in the graphics area one by one, see Figure 12.61. After selecting the cylindrical faces, click on the green tick mark in the PropertyManager. The universal joint mate is applied between the components and now you can review the universal joint mechanism by dragging the components.

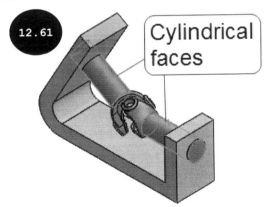

Moving and Rotating Individual Components

In SOLIDWORKS, you can move and rotate individual components of an assembly about their free degrees of freedoms by using the **Move Component** and **Rotate Component** tools of the **Assembly CommandManager**, see Figure 12.62. Both the tools are as follows:

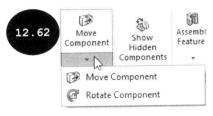

Moving a Component by using the Move Component Tool

In SOLIDWORKS, you can move individual components of an assembly along their free degrees of freedoms by using the **Move Component** tool. To move a component of an assembly, click on the **Move Component** tool in the **Assembly CommandManager**. The **Move Component PropertyManager** appears, see Figure 12.63. By default, the **Free Drag** option is selected in the **Move** drop-down list of the **Move** rollout in the PropertyManager. As a result, you can move the component freely along its free degrees of freedom. Select the component to be moved and then drag the cursor by pressing and holding the left mouse button. The selected component starts moving along with the cursor. To stop the movement of the component, release the left mouse button. The other options in the **Move** drop-down list are **Along Assembly XYZ**, **Along Entity**, **By Delta XYZ**, and **To XYZ Position**, see Figure 12.64. All these options are as follows:

Note: A component cannot move along its fixed or restricted degrees of freedom. For example, if the translational degree of freedom along the X axis of the component is fixed by applying mates then you cannot move the component along the X axis direction.

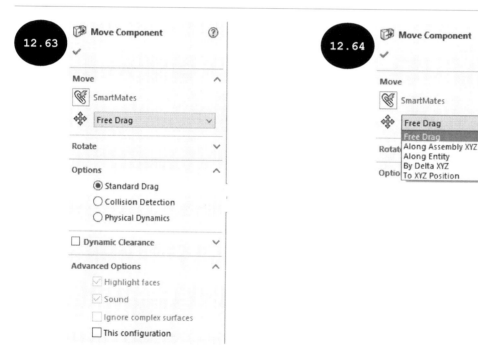

Along Assembly XYZ
On selecting the **Along Assembly XYZ** option, you can move a component along the X, Y, or Z axis of the assembly coordinate system.

Along Entity
On selecting the **Along Entity** option; the **Selected item** field appears in the **Move** rollout, see Figure 12.65. This field is used to select an entity as the direction along which the selected component has to be moved. You can select a linear edge, a sketch line, or an axis as the entity to define the direction along which the component has to be moved. After selecting the entity, select the

component to be moved and then drag the cursor. The selected component starts moving along the direction of the entity selected.

By Delta XYZ

On selecting the **By Delta XYZ** option, the **Delta X**, **Delta Y**, and **Delta Z** fields appear, see Figure 12.66. In these fields, you can specify the X, Y, and Z distance values for moving the component with respect to the current location of the component. After specifying the X, Y, and Z distance values in the respective fields, select the component to be moved and then click on the **Apply** button. The selected component moves with respect to the specified distance value.

To XYZ Position

On selecting the **To XYZ Position** option, the **X Coordinate**, **Y Coordinate**, and **Z Coordinate** fields get enabled in the PropertyManager, see Figure 12.67. These fields are used to specify the X, Y, and Z coordinates of the location where you want to move the selected component. After specifying the coordinate, click on the **Apply** button. The origin of the selected component is moved to the specified coordinate. Note that if you select a vertex or a point of the component to be moved then after clicking on the **Apply** button, the selected vertex or point of the component is moved to the specified coordinate location.

Note that by default the movement of the component is not prevented from any interference or collision occurred with other components of an assembly. It means the component moves continuously even if any other component comes across its way. This is because the **Standard Drag** radio button is selected in the **Options** rollout of the **Move Component PropertyManager**, see Figure 12.68. By selecting the **Collision Detection** or **Physical Dynamics** radio button, you can detect collisions or analyze the motion between components of an assembly. The methods of detecting collision and analyzing motion between components by using the **Collision Detection** and **Physical Dynamics** radio buttons are as follows:

Detecting Collision between Components

You can detect the collision between components of an assembly while moving a component by using the **Collision Detection** radio button. To detect collision between components, select the **Collision Detection** radio button in the **Options** rollout of the PropertyManager. The **All components** and **These components** radio buttons as well as the **Stop at collision** and **Dragged part only** check boxes appear in the **Options** rollout of the PropertyManager, see Figure 12.69.

By default, the **All components** radio button is selected. As a result, collision is detected when the moveable component collides with any other component of the assembly. Note that as soon as collision is detected between the components, the components are highlighted in the graphics area, see Figure 12.70. If the **Stop at collision** check box is selected in the rollout then the movement of the component is stopped as soon as it collides with other component of the assembly.

On selecting the **These components** radio button, the **Components for Collision Check** field appears in the PropertyManager. This field is used to select components for the detection of collision. After selecting the components for the detection of collision, click on the **Resume Drag** button and then drag the component to be moved. Note that the collision is detected only when the component being moved touches any of the selected components of the assembly. Note that the components which are not listed in the **Components for Collision Check** field are ignored by the moveable component.

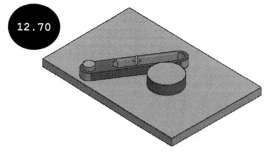

When the **Dragged part only** check box is selected in the **Options** rollout, collision is checked only for the component which is selected to be moved. However, if this check box is cleared then the collision is even checked for the components that move because of the mates with the moveable component.

Detecting Collision and Analyzing Motion between Components

Similar to the **Collision Detection** radio button, the **Physical Dynamics** radio button is also used to detect collision with the only difference that it forces the components to move along with the component, when the collision gets detected between them. In other words, by selecting the **Physical Dynamics** radio button, you can analyze the motion between the components of an assembly. Note that components can only move or rotate within their free degrees of freedom.

Note: In addition to moving individual components and detecting collision, you can also rotate components by using the **Rotate Component PropertyManager**. You can invoke the **Rotate Component PropertyManager** by expanding the **Rotate** rollout of the **Move Component PropertyManager** or by clicking on the **Rotate Component** tool in the **CommandManager**. The options of the **Rotate Component PropertyManager** are discussed next.

Rotating a Component by using the Rotate Component Tool

Similar to moving individual components, you can rotate individual components of an assembly about their free degrees of freedom by using the **Rotate Component** tool. To rotate a component of an assembly, click on the **Rotate Component** tool in the **Assembly CommandManager**, see Figure 12.71. The **Rotate Component PropertyManager** appears, see Figure 12.72.

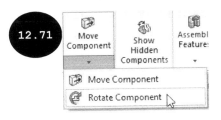

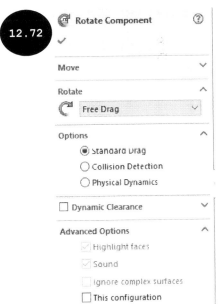

By default, the **Free Drag** option is selected in the **Rotate** drop-down list of the **Rotate** rollout in the PropertyManager. As a result, you can rotate a component freely about any axis by dragging the component. Select the component to be rotated in the graphics area and then drag the cursor about its degree of freedom by pressing and holding the left mouse button. The selected component starts rotating about the axis of rotation. Once you have rotated the component, release the left mouse button. All the options in the **Rotate Component PropertyManager** are the same as those discussed earlier while moving the component by using the **Move Component PropertyManager**.

Working with SmartMates

SmartMates is a smart method of applying standard mates such as coincident, parallel, and perpendicular between the components of an assembly. By using this method, you can save time and the designing process becomes faster. The SmartMates method of applying mates can be invoked by clicking on the **SmartMates** button in the **Move Component PropertyManager**. Note that as soon as you click on the **SmartMates** button, the **SmartMates PropertyManager** appears, see Figure 12.73. You can invoke the **Move Component PropertyManager** by clicking on the **Move Components** tool in the Assembly CommandManager.

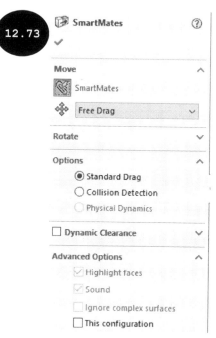

Once the **SmartMates PropertyManager** has been invoked, double-click on an entity of the component for applying a mate. The selected entity gets highlighted and the component becomes transparent in the graphics area, see Figure 12.74. Next, click on an entity of the other component of the assembly for applying the mate. The **Mate** Pop-up toolbar appears with the most suitable mate tool activated in it, by default. Also, the preview appears such that the most suitable mate is applied between the selected entities of the components, see Figure 12.75. You can apply mate by clicking the respective tool in the Pop-up tool. Next, click on the green tick mark ✓ in the toolbar. The selected mate is applied between the entities of the components.

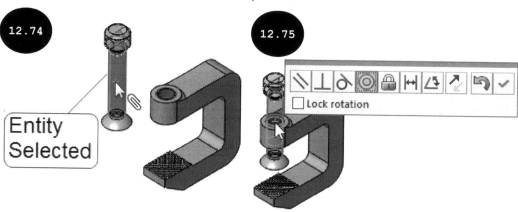

> **Note:** You can also press the ALT key and then drag a component toward the other component for applying a standard mate without invoking the **SmartMates PropertyManager**.

Tutorial 1

Create the assembly shown in Figure 12.76. For different views and dimensions of the components of the assembly, see Figures 12.77 through 12.83.

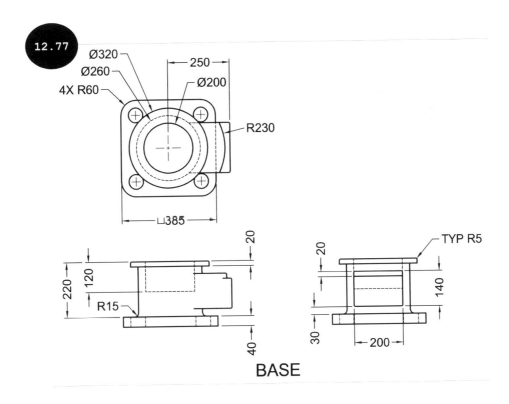

BASE

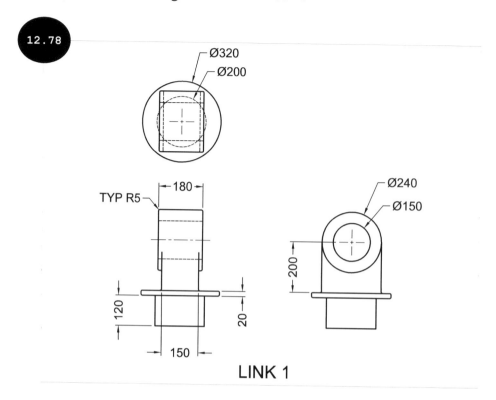

LINK 1

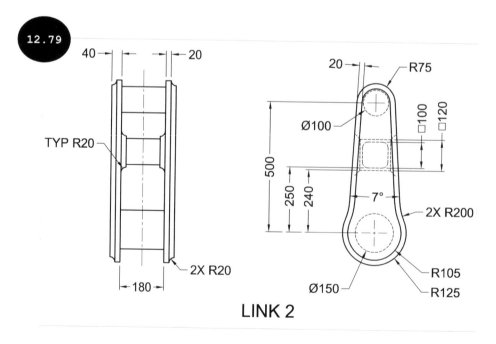

LINK 2

12.80

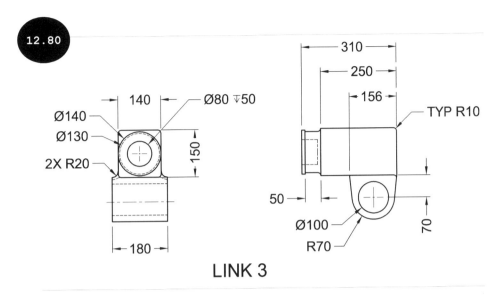

LINK 3

12.81

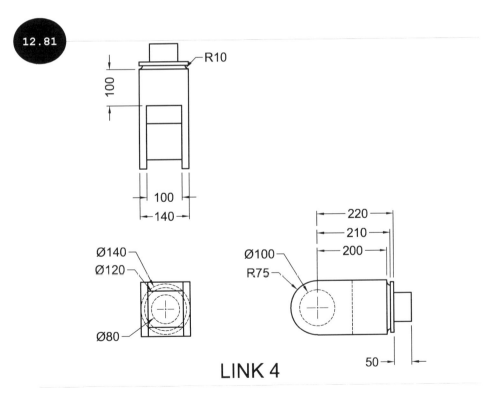

LINK 4

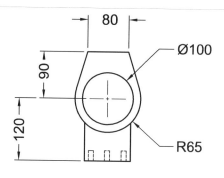

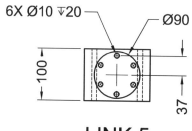

LINK 5

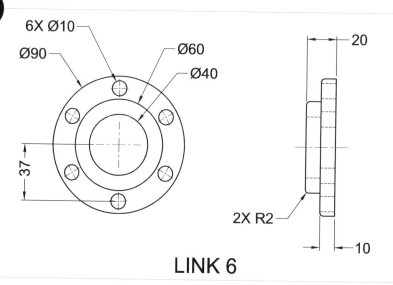

LINK 6

Section 1: Starting SOLIDWORKS and Creating Assembly Components

In this section, you will create all the components of the assembly in the Part modeling environment one by one.

1. Start SOLIDWORKS by double-clicking on the SOLIDWORKS icon on your desktop.

2. Create all components of the assembly one by one in the Part modeling environment. Refer to Figures 12.77 through 12.83 for the dimensions of each component. After creating components, save them in the *Tutorial 1* folder of the *Chapter 12* folder. You need to create these folders in the *SOLIDWORKS* folder.

> **Note:** You can also download all the components of the assembly from *www.cadartifex.com*. If you are a first time user, you need to register yourself to access the online resources.

Section 2: Invoking the Assembly Environment

After creating all the components, you need to assemble them in the Assembly environment.

1. Click on the **New** tool in the **Standard** toolbar. The **New SOLIDWORKS Document** dialog box appears.

2. Click on the **Assembly** button and then click on the **OK** button in the dialog box. The Assembly environment is invoked and the **Open** dialog box appears along with the **Begin Assembly PropertyManager**, see Figure 12.84.

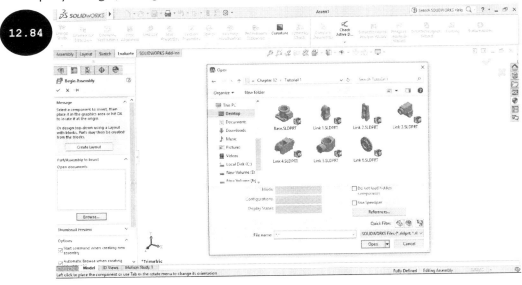

> **Note:** On invoking the Assembly environment, the **Open** dialog box appears, automatically along with the **Begin Assembly PropertyManager**, if none of the components are opened in the current session of SOLIDWORKS. If the **Open** dialog box does not appear, then click on the **Browse** button in the **Begin Assembly PropertyManager** to open it.

616 Chapter 12 > Working with Assemblies - I

Section 3: Inserting the First Component

1. Browse to the location where all the components of the assembly are saved (\SOLIDWORKS\ Chapter 12\Tutorial 1) by using the Open dialog box.

2. Select the *Base* component and then click on the Open button in the dialog box. The selected component is attached to the cursor, see Figure 12.85. Also, the Rotate Context toolbar appears in the graphics area, see Figure 12.85.

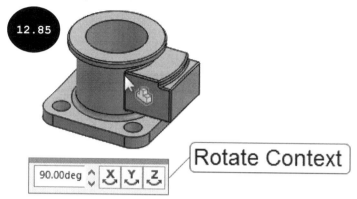

3. Click anywhere in the graphics area, the attached component moves toward the origin of the assembly and becomes the fixed component.

Section 4: Inserting the Second Component

1. Click on the Insert Components tool in the Assembly CommandManager. The Open dialog box appears, automatically along with the Insert Component PropertyManager. Note that the Open dialog box appears only if none of the components are opened in the current session of SOLIDWORKS. If the Open dialog box does not appear, automatically then click on the Browse button in the Insert Component PropertyManager to open the Open dialog box.

2. Browse to the location where all the components of the assembly are saved and then select the *LINK 1* component. Next, click on the Open button in the dialog box. The selected component is attached to the cursor, see Figure 12.86. Also, the Rotate Context toolbar appears in the graphics area, see Figure 12.86.

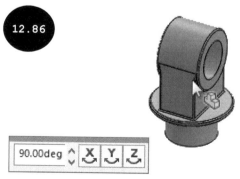

3. Enter **300** in the **Angle** field of the **Rotate Context** toolbar as the angle value to rotate the component. Next, click on the **X** tool in the **Rotate Context** toolbar. The component is rotated at 300-degree about the X axis in the graphics area, see Figure 12.87.

4. Click anywhere in the graphics area to specify the placement point for the second component (*LINK 1*). The component (*LINK 1*) is placed in the specified location, see Figure 12.88. Make sure that you specify the placement point such that the inserted component does not intersect the first component of the assembly.

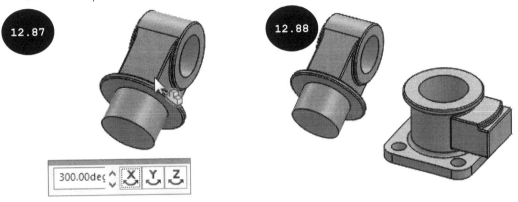

Note: By default, all degrees of freedom of the second component are free, which means the second component is free to translate and rotate along and about its axes. You need to apply the required mates to fix its required degrees of freedom with respect to the first component of the assembly.

Section 5: Assembling the Second Component

Before you insert the third component in the Assembly environment, it is recommended to first assemble the second component with the first component of the assembly.

1. Click on the **Mate** tool in the **Assembly CommandManager**. The **Mate PropertyManager** appears.

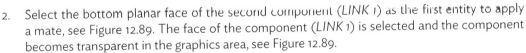

2. Select the bottom planar face of the second component (*LINK 1*) as the first entity to apply a mate, see Figure 12.89. The face of the component (*LINK 1*) is selected and the component becomes transparent in the graphics area, see Figure 12.89.

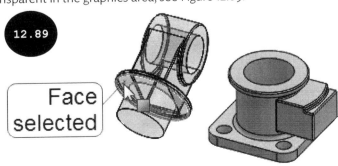

3. Select the top planar face of the first component (Base) as the second entity to apply the mate, see Figure 12.90. The Pop-up toolbar appears with the **Coincident** tool activated in it, by default. Also, the selected faces of the components become coincident to each other, see Figure 12.91.

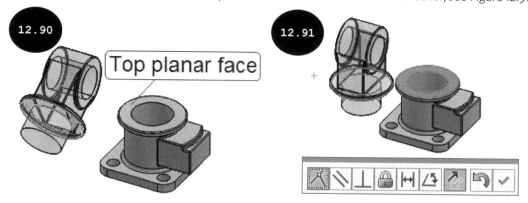

4. Click on the green tick mark button in the Pop-up toolbar. The coincident mate is applied between the selected faces of the components.

5. Select the cylindrical face of the second component (LINK 1) as the first entity to apply the concentric mate, see Figure 12.92. The cylindrical face of the component (LINK 1) is selected and the component becomes transparent in the graphics area, see Figure 12.92.

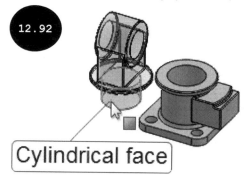

6. Select the inner circular face of the first component (Base) as the second entity to apply the concentric mate, see Figure 12.93. The Pop-up toolbar appears with the **Concentric** tool activated in it, by default. Also, the selected faces of the components become concentric to each other, see Figure 12.94.

7. Click on the green tick mark button in the Pop-up toolbar. The concentric mate is applied between the selected faces of the components. Next, exit the **Mate PropertyManager** by clicking on its green tick mark.

Note: After applying the coincident and concentric mate, the second component (LINK 1) cannot translate in any direction. However, it can rotate about its axis. This is because the rotational degree of freedom of the component has not been restricted.

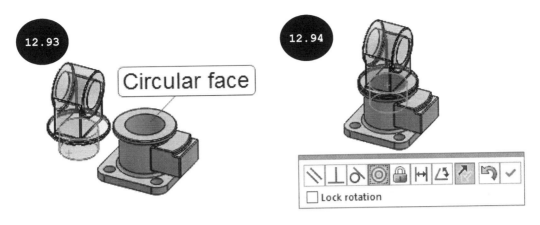

Section 6: Inserting the Third Component

1. Click on the **Insert Components** tool in the **Assembly CommandManager**. The **Open** dialog box appears along with the **Insert Component PropertyManager**. If the **Open** dialog box does not appear, automatically then click on the **Browse** button in the **Insert Component PropertyManager** to open the **Open** dialog box.

2. Select the third component (*LINK 2*) and then click on the **Open** button in the dialog box. The third component (*LINK 2*) is attached to the cursor, see Figure 12.95.

3. Click anywhere in the graphics area to specify the placement point for the third component (*LINK 2*). The component is placed in the specified location. Make sure that you specify the placement point such that the inserted component does not intersect the other components of the assembly.

Section 7: Assembling the Third Component

1. Click on the **Mate** tool in the **Assembly CommandManager**. The **Mate PropertyManager** appears.

2. Select the bottom cylindrical face of the third component (*LINK 2*) as the first entity to apply the concentric mate, see Figure 12.96. The cylindrical face of the component (*LINK 2*) is selected and the component becomes transparent in the graphics area, see Figure 12.96.

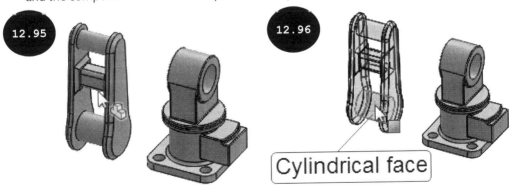

3. Select the inner circular face of the second component (LINK 1) as the second entity to apply the concentric mate, see Figure 12.97. The Pop-up toolbar appears with the **Concentric** tool activated in it, by default. Also, the selected faces of the components become concentric to each other, see Figure 12.98.

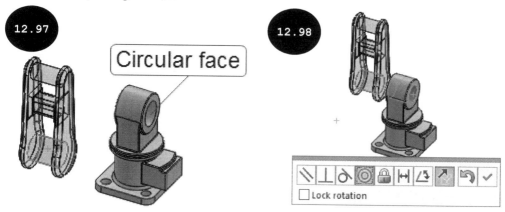

4. Click on the green tick mark button in the Pop-up toolbar. The concentric mate is applied between the selected faces of the components.

5. Select the inner planar face of the third component (LINK 2) as the first entity to apply the coincident mate, see Figure 12.99. Note that to select the inner planar face of the third component as shown in Figure 12.99, you need to rotate the assembly by dragging the cursor after pressing and holding the middle mouse button. Alternatively, you can use the **Rotate** tool to rotate the assembly. After selecting the inner planar face of the third component (LINK 2), you can change the orientation of the assembly back to isometric.

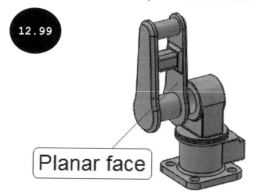

6. Select the right planar face of the second component (LINK 1) as the second entity to apply the coincident mate, see Figure 12.100. The Pop-up toolbar appears with the **Coincident** tool activated in it, by default. Also, the selected faces of the components become coincident to each other, see Figure 12.101.

7. Click on the green tick mark button in the Pop-up toolbar. The coincident mate is applied between the selected faces of the components. Next, exit the **Mate PropertyManager**.

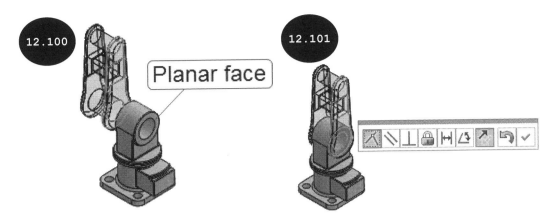

Section 8: Inserting the Fourth Component

1. Click on the **Insert Components** tool in the **Assembly CommandManager**. The **Open** dialog box appears along with the **Insert Component PropertyManager**. If the **Open** dialog box does not appear, automatically then click on the **Browse** button in the **Insert Component PropertyManager** to open the **Open** dialog box.

2. Select the fourth component (*LINK 3*) and then click on the **Open** button in the dialog box. The fourth component (*LINK 3*) is attached to the cursor.

3. Click anywhere in the graphics area to specify the placement point for the fourth component (*LINK 3*). The component (*LINK 3*) is placed in the specified location, see Figure 12.102.

Section 9: Assembling the Fourth Component

1. Click on the **Mate** tool in the **Assembly CommandManager**. The **Mate PropertyManager** appears.

2. Select the inner circular face of the fourth component (*LINK 3*) as the first entity to apply the concentric mate, see Figure 12.103. The circular face of the component (*LINK 3*) is selected and the component becomes transparent in the graphics area, see Figure 12.103.

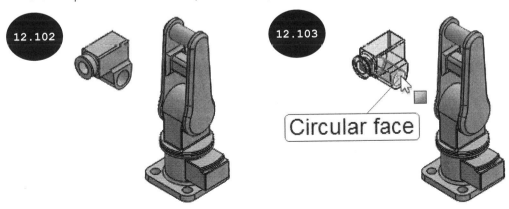

3. Select the upper cylindrical face of the third component (LINK 2) as the second entity to apply the concentric mate, see Figure 12.104. The Pop-up toolbar appears with the **Concentric** tool activated in it, by default. Also, the selected faces of the components become concentric to each other.

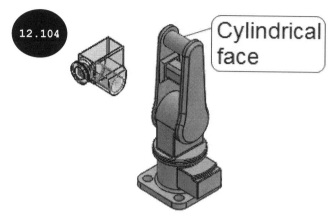

4. Click on the green tick mark ✓ in the Pop-up toolbar. The concentric mate is applied between the selected faces of the components.

5. Select the right planar face of the fourth component (LINK 3) as the first entity to apply the coincident mate, see Figure 12.105. The face of the component (LINK 3) is selected and the component becomes transparent in the graphics area, see Figure 12.105.

6. Select the inner planar face of the third component (LINK 2) as the second entity to apply the coincident mate, see Figure 12.106. The Pop-up toolbar appears with the **Coincident** tool activated in it. Also, the selected faces of the components become coincident to each other. Note that to select the inner planar face of the third component as shown in Figure 12.106, you need to rotate the assembly. After selecting the face, you can change the orientation of the assembly back to isometric.

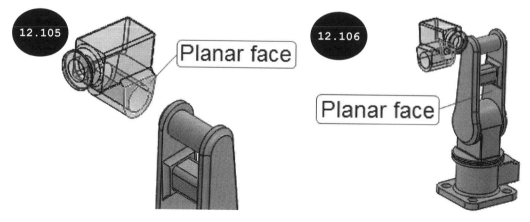

7. Click on the green tick mark ✓ in the Pop-up toolbar. The coincident mate is applied between the selected faces of the components. Next, exit the **Mate PropertyManager**.

Section 10: Inserting the Fifth Component

1. Click on the **Insert Components** tool in the **Assembly CommandManager**. The **Open** dialog box appears along with the **Insert Component PropertyManager**. If the **Open** dialog box does not appear, automatically then click on the **Browse** button in the **Insert Component PropertyManager** to open the **Open** dialog box.

2. Select the fifth component (*LINK 4*) and then click on the **Open** button in the dialog box. The fifth component (*LINK 4*) is attached to the cursor. Also, the **Rotate Context** toolbar appears in the graphics area.

3. Enter **90** in the **Angle** field of the **Rotate Context** toolbar as the angle value to rotate the component. Next, click on the **Z** tool in the **Rotate Context** toolbar. The component is rotated at 90-degree about the Z axis in the graphics area, see Figure 12.107.

4. Click anywhere in the graphics area to specify the placement point for the fifth component (*LINK 4*). The component (*LINK 4*) is placed in the specified location, see Figure 12.107.

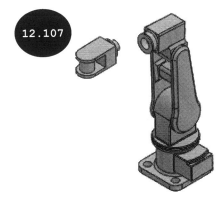

12.107

Section 11: Assembling the Fifth Component

1. Invoke the **Mate PropertyManager** by clicking on the **Mate** tool.

2. Select the back planar face of the fifth component (*LINK 4*) as the first entity to apply the coincident mate, see Figure 12.108. The face of the component is selected and the component becomes transparent in the graphics area. Note that to select the back planar face of the fifth component as shown in Figure 12.108, you need to rotate the assembly. After selecting the face, you can change the orientation of the assembly back to isometric.

3. Select the inner planar face of the fourth component (*LINK 3*) as the second entity, see Figure 12.109. The Pop-up toolbar appears with the **Coincident** tool activated in it, by default. Also, the selected faces of the components become coincident to each other.

4. Click on the green tick mark ✓ in the Pop-up toolbar. The coincident mate is applied between the selected faces of the components.

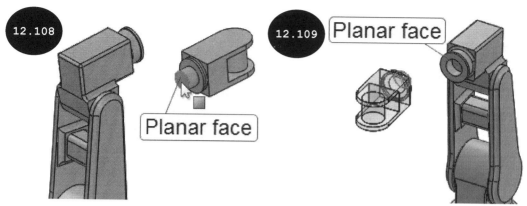

5. Select the back cylindrical face of the fifth component (LINK 4) as the first entity, see Figure 12.110.

6. Select the inner circular face of the fourth component (LINK 3) as the second entity, see Figure 12.111. The Pop-up toolbar appears with the **Concentric** tool activated in it. Also, the selected faces of the components become concentric to each other.

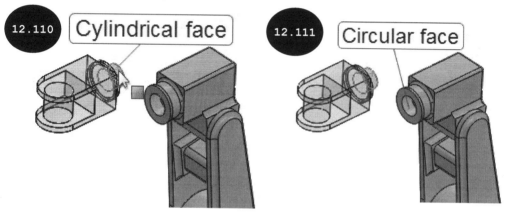

7. Click on the green tick mark in the Pop-up toolbar. The concentric mate is applied between the selected faces of the components. Next, exit the **Mate PropertyManager**.

Note: You may need to move components to select their faces for applying mates. To move a component, press and hold the left mouse button over the component to be moved and then drag the cursor.

Section 12: Inserting the Sixth Component

1. Click on the **Insert Components** tool in the **Assembly CommandManager**. The **Open** dialog box appears along with the **Insert Component PropertyManager**.

2. Select the sixth component (LINK 5) and then click on the **Open** button in the dialog box. The sixth component (LINK 5) is attached to the cursor.

3. Click anywhere in the graphics area to specify the placement point for the sixth component (*LINK 5*). The component (*LINK 5*) is placed in the specified location.

Section 13: Assembling the Sixth Component

1. Click on the **Mate** tool. The **Mate PropertyManager** appears.

2. Select the upper planar face of the sixth component (*LINK 5*) as the first entity, see Figure 12.112.

3. Select the planar face of the fifth component (*LINK 4*) as the second entity, see Figure 12.113. The Pop-up toolbar appears with the **Coincident** tool activated in it. Also, the selected faces of the components become coincident to each other.

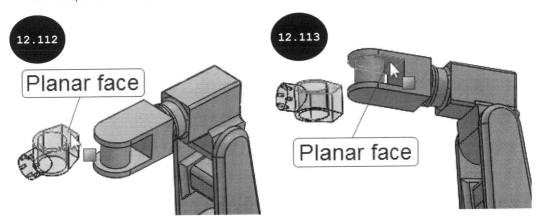

4. Click on the green tick mark ✔ in the Pop-up toolbar. The coincident mate is applied between the selected faces of the components.

5. Select the inner circular face of the sixth component (*LINK 5*) as the first entity, see Figure 12.114.

6. Select the cylindrical face of the fifth component (*LINK 4*) as the second entity, see Figure 12.115. The Pop-up toolbar appears and the selected faces become concentric.

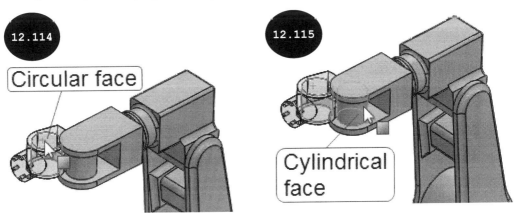

7. Click on the green tick mark ✓ in the Pop-up toolbar. The concentric mate is applied between the selected faces of the components. Next, exit the **Mate PropertyManager**.

Section 14: Inserting and Assembling the Seventh Component
1. Similarly insert the seventh component (*LINK 6*) and assemble it with the assembly by applying the mates, see Figure 12.116.

Section 15: Saving the Model
1. Click on the **Save** tool of the **Standard** toolbar. The **Save As** dialog box appears.

2. Browse to the *Tutorial 1* folder of the *Chapter 12* folder and then save the assembly with the name Tutorial 1.

Tutorial 2

Create the assembly shown in Figure 12.117. The exploded view of the assembly is shown in Figure 12.118 for your reference only. Different views and dimensions of individual components of the assembly are shown in Figures 12.119 through 12.127.

12.118

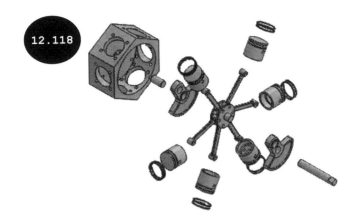

12.119

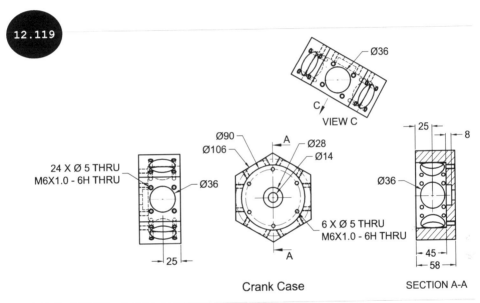

Crank Case

SECTION A-A

12.120

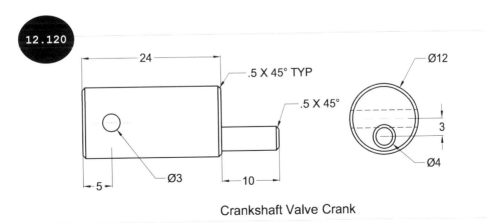

Crankshaft Valve Crank

12.121

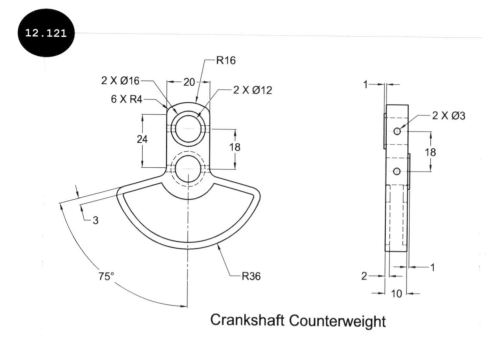

Crankshaft Counterweight

12.122

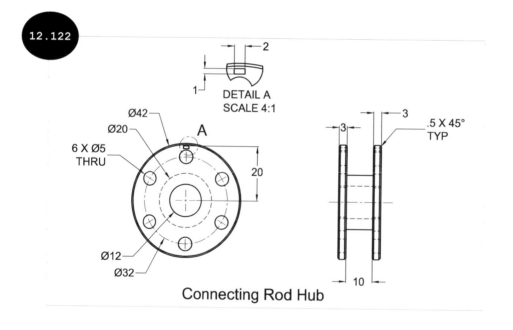

Connecting Rod Hub

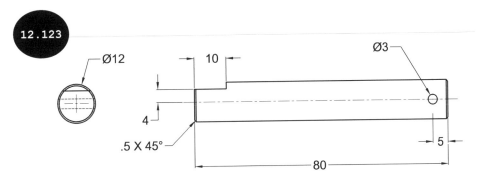

Crankshaft

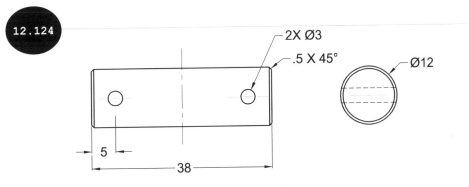

Crankshaft Pin

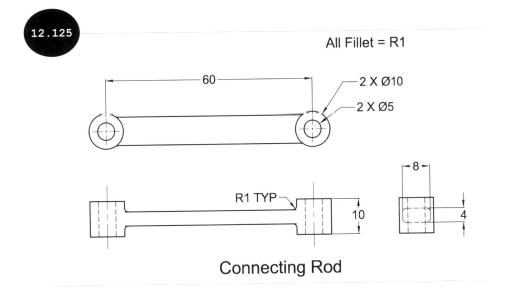

Connecting Rod

12.126

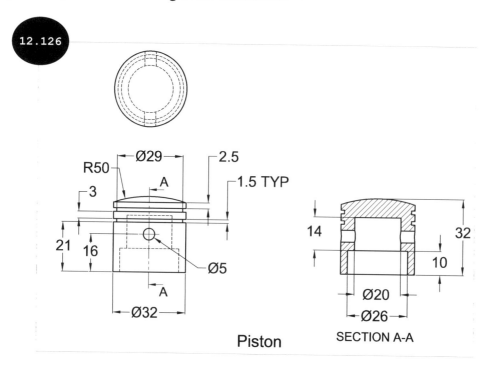

Piston

SECTION A-A

12.127

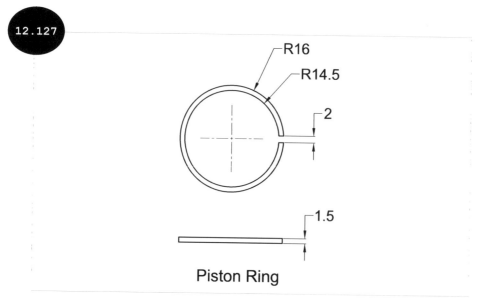

Piston Ring

Section 1: Starting SOLIDWORKS and Creating Assembly Components

In this section, you will create all components of the assembly.

1. Start SOLIDWORKS by double-clicking on the SOLIDWORKS icon on your desktop.

2. Create all the components of the assembly one by one in the Part modeling environment. Refer to Figures 12.119 through 12.127 for the dimensions of each component. After creating all the components of the assembly, save them in the *Tutorial 2* folder of the *Chapter 12* folder. You need to create these folders in the SOLIDWORKS folder, if not created in Tutorial 1.

Note: You can also download all the components of the assembly from www.cadartifex.com. If you are a first time user, you need to register yourself to access the online resources.

Section 2: Invoking the Assembly Environment

1. Click on the **New** tool in the **Standard** toolbar of SOLIDWORKS. The **New SOLIDWORKS Document** dialog box appears.

2. Double-click on the **Assembly** button in the dialog box. The Assembly environment is invoked and the **Open** dialog box appears along with the **Begin Assembly PropertyManager**, see Figure 12.128.

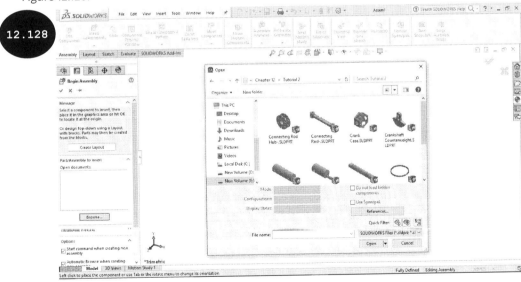

12.128

Note: On invoking the Assembly environment, the **Open** dialog box appears, automatically along with the **Begin Assembly PropertyManager**, if none of the components are opened in the current session of SOLIDWORKS. If the **Open** dialog box does not appear, then click on the **Browse** button in the **Begin Assembly PropertyManager** to open it.

Section 3: Creating the Piston Sub-Assembly

In this section, you will create the Piston sub-assembly.

1. Browse to the *Tutorial 2* folder of *Chapter 12*, where all the components of the assembly have been saved by using the **Open** dialog box.

2. Select the first component (*Piston*) and then click on the **Open** button in the dialog box. The first component (*Piston*) is attached to the cursor. Also, the **Rotate Context** toolbar appears in the graphics area.

3. Click anywhere in the graphics area. The first component (*Piston*) moves toward the origin of the assembly and becomes the fixed component automatically, see Figure 12.129.

   Now, you need to insert the second component of the Piston sub-assembly in the Assembly environment.

4. Click on the **Insert Components** tool in the **Assembly CommandManager**. The **Open** dialog box appears along with the **Insert Component PropertyManager**. If the **Open** dialog box does not appear, automatically then click on the **Browse** button in the **Insert Component PropertyManager** to open the **Open** dialog box.

5. Browse to the location where all components of the assembly have been saved and then select the second component (*Piston Ring*). Next, click on the **Open** button in the dialog box. The second component (*Piston Ring*) is attached to the cursor.

6. Click anywhere in the graphics area to specify the placement point of the second component (*Piston Ring*). The component (*Piston Ring*) is placed in the graphics area, see Figure 12.130. Make sure that you specify the placement point such that the component does not intersect with the first component of the assembly.

Note: By default, all degrees of freedom of the second component are free, which means the second component is free to translate and rotate along and about its axis. You need to apply the required mates to fix its required degrees of freedom with respect to the first component of the assembly.

Now, you need to assemble the second component (*Piston Ring*) with the first component (*Piston*) by applying the required mates between them.

7. Click on the **Mate** tool in the **Assembly CommandManager**. The **Mate PropertyManager** appears.

8. Select the bottom planar face of the second component (*Piston Ring*) as the first entity to apply a mate, see Figure 12.131. The bottom face of the component (Piston Ring) is selected and the component becomes transparent in the graphics area. Note that to select the bottom face of the second component (Piston Ring), you need to rotate the assembly. After selecting the face, you can change the orientation of the assembly back to isometric.

9. Select the planar face of the first component (*Piston*) as the second entity to apply the mate, see Figure 12.132. The Pop-up toolbar appears with the **Coincident** tool activated in it, by default. Also, the selected faces of the components become coincident to each other.

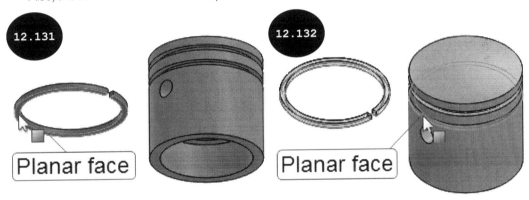

Note: To select the faces of components for applying mates, you may also need to rotate individual components of an assembly. You can rotate individual components by using the **Rotate Components** tool.

10. Click on the green tick mark ✓ in the Pop-up toolbar. The coincident mate is applied between the selected faces of the components.

11. Select the inner circular face of the second component (*Piston Ring*) as the first entity to apply a mate, see Figure 12.133.

12. Select the outer cylindrical face of the first component (*Piston*) as the second entity to apply the mate, see Figure 12.134. The Pop-up toolbar appears with the **Concentric** tool activated in it. Also, the selected faces of the components become concentric to each other.

13. Click on the green tick mark ✓ in the Pop-up toolbar. The concentric mate is applied between the selected faces of the components. Next, exit the **Mate PropertyManager** by clicking on its green tick mark button.

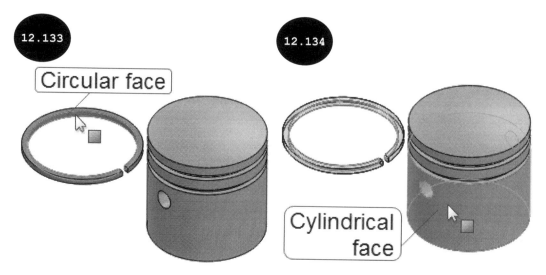

Figure 12.133, Figure 12.134

Now, you need to insert the second instance of the *Piston Ring* component in the Assembly environment and assemble it with the first component (*Piston*).

14. Move the cursor over the name of the second component (*Piston Ring*) in the FeatureManager Design Tree and then press and hold the left mouse button and the CTRL key. Next, drag the cursor toward the graphics area. The second instance of the *Piston Ring* component appears attached to the cursor in the graphics area, see Figure 12.135.

15. Release the left mouse button and then the CTRL key. The second instance of the *Piston Ring* component is inserted in the Assembly environment.

16. Invoke the **Mate PropertyManager** and then assemble the second instance of the *Piston Ring* component with the first component (*Piston*) by applying the coincident and concentric mates between them, see Figure 12.136. After assembling the second instance of the *Piston Ring* component, exit the **Mate PropertyManager**.

Figure 12.135, Figure 12.136

Note: You can also insert the second instance of a component by using the **Insert Components** tool of the **Assembly CommandManager**.

Section 4: Saving the Piston Sub-Assembly

1. Click on the **Save** tool in the **Standard** toolbar. The **Save As** dialog box appears.

2. Browse to the *Tutorial 2* folder of the *Chapter 12* folder and then save the assembly with the name Piston Sub-Assembly.

3. Close the Piston Sub-Assembly file by clicking on the **File** > **Close** in the SOLIDWORKS menus.

Section 5: Creating the Main Assembly - Radial Engine

In this section, you need to create the main assembly (*Radial Engine*).

1. Click on the **New** tool in the **Standard** toolbar. The **New SOLIDWORKS Document** dialog box appears.

2. Double-click on the **Assembly** button in the dialog box. The Assembly environment is invoked and the **Open** dialog box appears along with the **Begin Assembly PropertyManager**. If the **Open** dialog box does not appear, automatically then click on the **Browse** button in the **Begin Assembly PropertyManager** to open the **Open** dialog box.

3. Select the first component (*Crank Case*) of the main assembly (*Radial Engine*) and then click on the **Open** button in the dialog box. The first component (*Crank Case*) is attached to the cursor. Also, the **Rotate Context** toolbar appears in the graphics area.

4. Click anywhere in the graphics area. The first component (*Crank Case*) moves toward the origin of the assembly and becomes the fixed component, see Figure 12.137.

Section 6: Inserting and Assembling the Second Component

Now, you need to insert the second component (*Crankshaft Valve Crank*) of the main assembly (*Radial Engine*) in the Assembly environment.

1. Click on the **Insert Components** tool in the **Assembly CommandManager**. The **Open** dialog box appears along with the **Insert Component PropertyManager**. If

636 Chapter 12 > Working with Assemblies - I

the **Open** dialog box does not appear, automatically then click on the **Browse** button in the PropertyManager to open the **Open** dialog box.

2. Select the second component (*Crankshaft Valve Crank*) and then click on the **Open** button. The second component (*Crankshaft Valve Crank*) is attached to the cursor, see Figure 12.138. Also, the **Rotate Context** toolbar appears in the graphics area.

3. Enter **180** in the **Angle** field in the **Rotate Context** toolbar and then click on the **Y** tool in the **Rotate Context** toolbar. The orientation of the component is changed similar to the one shown in Figure 12.139.

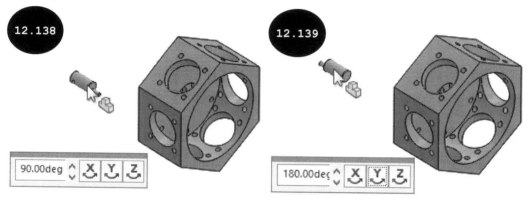

4. Click anywhere in the graphics area. The second component (*Crankshaft Valve Crank*) is placed in the specified location.

   Now, you need to assemble the second component (*Crankshaft Valve Crank*) with the first component of the assembly.

5. Invoke the **Mate PropertyManager**. Next, select the circular face of the second component (*Crankshaft Valve Crank*) and the circular face of the hole of the first component (*Crank Case*), see Figure 12.140 to apply the concentric mate. The Pop-up toolbar appears with the **Concentric** tool activated in it. Note that to select the faces of the components, you need to rotate the assembly such that the faces can be viewed.

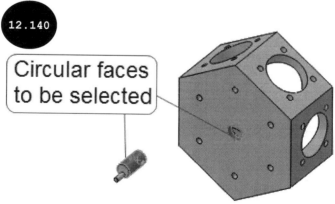

6. Click on the green tick mark ✓ in the Pop-up toolbar. The concentric mate is applied between the selected faces of the components.

7. Select the planar face of the second component (*Crankshaft Valve Crank*) and the planar face of the first component (*Crank Case*), see Figure 12.141. The Pop-up toolbar appears with the **Coincident** tool activated in it.

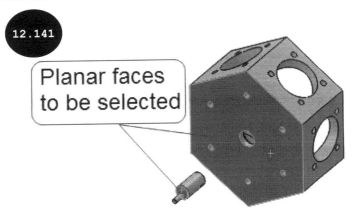

8. Click on the green tick mark ✓ in the Pop-up toolbar. The coincident mate is applied between the selected faces of the components.

9. Exit the **Mate PropertyManager** and then change the orientation of the assembly to isometric.

Section 7: Inserting and Assembling the Third Component

1. Insert the third component (*Crankshaft Counterweight*) in the Assembly environment by using the **Insert Components** tool, see Figure 12.142.

2. Hide the first component (*Crank Case*) so that you can easily select the faces of components for applying mates, see Figure 12.143. To hide the first component, click on the first component (*Crank Case*) in the graphics area. A Pop-up toolbar appears. In this Pop-up toolbar, click on the **Hide Components** tool.

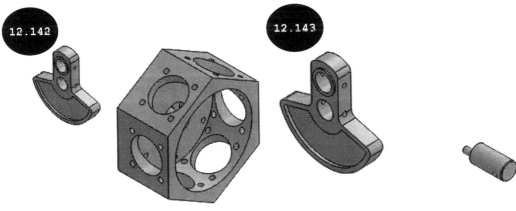

638 Chapter 12 > Working with Assemblies - I

Now, you need to assemble the third component (*Crankshaft Counterweight*).

3. Invoke the **Mate PropertyManager** and then select the outer circular face of the second component (*Crankshaft Valve Crank*) and the inner circular face of the third component (*Crankshaft Counterweight*) as the entities to apply a mate, see Figure 12.144. The Pop-up toolbar appears with the **Concentric** tool activated in it, by default. Also, the selected faces of the components become concentric to each other in the graphics area, see Figure 12.145.

4. Click on the **Flip Mate Alignment** tool in the Pop-up toolbar, if the alignment of the third component (*Crankshaft Counterweight*) does not appear similar to the one shown in Figure 12.145.

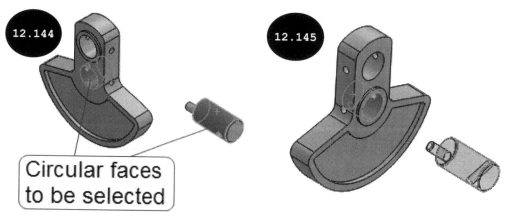

5. Click on the green tick mark in the Pop-up toolbar. The concentric mate is applied between the selected faces of the components.

6. Select the circular face of the bottom hole of the third component (*Crankshaft Counterweight*) and the circular face of the hole of the second component (*Crankshaft Valve Crank*), see Figure 12.146. The Pop-up toolbar appears with the **Concentric** tool activated in it.

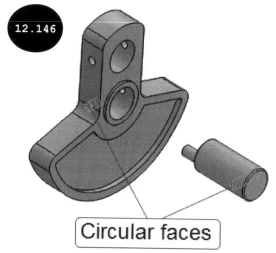

7. Click on the green tick mark ✓ in the Pop-up toolbar. The concentric mate is applied between the selected faces of the components, see Figure 12.147. Next, exit the **Mate PropertyManager**.

Section 8: Inserting and Assembling the Fourth Component

1. Insert the fourth component (*Crankshaft Pin*) in the Assembly environment by using the **Insert Components** tool, see Figure 12.148.

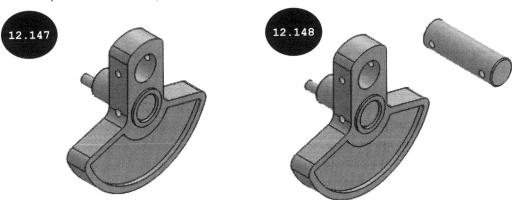

2. Select the inner circular face of the third component (*Crankshaft Counterweight*) and the circular face of the fourth component (*Crankshaft Pin*) by pressing the CTRL key, see Figure 12.149. Next, release the CTRL key. The Pop-up toolbar appears, see Figure 12.149.

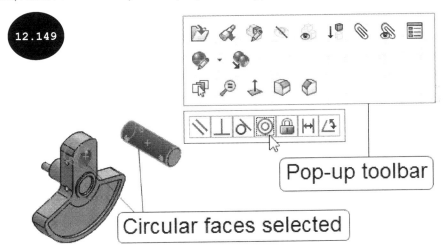

3. Click on the **Concentric** tool in the Pop-up toolbar, see Figure 12.149. The selected faces of the components become concentric to each other.

4. Similarly, select the circular face of the hole of the third component (*Crankshaft Counterweight*) and the circular face of the hole of the fourth component (*Crankshaft Pin*) by pressing the CTRL key, see Figure 12.150. Next, release the CTRL key. The Pop-up toolbar appears.

Note: To select the faces of components which are not visible, you may need to move the components. You can move a component by dragging it after pressing and holding the left mouse button.

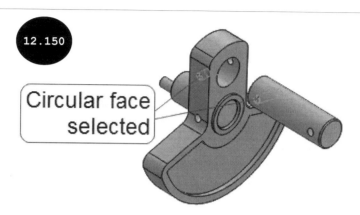

12.150 Circular face selected

5. Click on the **Concentric** tool in the Pop-up toolbar. The selected faces of the components become concentric to each other.

Section 9: Inserting and Assembling the Fifth Component

1. Insert the fifth component (*Crankshaft Counterweight*) in the Assembly environment by using the **Insert Components** tool, see Figure 12.151.

2. Invoke the **Mate PropertyManager** and then assemble the fifth component (*Crankshaft Counterweight*) with the fourth component (*Crankshaft Pin*) by applying two concentric mates, see Figure 12.152. After applying the mates, exit the **Mate PropertyManager**.

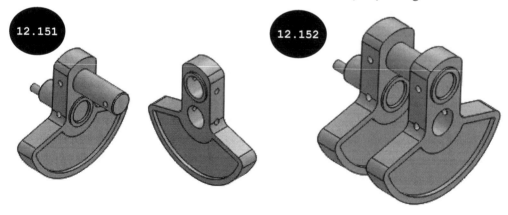

12.151 12.152

Section 10: Inserting and Assembling the Sixth Component

1. Insert the sixth component (*Crankshaft*) in the Assembly environment, see Figure 12.153. You need to change the orientation of the component (*Crankshaft*) similar to the one shown in Figure 12.153 by using the **Rotate Context** toolbar.

2. Invoke the **Mate PropertyManager**. Next, select the circular face of the sixth component (*Crankshaft*) and the inner circular face of the bottom hole of the fifth component (*Crankshaft Counterweight*) as the entities to apply a mate, see Figure 12.154. The Pop-up toolbar appears with the **Concentric** tool activated in it and the selected faces of the components become concentric to each other, see Figure 12.154.

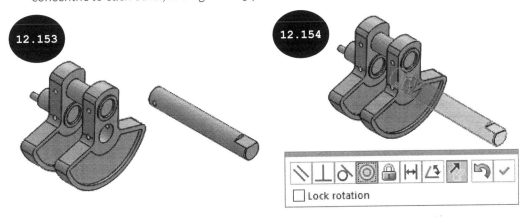

3. Click on the green tick mark ✓ in the Pop-up toolbar. The concentric mate is applied between the selected faces of the components.

4. Similarly, apply the concentric mate between the circular face of the hole of the fifth component (*Crankshaft Counterweight*) and the circular face of the hole of the sixth component (*Crankshaft*), see Figure 12.155. After applying the mate, exit the **Mate PropertyManager**.

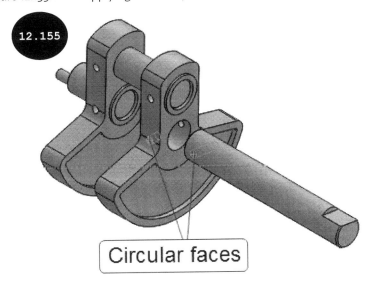

Section 11: Inserting and Assembling the Seventh Component

1. Insert the seventh component (*Connecting Rod Hub*) in the Assembly environment by using the **Insert Components** tool, see Figure 12.156.

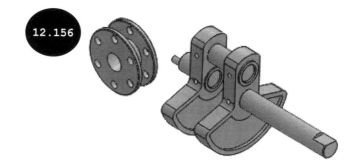

2. Invoke the **Mate PropertyManager**. Next, select the inner circular face of the seventh component (*Connecting Rod Hub*) and the circular face of the fourth component (*Crankshaft Pin*), see Figure 12.157. The Pop-up toolbar appears with the **Concentric** tool activated in it.

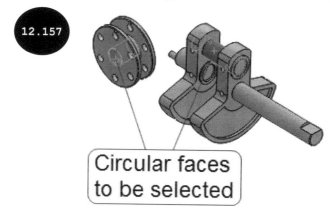

3. Click on the green tick mark ✓ in the Pop-up toolbar. The concentric mate is applied between the selected faces of the components.

4. Select the back planar face of the seventh component (*Connecting Rod Hub*) and the front planar face of the third component (*Crankshaft Counterweight*) as the entities to apply a mate, see Figure 12.158. The Pop-up toolbar appears with the **Coincident** tool activated in it.

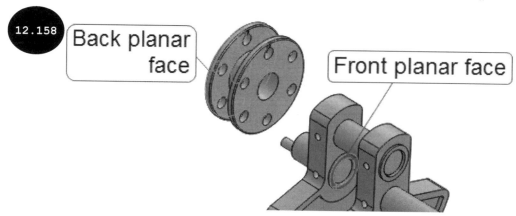

5. Click on the green tick mark ✓ in the Pop-up toolbar. The coincident mate is applied between the selected faces of the components. Next, exit the **Mate PropertyManager**.

Section 12: Inserting and Assembling the Eighth Component

1. Insert the eighth component (*Connecting Rod*) in the Assembly environment, see Figure 12.159. Note that you need to change the orientation of the eighth component (*Connecting Rod*) similar to the one shown in Figure 12.159 by using the **Rotate Context** toolbar.

2. Invoke the **Mate PropertyManager**. Next, select the circular face of the bottom hole of the eighth component (*Connecting Rod*) and the circular face of a hole of the seventh component (*Connecting Rod Hub*) as the entities to apply a mate, see Figure 12.160. The Pop-up toolbar appears with the **Concentric** tool activated in it.

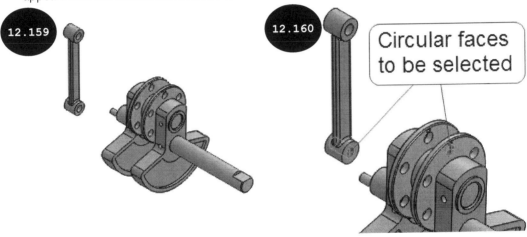

3. Click on the green tick mark ✓ in the Pop-up toolbar. The concentric mate is applied between the selected faces of the components.

4. Select the back planar face of the eighth component (*Connecting Rod*) and the inner planar face of the seventh component (*Connecting Rod Hub*), see Figure 12.161. The Pop-up toolbar appears with the **Coincident** tool activated in it.

5. Click on the green tick mark ✓ in the Pop-up toolbar. The coincident mate is applied between the selected faces of the components, see Figure 12.162. Next, exit the PropertyManager.

Section 13: Inserting and Assembling the Remaining Connecting Rods

1. Similarly, insert and assemble the five more instances of the *Connecting Rod* component with the remaining holes of the seventh component (*Connecting Rod Hub*), see Figure 12.163.

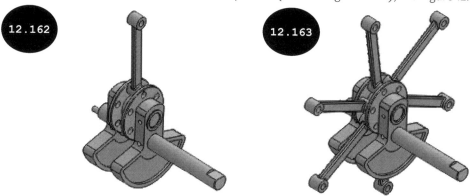

Note: To arrange the *Connecting Rod* components similar to the one shown in Figure 12.163, you need to fix the seventh component (*Connecting Rod Hub*). To fix the seventh component (*Connecting Rod Hub*), right-click on the seventh component (*Connecting Rod Hub*) in the graphics area. A shortcut menu appears. Next, click on the **Fix** option in the shortcut menu. Once the seventh component (*Connecting Rod Hub*) has been fixed, you can arrange the *Connecting Rod* components one by one by dragging them after pressing and holding the left mouse button. After arranging the *Connecting Rod* components, you need to make the seventh component (*Connecting Rod Hub*) back to the floating component. To make the component (*Connecting Rod Hub*) floating, right-click on the component in the graphics area and then click on the **Float** option in the shortcut menu appeared.

Section 14: Inserting and Assembling Piston Sub-Assembly

1. Insert the *Piston Sub-Assembly* in the Assembly environment by using the **Insert Components** tool, see Figure 12.164.

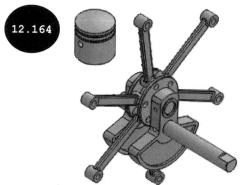

Tip: When you insert a sub-assembly in the Assembly environment, the sub-assembly becomes rigid and act as a single component in the Assembly environment. You can change a rigid sub-assembly to a flexible sub-assembly, whose all components are free to move individually in their free degrees of freedom. To change a rigid sub-assembly to a flexible, click on a rigid sub-assembly in the FeatureManager Design Tree. A Pop-up toolbar appears. In this Pop-up toolbar, click on the **Component Properties** tool. The **Component Properties** dialog box appears. In this dialog box, select the **Flexible** radio button in the **Solve as** area of the dialog box. Next, click the **OK** button.

2. Invoke the **Mate PropertyManager**. Next, select the inner circular face of the hole of the *Piston Sub-Assembly* and the inner circular face of the upper hole of a *Connecting Rod* component as the entities to apply a mate, see Figure 12.165. The Pop-up toolbar appears with the **Concentric** tool activated in it.

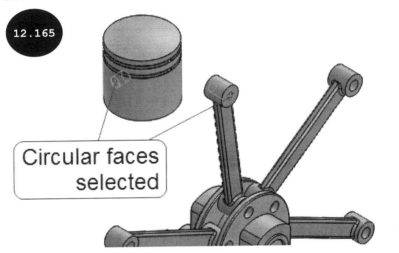

3. Click on the green tick mark in the Pop-up toolbar. The concentric mate is applied between the selected faces of the components.

4. Expand the **Advanced Mates** rollout of the **Mate PropertyManager** and then click on the **Width** button in it. The **Width selections** and the **Tab selections** fields are enabled in the **Mate Selections** rollout of the PropertyManager.

5. Select the front and back planar faces of the *Connecting Rod* component as the width selection set, see Figure 12.166. Next, select the outer circular face of the *Piston Sub-Assembly* as the tab selection, see Figure 12.166. The axis of the tab selection is centered to the width selection set in the graphics area.

6. Click on the green tick mark in the PropertyManager. The width mate is applied between the selected faces of the components. Next, exit the **Mate PropertyManager**.

646 Chapter 12 > Working with Assemblies - I

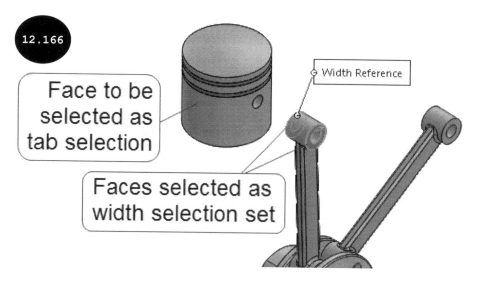

Figure 12.166

Section 15: Inserting and Assembling the Remaining Piston Sub-Assemblies

1. Similarly, insert and assemble the five more instances of the *Piston Sub-Assembly* with the remaining *Connecting Rod* components, see Figure 12.167.

2. Turn on the visibility of the first component (*Crank Case*), see Figure 12.168. To turn on the visibility or display of the first component (*Crank Case*) in the graphics area, click on its name (*Crank Case*) in the FeatureManager Design Tree. A Pop-up toolbar appears. Next, click on the **Show Components** tool in the Pop-up toolbar.

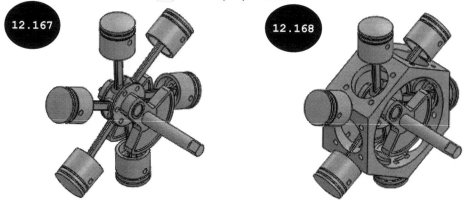

Now, you need to apply the concentric mate between each *Piston Sub-Assembly* and the first component (*Crank Case*).

3. Invoke the **Mate PropertyManager**. Next, select the outer circular face of a *Piston Sub Assembly* and the inner circular face of the respective hole of the first component (*Crank Case*), see Figure 12.169. The Pop-up toolbar appears with the **Concentric** tool activated in it.

4. Click on the green tick mark in the Pop-up toolbar. The concentric mate is applied between the selected faces of the components.

5. Similarly, apply the concentric mate between the remaining instance of *Piston Sub-Assembly* and the respective hole of the first component (*Crank Case*), see Figure 12.170.

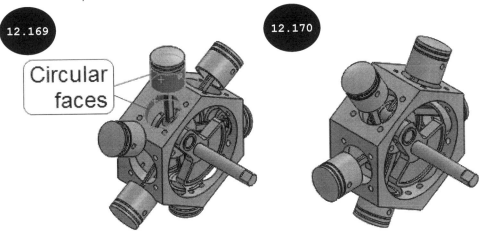

Now, you need to apply the parallel mate between the face of the rectangular cut in the seventh component (*Connecting Rod Hub*) and the respective outer planar face of the first component (*Crank Case*).

6. Click on the **Parallel** button in the **Mate PropertyManager**. Next, select a planar face of the rectangular cut in the seventh component (*Connecting Rod Hub*), see Figure 12.171 and then select the respective outer planar face of the first component (*Crank Case*), see Figure 12.172. The Pop-up toolbar appears with the **Parallel** tool activated in it.

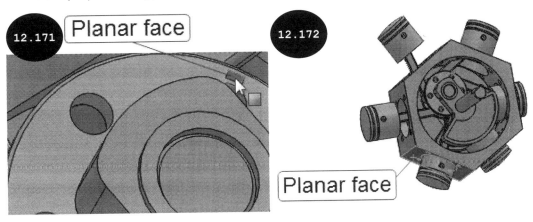

7. Click on the green tick mark ✓ in the Pop-up toolbar. The parallel mate is applied between the selected faces of the components. Next, exit the **Mate PropertyManager**. Figure 12.173 shows the final assembly after assembling all its components.

Tip: You can review the motion of the assembly by dragging the *Crankshaft* component of the assembly after pressing and holding the left mouse button.

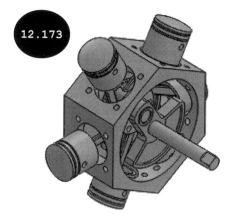

12.173

Section 16: Saving the Model

1. Click on the **Save** tool in the **Standard** toolbar. The **Save As** dialog box appears.

2. Browse to the *Tutorial 2* folder of the *Chapter 12* folder and then save the assembly with the name Tutorial 2.

Hands-on Test Drive 1

Create the assembly shown in Figure 12.174. Different views and dimensions of individual components of the assembly are shown in Figures 12.175 through 12.182.

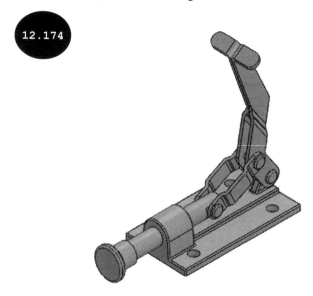

12.174

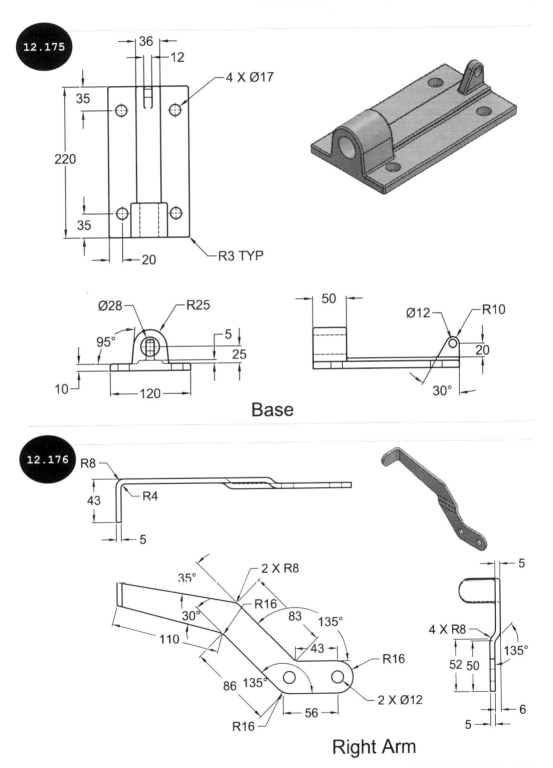

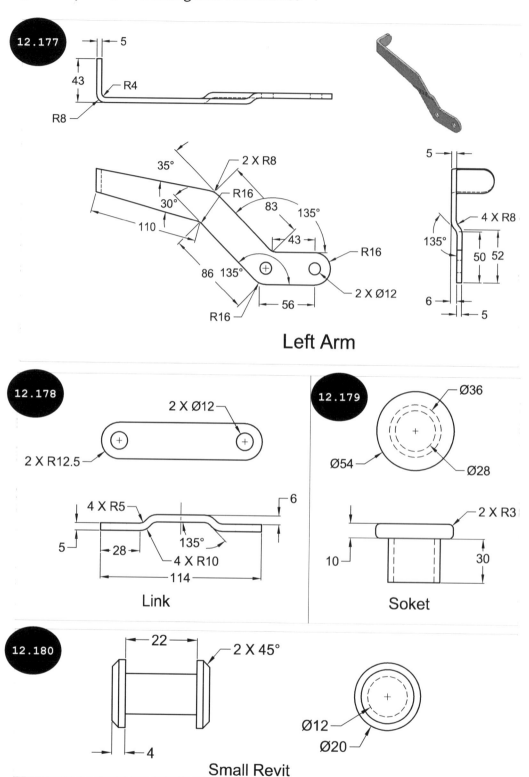

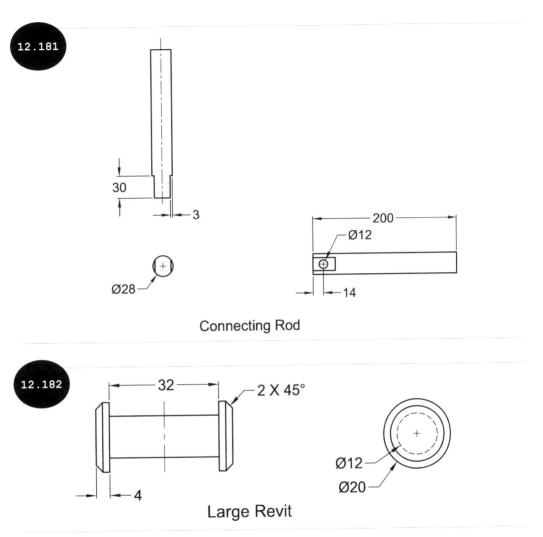

12.181

Connecting Rod

12.182

Large Revit

Summary

In this chapter, you have learned about creating assemblies by using the bottom-up assembly approach. In the bottom-up assembly approach, you first create all components in the Part modeling environment one by one and then assemble by applying mates/relations in the Assembly environment. In SOLIDWORKS, you can apply standard, advanced, and mechanical mates to assemble components with respect to each other. Note that a free component within the Assembly environment has six degrees of freedom: three translational and three rotational. Therefore, to assemble a component, you need to fix its degrees of freedom by applying the required mates. Additionally, you have also learned how to move and rotate the individual component within the Assembly environment. You have also learned about detecting collisions between the components of an assembly and applying standard mates by using the SmartMates method.

Questions

- In SOLIDWORKS, you can create assemblies by using the _____ and _____ approaches.

- If you make any change in a component in the Part modeling environment, the same change is automatically reflected in the assembly environment and vice-versa. This is because of the _____ property of SOLIDWORKS.

- The _____ toolbar allows you to change the orientation of a component before defining its placement point in the Assembly environment.

- A free component within the Assembly environment has _____ degrees of freedom.

- The _____ mate is used to center-align two rectangular profiles, two circular profiles, or a rectangular profile and a circular profile with each other.

- The _____ mate allows two components to rotate relative to each other and form a gear mechanism.

- The _____ mate is used to translate linear motion into rotational motion from one component to another and vice versa.

- The _____ mate allows a component to move along the defined path.

- You can move the individual components of an assembly along its degrees of freedom. (True/False).

- You can apply the mechanical mates by using the SmartMates method. (True/False).

- In SOLIDWORKS, you can detect collisions between the components of an assembly. (True/False).

CHAPTER 13

Working with Assemblies - II

In this chapter, you will learn the following:

- Creating Assembly by using the Top-down Approach
- Editing Assembly Components
- Editing Mates
- Patterning Assembly Components
- Creating a Pattern Driven Component Pattern
- Creating a Chain Component Pattern
- Mirroring Components of an Assembly
- Creating Assembly Features
- Suppressing or Unsuppressing Components
- Inserting the Parts having Multiple Configurations
- Creating and Dissolving Sub-Assemblies
- Creating an Exploded View
- Collapsing an Exploded View
- Animating an Exploded View
- Editing an Exploded View
- Adding Explode Lines in an Exploded View
- Creating Bill of Material (BOM) of an Assembly

In the previous chapter, you have learned about creating assemblies by using the Bottom-up Assembly Approach. You have also learned about different types of mates and how to move or rotate individual components of an assembly. In this chapter, you will learn about creating assemblies by using the Top-down Assembly Approach, editing assembly components, patterning and mirroring assembly components, creating assemblies features, exploding assemblies, and so on.

Creating Assembly by using the Top-down Approach

In the Top-down Assembly Approach, all components of an assembly are created within the Assembly environment itself. Creating components in the Assembly environment helps in taking reference from the existing components of the assembly. By using this approach, you can create concept-based design, where new components of an assembly can be created by taking reference from the existing components and maintain the relationships between them. The procedure for creating assembly by using the Top-down Assembly Approach is as follows:

Procedure for Creating Assembly by using the Top-down Approach

1. Invoke the Assembly environment by using the **New** tool of the **Standard** toolbar, see Figure 13.1. Note that the **Open** dialog box appears along with the **Begin Assembly PropertyManager** in the initial screen of the Assembly environment, by default.

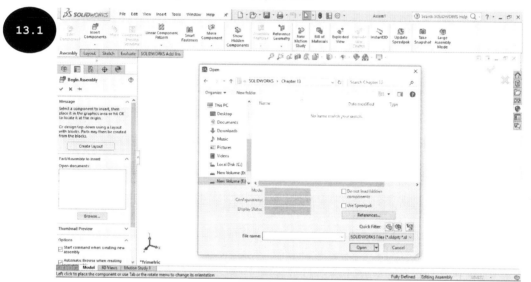

2. Close the **Open** dialog box by clicking on the **Close** button and then close the **Begin Assembly PropertyManager** by clicking on the red cross mark ⊠ available at its top. The reason behind closing the **Open** dialog box and the PropertyManager is to create components in the Assembly environment itself instead of importing them.

3. Click on the arrow at the bottom of the **Insert Components** tool in the Assembly **CommandManager**. A flyout appears, see Figure 13.2.

4. Click on the **New Part** tool in the flyout. A new empty part is inserted in the Assembly environment and its default name appears in the FeatureManager Design Tree, see Figure 13.3. Also, a green color tick mark appears attached to the cursor in the graphics area.

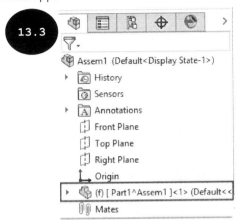

5. Click on a reference plane in the FeatureManager Design Tree. The Sketching environment is invoked within the Assembly environment such that the selected reference plane becomes the sketching plane for creating the base feature of the part, see Figure 13.4.

Note: You can click anywhere in the graphics area to define the position of the part instead of selecting a reference plane. On clicking anywhere in the graphics area, the position of the part gets defined such that the origin of the part becomes coincident to the origin of the assembly. But, the Sketching environment for creating the base feature is not invoked. In this case, to invoke the Sketching environment, click on the name of the part in the FeatureManager Design Tree and then click on the **Edit Component** tool in the **Assembly CommandManager**. Next, click on the **Sketch** tool in the **Sketch CommandManager** and then select a plane or a planar face as the sketching plane for creating the base feature.

6. Press CTRL + 8 to change the current orientation of the model as normal to the viewing direction. Alternatively, click on the **Normal To** tool in the **View Orientation** flyout, see Figure 13.5.

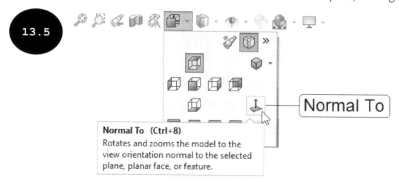

7. Draw the sketch of the base feature by using the sketching tools of the **Sketch CommandManager**, refer to Figure 13.6.

   After creating the sketch, you need to covert it into a solid feature by using the solid modeling tools.

8. Click on the **Features** tab in the CommandManager. The tools of the **Features CommandManager** are displayed. Now, by using the tools such as **Extruded Boss/Base** or **Revolved Boss/Base**, you can convert the sketch into a solid feature, refer to Figure 13.7. In this figure, the sketch is extruded to the depth of 15 mm by using the **Extruded Boss/Base** tool.

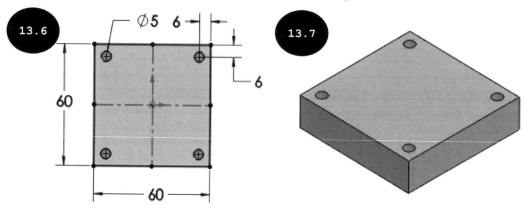

You need to create the second feature of the component.

9. Invoke the Sketching environment again by selecting a planar face or a plane as the sketching plane for creating the second feature of the component.
10. Create the sketch of the second feature, refer to Figure 13.8 and then convert it into a feature by using the solid modeling tools of the **Features CommandManager**, refer to Figure 13.9. In Figure 13.9, the sketch is extruded to the depth of 75 mm by using the **Extruded Boss/Base** tool. Similarly, you can create the remaining features of the part one after another.

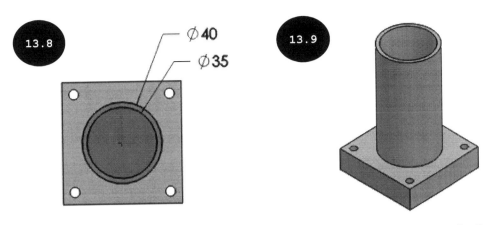

11. Once all the features of the component have been created, click on the **Edit Component** tool in the **Features CommandManager**. The first component is created and the Assembly environment is invoked.

Note: By default, the components created in the Assembly environment are fixed components and their degrees of freedom are restricted. This is because the Inplace mate is applied automatically between the plane of the component and the plane of the assembly. You can convert a fixed component into a floating component by deleting the Inplace mate. To delete the Inplace mate, expand the **Mates** node in the FeatureManager Design Tree and then select the InPlace mate to be deleted. Next, press the DELETE key.

If you have defined the placement of a component in the Assembly environment by clicking in the graphics area instead of selecting a plane then the component becomes fixed in the Assembly environment without applying the Inplace mate. In such case, to convert a fixed component into a floating component, select the component from the FeatureManager Design Tree and then right-click to display a shortcut menu. Next, click on the **Float** option in the shortcut menu.

After creating the first component, you can create the second component of the assembly.

12. Click on the arrow at the bottom of the **Insert Components** tool to invoke a flyout, see Figure 13.10. Next, click on the **New Part** tool in this flyout. A new empty part is inserted in the Assembly environment and its default name appears in the FeatureManager Design Tree.

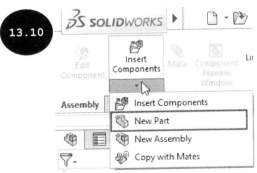

13. Click anywhere in the graphics area. The position of the part gets defined such that the origin of the part becomes coincident to the origin of the assembly.
14. Click on the name of the newly inserted component in the FeatureManager Design Tree. A Pop-up toolbar appears, see Figure 13.11.

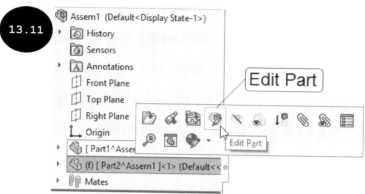

15. Click on the **Edit Part** tool in the Pop-up toolbar, see Figure 13.11. The Part modeling environment is invoked within the Assembly environment for creating the second component. Also, the first component becomes transparent so that you can easily create the second component and take the reference of the first component while creating the second component, refer to Figure 13.12.
16. Invoke the Sketching environment by selecting a plane or a planar face of the first component as the sketching plane for creating the base feature of the second component.
17. Create the sketch of the base feature of the second component by taking the reference of the first component, refer to Figure 13.13. In this figure, the rectangle and the four circles of the sketch have been created by projecting the edges of the first component onto the sketching plane.

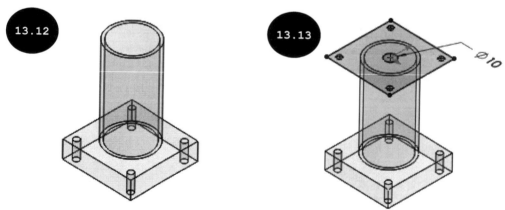

18. Convert the sketch into a feature by using the tools of the **Features CommandManager**, refer to Figure 13.14. In this figure, the sketch is extruded to the depth of 15 mm by using the **Extruded Boss/Base** tool. Similarly, you can create the remaining features of the second component one by one.

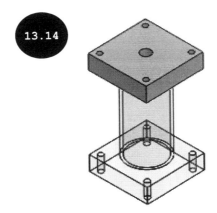

13.14

19. Once all the features of the second component have been created, click on the **Edit Component** tool in the **Features CommandManager**. The second component is created and the Assembly environment is invoked. Also, all components of the assembly appear in the shaded display style, refer to Figure 13.15.
20. Similarly, create the remaining components of the assembly one after another. Figure 13.16 shows an assembly whose all components are created one after another in the Assembly environment itself by using the Top-down Assembly Approach.

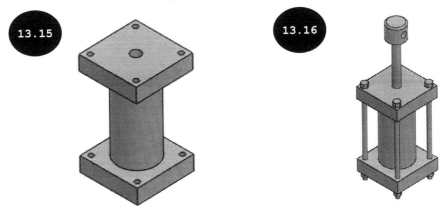

13.15 13.16

Note: As discussed, the components created by using the Top-down Assembly Approach become fixed in the Assembly environment. You can make these components floating components by deleting their respective Inplace mates or by selecting the **Float** option from the shortcut menu, which appears on right-clicking on the component. A floated component can translate and rotate in all directions, which means its all degrees of freedom are free. You can restrict the required degrees of freedom of a floated component and assemble it with the other components of the assembly by applying the required mates. The method of applying mates between the components, which are created by using the Top-down Assembly Approach is the same as discussed in the earlier chapter.

660 Chapter 13 > Working with Assemblies - II

After creating all the components of an assembly, you can save the assembly file and its components externally or internally in the assembly file.

21. Click on the **Save** button in the **Standard** toolbar. The **Save Modified Documents** dialog box appears, see Figure 13.17.

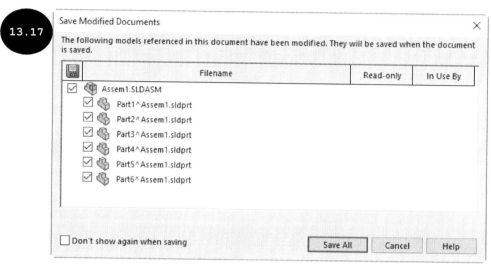

22. Click on the **Save All** button in the dialog box. The **Save As** dialog box appears. Next, browse to the location where you want to save the assembly.
23. Enter the name of the assembly in the **File name** field of the dialog box and then click on the **Save** button. The another **Save As** dialog box appears, see Figure 13.18.

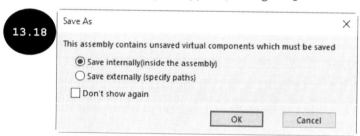

By default, the **Save internally (inside the assembly)** radio button is selected in the **Save As** dialog box, see Figure 13.18. As a result, all the components of the assembly will be saved internally in the assembly file. On selecting the **Save externally (specify paths)** radio button, all the components of the assembly will be saved externally as individual components in the same folder, where the assembly file is saved.

24. Select the **Save externally (specify paths)** radio button and then click on the **OK** button. All the components of the assembly and the assembly file are saved in the specified folder, individually.

Editing Assembly Components

In the process of creating an assembly, you may need to edit it components several times depending upon the changes in the design, revisions, or validate the design. SOLIDWORKS allows you to edit each component of an assembly within the Assembly environment as well as in the Part modeling environment. Different methods of editing assembly components are as follows:

Editing Assembly Components within the Assembly Environment

To edit a component of an assembly within the Assembly environment, select the component to be edited either from the graphics area or from the FeatureManager Design Tree. A Pop-up toolbar appears, see Figure 13.19.

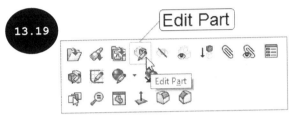

13.19

In this Pop-up toolbar, click on the **Edit Part** tool. The editing mode to edit the selected component is invoked within the Assembly environment itself, see Figure 13.20. Also, the other components of the assembly becomes transparent and the name of the component selected for editing appears blue in the FeatureManager Design Tree, see Figure 13.20.

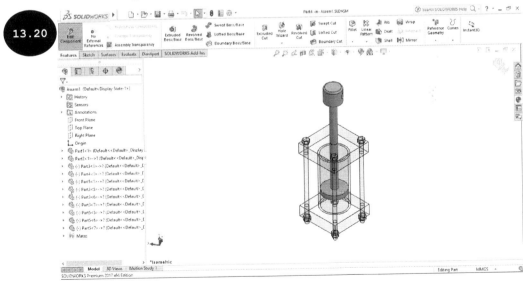

13.20

Expand the node of the component being edited in the FeatureManager Design Tree to list all its features, see Figure 13.21. Next, select the feature to be edited from the expanded node in the FeatureManager Design Tree. A Pop-up toolbar appears, see Figure 13.21. Next, click on the **Edit Feature** tool in the Pop-up toolbar for editing the feature parameters such as extrusion depth and end condition. If you want to edit the sketch of the feature then click on the **Edit Sketch** tool in the Pop-up toolbar, see Figure 13.21. Depending upon the tool selected (**Edit Feature** or **Edit Sketch**),

662 Chapter 13 > Working with Assemblies - II

the respective environment gets invoked for editing the selected feature or sketch of the component. In addition to editing the existing feature of a component, you can also create new features in the component by using the tools of the **Features CommandManager**. Once all the required editing operations have been performed on the component, click on the **Edit Component** tool in the **Features CommandManager** to exit the editing mode and switch back to the Assembly environment. Alternatively to exit the editing mode, click on the confirmation corner, which is available at the upper right corner of the graphics area.

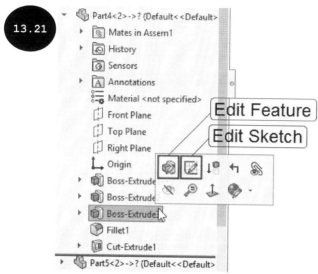

Editing Assembly Components in the Part Modeling Environment

In addition to editing the components of an assembly in the Assembly environment, you can also open a component of an assembly in the Part modeling environment and then perform the editing operations. To edit a component of an assembly in the Part modeling environment, click on the component to be edited either in the FeatureManager Design Tree or in the graphics area. A Pop-up toolbar appears, see Figure 13.22. Next, click on the **Open Part** tool in the Pop-up toolbar, see Figure 13.22. The selected component is opened the Part modeling environment. Now, you can edit the component by editing its features and sketch. To edit a feature, click on the feature to be edited in the FeatureManager Design Tree and then click on the **Edit Feature** tool in the Pop-up toolbar appeared. To edit the sketch of a feature, click on the **Edit Sketch** tool in the Pop-up toolbar. Depending upon the tool selected (**Edit Feature** or **Edit Sketch**), the respective environment gets invoked, which allows you to edit the selected feature. You can also create new features in the component by using the tools of the **Features CommandManager**.

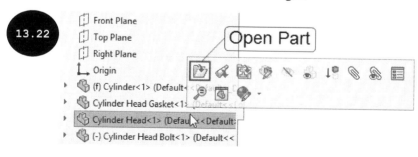

Once you have edited the component by using the tools of the Part modeling environment, click on the **Save** tool in the **Standard** toolbar to save the modified component. Next, click on **Window > *name of the assembly*** in the SOLIDWORKS menus to switch to the Assembly environment. The **SOLIDWORKS** message window appears. Click on the **Yes** button in this window. The process of updating the assembly starts and once the assembly has been updated, the updated assembly with the modified component appears in the Assembly environment. Note that the modifications made in the component are also reflected in the Assembly environment.

Note: SOLIDWORKS has bi-directional associative properties, which means the modifications made into a component in any environment are also reflected in other environments of SOLIDWORKS.

Editing Mates

In SOLIDWORKS, you can edit existing mates of an assembly, which are applied between the components. To edit existing mates, expand the **Mates** node available at the bottom of the FeatureManager Design Tree, see Figure 13.23. The **Mates** node consists of a list of all mates applied between components of an assembly. Next, click on the mate to be edited in the expanded **Mates** node of the FeatureManager Design Tree. A Pop-up toolbar appears, see Figure 13.24. Also, the entities between which the selected mate is applied get highlighted in the graphics area. Next, click on the **Edit Feature** tool in the Pop-up toolbar, see Figure 13.24. The PropertyManager appears depending upon the type of mate selected. By using the options of the PropertyManager, you can select new entities for the mate, change the type of mate, type of mate alignment, and so on. Once the editing has been done, click on the green tick mark ✓ in the PropertyManager to accept the change and to exit the PropertyManager.

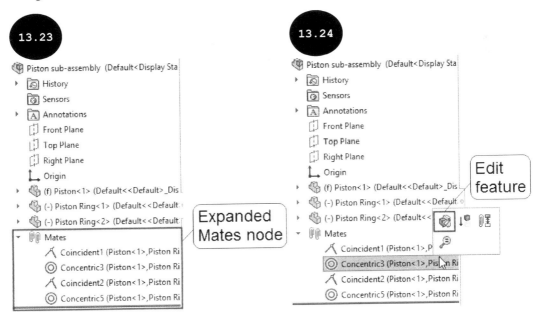

Patterning Assembly Components

Similar to patterning a feature of a component in the Part modeling environment, you can also pattern a component or components of an assembly in the Assembly environment, see Figure 13.25. In this figure, two components of the assembly are patterned to create their other instances.

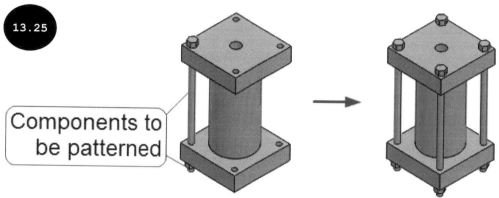

In the Assembly environment, you can create different types of patterns such as linear component pattern, circular component pattern, sketch driven component pattern, curve driven component pattern, pattern driven component pattern, and chain component pattern by using the respective tools available in the **Pattern** flyout of the **Assembly CommandManager**, see Figure 13.26. The method of creating linear component pattern, circular component pattern, sketch driven component pattern, and curve driven component pattern by using the respective tool is the same as discussed earlier while creating patterns in the Part modeling environment with the only difference that in the Part modeling environment, you pattern features to create their multiple instances. However, in the Assembly environment, you pattern components to create their multiple instances. The method of creating remaining types of patterns are as follows:

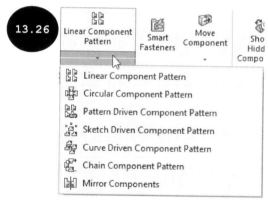

Creating a Pattern Driven Component Pattern

A pattern driven component pattern is created by patterning a component in an assembly with respect to a pattern feature of another component. In this type of pattern, the component to be patterned in the assembly drives by a pattern feature of another component. Consider a case of an assembly shown in Figure 13.27, which has three components: Component 1, Component 2, and Component 3.

The Component 3 is the component to be patterned with respect to the circular pattern feature of the Component 2. Figure 13.28 shows the resultant assembly, in which a pattern driven component pattern is created by patterning the Component 3 with respect to the circular pattern feature of the Component 2. Note that on modifying the number of instances of the pattern feature, the number of instances of the pattern driven component pattern are also modified, automatically. This is because, the instances of the pattern driven component pattern are driven by the instances of the pattern feature.

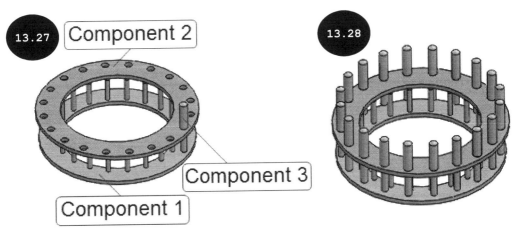

To create a pattern driven component pattern, invoke the **Pattern** flyout and then click on the **Pattern Driven Component Pattern** tool, refer to Figure 13.26. The **Pattern Driven PropertyManager** appears, see Figure 13.29. The options of the PropertyManager are as follows:

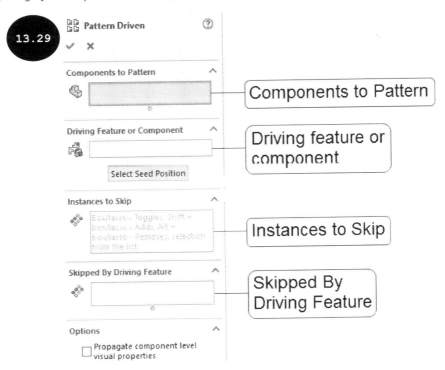

Components to Pattern
The **Components to Pattern** field is used to select components to be patterned. By default, this field is activated. As a result, you can select components to be patterned either from the graphics area or from the FeatureManager Design Tree.

Driving feature or component
The **Driving feature or component** field is used to select an instance of a pattern feature of a component as the driving feature, see Figure 13.30. To select a pattern instance (driving feature), click on this field in the PropertyManager and then select a pattern instance of a pattern. After selecting the component to be patterned and a pattern instance (driving feature), the preview of the pattern driven component pattern appears in the graphics area, see Figure 13.31.

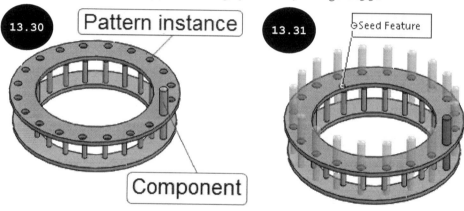

Note: By default, the position of the seed/parent instance of the pattern is taken as the position of the component being patterned. You can change the default position of the seed pattern instance by using the **Select Seed Position** button of the **Driving Feature or Component** rollout. On clicking the **Select Seed Position** button, a blue dot appears in the preview of the each pattern instance in the graphics area. You can click on the blue dot of the pattern instance to select it as the seed feature of the pattern.

Instances to Skip
The **Instances to Skip** field is used to skip pattern instances of the pattern. To skip pattern instances, click on the **Instances to Skip** field in the rollout. A pink dot appears on each pattern instance in the graphics area, see Figure 13.32. Move the cursor over the instance to be skipped and then click on it.

Skipped By Driving Feature
The **Skipped By Driving Feature** field is used to display the list of pattern instances, which are skipped in the pattern feature (driving) of the component.

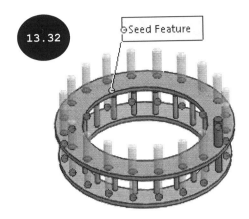

Procedure for Creating the Pattern Driven Component Pattern
1. Invoke the **Pattern** flyout in the **Assembly CommandManager**.
2. Click on the **Pattern Driven Component Pattern** tool in the **Pattern** flyout.
3. Click on the component to be patterned in the graphics area.
4. Click on the **Driving feature or component** field and then click on an instance of a pattern feature of the component as the driving feature.
5. If needed, you can skip the pattern instances by using the **Instances to Skip** rollout.
6. Click on the green tick mark ✓ in the PropertyManager. The pattern driven component pattern is created.

Creating a Chain Component Pattern
A chain component pattern is created by patterning a component along an open or a closed path to simulate the chain drive or cable carrier mechanism, dynamically in an assembly, see Figure 13.33. In SOLIDWORKS, you can create a chain component pattern by using the **Chain Component Pattern** tool.

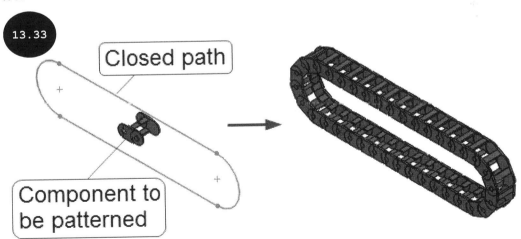

In the chain component pattern, the component drives along an open or closed path such that you can simulate its motion dynamically by dragging the pattern instances. To create a chain component pattern, invoke the **Pattern** flyout, see Figure 13.34 and then click on the **Chain Component Pattern** tool. The **Chain Pattern PropertyManager** appears, see Figure 13.35.

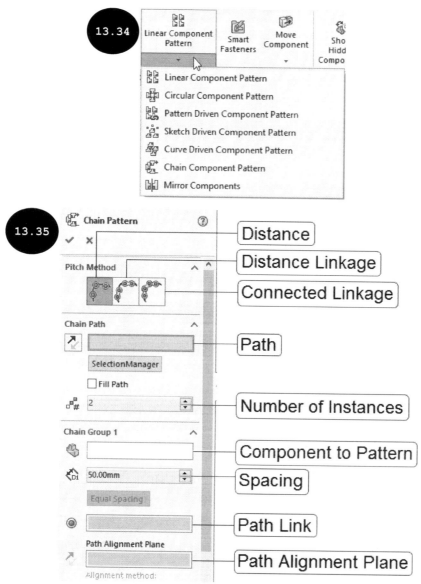

The **Chain Pattern PropertyManager** is used to create three types of chain patterns: Distance, Distance Linkage, and Connected Linkage. The Distance chain pattern is used to pattern a component with a single link among the pattern instances along a chain path. The Distance Linkage chain pattern is used to pattern a component with two non-connected links among the pattern instances along the path. The Connected Linkage chain pattern is used to pattern a component with connected links among the pattern instances along the path. The procedure of creating different types of chain patterns are as follows:

Procedure for Creating the Distance Chain Pattern

1. Click on the **Chain Component Pattern** tool in the **Pattern** flyout. The **Chain Pattern PropertyManager** appears.
2. Make sure the **Distance** button is selected in the **Pitch Method** rollout of the PropertyManager.
3. Click on the **SelectionManager** button in the **Chain Path** rollout. The **Selection** toolbar appears, see Figure 13.36.

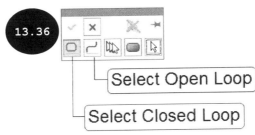

4. Click on the **Select Closed Loop** or **Select Open Loop** button in the **Selection** toolbar, depending upon the type of path (closed or open) to be selected.
5. Click on the path to be selected in the graphics area, see Figure 13.37. Next, click on the green tick mark ✓ in the **Selection** toolbar. The path is selected.
6. Either select the **Fill Path** check box in the **Chain Path** rollout to fill in the path with pattern instances or specify the number of instances to be created in the **Number of Instances** field.
7. Click on the **Component to Pattern** field in the **Chain Group 1** rollout to activate it.
8. Click on the component to be patterned in the graphics area, see Figure 13.37.
9. Click on the **Path Link** field in the **Chain Group 1** rollout to activate it.
10. Click on a cylindrical face, a circular edge, a linear edge, or a reference axis as the link among the pattern instances in the graphics area, see Figure 13.37.
11. Select a plane or a planar face as the alignment plane for aligning the pattern instances along the path, see Figure 13.37. The preview of the chain pattern appears, see Figure 13.38.
12. Specify the spacing between the pattern instances in the **Spacing** field.

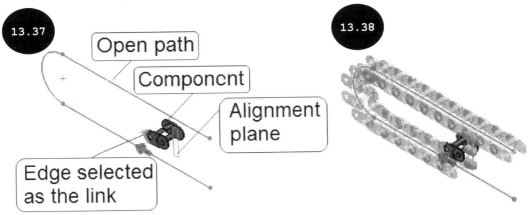

13. Click on the green tick mark ✓ in the PropertyManager. The chain component pattern is created, see Figure 13.39.

670 Chapter 13 > Working with Assemblies - II

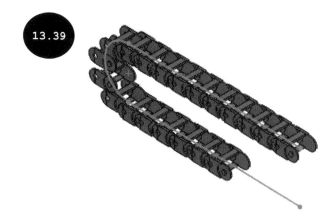

13.39

Procedure for Creating the Distance Linkage Chain Pattern

1. Click on the **Chain Component Pattern** tool in the **Pattern** flyout. The **Chain Pattern PropertyManager** appears.
2. Click on the **Distance Linkage** button in the **Pitch Method** rollout of the PropertyManager.
3. Click on the **SelectionManager** button in the **Chain Path** rollout. The **Selection** toolbar appears.
4. Click on the **Select Closed Loop** or **Select Open Loop** button in the **Selection** toolbar, depending upon the type of path (closed or open) to be selected.
5. Click on the path to be selected in the graphics area, see Figure 13.40. Next, click on the green tick mark ✓ in the **Selection** toolbar. The path is selected.
6. Either specify the number of pattern instances to be created along the path in the **Number of Instances** field or select the **Fill Path** check box to fill in the path with pattern instances.
7. Click on the **Component to Pattern** field in the **Chain Group 1** rollout to activate it.
8. Click on the component to be patterned in the graphics area.
9. Click on the **Path Link 1** field in the **Chain Group 1** rollout to activate it.
10. Click on a cylindrical face, a circular edge, a linear edge, or a reference axis as the link 1 among the pattern instances in the graphics area, see Figure 13.40.
11. Click on a cylindrical face, a circular edge, a linear edge, or a reference axis as the link 2 among the pattern instances, see Figure 13.40.
12. Click on a plane or a planar face as the alignment plane, see Figure 13.40. The preview of pattern appears, see Figure 13.41.

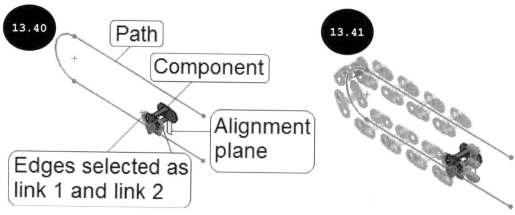

13. Specify the spacing between the pattern instances in the **Spacing** field.
14. Click on the green tick mark ✓ in the PropertyManager. The distance linkage chain pattern is created, see Figure 13.42.

13.42

Note: In the **Options** rollout of the **Chain Pattern PropertyManager**, the **Dynamic** radio button is selected by default, see Figure 13.43. As a result, you can drag any pattern instance to move the chain. On selecting the **Static** radio button, you can move the chain only by dragging the parent or seed component of the pattern. The **Static** radio button helps in improving the overall performance of the system for large assemblies.

13.43

Procedure for Creating the Connected Linkage Chain Pattern

1. Click on the **Chain Component Pattern** tool in the **Pattern** flyout to invoke the **Chain Pattern PropertyManager**.
2. Click on the **Connected Linkage** button in the **Pitch Method** rollout of the PropertyManager.
3. Select an open or a closed path from the graphics area by using the **SelectionManager** button of the **Chain Path** rollout, see Figure 13.44.
4. Either specify the number of pattern instances to be created along the path in the **Number of Instances** field or select the **Fill Path** check box to fill in the path with pattern instances.
5. Click on the **Component to Pattern** field in the **Chain Group 1** rollout to activate it.
6. Click on the component to be patterned in the graphics area.
7. Click on the **Path Link 1** field in the **Chain Group 1** rollout to activate it.
8. Click on a cylindrical face, a circular edge, a linear edge, or a reference axis as the link 1 between the pattern instances in the graphics area, see Figure 13.44.
9. Click on a cylindrical face, a circular edge, a linear edge, or a reference axis as the link 2 between the pattern instances, see Figure 13.44.
10. Click on a plane or a planar face as the alignment plane, see Figure 13.44. The preview of the pattern appears, see Figure 13.45. If the pattern preview does not appear in the graphics area, you need to reverse the direction of the pattern by clicking on the arrow appeared along the path in the graphics area.

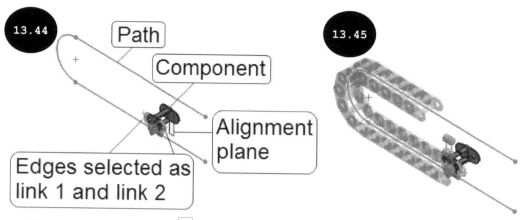

11. Click on the green tick mark ✓ of the PropertyManager. The connected linkage chain pattern is created, see Figure 13.46.

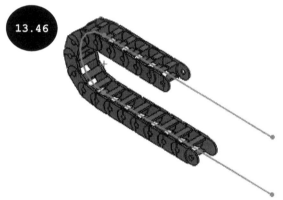

Mirroring Components of an Assembly

Similar to mirroring features in the Part modeling environment, you can also mirror components in the Assembly environment by using the **Mirror Components** tool of the **Pattern** flyout, see Figure 13.47.

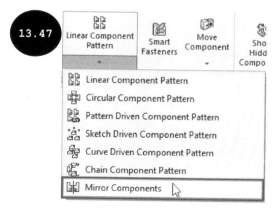

To mirror components of an assembly, invoke the **Pattern** flyout and then click on the **Mirror Components** tool, see Figure 13.47. The **Mirror Components PropertyManager** appears, see Figure 13.48. The options of the PropertyManager are as follows:

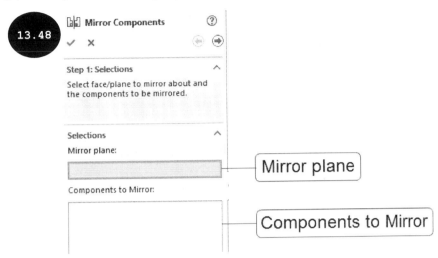

Mirror plane
The **Mirror plane** field is used to select a mirroring plane for mirroring the selected components of an assembly. By default, this field is activated. As a result, you can select a plane or a planar face as the mirroring plane, see Figure 13.49.

Components to Mirror
The **Components to Mirror** field is used to select components to be mirrored about the mirroring plane. This field gets activated as soon as you select the mirroring plane. Select a component or components to be mirrored either from the graphics area or from the FeatureManager Design Tree, see Figure 13.49.

After selecting the mirroring plane and a component to be mirrored, click on the green tick mark ✓ in the PropertyManager. The selected component is mirrored about the mirroring plane, see Figure 13.50.

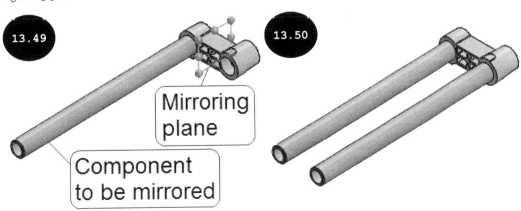

Note: You can also change the orientation of the mirrored component. To change the orientation of the mirrored component, click on the **Next** button in the **Mirror Components PropertyManager**. Next, click on the double arrow in the **Reorient components** area of the PropertyManager to view the second or next possible orientation of the mirrored component. You can cycle through four possible orientations of the mirrored component by clicking on this double arrow in the **Reorient components** area.

If you have selected a flexible sub-assembly as the component to be mirrored then you can synchronize the movement of the components of the mirrored sub-assembly with respect to the movement of the parent sub-assembly (flexible) by selecting the **Synchronize movement of flexible subassembly components** check box of the PropertyManager. After selecting this check box, if you move the components of the flexible sub-assembly (parent), the respective components of the mirrored sub-assembly are also moved, respectively, and vice versa. Note that this check box is enabled only if the selected sub-assembly to be mirrored is a flexible sub-assembly and the **Create opposite hand version** button is activated in the PropertyManager. The **Create opposite hand version** button is used to create the mirror image (opposite version) of the selected component.

Procedure for Mirroring Components of an Assembly

1. Invoke the **Pattern** flyout in the **Assembly CommandManager**.
2. Click on the **Mirror Components** tool in the **Pattern** flyout.
3. Select a plane or a planar face as the mirroring plane.
4. Select a component or components to be mirrored about the mirroring plane.
5. Click on the green tick mark in the PropertyManager. The selected components are mirrored.

Creating Assembly Features

In a manufacturing unit or a shop floor, after assembling all components of an assembly, several cut operations may take place in components in order to give final touch-up and align components perfectly with respect to each other. For this, SOLIDWORKS has tools to create cut features in the Assembly environment. Cut features created in the Assembly environment are known as assembly features and do not affect the original geometry of the components. For example, if you create an assembly feature (cut feature) on a component of an assembly in the Assembly environment; the assembly feature created will exist only in the assembly and if you open the same component in the Part modeling environment, you will not find the existence of the assembly feature. It means the assembly features exist in the assembly only and will not affect the original geometry of the component.

In SOLIDWORKS, you can create assembly features such as holes, extruded cut, revolved cut, swept cut, and fillets. The tools to create assembly features are provided in the **Assembly Features** flyout, see Figure 13.51. To invoke the **Assembly Features** flyout, click on the arrow at the bottom of the **Assembly Features** tool in the **Assembly CommandManager**. The procedure of creating assembly features is the same as creating features in the Part modeling environment. For example, to create an extruded cut feature, click on the **Extruded Cut** tool in the **Assembly Features** flyout. The **Extrude PropertyManager** appears. Select a plane or a planar face as the sketching plane. The Sketching environment is invoked. Create the sketch of the extruded cut feature and then exit the Sketching environment. As soon as you exit from the Sketching environment, the preview of the cut feature appears in the graphics area. Specify the required

parameters for the extrusion in the PropertyManager and then click on the green tick mark. The extruded cut feature is created in the Assembly environment.

Note: You can also invoke the tools for creating the assembly features by clicking on **Insert > Assembly Feature** in the SOLIDWORKS menus. In addition to creating the assembly features (cut features), you can mirror the assembly features about a mirroring plane by using the **Mirror** tool of the **Assembly Features** flyout. You can also create a linear pattern, circular pattern, table driven pattern, sketch driven pattern, and so on of the assembly features by using the respective tools available in the **Assembly Features** flyout. The tools to create mirror and pattern features become available in the **Assembly Features** flyout only after creating an assembly feature in the Assembly environment.

Suppressing or Unsuppressing Components

In SOLIDWORKS, you can suppress or unsuppress components of an assembly. A suppressed component is removed from the assembly and does not appear in the graphics area. Also, the name of the suppressed component appears in gray color in the FeatureManager Design Tree. Note that a suppressed component is not deleted from the assembly, it is only removed or disappeared such that it is not loaded into the RAM (random access memory) while rebuilding the assembly. This helps you speed up the overall performance of the system when you are working with large assemblies.

To suppress a component of an assembly, select the component to be suppressed either from the graphics area or from the FeatureManager Design Tree. A Pop-up toolbar appears, see Figure 13.52. In this Pop-up toolbar, click on the **Suppress** tool. The selected component is suppressed.

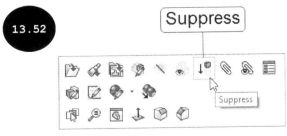

676 Chapter 13 > Working with Assemblies - II

To unsuppress a suppressed component, select the suppressed component from the FeatureManager Design Tree. A Pop-up toolbar appears. Next, click on the **Unsuppress** tool in the Pop-up toolbar. The component is now unsuppressed and appears in the assembly.

Inserting the Parts having Multiple Configurations

In SOLIDWORKS, you can choose a configuration of a component to be inserted in the Assembly environment. To choose a configuration of a component to be inserted in the Assembly environment, click on the **Insert Components** tool in the **Assembly CommandManager**. The **Open** dialog box appears along with the **Insert Component PropertyManager**, automatically. Note that if the **Open** dialog box does not appear then click on the **Browse** button in the **Part/Assembly to Insert** rollout of the PropertyManager to open the **Open** dialog box. In the **Open** dialog box, browse to the location where the component to be inserted has been saved. Next, select the component that has multiple configurations and then invoke the **Configurations** drop-down list in the **Open** dialog box, see Figure 13.53. Now, select the required configuration of the component from this drop-down list that is to be inserted in the Assembly environment. Next, click on the **Open** button in the dialog box. The selected configuration of the component is attached to the cursor. Now, click in the graphics area to specify the position of the component.

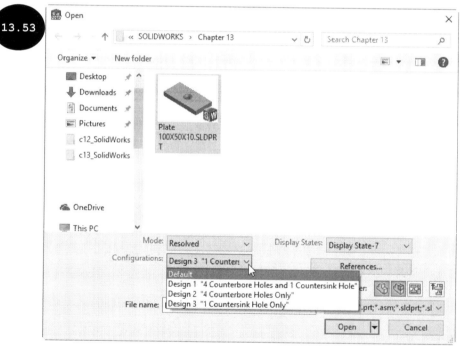

13.53

Note: In SOLIDWORKS, you can create multiple configurations of a component in the Part modeling environment. For example, if a bolt of same geometry has to be used in an assembly several times with the difference in its diameter, then you can create a single bolt with multiple configurations having different diameters. The different methods of creating multiple configurations are discussed in Chapter 11.

You can also choose a configuration of a component to be inserted in the Assembly environment by using the **Configuration** drop-down list of the **Insert Component PropertyManager** or the **Begin Assembly PropertyManager**. Additionally, you can change the configuration of a component even after inserting it in the Assembly environment. To change the configuration of an already inserted component, click on the component whose configuration has to be changed. A Pop-up toolbar appears with the **Configuration** drop-down list, see Figure 13.54. Next, invoke the **Configuration** drop-down list by clicking on its down arrow and then select the required configuration of the component. Next, click on the green tick mark appeared in front of the drop-down list to confirm the selection of the configuration. The configuration of the component changes to the selected configuration in the Assembly environment.

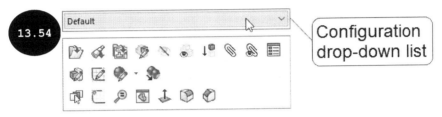

Creating and Dissolving Sub-Assemblies

SOLIDWORKS allows you to create sub-assemblies from the components of an assembly within the Assembly environment. To create a sub-assembly, select components to be included in the sub-assembly from the FeatureManager Design Tree by pressing the CTRL key and then right-click. A shortcut menu appears. In this shortcut menu, click on the **Form New Subassembly** option, see Figure 13.55. As soon as you select this option, a sub-assembly is created with a default name and the selected components become the part of the sub-assembly. In case, the **Assembly Structure Editing** window appears after selecting the **Form New Subassembly** option then click on the **Move** button. You can also include patterned and mirrored components in the sub-assembly. To rename the sub-assembly, select the sub-assembly in the FeatureManager Design Tree and then right-click. Next, click on the **Rename Assembly** option in the shortcut menu appeared. The name of the sub-assembly appears in an edit field. Now, you can enter a new name for the sub-assembly.

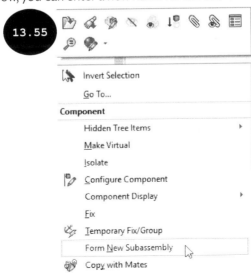

678 Chapter 13 > Working with Assemblies - II

You can also dissolve the created sub-assembly in the Assembly environment. To dissolve the sub-assembly, select the sub-assembly to be dissolved from the FeatureManager Design Tree and then right-click to display a shortcut menu. Next, click on the **Dissolve Subassembly** option in the shortcut menu. The selected sub-assembly is dissolved and its components become the individual components of the main assembly.

Creating an Exploded View

Creating an exploded view of an assembly is important from the presentation point of view. Also, an exploded view of an assembly helps you easily identify the position of each component of an assembly. Moreover, an exploded view helps in making technical documentation as well as it helps technical and non-technical clients easily understand about various components of the assembly. Figure 13.56 shows an assembly and Figure 13.57 shows the exploded view of the assembly.

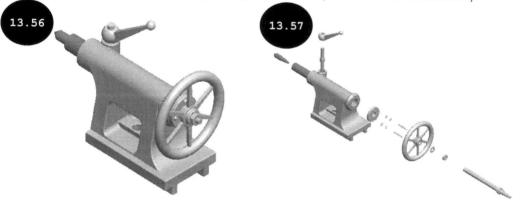

To create an exploded view of an assembly, click on the **Exploded View** tool in the **Assembly CommandManager**, see Figure 13.58. The **Explode PropertyManager** appears, see Figure 13.59. The options of the PropertyManager are as follows:

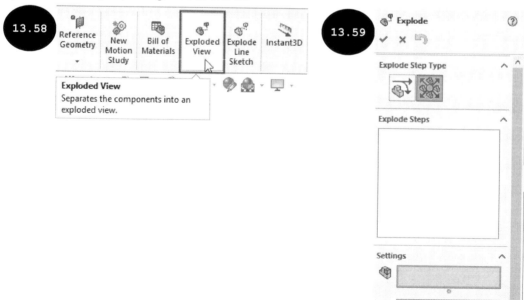

Explode Step Type

The **Explode Step Type** rollout of the PropertyManager is used to choose the type of exploded step to be created. By activating the **Regular step** button in the **Explode Step Type** rollout, you can explode the components of an assembly by translating and rotating them along and about an axis, see Figure 13.60. By activating the **Radial step** button, you can explode the components of an assembly by aligning them radially or cylindrically about an axis, see Figure 13.61.

Explode Steps

The **Explode Steps** rollout displays the list of exploded steps created for an exploded assembly, see Figure 13.62. Note that to create an exploded assembly, you may need to create multiple exploded steps (regular and radial steps). In each exploded step, one or more than one component can be exploded.

Settings

The options in the **Settings** rollout are used to create exploded steps. Note that the availability of the options in this rollout depends on the button (**Regular step** or **Radial step**) selected in the **Explode Step Type** rollout. Figure 13.63 shows the **Settings** rollout when the **Regular step** button is selected. The options of the **Settings** rollout are as follows:

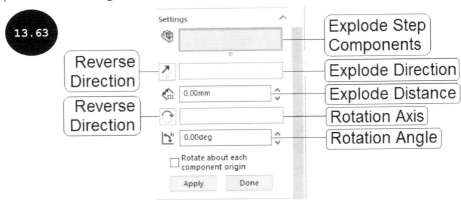

Explode Step Components

The **Explode Step Components** field is used to select components of the assembly to be exploded in the exploded step. You can select one or more than one component to be exploded in an exploded step from the graphics area. As soon as you select the components to be exploded, three rotation handles and three translation handles appear in the graphics area, see Figure 13.64. Note that these handles (three rotation and three translations) appear in the case of creating regular exploded step by using the **Regular step** button. In the case of creating the radial exploded step by using the **Radial step** button, one rotation handle and one translation handle appears in the graphics area as soon as you select the components to be exploded, see Figure 13.65.

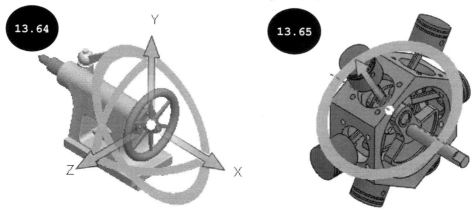

You can drag the required rotation handle or translation handles for creating the exploded step. A translation handle is used to translate the selected components along its respective direction, whereas a rotation handle is used to rotate the components about its respective axis.

Tip: For translation movement, move the cursor over the required translation handle and then drag it by pressing and holding the left mouse button. The selected component starts translating along the direction of translation handle. Once the desired location has been achieved, release the left mouse button. An explode step is created and appears in the **Explode Steps** rollout.

For rotational movement, move the cursor over the required rotation handle and then drag it by pressing and holding the left mouse button. The selected component starts rotating about the axis of the rotational handle. Next, release the left mouse button. An exploded step is created.

Explode Direction

The **Explode Direction** field displays, translation direction along which selected components can translate. Note that the display of exploded direction depends upon the translation handle selected.

Explode Distance

The **Explode Distance** field is used to specify translation distance value for translating the selected components along with the translation direction. After specifying translation distance value in this field, click on the **Apply** button and then on the **Done** button in the **Settings** rollout of the PropertyManager. Note that if you translate the components by dragging the translation handle, then the translation distance value updates automatically in this field.

Rotation Axis
The **Rotation Axis** field displays rotation axis about which the selected components are to be rotated. The display of the rotational axis depends upon the selection of rotation handle.

Rotation Angle
The **Rotation Angle** field is used to specify a rotation angle value for rotating the selected components. After entering a rotation angle value in this field, click on the **Apply** button and then on the **Done** button. Note that if you rotate the components by dragging the rotation handle, then the rotational angle value updates automatically in this field.

Rotate about each component origin
On selecting the **Rotate about each component origin** check box, the selected components rotate about the origin of the component. This check box is available only when the **Regular Step** button is activated in the **Explode Step Type** rollout of the PropertyManager.

Diverge from axis
On selecting the **Diverge from axis** check box, the selected components explode away from an axis. This check box is available only when the **Radial Step** button is activated in the **Explode Step Type** rollout of the PropertyManager.

Apply
The **Apply** button is used to apply the exploded parameters and display the preview of exploded step.

Done
The **Done** button is used to accept the preview of exploded step and create an exploded step.

Options
The options in the **Options** rollout control the exploded step, see Figure 13.66. Note that the availability of the options in this rollout depends upon the button (**Regular step** or **Radial step**) selected in the **Explode Step Type** rollout of the PropertyManager. Figure 13.66 shows the **Options** rollout when the **Regular step** button is selected. The options of the **Options** rollout are as follows:

Auto-space components on drag
The **Auto-space components on drag** check box is used to translate or rotate a set of selected components with equal spacing, automatically on exploding the components along or about the selected direction. Note that the equal spacing value for exploding a set of selected components

with equal spacing can be increased or decreased by using the **Adjust the spacing between chain components** slider.

Adjust the spacing between chain components
The **Adjust the spacing between chain components** slider is used to adjust the spacing between a set of selected components for exploding them, equally.

Show rotation rings
By default, the **Show rotation rings** check box is selected. As a result, the rotation handles/rings appear in the graphics area by selecting the components to be exploded. If you uncheck this check box, the display of rotation handles/rings is disabled.

Select the subassembly's parts
By selecting the **Select the subassembly's parts** check box, you can select individual components of a sub-assembly for explosion.

Reuse Subassembly Explode
The **Reuse Subassembly Explode** button is used to explode components by using the previously defined exploded step for a sub-assembly.

Note: By default, the selected components can only explode along the X, Y, and Z axes by using the handles appeared in the graphics area. To translate the component other than X, Y, and Z axes, move the cursor over a translation handle appeared in the graphics area and then right-click. A shortcut menu appears, see Figure 13.67. In this shortcut menu, click on the **Align with selection** or **Align to selection** option. Next, select a linear edge of a component. The selected handle is aligned along the direction of the selected linear edge. Now, you can drag the aligned handle to translate the components along the direction of the aligned handle.

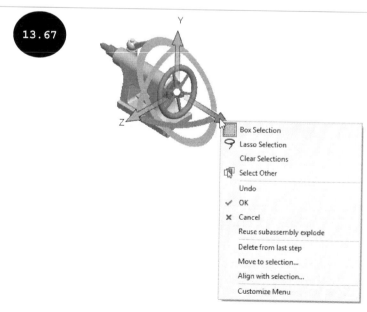
13.67

Procedure for Creating the Regular Exploded View

1. Click on the **Exploded View** tool. The **Explode PropertyManager** appears.
2. Make sure that the **Regular step** button is selected in the **Explode Step Type** rollout.
3. Select a set of components to be exploded as the first regular exploded step.
4. Drag a translation handle or a rotation handle appeared in the graphics area by pressing and holding the left mouse button. Alternatively, enter the translation distance or rotational angle value in the respective fields of the **Settings** rollout and then click on the **Apply** button and the **Done** button to create the first exploded step.
5. Similarly, create the other exploded steps for the assembly.
6. Click on the green tick mark button in the PropertyManager. The exploded view of the assembly is created.

Procedure for Creating the Radial Exploded View

1. Click on the **Exploded View** tool. The **Explode PropertyManager** appears.
2. Make sure that the **Radial step** button is selected in the **Explode Step Type** rollout.
3. Select a set of components to be exploded as the first exploded step.
4. Drag the translation handle or the rotation handle to a required distance by pressing and holding the left mouse button. Alternatively, enter the translation distance or rotation angle value in the respective fields of the **Settings** rollout and then click on the **Apply** button and then the **Done** button to create the first exploded step.
5. Similarly, create the other exploded steps for the assembly.
6. Click on the green tick mark in the PropertyManager. The exploded view of the assembly is created.

Note: You can create exploded view of an assembly with the combination of the regular and radial exploded steps.

Collapsing an Exploded View

After creating an exploded view of an assembly, you can restore the components of the assembly back to their original positions by collapsing the exploded view. To collapse the exploded view of an assembly, select the name of the assembly from the FeatureManager Design Tree and then right-click. A shortcut menu appears, see Figure 13.68. In this shortcut menu, click on the **Collapse** option.

After the collapsed view of an assembly has been displayed, you can display the exploded view again. To display the exploded view of an assembly again, select the name of the assembly from the FeatureManager Design Tree and then right-click to display a shortcut menu. In this shortcut menu, click on the **Explode** option. The exploded view of the assembly is displayed.

Animating an Exploded View

After creating an exploded view of an assembly, you can animate the components of the assembly to display its collapsed and exploded views. To animate the collapsed or exploded view of an assembly, select the name of the assembly from the FeatureManager Design Tree and then right-click to display a shortcut menu. Next, click on the **Animate collapse** or **Animate explode** option in the shortcut menu. The components start animating and the **Animation Controller** toolbar appears, see Figure 13.69. By using the **Animation Controller** toolbar, you can control the animation of the components. You can also record the animation and save it as a .avi, .bmp, and .tga file.

Note: The availability of the **Animate collapse** or **Animate explode** option in the shortcut menu depends upon the current state of the assembly. If the assembly appears in its exploded view in the graphics area, then the **Animate collapse** option is available in the shortcut menu. If the assembly appears in its collapsed view, then the **Animate explode** option is available in the shortcut menu.

Editing an Exploded View

You can edit the existing exploded view of an assembly to make necessary changes in its existing exploded steps and to create new exploded steps. To edit the exploded view of an assembly, invoke the ConfigurationManager by clicking on the **ConfigurationManager** tab, see Figure 13.70. The ConfigurationManager displays the list of all configurations of the assembly. Figure 13.70 shows the default configuration of the assembly (**Default** [*name of the assembly*]). Expand the configuration of the assembly by clicking on the arrow that appears in its front, see Figure 13.71.

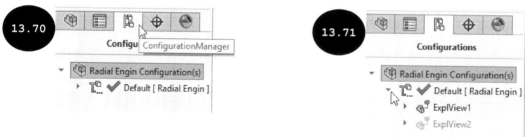

Figure 13.71 shows the two exploded views: **ExplView1** and **ExplView2** created for the assembly and out of which the **ExplView1** is activated, by default. You can activate the required exploded view by double-clicking on its name. To edit an exploded view, select the exploded view to be edited and then right-click to display a shortcut menu, see Figure 13.72. Next, click on the **Edit Feature** option

in the shortcut menu. The **Explode PropertyManager** appears. Now, by using the options of this PropertyManager, you can edit the exploded view, as required.

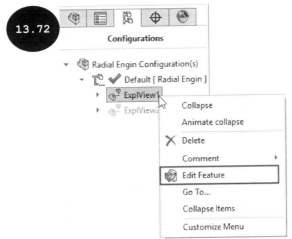

Adding Explode Lines in an Exploded View

After creating an exploded view of an assembly, you can add exploded lines in it. Figure 13.73 shows an assembly and Figure 13.74 shows an exploded view of the assembly with exploding lines.

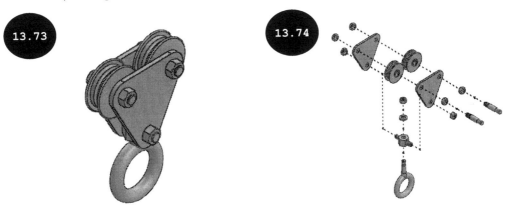

Exploded lines are used to show relationships between components in an exploded view. You can create exploded lines in an exploded view by using the **Explode Line Sketch** tool of the **Assembly CommandManager**. The procedure to create exploded lines in an exploded view of an assembly is as follows:

Procedure for Creating Exploded Lines

1. Click on the **Explode Line Sketch** tool in the **Assembly CommandManager**. The **Route Line PropertyManager** appears, see Figure 13.75.
2. Select faces, circular edges, straight edges, or planar faces of the components having same assembly line one after another to connect them with a single route line.
3. Select the **Reverse** check box to reverse the direction of route line, if needed. Also, you can select the **Alternate Path** check box to see the alternate route between the selected components.

4. Click on the green tick mark ✓ in the PropertyManager. A route line is created among the selected components, which represents the assembly line of the components.
5. Similarly, create route lines for remaining sets of components having the same assembly line.
6. Once you have created all the exploded lines, click on the green tick mark in the PropertyManager.

Creating Bill of Material (BOM) of an Assembly

A Bill of Material (BOM) is one of the important features of any drawing. It contains information related to the number of components, material, quantity, and so on. In addition to creating Bill of Material (BOM) in a drawing, SOLIDWORKS also allows you to create BOM in the Assembly environment. You will learn about creating Bill of Material (BOM) in a drawing in chapter 14. To create BOM in the Assembly environment, click on the **Bill of Materials** tool in the **Assembly CommandManager**. The **Bill of Materials PropertyManager** appears, see Figure 13.76. Accept the default parameters specified in the PropertyManager for creating the BOM by clicking on the green tick mark ✓ in the PropertyManager. The Bill of Material (BOM) is attached to the cursor and as you move the cursor in the graphics area, the BOM moves accordingly. Now, you need to specify the location for the BOM in the graphics area. Click in the graphics area. The BOM is placed on the specified location, see Figure 13.77.

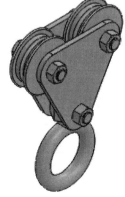

ITEM NO.	PART NUMBER	DESCRIPTION	QTY.
1	Metal Sheet Piece		2
2	Dowel Pin		2
3	Pulley		2
4	Hook Holder		1
5	Round Hook		1
6	Nut		7
7	Washer		1

Tutorial 1

Create the assembly shown in Figure 13.78 by using the Top-down Assembly approach. Different views and dimensions of the each assembly component are shown in Figures 13.79 through 13.81.

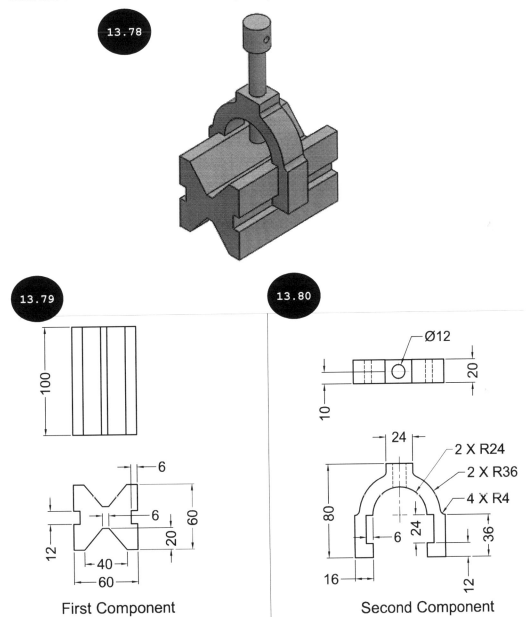

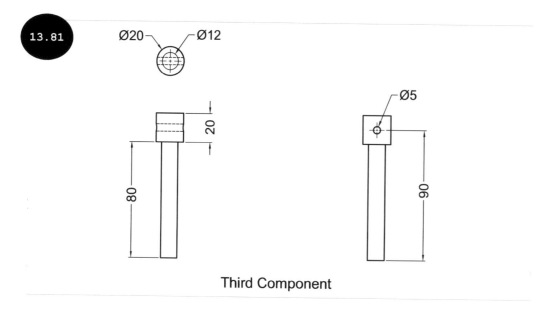

Third Component

Section 1: Starting SOLIDWORKS
1. Double-click on the SOLIDWORKS icon on your desktop to start SOLIDWORKS.

Section 2: Invoking the Assembly Environment
1. Click on the **New** tool in the **Standard** toolbar. The **New SOLIDWORKS Document** dialog box appears.

2. Click on the **Assembly** button and then click on the **OK** button in the dialog box. The assembly environment is invoked with the display of the **Open** dialog box along with the **Begin Assembly PropertyManager**, by default.

Section 3: Creating the First Component
1. Close the **Open** dialog box by clicking on the **Close** button and then close the **Begin Assembly PropertyManager** by clicking on the red cross mark ⊠ available at its top. This is because, in this tutorial, you need to create all components of the assembly within the Assembly environment itself.

2. Click on the arrow at the bottom of the **Insert Components** tool. A flyout appears, see Figure 13.82.

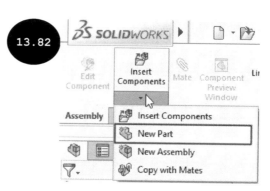

3. Click on the **New Part** tool in the flyout. A new empty part is added in the Assembly environment and appears in the FeatureManager Design Tree with its default name, see Figure 13.83. Also, a green color tick mark appears attached to the cursor

in the graphics area and you are prompted to define the placement for the newly added component in the graphics area.

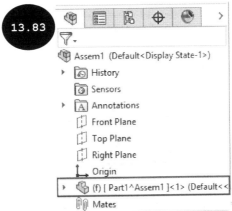

4. Click anywhere in the graphics area to define the position of the first component with respect to the origin of the assembly.

Note: If you select a plane or a planar face to define the position of the first component, then the Sketching environment is invoked such that the selected plane or the planar face becomes the sketching plane for creating the base feature of the component. Also, the Inplace mate is applied between the selected plane and the plane of the component.

5. Click on the newly added component in the FeatureManager Design Tree. A Pop-up toolbar appears, see Figure 13.84.

6. Click on the **Edit Part** tool in the Pop-up toolbar, see Figure 13.84. The Part modeling environment is invoked within the Assembly environment.

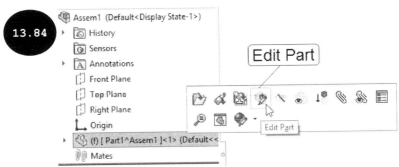

7. Click on the **Extruded Boss/Base** tool in the **Features CommandManager**. The **Extrude PropertyManager** appears.

8. Expand the FeatureManager Design Tree, which is now available at the top left corner of the graphics area and then expand the **Part1** node in it, which appears in blue color, see Figure 13.85.

9. Click on the **Front Plane** available under the expanded **Part1** node in the FeatureManager Design Tree as the sketching plane, see Figure 13.85. The Sketching environment is invoked.

10. Press CTRL + 8 to change the orientation of the model as normal to the viewing direction.

11. Click on the **Sketch** tab in the CommandManager to display the tools of the **Sketch CommandManager**.

12. Create the sketch of the base feature of the component by using the sketching tools, see Figure 13.86.

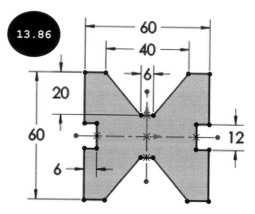

13. After creating the sketch of the base feature, click on the **Exit Sketch** tool in the Sketch CommandManager to exit the Sketching environment. The **Boss-Extrude** PropertyManager and the preview of the extruded feature appear.

14. Change the orientation of the model to isometric.

15. Invoke the **End Condition** drop-down list of the **Direction 1** rollout in the **Boss-Extrude** PropertyManager and then click on the **Mid Plane** option in it.

16. Enter **100** in the **Depth** field of the **Direction 1** rollout of the PropertyManager.

17. Click on the green tick mark ✓ in the PropertyManager. The component is created, see Figure 13.87.

18. Click on the **Edit Component** tool in the CommandManager to exit the Part modeling environment and switch to the Assembly environment.

Section 4: Creating the Second Component

1. Click on the arrow at the bottom of the **Insert Components** tool. A flyout appears, see Figure 13.88.

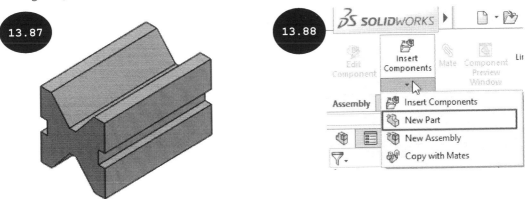

2. Click on the **New Part** tool in the flyout. A new empty part is added in the Assembly environment and appears in the FeatureManager Design Tree with its default name.

3. Click anywhere in the graphics area to define the position of the second component with respect to the origin of the assembly.

4. Click on the name of the newly added component (*Part2*) in the FeatureManager Design Tree. A Pop-up toolbar appears, see Figure 13.89.

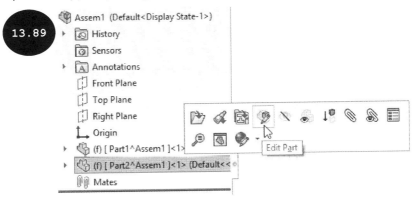

5. Click on the **Edit Part** tool in the Pop-up toolbar, see Figure 13.89. The Part modeling environment is invoked and the first component of the assembly becomes transparent in the graphics area.

6. Click on the **Extruded Boss/Base** tool in the **Features CommandManager**. The **Extrude PropertyManager** appears.

7. Expand the FeatureManager Design Tree, which is now at the top left corner of the graphics area. Next, expand the **Part 2** node of the FeatureManager Design Tree, which appears in blue color.

8. Click on the **Front Plane** of the second component as the sketching plane in the FeatureManager Design Tree. The Sketching environment is invoked.

9. Click on the **Sketch** tab in the CommandManager to display the tools of the **Sketch CommandManager**.

10. Press CTRL + 8 to change the orientation of the model as normal to the viewing direction.

11. Create the sketch of the first feature of the second component, see Figure 13.90.

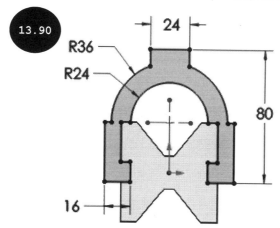

Note: To create the sketch of the base feature of the second component shown in Figure 13.90, you can take the reference of the edges of the first component.

12. After creating the sketch of the base feature of the second component, click on the **Exit Sketch** tool in the **Sketch CommandManager** to exit the Sketching environment. The **Boss-Extrude PropertyManager** and the preview of the extruded feature appear.

13. Change the orientation of the model to isometric.

14. Invoke the **End Condition** drop-down list of the **Direction 1** rollout in the **Boss-Extrude PropertyManager** and then click on the **Mid Plane** option in it.

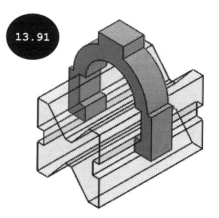

15. Enter 20 in the **Depth** field of the **Direction 1** rollout of the PropertyManager and then press ENTER.

16. Click on the green tick mark in the PropertyManager. The base feature of the second component is created, see Figure 13.91.

Now, you need to create the second feature of the second component.

17. Click on the **Extruded Cut** tool in the **Features CommandManager** and then click on the top planar face of the base feature of the second component as the sketching plane.

18. Press CTRL + 8 to change the orientation of the model as normal to the viewing direction.

19. Create a circle of diameter 12 mm as the sketch of the second feature, see Figure 13.92.

20. After creating the sketch of the second feature, click on the **Exit Sketch** tool in the **Sketch CommandManager** to exit the Sketching environment. The **Cut-Extrude PropertyManager** and the preview of the cut feature appear.

21. Change the orientation of the model to isometric.

22. Invoke the **End Condition** drop-down list of the **Direction 1** rollout and then click on the **Up To Next** option in it.

23. Click on the green tick mark in the PropertyManager. The second feature of the second component is created, see Figure 13.93.

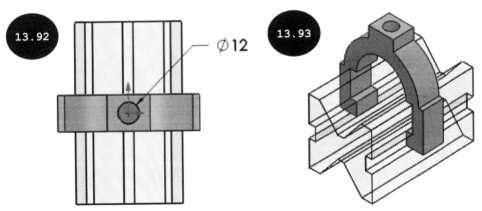

Now, you need to create the third feature of the second component.

24. Click on the **Fillet** tool in the **Features CommandManager**. The **Fillet PropertyManager** appears.

25. Make sure that the **Constant Size Fillet** button is selected in the **Fillet Type** rollout.

26. Enter **4** in the **Radius** field of the **Fillet Parameters** rollout in the PropertyManager.

27. Click on the required edges (4 edges) of the second component one by one as the edges to create the fillet. The preview of the fillet appears, see Figure 13.94.

694   Chapter 13 > Working with Assemblies - II

28. Click on the green tick mark ✓ in the PropertyManager. The third feature of the second component is created.

29. After creating all features of the second component, click on the **Edit Component** tool in the CommandManager to exit the Part modeling environment and switch to the Assembly environment. Figure 13.95 shows the assembly after creating its two components.

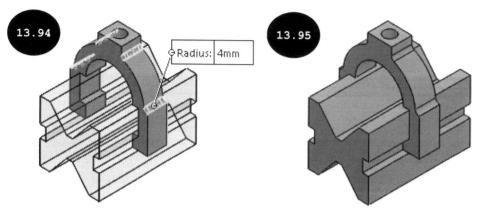

Section 5: Creating the Third Component

1. Click on the arrow at the bottom of the **Insert Components** tool. A flyout appears.

2. Click on the **New Part** tool in the flyout. A new empty part is added in the assembly and its default name gets added in the FeatureManager Design Tree.

3. Click on the top planar face of the second component as the sketching plane for creating the base feature of the third component. The Sketching environment is invoked and the top planar face of the second component becomes the sketching plane.

4. Press CTRL + 8 to change the orientation of the model as normal to the viewing direction.

5. Create a circle of diameter 12 mm as the sketch of the base feature of the third component, see Figure 13.96.

   Note: To create the circle of diameter 12 mm as shown in Figure 13.96, you can take the reference of the circular edge of the second component and apply the coradial relation between them. Alternatively, you can use the **Convert Entities** tool to project the circular edge of the second component for creating the circle of diameter 12 mm.

6. Click on the **Extruded Boss/Base** tool in the Features CommandManager. The Boss-Extrude PropertyManager appears.

7. Change the orientation of the model to isometric.

8. Invoke the **End Condition** drop-down list of the **Direction 1** rollout and then click on the **Mid Plane** option in it.

9. Enter **80** in the **Depth** field of the **Direction 1** rollout.

10. Click on the green tick mark ✓ in the PropertyManager. The base feature of the third component is created, see Figure 13.97.

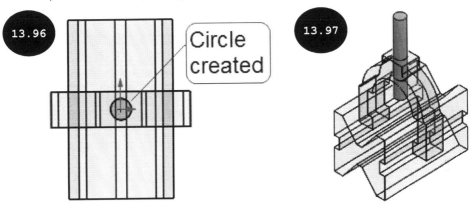

Now, you need to create the second feature of the third component.

11. Click on the **Extruded Boss/Base** tool in the **Features CommandManager** and then click on the top planar face of the base feature of the third component as the sketching plane.

12. Press CTRL + 8 to change the orientation of the model as normal to the viewing direction.

13. Create a circle of diameter 20 mm as the sketch of the second feature, see Figure 13.98.

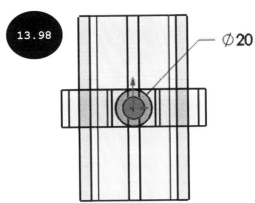

14. Click on the **Exit Sketch** tool in the **Sketch CommandManager** to exit the Sketching environment. The **Boss-Extrude PropertyManager** and the preview of the extruded feature appear.

696 Chapter 13 > Working with Assemblies - II

15. Change the orientation of the model to isometric.

16. Enter **20** in the **Depth** field of the **Direction 1** rollout in the PropertyManager.

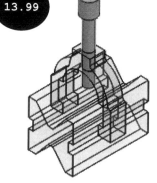

17. Click on the green tick mark in the PropertyManager. The second feature of the third component is created, see Figure 13.99.

    Now, you need to create the third feature of the third component.

18. Click on the **Extruded Cut** tool in the **Features CommandManager**. The **Extrude PropertyManager** appears.

19. Expand the FeatureManager Design Tree, which is now at the top left corner of the graphics area. Next, expand the **Part 3** node, which appears in blue color in the FeatureManager Design Tree.

20. Click on the **Right Plane** of the **Part 3** node in the FeatureManager Design Tree as the sketching plane. The Sketching environment is invoked. Next, press CTRL + 8 to change the orientation of the model as normal to the viewing direction.

21. Create a circle of diameter 5 mm as the sketch of the third feature, see Figure 13.100.

22. Click on the **Exit Sketch** tool in the **Sketch CommandManager** to exit the Sketching environment. The **Cut-Extrude PropertyManager** and the preview of the cut feature appear. Next, change the orientation of the model to isometric.

23. Invoke the **End Condition** drop-down list of the **Direction 1** rollout and then click on the **Through All - Both** option in it.

24. Click on the green tick mark in the PropertyManager. The third feature of the third component is created, see Figure 13.101.

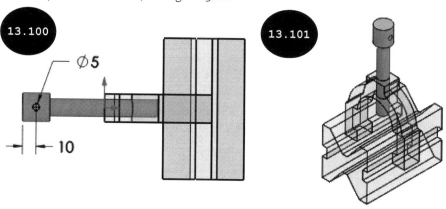

25. After creating all the features of the third component, click on the **Edit Component** tool in the CommandManager to exit the Part modeling environment and switch back to the Assembly environment. Figure 13.102 shows the final assembly after creating all the components.

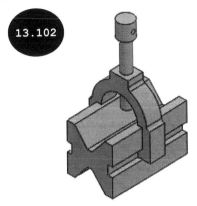

> **Note:** By default, the components created by using the Top-down approach become fixed components in the Assembly environment. You can make the components float and then apply required mates between the components of the assembly.

Section 6: Saving Assembly and its Component

1. Click on the **Save** button. The **Save Modified Documents** dialog box appears.

2. Click on the **Save All** button in the dialog box. The **Save As** dialog box appears. Browse to the *Tutorial* folder of the *Chapter 13* folder to save the assembly file. You need to create these folders in the *SOLIDWORKS* folder.

3. Enter **Tutorial 1** in the **File name** field of the dialog box as the name of the assembly and then click on the **Save** button in the dialog box. The another **Save As** dialog box appears, see Figure 13.103.

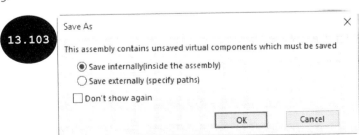

4. Select the **Save externally (specify paths)** radio button and then click on the **OK** button in the dialog box. All the components and the assembly file are saved in the specified location, individually.

Hands-on Test Drive 1

Create the assembly shown in Figure 13.104 by using the Top-down approach. Different views and dimensions of the individual components of the assembly are shown in Figures 13.105 through 13.108.

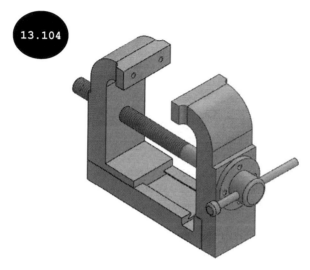

13.104

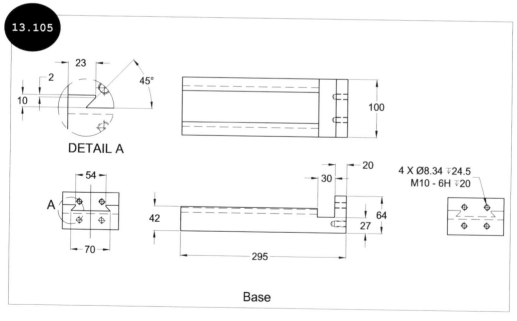

13.105

DETAIL A

Base

13.106

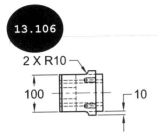

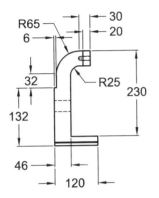
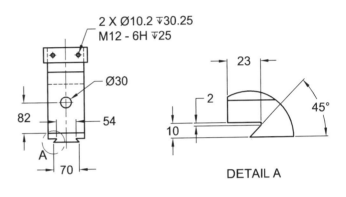

Moving Jaw

13.107

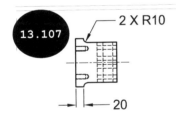

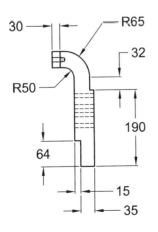
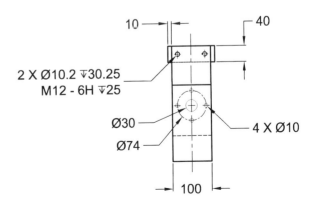

Fixed Jaw

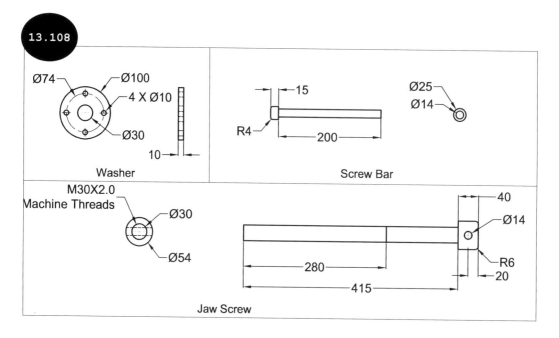

Summary

In this chapter, you have learned about creating assemblies by using the Top-down assembly approach. In the Top-down assembly approach, you can create all the components of an assembly in the Assembly environment itself. Once the assembly has been created, you can edit its components within the Assembly environment or by opening the component to be edited in the Part modeling environment. You can also edit the existing mates applied between the components of an assembly. Also, you have learned how to create different types of patterns such as a linear component pattern, pattern driven component pattern, and chain component pattern in the Assembly environment. Similar to mirroring features in the Part modeling environment, you can also mirror components in the Assembly environment by using the **Mirror Components** tool. In addition, you have learned about creating assembly features, suppressing or unsuppressing the components of an assembly, and inserting components having multiple configurations in the Assembly environment.

Moreover, you can create sub-assemblies of the components of an assembly within the Assembly environment. You can also dissolve the already created sub-assemblies into the individual components of an assembly. You have also learned how to create, edit, or collapse the exploded view of an assembly. You can also animate the exploded/collapse view of an assembly. Additionally, you have learned how to add exploded lines in an exploded view and create the Bill of Material (BOM) of an assembly.

Questions

- In the _____ approach, you create all the components of an assembly in the Assembly environment.

- In the _____ pattern, the pattern components drive by the pattern instances of the other components of an assembly.

- The _____ pattern allows you to dynamically simulate a chain drive or a cable carrier in an assembly.

- In SOLIDWORKS, you can create three types of chain patterns: _____, _____, and _____.

- The _____ tool is used to create an exploded view of an assembly.

- In SOLIDWORKS, you can create _____ and _____ types of exploded views.

- The _____ tool is used to create exploded lines in an exploded view.

- You can edit the components of an assembly within the Assembly environment. (True/False).

- In SOLIDWORKS, you can create cut features in the Assembly environment. (True/False).

- In SOLIDWORKS, you cannot create sub-assemblies from the components of an assembly. (True/False).

CHAPTER 14

Working with Drawings

In this chapter, you will learn the following:

- Invoking Drawing Environment by using the New tool
- Creating the Base/Model View of a Model
- Invoking Drawing Environment from the Part or the Assembly Environment
- Creating a Model View
- Creating a Projected View
- Creating 3 Standard Views
- Working with Angle of Projection
- Defining the Angle of Projection
- Editing the Sheet Format
- Creating a Section View
- Creating an Auxiliary View
- Creating a Detail View
- Creating a Broken-out Section View
- Creating a Break view
- Creating a Crop View
- Creating the Alternate Position View
- Applying Dimensions
- Modifying the Driving Dimension
- Controlling the Dimension and the Arrow Style
- Adding Notes
- Adding the Surface Finish Symbol
- Adding the Weld Symbol
- Adding the Hole Callout
- Adding the Center Mark
- Adding Centerlines
- Creating the Bill of Material (BOM)
- Adding Balloons

After creating parts and assemblies, you need to generate 2D drawings. 2D drawings are the technical drawings, which are used to fully and clearly communicate the information about the end product to be manufactured. 2D drawing is not only a drawing, but also a language of engineers that communicates ideas and information about engineered products with each other. By using 2D drawings, a designer can communicate the information about the component to be manufactured to the engineers on the shop floor. Underscoring importance of 2D drawings from the designers and engineers point of views, the role of designers is very important in generating accurate or error-free drawings for production. Inaccurate or missing information about a component in drawings can lead to wrong production. Keeping this in mind, SOLIDWORKS provides you with an environment that allows you to generate error-free 2D drawings. This environment is known as Drawing environment.

You can invoke the Drawing environment for generating 2D drawings by using the **New** tool available in the **Standard** toolbar as well as in the **File** menu of the SOLIDWORKS menus. You can also invoke the Drawing environment by using the **Make Drawing from Part/Assembly** tool, which is available within the Part and Assembly environments. Different methods of invoking Drawing environment are discussed next.

Invoking Drawing Environment by using the New Tool

To invoke the Drawing environment by using the **New** tool, click on the **New** tool in the **Standard** toolbar. The **New SOLIDWORKS Document** dialog box appears, see Figure 14.1. Click on the **Drawing** button in this dialog box and then click on the **OK** button. The **Sheet Format/Size** dialog box appears, see Figure 14.2. The options in this dialog box are used to select sheet size/format to be used for creating drawings. The options are as follows:

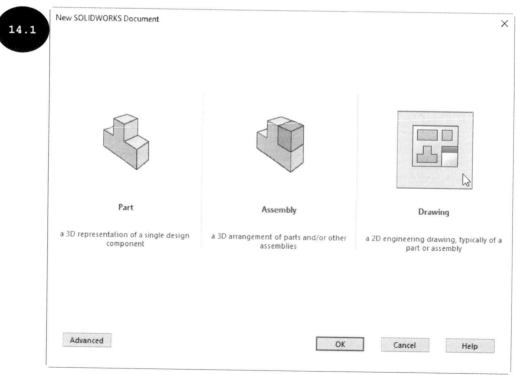

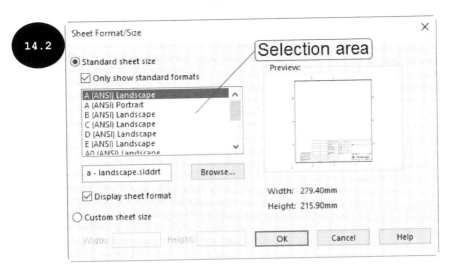

Figure 14.2

Standard sheet size

By default, the **Standard sheet size** radio button is selected in the **Sheet Format/Size** dialog box. As a result, a list of standard sheet sizes appears in the **Selection** area of the dialog box, see Figure 14.2. You can select a required standard sheet size from this area for creating drawing views. Note that if the **Only show standard formats** check box is selected in the dialog box, then the list of standard sheet sizes appears in the **Selection** area as per the current drawing standard only, see Figure 14.2. If this check is unchecked, all the standard sheet sizes are listed in this area.

Display sheet format

By default, the **Display sheet format** check box is selected in the dialog box. As a result, a drawing sheet will be displayed with the default standard sheet format. You can also select a sheet format other than the default one by clicking on the **Browse** button in the dialog box. When you click on the **Browse** button, the **Open** dialog box appears. In this dialog box, select the required sheet format and then click on the **Open** button. The preview of the sheet format appears in the **Preview** area of the dialog box. If you uncheck the **Display sheet format** check box, a blank drawing sheet will be displayed for creating drawings. Note that the **Display sheet format** check box is enabled only if the **Standard sheet size** radio button is selected in the dialog box.

Custom sheet size

On selecting the **Custom sheet size** radio button in the dialog box, the **Width** and **Height** fields are enabled and the other options in the dialog box are disabled, see Figure 14.3. In the **Width** and **Height** fields, you can specify the custom width and height values for the drawing sheet.

706 Chapter 14 > Working with Drawings

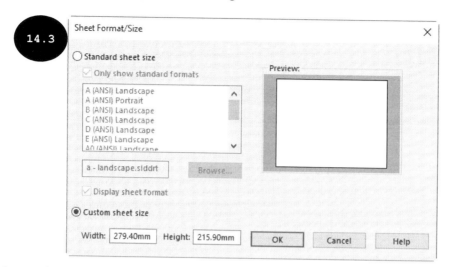

14.3

After selecting the required sheet size by using the options of the **Sheet Format/Size** dialog box, click on the **OK** button. The Drawing environment is invoked with the drawing sheet of specified size/format. Also, the **Model View PropertyManager** appears on its left, see Figure 14.4.

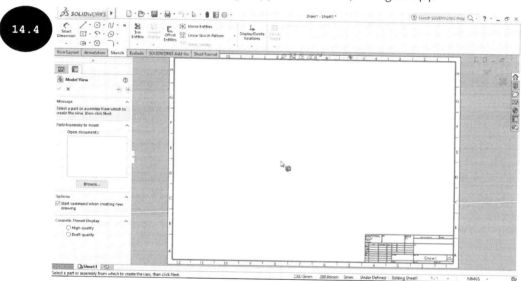

14.4

The options of the **Model View PropertyManager** are used to create the base/model view of a component or an assembly. The method of creating the base/model view of a component or an assembly by using this PropertyManager is as follows:

Note: The **Model View PropertyManager** appears each time on invoking the Drawing environment. This is because, in the **Options** rollout of the **Model View PropertyManager**, the **Start command when creating new drawing** check box is selected, by default, see Figure 14.4. If you uncheck this check box, next time when you invoke the Drawing environment, the **Model View PropertyManager** will not appear. In such a case, you can invoke the **Model View PropertyManager** by clicking on the **Model View** tool.

Creating the Base/Model View of a Model [Updated]

To create the base view of a model, click on the **Browse** button in the **Part/Assembly to Insert** rollout of the **Model View PropertyManager**. The **Open** dialog box appears. In this dialog box, browse to the location where the model, whose drawing view is to be created, has been saved and then select it. Next, click on the **Open** button in the dialog box. A rectangular box representing the base/model view of the model is attached to the cursor, see Figure 14.5. Also, the options of the PropertyManager are modified. The options are as follows:

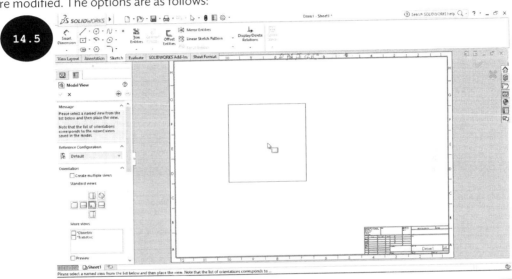

Tip: You can also select a component or an assembly, whose drawing views is to be created from the **Open documents** field of the **Part/Assembly to Insert** rollout in the PropertyManager. Note that only the models, which are opened in the current session of SOLIDWORKS are displayed in the **Open documents** field of the PropertyManager. To select a model from the **Open documents** field, double-click on the name of the model in this field.

Reference Configuration

The drop-down list in the **Reference Configuration** rollout of the PropertyManager contains a list of all the configurations of the selected model. You can select the required configuration of the model for creating its drawing views. Note that if the selected model does not have any configuration created, then only the **Default** option is available in this drop-down list, see Figure 14.6.

Orientation

The options in the **Standard views** area of the **Orientation** rollout are used to select a standard view of the model to be created. By default, the **Front** button is activated in the **Standard views** area, see Figure 14.6. You can click on the required button in this area to create the respective front, top, right, left, back, bottom, or isometric drawing view.

You can also create dimetric or trimetric drawing view of the model by using the **More views** field of this rollout, see Figure 14.6. To create the dimetric or the trimetric view, select the respective check box in the **More views** field of the rollout.

By default, the **Preview** check box of the **Orientation** rollout is unchecked, see Figure 14.6. As a result, an empty rectangular box appears attached to the cursor, which represents the selected view of the model. On selecting this check box, the preview of the selected standard view appears in the rectangular box.

You can also create multiple drawing views of the selected component or the assembly by selecting the **Create multiple views** check box of this rollout, see Figure 14.6.

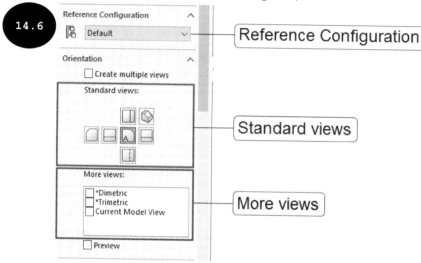

Import Options
The options in the **Import options** rollout are used to import annotations of the model into the drawing view, see Figure 14.7. On selecting the **Import annotations** check box, the **Design annotations**, **DimXpert annotations**, and **Include items from hidden features** check boxes are enabled in the rollout. Depending upon the check boxes selected in this rollout, the annotations of the model are imported into the drawing view.

Options
By default, the **Auto-start projected view** check box is selected in the **Options** rollout, see Figure 14.7. As a result, soon after creating the base/model view, the **Projected View PropertyManager** appears automatically. Also, a projected view of the model is attached to the cursor. The **Projected View PropertyManager** is used to create the projected views of the model. You will learn more about projected views later in this chapter.

Display Style
The options in the **Display Style** rollout are used to select the type of display for the drawing view, see Figure 14.7. On selecting the **Wireframe** button, all the visible and hidden edges of the model appear as continued lines in the drawing view, see Figure 14.8 (a). If you select

the **Hidden Lines Visible** button, the visible edges appear as continued lines and the hidden edges appear as dotted lines in the drawing view, see Figure 14.8 (b). On selecting the **Hidden Lines Removed** button, only the visible edges of the model appear in the drawing view as continued lines, see Figure 14.8 (c). On selecting the **Shaded With Edges** button, the drawing view is displayed in the shaded display style with the appearance of visible edges, see Figure 14.8 (d). If you select the **Shaded** button, the drawing view is displayed in the shaded model with the appearance of visible and hidden edges turned off, see Figure 14.8 (e).

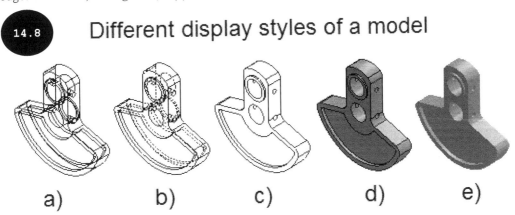

Figure 14.8 Different display styles of a model

Mirror

The **Mirror** rollout of the PropertyManager is used to create the horizontal or vertical mirror view of the model relative to the selected standard view. To create the horizontal or vertical mirror view of the model, expand the **Mirror** rollout of the PropertyManager and then select the **Mirror view** check box, see Figure 14.9. Next, select the **Horizontal** or **Vertical** radio button to create the respective mirror view of the model relative to the selected standard view.

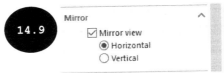

Figure 14.9

Scale

By default, the **Use sheet scale** radio button is selected in the **Scale** rollout, see Figure 14.10. As a result, the scale of the drawing view is the same as that of the scale of the drawing sheet. On selecting the **Use custom scale** radio button, the **Scale** drop-down list is enabled. By using this drop-down list, you can select a pre-defined scale value of the drawing view. Also, if you select the **User defined** option from the **Scale** drop-down list, then the **Scale** field gets enabled. In this field, you can specify the user-defined scale value of the drawing view.

Figure 14.10

Dimension Type

The **Dimension Type** rollout is used to specify the type of dimensions: true or projected for the drawing view. The projected dimensions appear as 2D dimensions in an isometric drawing view. It is mainly used in orthogonal views such as front, top, and right, see Figure 14.11. The true dimensions appear as accurate model dimensions in an isometric, dimetric, and trimetric drawing views, see Figure 14.12.

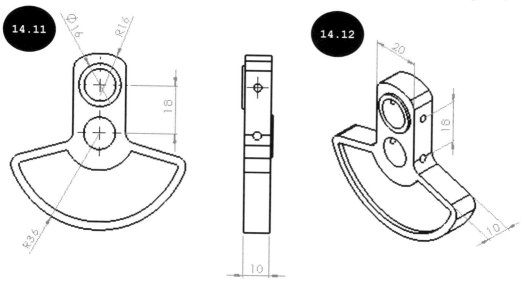

Cosmetic Thread Display

The **High quality** and **Draft quality** radio buttons of the **Cosmetic Thread Display** rollout are used to control the display of cosmetic threads in the drawing view. On selecting the **High quality** radio button, the cosmetic threads appear in precise line fonts. On selecting the **Draft quality** radio button, the cosmetic threads appear with less detail in the drawing views.

After specifying the required settings for creating the base view such as type of view, display style, and scale factor, click on the drawing sheet to position the drawing view. The drawing view is created and placed in the specified position on the drawing sheet. Also, the **Projected View PropertyManager** appears, automatically. Notice that on moving the cursor, a projected view appears attached to the cursor. You can create projection views by specifying the placement points in the drawing sheet. Most of the options of the **Projected View PropertyManager** are the same as those discussed earlier and are used to specify the settings for the projected views. Figure 14.13 shows different projected views that can be created from the base view. Once you have created the required projected views, press the ESC key to exit the creation of projection views.

> **Note:** You can also control or modify the settings such as display style and scale factor for a drawing view that has been already placed in the drawing sheet. To modify the settings of a drawing view, click on the drawing view in the drawing sheet. The **Drawing View PropertyManager** appears. By using the options of this PropertyManager, you can control the settings of the selected drawing view. All options of this PropertyManager are the same as those discussed earlier.

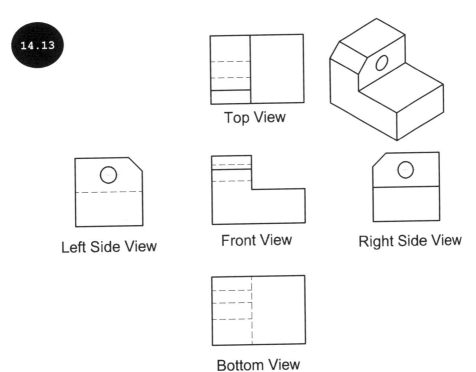

Third Angle of Projection

Invoking Drawing Environment from the Part or the Assembly Environment

Similar to invoking the Drawing environment by using the **New** tool and creating different drawing views of a model, you can also invoke the Drawing environment from the Part modeling environment or the Assembly environment. If you are in the Part modeling environment or in the Assembly environment, you can directly invoke the Drawing environment from there and start creating drawing views of the model, which is currently available in the respective environment. To invoke the Drawing environment from the Part modeling environment or the Assembly environment, click on the down arrow available next to the **New** tool in the **Standard** toolbar. A flyout appears, see Figure 14.14.

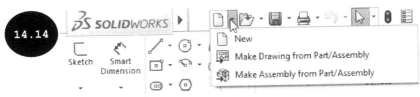

Click on the **Make Drawing from Part/Assembly** tool in this flyout. The **Sheet Format/Size** dialog box appears. The options in this dialog box are used to specify the required format/size of the drawing sheet and are same as those discussed earlier. After defining the format/size of the drawing sheet, click on the **OK** button. The Drawing environment is invoked with the display of **View Palette Task Pane** on the right of the drawing sheet, see Figure 14.15.

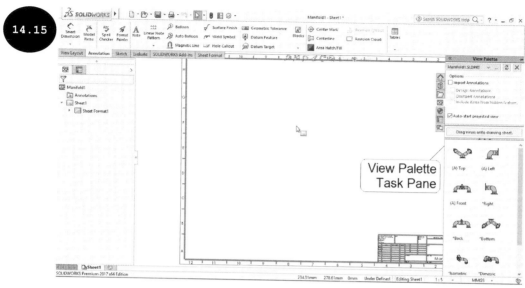

Note that the bottom half area of the **View Palette Task Pane** displays drawing views of the model that were opened in the Part modeling environment or the Assembly environment. By using this task pane, you can drag and drop the required drawing view of the model on the drawing sheet. The first placed view in the drawing sheet is known as a model, base, or parent view. As soon as you place the model/base view in the drawing sheet, the **Projected View PropertyManager** appears on the left of the drawing sheet. This is because the **Auto-start projected view** check box is selected in the upper half of the **View Palette Task Pane**, see Figure 14.15. Now, on moving the cursor in the drawing sheet, a projected view appears and attaches with the cursor, automatically. You can click on the drawing sheet to specify the position of the projected view. You can create multiple projected views one after another by clicking the left mouse button. Once you have created the required projected views, press the ESC key to exit the creation of projection views.

Creating a Model View

A model view is an independent view of a model. It is also known as base, first or parent view. You can create a model view of a model by using the **Model View PropertyManager** and the **View Palette Task Pane**, which appears automatically on invoking the Drawing environment, as discussed earlier. Moreover, you can also invoke the **Model View PropertyManager** by clicking on the **Model View** tool in the **View Layout CommandManager** for creating the model/base view of a model, see Figure 14.16.

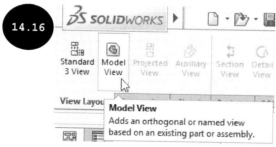

Procedure for Creating a Model/Base View

1. Invoke the **Model View PropertyManager** by clicking on the **Model View** tool, if not invoked, by default.
2. Click on the **Browse** button in the **Part/Assembly to Insert** rollout of the PropertyManager.

> **Tip:** If the component or the assembly whose drawing views is to be created appears in the **Open documents** field of the **Part/Assembly to Insert** rollout in the PropertyManager then you can directly select it from this field by double-clicking on it for creating the model view. The **Open documents** field displays a list of models, which are opened in the current session of SOLIDWORKS.

3. Select a part or an assembly, whose drawing views are to be created and then click on the **Open** button in the dialog box. A rectangular box appears attached to the cursor, which represents the model/base view of the selected part or assembly.
4. Specify the required settings such as standard view, display style, and scale factor for the drawing view by using the options in the PropertyManager.
5. Click on the drawing sheet to specify the position for the model/base view in the drawing sheet. The model view is created. Also, the **Projected View PropertyManager** appears. By using the **Projected View PropertyManager**, you can create the projected views of the model.
6. After creating the required views, press the ESC key to exit the creating of drawing views.

Creating a Projected View

Projected views are orthogonal views of an object, which are created by viewing the object from its different projection sides such as top, front, and side. Figure 14.17 and Figure 14.18 shows different projected views of an object.

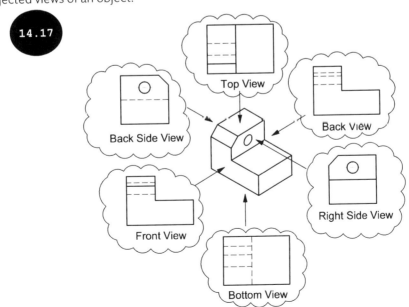

Projected Views

714 Chapter 14 > Working with Drawings

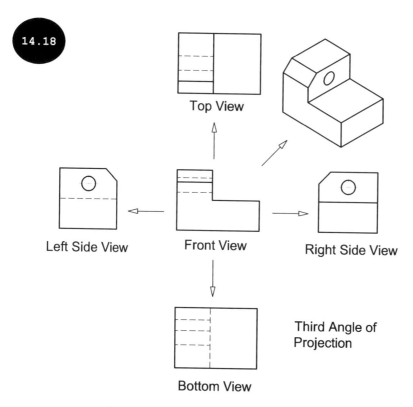

14.18

You can create projected views by using the **Projected View PropertyManager**. As discussed earlier, the **Projected View PropertyManager** is invoked automatically as soon as you create the model/base view of a model by using the **Model View PropertyManager**. You can also invoke this PropertyManager by clicking on the **Projected View** tool in the **View Layout CommandManager**. The options in the **Projected View PropertyManager** are the same as those discussed earlier and are used to create the projected views of a selected model/base view.

Procedure for Creating Projected Views

1. Invoke the **Projected View PropertyManager** by clicking on the **Projected View** tool.
2. Select a view as the model/base view whose projected views are to be created.

> **Note:** If only one drawing view is available in the drawing sheet then it is automatically selected for creating its projected views. Also, the preview of the projected view is attached to the cursor. However, if two or more than two views are available in the drawing sheet, then you need to select a view whose projected views are to be created.

3. Move the cursor to the required location in the drawing sheet and then click to specify the placement point for the projected view attached. You can continue creating other projected views by clicking the left mouse button in the drawing sheet.
4. Once you have created the projected views, press the ESC key.

Creating 3 Standard Views

In addition to creating drawing views by using the **Model View PropertyManager** and the **Projected View PropertyManager**, you can create three standard orthogonal views: front, top, and side by using the **Standard 3 View** tool of the **View Layout CommandManager**. On clicking this tool, the **Standard 3 View PropertyManager** appears. If the part or assembly, whose drawing views are to be created is displayed in the **Open documents** field of the PropertyManager then double-click on it. The three standard views are created automatically in the drawing sheet, see Figure 14.19. If the model is not displayed in the **Open documents** field, then click on the **Browse** button. The **Open** dialog box appears. In this dialog box, browse to the location where the required part or assembly has been saved and then select it. Next, click on the **Open** button in the dialog box.

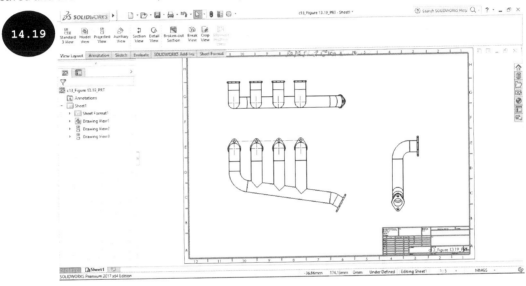

14.19

Note: The creation of standard views depends upon the angle of projection defined for the drawing sheet. You can define the first angle of projection or the third angle of projection for creating the standard drawing views. The concept of angle of projection and the procedure to define the angle of projection for the drawing are discussed next.

Working with Angle of Projection

Engineering drawings follow two types of angle of projection: first angle of projection and the third angle of projection. In the first angle of projection, the object is assumed to be kept in the first quadrant and the viewer views the object from the direction shown in Figure 14.20. As the object has been kept in the first quadrant, its projections of views are on the respective planes as shown in Figure 14.20. Now on unfolding the planes of projections, the front view appears on the upper side and the top view appears on the bottom side. Also, the right side view appears on the left and the left side view appears on the right side of the front view, see Figure 14.21. Similarly, in the third angle of projection, the object is assumed to be kept in the third quadrant, see Figure 14.20 and the projection of the front view appears on the bottom and the projection of the top view appears on the top side in the drawing. Also, the right side view appears on the right and the left side view appears on the left of the front view, see Figure 14.22.

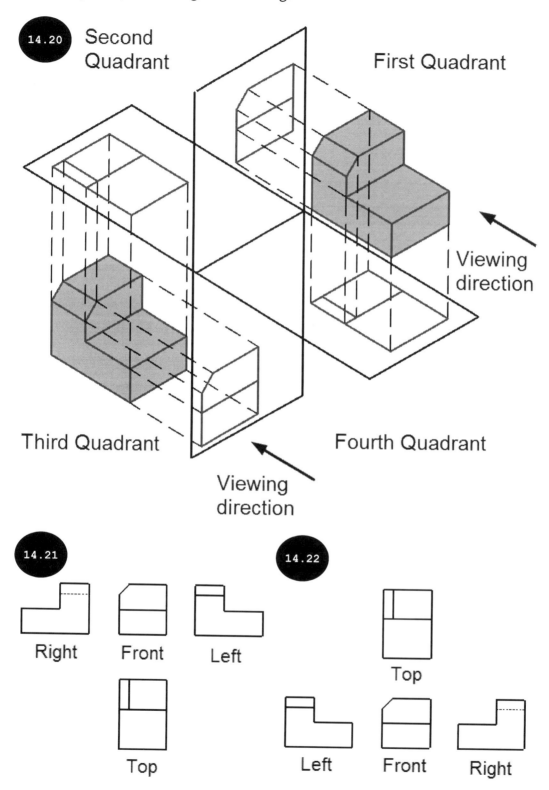

14.20 Second Quadrant / First Quadrant / Third Quadrant / Fourth Quadrant / Viewing direction

14.21 Right / Front / Left / Top

14.22 Top / Left / Front / Right

Defining the Angle of Projection

In SOLIDWORKS, to define the required angle of projection for creating drawing views, select the **Sheet** node from the FeatureManager Design Tree and then right-click. A shortcut menu appears, see Figure 14.23. Next, click on the **Properties** option in the shortcut menu. The **Sheet Properties** dialog box appears, see Figure 14.24. In this dialog box, you can select the type of projection to be followed for creating drawing views by selecting the respective radio button from the **Type of projection** area of the dialog box. Next, click on the **OK** button to accept the change and to exit the dialog box.

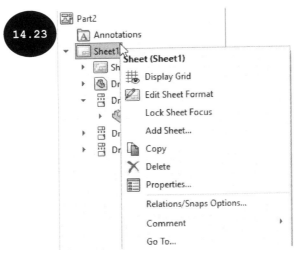

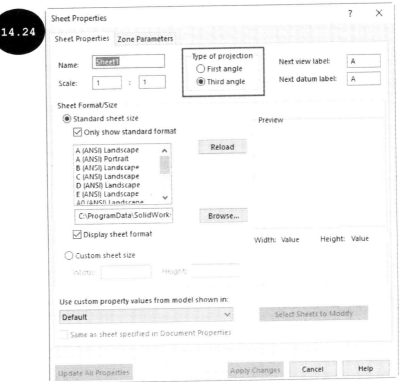

Editing the Sheet Format

While invoking the Drawing environment, you can select the required sheet size and sheet format. Note that the sheet format contains title block, which has drawing information such as project name, drawn by, checked by, approved by, date, sheet number, and so on. You can create or edit the sheet format such that it matches the standard format of your company. To edit the sheet format of a sheet, select the **Sheet** node in the FeatureManager Design Tree and then right-click to display a shortcut menu, refer to Figure 14.23. Next, click on the **Edit Sheet Format** option in the shortcut menu. The editing mode for editing sheet format is invoked, see Figure 14.25. Now, you can edit or modify the existing text and lines of the title block. Also, you can add new lines and text in the title block by using the sketching tools of the **Sketch CommandManager**. To delete existing lines and text, select the lines and text of the title block to be deleted and then press the DELETE key. To edit the existing text, double-click on the text to be edited. The editing mode is invoked such that the text appears in the edit field. Now, you can write new text in the edit field. Once you have edited the sheet format, click on the confirmation corner on the upper right corner of the drawing area to exit the editing mode and switch back to the drawing sheet.

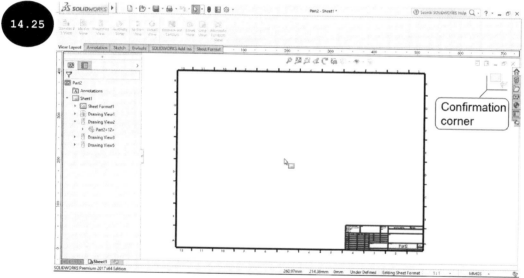

After modifying the sheet format or creating a new sheet format, as per the requirement, you can also save it for future use in other drawings. To save the sheet format, click on **Files > Save Sheet Format** in the SOLIDWORKS menus. The **Save Sheet Format** dialog box appears. In this dialog box, specify the name and location for the sheet format and then click on the **Save** button.

Creating other Drawing Views

In SOLIDWORKS, in addition to creating orthogonal views such as front, top, and right of an object, you can also create the following types of drawing views:

- Section View
- Aligned Section View
- Auxiliary View
- Detail View

- Broken View
- Crop View
- Alternate Position View
- Broken-out Section View

Creating a Section View Updated

A section view is created by cutting an object by using an imaginary cutting plane or a section line and then viewing the object from the direction normal to the cutting plane. Figure 14.26 shows a section view created by cutting an object using a cutting plane. A section view is used to illustrate internal features of the object clearly. It also reduces the number of hidden-detail lines, facilitates the dimensioning of internal features, shows cross-section, and so on. In SOLIDWORKS, you can create full section view and half section view by using the **Section View** tool of the **View Layout** CommandManager.

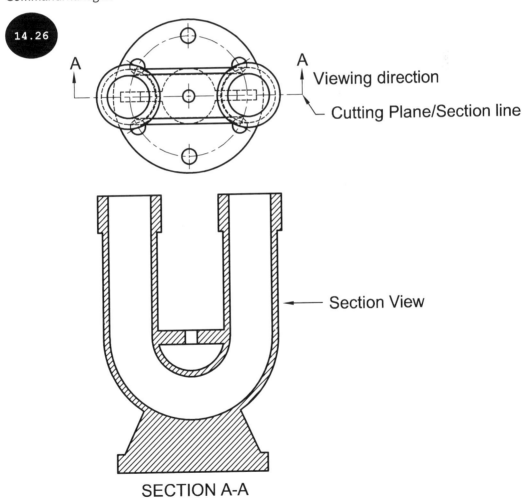

Creating a Full Section View

Full section views are the most widely used section views in engineering drawings. In a full section view, an object is assumed to be cut through all its length by an imaginary cutting plane or a section line, refer to Figure 14.26. In SOLIDWORKS, you can create four types of full section views: horizontal, vertical, auxiliary, and aligned by using the **Section View** tool.

To create a full section view, click on the **Section View** tool in the **View Layout** CommandManager. The **Section View Assist PropertyManager** appears, see Figure 14.27.

Note: In the **Section View Assist PropertyManager**, two tabs are available on its top: **Section** and **Half Section**. Out of which the **Section** tab is activated, by default. As a result, the options to create a full section view appear in the PropertyManager. On activating the **Half Section** tab, the options to create a half section view appears. You can learn more about creating half section views later in this chapter.

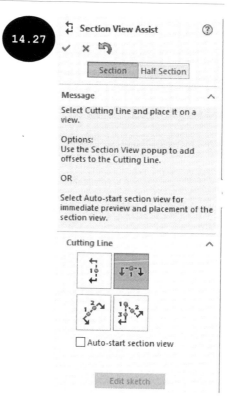

14.27

The **Cutting Line** rollout of the PropertyManager is used to select the type of cutting line for creating the respective full section view. You can create a vertical section view, horizontal section view, auxiliary section view, and aligned section view by using the respective buttons of the **Cutting Line** rollout. Different types of full section views are as follows:

Creating a Horizontal/Vertical Section View

To create a horizontal section view, click on the **Horizontal** button in the **Cutting Line** rollout of the PropertyManager. A horizontal cutting line attached to the cursor appears. Next, select the **Auto-start section view** check box in the **Cutting Line** rollout. Now, move the cursor toward an existing drawing view and then click to specify the placement point for the horizontal cutting line. The preview of the horizontal section view appears attached to the cursor. Also, the **Section View PropertyManager** appears with additional options. Note that the direction of the arrows of the cutting section line represents the viewing direction. You can reverse the viewing direction by clicking on the **Flip Direction** button in the PropertyManager.

In SOLIDWORKS 2017, you can emphasize the outlines of the cutting faces such that they appear thicker than the object lines in the section view by selecting the **Emphasize outline** check box in the **Section View** rollout of the PropertyManager. Also, if needed, you can scale the hatch pattern of the section view by selecting the **Scale Hatch Pattern** check box of the **Section View** rollout in the PropertyManager. Next, click to specify the placement point for the horizontal section view at the required location on the drawing sheet. The horizontal section view is created, refer to Figure 14.26.

Note: If the **Auto-start section view** check box in the **Cutting Line** rollout is unchecked, the **Section View** Pop-up toolbar appears soon after defining the placement point for the section line in a drawing view, see Figure 14.28. By using the tools of this Pop-up toolbar, you can modify or edit the section line, as required. Once you have edited or modified the section line, click on the green tick mark in the Pop-up toolbar. The preview of the section view appears attached to the cursor based on the modified section line. Now, you can specify the placement point for the section view in the drawing sheet.

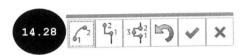

Similar to creating a horizontal section view, you can create a vertical section view by using the **Vertical** button of the **Cutting Line** rollout. Figure 14.29 shows a vertical section view created.

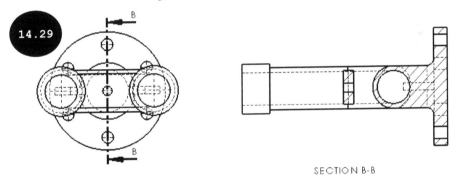

Note that if you are creating a section view of an assembly or a component having rib features, then soon after specifying the placement point for the section line, the **Section View** dialog box appears, see Figure 14.30.

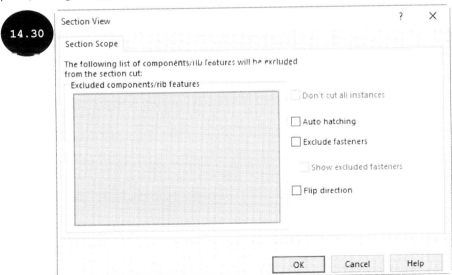

In the **Section View** dialog box, the **Excluded components/rib features** field is activated. As a result, you can select components like fasteners to be excluded from the section cut. You can also select features like ribs to be excluded from the section cut. Once you have selected components/features to be excluded, click on the **OK** button in the dialog box. The preview of the section view appears attached to the cursor, without cutting the selected components/features. Next, click to specify the placement point for placing the section view in the drawing sheet.

Tip: You can set the line font for the emphasized outlines of the cutting faces in the section view. To set the font for the emphasized outlines, click on the **Options** tool in the **Standard** toolbar to invoke the **System Options** dialog box. Next, click on the **Document Properties** tab in the dialog box and then click on the **Line Font** option. Next, select the **Emphasized Section Outline** option in the **Type of edge** area of the dialog box and then set the font/style for the emphasized outlines using the options that appear in the dialog box.

Creating a Auxiliary Section View

An auxiliary section view is created by cutting an object using a sight line which is not parallel to any of the principal projection planes: frontal, horizontal, or profile and then viewing the object from the direction normal to the sight line, see Figure 14.31.

To create an auxiliary section view, click on the **Section View** tool to invoke the **Section View Assist PropertyManager**. Next, click on the **Auxiliary** button in the **Cutting Line** rollout. A section line is attached to the cursor. Move the cursor to an existing drawing view and then click to specify the placement point. The preview of the auxiliary section view is attached to the cursor. If the **Section View** Pop-up toolbar appears soon after specifying the placement point then click on its green tick mark to display the preview of the auxiliary section view. You can reverse the default viewing direction by clicking on the **Flip Direction** button in the PropertyManager. Next, click to specify the placement point for the auxiliary section view at the required location in the drawing sheet. The auxiliary section view is created, see Figure 14.31.

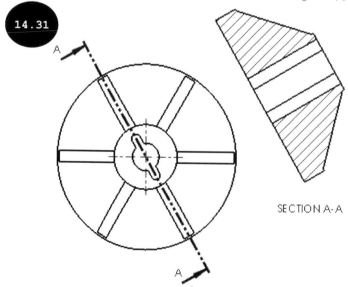

14.31

Creating a Aligned Section View

An aligned section view is created by cutting an object using the cutting section line, which comprises of two non-parallel lines and then straightening the cross-section by revolving it around the center point of the section line, see Figure 14.32.

Procedure for Creating a Aligned Section View

1. Invoke the **Section View Assist PropertyManager** by clicking on the **Section View** tool.
2. Click on the **Aligned** button in the **Cutting Line** rollout. A cutting section line, which comprises of two non-parallel lines is attached to the cursor.
3. Move the cursor toward an existing drawing view as the parent view for creating the aligned section view.
4. Click to specify the center point for the cutting section line, see Figure 14.32.
5. Move the cursor for a little distance and then click to specify the position for the first cutting line, see Figure 14.32.
6. Move the cursor for a little distance and then click to specify the position for the second cutting line, see Figure 14.32. The preview of the aligned section view is attached to the cursor.
7. Move the cursor to the required location and then click to specify the placement point for the aligned section view in the drawing sheet, see Figure 14.32.
8. Press ESC to exit.

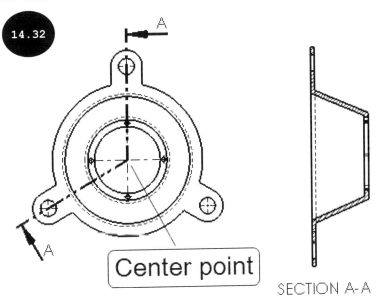

Creating a Half Section View

A half section view is created by cutting an object using an imaginary cutting plane or section line that passes halfway through the object, see Figure 14.33. In SOLIDWORKS, you can create half section view by using the **Section View** tool.

724 Chapter 14 > Working with Drawings

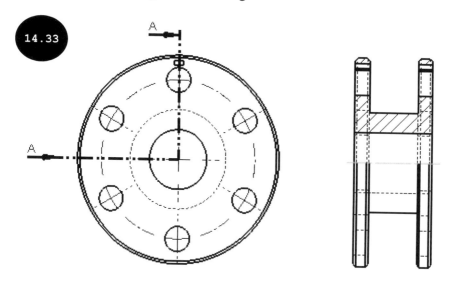

14.33

SECTION A-A

Procedure for Creating a Half Section View

1. Click on the **Section View** tool. The Section View Assist PropertyManager appears.
2. Click on the **Half Section** tab available at the top of the PropertyManager, see Figure 14.34. The options to create pre-defined shape of half section views appears in the PropertyManager.
3. Click on the required button in the **Half Section** rollout of the PropertyManager. The respective half section cutting line is attached to the cursor.
4. Move the cursor over an existing view in the drawing sheet and then click to specify the placement point for the half section cutting line at the required location. The preview of the half section view is attached to the cursor.
5. If you want to flip the viewing direction, click on the **Flip Direction** button in the **Section Line** rollout of the PropertyManager, else skip this step.
6. Click to specify the position for the half section view at the required location in the drawing sheet. The half section view is created. Next, press the ESC key.

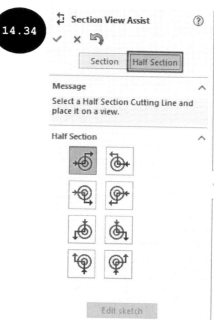

14.34

Creating an Auxiliary View

An auxiliary view is a projected view, which is created by projecting the edges of an object normal to the edge of an existing drawing view, see Figure 14.35. You can create an auxiliary view by using the **Auxiliary View** tool in the **View Layout CommandManager**.

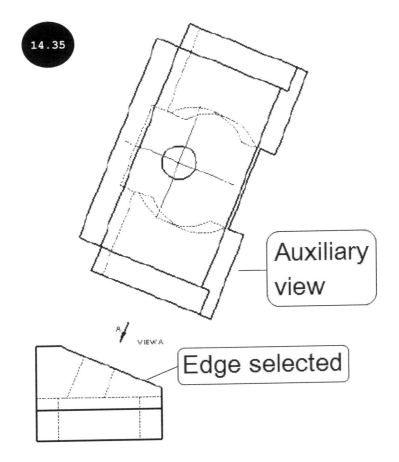

Figure 14.35

Procedure for Creating an Auxiliary View
1. Click on the **Auxiliary View** tool in the **View Layout CommandManager**.
2. Select an edge of an existing drawing view, see Figure 14.35. The preview of the auxiliary view is attached to the cursor.
3. Click to specify the position of the auxiliary view in the drawing sheet, see Figure 14.35.
4. Press ESC to exit.

Creating a Detail View *Updated*

A detail view is used to show a portion of an existing drawing view in an enlarged scale, see Figure 14.36. You can define the portion of an existing drawing view to be enlarged by creating a circle or a closed sketch. You can create the detail view of a portion of an existing view by using the **Detail View** tool.

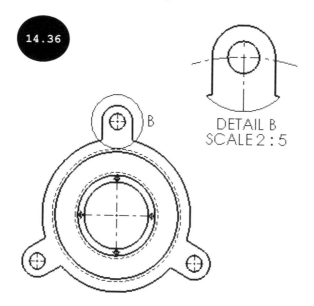

14.36

DETAIL B
SCALE 2 : 5

Procedure for Creating a Detail View

1. Click on the **Detail View** tool in the **View Layout CommandManager**. The **Detail View PropertyManager** appears. Also, you are promoted to draw a circle to define the portion of an existing drawing view to be enlarged.
2. Draw a circle around the portion of an existing view to be enlarged. The enlarged view of the portion of the existing view is attached to the cursor. Also, the **Detail View PropertyManager** appears with additional options.
3. You can increase or decrease the default scale factor for the attached detail view by using the options of the **Scale** rollout in the PropertyManager, as required.

Note: In SOLIDWORKS 2017, you can display the detail view with full outline around it by selecting the **Full outline** check box in the **Detail View** rollout of the PropertyManager, see Figure 14.37. Also, you can display the detail view with no outline by selecting the **No outline** check box in the **Detail View** rollout of the PropertyManager, see Figure 14.37. Moreover, in SOLIDWORKS 2017, you can also display the detail view with a jagged outline by selecting the **Jagged outline** check box in the **Detail View** rollout, see Figure 14.37.

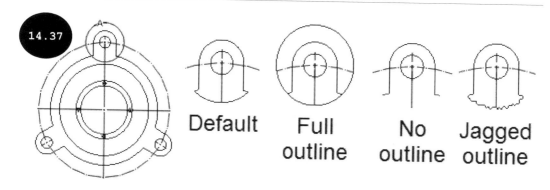

14.37

Default — Full outline — No outline — Jagged outline

4. After specifying the required properties for the detail view in the PropertyManager, move the cursor to the required location in the drawing sheet and then click to specify the placement point in the drawing sheet. The detail view is created.
5. Press the ESC key to exit.

Note: In addition to defining the portion of a view to be enlarged by drawing a circle, you can also use a closed sketch, which defines the portion of a view to be enlarged. To do so, before invoking the **Detail View** tool, first select an existing view and then draw a closed sketch by using the sketching tools of the **Sketch CommandManager**. Once the closed sketch has been drawn, select it and then click on the **Detail View** tool. Figure 14.38 shows the detail view created by a closed sketch, which is drawn by using the **Spline** tool.

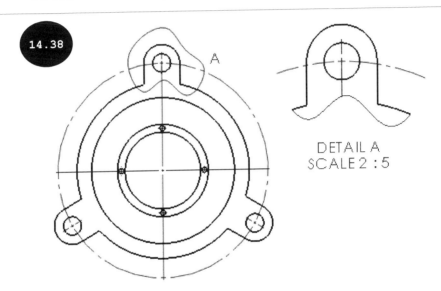

Creating a Broken-out Section View

A broken-out section view is created by removing the portion of an existing view up to a specified depth in order to view inner details of the object, see Figure 14.39. You can define the portion of an existing view to be removed by drawing a closed sketch.

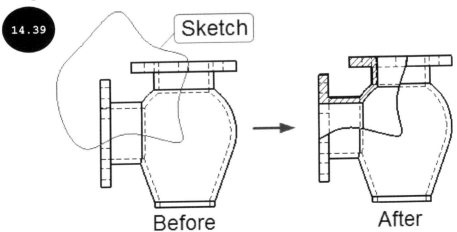

Procedure for Creating a Broken-out Section

1. Click on the **Broken-out Section** tool in the **View Layout CommandManager**. The **Spline** tool is invoked to create a closed sketch for defining the portion to be removed.
2. Move the cursor over the existing drawing view whose portion is to be removed up to a specified depth.
3. Draw a closed profile around the portion to be removed. As soon as you draw a closed profile, the **Broken-out Section PropertyManager** appears.
4. Enter the depth value in the **Depth** field of the PropertyManager up to which the material is to be removed. Alternatively, you can select an edge or an axis of the view to define the depth by using the **Depth Reference** field of the PropertyManager.
5. Select the **Preview** check box to display the preview of the broken-out section view in the drawing sheet.
6. Click on the green tick mark ✓ in the PropertyManager to accept the defined settings and to exit the PropertyManager. The broken-out section view is created, refer to Figure 14.39.

Creating a Break View Updated

A break view is created by breaking an existing view using a pair of break lines such that the portion existing between the breaking lines is removed, see Figure 14.40. A break view is used to display a large scaled view on a small scale sheet by removing a portion of the view that has the same cross-section, see Figure 14.40.

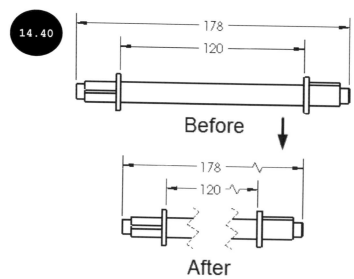

14.40

Note: The dimension applied to a break view represents its actual dimension, see Figure 14.40. It is evident from this figure that even on breaking the view, the dimension value associated with it remains the same. You will learn more about applying dimensions later in this chapter.

Procedure for Creating a Break View

1. Click on the **Break View** tool. The **Broken View PropertyManager** appears.

2. Move the cursor over an existing drawing view to be broken and then click on it. The first vertical or horizontal break line is attached to the cursor.

Note: The display of break line (vertical or horizontal) depends upon whether the **Add vertical break line** or the **Add horizontal break line** button is activated in the PropertyManager. If the **Add vertical break line** button is activated, a vertical break line appears and if the **Add horizontal break line** button is selected, a horizontal break line appears.

3. Make sure that the required button: **Add vertical break line** or **Add horizontal break line** is activated in the **Broken View PropertyManager**.
4. Specify the placement point for the first break line by clicking the left mouse button on the required location of the drawing view. The second break line is attached to the cursor.
5. Specify the placement point for the second break line in the view. The view is broken and the portion inside the break lines is removed, refer to Figure 14.40.

Note: You can also control the gap between the break lines by using the **Gap size** field of the PropertyManager. You can also select a required style or type for break lines by selecting the required button in the **Break line style** area of the PropertyManager. In SOLIDWORKS 2017, you can also use the jagged break lines for breaking the view by selecting the **Jigged Cut** button in the **Break line style** area of the PropertyManager.

6. Click on the green tick mark ✓ in the PropertyManager to confirm the creation of break view and to exit the PropertyManager.

Creating a Crop View `Updated`

A crop view is created by cropping an existing view by using a closed sketch in such a way that only the portion that is lying inside the closed sketch is retained in the view, see Figure 14.41. You can create a crop view by using the **Crop View** tool. Note that to create a crop view, you first need to create a closed sketch by using the sketching tools of the **Sketch CommandManager**.

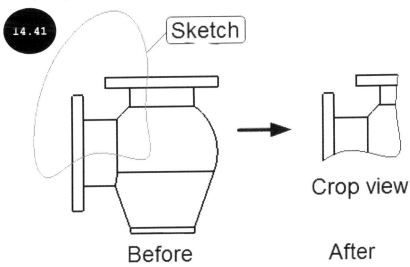

Procedure for Creating a Crop View

1. Select the view to be cropped.
2. Draw the closed sketch around the portion of the view to be cropped, refer to Figure 14.41.
3. Make sure that the sketch created is selected.
4. Click on the **Crop View** tool. The crop view is created by retaining only the portion that lies inside the closed sketch. Next, press the ESC key.

Note: In SOLIDWORKS 2017, after creating a crop view, you can display it with no outline or with jagged outline. To display a crop view with no outline or jagged outline, select the crop view in the drawing sheet. The **Drawing View PropertyManager** appears. In this PropertyManager, expand the **Crop View** rollout and then select the required check box: **No outline** or **Jagged outline**.

Creating the Alternate Position View

In SOLIDWORKS, you can show or create the alternate position of an assembly in a drawing view by using the **Alternate Position View** tool, see Figure 14.42. You can also create multiple positions of an assembly in a drawing view by using this tool.

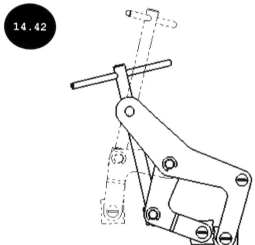

14.42

Procedure for Creating the Alternative View

1. Click on the **Alternative Position View** tool in the **View Layout CommandManager**. The **Alternate Position PropertyManager** appears.
2. Select a drawing view of an assembly. The **Alternate Position PropertyManager** is modified.

Note: In the **Configuration** rollout of the PropertyManager, the **New configuration** radio button is selected, by default. As a result, you can create a new alternative position for the assembly. Also, the default name for the alternate position appears in the **New Configuration Name** field. You can accept the default name or enter a new name in this field. The **Existing configuration** radio button is used to select the existing configuration of an assembly as the alternative view.

3. Make sure that the **New configuration** radio button is selected in the **Configuration** rollout.
4. Accept the default settings and then click on the green tick mark ✓ in the PropertyManager. The Assembly environment is invoked with the display of the **Move Component** PropertyManager on the left of the graphics area.

Note: In the Move Component PropertyManager, the **Free Drag** option is selected, by default. As a result, you can freely drag the components of the assembly to the desired position.

5. Drag to rotate or move the components of the assembly whose alternate position is to be created to the desired position.
6. Once the desired position of the assembly components has been achieved, click on the green tick mark ✓ in the **Move Component PropertyManager**. The Drawing environment is invoked again and the alternative position of the assembly components is created in the drawing view, refer to Figure 14.42. Note that the alternative position of the components is displayed in dotted lines.

Applying Dimensions

After creating various drawing views of a part or an assembly, you need to apply dimensions to them. In SOLIDWORKS, you can apply two types of dimensions: reference dimensions and driving dimensions. Reference dimensions are applied manually by using the dimension tools such as **Smart Dimension**, **Horizontal Dimension**, and **Vertical Dimension** whereas driving dimensions are generated automatically by retrieving the model dimensions. You can apply driving dimensions by using the **Model Items** tool of the **Annotation CommandManager**. The methods of applying both types of dimensions are as follows:

Applying Reference Dimensions

You can apply reference dimensions by using the dimension tools such as **Smart Dimension**, **Horizontal Dimension**, and **Vertical Dimension** available in the **Dimension** flyout of the **Annotation CommandManager**, see Figure 14.43.

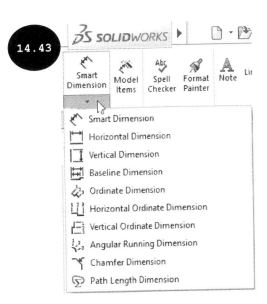

Applying reference dimension is the manual method of applying dimensions to drawing views and is same as discussed in the Sketching environment while dimensioning sketch entities. For example, to apply dimension to a linear edge in a view, click on the **Smart Dimension** tool and then select the edge. The dimension value of the selected edge is attached to the cursor. Next, place the dimension to the required location in the drawing sheet.

Applying Driving Dimensions

Driving dimensions are applied automatically in drawing views by retrieving the model dimensions, which are applied in the sketches and features of the model. Note that on modifying a driving dimension, the respective sketch or feature of the model is also modified and vice-versa.

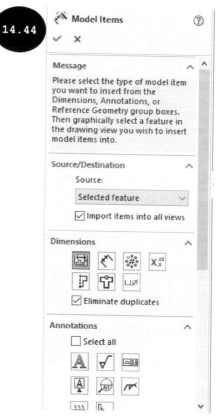

To apply driving dimensions, click on the **Model Items** tool in the **Annotation CommandManager**. The **Model Items PropertyManager** appears, see Figure 14.44. By using the options in the PropertyManager, you can retrieve dimensions, symbols, annotations, and other elements of the model in the drawing views. Some of the options of this PropertyManager are as follows:

Source/Destination

The options in the **Source/Destination** rollout of the PropertyManager are used to select features or the model as the source and destination for retrieving and applying dimensions, symbols, annotations. By default, the **Selected feature** option is selected in the **Source** drop-down list. As a result, you can select a feature of the model in a drawing view as the source and destination for retrieving and applying dimensions, respectively. As soon as you select a feature in a drawing view, the dimensions of the selected feature are retrieved and applied in the drawing views. In Figure 14.45, the driving dimensions are applied to a hole feature by selecting it as the source and destination feature in the drawing view.

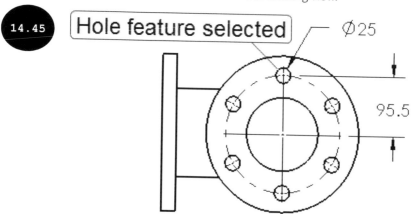

On selecting the **Entire model** option in the **Source** drop-down list, all dimensions, symbols, and annotations, which are applied in the model, get retrieved and applied in the drawing views. By default, the **Import items into all views** check box is selected in the **Source/Destination** rollout. As a result, items such as dimensions and annotations apply to all views present in the drawing sheet.

Dimensions

The buttons in the **Dimensions** rollout of the PropertyManager are used to select the type of dimensions to be retrieved from the model and applied in the drawing view. On selecting the **Eliminate duplicates** check box in this rollout, applying duplicate dimensions in the drawing views will be eliminated.

Annotations

The buttons in the **Annotations** rollout are used to select the type of annotations to be retrieved from the model and applied in the drawing view. You can click on the buttons to activate them in order to retrieve respective annotations in the drawing views. If you select the **Select all** check box, all the buttons of this rollout get activated, automatically.

Reference Geometry

The buttons in the **Reference Geometry** rollout are used to select the type of reference geometry such as planes, axis, and origin to be retrieved from the model and applied in the drawing views.

After selecting the required options in the **Model Items PropertyManager**, click on the green tick mark in the PropertyManager. The respective dimensions, annotations, and reference geometries are retrieved and applied in the drawing views, see Figure 14.46.

Note: Sometimes the driving dimensions applied in the drawing views do not appear in the required position, nor does they maintain uniform spacing in the drawing views. You can drag the dimensions and place in the required position for maintaining proper spacing between them.

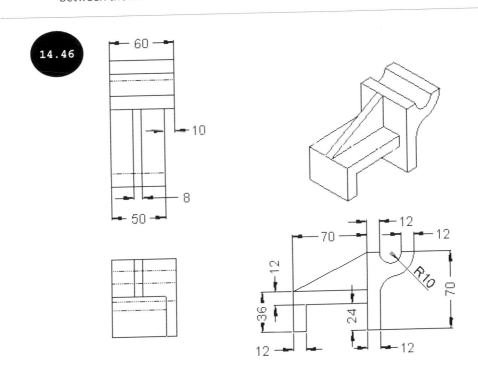

14.46

Modifying the Driving Dimension

On modifying a driving dimension in the Drawing environment, the same modification is reflected in the model as well. To modify a driving dimension, double-click on it in the drawing view. The **Modify** dialog box appears, see Figure 14.47. Enter the new dimension value in the field of this dialog box and then click on the green tick mark. The respective dimension and feature of the model are modified accordingly.

Controlling the Dimension and the Arrow Style

In SOLIDWORKS, you can control dimension and arrow styles such as dimension font, dimension height, and arrow height by using the options in the **Document Properties - Dimensions** dialog box. To invoke this dialog box, click on the **Options** tool in the **Standard** toolbar. The **System Options - General** dialog box appears. Next, click on the **Document Properties** tab in the dialog box and then click on the **Dimensions** option. The **Document Properties - Dimensions** dialog box appears, see Figure 14.48.

In this dialog box, click on the **Font** button in the **Text** area. The **Choose Font** dialog box appears. By using this dialog box, you can specify the required font, style, and height for dimensions text. Next, click on the **OK** button in the **Choose Font** dialog box.

You can control the dimension arrow height by using the options in the **Arrows** area of the **Document Properties - Dimensions** dialog box, see Figure 14.48.

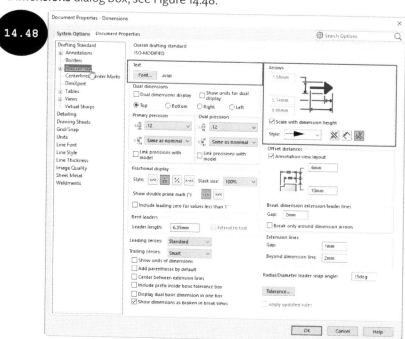

Adding Notes

In SOLIDWORKS, you can add notes on a drawing sheet by using the **Note** tool. Generally, adding notes in drawings is used to convey/provide additional information that are not available in the drawing views.

To add a note, click on the **Note** tool in the **Annotation CommandManager**. The **Note PropertyManager** appears, see Figure 14.49. Also, a rectangular box is attached to the cursor. Now, specify the required settings such as text style, text format, type of leader, leader style, so on for the note by using the options in the PropertyManager. Once the required settings for the note have been specified, move the cursor over an entity of a drawing view to add the note. The preview of the note with the leader attached to the entity of the drawing view appears in the drawing sheet. Next, click on the entity for adding the note. The leader arrow is attached to the selected entity. Now, move the cursor to the required location and then click to place the note. An edit box and the **Formatting** toolbar appear. Now, you can write text as note in the edit box. You can use the **Formatting** toolbar to control the formatting of the text such as font, style, height, and alignment. Next, click anywhere on the drawing sheet. The note is added in the selected entity of the drawing view, see Figure 14.50. You can also add note anywhere in the drawing sheet without selecting any entity.

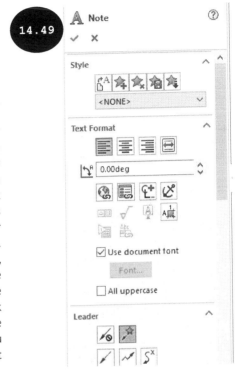

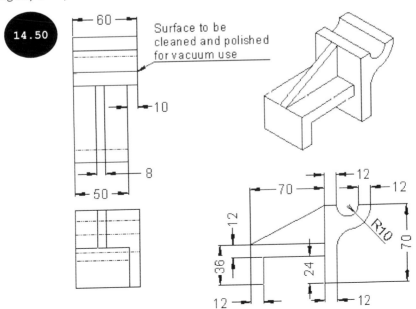

Adding the Surface Finish Symbol

In SOLIDWORKS, you can add surface finish symbol to specify the surface texture/finish for a face of a model. A surface finish symbol has three components: surface roughness, waviness, and lay, see Figure 14.51. Specifications for the surface finish given in a surface finish symbol are used to machine the respective surface of the object. You can add surface finish symbol to an edge of a surface in a drawing view by using the **Surface Finish** tool.

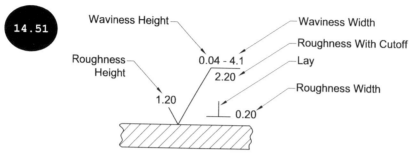

To add a surface finish symbol, click on the **Surface Finish** tool in the **Annotation CommandManager**. The **Surface Finish PropertyManager** appears, see Figure 14.52. Also, the default selected surface finish symbol is attached to the cursor. Select the required type of surface finish symbol to be added from the **Symbol** rollout of the PropertyManager. Next, in the **Symbol Layout** rollout, specify the required specification for the surface finish (roughness, waviness, and lay) in the respective fields.

If needed, you can rotate the surface finish symbol at an angle by using the options in the **Angle** rollout of the PropertyManager. By using the options of the **Leader** rollout, you can select the type of leader to be attached to the surface finish symbol. Once you have specified the surface finish specification, move the cursor over the required edge in a drawing view for applying the surface finish symbol and then click on the edge when it highlights. The surface finish symbol is applied and attached to the selected edge, see Figure 14.53.

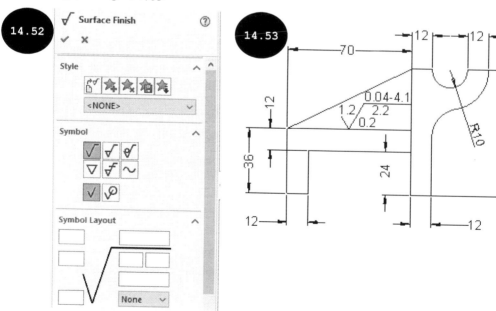

Adding the Weld Symbol

A weld symbol is added in a drawing view in order to represent the welding specification used while welding two parts of a model. To add a weld symbol, click on an edge of a model in the drawing view for adding a welding symbol, and then click on the **Weld Symbol** tool in the **Annotation CommandManager**. The **Properties** dialog box appears, see Figure 14.54. Also, the **Weld Symbol PropertyManager** appears on the left of the drawing sheet. By using the **Properties** dialog box, you can specify the welding properties to be included in the weld symbol. Note that the availability of options in the **Properties** dialog box for specifying the welding properties depends upon the type of drafting standard selected in the **Document Properties - Drafting Standard** dialog box. Once you have specified the welding properties, click on the **OK** button in the dialog box. The weld symbol is added in the selected edge of the model, see Figure 14.55.

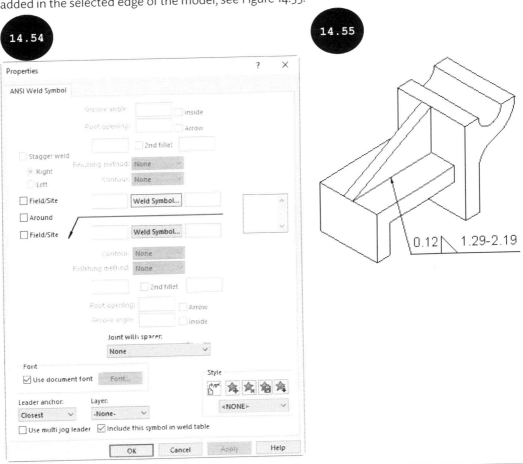

Tip: To invoke the **Document Properties - Drafting Standard** dialog box for specifying the drafting standard, click on the **Options** button in the **Standard** toolbar. The **System Options - General** dialog box appears. In this dialog box, click on the **Document Properties** tab. The **Document Properties - Drafting Standard** dialog box appears. Now, by using the **Overall drafting standard** drop-down list of the dialog box, you can select the required type of drafting standard to be followed in the drawing.

Adding the Hole Callout Updated

In SOLIDWORKS, you can add the hole callout to a hole in a drawing view. A hole callout contains hole specifications such as diameter and type of hole, see Figure 14.56. Note that on modifying the hole parameters of a model in the Part modeling environment, the respective hole callout gets updated accordingly in the Drawing environment.

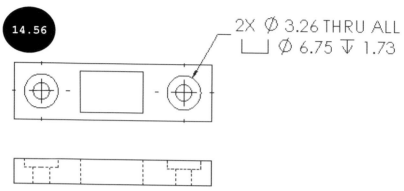

To add a hole callout to a hole in a drawing view, click on the **Hole Callout** tool in the **Annotation CommandManager**. The symbol of hole callout is attached to the cursor. Move the cursor over the hole for adding the hole callout in a drawing view and then click the left mouse button on the hole when it highlights. The preview of the hole callout is attached to the cursor. Now, move the cursor to the required location and then click to specify the placement point for the hole callout, see Figure 14.56. In SOLIDWORKS 2017, a hole callout also includes mirrored holes in the count.

Adding the Center Mark

Center marks are used as references for dimensioning circular edges, slot edges, or circular sketch entities in drawing views. You can add center marks on circular edges, slot edges, or circular sketch entities by using the **Center Mark** tool. To add center marks, click on the **Center Mark** tool in the **Annotation CommandManager**. The **Center Mark PropertyManager** appears, see Figure 14.57. By using this PropertyManager, you can add center marks automatically as well as manually in a drawing view.

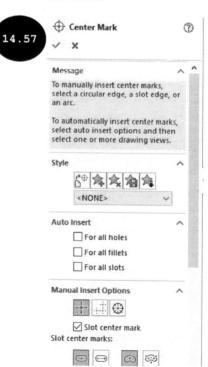

To add center marks automatically to all holes, fillets, slots, or all of them in a drawing view, select the respective check box or check boxes such as **For all holes** and **For all fillets** in the **Auto Insert** rollout of the PropertyManager. Next, select a drawing view for adding center marks. The center marks are added automatically in the drawing view, depending upon the check box or check boxes selected. In the automatic method of adding center marks, you can further control the connection among center marks by using the check boxes: **Connection lines**, **Circular lines**, **Radial lines**, and **Base center mark** in the **Options** area of the **Auto Insert** rollout, see Figures 14.58 through 14.61. Note that the **Options** area appears as soon as you select a check box in the **Auto Insert** rollout of the PropertyManager, see Figure 14.62.

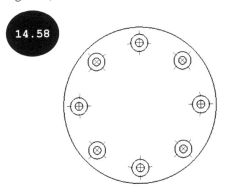
Center mark with connection lines

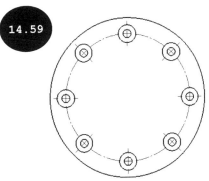
Center mark with circular lines

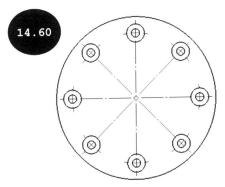
Center mark with radial lines

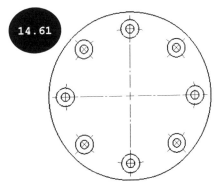
Center mark with base center mark

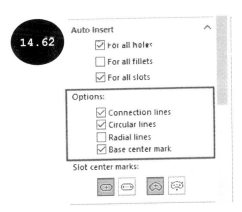

To add center marks manually, invoke the **Center Mark PropertyManager** and then move the cursor over a circular edge, a slot edge, or a circular sketch entity in a drawing view. Next, click on the entity when it highlights. The center mark is added. Similarly, you can add center marks to the other entities of drawing views manually. In the manual method of adding center marks, you can select the type of center marks to be added by activating the respective button in the **Manual Insert Options** rollout of the PropertyManager, see Figure 14.63.

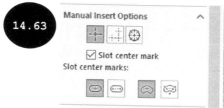

Once you have added center marks either by manual or automatic method, click on the green tick mark in the PropertyManager.

Adding Centerlines

Centerlines are used as references for dimensioning circular cut features and hole features in drawing views, see Figure 14.64. In SOLIDWORKS, you can add centerline between two linear edges that represent the edges of a circular cut or hole feature in a drawing view by using the **Centerline** tool, see Figure 14.64.

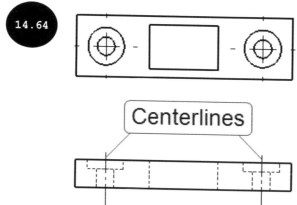

To add center lines, click on the **Centerline** tool in the **Annotation CommandManager**. The **Centerline PropertyManager** appears. Select two linear edges one by one by clicking the left mouse button. The centerline is added at the center of the two selected edges, see Figure 14.64. You can also select two sketch segments, or a single cylindrical, conical, toroidal, or swept feature for adding centerline.

Creating the Bill of Material (BOM)

After creating all the required drawing views of an assembly in the Drawing environment, you need to create Bill of Material. A Bill of Material (BOM) contains all the required information such as the number of parts used in an assembly, part number, quantity of each part, material, and so on of an assembly. Since Bill of Material (BOM) contains all the information, it serves as a primary source of communication between the manufacturer and the vendors as well as the suppliers.

To create Bill of Material (BOM), click on the down arrow below the **Tables** tool in the **Annotation CommandManager**. A flyout appears, see Figure 14.65. In this flyout, click on the **Bill of Materials** tool. The **Bill of Materials PropertyManager** appears. Next, click on the drawing view of the assembly whose Bill of Material has to be created. The **Bill of Materials PropertyManager** gets modified and appears as shown in Figure 14.66. The options of this PropertyManager are used to set the parameters for the Bill of Material. Some of the options of this PropertyManager are as follows:

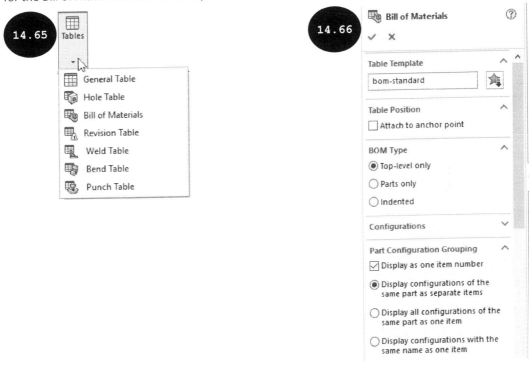

Tip: If a drawing view of an assembly is selected before invoking the **Bill of Materials** tool, then the modified **Bill of Material PropertyManager** appears, directly as shown in Figure 14.66.

Table Template
The **Table Template** rollout is used to specify template for the Bill of Material (BOM). By default, **bom-standard** template is selected in this rollout. You can select the template other than the default one by clicking on the **Open table template for Bill of Materials** button of this rollout. As soon as you click on this button, the **Open** dialog box appears such that all the template files are displayed in it. You can select a required template for the BOM in this dialog box and then click on the **Open** button.

Table Position
The **Table Position** rollout is used to specify the position for the BOM table in the drawing sheet. By default, the **Attach to anchor point** check box is unchecked in this rollout. As a result, on clicking the green tick mark of the PropertyManager, the BOM gets attached to the cursor and you need to

define its position in the drawing sheet by specifying the placement point. However, on selecting the **Attach to anchor point** check box, the BOM is placed directly in the drawing sheet such that the top left corner of the BOM is attached to the anchor point present in it.

Note: You can define the position of the anchor point in the drawing sheet, as required. To define the anchor point position in the drawing sheet, select the **Sheet** node in the FeatureManager Design Tree and then right-click to display a shortcut menu. Next, click on the **Edit Sheet Format** option in the shortcut menu. The editing mode for defining the anchor point location is invoked, see Figure 14.67. Now, click on an existing vertex or a point of the drawing sheet, see Figure 14.67 and then right-click to display a shortcut menu. In this shortcut menu, select **Set as Anchor > Bill of Materials**, see Figure 14.68. The selected vertex/point is defined as the anchor point for the BOM. In addition to selecting an existing vertex or a point, you can create a new sketch point by using the **Point** tool of the **Sketch CommandManager** and then define that point as the anchor point. Once you have defined the anchor point, exit the exiting mode by clicking on the confirmation corner available at the upper right corner of the drawing sheet.

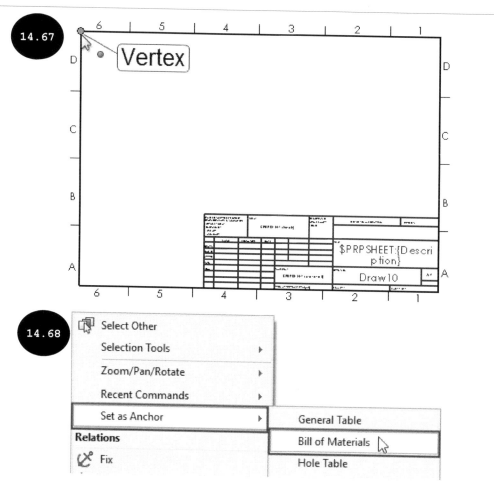

Item Number

The **Start at** field of the **Item Numbers** rollout in the PropertyManager is used to specify the start number for the count of components, see Figure 14.69. By default, 1 is entered in this field. As a result, the counting of components starts from number 1 in the BOM. In the **Increment** field, you can specify the incremental value for the count of components. Note that on selecting the **Do not change item numbers** button of this rollout, the components count/numbers assigned are locked.

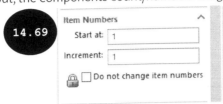

Border

The options of the **Border** rollout of the PropertyManager are used to define the thickness of the Bill of Material (BOM) border, see Figure 14.70.

Accept the default parameters specified in the PropertyManager and then click on the green tick mark ✓ in the PropertyManager. The Bill of Material (BOM) is attached to the cursor. Next, click on the drawing sheet to specify the position for the Bill of Material (BOM). The Bill of Material (BOM) is placed at the specified position in the drawing sheet, see Figure 14.71.

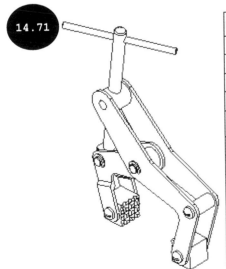

ITEM NO.	PART NUMBER	DESCRIPTION	QTY.
1	Clamp Base		2
2	Clamp Spacer		1
3	Clamp foot		2
4	Clamp Left Elbow		1
5	Clamp Right Elbow		1
6	Clamp Tee		1
7	Clamp Rod		1
8	Clamp Hinge		1
9	Clamp Support		1
10	Clamp Lever		1
11	Clamp Screw		6
12	Clamp Waser		4

Procedure for Creating Bill of Material (BOM)

1. Click on the down arrow below the **Tables** tool in the **Annotation CommandManager**. A flyout appears.
2. Click on the **Bill of Materials** tool in the flyout. The **Bill of Materials PropertyManager** appears.
3. Click on a drawing view of the assembly in the drawing sheet.
4. Accept the default parameters specified in the PropertyManager and then click on the green tick mark ✓ in the PropertyManager. The Bill of Material (BOM) is attached to the cursor.
5. Click to specify the placement point for the Bill of Material (BOM) in the drawing sheet.

Adding Balloons

A Balloon is attached to a component with a leader line and displays the respective part number assigned in the Bill of Material (BOM), see Figure 14.72. In the drawings, balloons are generally added to the individual components of an assembly in order to identify them easily with respect to the part number assigned in the Bill of Materials (BOM).

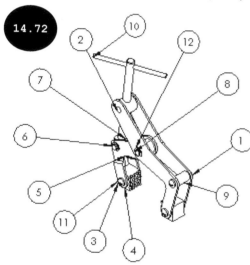

ITEM NO.	PART NUMBER	DESCRIPTION	QTY.
1	Clamp Base		2
2	Clamp Spacer		1
3	Clamp foot		2
4	Clamp Left Elbow		1
5	Clamp Right Elbow		1
6	Clamp Tee		1
7	Clamp Rod		1
8	Clamp Hinge		1
9	Clamp Support		1
10	Clamp Lever		1
11	Clamp Screw		6
12	Clamp Waser		4

In SOLIDWORKS, you can add balloons to the components of an assembly by using two methods: Automatic and Manual. In the Automatic method, balloons are added automatically to all the components of an assembly with respect to the part number assigned in the BOM. Whereas, in the Manual method, you need to add balloons manually to the components of an assembly one by one. Both these methods of adding balloons are as follows:

Adding Balloons Automatically

To add balloons automatically to the components of an assembly, click on the **Auto Balloon** tool in the **Annotation CommandManager**. The **Auto Balloon PropertyManager** appears, see Figure 14.73. The options of this PropertyManager are used to set parameters for balloons. Some of these options are as follows:

Balloon Layout

The **Balloon Layout** rollout is used to define the type of layout for balloons. The options of this rollout are as follows:

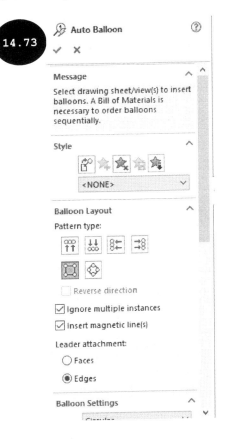

Pattern type
The buttons in the **Pattern type** area of the **Balloon Layout** rollout are used to select the required type of layouts (Square, Circular, Top, Bottom, Left, and Right) for arranging balloons in the drawing sheet.

Ignore multiple instances
By default, the **Ignore multiple instances** check box is selected in the **Balloon Layout** rollout. As a result, the duplicates are avoided by not adding balloons to all the instances of a component.

Insert magnetic line(s)
By default, the **Insert magnetic line(s)** check box is selected in the rollout. As a result, magnetic lines are inserted along with balloons such that balloons are aligned to each other. Note that this check box is not enabled if the **Layout Balloons to Circular** button is selected in the **Pattern type** area of the rollout.

Leader attachment
By default, the **Edges** radio button is selected in the **Leader attachment** area of the rollout. As a result, the leader lines of balloons are attached to the edges of components. On selecting the **Faces** radio button, balloons are attached to the faces of components through leader lines.

Balloon Settings

The **Balloon Settings** rollout is used to define the settings for balloons such as balloon style, balloon size, and balloon text. The options of this rollout are as follows:

Style
The **Style** drop-down list in the **Balloon Settings** rollout is used to select the required type of style for the border of balloons. By default, the **Circular** option is selected in this drop-down list. As a result, balloons appear with circular borders, refer to Figure 14.72. You can select a style such as triangle, hexagon, and diamond from this drop-down list. Note that on selecting the **None** option, balloons appear without borders, see Figure 14.74. If you select the **Circular Split Line** option, the border of balloons appears such that the circles are split into two areas, see Figure 14.75. By default, its upper area displays part number information and the lowest area displays information about the quantity of component.

746 Chapter 14 > Working with Drawings

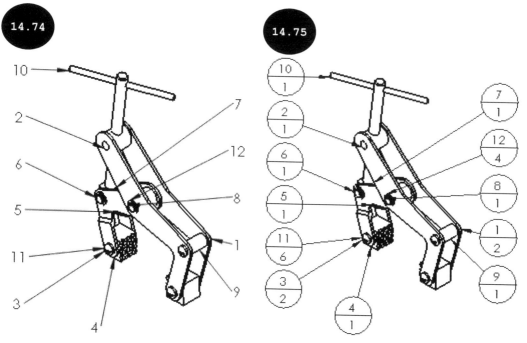

Size
The **Size** drop-down of the **Balloon Settings** rollout is used to select a required pre-defined size for balloons. In addition to selecting a pre-defined size, you can also select the **User Defined** option from this drop-down list and specify the value for the required size of balloons in the **User defined** field of the rollout.

Balloon text
The **Balloon text** drop-down list is used to select a required text to be displayed in balloons. By default, the **Item Number** option is selected. As a result, balloons appear with part numbers.

Lower text
The **Lower text** drop-down list is used to select a required text to be displayed in the lower area of the balloons. Note that this drop-down list is available only if the **Circular Split Line** option has been selected in the **Style** drop-down list. By default, the **Quantity** option is selected in the **Lower text** drop-down list. As a result, the lower area of balloons displays the quantity information, refer to Figure 14.75.

After specifying the required parameters for balloons, click on the green tick mark ✓ in the PropertyManager. The balloons are attached to the components of the assembly in the drawing view.

Procedure for Adding Balloons Automatically
1. Click on the **Auto Balloon** tool in the **Annotation CommandManager**. The **Auto Balloon** PropertyManager appears.
2. Click on the drawing view of an assembly, if not selected.

3. Define the pattern layout (square, circular, top, bottom, left, or right) by clicking on the required button in the **Pattern type** area of the **Balloon Layout** rollout.
4. Accept the other default settings in the PropertyManager.
5. Click on the green tick mark ✓ in the PropertyManager. The balloons are added automatically to the components.

Adding Balloons Manually

To add balloons manually to the components of an assembly, click on the **Balloon** tool in the **Annotation CommandManager**. The **Balloon PropertyManager** appears, see Figure 14.76. The options in this PropertyManager are the same as those discussed earlier. By using this PropertyManager, you can add balloons to the components of an assembly one by one by selecting them in the drawing view. As soon as you click on a component in the drawing view, the leader line of the balloon is attached to the component. Next, move the cursor to the required location and then click to specify the location for the balloon in the drawing sheet. Similarly, you can add balloons to all the components of the assembly one by one. Once you have added balloons to all the components, click on the green tick mark ✓ in the PropertyManager.

Procedure for Adding Balloons Manually

1. Click on the **Balloon** tool in the **Annotation CommandManager**.
2. Click on a component of the assembly in a drawing view.
3. Move the cursor to the required location and then click to specify the placement point for the balloon. The balloon is added to the component selected.
4. Similarly, add balloons to the remaining components of the assembly one by one.
5. Click on the green tick mark ✓ in the PropertyManager.

Tutorial 1

Open the model created in Tutorial 2 of Chapter 7 and then create different drawing views: front, top, side, isometric, section, and detail as shown in Figure 14.77 in the **A3 (ANSI) Landscape** sheet size. You also need to apply driving dimensions to the front, top, and right side drawing views of the model.

748 Chapter 14 > Working with Drawings

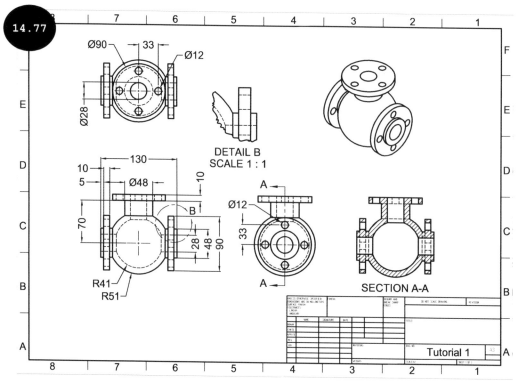

Section 1: Starting SOLIDWORKS
1. Double-click on the SOLIDWORKS icon on your desktop to start SOLIDWORKS.

Section 2: Opening and Saving Model Created in Tutorial 2 of Chapter 7
1. Open the model created in Tutorial 2 of Chapter 7 by using the Open button of the Standard toolbar, see Figure 14.78.

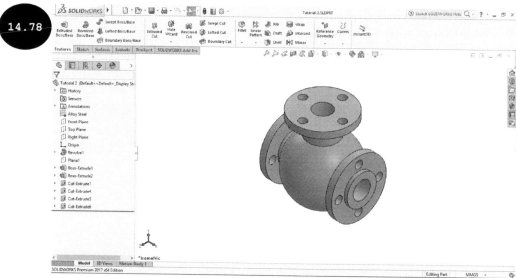

2. Click on **File > Save As** in the SOLIDWORKS menus and then save the model with the name Tutorial 1 inside the *Tutorial* folder of *Chapter 14*. Note that you need to create these folders inside the SOLIDWORKS folder.

Section 3: Invoking Drawing Environment

1. Click on the arrow next to the **New** tool in the **Standard** toolbar. A flyout appears, see Figure 14.79.

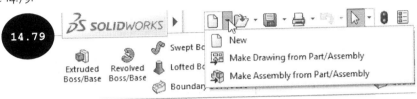

2. Click on the **Make Drawing from Part/Assembly** tool in the flyout. The **Sheet Format/Size** dialog box appears, see Figure 14.80.

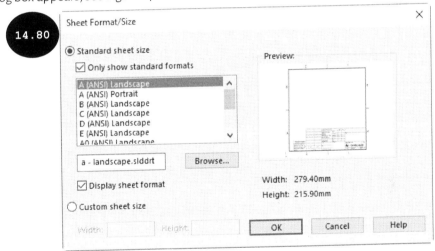

3. Make sure that the **Standard sheet size** radio button is selected in this dialog box, see Figure 14.80.

4. Select the **A3 (ANSI) Landscape** sheet size from the **Selection** area of the dialog box. If the A3 (ANSI) Landscape sheet size is not available in the **Selection** area of the dialog box, then you need to uncheck the **Only show standard formats** check box of the dialog box.

5. Make sure that the **Display sheet format** check box is selected in the dialog box.

6. Click on the **OK** button in the dialog box. The Drawing environment is invoked with the display of the **View Palette Task Pane** on the right of the drawing sheet, see Figure 14.81.

750   Chapter 14 > Working with Drawings

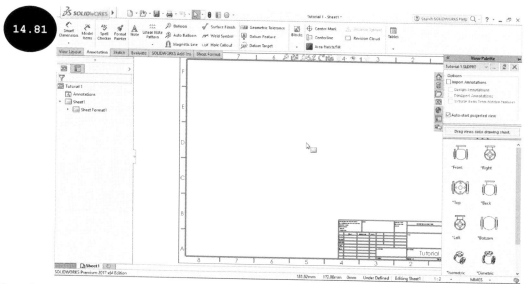

Figure 14.81

Section 4: Creating Front, Top, and Right Views

1. Drag and drop the front view of the model on the lower left corner of the drawing sheet from the **View Palette Task Pane** by pressing and holding the left mouse button, see Figure 14.82.

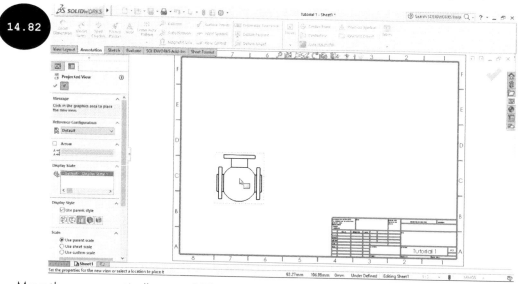

Figure 14.82

2. Move the cursor vertically upward. The projected view (top view) is attached to the cursor.

3. Click on the drawing sheet to specify the position for the top view, see Figure 14.83.

4. Move the cursor horizontally toward right. The projected view (right side view) of the model is attached to the cursor.

5. Click on the drawing sheet to specify the position for the right side view of the model, see

Figure 14.83. Next, click on the green tick mark ✓ in the PropertyManager or press ESC. The front, top and right side views of the model are created.

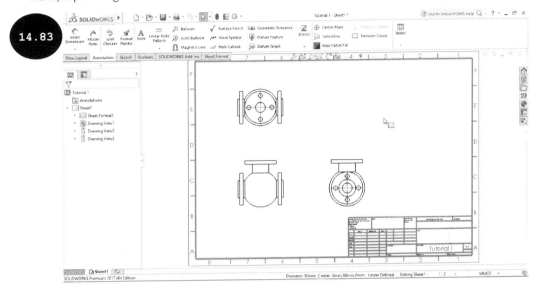

Section 5: Creating the Vertical Section View

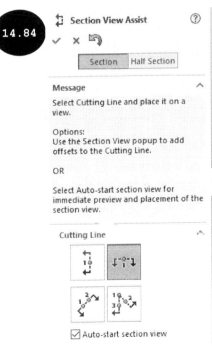

1. Click on the **Section View** tool in the **View Layout CommandManager**. The **Section View Assist PropertyManager** appears, see Figure 14.84.

2. Click on the **Vertical** button in the **Cutting Line** rollout of the PropertyManager to activate it. Note that on activating the **Vertical** button, the vertical section line appears attached to the cursor in the drawing sheet.

3. Move the cursor over the right side view of the model in the drawing sheet.

4. Click to specify the placement point for the vertical section line when the cursor snaps to the center point of the right side view of the model, see Figure 14.85. The preview of the section view appears attached to the cursor. If the **Section View** Pop-up toolbar appears, click on the green tick mark ✓ in the **Section View** Pop-up toolbar to display the preview of the section view.

Tip: The **Section View** Pop-up toolbar appears, if the **Auto-start section view** check box is unchecked in the PropertyManager. By using the tools of the **Section View** Pop-up toolbar, you can modify or edit the section line, as required.

752 Chapter 14 > Working with Drawings

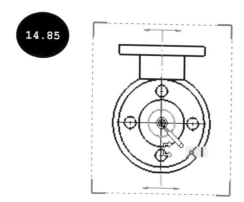

14.85

5. Move the cursor horizontally toward the right and then click on the drawing sheet to specify the placement point for the section view, see Figure 14.86.

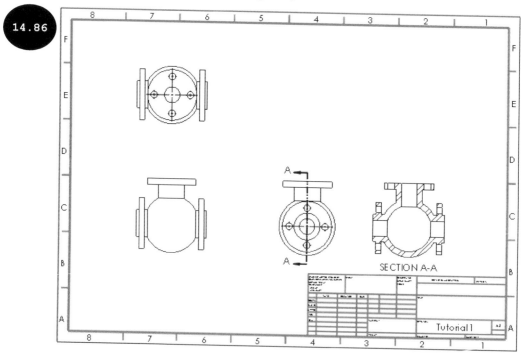

14.86

Section 6: Creating the Detail View

1. Click on the **Detail View** tool in the **View Layout CommandManager**. The **Detail View PropertyManager** appears. Also, you are prompted to specify the center point of the circle.

2. Move the cursor over the right vertical edge of the model in the front view, see Figure 14.87 and then click to specify the center point of the circle.

3. Move the cursor for a little distance and then click to define the radius of the circle, see Figure 14.88. The preview of the detail view is attached to the cursor.

SOLIDWORKS 2017: A Power Guide > 753

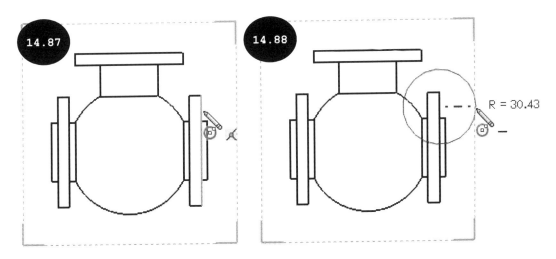

4. Select the **Jagged outline** check box in the **Detail View** rollout of the PropertyManager.

5. Click on the drawing sheet to define the placement point for the detail view, see Figure 14.89. The detail view is placed in the drawing sheet on the defined position.

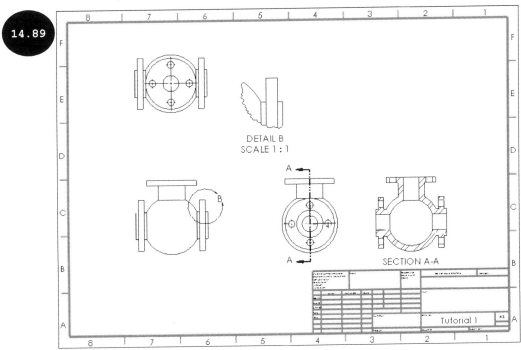

Section 7: Creating the Isometric View

1. Click on the **Model View** tool in the **View Layout CommandManager**. The **Model View PropertyManager** appears.

754 Chapter 14 > Working with Drawings

2. Double-click on the **Tutorial 1** model in the **Open documents** area of the **Part/Assembly to Insert** rollout in the PropertyManager. A rectangular box representing the model view is attached to the cursor. Also, the options of the PropertyManager get modified.

3. Click on the **Isometric** button in the **Standard views** area of the **Orientation** rollout to create an isometric view of the model.

4. Move the cursor toward the upper right corner of the drawing sheet and then click to specify the placement point for the isometric view, see Figure 14.90. Next, click anywhere in the drawing sheet.

Section 8: Changing the Display Styles

1. Click on the front view of the model in the drawing sheet. The **Drawing View PropertyManager** appears.

2. Click on the **Hidden Lines Visible** button in the **Display State** rollout of the PropertyManager to display the hidden lines of the model in the drawing views, see Figure 14.90.

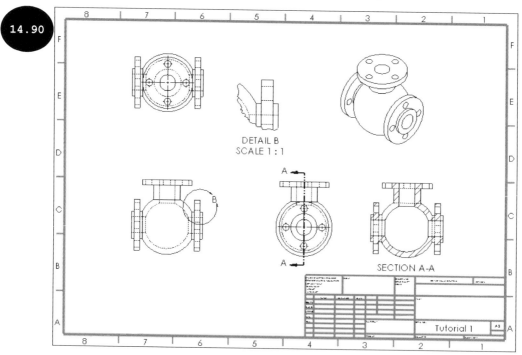

14.90

Section 9: Applying Driving Dimensions

1. Click on the **Annotation** tab in the CommandManager. The tools of the **Annotation CommandManager** are displayed.

2. Click on the **Model Items** tool in the Annotation CommandManager. The **Model Items PropertyManager** appears.

3. Make sure that the **Entire model** option is selected in the **Source** drop-down list of the **Source/Destination** rollout, see Figure 14.91.

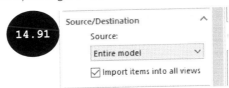

4. Uncheck the **Import items into all views** check box in the **Source/Destination** rollout. The **Destination view(s)** field appears in the rollout.

5. Click on the front, top, and right side views of the model one by one in the drawing sheet as the views to import driving dimensions.

6. Click on the green tick mark ✓ in the PropertyManager. The driving dimensions are applied to the selected drawing views, see Figure 14.92. Note that the applied dimensions are not placed in the proper locations nor do they maintain uniform spacing. You will learn about arranging driving dimensions in the next section of this tutorial.

Section 10: Arranging Driving Dimensions

1. Select all driving dimensions by dragging the cursor over the front, top, and right side views after pressing and holding the left mouse button, see Figure 14.92. Next, release the left mouse button, the **Dimension Palette Rollover** button appears in the drawing sheet.

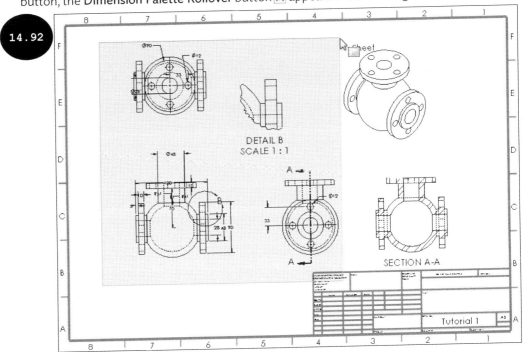

2. Move the cursor over the **Dimension Palette Rollover** button in the drawing sheet. The **Dimension Palette** appears, see Figure 14.93.

756   Chapter 14 > Working with Drawings

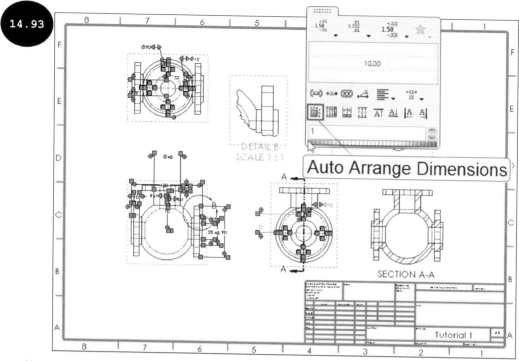

14.93

3. Click on the **Auto Arrange Dimensions** button in the **Dimension Palette**, see Figure 14.93. All the dimensions are arranged automatically in the drawing sheet, see Figure 14.94. You can further drag individual dimensions and place them on the required location, see Figure 14.94. Next, click anywhere in the drawing sheet.

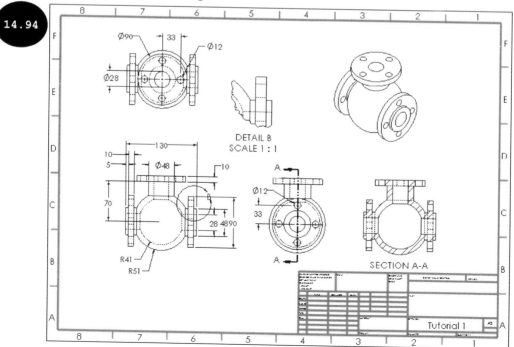

14.94

Section 11: Saving the Model

1. Click on the **Save** tool in the **Standard** toolbar. The **Save As** dialog box appears.

2. Browse to the *Tutorial* folder of *Chapter 14* folder and then save the drawing with the name Tutorial 1.

Hands-on Test Drive 1

Open the assembly created in Hands-on Test Drive 1 of Chapter 12 and then create different drawing views as shown in Figure 14.95. Also, you need to add balloons in the isometric view of the assembly and create the Bill of Material (BOM), see Figure 14.95. In addition to creating different views and BOM, you need to create alternative view of the assembly in the front view, see Figure 14.95.

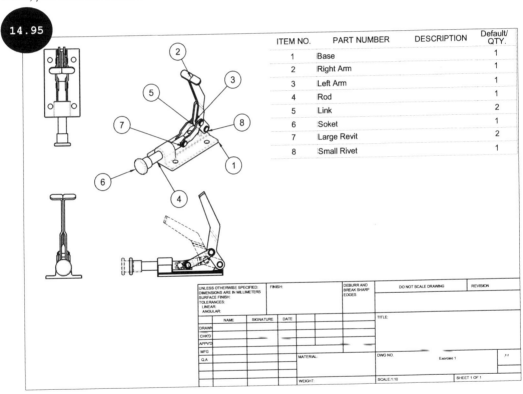

14.95

Summary

In this chapter, you have learned about creating 2D drawings from parts and assemblies. The 2D drawings are extremely important in order to manufacture components. In SOLIDWORKS, you can create 2D drawings in the Drawing environment. You can create various drawing views such as model/base views, projected views, section views, auxiliary views, and detail views of a component or an assembly by using the respective tools. You have also learned about the concept of angle of projections, defining the angle of projection for a drawing, and editing the sheet format. After creating the required drawing views of a component or an assembly, you can apply reference and driving dimensions. Note that on modifying driving dimensions in the Drawing environment, the same modifications are reflected in the model as well and vice versa.

In addition, you have learned about, adding notes on a drawing sheet in order to share additional information which are not present in a drawing. You can also add surface finish symbol for specifying surface texture/finish to the face of a model, weld symbols for representing welding specification, and hole callout to a hole. Also, you have learned about adding center mark and centerlines in drawing views. At last, in this chapter, you have learned about adding a Bill of Material (BOM) and balloons. In SOLIDWORKS, you can add balloons to different components of an assembly by using the automatic and manual methods.

Questions

- By using the _____ environment of SOLIDWORKS, you can generate error-free 2D drawings of a component or an assembly.

- The _____ PropertyManager is invoked automatically on invoking the Drawing environment.

- A _____ view is an independent first drawing view.

- The **Standard 3 View** tool is used to create three standard orthogonal views: _____, _____, and _____.

- Engineering drawings follow the _____ and the _____ angle of projections.

- A _____ view is created by cutting an object with an imaginary cutting plane and viewing the object from the direction normal to the cutting plane.

- A _____ view is created in order to show the portion of an existing view at an enlarged scale.

- The _____ view is created by removing the portion of an existing view up to a specified depth in order to view its inner details.

- In SOLIDWORKS, you can show/create the alternate position of an assembly component by using the _____ tool.

- In SOLIDWORKS, you can apply the _____ and _____ dimensions in a view.

- A surface finish symbol has three components: _____, _____, and _____.

- In SOLIDWORKS, you can add balloons by using the automatic and manual methods. (True/False).

- On modifying reference dimensions in a drawing view, respective modifications are also reflected in a model. (True/False).

- In SOLIDWORKS, you can select standard or custom sheet size for creating drawing views. (True/False).

INDEX

Symbols
3 Point Arc Slot Tool 77
3 Point Arc Tool 71
3 Point Center Rectangle Tool 66
3 Point Corner Rectangle Tool 65
3D Sketch Tool 390
3D Sketching Environment 390

A
Add Configuration Option 561
Add Configuration PropertyManager 561
Add Horizontal Break Line Button 729
Add or Update a Style 169
Add Relation Tool 156
Add Relations PropertyManager 156
Add Vertical Break Line Button 729
Adding Balloons 744
Adding Balloons Automatically 744
Adding Balloons Manually 747
Adding Centerlines 740
Adding Cosmetic Threads 496
Adding Explode Lines in an Exploded View 685
Adding Notes 735
Adding the Center Mark 738
Adding the Hole Callout 738
Adding the Surface Finish Symbol 736
Adding the Weld Symbol 737
Adjust the Spacing between Chain Components Slider 682

Advanced Hole PropertyManager 492
Advanced Hole Tool 492
Advanced Mates 590
Align to Seed 450
Align to Selection Option 682
Align with End Faces 351
Align with Selection Option 682
Alignment Method 450
Along Assembly XYZ Option 606
Along Entity Option 606
Alternate Position PropertyManager 730
Alternate Position View Tool 730
Ambient Occlusion Tool 232
Analytical 529
Angle Distance Chamfer 519
Angle Mate 589, 597
Animate Collapse Option 684
Animate Explode Option 684
Animating an Exploded View 684
Animation Controller Toolbar 684
Annotation CommandManager 34
Appearances, Scenes, and Decals 31, 300
Applying Aligned Dimension by using the Smart Dimension Tool 162
Applying Angular Dimension by using the Smart Dimension Tool 163
Applying Diameter Dimension by using the Smart Dimension Tool 164
Applying Dimensions 158, 731

Applying Driving Dimensions 732
Applying Geometric Relation by using the Add Relation Tool 156
Applying Geometric Relation by using the Pop-up Toolbar 157
Applying Horizontal Dimension by using the Smart Dimension Tool 161
Applying Linear Diameter Dimension by using the Smart Dimension Tool 165
Applying Material 305
Applying Radius Dimension by using the Smart Dimension Tool 164
Applying Reference Dimensions 731
Applying Relations or Mates 584
Applying Vertical Dimension by using the Smart Dimension Tool 162
Assembly CommandManager 32
Assembly Features Tool 675
Assigning Appearance/Texture 300
Assigning Customized Appearance 302
Auto Balloon PropertyManager 744
Auto Balloon Tool 744
Automatic Browse when Creating New Assembly 578, 582
Auto-space Components on Drag 681
Auto-start Projected View 708, 712
Auto-start Section View 720, 721
Auxiliary View Tool 724
Axis PropertyManager 252
Axis Tool 252

B

Balloon PropertyManager 747
Balloon Settings 745
Balloon Text 746
Balloon Tool 747
Base Center Mark 739
Begin Assembly PropertyManager 580
Bill of Materials Options 561
Bill of Materials PropertyManager 686, 741
Bill of Materials Tool 686, 741
Blind Option 213, 221
Boss - Extrude PropertyManager 210
Bottom-up Assembly Approach 578
Boundary Boss/Base Tool 369
Boundary Cut Tool 374
Boundary PropertyManager 369

Break View Tool 728
Broken View PropertyManager 728
Broken-out Section PropertyManager 728
Broken-out Section Tool 728
By Delta XYZ Option 607

C

Calculating Mass Properties 308
Cam Mate 598
Cartoon Tool 232
Center Mark PropertyManager 738, 739
Center Mark Tool 738
Center Rectangle Tool 65
Centerline Parameters 365
Centerline PropertyManager 740
Centerline Tool 61, 740
Centerpoint Arc Slot Tool 78
Centerpoint Arc Tool 70
Centerpoint Straight Slot Tool 77
Centroid 453
Chain Component Pattern Tool 667
Chain Pattern PropertyManager 668
Chamfer PropertyManager 518
Chamfer Tool 518
Changing the View of a Model 231
Choose Font Dialog box 734
Circle Tool 68
Circular Pattern PropertyManager 120
Circular Pattern Tool 444
Circular Profile 342
Circular Sketch Pattern 120
Circumscribed Circle 74
CirPattern PropertyManager 444
Close Loft Check box 366
Close Sketches 285
Coincident Mate 586
Coincident Relation 154
Collapsing an Exploded View 683
Collinear Relation 154
Collision Detection Radio button 608
Color PropertyManager 302
CommandManager 25
Composite Curve PropertyManager 385
Composite Curve Tool 385
Concentric Mate 588
Concentric Relation 155
Configuration Properties 561

ConfigurationManager 560, 684
Configurations Drop-down list 676
Conic Radius 508
Conic Rho 508
Conic Tool 82
Connected Linkage Button 671
Connected Linkage Chain Pattern 671
Constant Size Fillet Button 505
Construction Geometry Tool 69
Context Toolbar 34
Contour Select Tool 289
Controlling the Dimension and the Arrow Style 734
Controlling the Display of Geometric Relations 158
Convert Entities PropertyManager 293
Convert Entities Tool 292
Coordinate System Tool 254
Copy Entities Tool 128
Copy PropertyManager 128
Coradial Relation 155
Corner Rectangle Tool 63
Cosmetic Thread 496
Cosmetic Thread Display 710
Cosmetic Thread PropertyManager 496
Create Center of Mass feature 311
Create Opposite Hand Version Button 674
Create Pattern Table 462
Create Seed Cut Radio button 458
Creating a Parallel Plane 248
Creating a Plane at an Angle 248
Creating a Plane at an Offset Distance 247
Creating a Plane at the Middle of Two Faces/Planes 249
Creating a Plane Normal to a Curve 249
Creating a Plane Parallel to the Screen 250
Creating a Plane Passing through Three Points/Vertices 248
Creating a Plane Tangent to a Cylindrical Face 250
Creating a Projected Plane onto a Non-Planar Face 251
Creating a Projected View 713
Creating a Reference Axis 252
Creating a Reference Coordinate System 254
Creating a Reference Point 256

Creating a Revolved Feature 218
Creating a Section View 719
Creating a Sketch Chamfer 125
Creating a Sketch Driven Pattern 452
Creating a Sketch Fillet 123
Creating a Sweep Cut Feature 355
Creating a Sweep Feature 339
Creating a Table Driven Pattern 454
Creating a Variable Pattern 460
Creating a Variable Radius Fillet 511
Creating Advanced Holes 492
Creating an Auxiliary View 724
Creating an Exploded View 678
Creating an Extruded Feature 210
Creating and Dissolving Sub-Assemblies 677
Creating Assembly by using Bottom-up Approach 578
Creating Assembly by using the Top-down Approach 654
Creating Assembly Features 674
Creating Bill of Material (BOM) 686, 740
Creating Chamfers 518
Creating Configurations by using the Design Table 564
Creating Configurations by using the Manual Method 559
Creating Curves 374
Creating Curves by Selecting Reference Points 384
Creating Curves by Specifying XYZ Points 382
Creating Cut Features 282
Creating Extruded Cut Features 282
Creating Fillets 504
Creating Helical and Spiral Curves 377
Creating Projected Curves 374
Creating Reference Planes 244
Creating Revolved Cut Features 283
Creating Rib Features 523
Creating Shell Features 525
Creating the Alternate Position View 730
Creating the Base/Model View 707
Creating Threads 499
Creating Wrap Features 528
Crop View Tool 729
Curvature Combs Check box 373

762 INDEX

Curvature Continuous 508
Curvature To Face Option 362
Curve Driven Pattern PropertyManager 447
Curve Driven Pattern Tool 447
Curve File Dialog box 382
Curve Through Reference Points PropertyManager 384
Curve Through Reference Points Tool 384
Curve Through XYZ Points Tool 382
Custom Sheet Size Radio button 705
Custom Text Position 177
Customize Dialog box 35, 36, 37
Customize Tool 36
Customizing the CommandManager 36
Customizing the Context Toolbar of the Shortcut Menu 35
Cut Thread Radio button 502
Cut-Extrude PropertyManager 282
Cut-Revolve PropertyManager 284
Cut-Sweep PropertyManager 356

D

Deboss 528
Defining the Angle of Projection 717
Delete a Style 169
Design Library 31
Design Table 564
Design Table PropertyManager 564, 565
Detail View PropertyManager 726
Detail View Tool 725
Detecting Collision and Analyzing Motion between Components 609
Detecting Collision between Components 608
Dimension Input Value 167
Dimension PropertyManager 168
Direction of Extrusion 214
Direction Vector Option 360
Display As Diameter 165
Display As Radius 164
Display Sheet Format Check box 705
Displaying Shaded Sketch Contours 292
Dissolve Subassembly Option 678
Distance Along Path Option 595
Distance Chain Pattern 669
Distance Distance Chamfer 519
Distance Linkage Button 670

Distance Linkage Chain Pattern 670
Distance Mate 588, 596
Diverge from Axis Check box 681
Do not Change Item Numbers Button 743
Draft On/Off 214, 525
Draft Quality Radio button 710
Drag Sketch Button 366
Dragged Part Only Check box 608, 609
Drawing a Centerline 61
Drawing a Circle 68
Drawing a Line Entity 49
Drawing a Midpoint Line 62
Drawing a Parabola 81
Drawing a Polygon 73
Drawing a Rectangle 62
Drawing a Slot 75
Drawing a Spline 83
Drawing an Arc 70
Drawing an Arc by Using the Line Tool 55
Drawing an Ellipse 79
Drawing an Elliptical Arc 80
Drawing Conic Curves 82
Dynamic Mirror Tool 115

E

Edit Appearance Tool 302
Edit Component Tool 655
Edit Feature Tool 295, 662
Edit Part Tool 661
Edit Sheet Format Option 718
Edit Sketch Tool 295, 661, 662
Edit Table Option 568
Editing a Spline 90
Editing an Exploded View 684
Editing Assembly Components 661
Editing Mates 663
Editing the Sheet Format 718
Ellipse Tool 79
Emboss 528
Emphasize Outline Check box 720
Emphasized Section Outline Option 722
End Condition Drop-down list 213, 279
End Tangency Type 353
Entire Model Option 732
Equal Curve Length Relation 155
Equal Relation 155
Equation Driven Curve PropertyManager 84

Equation Driven Curve Tool 84
Evaluate CommandManager 26
Existing Configuration Radio button 730
Explicit 85
Explode Line Sketch Tool 685
Explode PropertyManager 678, 685
Explode Step Type 679
Exploded View Tool 678
Extend Entities Tool 109
Extending Sketch Entities 109
Extrude Thread Radio button 502
Extruded Boss/Base Tool 210
Extruded Cut Tool 282

F

Face Face Chamfer 522
Face Fillet Button 514
Face for Wrap Sketch 530
Far Side Countersink Check box 488
FeatureManager Design Tree 29
Features CommandManager 25
Fill Boundary 458
Fill Pattern PropertyManager 457
Fill Pattern Tool 457
Fillet Parameters 507
Fillet PropertyManager 505, 514
Fillet Tool 505
Fit Spline Tool 87
Fix Relation 155
Flip Mate Alignment Tool 586
Flip Material Side 525
Flip Side to Cut Check box 282
Float Option 581
Follow First and Second Guide Curve 349
Follow Path and First Guide Curve 348
Follow Path Option 344
For all Fillets 738
For all Holes 738
Form New Subassembly Option 677
Formatting Toolbar 735
Free Drag Option 606, 610
From Drop-down list 278
Full Outline Check box 726
Full Round Fillet Button 516
Fully Defined Sketch 180

G

Gear Mate 602
Geometric Relations 153, 156
Geometry Pattern 439, 465
Getting Started with SOLIDWORKS 20
Global Option 365
Graphics Area Toolbar 35
Grids and Snaps Settings 47
Guide Curves 364

H

Head Clearance Check box 488
Height and Pitch Option 379
Height and Revolution Option 379
Helix and Spiral Tool 377
Helix/Spiral PropertyManager 377
Hidden Lines Removed Tool 230
Hidden Lines Visible Tool 230
High Quality Radio button 710
Hinge Mate 601
Hole Callout Tool 738
Hole Specification PropertyManager 485
Hole Specifications 487
Hole Wizard Tool 485
Horizontal Dimension Tool 165
Horizontal Ordinate Dimension Tool 167
Horizontal Relation 154

I

Identifying SOLIDWORKS Documents 24
Ignore Multiple Instances Check box 745
Import Annotations Check box 708
Import Items into all Views Check box 732
Inscribed Circle 71
Insert Component PropertyManager 582
Insert Components Tool 582, 676
Insert Line PropertyManager 49
Insert Magnetic Line(s) Check box 745
Inserting the Parts having Multiple Configurations 676
Installing SOLIDWORKS 20
Instances to Skip 118, 122, 437
Instances to Vary 440
Instant2D Tool 168
Intersecting Sketch 287
Intersection Radio button 387

764 INDEX

Invoking a Shortcut Menu 34
Invoking Drawing Environment by using the New Tool 704
Invoking Drawing Environment from the Part or the Assembly Environment 711
Invoking the Assembly Environment 31
Invoking the Part Modeling Environment 24, 41
Invoking the Sketching Environment 43

J
Jagged Outline Check box 726

K
Keep Features Check box 510
Keep Normal Constant Option 344
Keep Visible Icon 582, 583

L
Layout Balloons to Circular Button 745
Leader/Dimension Line Style 177
Left-hand Thread Radio button 502
Line Tool 49
Linear Diameter Dimension 165
Linear Pattern PropertyManager 116, 433
Linear Pattern Tool 433
Linear Sketch Pattern 116
Linear/Linear Coupler Mate 595
Load Style 170
Lock Mate 590
Loft PropertyManager 358
Lofted Boss/Base Tool 358
Lofted Cut Tool 368

M
Make Drawing from Part/Assembly Tool 711
Make First Selection Transparent Check box 584
Manipulating View Orientation by Using Reference Triad 229
Manipulating View Orientation by Using the Orientation Dialog box 227
Manipulating View Orientation by Using the View Orientation Flyout 226
Manipulating View Orientation by Using the View Selector Cube 228

Mass Properties Dialog box 308
Mass Properties Tool 308
Mate PropertyManager 584, 590
Mate Tool 584, 590
Material Dialog box 306
Mates Node 663
Measure Tool 296
Measure Units/Precision Dialog box 298
Measurement History 299
Measuring the Distance between Entities/Faces 296
Mechanical Mates 598
Merge Relation 155
Merge Result Check box 281, 350
Merge Smooth Faces 352
Merge Tangent Faces 350, 366
Mesh Preview Check box 373
Mid Plane Option 213, 221
Midpoint Line Tool 62
Midpoint Relation 155
Minimum Twist Option 348
Mirror Components PropertyManager 673
Mirror Components Tool 672
Mirror Entities Tool 113
Mirror PropertyManager 464
Mirror Tool 464
Mirroring a Feature 464
Mirroring Components of an Assembly 672
Mirroring Sketch Entities 113
Model Items PropertyManager 732
Model Items Tool 732
Model View PropertyManager 706, 707, 712
Modify Dialog box 159, 734
Modifying Dimension Properties 168
Modifying the Driving Dimension 734
Modifying/Editing Dimensions 167
Mouse Gestures 37
Move Component PropertyManager 606
Move Component Tool 606
Move Entities Tool 126
Move PropertyManager 126
Moving a Sketch Entity 126
Moving and Rotating Individual Components 605
Multiple Radius Fillet 508
Multi-thickness Faces 527
Multi-thickness Settings 527

N

Natural Option 348
Navigating a 3D Model 223
Near And Far Side Faces 492
Near Side Countersink Check box 488
Nested Sketches 285
New Configurations Check box 565
New Document Tool 22
New Parameters Check box 565
New Part Tool 655
New SOLIDWORKS Document
    Dialog box 22
New Tool 22
New View Tool 227
No Outline Check box 726
None Option 345
Normal To Profile Option 362
Normal to Sketch 524
Normal To Tool 226
Note PropertyManager 735
Note Tool 735

O

Offset Curve 450
Offset Entities PropertyManager 110
Offset Entities Tool 110
Offset Face Chamfer 521
Offset From Surface Option 280
Offset Option 212
Offsetting Sketch Entities 110
One-Direction Option 216
Only Show Standard Formats
    Check box 705
Open Sketches 285
Open Table Template for Bill of
    Materials 741
Opening Existing Documents 38
Ordinate Dimension Tool 166
Orientation Dialog box 227
Over Defined Sketch 180
Override Mass Properties 310

P

Pan 225
Parabola Tool 81
Parallel Mate 587
Parallel Relation 154
Parallel to Sketch 524
Parallelogram Tool 67
Parametric 85
Partial Ellipse Tool 80
Path Mate 594
Pattern Driven Component Pattern Tool 665
Pattern Driven PropertyManager 665
Pattern Layout 459
Pattern Seed Only Check box 437
Pattern Table Dialog box 462
Patterning Assembly Components 664
Patterning Features/Faces/Bodies 431
Patterning Sketch Entities 116
Percent Along Path Option 595
Perimeter Circle Tool 69
Perpendicular Mate 587
Perpendicular Relation 154
Perspective Tool 231
Physical Dynamics Radio button 608, 609
Pierce Relation 155
Pin/Unpin the Dialog 227
Pitch and Revolution Option 379
Pitch/Yaw Control Drop-down list 595
Plane PropertyManager 244
Plane Tool 244
Point PropertyManager 256
Point Tool 256
Polygon PropertyManager 73
Polygon Tool 73
Power Trim 106
Previous View Tool 228
Profile Center Mate 590
Profile Orientation Drop-down list 344
Profile Twist Drop-down list 345
Project Curve Tool 374
Projected Curve PropertyManager 375
Projected View PropertyManager 714
Projected View Tool 714
Projecting Edges onto the Sketching
    Plane 292
Projection Radio button 386
Propagate Visual Properties 440
Properties Dialog box 737

R

Rack Pinion Mate 603
Radial Lines 739

Radial Step Button 680
Radians Option 346
Reference Geometry to Drive Seeds 461
Reference Sketch 453
Region Parameters Table 380
Regular Step Button 679, 680
Rename Assembly Option 677
Reset Spin Increment Value 160
Reset Standard Views Tool 228
Resume Drag Button 608
Reuse Subassembly Explode Button 682
Reverse the Sense of the Dimension 161
Revolutions/mm Radio button 604
Revolve PropertyManager 219
Revolve Type Drop-down list 221
Revolved Boss/Base Tool 218
Revolved Cut Tool 283
Rho Field 508
Rho Value 83
Rib PropertyManager 523
Rib Thickness 524
Rib Tool 523
Right-hand Thread Radio button 502
Roll Control Drop-down list 595
Rotate about each Component Origin Check box 681
Rotate Component PropertyManager 609
Rotate Component Tool 609
Rotate Context Toolbar 580
Rotate Entities Tool 128
Rotate PropertyManager 128
Route Line PropertyManager 685

S

Save a Style 169
Save Externally (Specify Paths) Radio button 660
Save Internally (Inside the Assembly) Radio button 660
Save Modified Documents Dialog box 660
Save Sheet Format Dialog box 718
Save the Current Value and Exit the Dialog 161
Saving Documents 38
Scale Entities Tool 130
Scale Hatch Pattern Check box 720
Scale PropertyManager 130
Scaling Sketch Entities 130
Screw Mate 603
Section View Assist PropertyManager 720
Section View Dialog box 721
Section View Pop-up Toolbar 722
Section View Tool 719
Select Seed Position Button 666
Select the Subassembly's Parts Check box 682
Select Through Faces 510
Selected Contours 217, 223
Set a Current Style 170
Set Unassigned 513
Setback Distances 509
Setback Parameters 509
Shaded Cosmetic Threads 499
Shaded Sketch Contours Tool 292
Shaded Tool 230
Shaded With Edges Tool 229
Shadows In Shaded Mode Tool 231
Sheet Format/Size Dialog box 704
Sheet Metal CommandManager 28
Sheet Node 718
Sheet Properties Dialog box 717
Shell Outward 527
Shell PropertyManager 526
Shell Tool 526
Show All Connectors Option 359
Show Configuration 564
Show Custom Sizing Check box 487
Show Rotate Context Toolbar Check box 580
Show Rotation Rings Check box 682
Show Sections 352
Silhouette Radio button 389
Sketch Chamfer PropertyManager 125
Sketch Chamfer Tool 125
Sketch CommandManager 26
Sketch Driven Pattern PropertyManager 452
Sketch Driven Pattern Tool 452
Sketch Fillet PropertyManager 123
Sketch Fillet Tool 123
Sketch on Faces 375
Sketch on Sketch 376
Sketch Profile 341
Skipped By Driving Feature 666
Slot Mate 599
Slot PropertyManager 75
Smart Dimension Tool 159, 731

SmartMates Button 610
SmartMates PropertyManager 610
Solid Profile Radio button 356
SOLIDWORKS Menus 21
SOLIDWORKS Resources 30
SOLIDWORKS Search 22
Spacing and Instances Radio button 435
Specify Direction Vector Option 347
Specify Twist Value Option 345
Specifying Grids and Snaps Settings 47
Specifying Units 45
Spiral Option 379
Spline Surface 529
Spline Tool 83
Split Line PropertyManager 386
Split Line Tool 386
Splitting Faces of a Model 386
Standard 3 View PropertyManager 715
Standard 3 View Tool 715
Standard Mates 586
Standard Sheet Size Radio button 705
Standard Toolbar 21
Start and End Tangency 353
Start Command when Creating New Assembly Check box 580, 583
Start Command When Creating New Drawing Check box 706
Start Condition Drop-down list 212
Status Bar 30
Stop at Collision and Dragged Part Only Check box 608
Straight Slot Tool 75
Stretch Entities Tool 131
Stretch PropertyManager 131
Stretching an Entity 131
Style Spline Tool 86
Suppress Tool 569, 675
Suppressing and Unsuppressing Features 569
Suppressing or Unsuppressing Components 675
Surface Finish PropertyManager 736
Surface Finish Tool 736
Surface/Face/Plane Option 278
Surfaces CommandManager 27
Sweep PropertyManager 340
Swept Boss/Base Tool 340

Swept Cut Tool 355
Symmetric Mate 592
Symmetric Relation 155
Synchronize Movement of Flexible Subassembly Components 674

T
Table Driven Pattern Dialog box 454
Table Driven Pattern Tool 454
Table Position 741
Table Template 741
Tables Tool 741
Tangency To Face Option 362
Tangent Arc Tool 71
Tangent Mate 588
Tangent Propagation Check box 506
Tangent Relation 154
Tangent to Adjacent Faces Option 348
Tangent to Curve 450
Taper Helix 381
Task Pane 21, 30
Text Fonts 179
Thin Feature 216, 222, 353, 367, 372
Thread Callout 498
Thread Class 490
Thread Location 500
Thread Options 502
Thread PropertyManager 500
Thread Settings 497
Thread Tool 500
Thumbwheel 160
To Next Edge Option 365
To Next Guide Option 364
To Next Sharp Option 364
To XYZ Position Option 607
Tolerance/Precision 170
Tool Body 356
Top-down Assembly Approach 578, 654
Transform Curve 449
Trim away Inside 108
Trim away Outside 108
Trim by Direction 1 371
Trim Entities Tool 106
Trim PropertyManager 106
Trim to Closest 108
Trim with End Face Check box 503
Trim with Start Face Check box 503

Trimming Sketch Entities 106
Twist Control Drop-down list 346
Two-Direction Option 217
Type of Projection 717

U

Under Defined Sketch 179
Under Head Countersink Check box 489
Units 45
Units and Dimension Standard Dialog box 22
Universal Joint 605
Unsuppress Tool 569, 676
Up To Body Option 280
Up to Reference Radio button 435
Up To Surface Option 280
Up To Vertex Option 279
Update Standard Views Tool 228
Use Sheet Scale Radio button 709

V

Variable Pattern PropertyManager 461
Variable Pattern Tool 460
Variable Pitch 380
Variable Radius Parameters 512
Variable Size Fillet Button 511
Vary Sketch 438
Vertex Chamfer 520
Vertical Dimension Tool 166
Vertical Ordinate Dimension Tool 167
Vertical Relation 154
View (Heads-Up) Toolbar 30
View Center of Mass Tool 311
View Layout CommandManager 33
View Orientation Tool 226
View Palette Task Pane 712
View Selector Cube 227, 228
View Selector Tool 226
View Sketch Relations Tool 158

W

Weld Symbol PropertyManager 737
Weld Symbol Tool 737
Weldments CommandManager 29
Width Mate 592
Wireframe Tool 230

Working with Advanced Mates 590
Working with Angle of Projection 715
Working with Contours of a Sketch 287
Working with Degrees of Freedom 584
Working with Different States of a Sketch 179
Working with Different Types of Sketches 285
Working with Geometric Relations 153
Working with Hole Wizard 485
Working with Mechanical Mates 598
Working with Selection of Planes 45
Working with Smart Dimension Tool 159
Working with SmartMates 610
Working with Standard Mates 586
Wrap Method 529
Wrap Parameters 529
Wrap PropertyManager 528
Wrap Tool 528
Wrap Type 528

Z

Zebra Stripes Check box 373
Zoom In/Out 223
Zoom to Area 224
Zoom To Fit 224
Zoom to Selection 225

Made in the USA
Middletown, DE
19 June 2017